THE LANAHAN READINGS IN THE PSYCHOLOGY OF WOMEN

Second Edition

THE LANAHAN READINGS IN THE PSYCHOLOGY OF WOMEN

Second Edition

edited by
Tomi-Ann Roberts
THE COLORADO COLLEGE

LANAHAN PUBLISHERS, INC. *Baltimore*

Copyright © 1997, 2004 by LANAHAN PUBLISHERS, INC.

All Rights Reserved
Printed in the United States of America

Since this page can not legibly accommodate
all copyright notices, pages 605 through 608
constitute a continuation of this copyright page.

The text of this book was composed in Bembo
with display type set in
Garamond and Bernhard Modern Roman.
Composition by Bytheway Publishing Services
Manufacturing by Victor Graphics, Inc.

ISBN 1-930398-04-2

LANAHAN PUBLISHERS, INC.
324 Hawthorn Road, Baltimore, MD 21210
1-866-345-1949 (toll free)

1 2 3 4 5 6 7 8 9 0

CONTENTS

PART THREE
The Developing Science

PREFACE

My experience teaching the psychology of women is by far and away the most rewarding of all the many things I do as a professor of psychology. One hallmark of this kind of women's studies course is the integration of personal experience with course material. Along with the sharing of information among all members of the class come new insights—new insights about my students and myself, and about my daughters, my sister, my mother, and my grandmothers. Despite the distinctiveness of each class I have taught, based on its unique combination of race, class, and age among the members, there is almost always a universal sense of excitement and wonder about coming together to learn about *women's* lives.

In fact, I have taught on two very different campuses—the very conservative Brigham Young University and the quite liberal Colorado College. Even though my experiences on each campus have been as different as anyone could imagine, my women's studies classes at each have shared some special common features. For example, I have had one or two students find particular readings that so move them or alter their view of the world, that they feel they can never go back to being the person they were before. Each time too, the group seems to bond in a way that doesn't happen often in the other classes I teach. The bonding comes perhaps from the sharing of personal experience with emotionally laden topics. It comes perhaps from the intellectual distance many travel to get to an understanding of feminism. And it often solidifies in a commitment to social action toward a better, less sexist world.

When I teach any women's studies class I find it essential not only to have my students read textbook-style material, but also to explore more primary sources of research, theory, and creative writing. This book provides such sources and is essentially the collection of readings I have been using in my own teaching; in effect, I have been class testing the book for the past twelve years.

Although the focus of this book is decidedly *psychological*, there are many different kinds of voices represented here, so it is appropriate not only for psychology of women classes, but also for classes in psychology of gender, as well as introductory interdisciplinary courses in gender studies and women's studies. In nearly all sections of the book, I have included what are now thought of as "classic" papers on that topic, as well as very recent works. In this way, I have tried to represent both where research in psychology of women has come from and where it is going. In addition, this book includes a number of creative pieces, personal statements, and news articles as a way of placing some of the research issues in more applied contexts.

The Second Edition represents a substantial revision. Over one-third of the essays are new to this edition, and as with the retained essays, they come from a wide variety of sources and are written by a diverse group of authors. For this edition I have added a new chapter entitled "Embodied Selves" (chapter two). Three of its four essays are new, and they consider the female body—how it is understood, how it is portrayed in the media, and how it reflects our culture. I have also expanded the section on women's mental health (chapter seven). There is an entirely new group of readings on violence against women (chapter eight). To make room for the new material, I have combined some First Edition chapters into one chapter: Chapter One, "Growing Up and Growing Old" combines previous chapters one ("Growing Up in a Society of Gender Differences") and five ("Women Aging"); new chapter four, "Reproductive Health" combines previous chapters two ("Biological and Social Aspects of Menstruation") and four ("Pregnancy and Motherhood").

In preparing the Second Edition, I relied greatly on my students—what they enjoyed reading, what they could handle, what they learned from—as I had done with the First Edition. A number of the new essays for this edition have in effect been student-tested. But the Second Edition also profits from having been "out there" in the so-called marketplace.

Many of my colleagues in the field have relayed their experiences using the First Edition with their students—and in some cases, some have shared their reasons for *not* assigning the book. Others, mentioned later, provided more formal reviews of the project. The new edition reflects all of these diverse influences, as well as my own experience teaching the course I love to teach.

The LANAHAN *Readings in the Psychology of Women* is divided into three main headings: "The Developing Woman," "Women in Society," and "The Developing Science." In Part I, the readings explore women's lifespan developmental issues—from early childhood through old age. Part II considers issues of women's relationships with one another and with men, achievement and work, and mental health. In Part III are feminist philosophical and methodological pieces, as well as the various theoretical approaches to the question of gender differentiation within psychology.

The order in which the three main headings of the book appear is arbitrary, therefore instructors using the book may approach it any number of ways. For example, some may wish to begin by having students read the pieces in Part III, "The Developing Science" first, as a way of setting the stage with feminist theory and research methodology before students actually read about development or social issues. Others, however, may wish to have students read this section last, with the perspective that, once they have read exemplary articles and essays in the psychology of women, they are in a better position to explore feminist theoretical and methodological critiques.

Each of the eleven chapters begins with a detailed introduction. These introductory sections not only orient students to each of the readings, but they also provide important background material and context for the broad topic of that section. I have written them with a special eye to students who are interested in how these readings and other research fit together. Because the introductions place the readings in context and provide broad research-based conclusions in various topic areas, the collection can be used either in addition to a textbook in psychology of women and other women's studies courses, or it could well stand on its own as the main text.

As I mentioned, students in my classes have reflected the racial and ethnic diversity of our society. This has made the context of my classes richer. For that reason, I have included issues of women's diversity throughout the collection, incorporating the research, stories, and critiques of women of color within the various developmental and topical sections of the book.

The writings in this book have been informative and inspirational to both me and my students. It is my hope that this book will instill in all readers an excitement about the psychology of women.

Acknowledgments

I have a number of people to thank for helping this book grow. First, I must thank my editor at LANAHAN PUBLISHERS, INC., Don Fusting, for his enthusiasm for this project, despite its many fits and starts. He convinced me a long time ago that I had something to contribute to the teaching of psychology of women beyond my own classroom, and all along he has helped shape and nurture my ideas. He has become, and will remain, a good friend.

Thanks go to Susan Nolen-Hoeksema of the University of Michigan and to Laura Carstensen of Stanford University for being my mentors in graduate school, and for providing inspiring examples of how to teach students and to conduct research in the psychology of women. Several of the articles in this book came directly from classes they taught me many years ago.

For the stimulating, woman-friendly environment of the Nag's Heart Conferences of years ago, I thank Faye Crosby, then at Smith College, now at the University of California, Santa Cruz. My discussions with fascinating women scholars at Faye's house during those summers shaped many of the ideas included in this book.

Also, for their insightful comments, I thank Tamara Beauboeuf of DePauw University, Karen Howe of The College of New Jersey, Esther Rothblum of the University of Vermont,and Kim Vaz of the University of South Florida.

I am grateful to all the students over the years who have commented on the selections in this collection. By their enthusiasm for some readings—and their clear rejection of other selections—they all have been my editor.

Most of all, I thank my husband Bill Davis for his patience and support during the many long hours I've spent on this project. Our conversations challenge and nourish me, and the quality of my work is a reflection of the always-exciting intellectual space we share.

This book is for Karin Gabrielsson, Asta Gabrielsson Roberts, Lisen Christina Roberts, Annika Karin Davis, and Mia Christina Davis—my grandmother, mother, sister, and daughters. Embraced by you and embracing you, my life is rich.

Tomi–Ann Roberts
Colorado Springs

PART ONE

The Developing Woman

CHAPTER ONE

Growing Up and Growing Old

Some years ago, I watched a network television special, hosted by John Stossel, titled "Men, Women, and the Sex Difference." I, of course, was eager to see which of my colleagues in psychology of women would be interviewed about their gender research. About ten minutes into the hour-long show, I realized I probably wasn't going to see any. What was so disappointing to me about this program was its perspective, first, that feminists have had as their goal to try to convince us that there are absolutely no differences at all between men and women, and second, that "good" scientists have been working diligently to demonstrate what we all know to be true—that there are indeed deep, immutable, biologically-determined differences between us from the time we are very young children. This false dichotomy was made even more vivid by the guests the show presented in its opposing-sides format: several biological scientists studying brain differences between males and females on the "pro-sex-differences" side, and one feminist activist (Gloria Steinem) on the other. Unfortunately, this dichotomy still seems representative of American culture's current view.

In addition to the scientific evidence, the program also presented evidence that policies based on a "there are no sex differences at all" perspective (what the host called the "feminist perspective") are failing. For example, Los Angeles fire department footage was shown of women firefighters in training unable to climb over large walls and having great difficulty lifting heavy hoses. (It was interesting that there was no footage of male nurses having difficulty soothing their patients or of male secretaries unable to type 60 words per minute.)

This show was by no means an anomaly. We as a culture are fascinated with the question of gender differences, and a visit to any newsstand or psychology section of a bookstore will convince the skeptic. Why are we so interested in this question? Perhaps it is because there are profound socio-political implications involved in figuring out the answer. If women really are poorer at math, why should we include them in affirmative action efforts to increase their enrollments in engineering programs? If men really can't nurture infants as well as women, why should we give them paternity leave from work?

The problem is that the answers are complicated! There are actually two steps in gender difference research. One is finding out what, if any, differences exist between women and men, girls and boys. The second is much harder: figuring out why such differences exist, and what they mean—and whether they matter at all in the twenty-first century. What most of the television specials and magazine features leave out is the critical second step. This is because we are far from understanding the complexity of both biological and environmental influences on human behavior, thought, and emotion. We are also just beginning to appreciate the subtle but important ways that our biological makeup and cultural conditioning interact to produce who we are. The papers in this section explore the process of gender through childhood, adolescence, and old age.

Those interested in exploring the age-old "nature versus nurture" question with respect to gender differences pay close attention to infant research, for the earlier one can document differences between boys and girls, the more compelling a biological explanation becomes. For the most part, very few if any behavioral differences exist between the genders in infancy. Instead, what has been consistently documented is the powerful difference gender seems to make to *observers* of small infants. I remember once when my bald-headed first daughter, then about five months old, and I were in a store, a woman commented on my "strong, big boy." I corrected her and said she was a girl. The woman immediately came back with, "oh, yes, I should have known. Her features really are so delicate!"

The first paper in this section, by Jeffrey Rubin and his colleagues, "The Eye of the Beholder: Parents' Views on Sex of Newborns," is now a classic illustration of the power of gender as a social stimulus. Their study involved thirty parents of newborn infants, who were asked a series of questions about their babies within the first twenty-four hours after birth. Although the thirty babies did not differ significantly from one another physically, you will read that the parents made quite different ratings of boy versus girl babies. Also, the strength of these ratings differed by sex of the observer. The implications of this study are fascinating to contemplate: sex-role socialization is already at work in the first hours of an infant's life. The labels that are then given to the baby, based on its sex, may affect expectations about how that baby ought to behave, and these in turn may indeed affect the child's behaviors. Perhaps, then, the most important message of this study is that untangling "nature" from "nurture" in terms of their contributions to gender differences is practically an exercise in futility.

Next, Barrie Thorne presents her fascinating research on the playground culture of childhood in her article, "Girls and Boys Together . . . But Mostly Apart: Gender Arrangements in Elementary School." Her research reveals how gender is not only a property of individuals (we possess either femaleness or maleness), but also a *social process* involving groups, and one that is highly dependent on context (playground, classroom, neighborhood, etc.). One of the most fundamental and easy-to-spot qualities of young children's social time is that it is highly gender segregated. With her naturalistic observational method, Thorne was able to see the ways in which boys and girls do this themselves, and how such self-segregation is greatest in contexts that have not been structured by adults, like the playground or the lunch room. Does it matter that girls and boys inhabit largely separate worlds in elementary school? Thorne tries to answer several questions about boys' and girls' play arrangements in the elementary years: 1) Who gets entitled to more space? 2) Who has the unreciprocated right to interrupt and invade the others' activities? 3) Who ends up needing more adult protection? and, 4) Who are lower in status, more often defined as "polluting," and defined more sexually?

What is clear from these papers is that differences between the genders certainly do develop in childhood, but for the most part these differences are a complex product of biological givens, social expectations, self-selection, status, power distinctions, and much, much more. This makes the question of what the differences *mean* in terms of the opportunities and roles adult men and women ought to be able to have in society much harder to answer than my television special would have us believe.

And what of the transition from girlhood to young womanhood? For the most part, adolescent girls have been ignored by psychological research. Virtually all of the major theories of human development were devised from research with samples of boys and men only. Fortunately, this is beginning to change. Unfortunately, what we are learning about the transition of becoming a woman is not always positive. During the teenage years, many girls show increasing problems with eating and body image, increasing depressive disorders, and troubled self-confidence. More and more face pregnancy. What can be done to guide girls away from these negative experiences as they make the transition to adult womanhood? Further research will help us answer this question, but one thing seems clear: the more an adolescent girl today can avoid having to face the agonizing either-or dichotomies that have traditionally been given to girls (be athletic versus be pretty, be popular versus be smart, pursue a career versus pursue a family), the better off she'll be.

In Becky Thompson's article "Childhood Lessons: Culture, Race, Class and Sexuality," the intersections of race, culture, and class are explored in understanding girls' experience of adolescence. This piece focuses on the lessons girls learn about their body sizes and appearance, and argues that one of the few experiences common to all growing girls in the United States is the pressure to diet. However, this pressure is shaped by race, class, ethnicity, and religion. That is, the "culture of thinness," although widespread and media-driven, must be considered along with other destructive social forces that impact adolescent girls.

Thompson presents fascinating qualitative data from Latina, African-American, working-class, rural, white, and Jewish families, painting a tapestry of the many unique cultural influences on growing girls regarding their changing bodies. Pressures of assimilation may account for some parents' strong messages to their girls to become thin. Other parents may find that, although they cannot protect their daughters from racism, they can encourage thinness as a shield at least from discrimination against fat people. And still other parents may present confusing messages to their daughters if cultural traditions encourage nurturing through food, yet mainstream American cultural images presented via the media emphasize thinness.

In other words, standards of physical beauty for women are not just gendered. There are other important influences on girls' opinions of their bodies. Exploring the power of racism and classism to impact messages about standards of appearance helps expand our understanding of girls' identity development and, in the words of Becky Thompson, "paves the way for seeing why girls—across race, class, religion, and ethnicity—may turn to food as a reaction to injustice.

From the young women in Becky Thompson's article, we jump a couple decades to the mature, aging woman. Consider the stereotypes of aging. To grow old has been associated with growing frail, foolish, grumpy, and ugly. Indeed the culture is full of euphemisms for the word "old," illustrating that describing people with this adjective is, in and of itself, an insult. We have senior citizens, "golden girls," and retirees. Furthermore, many have argued that there is a "double standard" of aging in our culture. That is, we view the aging of men and women quite differently. As men approach middle age and beyond, they may grow more handsome and "distinguished." Women, in contrast, "lose their looks," and are complimented only if they successfully cover up their age and appear younger than they are.

One year in my psychology of women class, a group of students designed a research project that investigated these popular stereotypes of aging in the context of advertising. They collected images of adult male and female faces of three different age categories from magazines: young, middle aged, and old. (The last actually turned out to be one of the hardest parts of their project! There are so precious few images of old women in print media, they had a terrible time finding a picture for that category.) They then formulated a list of products, including such things as cars, beer, cosmetics, household cleansers, and insurance. The study simply involved having students imagine that they were advertisers, view the various faces, and make judgments of what each would be best suited to advertise. What they found was that age mattered much less in the selection of items suited for the male images than it did for the female images. That is, the male faces of all three age categories were associated with "masculine" products, such as cars, alcohol, and insurance. For the female faces, in contrast, there were very clear distinctions made among the products—the young woman was associated with cosmetics, the middle-aged woman with cleaning products, and the old woman with items such as Geritol and undergarments for incontinence! A quite persuasive illustration of the double standard of aging.

In "Women of a Certain Age," Laura Carstensen and Monisha Pasupathi argue that aging is a feminist issue. Why? Because a great majority of the old and very old in the United States are women. Indeed at age sixty-five, women outnumber men by 100 to 83, and by age eighty-five they outnumber men by 100 to 39. This fact is largely ignored by policy makers for the elderly, and by the media, which often portrays older people as wielding more power than any other age group. However, the power that age can bring is clearly not distributed evenly between men and women, or among various class and ethnic groups. In this article, the authors review a number of sobering facts that distinguish older women from older men. Women are far more likely than men to be widowed in old age, and widowhood provides a health risk. Widowed women are more likely to live alone and to suffer various negative outcomes associated with this, than other older people. Seventy-five percent of nursing home residents are female. Elderly women are more likely to be poor, and they are very likely to be burdened by the responsibilities of caregiving for ill and disabled elderly spouses or relatives. Carstensen and Pasupathi provide an eye-opening case study to illustrate these all-too-common negative life events for women in old age. They impress upon readers the importance of realizing that such an extreme-sounding case could happen to them.

What is perhaps most fascinating about older women is that, despite the many problems they face, they are not more likely to be depressed or lonely than younger people. Instead, women who reach old age appear to be especially resilient, despite life-long discrimination. Researchers and policy makers need to listen more carefully to them, for they truly are the survivors among us.

1 The Eye of the Beholder: Parents' Views on Sex of Newborns

JEFFREY Z. RUBIN

FRANK J. PROVENZANO

ZELLA LURIA

As Schaffer[10] has observed, the infant at birth is essentially an asocial, largely undifferentiated creature. It appears to be little more than a tiny ball of hair, fingers, toes, cries, gasps, and gurgles. However, while it may seem that "if you've seen one, you've seen them all," babies are *not* all alike—a fact that is of special importance to their parents, who want, and appear to need, to view their newborn child as a creature that is special. Hence, much of early parental interaction with the infant may be focused on a search for distinctive features. Once the fact that the baby is normal has been established, questions such as, "Who does the baby look like?" and "How much does it weigh?" are asked.

Of all the questions parents ask themselves and each other about their infant, one seems to have priority: "Is it a boy or a girl?" The reasons for and consequences of posing this simple question are by no means trivial. The answer, "boy" or "girl," may result in the parents' organizing their perception of the infant with respect to a wide variety of attributes—ranging from its size to its activity, attractiveness, even its future potential. It is the purpose of the present study to examine the kind of verbal picture parents form of the newborn infant, as a function both of their own and their infant's gender.

As Asch[2] observed years ago, in forming our impressions of others, we each tend to develop a *Gestalt*—a global picture of what others are like, which permits us to organize our perceptions of the often discrepant, contradictory aspects of their behavior and manner into a unified whole. The awareness of another's status,[13] the belief that he is "warm" or "cold,"[2,5] "extroverted" or "introverted,"[6] even the apparently trivial knowledge of another's name[4]—each of these cues predisposes us to develop a stereotypic view of that other, his underlying nature, and how he is likely to behave. How much more profound, then, may be the consequences of a cue as prominent in parents' minds as the gender of their own precious, newborn infant.

The study reported here is addressed to parental perceptions of their infants at the point when these infants first emerge into the world. If it can be demonstrated that parental sex-typing has already begun its course at this earliest of moments in the life of the child, it may be possible to understand better one of the important antecedents of the complex process by which the growing child comes to view itself as boy-ish or girl-ish.

Based on our review of the literature, two forms of parental sex-typing may be expected to occur at the time of the infant's birth. First, it appears likely that parents will view and label their newborn child differentially, as a simple function of the infant's gender. Aberle and Naegele[1] and Tasch,[12] using only fathers as subjects, found that they had different expectations for sons and daughters: sons were expected to be aggressive and athletic, daughters were expected to be pretty, sweet, fragile, and delicate. Rebelsky and Hanks[9] found that fathers spent more time talking to their daughters than their sons during the first three months of life. While the sample size was too small for the finding to be significant, they suggest that the role of father-of-daughter may be perceived as requiring greater nurturance. Similarly, Pedersen and Robson[8] reported that the fathers of infant daughters exhibited more behavior labeled (by the authors) as "apprehension over well being" than did the fathers of sons.

A comparable pattern emerges in research using mothers as subjects. Sears, Maccoby and Levin,[11] for example, found that the mothers of kindergartners reported tolerating more aggression from sons than daughters, when it was directed toward parents and peers. In addition, maternal nurturance was seen as more important for the daughter's than the son's development. Taken together, the findings in this body of research lead us to expect parents (regardless of their gender) to view their newborn infants differentially—labeling daughters as weaker, softer, and therefore in greater need of nurturance, than sons.

The second form of parental sextyping we expect to occur at birth is a function both of the infant's gender *and* the parent's own gender. Goodenough[3] interviewed the parents of nursery school children, and found that mothers were less concerned with sex-typing their child's behavior than were fathers. More recently, Meyer and Sobieszek[7] presented adults with videotapes of two seventeen-month-old children (each of whom was sometimes described as a boy and sometimes as a girl), and asked their subjects to describe and interpret the children's behavior. They found that male subjects, as well as those having little contact with small children, were more likely (although not always significantly so) to rate the children in sex-stereotypic fashion—attributing "male qualities" such as independence, aggressiveness, activity, and alertness to the child presented as a boy, and qualities such as cuddliness, passivity, and delicacy of the "girl." We expect, therefore, that sex of infant and sex of parent will interact, such that it is fathers, rather than mothers, who emerge as the greater sex-typers of their newborn.

In order to investigate parental sex-typing of their newborn infants, and in order, more specifically, to test the predictions that sex-typing is a function of the infant's gender, as well as the gender of both infant and parent, parents of newborn boys and girls were studied in the maternity ward of a hospital, within the first 24 hours postpartum, to uncover their perceptions of the characteristics of their newborn infants.

Method

Subjects The subjects consisted of 30 pairs of primiparous parents, fifteen of whom had sons, and fifteen of whom had daughters. The subjects were drawn from the available population of expecting parents at a suburban Boston hospital serving local, predominantly lower-middle-class families.

All subjects participated in the study within the first 24 hours postpartum—the fathers almost immediately after delivery, and the mothers (who were often under sedation at the time of delivery) up to but not later than 24 hours later. The mothers typically had spoken with their husbands at least once during this 24 hour period.

There were no reports of medical problems during any of the pregnancies or deliveries, and all infants in the sample were full-term at time of birth. Deliveries were made under general anesthesia, and the fathers were not allowed in the delivery room. The fathers were not permitted to handle their babies during the first 24 hours, but could view them through display windows in the hospital nursery. The mothers, on the other hand, were allowed to hold and feed their infants. The subject participated individually in the study. The fathers were met in a small, quiet waiting room used exclusively by the maternity ward, while the mothers were met in their hospital rooms. Every precaution was taken not to upset the parents or interfere with hospital procedure.

Procedure After introducing himself to the subjects, and after congratulatory amenities, the experimenter (FJP) asked the parents: "Describe your baby as you would to a close friend or relative." The responses were tape-recorded and subsequently coded.

The experimenter then asked the subjects to take a few minutes to complete a short questionnaire. The instructions for completion of the questionnaire were as follows:

> On the following page there are 18 pairs of opposite words. You are asked to rate your baby in relation to these words, placing an "x" or a checkmark in the space that best describes your baby. The more a word describes your baby, the closer your "x" should be to that word.
>
> Example: Imagine you were asked to rate Trees.
>
> Good :__:__:__:__:__:__:__:__:__:__:__ Bad
> Strong :__:__:__:__:__:__:__:__:__:__:__ Weak
>
> If you cannot decide or your feelings are mixed, place your "x" in the center space. Remember, the more you think a word is a good description of your baby, the closer you should place your "x" to that word. If there are no questions, please begin. Remember, you are rating your baby. Don't spend too much time thinking about your answers. First impressions are usually the best.

Having been presented with these instructions, the subjects then proceeded to rate their baby on each of the eighteen following, eleven-point, bipolar adjective scales: firm-soft; large featured-fine featured; big-little; relaxed-nervous; cuddly-not cuddly; easy going-fussy; cheerful-cranky; good eater-poor eater; excitable-calm; active-inactive; beautiful-plain; sociable-unsociable; well coordinated-awkward; noisy-quiet; alert-inattentive; strong-weak; friendly-unfriendly; hardy-delicate.

Upon completion of the questionnaire, the subjects were thanked individually, and when both parents of an infant had completed their participation, the underlying purposes of the study were fully explained.

Hospital Data In order to acquire a more objective picture of the infants whose characteristics were being judged by the subjects, data were obtained from hospital records concerning each infant's birth weight, birth length, and Apgar scores. Apgar scores are typically assigned at five and ten minutes postpartum, and represent the physician's ratings of the infant's color, muscle tonicity, reflex irritability, and heart and respiratory rates. No significant differences between the male and female infants were found for birth weight, birth length, or Apgar scores at five and ten minutes postpartum.

Results There were *no* rating differences on the eighteen scales as a simple function of Sex of Parent: parents appear to agree with one another, on the average. As a function of Sex of Infant, however, several significant effects emerged: Daughters, in contrast to sons, were rated as significantly softer, finer featured, littler, and more inattentive. In addition, significant interaction effects emerged for seven of the eighteen scales: firm-soft, large featured-fine featured, cuddly-not cuddly, well coordinated-awkward, alert-inattentive, strong-weak, and hardy-delicate.

The meaning of these interactions becomes clear [when one notes that] fathers were more extreme in their ratings of *both* sons and daughters than were mothers. Thus, sons were rated as firmer, larger featured, better coordinated, more alert, stronger, and hardier—and daughters as softer, fine featured, more awkward, more inattentive, weaker, and more delicate—by their fathers than by their mothers. Finally, with respect to the other significant interaction effect (cuddly-not cuddly), a rather different pattern was found. In this case, mothers rated sons as cuddlier than daughters, while fathers rated daughters as cuddlier than sons—a finding we have dubbed the "oedipal" effect.

Responses to the interview question were coded in terms of adjectives used and references to resemblance. Given the open-ended nature of the question, many adjectives were used—healthy, for example, being a high frequency response cutting across sex of babies and parents. Sons were described as big more frequently than were daughters; daughters were called little more often than were sons. The "feminine" cluster—beautiful, pretty, and cute—was used significantly more often to describe daughters than sons. Finally, daughters were said to resemble mothers more frequently than were sons.

Discussion The data indicate that parents—especially fathers—differentially label their infants, as a function of the infant's gender. These results are particularly striking in light of the fact that our sample of male and female infants did *not* differ in birth length, weight, or Apgar scores. Thus, the results appear to be a pure case of parental labeling—what a colleague has described as "nature's first projective test" (personal communication, Leon Eisenberg). Given the importance parents attach to the birth of their first child, it is not surprising that such ascriptions are made.

But why should posing the simple question, "Is it a boy or a girl?", be so salient in parents' minds, and have such important consequences? For one thing, an infant's gender represents a truly *distinctive* characteristic. The baby is either a boy or a girl—there are no ifs, ands, or buts about it. A baby may be active sometimes, and quiet at others, for example, but it can always be assigned to one of two distinct classes: boy or girl. Secondly, an infant's gender tends to assume the properties of a *definitive* characteristic. It permits parents to organize their questions and answers about the infant's appearance and behavior into an integrated *Gestalt*. Finally, an infant's gender is often a *normative* characteristic. It is a property that seems to be of special importance not only to the infant's parents, but to relatives, friends, neighbors, and even casual passersby in the street. For each of these reasons, an infant's gender is a property of considerable importance to its parents, and is therefore one that is likely to lead to labeling and the investment of surplus meaning.

The results of the present study are, of course, not unequivocal. Although it was found, as expected, that the sex-typing of infants varied as a function of the infant's gender, as well as the gender of both infant and parent, significant differences did not emerge for all eighteen of the adjective scales employed. Two explanations for this suggest themselves. First, it may simply be that we have overestimated the importance of sex-typing at birth. A second possibility, however, is that sex-typing is more likely to emerge with respect to certain classes of attributes—namely, those which denote physical or constitutional, rather than "internal," dispositional, factors. Of the eight different adjective pairs for which significant main or interaction effects emerged, six (75%) clearly refer to external attributes of the infant. Conversely, of the ten adjective pairs for which no significant differences were found, only three (30%) clearly denote external attributes. This suggests that it is physical and constitutional factors that specially lend themselves to sex-typing at birth, at least in our culture.

Another finding of interest is the lack of significant effects, as a simple function of sex of parent. Although we predicted no such effects, and were therefore not particularly surprised by the emergence of "non-findings," the implication of these results is by no means trivial. If we had omitted the sex of the infant as a factor in the present study, we might have been led to conclude (on the basis of simply varying the sex of the parent) that *no* differences exist in parental descriptions of newborn infants—a patently erroneous conclusion! It is only when the infant's and the parent's gender are considered together, in interaction, that the lack of differences between overall parental mean ratings can be seen to reflect the true differences between the parents. Mothers rate both sexes closer together on the adjective pairs than do fathers (who are the stronger sex-typers), but *both* parents agree on the direction of sex differences.

An issue of considerable concern, in interpreting the findings of the present study appropriately, stems from the fact that fathers were not permitted to handle their babies, while mothers were. The question then becomes: is it possible that the greater sex-typing by fathers is simply attributable to their lesser exposure to their infants? This, indeed, may have been the case. However it seems worthwhile to consider some of the alternative possibilities. Might not the lesser exposure of fathers to their infants have led not to greater sex-typing, but to a data "wash out"—with no differences emerging in paternal ratings? After all, given no opportunity to handle their babies, and therefore deprived of the opportunity to obtain certain first-hand information about them, the fathers might have been expected to make a series of neutral ratings—hovering around the middle of each adjective scale. The fact that they did not do this suggests that they brought with them a variety of sex stereotypes that they then imposed upon their infants. Moreover, the fact that mothers, who were allowed to hold and feed their babies, made distinctions between males and females that were in keeping with cultural sex-stereotypes, suggests that even if fathers had had the opportunity of holding their infants, similar results might have been obtained. We should also not lose sight of the fact that father-mother differences in exposure to infants continue well into later years. Finally, one must question the very importance of the subjects' differential exposure on the grounds that none of the typical "exposure" effects reported in the social psychological literature[14] were observed. In particular, one might have expected mothers to have come to rate their infants more favorably than fathers, simply as a result of greater exposure. Yet such was not the case.

The central implication of the study, then, is that sex-typing and sex-role socialization appear to have already begun their course at the time of the infant's birth, when information about the infant is minimal. The *Gestalt* parents develop, and the labels they ascribe to their newborn infant, may well affect subsequent expectations about the manner in which their infant ought to behave, as well as parental behavior itself. This parental behavior, moreover, when considered in conjunction with the rapid unfolding of the infant's own behavioral repertoire, may well lead to a modification of the very labeling that affected parental behavior in the first place. What began as a one-way street now bears traffic in two directions. In order to understand the full importance and implications of our findings, therefore, research clearly needs to be conducted in which delivery room stereotypes are traced in the family during the first several months after birth, and their impact upon parental behavior is considered. In addition, further research is clearly in order if we are to understand fully the importance of early paternal sex-typing in the socialization of sex-roles.

References

1. Aberle, D. and Naegele, K. 1952. Middleclass fathers' occupational role and attitudes toward children. *Amer. J. Orthopsychiat.* *22*(2):366–378.

2. Asch, S. 1946. Forming impressions of personality. *J. Abnorm. Soc Psychol.* *41*:258–290.

3. Goodenough, E. 1957. Interest in persons as an aspect of sex differences in the early years. *Genet. Psychol. Monogr.* *55*:287–323.

4. Harari, H. and McDavid, J. Name stereotypes and teachers' expectations. *J. Educ. Psychol.* (in press).

5. Kelley, H. 1950. The warm-cold variable in first impressions of persons. *J. Pers.* *18*:431–439.

6. Luchins, A. 1957. Experimental attempts to minimize the impact of first impressions. *In The Order of Presentation in Persuasion*, C. Hovland, ed. Yale University Press, New Haven, Conn.

7. Meyer, J. and Sobieszek, B. 1972. Effect of a child's sex on adult interpretations of its behavior. *Developm. Psychol.* *6*:42–48.

8. Pedersen, F. and Robson, K. 1969. Father participation in infancy. *Amer. J. Orthopsychiat.* *39*(3):466–472.

9. Rebelsky, F. and Hanks, C. 1971. Fathers' verbal interaction with infants in the first three months of life. *Child Developm.* *42*:63–68.

10. Schaffer, H. 1971. *The Growth of Sociability*. Penguin Books, Baltimore.

11. Sears, R., Maccoby, E. and Levin, H. 1957. *Patterns of Child Rearing*. Row, Peterson, Evanston.

12. Tasch, R. 1952. The role of the father in the family. *J. Exper. Ed.* *20*:319–361.

13. Wilson, P. 1968. The perceptual distortion of height as a function of ascribed academic status. *J. Soc. Psychol.* 74:97–102.

14. Zajonc, R. 1968. Attitudinal effects of mere exposure. *J. Pers. Soc. Psychol. Monogr.* Supplement *9*:1–27.

2 Girls and Boys Together . . . But Mostly Apart: Gender Arrangements in Elementary Schools

BARRIE THORNE

Throughout the years of elementary school, children's friendships and casual encounters are strongly separated by sex. Sex segregation among children, which starts in preschool and is well established by middle childhood, has been amply documented in studies of children's groups and friendships (e.g., Eder and Hallinan 1978; Schofield 1981) and is immediately visible in elementary school settings. When children choose seats in classrooms or the cafeteria, or get into line, they frequently arrange themselves in same-sex clusters. At lunchtime, they talk matter-of-factly about "girls' tables" and "boys' tables." Playgrounds have gendered turfs, with some areas and activities, such as large playing fields and basketball courts, controlled mainly by boys, and others (smaller enclaves like jungle-gym areas and concrete spaces for hopscotch or jumprope) more often controlled by girls. Sex segregation is so common in elementary schools that it is meaningful to speak of separate girls' and boys' worlds.

Studies of gender and children's social relations have mostly followed this "two worlds" model, separately describing and comparing the subcultures of girls and of boys (e.g., Lever 1976; Maltz and Borker 1983). In brief summary: Boys tend to interact in larger, more age-heterogeneous groups (Lever 1976; Waldrop and Halverson 1975; Eder and Hallinan

1978). They engage in more rough and tumble play and physical fighting (Maccoby and Jacklin 1974). Organized sports are both a central activity and a major metaphor in boys' subcultures; they use the language of "teams" even when not engaged in sports, and they often construct interaction in the form of contests. The shifting hierarchies of boys' groups (Savin-Williams 1976) are evident in their more frequent use of direct commands, insults, and challenges (Goodwin 1980).

Fewer studies have been done of girls' groups (Foot, Chapman and Smith 1980; McRobbie and Garber 1975), and—perhaps because categories for description and analysis have come more from male than female experience—researchers have had difficulty seeing and analyzing girls' social relations. Recent work has begun to correct this skew. In middle childhood, girls' worlds are less public than those of boys; girls more often interact in private places and in small groups or friendship pairs (Eder and Hallinan 1978; Waldrop and Halverson 1975). Their play is more cooperative and turn-taking (Lever 1976). Girls have more intense and exclusive friendships, which take shape around keeping and telling secrets, shifting alliances, and indirect ways of expressing disagreement (Goodwin 1980; Lever 1976; Maltz and Borker 1983). Instead of direct commands, girls more often use directives which merge speaker and hearer, such as "let's" or "we gotta" (Goodwin 1980).

Although much can be learned by comparing the social organization and subcultures of boys' and of girls' groups, the separate worlds approach has eclipsed full, contextual understanding of gender and social relations among children. The separate worlds model essentially involves a search for group sex differences, and shares the limitations of individual sex difference research. Differences tend to be exaggerated and similarities ignored, with little theoretical attention to the integration of similarity and difference (Unger 1979). Statistical findings of difference are often portrayed as dichotomous, neglecting the considerable individual variation that exists; for example, not all boys fight, and some have intense and exclusive friendships. The sex difference approach tends to abstract gender from its social context, to assume that males and females are qualitatively and permanently different (with differences perhaps unfolding through separate developmental lines). These assumptions mask the possibility that gender arrangements and patterns of similarity and difference may vary by situation, race, social class, region, or subculture.

Sex segregation is far from total, and is a more complex and dynamic process than the portrayal of separate worlds reveals. Erving Goffman (1977) has observed that sex segregation has a "with-then-apart" structure; the sexes segregate periodically, with separate spaces, rituals, and groups, but they also come together and are, in crucial ways, part of the same world. This is certainly true in the social environment of elementary schools. Although girls and boys do interact as boundaried collectivities, an image suggested by the separate worlds approach, there are other occasions when they work or play in relaxed and integrated ways. Gender is less central to the organization and meaning of some situations than others. In short, sex segregation is not static, but is a variable and complicated process.

To gain an understanding of gender which can encompass both the "with" and "apart" of sex segregation, analysis should start not with the individual, nor with a search for sex differences, but with social relationships. Gender should be conceptualized as a system of relationships rather than as an immutable and dichotomous given. Taking this approach, I have organized my research on gender and children's social relations around questions like the following: How and when does gender enter into group formation? In a given situation, how is gender made more or less salient or infused with particular meanings? By what rituals, processes, and forms of social organization and conflict do "with-then-apart" rhythms get enacted? How are these processes affected by the organization of institutions (different types of schools, neighborhoods, or summer camps, for example), varied settings (such as the constraints and possibilities governing interaction on playgrounds versus classrooms), and particular encounters?

Methods and Sources of Data

This study is based on two periods of participant observation. In 1976–77 I observed for eight months, in a largely working-class elementary school in California, a school with 8 percent black and 12 percent Chicana/o students. In 1980 I did field work for three months in a Michigan elementary school of similar size (around 400 students), social class, and racial composition. I observed in several classrooms (a kindergarten, a second grade, and a combined fourth-fifth grade) and in school hallways, cafeterias, and playgrounds. I set out to follow the round of the school day as children experience it, recording their interactions with one another, and with adults, in varied settings. . . .

Daily Processes of Sex Segregation

Sex segregation should be understood not as a given, but as the result of deliberate activity. The outcome is dramatically visible when there are separate girls' and boys' tables in school lunchrooms, or sex-separated groups on playgrounds. But in the same lunchroom one can also find tables where girls and boys eat and talk together, and in some playground activities the sexes mix. By what processes do girls and boys separate into gender-defined and relatively boundaried collectivities? In what contexts, and through what processes, do boys and girls interact in less gender-divided ways?

In the school settings I observed, much segregation happened with no mention of gender. Gender was implicit in the contours of friendship, shared interest, and perceived risk which came into play when children chose companions—in their prior planning, invitations, seeking-of-access, saving-of-places, denials of entry, and allowing or protesting of "cuts" by those who violated the rules for lining up. Sometimes children formed mixed-sex groups for play, eating, talking, working on a classroom project, or moving through space. When adults or children explicitly invoked gender (and this was nearly always in ways which separated girls and boys) boundaries were heightened and mixed-sex interaction became an explicit arena of risk.

In the schools I studied, the physical space and curriculum were not formally divided by sex, as they have been in the history of elementary schooling (a history evident in separate entrances to old school buildings, where the words *Boys* and *Girls* are permanently etched in concrete). Nevertheless, gender was a visible marker in the adult-organized school day. In both schools, when the public address system sounded, the principal inevitably opened with "Boys and girls . . . " and in addressing clusters of children, teachers and aides regularly used gender terms ("Heads down, girls"; "The girls are ready and the boys aren't"). The forms of address made gender visible and salient, conveying an assumption that the sexes are separate social groups.

Teachers and aides sometimes drew upon gender as a basis for sorting children and organizing activities. Gender is an embodied and visual social category which roughly divides the population in half, and the separation of girls and boys permeates the history and lore of schools and playgrounds. In both schools (although through awareness of Title IX, many teachers had changed this practice) one could see separate girls' and boys' lines moving, like caterpillars, through the school halls. In the fourth-fifth grade classroom the teacher frequently pitted girls against boys for spelling and math contests. On the playground in the Michigan school, aides regarded the space close to the building as girls' territory, and the playing fields "out there" as boys' territory. They sometimes shooed children of the other sex away from those spaces, especially boys who ventured near the girls' area and seemed to have teasing in mind.

In organizing their activities, both within and apart from the surveillance of adults, children also explicitly invoked gender. During my fieldwork in the Michigan school, I kept a daily record of who sat where in the lunchroom. The amount of sex segregation varied: it was least at the first-grade tables and almost total among sixth-graders. There was also variation from classroom to classroom within a given age, and from day to day. Sometimes, particular actions heightened the gender divide. In the lunchroom, when the two second-grade tables were filling, a high-status boy walked by the inside table, which had a scattering of both boys and girls, and said loudly, "Oooo, too many girls," as he headed for a seat at the far table. The boys at the inside table picked up their trays and moved, and no other boys sat at the inside table, which the pronouncement had effectively made taboo. In the end, that day (which was not the case every day), girls and boys ate at separate tables.

Eating and walking are not sex-typed activities, yet in forming groups in lunchrooms and hallways children often separated by sex. Sex segregation assumed added dimensions on the playground, where spaces, equipment, and activities were infused with gender meanings. My inventories of activities showed similar patterns in both schools: boys controlled the large, fixed spaces designated for team sports (baseball diamond, grassy fields used for football or soccer); girls more often played closer to the building, doing tricks on the monkey bars (which, for sixth-graders, became an area for sitting and talking) and using cement areas for jump-rope, hopscotch, and group games like four-square. Lever (1976) provides a good analysis of sex-divided play. Girls and boys most often played together in kickball and group (rather than team) games like four-square, dodgeball, and handball. When children used gender to exclude others from play, they often drew upon beliefs connecting boys to some activities and girls to others. A first-grade boy, for example, avidly watched an all-female game of jumprope. When the girls began to shift positions, he recognized a means of access to the play and he offered, "I'll swing it." A girl responded, "No way, you don't know how to do it, to swing it. You gotta be a girl." He left without protest. Although children sometimes ignored pronouncements about what each could or could not do, I never heard them directly challenge such claims.

When children had explicitly defined an activity or a group as gendered, those who crossed the boundary—especially boys who moved into female-marked space—risked being teased: "Look! Mike's in the girls' line!"; "That's a girl over there," a girl said loudly, pointing to a boy sitting at an otherwise all-female table in the lunchroom. Children, and occasionally adults, used teasing, especially the tease of "liking" someone of the other sex, or of "being" that sex by virtue of being in their midst, to police gender boundaries. Much of the teaching drew upon heterosexual romantic definitions, making cross-sex interaction risky, and increasing the social distance between boys and girls.

Relationships between the Sexes

Because I have emphasized the "apart" and ignored the occasions of "with" in this analysis of sex segregation, I have perhaps falsely implied that there is little contact between girls and boys in daily school life. In fact, relationships between girls and boys (which should be studied as fully as, and in connection with, same-sex relationships) are of several kinds:

1. "Borderwork," or forms of cross-sex interaction which are based upon and reaffirm boundaries and asymmetries between girls' and boys' groups;
2. Interactions which are infused with heterosexual meanings;
3. Occasions where individuals cross gender boundaries to participate in the world of the other sex; and
4. Situations where gender is not predominant, and girls and boys interact in more relaxed ways.

Borderwork In elementary school settings boys' and girls' groups are sometimes spatially set apart. Same-sex groups sometimes claim fixed territories such as the basketball court, the bars, or specific lunchroom tables. However, in the crowded, multifocused, and adult-controlled environment of the school, groups form and disperse at a rapid rate and can never stay totally apart. Contact between girls and boys sometimes lessens sex segregation, but gender-defined groups also come together in ways which emphasize their boundaries.

"Borderwork" refers to interaction across, yet based upon and even strengthening, gender boundaries. I have drawn this notion from Fredrik Barth's (1969) analysis of social relations which are maintained across ethnic boundaries without diminishing dichotomized ethnic status.[1] His focus is on more macro, ecological arrangements; mine is on face-to-face behavior. But the insight is similar: groups may interact in ways which strengthen their borders, and the maintenance of ethnic (or gender) groups can best be understood by examining the boundary that defines the group, "not the cultural stuff that it encloses" (Barth 1969, p. 15). In elementary schools there are several types of borderwork: contests or games where gender-defined teams compete; cross-sex rituals of chasing and pollution; and group invasions. These interactions are asymmetrical, challenging the separate-but-parallel model of "two worlds."

Contests Boys and girls are sometimes pitted against each other in classroom competitions and playground games. The fourth-fifth grade classroom had a boys' side and a girls' side, an arrangement that re-emerged each time the teacher asked children to choose their own desks. Although there was some within-sex shuffling, the result was always a spatial moiety system—boys on the left, girls on the right—with the exception of one girl (the "tomboy" whom I'll describe later), who twice chose a desk with the boys and once with the girls. Drawing upon and reinforcing the children's self-segregation, the teacher often pitted the boys against the girls in spelling and math competitions, events marked by cross-sex antagonism and within-sex solidarity.

The teacher introduced a math game, for example; she would write addition and subtraction problems on the board, and a member of each team would race to be the first to write the correct answer. She wrote two score-keeping columns on the board: "Beastly Boys" and "Gossipy Girls." The boys yelled out, as several girls laughed, "Noisy girls!" "Gruesome girls!" The girls sat in a row on top of their desks; sometimes they moved collectively, pushing their hips or whispering "Pass it on." The boys stood along the wall, some reclining against desks. When members of either group came back victorious from the front of the room, they would do the "giving five" hand-slapping ritual with their team members.

On the playground a team of girls occasionally played against a team of boys, usually in kickball or team two-square. Sometimes these games proceeded matter-of-factly, but if gender became the explicit basis of team solidarity, the interaction changed, becoming more antagonistic and unstable. On one occasion, two fifth-grade girls played against two fifth-grade boys in a team game of two-square. The game proceeded at an even pace until an argument ensued about whether the ball was out or on the line. Karen, who had hit the ball, became annoyed, flashed her middle finger at the other team, and called to a passing girl to join their side. The boys then called out to other boys, and cheered as several arrived to play. "We got five and you got three!" Jack yelled. The game continued, with the girls yelling, "Bratty boys!" "Sissy boys!" and the boys making noises—"weee haw" "ha-ha-ha"—as they played.

Chasing Cross-sex chasing dramatically affirms boundaries between girls and boys. The basic elements of chase and elude, capture and rescue (Sutton-Smith 1971) are found in various kinds of tag with formal rules, and in informal episodes of chasing which punctuate life on playgrounds. These episodes begin with provocation (taunts like "You can't get me!" or "Slobber monster!", bodily pokes, or the grabbing of possessions). A provocation may be ignored, or responded to by chasing. Chaser and chased may then alternate roles. In an ethnographic study of chase sequences on a school playground, Christine Finnan (1982) observes that chases vary in number of chasers to chased (for example, one chasing one, or five chasing two); form of provocation (a taunt or a poke); outcome (an episode may end when the chased outdistances the chaser, or with a brief touch, being wrestled to the ground, or the recapturing of a hat or a ball); and in use of space (there may or may not be safety zones).

Like Finnan (1982), and Sluckin (1981), who studied a playground in England, I found that chasing has a gendered structure. Boys frequently chase one another, an activity which often ends in wrestling and mock fights. When girls chase girls, they are usually less physically aggressive; they less often, for example, wrestle one another to the ground.

Cross-sex chasing is set apart by special names—"girls chase the boys"; "boys chase the girls"; "chasers"; "chase and kiss"; "kiss chase"; "kissers and chasers"; "kiss or kill"—and by children's animated talk about the activity. The names vary by region and school, but contain both gender and sexual meanings (this form of play is mentioned, but only briefly analyzed, in Finnan 1982; Sluckin 1981; Parrott 1972; and Borman 1979).

In "boys chase the girls" and "girls chase the boys" (the names most frequently used in both the California and Michigan schools) boys and girls become, by definition, separate teams. Gender terms override individual identities, especially for the other team ("Help, a girl's chasin' me!"; "C'mon Sarah, let's get that boy"; "Tony, help save me from the girls"). Individuals may call for help from, or offer help to, others of their sex. They may also grab someone of their sex and turn them over to the opposing team: Ryan grabbed Billy from behind, wrestling him to the ground. "Hey girls, get 'im," Ryan called.

Boys more often mix episodes of cross-sex with same-sex chasing. Girls more often have safety zones, places like the girls' restroom or an area by the school wall, where they retreat to rest and talk (sometimes in animated post-mortems) before new episodes of cross-sex chasing begin.

Early in the fall in the Michigan school, where chasing was especially prevalent, I watched a second-grade boy teach a kindergarten girl how to chase. He slowly ran backwards, beckoning her to pursue him, as he called, "Help, a girl's after me." In the early grades chasing mixes with fantasy play, like a first-grade boy who played "sea monster," his arms out-flung and his voice growling, as he chased a group of girls. By third grade, stylized gestures—exaggerated stalking motions, screams (which only girls do), and karate kicks—accompany scenes of chasing.

Names like "chase and kiss" mark the sexual meanings of cross-sex chasing, a theme to which I shall return later. The threat of kissing (most often girls threatening to kiss boys) is a ritualized form of provocation. Cross-sex chasing among sixth-graders involves elaborate patterns of touch and touch avoidance, which adults see as sexual. The principal told the sixth-graders in the Michigan school that they were not to play "pom-pom," a complicated chasing game, because it entailed "inappropriate touch."

Rituals of Pollution Cross-sex chasing is sometimes entwined with rituals of pollution, as in "cooties," where specific individuals or groups are treated as contaminating or carrying "germs." Children have rituals for transferring cooties (usually touching someone else and shouting "You've got cooties!"), for immunization (such as writing "CV" for "cootie vaccination" on their arms), and for eliminating cooties (saying "no gives," for example, or using "cootie catchers" made of folded paper, which is described in Knapp and Knapp, 1976). While girls may give cooties to girls, boys do not generally give cooties to one another (Samuelson 1980).

In cross-sex play, either girls or boys may be defined as having cooties, which they transfer through chasing and touching. Girls give cooties to boys more often than vice versa. In Michigan, one version of cooties is called "girl stain"; the fourth-graders whom Karkau (1973) describes used the phrase "girl touch." "Cootie queens" or "cootie girls" (there are no "kings" or "boys") are female pariahs, the ultimate school untouchables, seen as contaminating not only by virtue of gender, but also through some added stigma such as being overweight or poor.[2] That girls are seen as more polluting than boys is a significant asymmetry, which echoes cross-cultural patterns, although in other cultures female pollution is generally connected with menstruation, and not applied to prepubertal girls.

Invasions Playground invasions are another asymmetric form of borderwork. On a few occasions I saw girls invade and disrupt an all-male game, most memorably, a group of tall sixth-grade girls who ran on to the playing field and grabbed a football which was in play. The boys were surprised and frustrated and, unusual for boys this old, finally tattled to the aide. In the majority of cases, however, boys disrupt girls' activities rather than vice versa. Boys grab the ball from girls playing four-square, stick feet into a jumprope and stop an ongoing game, and dash through the area of the bars, where girls are taking turns performing, sending the rings flying. Sometimes boys ask to join in a girls' game and then, after a short period of seemingly earnest play, disrupt the game. Two second-grade boys, for example, begged to "twirl" the jumprope for a group of second-grade girls who had been jumping for some time. The girls agreed, and the boys began to twirl. Soon, without announcement, the boys changed from "seashells, cockle bells" to "hot peppers" (spinning the rope very fast), and tangled the jumper in the rope. The boys ran away laughing.

Boys disrupt girls' play so often that girls have developed almost ritualized responses: they guard their ongoing play, chase boys away, and tattle to the aides. In a playground cycle which enhances sex segregation, aides who try to spot potential trouble before it occurs sometimes shoo boys away from areas where girls are playing. Aides do not anticipate trouble from girls who seek to join groups of boys, with the exception of girls intent on provoking a chase sequence. Indeed, if they seek access to a boys' game, girls usually play with boys in earnest rather than breaking up the game.

A close look at the organization of borderwork, or boundaried interactions between the sexes, shows that the worlds of boys and girls may be separate, but they are not parallel, nor are they equal. The worlds of girls and boys articulate in several asymmetric ways:

1. On the playground, boys control as much as ten times more space than girls, when one adds up the area of large playing fields and compares it with the much smaller areas where girls predominate. Girls, who play closer to the building, are more often watched over and protected by the adult aides.
2. Boys invade all-female games and scenes of play much more than girls invade boys. This, and boys' greater control of space, correspond with other findings about the organization of gender, and inequality, in our society: compared with men and boys, women and girls take up less space, and their space, and talk, are more often violated and interrupted (Grief 1982; Henley 1977; West and Zimmerman 1983).
3. Although individual boys are occasionally treated as contam-

> inating (like a third-grade boy who both boys and girls said was "stinky" and "smelled like pee"), girls are more often defined as polluting. This pattern ties to themes that I shall discuss later. It is more taboo for a boy to play with (as opposed to invade) girls, and girls are more sexually defined than boys.

A look at the boundaries between the separated worlds of girls and boys illuminates within-sex hierarchies of status and control. For example, in the sex-divided seating in the fourth-fifth grade classroom, several boys recurrently sat near "female space": their desks were at the gender divide in the classroom, and they were more likely than other boys to sit at a predominantly female table in the lunchroom. These boys (two nonbilingual Chicanos and an overweight "loner" boy who was afraid of sports) were at the bottom of the male hierarchy. Gender is sometimes used as a metaphor for male hierarchies; the inferior status of boys at the bottom is conveyed by calling them "girls." Once, when seven boys and one girl were playing basketball, two younger boys came over and asked to play. While the girl silently stood, fully accepted in the company of the players, one of the older boys disparagingly said to the younger boys, "You girls can't play."[3]

In contrast, the girls who more often travel in the boys' world, sitting with groups of boys in the lunchroom or playing basketball, soccer, and baseball with them, are not stigmatized. Some have fairly high status with other girls. The worlds of girls and boys are asymmetrically arranged, and spatial patterns map interacting forms of inequality.

Heterosexual Meanings The organization and meanings of gender (the social categories "woman/man," "girl/boy") and of sexuality vary cross-culturally (Ortner and Whitehead 1981) and, in our society, across the life course. Harriet Whitehead (1981) observed that in our (Western) gender system, and that of many traditional North American Indian cultures, one's choice of a sexual object, occupation, and one's dress and demeanor are closely associated with gender. However, the "center of gravity" differs in the two gender systems. For Indians, occupational pursuits provide the primary imagery of gender; dress and demeanor are secondary, and sexuality is least important. In our system, at least for adults, the order is reversed: heterosexuality is central to our definitions of "man" and "woman" ("masculinity" "feminity") and the relationships that obtain between them, whereas occupation and dress/demeanor are secondary.

Whereas erotic orientation and gender are closely linked in our definitions of adults, we define children as relatively asexual. Activities and dress/demeanor are more important than sexuality in the cultural meanings of "girl" and "boy." Children are less heterosexually defined than adults, and we have nonsexual imagery for relations between girls and boys. However, both children and adults sometimes use heterosexual language—"crushes," "like," "goin' with," "girlfriends," and "boyfriends"—to define cross-sex relationships. This language increases through the years of elementary school; the shift to adolescence consolidates a gender system organized around the institution of heterosexuality.

In everyday life in the schools, heterosexual and romantic meanings infuse some ritualized forms of interaction between groups of boys and girls (such as "chase and kiss") and help maintain sex segregation. "Jimmy likes Beth," "Beth likes Jimmy" is a major form of teasing, which a child risks in choosing to sit by or walk with someone of the other sex. The structure of teasing, and children's sparse vocabulary for relationships between girls and boys, are evident in the following conversation which I had with a group of third-grade girls in the lunchroom. Susan asked me what I was doing, and I said I was observing the things children do and play. Nicole volunteered. "I like running, boys chase all the girls. See Tim over there? Judy chases him all around the school. She likes him." Judy, sitting across the table, quickly responded, "I hate him. I like him for a friend." "Tim loves Judy," Nicole said in a loud, sing-song voice.

In the younger grades, the culture and lore of girls contains more heterosexual romantic themes than that of boys. In Michigan, the first-grade girls often jumped rope to a rhyme which began:

> Down in the valley where the green grass grows,
> There sat Cindy [name of jumper], as sweet as a rose.
> She sat, she sat, she sat so sweet.
> Along came Jason, and kissed her on the cheek . . .
> First comes love, then comes marriage,
> Then along comes Cindy with a baby carriage . . .

Before a girl took her turn at jumping, the chanters asked her "Who do you want to be your boyfriend?" The jumper always proffered a name, which was accepted matter-of-factly. In chasing, a girl's kiss carried greater threat than a boy's kiss; "girl touch," when defined as contaminating, had sexual connotations. In short, starting at an early age, girls are more sexually defined than boys.

Through the years of elementary school, and increasing with age, the idiom of heterosexuality helps maintain the gender divide. Cross-sex interactions, especially when children initiate them, are fraught with the risk of being teased about "liking" someone of the other sex. I learned of several close cross-sex friendships, formed and maintained in neighborhoods and church, which went underground during the school day.

By the fifth grade a few children began to affirm, rather than avoid, the charge of having a girlfriend or a boyfriend; they introduced the heterosexual courtship rituals of adolescence. For example, in the lunchroom in the Michigan school, as the tables were forming, a high-status fifth-grade boy called out from his seat at the table: "I want Trish to sit by me." Trish came over and, almost like a king and queen, they sat at the gender divide—a row of girls down the table on her side, a row of boys on his. In this situation, which inverted earlier forms, it was not a loss but a gain in status publicly to choose a companion of the other sex. By affirming his choice, the boy became unteasable (note the familiar asymmetry of heterosexual courtship rituals: the male initiated). This incident signals a temporal shift in arrangements of sex and gender.

Traveling in the World of the Other Sex Contests, invasions, chasing, and heterosexually-defined encounters are based upon and reaffirm boundaries between girls and boys. In another type of cross-sex interaction, individuals (or sometimes pairs) cross gender boundaries, seeking acceptance in a group of the other sex. Nearly all the cases I saw of this were tomboys, girls who played organized sports and frequently sat with boys in the cafeteria or classroom. If these girls were skilled at activities central in the boys' world, especially games like soccer, baseball, and basketball, they were pretty much accepted as participants.

Being a tomboy is a matter of degree. Some girls seek access to boys' groups but are excluded; other girls limit their "crossing" to specific sports. Only a few (such as the tomboy I mentioned earlier, who chose a seat with the boys in the sex-divided fourth-fifth grade) participate fully in the boys' world. That particular girl was skilled at the various organized sports which boys played in different seasons of the year. She was also adept at physical fighting and at using the forms of arguing, insult, teasing, naming, and sports-talk of the boys' subculture. She was the only black child in her classroom, in a school with only 8 percent black students; overall that token status, along with unusual athletic and verbal skills, may have contributed to her ability to move back and forth across the gender divide. Her unique position in the children's world was widely recognized in the school. Several times, the teacher said to me, "She thinks she's a boy."

I observed only one boy in the upper grades (a fourth-grader) who regularly played with all-female groups, as opposed to "playing at" girls' games and seeking to disrupt them. He frequently played jumprope and took turns with girls doing tricks on the bars, using the small gestures (for example, a helpful push on the heel of a girl who needed momentum to turn her body around the bar) which mark skillful and earnest participation. Although I never saw him play in other than an earnest spirit, the girls often chased him away from their games and both girls and boys teased him. The fact that girls seek and have more access to boys' worlds than vice versa, and the fact that girls who travel with the other sex are less stigmatized for it, are obvious asymmetries, tied to the asymmetries previously discussed.

Relaxed Cross-sex Interactions Relationships between boys and girls are not always marked by strong boundaries, heterosexual definitions, or by interacting on the terms and turfs of the other sex. On some occasions girls and boys interact in relatively comfortable ways. Gender is not predominant nor explicitly invoked, and girls and boys are not organized into boundaried collectivities. These "with" occasions have been neglected by those studying gender and children's relationships, who have emphasized either the model of separate worlds (with little attention to their articulation) or heterosexual forms of contact.

Occasions where boys and girls interact without strain, where gender wanes, rather than waxes in importance, frequently have one or more of the following characteristics:

1. The situations are organized around an absorbing task, such as a group art project or creating a radio show, which encourages cooperation and lessens attention to gender. This pattern accords with other studies finding that cooperative activities reduce group antagonism (e.g., Sherif and Sherif, 1953, who studied divisions between boys in a summer camp; and Aronson et al. 1978, who used cooperative activities to lessen racial divisions in a classroom).
2. Gender is less prominent when children are not responsible for the formation of the group. Mixed-sex play is less frequent in games like football, which require the choosing of teams, and more frequent in games like handball or dodgeball which individuals can join simply by getting into a line or a circle. When adults organize mixed-sex encounters—which they frequently do in the classroom and in physical education periods on the playground—they legitimize cross-sex contact. This removes the risk of being teased for choosing to be with the other sex.
3. There is more extensive and relaxed cross-sex interaction

when principles of grouping other than gender are explicitly invoked—for example, counting off to form teams for spelling or kickball, dividing lines by hot lunch or cold lunch, or organizing a work group on the basis of interests or reading ability.

4. Girls and boys may interact more readily in less public and crowded settings. Neighborhood play, depending on demography, is more often sex and age integrated than play at school, partly because with fewer numbers one may have to resort to an array of social categories to find play partners or to constitute a game. And in less crowded environments there are fewer potential witnesses to "make something of it" if girls and boys play together.

Relaxed interactions between girls and boys often depend on adults to set up and legitimize the contact.[4] Perhaps because of this contingency (and the other, distancing patterns which permeate relations between girls and boys) the easeful moments of interaction rarely build to close friendship. Schofield (1981) makes a similar observation about gender and racial barriers to friendship in a junior high school.

Implications for Development

I have located social relations within an essentially spatial framework, emphasizing the organization of children's play, work, and other activities within specific settings, and in one type of institution, the school. In contrast, frameworks of child development rely upon temporal metaphors, using images of growth and transformation over time. Taken alone, both spatial and temporal frameworks have shortcomings; fitted together, they may be mutually correcting. . . .

A full understanding of gender and social relations should encompass cross-sex as well as within-sex interactions. "Borderwork" helps maintain separate gender-linked subcultures, which, as those interested in development have begun to suggest, may result in different milieus for learning. Daniel Maltz and Ruth Borker (1983), for example, argue that because of different interactions within girls' and boys' groups, the sexes learn different rules for creating and interpreting friendly conversation, rules which carry into adulthood and help account for miscommunication between men and women. Carol Gilligan (1982) fits research on the different worlds of girls and boys into a theory of sex differences in moral development. Girls develop a style of reasoning, she argues, which is more personal and relational; boys develop a style which is more positional, based on separateness. Eleanor Maccoby (1985), also following the insight that because of sex segregation, girls and boys grow up in different environments, suggests implications for gender-differentiated prosocial and antisocial behavior.

This separate worlds approach, as I have illustrated, also has limitations. The occasions when the sexes are together should also be studied, and understood as contexts for experience and learning. For example, asymmetries in cross-sex relationships convey a series of messages: that boys are more entitled to space and to the nonreciprocal right of interrupting or invading the activities of the other sex; that girls are more in need of adult protection, and are lower in status, more defined by sexuality, and may even be polluting. Different types of cross-sex interaction—relaxed, boundaried, sexualized, or taking place on the terms of the other sex—provide different contexts for development. . . .

Overall, I am calling for more complexity in our conceptualizations of gender and of children's social relationships. Our challenge is to retain the temporal sweep, looking at individual and group lives as they unfold over time, while also attending to social structure and context, and to the full variety of experiences in the present.

Notes

1. I am grateful to Frederick Erickson for suggesting the relevance of Barth's analysis.
2. Sue Samuelson (1980) reports that in a racially mixed playground in Fresno, California, Mexican-American, but not Anglo children gave cooties. Racial, as well as sexual, inequality may be expressed through these forms.
3. This incident was recorded by Margaret Blume, who, for an undergraduate research project in 1982, observed in the California school where I earlier did fieldwork. Her observations and insights enhanced my own, and I would like to thank her for letting me cite this excerpt.
4. Note that in daily school life, depending on the individual and the situation, teachers and aides sometimes lessened and at other times heightened sex segregation.

References

Aronson, E. et al. (1978) *The Jigsaw Classroom*, Beverly Hills, Sage.

Barth, F. (Ed.) (1969) *Ethnic Groups and Boundaries*, Boston, Little, Brown.

Borman, K. M. (1979) "Children's Interactions in Playgrounds," *Theory into Practice* 18, pp. 251–7.

Eder, D. and Hallinan, M. T. (1978) "Sex Differences in Children's Friendships," *American Sociological Review* 43, pp. 237–50.

Finnan, C. R. (1982) "The Ethnography of Children's Spontaneous Play," in Spindler, G. (Ed.) *Doing the Ethnography of Schooling*, pp. 358–80, New York, Holt, Rinehart & Winston.

Foot, H. C., Chapman, A. J. and Smith, J. R. (1980) *Friendship and Social Relations in Children*, pp. 1–14, New York, Wiley.

Gilligan, C. (1982) *In a Different Voice: Psychological Theory and Women's Development*, Cambridge, Harvard University Press.

Glaser, B. G. and Strauss, A. L. (1967) *The Discovery of Grounded Theory*, Chicago, Aldine.

Goffman, E. (1977) "The Arrangement Between the Sexes," *Theory and Society* 4, pp. 301–36.

Goodwin, M. H. (1980) "Directive-Response Speech Sequences in Girls' and Boys' Task Activities," in McConnell-Ginet, S., Borker, R. and Furman, N. (Eds.) *Women and Language in Literature and Society*, pp. 157–73, New York, Praeger.

Greif, E. B. (1982) "Sex Differences in Parent-Child Conversations," *Women's Studies International Quarterly* 3, pp. 253–8.

Henley, N. (1977) *Body Politics: Power, Sex, and Nonverbal Communication*, Englewood Cliffs, Prentice-Hall.

Karkau, K. (1973) *Sexism in the Fourth Grade*, Pittsburgh, KNOW, Inc. (pamphlet).

Katz, J. (1983) "A Theory of Qualitative Methodology: The Social System of Analytic Fieldwork," in Emerson, R. M. (Ed.) *Contemporary Field Research*, pp. 127–48, Boston, Little, Brown.

Knapp, M. and Knapp, H. (1976) *One Potato, New Potato, The Secret Education of American Children*, New York, W.W. Norton.

Lever, J. (1976) "Sex Differences in the Games Children Play," *Social Problems* 23, pp. 478–87.

Maccoby, E. (1985) "Social Groupings in Childhood: Their Relationship to Prosocial and Antisocial Behavior in Boys and Girls," in Olweus, D., Block, J. and Radke-Yarrow, M. *Development of Antisocial and Prosocial Behavior*, pp. 263–84, San Diego, Academic Press.

Maccoby, E. and Jacklin, C. (1974) *The Psychology of Sex Differences*, Stanford, Stanford University Press.

Maltz, D. N. and Borker, R. A. (1983) "A Cultural Approach to Male-Female Miscommunication," in Gumperz, J. J. (Ed.) *Language and Social Identity*, pp. 195–216, New York, Cambridge University Press.

McRobbie, A. and Garber J. (1975) "Girls and Subcultures," in Hall, S. and Jefferson, T. (Eds.) *Resistance Through Rituals*, pp. 209–23, London, Hutchinson.

Ortner, S. B. and Whitehead, H. (1981) *Sexual Meanings*, New York, Cambridge University Press.

Parrott, S. (1972) "Games children play: Ethnography of a second-grade recess," in Spradley, J. P. and McCarthy, D. W. (Eds.) *The Cultural Experience*, pp. 206–19, Chicago, Science Research Associates.

Rich, A. (1980) "Compulsory Heterosexuality and Lesbian Existence," *Signs* 5, pp. 631–60.

Samuelson, S. (1980) "The Cooties Complex," *Western Folklore*, 39, pp. 198–210.

Savin-Williams, R. C. (1976) "An Ethological Study of Dominance Formation and Maintenance in a Group of Human Adolescents," *Child Development* 47, pp. 972–9.

Schofield, J. W. (1981) "Complementary and Conflicting Identities: Images and Interaction in an Interracial School," in Asher, S. R. and Gottman, J. M. (Eds.) *The Development of Children's Friendships*, New York, Cambridge University Press.

Sherif, M. and Sherif, C. (1953) *Groups in Harmony and Tension*, New York, Harper.

Sluckin, A. (1981) *Growing Up in the Playground*, London, Routledge & Kegan Paul.

Speier, M. (1976) "The Adult Ideological Viewpoint in Studies of Childhood," in Skolnick, A. (Ed.) *Rethinking Childhood*, pp. 168–86, Boston, Little, Brown.

Sutton-Smith, B. (1971) "A Syntax for Play and Games," in Herron, R. E. and Sutton-Smith, B. (Eds.) *Child's Play*, pp. 298–307, New York, Wiley.

Unger, R. K. (1979) "Toward a Redefinition of Sex and Gender," *American Psychologist* 34, pp. 1085–94.

Waldrop, M. F. and Halverson, C. F. (1975) "Intensive and Extensive Peer Behavior: Longitudinal and Cross-Sectional Analysis," *Child Development* 46, pp. 19–26.

West, C. and Zimmerman, D. H. (1983) "Small Insults: A Study of Interruptions in Cross-Sex Conversations between Unacquainted Persons," in Thorne, B., Kramarae C. and Henley, N. (Eds.) *Language, Gender and Society*, Rowley, Newbury House.

Whitehead, H. (1981) "The Bow and the Burden Strap: A New Look at Institutionalized Homosexuality in Native America," in Ortner, S. B. and Whitehead, H. (Eds.) *Sexual Meanings*, pp. 80–115, New York, Cambridge University Press.

3 Childhood Lessons: Culture, Race, Class, and Sexuality

BECKY W. THOMPSON

If there is one story that is an integral part of the folklore of growing up female, it is the chronicle of the onset of menstruation. These accounts are often embarrassing—a thirteen-year-old girl has to ask her father to tell her what to do, another is sure that people can tell from her face what is going on in her body—and many, like that of the young teenager who gets a red cake with red candles from her mother to celebrate her first period, are funny. Usually told only in the company of other women, these stories of a rite of passage are often filled with pain, ingenuity, and humor—and sometimes joy.

Equally revealing stories about the development of female identity in the United States spring from lessons girls learn about their body sizes and appetites. Whether they are fat or thin, Latina or Jewish (or both), lesbian or heterosexual, girls are barraged by complicated messages about their bodies, skin, hair, and faces. Not surprisingly, girls who do not fit the standard mold—who look like tomboys, whose skin is dark, who have nappy hair, who are chubby or just plain big, who develop early or develop late—are most aware of negative assessments, and their stories are commonly filled with shame and confusion.

Although there is no single message to girls about weight and food that crosses regional, religious, and cultural lines in the United States, early lessons about weight and appetite often leave indelible marks on their lives. Growing up on a working farm may protect a girl from the pressure to diet, but she may learn elsewhere that a big appetite is not acceptable for girls and women. While being raised in the Dominican Republic may help a young girl value women of all sizes, if she emigrates to the United States, the pressures to assimilate culturally and linguistically may make her especially determined to be thin.

Increasingly, one of the few experiences common to growing girls in the United States is the pressure to diet. This pressure not only reveals strictures about body size, it also telegraphs complicated notions about race, culture, and class. A girl's body may become the battleground where parents and other relatives play out their own anxieties. Just as stories about a first menstruation tell us about a family's social traditions and the extent to which the girl's body is respected within them, lessons about weight and eating habits tell us an enormous amount about culture, race, religion, and gender. It is through these familial and cultural lenses that young girls make judgments about their bodies and their appetites. The nuances in the socialization of girls show why—across race, class, and religion—they may become vulnerable to eating problems and demonstrate how many girls begin to use food to cope with trauma.

Growing up Latina

By the year 2020 the single largest minority group in the United States will be Latino people—including the descendants of people who were in what is now the United States before it was "discovered," people who fled El Salvador and Guatemala in the 1970s and 1980s, Puerto Rican people, and a host of others. Latinos share a history of struggling against colonialism and racism, and they share a common language. Other generalizations are often erroneous.

There is no single Latino ethic about body size and eating patterns. . . . The notion that Latinas as a group are somehow protected from or ignorant of cultural pressure to be thin simply does not hold up in the face of their diversity. Nor can it be said that any particular group of women is isolated from the culture of thinness; the mass media have permeated even the most remote corners of the United States. The pressures of assimilation and racism may make some Latinas especially vulnerable to strictures about weight.

The task, then, is to identify both how ethnic, racial, and socioeconomic heterogeneity among Latinos and Latinas influences their socialization and how these factors may make Latinas susceptible to developing eating problems. One of the Latina women I interviewed, Elsa, was raised by German governesses in an upper-class family in Argentina. Another, Julianna, was cared for by her grandmother in a middle-class family in the Dominican Republic. The other three are Puerto Rican women who grew up in the United States and whose backgrounds ranged from working- to upper-middle-class; among these women, the degree of assimilation varied markedly depending on whether Spanish was their first language, the degree of contact with other Latinas, and the extent to which they identified as Puerto Ricans.

What the Latina women learned about weight and size was influenced by nationality. Julianna, who grew up in a small town in the Dominican Republic, was taught that

> people don't think that fat is bad. You don't undermine fat people. You just don't. . . . The picture of a woman is not a woman who has a perfect body that you see on TV. A woman is beautiful because she is a virgin or because she is dedicated to her husband or because she takes care of her kids; because she works at home and does all the things that her husband and family want her to do. But not because she is skinny or fat.

In the Dominican Republic, female beauty is closely linked to being a good wife and mother and obeying gendered expectations about virginity and monogamy. Thinness is not a necessary criterion for beauty, regardless of a woman's class. By contrast, the Argentinian woman, Elsa, said that a woman's weight was the primary criterion for judging her worth. The diets and exercise her father enforced among his wife and daughters were "oppressive and Nazi-like." But judgments about weight varied with class and degree of urbanization:

> The only people who see being fat as a positive thing in Argentina are the very poor or the very rural people who still consider it a sign of wealth or health. But as soon as people move to the bigger cities and are exposed to the magazines and the media, dieting and figures become incredibly important.

None of the Puerto Rican women I talked with benefited from the acceptance of size that the Dominican woman described. Laura, who lived in Puerto Rico with her family for four years when she was a child, recalls that "Latina women were almost expected to be more overweight.

Latin women living in Puerto Rico were not uncomfortable with extra weight. To them it wasn't extra. It wasn't an issue." This didn't help Laura appreciate her own chunky size because her family's disdain for fat people was much more influential. Her father was British and her mother liked to "hang out with wealthy white women," both factors that impeded Laura's ability to adopt the Puerto Rican community's values.

Another Puerto Rican woman, Vera, who grew up in Chicago, was chunky as a child and learned that the people around her disapproved of her size. Vera remembers painful scenes at school and in clothing stores that taught her she should be embarrassed by her body size. Although she was an amazingly limber and energetic student in her ballet class, her mother took her out of it because Vera wasn't thin enough.

African-American Girls and Community Life

Rosalee grew up in Arkansas in a rural African-American community where, as she described it, "home grown and healthy" was the norm. She remembers that her uncles and other men liked a "healthy woman": as they used to say, "They didn't want a neck bone. They liked a picnic ham." Among the people in her community, skin color and hair were more important than weight in determining beauty. Unlike most of the other women I interviewed, Rosalee didn't think about dieting as a way to lose weight until she was a teenager. Because her family didn't always have money, "there were times when we hardly had food anyway so we tended to slim down. And then . . . when the money was rolling in . . . we celebrated. We ate and ate and ate." When poverty is a constant threat, Rosalee explained, "dieting just isn't a household word." This did not stop Rosalee from developing an eating problem when she was four years old as a response to sexual abuse and being a witness to beatings. Trauma, not size, was the primary factor.

Carolyn, a middle-class woman who grew up in an urban area, remembered that her African-American friends considered African-American women of varying weights to be desirable and beautiful. By contrast, among white people she knew, the only women who were considered pretty were petite. Both the white and the African-American men preferred white girls who were petite.

The women who went to schools in which there were only a few African-American students remember thinness as dominant. By contrast, those who went to racially mixed or predominantly African-American schools saw more acceptance of both big and thin women. . . .

The women who attended private, predominantly white schools were sent by parents who hoped to open up opportunities unavailable in public schools. As a consequence, both Nicole and Joselyn were isolated from other African-American children. Their parents discouraged them from socializing with neighborhood African-American children, who in turn labeled them arrogant, thus furthering their isolation. Both were teased by neighborhood children for being chubby and light-skinned. At school they were teased for being fat and were excluded by white people in ways both subtle and overt. Racist administrators and teachers granted the girls neither the attention nor the dignity they deserved. Joselyn, who attended Catholic schools, remembered both racial and religious intolerance: "Sister Margaret Anna told me that, basically, what a black person could aspire to at that time was to Christianize the cannibals in Africa." Neither Nicole nor Joselyn had a public context in which her racial identity was validated. As Nicole said, "By second or third grade I was saying I wished I was white because kids at school made fun of me. I remember . . . getting on the bus and a kid called me a brown cow." As the women were growing up, their weight and their race were used to ostracize them.

Intersection of Race and Class

Most of the African-American and Latina women were pressured to be thin by at least one and often all of their family members. For some, these pressures were particularly virulent because they were laced with racism. Rosalee, who grew up on a farm in the South, got contradictory messages about weight and size from her family. Like most of the African-Americans in her community, Rosalee's mother thought thin women were sickly and took her young daughters to the doctor because they weren't gaining enough weight. But her father told her she "had better not turn out fat like her mother." Rosalee and her mother often bore the brunt of his disdain as he routinely told them that African-American women were usually fatter and less beautiful than white women. Rosalee says:

> I can remember fantasizing that "I wish I was white." . . . It seemed to be the thing to be if you were going to be anything. You know, [white women] were considered beautiful. That was reinforced a lot by my father, who happened to have a strong liking for white women. Once he left the South and he got in the army and traveled around and had

> more freedom, he became very fond of them. In fact, he is married to one now. He just went really overboard. I found myself wanting to be like that.

Although she was not familiar with dieting as a child, she feared weight gain and her father's judgments. At puberty, she began to diet. Her father's sexism and prejudice against black women meant that she was raised with contradictory messages about weight. At the same time, she was learning about the dominant standard of beauty that emphasizes a fair complexion, blue eyes, and straight hair. About the lessons many black girls learn about straightening their hair and using lightening creams, Rosalee says:

> It was almost as if you were chasing after an impossible dream. I can remember stories about parents pinching their children's noses so they don't get too big. I laugh about it when I am talking about it with other people but on the inside I don't laugh at all. There is nothing there to reinforce who you are, and the body image gets really confused.

Some of the Latinas' and African-Americans' relatives projected their own frustrations and racial prejudices onto the girls' bodies. Joselyn, an African-American woman, remembers her white grandmother telling her she would never be as pretty as her cousins because they had lighter skin. Her grandmother often humiliated Joselyn in front of others, making fun of Joselyn's body while she was naked and telling her she was fat. As a young child Joselyn began to think that although she couldn't change her skin color, she could at least try to be thin.

When Joselyn was young, her grandmother was the only family member who objected to her weight. Then her father also began to encourage his wife and daughter to be thin as the family's social status began to change. When Joselyn was very young, her family was what she called "aspiring to be middle class." For people of Joselyn's parents' generation, having chubby, healthy children was a sign the family was doing well. But, as the family moved up the social ladder, Joselyn's father began to insist that Joselyn be thin:

> When my father's business began to bloom and my father was interacting more with white businessmen and seeing how they did business, suddenly thin became important. If you were a truly well-to-do family, then your family was slim and elegant.

Her grandmother's racism and her father's determined fight to be middle class converged, and Joselyn's body became the playing field for their conflicts. While Joselyn was pressured to diet, her father still served her large portions and bought treats for her and the neighborhood children. These contradictory messages confused her. Like many girls, Joselyn was told she was fat from the time she was very young, even though she wasn't. And, like many of the women I interviewed, Joselyn was put on diet pills and diets before puberty, beginning a cycle of dieting, compulsive eating, and bulimia. She remembers her father telling her, "You know you have a cute face, but from the body down, you are shot to hell. You are built just like your old lady."

Another African-American woman also linked contradictory messages about food to her parents' internalized racism. As Nicole explains it, her mother operated under the "house-nigger mentality," in which she saw herself and her family as separate from and better than other African-American people. Her father shared this attitude, saying that being Cherokee made him different. Her parents sent Nicole to private schools and a "very white Anglican upper-class church" in which she was one of a few black children. According to Nicole, both parents "passed on their internalized racism in terms of judgments around hair or skin color or how a person talks or what is correct or proper."

Their commandments about food and body size were played out on Nicole's body in powerful ways. Nicole's father was from a working-class rural Southern family. Her mother, by contrast, was from a "petit bourgeois family," only one of three black families in a small New Hampshire town. While Nicole's father approved of her being, as he said, "solid," her mother restricted her eating to ensure that Nicole would grow up thin. Each meal, however, was a multicourse event. Like Joselyn, Nicole was taught that eating a lot was a dangerous but integral part of the family tradition:

> When I was growing up, I thought that breakfast was a four- or five-course meal the way you might think dinner is. I thought that breakfast involved fruit and maybe even juice and cereal and then the main course of breakfast, which was eggs and bacon and toast. On Sundays we had fancy breakfasts like fish and hominy grits and corn bread and muffins. So breakfast had at least three courses. That is how we ate. Dinner was mostly meat and potatoes and vegetables and bread. Then my father would cajole my mother into making dessert. There were lots of rewards that all had to do with food, like going to Howard Johnson or Dunkin' Donuts.

At the same time, Nicole's mother put her on a diet when she was three and tortured her about her weight. Nicole became terrified of going to the doctor because she was weighed and lectured about her weight. Yet, after each appointment, her mother took her to Dunkin' Donuts for a powdered jelly doughnut. When her father did the grocery shopping, he bought Nicole treats, which her mother snatched and hid, accusing her father of trying to make her fat. When she was left alone, Nicole spent hours trying to find the food. In her mother's view, Nicole's weight and curly hair were what kept her from being perfect: her body became the contested territory onto which her parents' pain was projected.

The confusion about body size and class expectations that troubled some of the African-American women paralleled the experiences of two Puerto Rican women. Vera attributed her eating problems partly to the stress of assimilation as her family moved from poverty to the working class. When Vera was three, she was so thin that her mother took her to a doctor who prescribed appetite stimulants. By the time she was eight, though, she remembered her mother comparing her to other girls who stayed on diets or were thin. Vera attributed her mother's change of heart to pressure from family members:

> Even though our family went from poverty to working class, there were members of my extended family who thought they were better than everyone else. As I grew up, the conversation was, "Who is going to college? Who has a job working for Diamonds?" It was always this one-upmanship about who was making it better than who. The one-upmanship centered on being white, being successful, being middle class . . . and it was always, "Ay, Bendito [Oh, God]! She is so fat! What happened?"

Vera's mother warned her that she would never make friends if she was fat. Her mother threatened to get a lock for the refrigerator door and left notes on it reminding Vera not to eat. While Vera's mother shamed her into dieting, she also felt ambivalent when Vera did not eat much. When Vera dieted, her mother would say, "You have to eat. You have to eat something. You can't starve yourself." The messages were always unclear.

Ruthie also remembers changes in the family ethic about size and eating that she attributes to assimilation with Anglo culture. In keeping with Puerto Rican tradition, Ruthie's mother considered chubby children a sign of health and well-being. According to Puerto Rican culture, Ruthie says, "If you are skinny, you are dying. What is wrong with you?" When Ruthie was ten to twelve years old, her mother made her take a food supplement and iron pills that were supposed to make her hungry. Ruthie did not like the supplement and felt fine about the size of her body. But how Ruthie looked was very important to her mother: "My mother used to get these dresses from Spain. She used to show everyone our closets. They were impeccable. Buster Brown shoes and dresses. She thought if I were skinny it would reflect badly on her." Ruthie questioned whether her mother cared about Ruthie or was actually worried about what the family and neighbors would say. When Ruthie became a teenager, her mother's attitude about weight changed:

> When I was little, it was not okay to be skinny. But then, at a certain age, it was not okay to be fat. She would say, "Your sister would look great in a bikini and you wouldn't." I thought maybe this was because I felt fat. . . . Being thin had become something she valued. It was a roller coaster.

Ruthie attributed this change to her mother's acceptance of Anglo standards, which she tried to enforce on Ruthie's eating and body size.

The women's experiences dispel the notion that African-American and Latina women—as a group—are less exposed to or influenced by a culturally imposed thinness than white women. The African-American women who saw community acceptance of different sizes did not escape pressure to be thin from family members. While growing up in a rural area and attending predominantly black schools did protect two of the girls from pressures to diet, childhood traumas resulted in eating problems. For the women of color whose parents' internalized racism, an emphasis on thinness was particularly intense. Rosalee explains:

> For a black woman dealing with issues of self-esteem, if you don't get it from your family, you [are punished] twice because you don't get self-esteem from society either. If you come from a dysfunctional or abusive family, there [are] just not a lot of places to go that will turn things around for you.

This reality underscores why some women of color may be more, rather than less, vulnerable than white women to eating problems.

White Girls in Their Families and Communities

As is true of the women of color, ethnic, religious, and national diversity among white women makes it difficult to generalize about a monolithic socialization process. With the exception of a Sephardic Jewish woman who grew up outside the United States, none of the white women

I talked with escaped pressure to diet and be thin. Ethnic and religious identity, however, did influence their eating patterns and their attitudes about their bodies. Anti-Semitism and ethnic prejudice shaped the way some of the girls interpreted strictures about weight and eating. Like most of the women of color, the white women had little access to communities in which women of different sizes were valued. Messages that white girls received both in their homes and in their communities promoted dieting and thinness.

All of the American Jewish women I interviewed were taught that they needed to be thin. Although none were fat as children, all had parents who were afraid they would become fat and took what they saw as precautions. One family bought only enough food for one day at a time, reasoning that they would not overeat if no "extra" food was available. Two Jewish women who went to predominantly Protestant schools said belonging to a religious minority exacerbated pressures about body size. Both felt like outsiders because they were Jewish, and their Protestant classmates perceived them as talking, dressing, and looking different.

As for many of the Latinas and African-American women, the discrimination Jewish children experienced was most overt when they were in the minority. Sarah learned that some of her Protestant classmates thought that Jewish people had horns. Both Sarah and Gilda were called names and excluded from friendship groups. Gilda, who is a Sephardic Jew, remembers that when she began to attend school in the United States, other children spit on her and called her "kike." . . . Children in the United States called her father the "Tasmanian devil" and made fun of her accent. The Jewish girls coped with discrimination by minimizing the ways they felt different from or inferior to others, including trying to hide their body sizes. Sarah explained that "in the school I attended, where I was only one of a handful of Jewish kids, I never felt like I fit in. I didn't have the right clothes, I didn't look the right way. I didn't come from the right family." When she was as young as eleven, Sarah began to feel "that I had to lose weight or that something wasn't right." Although she wasn't fat, in her mind, she was.

Of the five Jewish women, Gilda—who grew up in North Africa and France before settling in the United States—was the only one exposed to a wholehearted acceptance of food. For Gilda's father, who was raised in North Africa, family meals were a central, celebrated aspect of maintaining North African and Jewish culture:

> First of all food and Friday night and Shabbes. Friday night for my father is a very important time. . . . We have a traditional [North

> African] meal with vegetables and different salads and [North African] spices. The whole flavor, the whole mood of the evening is not American at all. On holidays, Passover, we read the Haggadah in French, Arabic, Hebrew, and English. By page thirty, you are ready to die of hunger and exhaustion.

Eating together as a family was an important aspect of this tradition. Although Gilda learned that being a very thin child was not acceptable and that eating was a primary way her father celebrated his culture and religion, she remembered her mother always being on a diet, even though she was never more than slightly overweight. Gilda's father became angry with her when, as an adolescent, Gilda refused to eat with the family and did not keep kosher meals. Contradictory messages from her father and mother and differences between North African and U.S. standards caused confusion about weight and size.

The white women who were raised in Christian families were taught that being thin was crucial for females. Dawn, a middle-class white woman raised in a strict Catholic family, was taught from a young age that "a woman's worth was in her size." Antonia's ideas about eating and weight were deeply affected by her Italian-American ethnic identity. Like some of the Jewish women and women of color, Antonia felt like an outsider at school from kindergarten on, a feeling that was compounded by thinking she was overweight. At school she learned that to be accepted socially, she had to look and act like the "WASPs"—to have straight blond hair and be passive and quiet. She remembers that "I used to get called loud. I talked a lot. Very active. And I was very aggressive. I used to wrestle with the boys a lot. I stood out from other people." Because she was fat, she was often humiliated by other children at school. One of the boys called her "taters" (a big potato). At a high school prom fund-raiser—a "slave auction," where girls were auctioned off—"when it was my turn, no one was bidding. To this day, . . . I can't even really remember the actual sequence of events. It was just the most humiliating thing in my life." When Antonia was eleven, her mother put her on a diet and a doctor prescribed amphetamines. During adolescence she tried to diet but her heart was not in it. In her mind, no amount of dieting would take away her assertive, emotional, and athletic ways, so what was the point in trying to lose weight anyway?

Grooming Girls to Be Heterosexual

While messages to girls about their bodies and appetites are shaped by race, class, ethnicity, and religion, no such diversity exists when it comes to learning about heterosexuality. In both subtle and overt ways, girls—across race, class, ethnicity, and religion—learn that being heterosexual is natural and inevitable. These expectations add up to what poet and writer Adrienne Rich has termed "compulsory heterosexuality": a largely invisible but enormously powerful force that orchestrates the range of what is considered acceptable female sexuality.[1] Elements of this enforced heterosexuality include pressure to marry and have children, male control of female sexuality, and an economic system that makes it difficult for many women to support themselves without marrying—plus prejudice and discrimination against gay men and lesbians and limitations on how emotionally close people of the same gender can be without facing reprisals. As girls reach their teenage years, they are punished if their friendships with other girls become intimate. They are also expected to show an interest in the opposite sex. As Johnnetta Cole writes, women in the United States are "being measured against an objectified notion of female sexuality which is eternally young, never fat but 'well developed,' heterosexual, submissive to 'her man,' and capable of satisfying him sexually. It is striking how this ideal image cuts across racial, ethnic and class lines."[2]

The idea that heterosexuality is a necessary condition of "normal development" is often not overt or explicit unless girls begin to show signs of not being sufficiently heterosexual. For example, a Puerto Rican lesbian told me:

> My mother would say, there is nothing you can't do, if you want. But yet, in other subtle ways, she would encourage me to be a nurse. She wouldn't come right out and say, you can't be a doctor. She'd say I was supposed to be ladylike.

Being ladylike and having a traditionally female career was a prerequisite for marriage. Being thin was also integral to this heterosexual expectation.

All of the women I interviewed were taught that heterosexuality was essential. Many traced strictures about their bodies and appetites partly to this imperative. Implicit messages were commonly conveyed in the form of how girls were expected to look, how they were permitted to use their bodies athletically, how they should dress, and how much they were allowed to eat. For many girls, these rules were most fiercely applied as they approached puberty. Tomboys who grew up riding bicycles, playing handball, and wrestling with boys were often summarily reprimanded as they approached puberty. As they were informed that they should start wearing dresses and go to the junior high dances, they were also encouraged to "eat like a lady" and pass up second helpings. In some families, boys were allowed to eat all they wanted while girls were not.

The rationale for this double standard was that girls should be smaller than boys in order to be attractive to the opposite sex. Some girls remembered hating these restrictions. They missed being physically active, and they resented having to get by with less food.

As they approached their teen years, many were taught that having boyfriends depended upon being thin. One African-American woman remembers initiating her first self-imposed diet because her boyfriend liked thin women. All of his sisters encouraged it, too. When an Argentinean woman was eleven years old her mother told her, "You should really make an effort and diet. You won't be popular around the boys. You are going to have trouble finding a husband. You look terrible. What a pity. You have a nice face but look at your figure." Laura, a Puerto Rican woman, remembers her mother and father both teaching her that she needed to lose weight or run the risk of being an "old maid." Integral to her socialization was the message that being successful heterosexually depended upon being thin:

> One day when I was eleven my parents and I were sitting on the beach in Puerto Rico. There was this blond woman walking down the beach with about ten men around her. She was in a bikini and my father and mother said, "She is not very attractive but she is thin. Look at all those men around her." They pointed out this other woman, who was heavy. She was by herself. She had a very beautiful face. They said, "See, she is beautiful. But she is not thin. She is by herself." It was right out front. That began at eleven years old. You are worthless unless you are thin.

The lessons about heterosexuality often went hand in hand with lessons about weight and dieting. Not surprisingly, those who questioned their heterosexuality at a young age were often best able to identify how these strictures reinforced each other. One of the characteristics of dominant ideology—including compulsory heterosexuality—is that it is understood as significant only when it is transgressed. This is also the power of dominant ideology, since it is often consciously felt only by those who contest it, who are encouraged—and sometimes forced—to accept it. For example, one woman who was not interested in boys during high school and had crushes on girls remembers that the "in group" of girls at school constantly talked about their boyfriends, diets, and losing weight. She partly wanted to be like them and thought that dieting would make her feel included in their friendship circle. Another woman's grandmother and mother taught her that "if you were thin, then all of your problems should be erased. You could be happily married, you could satisfy a man, anything you wanted could be yours if only you could be thin."

None of the girls grew up in homes where heterosexuality was questioned. This taken-for-granted aspect of their socialization meant that all the models for sexuality pivoted on attracting men; there were no alternatives. Consequently, there was no room for the idea that women's appetites and body sizes could be defined according to their own standards rather than norms based on rigid definitions of masculinity and femininity. . . .

American Dreams and Unsatisfied Hungers

The childhood lessons that African-American, Latina, and white women learn illuminate pressures about body size and appetites that have not yet been examined in research or focused on by the media. Jewish and black parents may assume that although they cannot protect their daughters from anti-Semitism and racism, encouraging thinness at least shields them from discrimination against fat people. An African-American or Latino parent who tells a child not to eat and then feeds her confuses the child as she learns to feed herself, yet the feeding may also indicate a cultural tradition of nurturing through food. When a Puerto Rican mother gives her five-year-old daughter a food supplement to make her gain weight, then ridicules her when she gains weight as an adolescent, pressures of assimilation may account for the mother's change of heart.

To understand why a girl's relatives want her to be thin, we need to know what forms of economic, racial, ethnic, and religious discrimination they have encountered. Underlying an attempt to make a girl thin is an often unspoken assumption that while the family might not be financially stable, or it cannot fully shield her from racism, or it does not speak English without an accent, her small size may make her life and theirs somewhat easier. Some African-American women and Latinas I interviewed related pressure to be thin to their parents' hopes to be middle class, and middle-class standing depended upon upholding this aesthetic. The dual strain of changing class expectations and racism may explain why some of the women of color linked an emphasis on thinness to class pressures while the white women did not. Class does not, by itself, determine whether or not the women were expected to be thin. Supposing that it does implies that poor women—both women of color and white women—are somehow culturally "out of the loop," an assumption that is both demeaning and inaccurate. But changes in class did fuel some parents' desire to control their daughters' appetites.

Pressures on parents do not justify their attempts to mold their daughters' bodies, but understanding why women across race and class develop eating problems requires clarifying what constitutes the "culture" in the culture-of-thinness model. Many people accept the notion that body size is, in fact, something that can be controlled, given enough self-discipline. This ideology makes dieting appear to be a logical strategy. When caretakers demand that their daughters be thin, some may do so believing that they have more control over weight than over other more complex and insidious forces that they have little power to change.

Doing justice to the social context in which eating problems arise also explains why the culture-of-thinness model needs to be considered along with other destructive social forces. Although thinness is an institutionally supported criterion for beauty, imperatives about age, color, and sexuality matter as well. An often-cited 1980 study documents the emergence of the culture of thinness by showing a marked decrease in the weight of centerfold models in *Playboy* magazine and the winners of the Miss America Pageant between 1959 and 1978.[3] This study quantifies a relationship between the social emphasis on thinness and the increase in eating problems but does not point out that, until recently, women in *Playboy* and the Miss America Pageant have been almost exclusively white, young, and heterosexual. Although the study shows that both the magazine and the pageant support a tyranny of slenderness, an integrated analysis would also elucidate tyranny based on the glorification of whiteness, youth, heterosexuality, and able-bodiedness. An expansive understanding of socialization requires scrutiny of the power of racism and classism as they inform standards of appearance. While white skin will not protect a fat woman from weight discrimination, it does protect her from racial discrimination. The resilience of the stereotype of the fat black "mammy" shows the futility and damage of considering standards of beauty as simply gendered. Interpreting socialization inclusively shows the myriad pressures affecting girls' opinions of their bodies. This approach also paves the way for seeing why girls—across race, class, religion, and ethnicity—may turn to food as a reaction to injustice.

Notes

1. Adrienne Rich, "Compulsory Heterosexuality and Lesbian Existence," in *Blood, Bread, and Poetry* (New York: Norton, 1986).
2. Johnnetta Cole, ed., *All American Women* (New York: Free Press, 1986), pp. 15–16.
3. D. Garner, P. Garfinkel, D. Schwartz, and M. Thompson, "Cultural Expectations of Thinness," *Psychological Reports* 47 (1980): 483–91.

4 Women of a Certain Age

LAURA L. CARSTENSEN

MONISHA PASUPATHI

> The whole meaning of our lives is in question. If we do not know what we are going to be, we cannot know what we are. Let us recognize ourselves in this old man or that old woman. It must be done if we are to take upon ourselves the entirety of our human state.[1]

Medicare, social security, national health insurance, nursing-home placement, and other pressing issues are receiving increasing attention in the media. Rarely do we hear them framed as "women's issues." On the contrary, age is treated as the great equalizer—men and women, rich and poor, regardless of background, escape old age only through premature death. It is true that both women and men suffer the biological deterioration that advanced age brings, and both men and women face ageist stereotypes and misconceptions. Both men and women experience loss with age.

Aging, however, is not a process that occurs evenly for women and men in the United States. In this chapter we will review briefly some basic facts that distinguish older women from older men, illustrate the impact of these differences in everyday life, and suggest ways people might modify the inevitability of deleterious outcomes and the course of their own aging process.

The Facts

The fact that our elderly population is rapidly growing has become common knowledge. During the twentieth century, the proportion of elderly people in the population grew from 3 percent to 12 percent.[2] By the year 2040, 23 percent of the population will be over 65.[3] However, the fact that *most* of these people are women is largely ignored. At 65, women outnumber men by 100 to 83; by 85, women outnumber men by 100 to 39.[4] The over-85 age segment is the fastest growing segment of the population. Indeed, "the world of the very old is a world of women."[5]

These population statistics reflect the fact that women outlive men by about seven years. For reasons as yet unknown, the survivability of females is greater than males from conception on. The average life expectancy for white women in the United States is 79; for men it is 72. For most ethnic minorities in the United States, life expectancy is lower. For black women, the average life expectancy is 73 years; for black men it is 64 years. The difference of roughly seven years between men and women in longevity holds across ethnic groups.

In part because of the difference in longevity and in part because women traditionally marry older men, women are far more likely than men to be widowed in old age. In fact, even though 95 percent of Americans marry at some point during their lives, only 35 percent of women over 65 are married. After 85, only 21 percent of women are married. Moreover, when men *are* widowed, they are four times more likely to remarry than women who are widowed. For women, the average length of widowhood is 15 years; once widowed, women are at high risk for a number of age-related problems.

It is important to note that the jeopardy widowed women face is not the result of being without a man, but from widowhood itself. Women who have always been single fare much better than widows in late life; they are better off financially[6] and less likely to be depressed or lonely. Very little is known about older lesbians, but they are included in statistics about single women. Also included among single women are women who live in religious communities. Nuns enjoy a life expectancy six years longer than the average woman in the United States. Thus, it is not being *single* that puts women at risk; it is, as we will illustrate, the result of a complex system of structural inequities that exploit all women and especially married women.

Living alone is a risk factor for a number of negative outcomes in old age and widowed women are far more likely to live alone than other older people. Most men live out their lives living with a spouse in the community. Among elderly men, 76 percent of whites, 66 percent of Hispanics, and 63 percent of blacks live with a spouse. Among elderly women, these percentages are substantially lower—41 percent of whites, 35 percent of Hispanics, and 27 percent of blacks live with a spouse.[7]

Twenty-five percent to 30 percent of older people will reside in nursing homes at some point in their lives.[8] These facilities are virtual worlds of women. Seventy-five percent of nursing-home residents are female.

Not surprisingly, older women are more likely than older men to be poor. Twenty-five percent of elderly white women are poor. Much higher poverty rates are found among minority women.

One more statistic—we hear a fair amount these days about caregivers of the elderly, what we don't hear is that the caregivers of the elderly are, for the most part, elderly women.

A Case Study

What do these numbers really mean for the lives of elderly women? Consider the following scenario, a story that is more common than most of us would like to admit.

Married since 1947, Helen and Paul—a white American, middle-class couple—are expecting to spend a relaxed and satisfying old age together. Paul retired from his engineering job a year ago with a good pension. Helen had worked on and off over the years in a day-care center. Because she worked only part time at a relatively low-paying job, she has not accrued any retirement benefits, but she does qualify for social security. Between Paul's pension and the couple's social-security benefits, they feel relatively secure and optimistic about their future. Their two sons, Michael and Robert, are both married and live out of state with children of their own. Both sons have jobs they like. Neither makes a lot of money, but they manage to make ends meet. Helen and Paul see their grandchildren once or twice a year and enjoy frequent telephone contact with them.

About one year after Paul retires, he begins to behave peculiarly. Always an active person, he now seems anxious in conversations with old friends and spends more and more time alone. One day Helen finds a note in Paul's pocket that gives directions from their house to the market only six blocks away. When she asks him what the instructions are for, he gets angry and accuses her of invading his privacy. During the next two months she finds him to be increasingly forgetful. Occasionally, he acknowledges problems in performing familiar tasks, but usually he claims that it is "just old age."

One day, the doorbell rings. The local police bring Paul home. They tell Helen that they found Paul wandering in a park and that, while he could tell them his name, he could not remember his address. After looking up the address at the police station, the officers brought Paul home. They suggest to Helen that she take him to a physician for a thorough medical evaluation.

Helen calls Dr. Frierson, their longtime physician, and makes an appointment. After a lengthy workup, he informs Helen that Paul appears to be in the early stages of Alzheimer's disease, a chronic debilitating disease that ultimately ends in death. Helen is devastated, but is determined to do the best she can to make sure that Paul lives out his life as comfortably as possible.

Paul gets worse and worse. He has difficulty with basic grooming and bathing. She can dress him, but cannot bathe him without assistance. Paul is a large man and Helen cannot physically lift him. She hires help to come in three times a week to help Paul shower, but the aides quit regularly and Helen is forced to hire new people and sometimes go without assistance. Besides, she is quickly spending their savings to pay aides. As time passes, Paul loses the ability to tell night from day. He gets up many times throughout the night and wakes Helen. During the day, he naps frequently, but Helen cannot do the same. It is unusual for Helen to sleep more than three hours a night. She feels that she cannot afford to hire someone to stay in the evenings. She becomes increasingly depressed and physically exhausted.

Helen rarely sees her friends. She cannot bring Paul out with her because he becomes agitated in unfamiliar places. Her friends feel for her, but are uncomfortable coming to the house. It's hard for them to see Paul and, in some ways, Helen prefers that they stay away. Michael and Robert call regularly. They are obviously concerned for her so she tries to minimize the gravity of the situation. Susan, her daughter-in-law, tries especially hard to help. She even stops working full-time so that she can visit once a month and alleviate some of the burden, but she has young children so she cannot stay more than a day or two.

When Paul becomes incontinent, Helen realizes that she can no longer manage him at home. She looks at several nursing homes. Some are horrible—understaffed and overcrowded. Eventually, she finds a nice place where the staff are kind, the food is good, and Paul can have a room with a view of the park. They had saved about $200,000 toward their retirement so Helen feels that she can afford a decent place for him. The cost of the nursing home is $40,000 a year. Helen assumes that her insurance will pay some of the nursing-home costs, but is told that less than 5 percent is covered. She decides that she has no choice, however, and admits Paul to the facility.

Helen visits every day even though Paul no longer recognizes her. She cannot stay away. She loves Paul very much and this is the only way left for her to show her love. Medicare pays for 80 percent of Paul's medical treatment, but virtually nothing toward the nursing-home expenses. She inquires about Medicaid, but is told that she has too much money to qualify for assistance. Rather, she must spend down their savings to $60,000 before Paul can qualify. Just a few years later, they qualify for Medicaid assistance. Seven years later, Paul dies.

Shortly after Paul's death Helen learns that Paul's pension pays only minimal survivor benefits. Helen, now 77 years old and alone, is living on far less income that she had anticipated. Her car engine fails one day. She decides to sell the car rather than pay the cost of repair. Then, one morning she slips on the sidewalk, breaks a hip, and is hospitalized. Her physician is pleased with her recovery progress and releases her after three weeks, but her cost of medical care, even with Medicare insurance, totals $40,000. Without savings to supplement her income, she can no longer make ends meet.

She considers asking her sons for financial assistance, but decides that the house is too big for her, anyway, and, after all, they have expenses of their own. She decides that if she sells the house, she can live more cheaply and perhaps leave some money for her grandchildren, as Paul had so hoped to do. She is surprised to see how high the rent is in her neighborhood. Eventually someone tells her about a housing unit, called the Rainbow House, in the center of the city and takes an apartment there.

In some ways, life is better now. Her financial concerns are somewhat alleviated and she is proud that she is not a burden on her children. She does not let them visit because she doesn't want them to see her apartment. It might concern them to see the neighborhood and she doesn't want to worry them. With her old furniture, her apartment is fairly comfortable, but the neighborhood is quite dangerous. Her friends from the old neighborhood telephone occasionally, but they do not visit. She leaves the building only when necessary. Unfortunately, Helen feels that she has nothing in common with the other tenants.

Helen's long-standing cardiac arrhythmia worsens. Normally, she would see her physician, but she can't get to Dr. Frierson without an expensive taxicab ride and she puts off finding a new physician in the neighborhood. Her diet is poor and, without exercise, her arthritis worsens.

One day, a worker from Adult Protective Services is called. A neighbor had reported that several newspapers had piled up outside Helen's door. The worker finds Helen weak and disoriented. She urges her to move into a state-funded nursing home nearby. When Michael and Robert find out how sick Helen is they want to help, but neither can afford to do very much. Michael visits once, but it breaks his heart to see his mother in the condition she is in and he never returns. Five years later, at the age of 85, Helen dies.

The Issues

Sound extreme? Probably the worst thing you can do is to think that this cannot happen to you. A major part of the problem is that, in our society, older women and their problems are invisible. We are just beginning to fully realize the problems older people face. Only rarely do we hear that these issues are especially relevant to women. Instead, we hear in the media that older people wield more power than any other age group, are draining the social-security system, and hold positions of power. True, the U.S. government is a gerontocracy, but it is extremely important to realize that the power age affords is not evenly distributed across gender, class, or ethnicity.

Even aspects of aging that on the surface affect men and women equally, do not. For example, the incidence of Alzheimer's disease is equal for men and women, but since the chances increase with age, and women live longer, more women develop it. Moreover, because husbands are typically older than wives, elderly women are far more likely to care for a spouse who has dementia.

As our case study illustrates, caregiving takes its toll in many ways, affecting both physical and mental health. A large amount of literature documents the considerable physical and mental strain of caregiving.[9] Luck and fate may have some impact on who gets ill in old age, but they do not determine who becomes a caregiver. The vast majority of unpaid caregivers are women.[10] Wives care for their husbands; elderly daughters care for elderly mothers. The path of responsibility does not just flow directly down through bloodlines and generations. In families where there are only sons, daughters-in-law provide care. When daughters-in-law are not available, the burden is likely to fall on a granddaughter or niece. Only rarely are caregiving responsibilities assumed by sons.[11]

Interestingly, when husbands do become caregivers, their experience is different from that of wives. For one, when husbands provide caregiving, they often receive help from other relatives and friends or hire professional help.[12] When women provide caregiving, they are reluctant to seek *any* help. Instead, they often try to protect other loved ones from the burden that they bear.[13] Subsequently, caregiving is typically more stressful for women than men.[14] The extent of the stress is evidenced in the fact that 50 percent of caregivers become clinically depressed.[15]

The cornerstone of the U.S. Department of Health and Human Services social policy is that caregiving falls in the private domain and is supported by the government *only as a last resort.*[16] Despite the fact that home-based care is relatively cheap, Congress imposes major restrictions on this funding, which forces families—in most cases, women—to provide an abundance of unpaid labor in order to provide home care. It is their only alternative to institutionalization of loved ones.[17]

In our story, Helen's daughter-in-law, Susan, helped her the most, compromising her career to do so. As noted above, this is common and occurs for a variety of reasons at different points in the life cycle. Young women often make career concessions by working part time or taking years off to care for children. Later in life, women often retire early to care for ailing spouses, parents, or siblings. Social security penalizes women for these work patterns. Because social-security benefits are based on income, working part time or taking years off reduces social-security entitlements.

The insidiousness of the disadvantages for women is apparent in two ways. First, since wives usually make less than husbands, they are the logical candidates for career compromises. Second, those compromises reduce the likelihood that they will accrue private pension benefits to supplement their already lower social security. Subsequently, elderly women are far more likely than elderly men to rely exclusively on minimal social security benefits. Elderly women receive approximately 24 percent less than elderly men in social-security benefits *and* have less private supplemental income.[18]

You can see the beginning of this process in our story when Susan begins working part time to help Helen. In the unwritten epilogue, Susan reaches old age having only worked part time. Subsequently, under current regulations, she will be entitled to lower social-security benefits. Moreover, as a widow, she will not have a private pension and will very likely live at poverty level. Sadly, even young women today who work for most of their lives, will receive comparable retirement benefits to their mothers who were never employed.[19]

With Paul's illness, Helen's financial difficulties worsened considerably. A couple's entire life savings can be quickly exhausted providing medical intervention for a spouse, leaving a widow destitute. When

Medicaid is required to pay for health care, as is the case in the vast majority of nursing-home placements, assets must be spent down before eligibility requirements are met.[20] Again, because of the shorter life span and accompanying morbidity of men, women are more likely to be left destitute after the death of their husbands. Interestingly, widowed women are worse off financially than single and divorced women.[21]

Many women come to old age poor, but others, like Helen, become poor for the first time in their lives in old age. A cogent argument can be made that public policy surrounding old age is inherently discriminatory because it fails to take into account the cumulative economic disadvantages women bring to old age. The poverty of old age is especially intractable due to very limited opportunities to generate more income.[22]

Among minorities, poverty is far more widespread than among whites. Over *half* of black and Hispanic elderly females not living with their families are living at or below poverty level.[23] These alarming statistics are not simply an artifact of past eras. It is estimated that 25 percent of young women today will live at or near the poverty level in old age.

Living alone increases the likelihood of institutionalization because no one is available to assist in daily care. Poverty drastically limits the available options for nursing homes or board-and-care facilities. Again, women are more likely than men to experience the consequences. In people 85 and over, one in four women lives in a nursing home, whereas only one in seven men lives in a nursing home.[24] The quality of nursing homes ranges from excellent to very poor and, not surprisingly, high quality care inevitably requires money. Here again we are confronted with the cumulative discrepancies between men and women in financial security garnered across the life span.

Less obvious are the combined ramifications of poverty and widowhood. For example, the health of low-income patients with heart disease is more likely to worsen[25] and, if they live alone, they are almost twice as likely to suffer another heart attack.[26] Once again, women are more likely to experience both risk factors.

Double jeopardy refers to being old and female; *triple jeopardy* refers to being a member of a minority group, as well. The terms are problematic because they imply that the problems are additive when, in fact, the problems older black women face are qualitatively different from those older white women face.[27] But they are fitting in suggesting that problems are greater for minority elderly. Reading the case study in this chapter, you may have felt that we were presenting the worst-case scenario. Not so. We provided you with a case study about people who had come to old age privileged in many ways. Helen and Paul were white and middle-class. They planned for their retirement, saved thousands of dollars, and enjoyed excellent health care. To many Americans, these are luxuries.

Virtually every risk factor we have discussed is greater for minority elderly. For example, non-Hispanic blacks and Puerto Ricans are the least likely groups to have private health insurance.[28] Sixty-four percent of black women living alone live below the poverty level.[29] Elderly blacks are twice as likely as elderly whites to report fair or less than fair health.[30]

In addition to problems that result from a lifetime of disadvantage, elderly minorities are more likely to face the disadvantages of more current social crises. In the midst of a drug epidemic, which is hitting the inner-city particularly hard, black grandmothers have become the most likely caregivers for grandchildren whose parents have become addicted to drugs.[31] Native American grandparents are also increasingly likely to assume primary caretaking roles for grandchildren, for reasons ranging from the desire to preserve native culture to the drug dependency of parents.[32]

The picture we have painted is, indeed, pessimistic. If there is a positive element to this at all it is that, despite the problems, older women are doing quite well psychologically. For some reason, they are less likely to be depressed[33] or lonely[34] than their younger counterparts. Instead, reading the literature on aging invokes the adage "what doesn't kill you makes you stronger." Older women appear to have impressive resilience despite the uneven odds.

The labeling of older women as a *special* or *needy* population is ironic. Older women, by and large, face the cumulative disadvantages of life-long discrimination and, *in spite of that*, cope reasonably well. The problem is not a needy population; rather, the problem stems from massive structural inequities. Government policy does not adequately address the concerns of minorities, women, or elderly people. Those inadequacies in policy translate into cumulative disadvantages that are dramatically evident in old age.

In theory, the inequities can be changed. The first step is to recognize the problem. Subsequent steps fall in two domains: personal planning and political restructuring. We offer the following suggestion: At the individual level, women must plan for their futures. Find out about health-insurance policies, survivor benefits, and retirement income. Plan for an old age without a spouse. Most women do not think about widowhood until they are nearing old age even though only a small minority of married women live out their lives with their spouses. Carefully think through alternative living arrangements. The second domain involves public policy. Write letters to state and local representatives. Insist on a national health-insurance plan. Affordable health care is possible if it is made a national priority. Medicaid laws can be changed to reduce the inherent discrimination toward women. We can reduce the likelihood of problems if we become informed about the future.

We need to act. Older women, who have a lifetime of experience on which to draw, may be our best spokespersons. We'll leave you with a last word from Maggie Kuhn, founder of the Gray Panthers:

> What can we do? Those of us who have survived to this advanced age? We can think and speak, we can remember. We can give advice, and make judgments. We can dial the phone, write letters and read. We may not be able to butter our bread, but we can still change the world.[35]

Notes

1. S. de Beauvoir, *The Coming of Aging* (New York: Putnam, 1972), 12.
2. National Center for Health Statistics, *Vital and Health Statistics: Current Estimates from the National Health Interview Survey, 1990* (DHHS Publication No. PHS 92-1509) (Washington, D.C.: U.S. Government Printing Office, 1991).
3. Special Committee on Aging, United States Senate, *Aging America: Trends and Projections* (Serial No. 101-E) (Washington, D.C.: U.S. Government Printing Office, 1989).
4. Ibid.
5. G. Hagestad, "The Family: Women and Grandparents as Kinkeepers," in *Our Aging Society: Paradox and Promise*, ed. A. Pifer and L. Bronte (New York: W. W. Norton, 1986), 147.
6. Special Committee on Aging, 1989.
7. Ibid.
8. C. Lesnoff-Caravaglia, "The Five Percent Fallacy," *International Journal of Aging and Human Development* 2 (1978–79): 187–192.
9. D. E. Biegel, E. Sales, and R. Schulz, *Family Caregiving in Chronic Illness* (Newbury Park, Calif.: Sage Publications, 1991); L. George and L. P. Gwyther, "Caregiver Well-being: A Multidimensional Examination of Family Caregivers of Demented Adults," *The Gerontologist* 26 (1986): 253–259; and D. Gallagher, J. Rose, P. Rivera, S. Lovett, and L. Thompson, "Prevalence of Depression in Family Caregivers," *The Gerontologist* 29 (1989): 449–456.
10. S. E. England, S. M. Keigher, B. Miller, and N. Linsk, "Community Care Policies and Gender Justice," in *Critical Perspectives on Aging: The Political and Moral Economy of Growing Old*, ed. M. Minkler and C. Estes (Amityville, N.Y.: Baywood Publishing, 1991), 227–244.
11. A. Horowitz, "Sons and Daughters as Caregivers to Older Parents:

Differences in Role Performance and Consequences," *The Gerontologist* 25 (1985): 612–617.
12. S. H. Zarit, N. K. Orr, and J. M. Zarit, *The Hidden Victims of Alzheimer's Disease: Families Under Stress* (New York: New York University Press, 1982).
13. Ibid.
14. A. S. Barusch and W. M. Spaid, "Gender Differences in Caregiving: Why Do Wives Support Greater Burden?" *The Gerontologist* 29 (1989): 667–675.
15. Gallagher et al., 1989.
16. England et al., 1991.
17. Ibid.
18. T. Arendell and C. Estes, "Older Women in the Post-Reagan Era," in *Critical Perspectives on Aging: The Political and Moral Economy of Growing Old*, ed. Minkler and Estes, 209–226.
19. Older Women's League, "Heading for Hardship: Retirement Income for American Women in the Next Century," *Mothers' Day Report*, 1991.
20. Spend-down rules have changed a great deal over the last few years. As of 1992, states vary considerably in the level of assets individuals are allowed to keep before they are eligible for Medicaid assistance.
21. Special Committee on Aging, 1989.
22. G. J. Duncan, *Years of Poverty, Years of Plenty: The Changing Economic Fortunes of American Workers and Families* (Ann Arbor: Institute for Social Research, University of Michigan, 1984).
23. Special Committee on Aging, 1989.
24. American Association of Homes for the Aging, "Fact Sheet: Nursing Homes" (Washington, D.C.: 1991).
25. R. B. Williams, J. C. Barefoot, R. M. Califf, T. L. Haney, W. B. Saunders, D. B. Pryor, M. A. Hlatky, I. C. Siegler, and D. B. Mark, "Prognostic Importance of Social and Economic Resources Among Medically Treated Patients with Angiographically Documented Coronary Artery Disease," *New England Journal of Medicine* 267(4) (1992): 520–524.
26. R. B. Case, A. J. Moss, N. Case, M. McDermott, and S. Eberly, "Living Alone After Myocardial Infarction: Impact on Prognosis," *New England Journal of Medicine* 267(4) (January 22/29, 1992): 515–519.
27. P. L. Dressel, "Gender, Race and Class: Beyond the Feminization of Poverty in Later Life," in *Critical Perspectives on Aging: The Political and Moral Economy of Growing Old*, ed. M. Minkler and C. Estes (Amityville, N.Y.: Baywood Publishing, 1991).
28. National Center for Health Statistics, *Health United States 1990* (DHHS Publication No. PHS 91-1232) (Washington, D.C.: U.S. Government Printing Office, 1991).
29. Special Committee on Aging, 1989.
30. U.S. Department of Health and Human Services, 1990.

31. M. Minkler, "Forgotten Caregivers: Grandparents Raising Infants and Young Children in the Crack Cocaine Epidemic," *Symposium Presented at the 44th Annual Scientific Meeting of the GSA*, San Francisco (1991).
32. J. Weibel-Orlando, "Grandparenting Styles: Native American Perspectives," in *The Cultural Context of Aging: Worldwide Perspectives*, ed. J. Sokolovsky (New York: Bergin & Garvey Publishers, 1991), 109–125.
33. D. Blazer, "Depression in Late Life: An Update," in *Annual Review of Geriatrics and Gerontology*, ed. M. P. Lawton (New York: Springer, 1989), 197–215.
34. T. A. Revenson, "Social and Demographic Correlates of Loneliness in Late Life," *American Journal of Community Psychology* 12 (1984): 338–342.
35. M. Kuhn, *No Stone Unturned: The Life and Times of Maggie Kuhn* (New York: Ballantine, 1991), 212–213.

CHAPTER TWO

Embodied Selves

How does living in a female body affect women's lives? One look at the magazine covers at your local newsstand ought to convince you, "a lot." Psychology has only recently begun to explore questions of the social construction and politics of bodies. That is, the body has mostly been relegated to the domain of biology or "nature," reflecting the kind of mind-body dualism that has been so prevalent in Western thought. The influence of feminism on social scientific thinking has begun to radically change that. We are, after all, "embodied selves" and the articles in this chapter provide a small sampling of the range of topics that become important in the psychology of women, once the body is placed front and center.

We can start with the fetus before she is even born to see how important the body is to our understanding of what it *means* to be female. In the most biological sense, the female is the prototype for human-beings. That is, during gestation, without exposure to androgens (such as testosterone), fetuses will become female. Natalie Angier's piece, "Default Line," manages to combine both real, useful information about women's bodies with discussion of the social constructions and attitudes surrounding them. What we learn is that we have been wrong to believe that Eve sprung from Adam's rib. The biological fact is quite the opposite. The male is derived from the ancestral female. Why should this matter? Angier convinces us that it matters a lot. Even today, negative attitudes about women's bodies have evolved directly out of early religious and medical misinformation about the secondary, "problematic" nature of our feminine body parts. In addition to learning about the fascinating history of attitudes toward the vagina and its effluvia, you might take seriously the one bit of medical advice Angier offers. "Don't douche, ever, period, end of squirt bottle." Read carefully to find out why.

The next piece is by my colleague Barbara Frederickson and me, and represents a comprehensive theoretical approach to understanding women's subjective experience and mental health risks by focusing on the ways these can be understood as consequences of the objectification of the female body. We argue that in a culture that sexually objectifies the female body, girls and women are coaxed to internalize an observer's perspective on their physical selves. Doing so, we believe, increases their opportunities for shame and anxiety, reduces their experiences of non-self-conscious "peak motivational states," and diminishes their awareness of their own internal bodily states. Accumulations of these experiences may then help to account for some of the mental health risks that disproportionately affect women, such as depression, eating disorders, and sexual dysfunction. We close by briefly offering suggestions for helping to bolster girls and women against the negative consequences of sexual objectification.

Anyone with anything resembling a critical eye would likely argue that the epicenter of sexual objectification in our culture is the media. And indeed, it's popular these days to say that the impossible images of female bodily beauty presented on television and in magazines are in some way responsible for the epidemic of eating disorders and body shame seen in young women. Many essays have been written and several important films have been made critiquing the media for its objectification of women's bodies. (I recommend, for example, Sut Jhally's documentary *Dreamworlds II*, which vividly documents the sexual objectification and degradation of women in music videos.) But there has been relatively little beyond anecdotal evidence to support claims that the message and images about ideal beauty and sexuality promulgated by the media are harmful to women.

In "Women and Weight: Gendered Messages on Magazine Covers," Amy Malkin, Kimberly Wornian and Joan Chrisler report on a fascinating content analysis of popular women's and men's magazines, which they explored for gendered messages related to bodily appearance. Think about the messages that men's magazines deliver to them about how they can improve their lives. Now think about the messages that women's magazines deliver. Their analyses reveal that the overwhelming message presented on the covers of women's magazines is about improving one's life by changing one's physical apperance. No such messages were seen in the men's magazines this group studied. Also, contradictory messages appear on women's magazine covers. How often have you seen a headline such as "Thinner thighs in one week!" right next to a photograph of a delicious-looking chocolate layer cake "(recipe on page 124)" on the cover of a magazine?

My students have pointed out to me and have brought several examples to class that there are some newer magazines on the stands lately that seem to be targeting men for feelings of insecurity about their bodies much in the same way that women's fashion magazines have done for decades. This new crop of magazines offers tips for "better abs" or a "six-pack," implying that men's bodies are not acceptable as they are. Interestingly, however, they also are chock-full of sexually objectified images of *women*—apparently the prizes for successful body alteration. Indeed, more often than not the cover image on these magazines is of an impossibly large-breasted, thin-waisted, luxurious-haired woman. What do you think of this new trend? Is turn-about fair play? Or will such messages, now that they are being delivered to men, awaken us as a culture to the harm that they can do? Are such magazines destined to be as damaging to men's feelings of body satisfaction as it seems women's magazines have been to theirs? Time will tell. And more good research in this area is needed.

The final piece in this chapter on feminine embodiment takes a very different approach and considers the ways in which gender development gets "under our skin," impacting not only our attitudes and emotions, but the very ways our bodies move in space. "Throwing Like a Girl," by Iris Marion Young, is a philosophical treatise, and one that I'm sure will not be easy to digest. She proposes that girls and women are "doubled." That is, when making movements, many women's attention is split between being *inside* the body that must accomplish the movement (such as throwing) and being *outside* of it, observing as if second-hand. In other words, many women experience their bodies as *things* as well as capacities. What is her thesis about why this is the case? The Fredrickson and Roberts article offers an answer: When you look around you, and examine the non-verbal expressions of women and men (the last reading in this book, by Henley and LaFrance provides some excellent examples), do you agree with Young's thesis? What do you think are some real-world consequences of women's "limited spatiality"?

I hope the pieces in this chapter convince you that to neglect the body in our understanding of women's psychology is to settle for a very limited understanding indeed. Perhaps these readings can motivate you and your class to think beyond them to the very question of the orthodox binary of sex itself. What exactly is a woman? And how is such a creature different from a man? How does our cultural commitment to two and only two "natural" genders impact gender relations? If the body is, as these articles attempt to argue, a social construction, then the answer to the question "What is a woman?" isn't as easy as it first appears. But it's worth contemplating.

References

Jhally, S. (2002). *Dreamworlds II: Desire, Sex, Power in Music Video.* Media Education Foundation, Northampton MA.

5 Default Line: Is the Female Body a Passive Construct?

NATALIE ANGIER

One of the first things I noticed as I began shopping during pregnancy for baby ballast is that three decades after the birth of the current feminist movement, there is still no escaping the binary coding by color. Whether you're looking at clothes for newborns, for six-month-olds, or for that relatively recent store category, preemies, everything is either pink or blue. Maybe it's because the promiscuous use of sonograms and prenatal tests means that most people know the sex of their baby ahead of time, so there's little need to hedge your purchase even when buying a gift for a prenate. Whatever the reason, the emphasis on sartorial sex distinctions seems stronger than ever before. Just try finding an item of infant clothing that isn't trimmed or beribboned or beanimaled in either pink or blue, and you'll realize how limited your fashion options are. Oh, here it is, the lone ungendered baby outfit: a yellow T-shirt with a picture of a duck on it. . . .

. . . [I]f there's one thing about the pink-blue dichotomy that annoys me, it's the unidirectional manner in which we sometimes let it slide. It's fine to dress a girl in blue, but think about pink on a boy. Think hard about subjecting your son to girl clothes. Think about dressing him in a pink T-shirt, and even you, my most rad-chic mother, will hesitate and, in compromise, reach instead for the yellow shirt with the duck on it. None of this is surprising or limited to babies, of course. A woman can wear stovepipe trousers or blue jeans or a farmer's bib or tails and a top hat and so what—she's just exercising her options as a consumer; but if a man puts on a skirt he'd better be ready to pick up a bagpipe and blow. We've known this for years, but it's still a nuisance to know it. "I guarantee that even if you were given a case of free diapers and they happened to be pink, you would use them for gift wrapping before you would put them on your firstborn *son*," Vicki Iovine writes in her very amusing book, *The Girlfriends' Guide to Pregnancy*. "It's an illness, I know, and we could all keep our therapists busy for weeks over this issue of gender stereotypes, but it's the truth." When I first read that line, I thought in irritation, She wouldn't say that about using a box of free *blue* diapers for your firstborn *daughter*; yet I knew that for all her flippant shoulder-shrugging, Iovine was right. You don't dress your first or second or twelfth-born son in pink diapers, unless you are a mother in a Hollywood horror movie who will soon be revealed as having Medea-sized intentions.

So what exactly are we afraid of when we fear polluting a boy with pink? Are we worried that we might turn him gay? The evidence strongly suggests that sexual orientation has little or nothing to do with one's upbringing, and in any event gay sons love their mothers, so what's the problem there? Is it the usual misogyny, the association of masculine with "fully human" and "quality controlled," and feminine with "circa human," the "chipped goods on the remainder table"? In part, yes, we're still very much a misogynist culture, and therefore the boys' stuff is good enough for girls—it may even, when used judiciously on daughters, reflect a certain parental panache—but never, ever vice versa. Girl goods are too silly, too icky and, let's not mince our words, too inferior for a boy.

This thought is familiar. It's disheartening. And since we're not about to change the pattern anytime soon, it's distinctly unhelpful. So in my ongoing campaign to sweeten brackish waters and to give a female-friendly twist to an old truism, let me suggest the following: our willingness to clothe females in male garb but not the opposite, and the concomitant acceptance of the tomboyish girl and distaste for the sissyish boy, indicate, albeit on an unconscious level, an awareness of who is the real primogenitor, the legitimate First Sex, and therefore which is ultimately the freer sex. Simone de Beauvoir may have been right about a lot of sociocultural inequities, but from a biological perspective women are not the runners-up; women are the original article. We are Chapter 1, lead paragraph, descendants of the true founding citizen of Eden, whom we may cheerfully think of as Lilith, Adam's first wife. Lilith is not mentioned in the canonical Old Testament, and in the sources where she does make an appearance—for example, the sixteenth-century *Alphabet of Ben Sira*—she is predictably described as having been created *after* Adam, designed for his companionship and erotic pleasure. In these accounts, the couple took to quarreling when Adam announced that he was partial to the missionary position. He liked it not so much for the way it felt as for the political point it made. "You are fit to be below me and I above you," he said to Lilith. His companion refused to acknowledge her subordinate status. "Why should I lie beneath you?" she demanded. "We are both equal because we both come from the earth." Lilith's act of rebellion cut short her tenure in the Garden and assured that all her children would be cursed by God ever after (then again, her more pliant replacement hardly fared much better). But in my unkosher retelling of the story, Lilith was outraged at Adam's pronouncements for their imperialist trash. She knew, even if he did not, bloody hell, *she* was there first.

By saying that Lilith preceded Adam, that she, not he, was the one with the rib to spare, I'm not being gratuitously contrarian. In a basic biological sense, the female is the physical prototype for an effective living being. . . . Fetuses are pretty much primed to become female unless the female program is disrupted by gestational exposure to androgens. If not instructed otherwise, the primordial genital buds develop into a vulva and at least a partial vagina. (The brain may also assume a female configuration, but this far fuzzier issue we will discuss later.) By the conventional reckoning of embryology, females are said to be the "default" or "neutral" sex, males the "organized" or "activated" sex. That is, a fetus will grow into a girl in the absence of a surge in fetal hormones, with no need for the impact of estrogen, the hormone we normally think of as the female hormone. Estrogen may be indispensable for building breasts and hips later in life, and for orchestrating the monthly menstrual cycle, but it doesn't seem to have much of a role in mapping out girlness to begin with. The male body plan, in contrast, is wrought when the little testes begin secreting testosterone, müllerian inhibiting factor, and other hormones. The hormones organize—or, more precisely, reorganize—the primordial tissue into a masculine format.

But the term *default sex* has such a passive ring to it, suggesting that girls just happen, that making them is as easy as unrolling a carpet downhill; you don't even have to kick it to get it going. A number of women in biology have objected to the terminology and the reasoning behind it. Anne Fausto-Sterling, of Brown University, has complained that the notion of female as default is an intellectual vestige of the male domination of developmental biology. The reason that nobody has found any of the chemical signals that activate the female blueprint, she argues, is that nobody has looked for them. From a man's perspective, the mechanism behind the growth of fallopian tubes simply can't hold the fascination of the recipe for a penis. Just because hormones don't appear to be responsible for female sex determination doesn't mean that *nothing* is responsible; other signaling systems exist and participate in fetal growth, though they're harder to find and study than a sharp and unmistakable burst of androgens.

What we can do is reformulate the principle of female first into something less simplistic and inert than the ho-hum default mode. David Crews, of the University of Texas, proposes a lovely system for discussing the sex determination of an animal: the female is the ancestral sex while the male is the derived sex. The female form came first, and eventually it gave rise to the male variant. Athena was said to have sprung from the skull of Zeus. Perhaps we might better imagine Apollo springing from the head of Hera.

What the notion of female as ancestral sex means, when stretched to its most interesting dimensions, is that males are more like females than females are like males. Males, after all, are derived from females; they have no choice but to hold in common those features—those girlish features, those pink pajamas!—that were modified in the making of them. But females have no such reliance on the male prototype to invent a sense of self. Self was there to begin with; we defined self. We don't need Adam's rib, we didn't use Adam's rib; our bones calcified and our pelvises hardened entirely without male assistance.

Crews arrived at his thesis through a couple of lines of reasoning. To begin with, he studies sex determination in reptiles rather than in mammals, so he sees a different system at work, from which he can extract novel principles to counter the conventional wisdom held by the warm-bloods. He has observed that the sex of a crocodile or a turtle is not dictated by an X or a Y chromosome, the SRY gene or the testes it can build. Instead, a baby reptile is sexualized by environmental elements, particularly the air or water temperature surrounding the egg while the creature is developing. All embryos begin with bisexual potential, and then, depending on whether it is mild or cold outside, they grow either ovaries or testes. (Generally, a colder temperature yields males, a warmer one yields females, and an intermediate temperature will give rise to a brood of 50 percent males and 50 percent females.) Importantly, neither sex is a "default" sex. A crocodile can't become a female just by not becoming a male. The pre-she must receive some kind of stimulus, pegged to temperature, that in turn sets off a physiological chain of events to build ovaries. So too to construct testes: the young reptile requires signals from the outside world to set the masculine protocol in motion. In other words, the business of sexualizing a reptile is active and multistep whatever the final outcome will be.

Reptiles are very different from mammals; nevertheless, the details of their sex determination program tempt us to question assumptions about the neutrality of the female. There may be much that we're overlooking in the embryonic establishment of sex. For example, a male fetus's testes release müllerian inhibiting factor to destroy the primitive ducts that otherwise would flower into the fallopian tubes, uterus, and vagina. Yet in addition to her müllerian ducts, a female embryo possesses until the ninth week of gestation what are called the wolffian ducts, structures that have the potential to become the seminal vesicle, the epididymides, and other elements of male anatomy. In the female, most of the wolffian ductal structures dissolve away during development, but has anybody ever found a wolffian inhibiting factor, a WIF? No. Supposedly no such factor exists. Supposedly the wolffian ducts disappear in the *absence* of a signal from the testes to persist and flourish. This is part of the female-as-default model. The wolffian ducts will self-destruct unless they're given a reason to live. This hypothesis is possible, but it is hardly plausible. We've seen with the development of eggs and brains that nature, Shiva-child that she is, creates abundance only to destroy the bulk of it. But does destruction just happen, or must it be initiated? If death is an active process—and the new creed of apoptosis claims it is—well, then, it needs activation. Somewhere there must be a wolffian inhibiting factor: not a hormone, not something easily isolated like a hormone, but a signal. A subtle set of teeth that eliminates one aspiration and gives the female principle the run of the shop, to shape the body temple so that Lilith might lie as she likes.

In fact, in 1993 scientists presented preliminary evidence that they had found an active ovarian initiator, that the construction of ovaries wasn't merely a question of a passive unfolding. They had identified a genetic signal that could aggressively override testosterone's actions and turn primordial fetal genitals into the female format—in this case, not because a signal was missing or because the tissue couldn't respond to androgens, as happens in androgen insensitivity syndrome, but because this factor, whatever it is, had become hyperactive and pushed the androgens out of the way. Eau d'Amazon! But none of this work has been replicated yet, nor explored in any detail, so whether we have found the long-sought girl growth factor, nobody can say.

Assuming, then, that it takes work to generate either a male or a female form and that there are active ovarian initiators out there able to do for gals what testosterone does for our brothers, why does Crews give ancestral primacy to the female while consigning the male to the status of the derivative? In this, his training as a herpetologist colors his worldview. Among mammals, sexual reproduction is obligatory. If a mammal is to have offspring, it must mate with a member of the opposite sex. There is no such thing as a parthenogenetic mammal in nature, a female who can spin out her own clones. But some lizards—and fish, and a few other types of vertebrates—breed through self-replication, almost always producing daughters only, no sons. Parthenogenesis is not a terribly common strategy, but it occurs. In fact, it tends to appear and disappear over evolutionary time. A species that once was a sexually reproducing one, requiring the existence of males and females, will for any number of reasons lose the male and turn parthenogenetic. In other cases, a parthenogenetic species will discover the benefits of having a fellow around—specifically, because sexual reproduction gives rise to enhanced genetic diversity and thus to children with sufficiently varied traits to withstand changing times. Desiring change, the formerly hymeneal females, the cold-blooded madonnas, retreat to the Garden of Eden and start bickering over who is to take on the role of the male and get to be on top. In either evolutionary scenario, males come and males go, but the female remains. There is no species where there is no female. The female, the great Mother, is never lost.

(You may wonder whether it's fair to call a parthenogenetic animal a female rather than a neuter, or even, just for the jazz of it, a male. The short answer is, of course it's fair. It's even accurate. A parthenogenetic lizard produces and lays eggs from which infant lizards eventually emerge, and a female animal, in her purest sense, is the animal with the eggs.)

"Males evolved only after the evolution of self-replicating (=female) organisms," Crews writes. "Males have been gained and lost, but females have remained. The male pattern is derived and imposed upon the ancestral female pattern." . . .

. . . Crews says that in conceptualizing the ancestral female and the derivative male, "the intriguing possibility emerges that males may be more like females than females are like males." If he is right, then it makes crude sense, in a monotheistic culture that insists on abandoning the pantheon and choosing one god to reign symbolically over a two-sexed species, for the god to be male; for the male incorporates the female, is like the female—in a sense, begins as an imitation of the female—but the female cannot say the same. The female does not incorporate the male, did not originally need the male. Who knows? She may not in the future need him again.

On his side, the male needs the female, as he needs the basal parts of himself. He cannot escape her, and so he coopts her greatest power, her generative capabilities. But being male and of a Roman cut, he goes her one better. Remember that a parthenogenetic female can give birth only to daughters. A male god, though, is reinvented as a super-parthenogen, able without assistance to create sons and daughters alike. Imagining, incorrectly but understandably, that he can thenceforth go it alone, he takes it upon himself to be the one god, a fabulist creature whose like can't be found in nature.

Deities have their problems and delusions, we humans have ours. If among gods males are likelier to encroach on female prerogatives than the reverse, among humans women feel more comfortable coopting the male than men do behaving in a manner that may be seen as womanish—or, worse, womanly. Freud suggested that men had to individuate by wrenching themselves free of the world of women—mothers, grandmothers, aunts, nursemaids—the monotonously, claustrophobically feminine habitat in which they spent their infancy and youth. Women threaten because women rule for so long. If men are to find autonomy, they must denounce femininity. Women do not need to pull themselves away to achieve womanhood; they do not need to reject the mother who cared for them and defined them.

Forget Freud. It could well be that men must pull away not from the external world of women but from the internal female template. Maybe men feel driven to emphasize their distinctiveness over their derivation, to escape the ancestral female as though escaping a dynastic hex, the femuncula within. We women therefore may have, at our core, an easier time with fluid sexuality. We can afford to play around with clothes and personas and attitudes, to be as ballsy as we want to be; still we will be women. Men's brief and much-derided foray into the land of sensitivity and Alan Alda suggests that men cannot say the same; to the contrary, their edges blur and their convictions become hesitant if they toy with androgyny too long. . . .

When Crews says that the male pattern is derived from and imposed on the ancestral female pattern, he is talking about many things: the pattern of hormone release and activity, the pattern of brain structures, the pattern of behaviors, and of course the pattern of the reproductive systems. It is our genitals that we think of as the clearest difference between male and female; it is our genitals that most fascinate us and inculcate notions of gender in us as children (along, of course, with our divergent styles of using the toilet). The reproductive system is supposedly what most clearly distinguishes a man from a woman.

Except that when you take a close look, you'll see that we're remarkably the same. If you look at a woman in stirrups, for example, you'll see that the plumpness of her labia and the way they fall slightly into the folds of her thighs are reminiscent of a man's scrotum. The ancients knew as much. Hippocrates, Galen, and other early anatomists and body philosophers knew as much. They were not saints. They were not gynophiles. In *Making Sex: Body and Gender from the Greeks to Freud*, Thomas Laqueur describes the ideas of Galen as "phallocentric," taking the male pattern as primary and describing the female from that reference point. The Greek doctors also made errors in their understanding of anatomy. Nevertheless, they were on to something. They thought that the human body was basically unisexual and that the two sexes were inside-out versions of each other. The ancients emphasized the homology between female and male organs.

"In the one-sex model, dominant in anatomical thinking for two thousand years, woman was understood as man inverted: the uterus was the female scrotum, the ovaries were testicles, the vulva was a foreskin, and the vagina was a penis," Laqueur writes. "Women were essentially men in whom a lack of vital heat—of perfection—had resulted in the retention, inside, of structures that in the male were visible without." Galen even used the same words to describe male and female structures, calling the ovaries *orcheis*, the Greek word for testes. (Orchid flowers also were named after testicles, because the water bulb at the base of the plant looks like a little wrinkled scrotum. So when Georgia O'Keeffe used the orchid to represent female genitals, she incidentally committed a minor act of conjoinment of maleness with femaleness.) Sexual parallelism was gospel; a fourth-century bishop said he realized that women had the same equipment as he, except "theirs are inside the body and not outside it."

Nor was it only the genitals that were assumed to be homologous; so too were the body's excretions. Semen was man's version of menstrual blood; milk and tears were as one. The ancients also saw no difference between men's and women's capacity for sexual pleasure and the necessity of mutual orgasm for conception. Galen proclaimed that a woman could not get pregnant unless she had an orgasm, and his view prevailed until the eighteenth century. This is a sweet thought, one of my favorite glaring errors of history, and a roundabout acknowledgment of the importance of the female climax to life as we know it. Unfortunately, the insistence that an expectant woman was a postorgasmic woman spelled tragedy for a number of our foresisters. Women who became pregnant after rape, for example, were accused of licentiousness and adultery, since their swollen bellies were evidence of their acquiescence and their pleasure, and they were routinely put to death. In more recent times, women have been advised that when rape is inevitable, they should just "lie back and enjoy it," and they also have been blamed in any number of ways for their predicament—why did you dress that way, why did you invite him back to your apartment, why did you go for a walk in the park after dark?

Galen was wrong about a number of things. The vulva is not a foreskin, though it may be treated as such in countries that practice female genital mutilation; and neither women nor men need to reach orgasm for a woman to conceive (men secrete sperm in their pre-ejaculates, and I knew a woman who became pregnant without having intercourse, when a smear of pre-ejaculate deposited on her thigh during a thrashabout of heavy petting migrated insidiously upward). But about the unisexual quality of the body he was prescient. The female may be the ancestral form, yet in our current bodies we develop bipotentially; the clay can be shaped either way. We are hermaphrodites, legatees of the son of Hermes and Aphrodite, who merged his body with that of the nymph of the Salmacis fountain. Male and female fetuses look identical until the ninth week of gestation, and our adult organs are analogous structures, male to female. Inside its apricot-sized body, the antesexual two-month-old fetus has a pair of immature seedpods, the primordial gonads, which become testes in males, ovaries in females. It has a set of wolffian and müllerian ducts, one of which will be chosen depending on whether the fetus is to develop a seminal duct system or fallopian tubes. Externally, each begins with an undifferentiated genital ridge, a bump of tissue above a small membrane-shielded slit. Starting in the third month, the nub of flesh either grows gracefully into a clitoris or grows more emphatically into the head of a penis. In girls, the membrane around the primordial slit dissolves, and the slit opens to form the vaginal lips, which will surround the vagina and the urethra, from which urine flows. In boys, androgens prompt the slit to fuse and push forward to generate the shaft of the penis.

As symbols go, the phallus is a yawn. Tubes that point and shoot, and there you have it. The obelisk pierces the heavens, the gun ejaculates bullets, the cigar puffs like a peacock, the hot rod screams, the hot dog is eaten. A phallus doesn't give you much to play with, metaphorically, and it doesn't lend itself to multiple interpretations. A hose is a hose is a hose.

But the vagina, now there's a Rorschach with legs. You can make of it practically anything you want, need, or dread. A vagina in its most simple-minded rendering is an opening, an absence of form, an inert receptacle. It is a four- to five-inch-long tunnel that extends at a forty-five-degree angle from the labia to the doughnut-shaped cervix. It is a pause between the declarative sentence of the outside world and the mutterings of the viscera. Built of skin, muscle, and fibrous tissue, it is the most obliging of passageways, one that will stretch to accommodate travelers of any conceivable dimension, whether they are coming (penises, speculums) or going (infants). I'm sure I'm not the only woman who dreamed during pregnancy that she was about to give birth to a baby whale, in my case an endangered blue whale. Oh, the human vagina in its role as birth canal can stretch, all right, and it must distend in proportion to the rest of us far more than the pelvis of a mother whale. You've heard, or experienced firsthand, how the cervix must dilate to ten centimeters, or four inches, before the laboring woman is given sanction to push. It must become as wide as the vagina is long. But those ten centimeters, oh grunting, flailing lady, are not the width of the baby's head. No, the average seven-pound baby has a head five inches across, and some fat-headed infants have skulls nearly six inches wide. While the baby's head does compress into something the shape of a keel as it rams and glides its way to the light—thank Ishtar for the sutures, fontanel, and ductile plates of the newborn's skull—nonetheless you can count on your vagina's stretching during delivery to proportions unimagined when you had trouble negotiating your first tampon insertion. So the vagina is a balloon, a turtleneck sweater, a model for the universe itself, which, after all, is expanding in all directions even as we sit here and weep. . . .

Beginning on the border of the vaginal environment, we come to a small mountain, the mons pubis, also called the mons veneris, which means "mountain of Venus," the Love Mount. But let's not get carried away with woozy romance; *veneris* also gives rise to the term *venereal disease*. The mons veneris is made mons by a thick pad of fatty tissue that cushions the pubic symphysis, the slightly movable joint between your left and right pubic bones. The joint, which is relatively delicate and easily bruised by a bad jolt on a bicycle, is further cushioned at adolescence when the carpet of pubic hair grows in (assuming that you have requisite responsiveness to androgens). The pubic hair serves other purposes as well. It traps and concentrates pelvic odors, which can be quite attractive to a mate if they are the odors of health, as I will discuss below. Moreover, the pubic hair is a useful visual cue for us primates, who are, after all, a visually oriented species. The hair showcases the genital area and allows it to stand out from the less significant landscape around it. . . .

Extending down from the mons veneris are two long folds of skin, the labia majora, or major lips. The outer sides of the labia are covered with pubic hair, while the inner sides have no follicles but are well supplied with oil and sweat glands. Beneath the skin of the labia majora is a crisscross of connective tissue and fat. The fat of the labia, like that of the breasts and hips—but unlike that of the mons veneris—is sensitive to estrogen, the hormone of sexual maturity. Thus the labia swell when adolescence sends a surge of estrogen through the body and retreat when the hormone subsides at menopause. Under the fat is erectile tissue, which is a spongy mesh that engorges with blood during sexual arousal. Because the labia absorb blood so readily, they also become incessantly engorged during pregnancy, when the volume of circulating blood doubles (at the same time, they can turn a coppery maroon color like the punkiest vampire shade of lipstick on the market).

The erotic and mythic taxonomy of our genitals continues. Inside the labia majora are the nymphae, named for the Greek maidens of the fountain, whose libidos were reputedly so robust that they gave birth to the concept of nymphomania.* The more pedestrian name for nymphae is labia minora, or little lips, the exquisite inner origami of flesh that enfolds the vagina and nearby urethral opening. The inner labia have no hair, but the sebaceous, or oil, glands within them can be felt through the thin skin as tiny bumps, like a subcutaneous scattering of grain. The nymphae are among the most variable part of female genitals, differing considerably in size from woman to woman and even between one labium and its partner. Like the labia majora, the labia minora swell with blood during sexual excitement, and to an even more emphatic extent, doubling or trebling their dimensions at peak arousal. Some of our primate relatives have very exaggerated labia minora, which they drag along the ground to dispense pheromones that advertise their ovulatory status. In the spring of 1996, scientists discovered a new species of marmoset in Brazil, whose most outstanding trait is the female's inner labia. Each flap of skin hangs down visibly, fusing at the bottom into a sort of genital garland.

*As Ethel Sloane points out in her excellent *Biology of Women*, "Everyone knows that a nymphomaniac is a woman with an excessive sex drive. Why is it that hardly anyone knows the same condition in males is satyriasis?" Is it because in women excessive lust is considered a disease worthy of a name tag, while in men the same drive is considered mandatory?

The marmoset's labia sound remarkably like the notorious Hottentot Apron, the absurdly pronounced inner labia that naturalists from Carolus Linnaeus on insisted were a defining feature (or deformity) of the women of South Africa. The best-known Hottentot woman was the so-called Hottentot Venus, who was taken to England and France in the nineteenth century and given the name Sarah Bartmann. In Europe she was paraded in front of curious spectators as a kind of circus animal—though a clothed one—and later she was made to strip naked in front of teams of zoologists and physiologists. After her death, her genitals were dissected and preserved in a jar of formalin. Georges Cuvier, the French anatomist who performed the autopsy, declared in his memoirs that his investigations "left no doubt about the nature of her apron." But as the historian Londa Schiebinger comments in *Nature's Body*, the prurient obsession that Western men of science had with Hottentot genitals had less to do with the reality of hypertrophied labia (never proved and rightfully doubted) than with the desire to place African women in a phylogenetic category closer to orangutan than to human.

Whatever the size of the labia, inner and outer, they sweat. The entire vulval area sweats, with the same insistence as the armpits. If you've ever worked out in a bodysuit, you've probably noticed after a good sweaty session that you have three fetching triangles staining your clothes, one under each arm and a third at the crotch. You probably have felt embarrassed and exposed, the Hottentot Venus in Lycra, or maybe you're worried that others will think you've peed in your pants. Don't be ashamed; be grateful. You need to wick away all that internal body heat if you're going to stay in the running, and frankly, a woman's armpits aren't as efficient as a man's at sweating. Be glad that the female crotch at least is more so.

The vulval area also secretes sebum, a blend of oils, waxes, fats, cholesterol, and cellular debris. The sebum serves as waterproofing, helping to repel with the efficiency of a duck's back the urine, menstrual blood, and pathogenic bacteria that might otherwise settle into the crevices of the mons veneris. The sebum gives the pelvis a sleek and slippery feel, as though everything, including the pubic hairs, had been dipped in a melted candle. Stationed at the outskirts of the genital habitat, the sebum acts as the first line of defense, the Great Wall of Vagina, to thwart disease organisms that seek to colonize the rich world within. . . .

. . . Sharon Hillier, a gynecologist at Magee-Women's Hospital in Pittsburgh, . . . is out to buff the image of the vagina. . . .

Hillier knows that people generally think of the vagina as dirty, in every sense of the term. The word *vagina* sounds both dirtier and more clinical than its counterpart, *penis*, while a curse like *cunt* has a much more violent sting to it than *prick* or *dick*, either of which would sound at home on primetime television. As we've seen, American doctors jestingly compare the vagina to the anus. "In Nairobi, the word for vaginal discharges translates as *dirt*," Hillier told me. "Almost all of the women there try to dry the vagina, because a moist, well-lubricated vagina is thought to be disgusting.

"But really, anywhere you go, the story is the same," she said. "Women are taught that their vaginas are dirty. In fact, a normal healthy vagina is the cleanest space in the body. It's much cleaner than the mouth, and much, much cleaner than the rectum." She sighed. "The negative training starts early. My five-year-old daughter came home from school the other day and said, 'Mommy, the vagina is full of germs.'" Part of the brainwashing involves a lot of big fish stories. The vagina is said to have a fishy odor, a source of great merriment to male comedians. "You've heard the jokes," Hillier said. "My favorite is the one about the blind man who passes by the fish store and says, 'Good morning, ladies.'" Ha-ha. I complained once to a male friend about a line in a movie when a gay male character, in the middle of a discussion about fellatio, turned to a woman and said, "Sorry, hon, I don't eat fish." Fish! I cried. It's not fishy! My friend replied, "Well, you've got to admit it's closer to tuna than to, say, roast beef." Yes, all analogies to meat must be reserved for a different sort of organ. In any event, men may well think of a vagina as smelling fishy, for as it happens, sperm is one of the ingredients that can make a good thing go bad.

The crux of the vaginal ecosystem, said Hillier, is symbiosis, a mutually advantageous and ongoing barter between macroenvironment and microorganism. Yes, the vagina is full of germs, in the sense of bacteria; it swims with life forms, and you hope it stays that way. But there are germs and germs. When conditions are healthy, the germs, or rather bacteria, in the vagina do a body good. They are lactobacilli, the same bacteria found in yogurt. "A healthy vagina is as clean and pure as a carton of yogurt," said Hillier. (Why do I suspect that we're not likely to see Dannon picking up on this slogan anytime soon?) And so the smell: "A normal vagina should have a slightly sweet, slightly pungent odor. It should have the lactic acid smell of yogurt." The contract is simple. We provide lactobacilli with food and shelter—the comfort of the vaginal walls, the moisture, the proteins, the sugars of our tissue. They maintain a stable population and keep competing bacteria out. Merely by living and metabolizing, they generate lactic acid and hydrogen peroxide, which are disinfectants that prevent colonization by less benign microbes. The robust vagina is an acidic vagina, with a pH of 3.8 to 4.5. That's somewhat more acidic than black coffee (with a pH of 5) but less piquant than a lemon (pH 2). In fact, the idea of pairing wine and women isn't a bad one, as the acidity of the vagina in health is just about that of a glass of red wine. This is the vagina that sings; this is the vagina with bouquet, with legs.

Nor is ordinary vaginal discharge anything to be mortified about. It is made up of the same things found in blood serum, the clear, thin, sticky liquid that remains behind when the solid components of blood, like clotting factors, are separated away. Vaginal discharge consists of water, albumin—the most abundant protein in the body—a few stray white blood cells, and mucin, the oily substance that gives the vagina and cervix their slippery sheen. Discharge is not dirt, certainly, and it is not a toxic waste product of the body in the sense of urine and feces. No, no, no. It is the same substance as what's inside the vagina, neither better nor worse, pulled down because we're bipedal and gravity exists, and because on occasion the cup runneth over. It is the lubricant beneath the illusion of carapace, reminding us that physiologically we are all aquatic organisms.

But, gals, there's no denying it: sometimes we stink, and we know it. Not like strawberry yogurt or a good Cabernet but like, alas, albacore. Or even skunk. How does this happen? If you haven't bathed for a week, I'll let you figure it out for yourself. But sometimes it's not a question of hygiene; it's a medical issue, a condition called bacterial vaginosis. For a number of reasons, the balance of flora within the vagina is upset, and the lactobacilli start to founder. In their stead, other organisms proliferate, particularly anaerobic bacteria, which thrive in the absence of oxygen. These microbes secrete a host of compounds, each fouler than the last. Here is where the unflattering comparison to seafood comes in. Distressingly, the microbes make trimethylamine, which is the same substance that gives day-old fish its fishy odor. They make putrescine, a compound found in putrifying meat. They make cadaverine, and I need not tell you from whence that chemical was named. The amount and combination of these rank byproducts depends on the severity of the vaginosis.

In other words, if you're having a problem with unspeakable "feminine odor," that syndrome so coyly referred to in all the ads for douches and feminine deodorants, you could have an infection, often a low-grade, chronic one, with no symptoms beyond the odiferous. Some of the causes of such infections are known. Among the biggest is . . . douching. In an effort to get fresh 'n' clean and to look like the dewy, virginal women pictured on the packages of Massengill, women can make themselves dirtier than ever. Douching kills off the beneficial lactobacilli and paves the way for infestation by anaerobes and their trails of cadaverine. So while I rarely dispense medical advice, this one is easy: don't douche, ever, period, end of squirt bottle.

Vaginosis can also arise in the wake of other infections, such as pelvic inflammatory disease. Moreover, some women are born with an unfortunate predisposition toward imbalances of vaginal flora, just as some women are susceptible to acne. Even the generally desirable lactobacilli differ in their potency, with certain strains more able than others to generate hydrogen peroxide and thus more efficiently fend off contending microorganisms. Some women have "lucky lactos," said Hillier, and some have so-so lactobacilli. The so-sos are more susceptible to vaginosis, as well as to infection with yeast, another type of microbe that thrives in highly anaerobic conditions.

To rectify any imbalance, you can try eating a lot of yogurt to derive the benefit of lactobacilli in yogurt culture, but very few ingested bacteria are likely to find their way to your genitalia, and any postprandial improvements in the pelvic ecosystem will probably be transitory. Chronic cases of vaginosis can be treated with antibiotics, the course of action usually suggested for pregnant women, in whom the infection raises the risk of a premature delivery. Better than antibiotics, which are indiscriminate when taken systemically, will be a type of suppository now under development, which can provide the lucky lactos exactly where they are needed.

Another cause of vaginosis is sleeping around with men who don't use condoms. Even a single shot of semen will temporarily disturb the ecosystem of the vagina. Sperm can't swim in the biting climate of a healthy vagina, so they're buffered in a solution of acid's biochemical yang, alkaline. Semen is highly alkaline, with a pH of 8. It is more alkaline than any other body fluid, including blood, sweat, spit, and tears. For several hours after intercourse, the overall pH of the vagina rises, momentarily giving unsavory bacteria the edge. Usually the change is fleeting and the woman's body has no trouble readjusting the pH thermostat back to status quo. The restoration is particularly easy when the sperm looks familiar—that is, when it belongs to the woman's regular partner. But in a woman who is exposed to the semen of multiple partners, the homeostatic mechanism sometimes falters, for reasons that remain unclear and probably have to do with an immunological reaction to all that strange sperm.

Thus, even though a woman with catholic tastes in sex may be exposed to no more semen overall than a woman who sleeps regularly with a husband, her vagina is at greater risk of becoming chronically alkaline. She loses her wine-and-yogurt tartness. So maybe it was not mere misogyny that prompted the authors of the *Kama Sutra* to describe licentious women as smelling like fish.

Are you a masochist? Do you like to look for patterns in life, morals to the story? You can think of this as another case of divine justice. If you sleep around a lot, your vagina becomes more alkaline. It becomes fishy, yes, but worse than that, an alkaline vagina is less able to defend itself against pathogens, including agents of venereal disease. Women with bacterial vaginosis are more susceptible to gonorrhea, syphilis, and AIDS. At the same time, if you sleep around a lot, you'll be exposed to a greater load of such venereal microbes. In sum, just when you need an acidic vagina the most, yours is turning alkaline. Is this not an argument for monogamy, or abstinence? Doesn't this suggest that Somebody is watching, keeping track of the notches on your lipstick case?

To me, the association is not fraught with moral or ironic underpinnings, but rather merely confirms what is ancient, prehominid news. Sex is dangerous. It always has been, for every species that engages in it. Courting and copulating animals are exposed animals, subject to greater risk of predation than animals who are chastely asleep in their burrow; not only do mating animals usually perform their rituals out in the open, but their attention is so focused on the particulars of fornication that they fail to notice the glint of a gaping jaw or the flap of a raptor's wings. Pregnancy, disease, threat of death by stoning—yes, sex has always been chancy. Momentum is chancy, and sex is nothing if not momentous. Let us not forget that. Let us not be so intimidated by overwork or familiarity or trimethylamines that we forget the exquisite momentum of sexual hunger.

The vagina is both path and journey, tunnel and traveler. Seeing beyond it requires invasion, which is why most women have only the vaguest sense of what their interior design is like, the appearance of the long-exalted, often-overrated womb and its tributaries. Again O'Keeffe has given us a visual translation of the uterus, fallopian tubes, and ovaries, evoking them through the cattle's skull and horns stripped bare on the desert floor, again a reverie of life-in-death. I think instead of water and coral reefs, where the rosy fingers of sea pens and feather anemones brush hungrily from side to side, enlivened as though with wills of their own.

References

Crews, David. (1993). The organizational concept and vertebrates without sex chromosomes. *Brain Behavior and Evolution, 42*, 202–214.

Fausto-Sterling, Anne (1992). *Myths of gender.* New York: Basic Books.

Hillier, Sharon. (1993). Diagnostic microbiology of bacterial vaginosis. *American Journal of Obstetrics and Gynecology, 169*, 455–459.

Laqueur, Thomas. (1990). *Making sex: Body and gender from the Greeks to Freud*. Cambridge, MA: Harvard University Press.

Sloane, Ethel. (1993). *The biology of women*. New York: Delmar.

6 Objectification Theory: Towards Understanding Women's Lived Experience and Mental Health Risks

BARBARA L. FREDRICKSON

TOMI-ANN ROBERTS

The body is the basis for the distinction between the sexes. Yet in the traditional debate between biological and environmental determinants of gender differences, the body has most often been explored in terms of its anatomical, genetic, or hormonal influences on personality, experience, and behavior. Feminists and others have been understandably suspicious of such perspectives for their deterministic flavor, and perhaps for this reason the body has been largely ignored in non-biological explanatory schemes for gender distinctions, which tend to focus more on sociocultural influences. Feminist and other sociocultural perspectives, for instance, have done a great deal to illuminate the ways in which many gender differences have little to do with the biological body, and much more to do with the differential socialization of boys and girls, and, perhaps even more profoundly, with the different social status and power held by women and men in society.

Yet, in doing so, much of the sociocultural tradition within the psychology of gender has underemphasized the fact that the body is constructed from more than just biology. Bodies exist within social and cultural contexts, and hence are also constructed through sociocultural practices and discourses. Theorists in a variety of disciplines have begun to explore the multiple ways that the body conveys social meaning and how these meanings shape gendered experience [e.g., Bordo (1993) and Foucault (1980) in philosophy; Martin (1987) in cultural anthropology; Shilling (1993) in sociology; Kaschak (1992) and Ussher (1989) in psychology]. We think it is time for psychology to broaden its understanding of women and gender by pushing further the analysis of bodies as social constructions.

In this paper, we propose *objectification theory*. This theoretical framework places bodies in sociocultural context with the aim of illuminating the lived experiences and mental health risks of girls and women who encounter sexual objectification. Like other forms of sexism, sexual objectification occurs with both "endless variety and monotonous similarity" (Rubin, 1975, cited in Fraser & Nicholson, 1990, p. 28). The common thread running through all forms of sexual objectification is the experience of being treated *as a body* (or collection of body parts) valued predominantly for its use to (or consumption by) others. Certainly not all women experience and respond to sexual objectification in the same way. Unique combinations of ethnicity, class, sexuality, age and other physical and personal attributes undoubtedly create unique sets of experiences across women, as well as experiences shared by particular subgroups. Yet amidst the heterogeneity evident among women, we suggest that having a reproductively mature female body can create a shared social experience—a vulnerability to sexual objectification—which in turn may create a shared set of psychological experiences. . . .

Part I: Objectification Theory

Women's Bodies Are Looked At, Evaluated, and Always Potentially Objectified

Our culture is saturated with heterosexuality. One marker of this, as Karen Horney indicated six decades ago, is "the socially sanctioned right of all males to sexualize all females, regardless of age or status" (Westkott, 1986, p. 95; see also Schur, 1983). The sexualizing of girls and women occurs on a continuum, with sexual violence at one extreme, and sexualized evaluation at the other (Fischer, Vidmar & Ellis, 1993; Hughes & Sandler, 1988; Kaschak, 1992; Reilly, Lott, Caldwell & DeLuca, 1992; Quina & Carlson, 1989; Stoltenberg, 1989). The most subtle and deniable way sexualized evaluation is enacted—and arguably the most ubiquitous—is through gaze, or visual inspection of the body (Kaschak,

1992). All along the sexualizing continuum, women are treated *as bodies*—and in particular, as bodies that exist for the use and pleasure of others. While the psychological repercussions of the extreme end of the continuum (i.e., sexual violence) have begun to capture substantial research attention (e.g., Herman, 1992; Russo, 1985; Trickett & Putnam, 1993), the more subtle and everyday end of this continuum (e.g., sexualized gazing) has gone understudied; this is an imbalance we seek to redress.

Always present in contexts of sexualized gazing is the *potential* for sexual objectification. Sexual objectification occurs whenever a woman's body, body parts, or sexual functions are separated out from her person, reduced to the status of mere instruments, or else regarded as if they were capable of representing her (Bartky, 1990). Certainly not all men sexually objectify women; indeed, many elect not to, and are likely to have richer relationships with women by consequence (Stoltenberg, 1989). But importantly, because sexually objectifying gaze is not under women's own control, few women can completely avoid potentially objectifying contexts (Kaschak, 1992).

Objectifying gaze is played out in three related arenas. First, it occurs within actual interpersonal and social encounters. Studies have shown that (a) women are gazed at more than men (for a review see Hall, 1984); (b) women are more likely to feel "looked at" in interpersonal encounters (Argyle & Williams, 1969); (c) men direct more non-reciprocated gaze toward women than vice versa, particularly in public places (Cary, 1978; Fromme & Beam, 1974; Henley, 1977); plus (d) men's gazing is often accompanied by evaluative commentary that highlights women's differential status (Gardner, 1980). Moreover, Henley (1977) has pointed out that our language provides specific verbs to connote men's staring at women's bodies, such as "ogle" or "leer," underscoring not only that this sexualized gazing occurs, but also that it is disquieting for women.

Second, sexually objectifying gaze also occurs in visual media that depict interpersonal and social encounters. Analyses of advertisements show that males are pictured looking directly at their female partner far more often than the reverse (Goffman 1979; Umiker-Sebeok, 1981). Goffman (1979), for instance, has described the "anchored drift," a common theme in advertising in which a male is depicted staring at or monitoring a female who is looking off into the distance, daydreaming, or otherwise mentally drifting from the scene.

The third, and perhaps most insidious manner in which objectifying gaze infuses American culture is in people's encounters with visual media that spotlight bodies and body parts and seamlessly align viewers with an implicit sexualizing gaze (Mulvey, 1975). This sexually objectifying treatment of women in the visual media is certainly not limited to pornography. Analyses of mainstream films (Kuhn, 1985; Mulvey, 1975; van Zoonen, 1994), visual arts (Berger, 1972), advertisements (Archer, Iritani, Kimes & Barrios, 1983; Goffman, 1979; Solely & Kurzbard, 1986), television programming (Copeland, 1989), women's magazines (Ferguson, 1978), and sports photography (Duncan, 1990) provide evidence that women's bodies are targeted for sexual objectification more often than men's. In mainstream print media and television, for example, men tend to be portrayed in a close-up style that focuses on their faces, and women tend to be portrayed in a long-shot style that focuses on their bodies (Archer et all, 1983). As Basow (1992) concludes, "the female body has been sexually objectified in most visual stimuli, from pornography to shoe advertisements" (p. 87).

Moreover, the mass media's proliferation of sexualized images of the female body is fast and thorough. Confrontations with these images, then, are virtually unavoidable in American culture. In sum, the sexual objectification of the female body has clearly permeated our cultural milieu; it is likely to affect most girls and women to some degree, no matter who their actual social contacts may be.[1]

A handful of theorists have ventured to explain *why* visual evaluations of the female body, which can lead to sexual objectification, are integral to male heterosexuality. Evolutionary theorists contend that women's physical attractiveness indirectly signals reproductive value, and so evaluating women's physical attributes has become an important criterion in men's mate selection (Buss, 1989; Singh, 1994). Others argue that the cultural practice of objectifying female bodies originated to create, maintain, and express patriarchy (Connell, 1987; Kuhn, 1985; Stoltenberg, 1989). Distinct from attempts to uncover *why* objectification occurs, objectification theory takes as a *given* that women exist in a culture in which their bodies are—for whatever reasons—looked at, evaluated, and always potentially objectified. The theory limits its aim to illuminating what we believe to be the experiential *consequences* that sexual objectification might have in many women's lives.

Internalizing an Observer's Perspective on Physical Self

Objectification theory posits that a cultural milieu of objectification functions to socialize girls and women to, at some level, treat *themselves* as objects to be looked at and evaluated.[2] In other words, as numerous feminist theorists have argued, women often adopt an observer's perspective on their physical selves (Bartky, 1990; Beauvoir, 1961; Berger, 1972;

Young, 1990). Psychological theory on socialization and the self can provide a possible explanation of how this internalization might come about. Effective socialization, Costanzo (1992) has argued, begins with compliance to minimally sufficient external pressures, proceeds through interpersonal identification, and ends with individuals claiming ownership of the socialized values and attitudes, often by incorporating them into their sense of self.

The external pressures that encourage women's preoccupation with their own physical appearance abound. Take, for example, the array of life benefits that physically attractive, or "eye-catching" women receive in American culture. Empirical research demonstrates that how a woman's body appears to others can determine her life experiences. Studies have demonstrated, for instance, that obesity negatively affects women's, but not men's, social mobility, with obese women showing lower educational and economic attainment than their parents. Compared to average weight or thin girls, overweight girls are also less likely to be accepted to college (Wooley & Wooley, 1980; Wooley, Wooley & Dyrenforth, 1979). In addition, job discrimination and hostile work environments are more frequently reported by overweight women than by overweight men (Snow & Harris, 1985). More generally, women deemed unattractive by their coworkers are described more negatively than comparably unattractive men (Bar-Tal & Saxe, 1976; Cash, Gillen, & Burns, 1977; Wallston & O'Leary, 1981). Additionally, a recent Supreme Court case (*Price Waterhouse v. Hopkins*) illustrates that women who aspire to high-status work positions may suffer job discrimination based on unfeminine appearance (Fiske, Bersoff, Borgida, Deaux & Heilman, 1991). Physical attractiveness has also been shown to correlate more highly with popularity, dating experience, and marriage opportunities for women than for men (Berscheid, Dion, Walster & Walster, 1971; Walster, Aronson, Abrahams, & Rottman, 1966; Margolin & White, 1987). Indeed studies of implicit cultural modes of gender relations suggest that both women and men discuss heterosexual relations as though women can "exchange" their relative attractiveness for good treatment in relationships (e.g., Holland & Skinner, 1987).

For these and other reasons, Unger (1979) argues that physical beauty can translate into power for women: Attractiveness functions as a prime currency for women's social and economic success. The value of this currency, however, may differ across subgroups of women. Arguably for instance, to be traded for economic power, a woman's beauty must appeal to the tastes of the dominant (white, male) culture. Given this standard, preoccupation with appearance may be most evident among white women and those seeking upward social mobility. Consistent with this view, Hurtado (1989) has argued that white women typically experience oppression through "seduction"—which we suggest is often enacted through sexual objectification masquerading as positively valanced admiration; women of color, Hurtado suggests, are more likely to be oppressed through "rejection" or negatively valanced social evaluations. The point here is that women of color, poor women, and lesbians face the negatively valanced oppressions of racism, classism, and homophobia. As such, for these subgroups of women, sexual objectification may not be a *primary* source of oppression. We recognize, then, that the effects of sexual objectification may be less salient among some subgroups of women. Even so, because sexual objectification infuses cross-gender relations—which most often may be *within-ethnicity* cross-gender relations—we suggest that the oppression objectification produces may be more or less shared among women across ethnic boundaries.

Given the evidence that women's social and economic prospects can be determined by their physical appearance, it behooves women to anticipate the repercussions of their appearance, or as Berger (1972) puts it, to be their own first surveyors. Therefore, women's attentiveness to their own physical appearance, which has often been interpreted as narcissism and vanity (Deutsch, 1944, 1945; Freud, 1933), might more appropriately be viewed as women's strategy for helping to determine how others will treat them (Silberstein, Steigel-Moore & Rodin, 1987). This strategy need not be conscious, or deliberately chosen. Instead, theories of socialization would predict that with repeated exposure to the array of subtle external pressures to enhance physical beauty, girls and women come to experience their efforts to improve their appearance as self-chosen, or even natural (Costanzo, 1992).

In a related vein, a core social psychological view of self holds that an individual's sense of self is a social construction, reflecting the ways that other people view and treat that individual (Cooley, 1902; Harter, 1987). Cooley (1902) captured this idea with the phrase "the looking-glass self," a term we appreciate because mirrors reflect the physical attributes that we argue can monopolize women's sense of self. Yet we believe that Cooley (and other self theorists who followed his lead) missed the opportunity to illuminate women's views of self by pronouncing that self "refers chiefly to opinions, purposes, desires, claims, and the like, concerning matters that involve no thought of the body" (1902/1990, p. 63). Recent empirical evidence indicates that such "disembodied" views of self are untenable. For instance, data gathered by Harter and colleagues demonstrate that physical appearance is the most important domain contributing to children and young adolescent's sense of self-worth (female and male alike), outpacing social acceptance, scholastic and athletic competence, and behavioral conduct (Harter, 1987). Similarly, data collected in multiple laboratories show that women's body image satisfaction is positively related to their sense of self (for a review, see Polivy, Herman & Pliner, 1990). Other data demonstrate that the body contributes to sense of self differently for women than for men: For women, positive self-concept hinges on perceived physical *attractiveness*, whereas for men, it hinges on perceived physical *effectiveness* (Lerner, Orlos & Knapp, 1976). These data suggest that the notion of the "looking-glass self" perhaps ought to be taken more literally when applied to women.

Even so, new data raise the possibility that the "looking-glass self" may not apply in comparable ways across ethnic subgroups. Crocker and colleagues, for instance, suggest that unlike white and Asian students, black students seem to separate how they privately feel about themselves from how they believe others (presumably non-blacks) evaluate them (Crocker, Luhtanen, Blaine & Broadnax, 1994). Crocker and colleagues interpret this result as an adaptive coping response by blacks to chronic and recurring experiences of racial oppression and prejudice. It may be, then, that psychological coping strategies that women of color develop to deal with racism may also buffer against some of the negative psychological repercussions of sexual objectification to some degree, perhaps regardless of whether this objectification is enacted within or across ethnic boundaries.

To summarize, then, a critical repercussion of being viewed by others in sexually objectifying ways is that individuals may be coaxed to internalize an observer's perspective on self. Girls and women, according to our analysis, may to some degree come to view themselves as objects or "sights" to be appreciated by others (Berger, 1972). This is a peculiar perspective on self, one that can lead to a form of self-consciousness characterized by habitual monitoring of the body's outward appearance. Again, self-conscious body monitoring can be viewed as a habit (or a strategy) that many women develop to help determine how other people will treat them, which has clear implications for their quality of life.

Yet this habit is not a trivial one. We propose that it can profoundly disrupt a woman's flow of consciousness. As Beauvoir wrote, when a girl becomes a woman she is "doubled; instead of coinciding exactly with herself, she . . . [also] exist[s] outside" (1961, p. 316). That is, significant portions of women's conscious attention can often be usurped by concerns related to real or imagined, present or anticipated, surveyors of their physical appearance. We posit that in a culture that objectifies the female body, whatever girls and women do, the potential always exists for their thoughts and actions to be interrupted by images of how their bodies appear. This habitual body monitoring, we believe, can create a predictable set of subjective experiences that may be essential to understanding the psychology of women.

Consequences for Subjective Experience

The psychological and experiential consequences that follow from internalizing an observer's perspective on physical self have not been fully explored, and in this section, we begin to do so. The consequences we discuss, however, ought not to be considered inevitable and chronic aspects of all women's experience. Instead, we conceptualize the emergence of gendered experience in objectifying cultures in a manner similar to Deaux and Major's (1987) conceptualization of the emergence of gendered behavior. That is, we emphasize the extent to which women's experience is variable, proximally caused, and context dependent (Deaux & Major, 1987). Throughout the course of a day, women enter into and exit from multiple contexts, some that protect them from the negative repercussions of objectification, and some that do not. To the extent that particular social contexts accentuate women's awareness of actual or potential observers' perspectives on their bodies, certain types of experiences are likely to ensue. Our framework, then, acknowledges both powerful situation-specific effects, as well as relatively stable individual differences across women in the experiential consequences of objectification. That is, some women may be dogged by observers' perspectives on their bodies in *most* of the contexts in which they find themselves, whereas others may only be made aware of these perspectives when, for example, they receive a "cat call" while walking down a busy street.

We propose psychological and experiential consequences of sexual objectification for (a) the emotion of shame, (b) the emotion of anxiety, (c) peak motivational states, and (d) the awareness of internal bodily states, offering objectification theory as a parsimonious explanation for known gender differences in these varied psychological experiences.

Shame Shame occurs when people evaluate themselves relative to some internalized or cultural ideal and come up short (M. Lewis, 1992; Darwin, 1872/1965). Darwin captured how the internalization of another's gaze is central to the experience of shame: "It is not the simple act of reflecting on our own appearance, but the thinking what others think of us, which excites a blush" (Darwin, 1872/1965, p. 325). Shame, then, results from a fusion of negative self evaluation with the potential for social exposure.

Empirical studies have documented that women experience more shame than men (H. Lewis, 1971; M. Lewis, 1992; Staply & Haviland, 1989; Silberstein et al., 1987). Understanding the messages women receive within our objectifying culture helps to explain this difference. First, in American culture, we are continually exposed to images of idealized female bodies (Wolf, 1991). These idealized images are invariably of youth, slimness, and whiteness. Indeed it is difficult to find media depictions of female beauty that are different from this western European ideal. The mass media's broad dispersion of these idealized images of women's bodies has all but universalized them.

Second, as we have seen, women's eagerness to approximate the cultural ideals is understandable given the rewards they reap for attractiveness in heterosexual relationships as well as work settings. Pointing out, however, that only 1 in 40,000 women actually meet the requirements of a model's size and shape, Wolf (1991) argues that the ideal female body is a myth, unrealistic, and impossible to attain. As such, the continual comparison a woman makes between her actual body and the mythic ideal is a recipe for shame. For instance, although only a minority of girls and women in our society are actually overweight, empirical studies report that the majority report feeling fat, and ashamed of this "failure" (Silberstein et al., 1987; see also Fallon & Rozin, 1985). Furthermore, Root (1990) has argued that pressure to look "perfect" (by the dominant culture's standards) is increasing among ethnic minority women. For those women of color who, in hopes of gaining the benefits of acceptance from the dominant culture, strive to match media-depicted body ideals, the resulting shame may be even deeper, given the media's tendency to equate beauty with whiteness.

Shame generates an intense desire to hide or escape the painful gaze of others (Darwin, 1872/1965; M. Lewis, 1992), a wish that may be reflected nonverbally as a hanging head and general body collapse. Intense shame can also compound an already fragmented state of consciousness. "Shame disrupts ongoing activity as the self focuses completely on itself, and the result is a state of confusion: inability to think clearly, inability to talk, and inability to act" (M. Lewis, 1992, p. 34). Interestingly, M. Lewis (1992) identifies this disruption as "adaptive," arguing that its function is to inhibit or change that which fails to live up to the person's internally or externally derived standards. Shame is thus considered a moral emotion, one that is used to socialize societal standards[3] (H. Lewis,

1989; M. Lewis, 1992). To the extent that "that which fails" is indeed changeable, as actions often are, shame may indeed be adaptive.

Yet bodies are harder to change than actions. Viewed in this light, women's ongoing efforts to change body and appearance through diet, exercise, surgery, fashion, beauty products, and, perhaps most dangerously, eating disorders reveal what may be a perpetual and hardly adaptive body-based shame. The extent to which body "correction" is motivated by shame elevates the task of meeting societal standards of beauty to a moral obligation. Women who fail to live up to this obligation have been deemed uncivilized and immoral. For instance, in discussing his own contempt for fat women, psychiatrist Irvin Yalom calls their bodies profane, asking "How dare they impose that body on the rest of us?" (Yalom, 1989, cited in Kaschak, 1992, p. 71; see also Crocker, Cornwell & Major, 1993, on the stigma of being overweight).

In sum, the habitual body monitoring encouraged by a culture that sexually objectifies the female body can lead women to experience shame that is recurrent, difficult to alleviate, and constructed as a matter of morality.

Anxiety People experience anxiety when they anticipate danger or threats to self; distinct from fear, however, these threats often remain ambiguous (Lazarus, 1991; Ohman, 1994). Motor tension, vigilance, and scanning are key manifestations of anxiety (DSM-IV, APA, 1994). Being female in a culture that objectifies the female body creates multiple opportunities to experience anxiety with its accompanying vigilance. We highlight two: appearance anxiety and safety anxiety.

Not knowing exactly when and how one's body will be looked at and evaluated can create anxiety about potential exposure. Indeed, empirical studies document that women experience more anxiety about their appearance than do men (Dion, Dion & Keelan, 1990). Data further show that women's appearance anxiety may have roots in negative early life social experiences, including histories of receiving negative appearance-related comments. Appearance anxiety is often manifested by concerns of checking and adjusting one's appearance (Keelan, Dion & Dion, 1992). Women's fashions arguably compound the opportunities for anxiety: Certain necklines and hemlines require regular body monitoring. In wearing these fashions a woman is forced to be chronically vigilant about whether undergarments or "too much skin" is (shamefully) exposed, all while maintaining the illusion that she is at ease dressed as she is.

Yet appearance anxiety is not just about so-called vanity. It is also fused with concerns about safety. Earlier we noted that women's beauty has been likened to power. Consistent with this view, Beneke (1982) has reported that some men who rape construe physically attractive women as personally threatening and therefore deserving of retaliation. For instance, those who suggest that a female victim of sexual assault "asked for it" often refer to her physical appearance. Women whose appearance is considered "striking" or "provocative" are thought to provoke their own rape, much as a punch in the nose provokes a fist fight (Beneke, 1982). Empirical studies also demonstrate that more attractive rape victims are assigned greater blame for their own rape than less attractive victims (e.g., Jacobson & Popovich, 1983).

This underscores the notion that sexual objectification lies on a continuum of dehumanizing experiences, with sexual violence at the extreme. Because to some degree all women in our culture face the possibility of sexual victimization, they need to be attentive to the potential for sexually-motivated bodily harm (Griffin, 1979; Brownmiller, 1975; Beneke, 1982; Pollitt, 1985). Empirical research shows that this attentiveness is a chronic and daily source of anxiety for many women, affecting both their personal and work lives (Gordon & Riger, 1989; Rozee, 1988). Feminists have argued that vigilance to safety may be the most fundamental difference between women's and men's subjective experiences (Griffin, 1979; Pollitt, 1985). For instance, when we have asked mixed-sex groups of students what they do on a given day to ensure their personal safety, we find that women dutifully identify multiple strategies (e.g., double-checking locks, carrying keys between fingers, checking the backseat of their car, jogging with a dog, staying in after dark, feigning deafness, etc.). Men, however, having few strategies to list, find it eye-opening to realize how women's daily experiences in the world differ so dramatically from their own.

In short, a culture that objectifies the female body presents women with a continuous stream of anxiety-provoking experiences, requiring them to maintain an almost chronic vigilance both to their physical appearance and to their physical safety.

Peak Motivational States Being fully absorbed in challenging mental or physical activity can be immensely rewarding and enjoyable. This state is what Csikszentmihalyi calls "flow" (1982, 1990), occurring "when a person's body or mind is stretched to its limits in a voluntary effort to accomplish something difficult and worthwhile" (1990, p. 3; see also Deci & Ryan, 1985b, for related work on *intrinsic motivation*). Csikszentmihalyi identifies flow as a prime source of optimal experience, those rare moments during which we feel we are truly living, uncontrolled by others, creative and joyful. Maximizing such experience, he argues, improves the quality of life.

We see at least two ways that being female in a culture that objectifies the female body can prevent or derail peak motivational states. First, and most obviously, a woman's activities are interrupted when actual others call attention to the appearance or functions of her body. As early as elementary school, in classrooms and on playgrounds, observational research shows that girls' activities and thoughts are more frequently disrupted by boys than vice versa (Thorne, 1993). Early on, these disruptions are often focused on "cooties" or "girl germs," fictitious pollutants associated with girls' bodies. Increasingly, these interruptions become infused with more direct overtones of heterosexuality, often drawing attention to a girl's appearance, weight, or breast development (Brownmiller, 1984; Thorne, 1993).

In addition, Csikszentmihalyi (1990) argues persuasively that a person must necessarily lose self-consciousness in order to achieve flow. Women's internalization of an observer's perspective on their bodies, by definition, creates a form of self-consciousness. This is the second way that women's peak motivational states are thwarted or limited. To be "doubled," as Beauvoir put it, is simply incompatible with the single-mindedness of flow states.

In her essay titled "Throwing Like a Girl," Young (1990) describes how habitual self-conscious body monitoring limits the flow to women's physical activities. We know from empirical work on nonverbal behavior that girls and women, relative to boys and men, restrict their bodily comportment and use of personal space (Hall, 1984; Henley, 1977). Young (1990) suggests two ways that this physical constriction can be linked to the practices of objectification. First, because movement itself draws attention to the body, it can increase a woman's potential for objectification. Second, and more critically, maintaining an observer's perspective of physical self forces women to simultaneously experience their bodies as "objects" as well as capacities: "[Women's] attention is often divided between the aim to be realized in motion and the body that must accomplish it" (Young, 1990, p. 146). Women's movement, by consequence, can grow timid, uncertain, and hesitant. These fits and starts apparent in women's movements may also infect women's mental concentration. This may pose a critical hindrance to women's attempts to become fully absorbed in any rewarding "flow" activity, whether physical or mental.

In sum, by limiting women's chances to initiate and maintain peak motivational states, the habitual body monitoring encouraged by a culture that objectifies the female body may reduce women's quality of life.

Awareness of Internal Bodily States Feminist poets and essayists have described women as alienated and distant from their own bodies and bodily sensations (e.g., Lerner, 1993; Orbach, 1982; Rich, 1979; Young, 1990). These ideas fit well within an objectification framework, which highlights the observer's perspective that women often adopt toward their own bodies.

Recent reviews of a wide range of empirical literatures argue that these poets and essayists may in fact be correct (Pennebaker & Roberts, 1992; Roberts & Pennebaker, 1995). Multiple studies suggest that, in the absence of relevant contextual cues, women are less accurate than men at detecting internal physiological sensations, such as heartbeat, stomach contractions, and blood glucose levels (e.g., Blascovich et al., 1992; Harver, Katkin & Bloch, 1993; Katkin, 1985; Katkin, Blascovich & Goldband, 1981). Consequently, women appear to make lesser use of these bodily cues than men in determining how they feel. For example, Laan and colleagues (e.g., Laan, Everaerd, van der Velde, & Geer, 1995; Laan & Everaerd, in press) have demonstrated that, unlike for men, the physiological changes associated with sexual arousal are only minimally predictive of women's subjective experience of sexual arousal. Rather, contextual stimuli appear to be more reliably related to women's feelings of sexual excitement (Laan, Everaerd, van Bellen, & Hanewald, 1994). Other findings from such diverse areas as sport psychology (e.g., Koltyn, O'Connor & Morgan, 1991) and emotion research (e.g., Levenson, Carstensen & Gottman, 1994) also demonstrate that physiological cues are relatively less important determinants of subjective experience for women than for men (see Roberts & Pennebaker, 1995 for a review of these literatures).

How might women's relative inattention to physiological cues come about? One possibility is suggested by research on dieting and restrained eating. Beginning in adolescence, dieting becomes a critical part of most women's lives in their efforts to achieve or maintain a slim body ideal (Dornbusch, Gross, Duncan & Ritter, 1987; Silberstein et al., 1987; Thornberry, Wilson & Golden, 1986). Importantly, dieting and restrained eating require active suppression of hunger cues. Some have argued that it may not be possible to selectively tune out hunger, and that the habits of restrained eaters may lead to a generalized insensitivity to internal bodily cues (Heatherton, Polivy & Herman, 1989; Polivy, et al., 1990).

A second possibility focuses on the self-conscious body monitoring that we have argued occupies women in a culture that objectifies the female body. Because women are vigilantly aware of their outer bodily appearance, they may be left with fewer perceptual resources available for attending to inner body experience. This limited resources perspective would predict that those particular social contexts that highlight women's awareness of observers' evaluations of their bodies would be associated with a corresponding muting of inner sensations. Arguably, repeated experiences in such contexts could lead to a more generalized loss of the privileged access people typically have to their own inner states.

In sum, by internalizing an observer's perspective as a primary view of physical self, women may lose access to their own inner physical experiences.

Part II: What Does Objectification Theory Offer to the Understanding of Women's Mental Health Risks?

So far, we have described multiple ways that being female in a culture that objectifies the female body may impact women's subjective experiences in negative ways. Recognizing that these negative experiences can accumulate and compound points to a possible contribution to a subset of women's mental health risks. In this section we explore three particular psychological disorders that, in American culture, are populated predominantly by females: unipolar depression, sexual dysfunction, and eating disorders.

Key to our framework is the idea that there are two main routes through which sexual objectification might contribute to poor mental health outcomes for women, one chronic and one more acute. The first follows from the experiences described in Part I: The potential for objectification fosters habitual body monitoring, leaving women with surpluses of shame and anxiety, a shortage of peak motivational states, and scant awareness of internal bodily states. We argue that the accumulation of such experiences could, for some women, result in pathology. The second route is more obvious and extreme, although just beginning to capture substantial research interest: actual sexual victimization, whether through rape, incest, battering, or even sexual harassment. With these forms of victimization, a woman's body is literally treated as a mere instrument or thing by her perpetrator. While our primary interest is in the first route—the mental health risks that may accumulate simply from being female in a culture that objectifies the female body—we also incorporate emerging evidence regarding the links between women's actual sexual victimization and poor mental health outcomes.

Objectification May Contribute to Women's Depression

Depressive episodes are characterized by prolonged depressed moods, loss of pleasure in most activities, or both (DSM-IV, APA, 1994). Experiences of depression—ranging from mild to severely debilitating—are common in both women and men (Eaton & Kessler, 1981; Robins et al., 1984). Even so, women are about twice as likely as men to become depressed (Nolen-Hoeksema, 1990). Although the lifetime prevalence of depression is lower among blacks than among whites and Hispanics, the 2-to-1 sex ratio holds across all three ethnic groups (Blazer, Kessler, McGonagle & Swartz, 1994). The lack of consensus across explanations for this sex difference leads us to explore what objectification theory might contribute to our understanding of depression in women.

Many theories have been advanced to explain the consistent sex difference in risk for depression (see Nolen-Hoeksema, 1990, for a review). These theories can be distilled into three classes of explanations. A first class of explanation focuses on female biology, attributing sex differences in depression to women's hormonal fluctuations and periodically low levels of estrogen. Puberty, pre-menstrual phases, post-partum and menopause are thus identified as times when women should be highly susceptible to depression. Empirical studies of these life phases, however, offer only mixed evidence, suggesting that the direct relationship between hormonal changes and depression is weak, at best temporary, and far from universal (Nolen-Hoeksema, 1990).

A second class of explanations for women's greater depression focuses on women's inferior social status and relative lack of power. The overt and covert discrimination women experience in relationships and in the workplace can make them feel powerless to achieve their goals and control important life outcomes. Learned helplessness theory (Seligman, 1975) explains how such powerlessness can lead to reduced motivation, sadness, and depression (Nolen-Hoeksema, 1990). As well, it may help to explain why women who are low-income single parents are particularly likely to become depressed (Russo, 1985). Power-status explanations, however, like biological explanations, at best offer partial explanations for women's depressions: Although nearly all women experience some forms of discrimination (and hormonal changes), most do not become depressed. Furthermore, given the multiple sources of oppression faced by women of color, a power/status explanation would predict that ethnic minority women ought to experience depression at higher rates than white women, and this appears not to be the case.

A third class of explanations better accounts for individual differences among women by describing how certain personality characteristics, more typical of women than men, can increase risk for depression. Many women are characterized as nurturant, emotional, nonassertive, self-sacrificing, and relationship-oriented. A range of theories have been offered to explain how women develop these traits and how these traits can compromise mental health (again, see Nolen-Hoeksema, 1990, for a review). As one example, Gilligan and others who emphasize women's relational style (Brown & Gilligan, 1992; Gilligan, Lyons & Hanmer, 1990; Jack, 1991) suggest that women's strivings for interpersonal intimacy, coupled with cultural prescriptions for being a "good woman," combine to create an experience women describe as loss of self (Gilligan, 1989; Jack, 1991). According to these theorists, loss of self (sometimes called silencing of self) results when, in efforts to smooth and protect valued relationships, women develop habits of censoring their own expression and restricting their own initiatives (Brown & Gilligan, 1992; Gilligan, 1989; Jack, 1991). In a depressed woman's words, "[I am] trying to be the way that other person wants me to be instead of the way I am" (Linda, quoted in Jack, 1991, p. 32). Over time, habitual self-censorship can lead to a duplicity of experience in which outer compliance is paired with inner confusion and frustration, often with ensuing depression (Jack, 1991). Although relational theorists sketch a compelling portrait of the depressed woman, they leave underspecified the mechanisms by which "loss of self" might lead to depression.

Objectification theory draws together strands of each of these classes of explanations for women's depression, yet reorients the focus toward the experience of being female in a culture that objectifies the female body. It builds on a view advanced by researchers in the biopyschosocial tradition which suggests that the influence hormones have on women's experiences is mediated by observable bodily changes: Hormones create conspicuous changes in the female body, which in turn alter the way girls and women interact with, and experience the social world (Brooks-Gunn & Peterson, 1983; Parlee, 1984). We articulated in Part I how living in a culture that objectifies the female body can disrupt women's flow of consciousness by doubling their perspectives of themselves. At an extreme, internalizing an observer's perspective on self might fully supplant a woman's own first-person perspective on self, a state that may resemble the "loss of self" described by relational theorists. Objectification theory further predicts that habitual body monitoring can generate recurrent shame and anxiety, and also curb the pleasure associated with peak motivational states. How repeated negative experiences such as these can spiral down into depression has garnered considerable attention in the depression literature. (The resulting theories, however, were not necessarily conceived to explain gender differences in depression.) Combining these existing theories with the explanatory framework offered by objectification theory can illuminate the mechanisms by which the "loss of self" inherent in being a "good woman" can increase risk for depression.

First, learned helplessness theory and other cognitive models of depression (Abramson, Seligman, & Teasdale, 1978; Beck, 1976) can explain how recurrent and uncontrollable experiences of shame and anxiety could lead to depression. The learned helplessness perspective suggests that depression ensues when people attribute their perceived failings to internal, stable, and global causes. We have argued that, because bodies are only partially alterable, women's body-based shame and anxiety cannot be readily overcome. Many women, then, may learn to feel helpless not only to correct their physical "failings" but also to control other people's reactions to their physical appearance. So, to the extent that a woman's body generates feelings of helplessness, it can also induce depression. Another perspective is that, because recurrent shame signals an unfixable *moral* shortcoming, it becomes so intolerable that women may be motivated to substitute shame with depression, which is thought to be more personally and socially acceptable (M. Lewis, 1992).

Second, as mentioned earlier, Csikszentmihalyi (1990) claims that because peak motivational states are intensely enjoyable, having few of them necessarily reduces the quality of life. Working from a behavioral perspective, Lewinsohn (1974) offers a compatible model of depression: He suggests that having few self-initiated positive experiences serves to extinguish active behavior, creating the motivational deficit characteristic of depression. Objectification theory adds that because women's prospects in relationships and in work often depend on others' evaluations of their appearance, women have less direct control over many of their own positive experiences. As such, women may have lean schedules of response-contingent positive reinforcement. According to Lewinsohn's model, this would put women at increased risk for depression.

And third, we underscore that objectification is part and parcel of the sexual victimization and harassment that women experience at much higher rates than men. Several theorists have recently argued that women's experiences of victimization may account for up to a third of the gender difference in depression (Cutler & Nolen-Hoeksema, 1991; Hamilton & Jensvold, 1992; Nolen-Hoeksema & Gergus, 1994).

In sum, by illuminating how women's emotional experiences can be shaped by the dictates of a culture that objectifies the female body, objectification theory can draw together disparate strands across current theories for sex difference in depression. Sexual objectification fosters a loss of self, accompanied by recurrent and perhaps uncontrollable shame and anxiety. These experiences, coupled with reduced opportunities for pleasure, may constitute one root cause of some women's depression. We wish to underscore, however, that like other theories for depression, objectification can only offer a partial explanation for the extent of depression evident among women in today's culture.

Objectification May Contribute to Women's Sexual Dysfunctions

Women report far more sexual dissatisfaction and dysfunction in heterosexual relations than do men (e.g., Frank, Anderson & Rubenstein, 1978; Hei man & Verhulst, 1982). Since research has shown that women and men are equally "sexual" in terms of their capacity for arousal and orgasm, purely physiological explanations for this difference are unsatisfactory (Heiman & Verhulst, 1982). Instead, several socialization theories have been offered, the most common and compelling of which focuses on cultural double-standards and the enactment of gender-role stereotypes in the sexual script (e.g., Tevlin & Leiblum, 1983). For example, heterosexual relations tend to focus on men's experience, and to be far more permissive of men's active, even aggressive sexuality. Women are more often expected to be passive, even asexual, saying either "yes" or "no" to men's sexual requests, rather than actively initiating sexual encounters. This passivity is perhaps most characteristic of adolescent girls and young women just beginning to be sexually "active" (Martin, in press). One consequence of this cultural attitude, some have argued, is that women's role in the sexual script is to give rather than take. This leads many women to fear appearing "selfish," (that is, unfeminine) and hence to focus not on their own desires and physical sensations, but rather on their male partner's.

Objectification theory offers a somewhat different explanation for women's sexual difficulties, focusing not simply on women's enactment of feminine roles, but rather on their self-conscious body monitoring and inattention to internal bodily states. As hypothesized in the section on peak motivational states, chronic attentiveness to one's own visual image may consume mental energy that might otherwise be spent on more satisfying and rewarding activity. Indeed sex researchers Masters and Johnson (1970) refer to the self-conscious body monitoring that occupies many women during sex as "spectatoring," and argue that this division of attention greatly hinders women's sexual satisfaction. Furthermore, sex researchers contend that orgasm (which we do not view as synonymous with subjective sexual pleasure) often requires attention and responsiveness to internal bodily signals of arousal (Adams, Haynes & Brayer, 1985; Hoon & Hoon, 1978; Wincze, Hoon & Hoon, 1976). We have argued that women's habitual attentiveness to external bodily appearance, combined with habits of restrained eating and dieting may lead to a generalized insensitivity to internal bodily cues. So, in addition to the divided attention associated with spectatoring, interoceptive insensitivity may be another obstacle to women's sexual pleasure.

Clearly the direct experience of sexual abuse, assault, or harassment also impacts women's enjoyment of sex. Research shows that for victims of such cruel and dehumanizing forms of objectification, sexual dysfunction and reductions in sexual enjoyment are common (e.g., Gordon & Riger, 1989; Martin, Warfield & Braen, 1983). One study showed that women's satisfaction with sex can remain lower than previous levels for up to seven years following sexual assault (Feldman-Summers, Gordon & Maegher, 1979).

Objectification May Contribute to Women's Eating Disorders

Perhaps the most obvious well-being risk for girls and women in a culture that objectifies the female body is eating disorders, for such problems are literally and visibly enacted on the body. Women overpopulate such disorders, comprising about 90 percent of those who suffer from bulimia and anorexia nervosa (Garfinkel & Garner, 1982; Johnson, Lewis & Hagman, 1984). Women are also more likely to be obese than men (Foreyt & Goodrick, 1982; Zegman, 1983). Contrary to a commonly-held stereotype that eating disorders are a "white, middle-class" phenomenon, substantial research now shows that they are becoming increasingly prevalent among women of color (e.g., Hsu, 1987; Root, 1990; Rosen, et al., 1988, Silber, 1986). Feminist research and theorizing on eating disorders has done much to illuminate the broad cultural influences on eating in an effort to answer the question of why eating disorders are almost uniquely a female problem in American culture.

Two distinct strands of feminist thought have been brought to bear on the causes of eating disorders. One of these perspectives points to the near universality of troubled attitudes toward eating among girls and women. This view argues that women's concerns with dieting and weight control are so pervasive that they reflect a "normative discontent" that women feel toward their bodies (Rodin, Silberstein & Striegel-Moore, 1984). Chronic dieting and restrained eating have been said to be a way of life for girls and women, one that is supported and encouraged by peers (Crandall, 1988) as well as parents (Costanzo & Woody, 1985).

From this perspective, eating disorders are seen merely as the extreme end of a continuum of this normative discontent. That is, women with anorexia and bulimia are argued simply to be resorting to more drastic means of manipulating the body (i.e., starvation and binging-and-purging vs. dieting and restrained eating) in order to attain the slim beauty ideal (e.g., Rodin, et al., 1984). Ironically, starvation and binging-and-purging, although clearly pathological, do function to alleviate body dissatisfaction to some degree, along with its associated shame and depression (McCarthy, 1990).

Another feminist perspective focuses on women's powerlessness by viewing eating disorders as political statements of protest against patriarchy. This view explains the sex difference in eating disorders by pointing out that women, having less power than men to influence through action, often use the one thing they can manipulate—their bodies—as a means of influence. For example, Orbach (1978) has argued that obesity in women can be viewed as a response to their social position: "Fat is a way of saying 'no' to powerlessness and self-denial, to a limiting sexual expression which demands that females look and act a certain way, and to an image of womanhood that defines a specific social role" (p. 21). Similarly, psychoanalytic theorists have pointed out that self-starvation represents a strategic regression considering that it prevents the girl's body from developing from childlike angularity to curvy young womanhood and can even prevent menses (e.g., Bruch 1973, 1978). Recently, Steiner-Adair (1990) has argued that anorexia can be viewed as a way of using the body as a political statement of rebellion, particularly in adolescence. She likens the prolonged fasting of the many anorexic teenage girls in our country to a "hunger strike undertaken by a group who have a vision of impending calamity and danger" (p. 175). Steiner-Adair (1990) argues that girls may choose to avoid entering the world of adulthood, because they see that world does not value feminine principles of caring and interrelatedness. This is symbolized, she argues, by the cultural idealization of thinness in women, and denial of the rounded, maternal female body.

Clearly, then, both feminist perspectives on eating disorders can be seen as fitting within an objectification framework. We have argued that comparing one's own body to cultural ideals, and knowing that one's body will be subject to such comparisons by others, is fundamental to women's experience. Whether an individual woman attempts to (a) meet such ideals, or (b) opt out of the system of objectification, she must do so with her body. Eating disorders may thus reflect either of these two strategies. On the one hand, they may function to relieve the discontent, shame, and anxiety that nearly all women feel about their bodies. On the other hand, eating disorders may function as resistance. While Steiner-Adair's hunger strike analogy is provocative, her suggestion that girls link the shape of the adult female body to feminine principles of caring and interrelatedness seems doubtful to us. We find it more parsimonious to link the shape of the adult female body to our culture's practices of sexually objectifying that body. The negative consequences that objectification has for women's life experiences gives girls reason enough to protest. In either case, however, eating disorders are passive, pathological strategies, reflecting girls' and women's lack of power to more directly control the objectification of their bodies. Moreover, studies show that victims of actual sexual assault and abuse often show severe body image disturbances and suffer from eating disorders at higher rates than others (Demitrack, Putnam, Brewerton, Brandt & Gold, 1990). This lends further sobering support to the idea that girl's and women's troubled attitudes toward eating can be intimately linked to the objectification of their bodies. . . .

Summary and Conclusions

Objectification theory represents our attempt to push further a sociocultural analysis of the female body within the psychology of women and gender. It provides a partial framework for organizing and understanding an array of experiences that appear to be uniquely female. Perhaps the most profound and pervasive of these experiences is the disruption in the flow of consciousness that results as girls and women internalize the culture's practices of objectification and habitually monitor their bodies' appearance. The repercussions of this habitual body monitoring, in turn, permeate a host of emotional, motivational, and attentional states. Collectively, these patterns of experience may be important contributors to women's mental health risks. . . . Beyond parsimoniously organizing a wide variety of preexisting empirical evidence regarding women's lives, objectification theory also presents specific predictions to guide empirical work yet to be done.

In summarizing the theory, however, it is critical to underscore that objectification does not affect all women equally. First, particular combinations of class, ethnicity, age, and sexuality, as well as personal and physical attributes, are likely to produce heterogeneity of experience across subgroups of women. Some of these sources of difference from the dominant culture may mitigate or protect certain subgroups of women against the negative psychological repercussions that we link to sexual objectification. For instance, the findings of Crocker and colleagues mentioned earlier suggest that a history of racial oppression may lead blacks to construct a sense of self that deflects rather than reflects others' appraisals (Crocker et al., 1994). However, as Root (1990) has argued, minority women are not immune to the pressure to look "perfect," particularly in the context of upward social mobility in which acceptance is sought from the dominant (white, male) culture that so clearly values thinness and "beauty" in women. The notion of "protective factors" among subgroups of women, therefore, should not be mistaken for complete invulnerability to the consequences of objectification.

In addition, sexual objectification is unlikely to affect any woman all of the time. The extent to which particular social contexts accentuate a woman's awareness of actual or potential observers' perspectives on her body will, in part, predict the degree and kind of negative repercussions that she may experience. Sociological research has shown that it is in certain spaces—namely public, mixed-gender, unstructured ones—that women's bodies are most subject to evaluative commentary by others (e.g., Gardner, 1980). These then are the contexts in which the experiential consequences of objectification are predicted to be most evident. Interestingly, many women take precautions either to avoid appearing alone in these sorts of contexts, or to fortify themselves for such appearances.

As well, not all women appear to internalize an observer's perspective on their bodies to the same degree. There are multiple ways that women of all walks of life are able to resist and subvert the culture's practices of objectification in their own lives. Changes in bodily presentation, for instance, appear to alter the extent to which women are open for evaluative attention. Many women adopt conscious strategies for stepping out of the "objectification limelight," ranging from wearing comfortable shoes and loose-fitting clothing, to not removing "unwanted" body hair nor wearing cosmetics. These seemingly trivial practices of self-presentation ought to be taken seriously by researchers as women's efforts to resist sexual objectification and thereby enhance their own psychological well-being within a culture that so vehemently objectifies the female body.

The evidence we have reviewed suggests that our culture's practices of objectification certainly do not serve women well. If future direct tests of objectification theory produce further evidence to support it, then the most important contribution of the theory may be to prompt individual and collective action to change, or at least diversify the meanings our culture assigns to the female body. One strategy is to take aim at our cultural practices, the visual media in particular. Another is to transform our educational efforts, both formal and informal, to fortify girls and women against the negative psychological repercussions of objectification and teach them to experience their bodies in more direct and positive ways. For example, encouraging sports participation—particularly in childhood and through the adolescent years—might help girls and women to experience their bodies as strong, active agents.

Seemingly innocuous, the sexual objectification of women and its psychological consequences have gone understudied by researchers for too long. Objectification theory is our effort to name one set of sociocultural barriers that diminish women's well-being and limit their potential.

Notes

1. We focus in this paper on the psychological consequences for women of the cultural practice of sexually objectifying female bodies. In doing so, we do not wish to convey that men are not also at times subjected to sexually objectifying treatment, nor that they do not also experience negative repercussions from such treatment. In fact, an analysis of the unique ways that men experience sexual objectification will certainly become necessary if our culture's mass media practices follow current trends toward equal treatment: Instead of eliminating objectifying portrayals of women, we've witnessed an upsurge of objectifying portrayals of men (Wernick, 1991; van Zoonen, 1994).
2. We also add that the cultural milieu of objectification encourages girls and women to treat *other girls and women* as objects to be looked at and evaluated. Although the ways that such treatment alter the relationships between and among girls deserves attention and study, they are beyond the scope of this introductory paper.
3. This implicit association between shame and moral shortcomings may explain why shame is often more difficult than other negative emotions to assess via direct self-report.

References

Abramson, L. Y., Seligman, M. E. P., & Teasdale, J. (1978). Learned helplessness in humans: Critique and reformulation. *Journal of Abnormal Psychology, 87*, 49–74.

Adams, A. E., Haynes, S. N. & Brayer, M. A. (1985). Cognitive distraction in female sexual arousal. *Psychophysiology, 22*, 689–96.

American Association of University Women. (1993). *Hostile Hallways: The AAUW Survey on Sexual Harassment in American Schools.* The AAUW Educational Foundation.

American Psychiatric Association. (1994). *Diagnostic and statistical manual of mental disorders* (4th ed.). Washington, DC: American Psychiatric Association.

Archer, D., Iritani, B., Kimes, D. D., & Barrios, M. (1983). Face-ism: Five studies of sex differences in facial prominence. *Journal of Personality and Social Psychology, 45*, 725–35.

Argyle, M. & Williams, M. (1969). Observer or observed: A reversible perspective in person perception. *Sociometry, 32*, 396–412.

Attie, I., & Brooks-Gunn, J. (1989). Development of eating problems in adolescent girls: A longitudinal study. *Developmental Psychology, 25*, 70–79.

Bar-Tal, D., & Saxe, L. (1976). Physical attractiveness and its relationship to sex role stereotyping. *Sex Roles, 2*, 123–33.

Bartky, S. L. (1990). *Femininity and domination: Studies in the phenomenology of Oppression.* New York: Routledge.

Basow, S. A. (1992). *Gender stereotypes and roles* (3rd ed.). Pacific Grove, CA: Brooks/Cole.

Beauvoir, S. (1952). *The second sex.* Translated by H. M. Parshley. New York: Knopf.

Beck, A. T. (1976). *Cognitive therapy and the emotional disorders.* New York: International University Press.

Beneke, T. (1982). *Men on rape.* New York: St. Martin's Press.

Berger, J. (1972). *Ways of seeing.* London: Penguin.

Berscheid, E., Dion, K., Walster, E., & Walster, G. W. (1971). Physical attractiveness and dating choice: A test of the matching hypothesis. *Journal of Experimental Social Psychology, 7*, 173–89.

Blascovich, J., Brennan, K., Tomaka, J., Kelsey, R. M., Hughes, P., Coad, M. L., & Adlin, R. (1992). Affect intensity and cardiac arousal. *Journal of Personality and Social Psychology, 63*, 164–74.

Blazer, D. G., Kessler, R. C., McGonagle, K. A., & Swartz, M. S. (1994). The prevalence and distribution of major depression in a national community sample: The National Comorbidity Survey. *American Journal of Psychiatry, 151*, 979–86.

Bordo, S. (1993). *Unbearable weight: Feminism, western culture, and the body.* Berkeley: University of California Press.

Brooks-Gunn, J., & Petersen, A. C. (1983). *Girls at puberty: Biological and psychosocial perspectives.* New York: Plenum.

Brown, L. M., & Gilligan, C. (1992). *Meeting at the crossroads: Women's psychology and girls' development.* Cambridge, MA: Harvard University Press.

Brownmiller, S. (1975). *Against our will: Men, women and rape.* New York: Simon & Schuster.

Brownmiller, S. (1984). *Femininity.* New York: Linden Press.

Bruch, H. (1973). *Eating disorders: Obesity, anorexia nervosa, and the person within.* New York: Basic Books.

Bruch, H. (1978). *The golden cage: The enigma of anorexia nervosa.* Cambridge: Harvard University Press.

Buss, D. (1989). Sex differences in human mate preferences: Evolutionary hypotheses tested in 37 cultures. *Behavioral and Brain Sciences, 12,* 1–49.

Cary, M. S. (1978). Does civil inattention exist in pedestrian passing? *Journal of Personality and Social Psychology, 36,* 1185–93.

Cash, T. F., Gillen, B., & Burns, D. S. (1977). Sexism and "beautyism" in personnel consultant decision making. *Journal of Applied Psychology, 62,* 301–10.

Connell, R. W. (1987). *Gender and power.* Stanford, CA: Stanford University Press.

Cooley, C. H. (1902/1990). Human nature and the social order. Excerpted in A. G. Halberstadt & S. L. Ellyson. eds. *Social psychology readings: A century of research* (pp. 61–67). New York: McGraw-Hill.

Copeland, G. A. (1989). Face-ism and prime-time television. *Journal of Broadcasting and Electronic Media, 33,* 209–14.

Costanzo, P. R. (1992). External socialization and the development of adaptive individuation and social connection. In D. N. Ruble, P. R. Costanzo, & M. E. Oliveri. eds. *The social psychology of mental health* (pp. 55–80). New York: Guilford.

Costanzo, P. R. & Woody, E. Z. (1985). Domain-specific parenting styles and their impact on the child's development of particular deviance: The example of obesity proneness. *Journal of Social and Clinical Psychology, 3,* 425–45.

Crandall, C. S. (1988). Social contagion of binge eating. *Journal of Personality and Social Psychology, 55,* 588–98.

Crocker, J., Cornwell, B., & Major, B. (1993). The stigma of overweight: Affective consequences of attributional ambiguity. *Journal of Personality and Social Psychology, 64,* 60–70.

Crocker, J., Luhtanen, R., Blaine, B., & Broadnax, S. (1994). Collective self-esteem and psychological well-being among white, black and Asian college students. *Personality and Social Psychology Bulletin, 20,* 503–13.

Csikszentmihalyi, M. (1982). Toward a psychology of optimal experience. In L. Wheeler. ed. *Review of personality and social psychology.* Beverly Hills, CA: Sage.

Csikszentmihalyi, M. (1990). *Flow.* New York: Harper Perennial.

Cutler, S. E., & Nolen-Hoeksema, S. (1991). Accounting for sex differences in depression through female victimization: Childhood sexual abuse. *Sex Roles, 24,* 425–38.

Darwin, C. (1965). *The expression of emotion in man and animals.* Chicago: University of Chicago Press. (Original work published 1872).

Deaux, K., & Major, B. (1987). Putting gender into context: An interactive model of gender-related behavior. *Psychological Review, 94,* 369–89.

Deci, E. L., & Ryan, R. M. (1985b). *Intrinsic motivation and self determination in human behavior.* New York: Plenum.

Demitrack, M. A., Putnam, F. W., Brewerton, T. D., Brandt, H. A., & Gold, P. W. (1990). Dissociative phenomena in eating disorders: Relationship to clinical variables. *American Journal of Psychiatry, 147*, 1184–88.

Deutsch, H. (1944). *The psychology of women: A psychoanalytic interpretation*, Vol. 1. New York: Grune & Stratton.

Deutsch, H. (1945). *The psychology of women: A psychoanalytic interpretation*, Vol. 2. New York: Grune & Stratton.

Dion, K. L., Dion, K. K., & Keelan, J. P. (1990). Appearance anxiety as a dimension of social-evaluative anxiety: Exploring the ugly duckling syndrome. *Contemporary Social Psychology, 14*, 220–24.

Dornbusch, S. M., Gross, R. T., Duncan, P. D., & Ritter, P. L. (1987). Stanford studies of adolescence using the national health examination survey. In R. M. Lerner & T. T. Foch, eds. *Biological-psychosocial interactions in early adolescence* (pp. 189–205). Hillsdale, NJ: Erlbaum.

Duncan, M. C. (1990). Sports photographs and sexual difference: Images of women and men in the 1984 and 1988 Olympic Games. *Sociology of Sport Journal*, 7, 22–43.

Eaton, W. W., & Kessler, L. G. (1981). Rates of symptoms of depression in a national sample. *American Journal of Epidemiology, 114*, 528–38.

Eccles, J. S., Jacobs, J. E., & Harold, R. D. (1990). Gender role stereotypes, expectancy effects, and parents' socialization of gender differences. *Journal of Social Issues, 46*, 183–201.

Fallon, A. E., & Rozin, P. (1985). Sex differences in perception of desirable body shape. *Journal of Abnormal Psychology, 94*, 102–105.

Feldman-Summers, S., Gordon, P. E., & Maegher, J. R. (1979). The impact of rape on sexual satisfaction. *Journal of Abnormal Psychology, 88*, 101–105.

Ferguson, M. (1978). Imagery and ideology: The cover photographs of traditional women's magazines. In G. Tuchman, A. K. Daniels, & J. Benet (Eds.), *Hearth and home: Images of women in the mass media* (pp. 97–115). New York: Oxford University Press.

Fine, M. (1988). Sexuality, schooling, and adolescent females: The missing discourse of desire. *Harvard Educational Review, 58*, 29–53.

Fischer, K., Vidmar, N., & Ellis, R. (1993). The culture of battering and the role of mediation in domestic violence cases. *SMU Law Review, 46*, 2117–74.

Fiske, S. T., Bersoff, D. N., Borgida, E., Deaux, K., & Heilman, M. E. (1991). Social science research on trial: Use of sex stereotyping research in Price Waterhouse v. Hopkins. *American Psychologist, 46*, 1049–60.

Fodor, I. G., & Franks, V. (1990). Women in midlife and beyond: The new prime of life? *Psychology of Women Quarterly, 14*, 445–49.

Foreyt, J. P., & Goodrick, G. K. (1982). Gender and obesity. In I. Al-Issa (Ed.), *Gender and psychopathology* (pp. 337–55). New York: Academic Press.

Foucault, M. (1980). *The history of sexuality* Vol. 1. New York: Vintage.

Frank, E., Anderson, C., & Rubenstein, D. (1978). The frequency of sexual dysfunction in "normal" couples. *New England Journal of Medicine, 299*, 111–15.

Fraser, N. & Nicholson, L. J. (1990). Social criticism without philosophy: An encounter between feminism and postmoderism. In L. J. Nicholson (Ed.), *Feminism/Postmoderism* (pp. 19–38). New York: Routledge.

Freud, S. (1933). Femininity. In Strachey, J. (Tr. and Ed.), *New introductory lectures on psychoanalysis*. New York: Norton.

Friedan, B. (1993). *The fountain of age*. New York: Simon & Schuster.

Fromme, D. K. & Beam, D. C. (1974). Dominance and sex differences in nonverbal responses to differential eye contact. *Journal of Research in Personality, 8*, 76–87.

Gardner, C. B. (1980). Passing by: Street remarks, address rights, and the urban female. *Sociological Inquiry, 50*, 328–56.

Garfinkel, P. E. & Garner, D. M. (1982). *Anorexia nervosa: A multidimensional perspective*. New York: Brunner/Mazel.

Gergen, M. M. (1990). Finished at 40: Women's development with the patriarchy. *Psychology of Women Quarterly, 14*, 471–93.

Gilligan, C. (1989). Teaching Shakespeare's sister: Notes from the underground of female adolescence. In C. Gilligan, N. P. Lyons, & T. J. Hanmer (Eds.), *Making connections: The relational worlds of adolescent girls at Emma Willard School* (pp. 6–29). Cambridge, MA: Harvard University Press.

Gilligan, C., Lyons, N. P., & Hanmer, T. J. (1990). *Making connections: The relational worlds of adolescent girls at Emma Willard School*. Cambridge, MA: Harvard University Press.

Goffman, E. (1979). *Gender advertisements*. Cambridge, MA: Harvard University Press.

Gordon, M. T. & Riger, S. (1989). *The female fear: The social cost of rape*. New York: Free Press.

Griffin, S. (1979). *Rape: The power of consciousness*. San Francisco, CA: Harper & Row.

Hall, J. A. (1984). *Nonverbal sex differences: Communication accuracy and expressive style*. Baltimore, MD: Johns Hopkins University Press.

Hamilton, J. A. & Jensvold, M. (1992). Personality, psychopathology, and depressions in women. In L. S. Brown & M. Ballou (Eds.), *Personality and psychopathology: Feminist reappraisals* (pp. 116–143). New York: Guilford.

Hancock, E. (1989). *The girl within*. New York: Fawcett Columbine.

Harter, S. (1987). The determinants and mediational role of global selfworth in children. In N. Eisenberg (Ed.), *Contemporary issues in developmental psychology* (pp. 219–42). New York: John Wiley.

Harver, A., Katkin, E. S., & Bloch, E. (1993). Signal-detection outcomes of heartbeat and respiratory resistance detection tasks in male and female subjects. *Psychophysiology, 30*, 223–30.

Heatherton, T. F., Polivy, J., & Herman, C. P. (1989). Restraint and

internal responsiveness: Effects of placebo manipulations of hunger on eating. *Journal of Abnormal Psychology, 98*, 89–92.
Heilbrun, C. G. (1988). *Writing a woman's life*. New York: Ballantine Books.
Heiman, J. R. & Verhulst, J. (1982). Gender and sexual functioning. In I. Al-Issa (Ed.), *Gender and psychopathology* (pp. 305–20). New York: Academic Press.
Henley, N. M. (1977). *Body politics: Power, sex and nonverbal communication*. New York: Touchstone.
Herman, J. L. (1992). *Trauma and recovery*. New York: Harper Perennial.
Holland, D., & Skinner, D. (1987). Prestige and intimacy: The cultural models behind Americans' talk about gender types. In D. Holland & N. Quinn (Eds.), *Cultural models in language and thought* (pp. 78–111). Cambridge: Cambridge University Press.
Hoon, E. F., & Hoon, P. W. (1978). Styles of sexual expression in women: Clinical implications of multivariate analysis. *Archives of Sexual Behavior, 7*, 105–16.
Hsu, L. K. G. (1987). Are eating disorders becoming more common in Blacks? *International Journal of Eating Disorders, 6*, 113–24.
Hughes, J. O. & Sandler, B. R. (1988). *Peer harassment: Hassles for women on campus*. Washington D.C.: Project on the Status and Education of Women, Association of American Colleges.
Hurtado, A. (1989). Relating to privilege: Seduction and rejection in the subordination of white women and women of color. *Signs, 14*, 833–55.
Itzin, C. (1986). Media images of women: The social construction of ageism and sexism. In S. Wilkinson (Ed.), *Feminist Social psychology: Developing theory and practice* (pp. 119–34). Philadelphia: Open University Press.
Jack, D. C. (1991). *Silencing the self: Women and depression*. New York: Harper Perennial.
Jacobson, M. B. & Popovich, P. M. (1983). Victim attractiveness and perceptions of responsibility in an ambiguous rape case. *Psychology of Women Quarterly, 8*, 100–104.
Johnson, C. L., Lewis, C., & Hagman, J. (1984). The syndrome of bulimia: Review and synthesis. *Psychiatric Clinics of North America, 7*, 247–73.
Kaschak, E. (1992). *Engendered Lives: A new psychology of women's experience*. New York: Basic Books.
Katkin, E. S. (1985). Blood, sweat and tears: Individual differences in autonomic self-perception. *Psychophysiology, 22*, 125–37.
Katkin, E. S., Blascovich, J., & Goldband, S. (1981). Empirical assessment of visceral self-perception: Individual and sex differences in the acquisition of heartbeat discrimination. *Journal of Personality and Social Psychology, 40*, 1095–101.
Keelan, J. P., Dion, K. K., & Dion, K. L. (1992). Correlates of appearance anxiety in late adolescence and early adulthood among young women. *Journal of Adolescence, 15*, 193–205.

Koss, & Harvey. (1987). *The rape victim: Clinical and community approaches to treatment.* Lexington, MA: Stephen Greene Press.

Kuhn, A. (1985). *The power of the image: Essays on representation and sexuality.* London: Routledge & Kegan Paul.

Laan, E. & Everaerd, W. (in press). Determinants of female sexual arousal: Psychophysiological theory and data. *Annual Review of Sex Research, 6.*

Laan, E., Everaerd, W., van Bellen, G. & Hanewald, G. (1994). Women's sexual and emotional responses to male- and female-produced erotica. *Archives of Sexual Behavior, 23*, 153–69.

Laan, E., Everaerd, W., van der Velde, J. & Geer, J. H. (1995). Determinants of subjective experience of sexual arousal in women: Feedback from genital arousal and erotic stimulus content. *Psychophysiology, 32*, 444–51.

Lazarus, R. S. (1991). *Emotion and adaptation.* New York: Oxford University Press.

Lerner, H. G. (1993). *The dance of deception: Pretending and truth-telling in women's lives.* New York: HarperCollins.

Lerner, R. M., Orlos, J. B., & Knapp, J. R. (1976). Physical attractiveness, physical effectiveness and self-concept in late adolescents. *Adolescence, 11*, 313–26.

Levenson, R. W., Carstensen, L. L., & Gottman, J. M. (1994). The influence of age and gender on affect, physiology and their interrelations: A study of long-term marriages. *Journal of Personality and Social Psychology, 67*, 56–68.

Lewinsohn, P. M. (1974). A behavioral approach to depression. In R. J. Friedman & M. M. Katz (Eds.), *The psychology of depression: Contemporary theory and research.* Washington, DC: Winston-Wiley.

Lewis, H. B. (1971). *Shame and guilt in neurosis.* New York: International Universities Press.

Lewis, H. B. (1989). Some thoughts on the moral emotions of shame and guilt. In L. Cirillo, B. Kaplan, & S. Wapner (Eds.), *Emotions in ideal human development* (pp. 35–51). Hillsdale, NJ: Lawrence Erlbaum.

Lewis, M. (1992). *Shame: The exposed self.* New York: Free Press.

Livson, F. B. (1976). Patterns of personality development in middle-aged women: A longitudinal study. *International Journal of Aging and Human Development,* 7, 107–15.

Margolin, L., & White, L. (1987). The continuing role of physical attractiveness in marriage. *Journal of Marriage and the Family, 49*, 21–27.

Martin, C. A., Warfield, M. C., & Braen, G. R. (1983). Physicians' management of the psychological aspects of rape. *Journal of the American Medical Association, 249*, 501–503.

Martin, E. (1987). *The woman in the body: A cultural analysis of reproduction.* Boston: Beacon Press.

Martin, K. (in press). *Puberty, sexuality, and the self: Boys and girls at adolescence.* New York: Routledge.

Masters, W. H. & Johnson, V. E. (1970). *Human sexual inadequacy*. Boston: Little, Brown & Company.

McCarthy, M. (1990). The thin ideal, depression and eating disorders in women. *Behavior Research and Therapy, 28*, 205–15.

Mitchell, V. & Helson, R. (1990). Women's prime of life: Is it the 50s? *Psychology of Women Quarterly, 14*, 451–70.

Mulvey, L. (1975). Visual pleasure and narrative cinema. *Screen, 16*, 6–18.

Neugarten, B. L., Wood, V., Kraines, R. J., & Loomis, B. (1963). Women's attitudes towards menopause. *Vita Humana, 6*, 140–51.

Nolen-Hoeksema, S. & Girgus, J. (1994). The emergence of gender differences in depression during adolescence. *Psychological Bulletin, 115*, 424–43.

Nolen-Hoeksema, S. (1990). *Sex differences in depression*. Stanford, CA: Stanford University Press.

Ohman, A. (1993). Fear and anxiety as emotional phenomena: Clinical phenomenology, evolutionary perspectives, and information-processing mechanisms. In M. Lewis & J. M. Haviland (Eds.), *Handbook of Emotions* (pp. 511–36). New York: Guilford.

Orbach, S. (1978). *Fat is a feminist issue: A self-help guide for compulsive eaters*. New York: Berkley Books.

Orbach, S. (1982). *Fat is a feminist issue II: A program to conquer compulsive eating*. New York: Berkley Books.

Parlee, M. B. (1984). Reproductive issues, including menopause. In G. Baruch & J. Brooks-Gunn (Eds.), *Women in midlife* (pp. 303–13). New York: Plenum.

Pennebaker, J. W. & Roberts, T-A. (1992). Toward a his and hers theory of emotion: Gender differences in visceral perception. *Journal of Social and Clinical Psychology, 11*, 199–212.

Polivy, J., Herman, C. P., & Pliner, P. (1990). Perception and evaluation of body image: The meaning of body shape and size. In J. M. Olson & M. P. Zanna (Eds.), *Self-Inference Processes: The Ontario Symposium, 6*, (pp. 87–114). Hillsdale, NJ: Lawrence Erlbaum Associates.

Pollitt, K. (1985, December 12). Hers. *New York Times*. p. C–2.

Quina, K. & Carlson, N. (1989). *Rape, incest, and sexual harassment*. New York: Greenwood.

Reilly, M. E., Lott, B., Caldwell, D., & DeLuca, L. (1992). Tolerance for sexual harassment related to self-reported sexual victimization. *Gender and Society, 6*, 122–38.

Rich, A. (1979). *On lies, secrets and silences*. New York: Norton.

Roberts, T-A., & Pennebaker, J. (1995). Gender differences in perceiving internal state: Toward a his and her model of perceptual cue use. *Advances in Experimental Social Psychology, 27*, 143–75.

Robins, L. N., Helzer, J. E., Weissman, M. M., Orvaschel, H., Gruenberg, E., Berke, J. D., & Regier, D. A. (1984). Lifetime prevalence of specific psychiatric disorders in three sites. *Archives of General Psychiatry, 41*, 949–58.

Rodeheaver, D. & Stohs, J. (1991). The adaptive misperception of age in older women: Sociocultural images and psychological mechanisms of control. *Educational Gerontology, 17*, 141–56.

Rodin, J., Silberstein, L. & Striegel-Moore, R. H. (1984). Women and weight: A normative discontent. In T. B. Sonderegger (Ed.), *Nebraska symposium on motivation 1984: Psychology and gender*, vol. 32 (pp. 267–307). Lincoln: University of Nebraska Press.

Root, M. P. P. (1990). Disordered eating in women of color. *Sex Roles, 22*, 525–36.

Rosen, L. W., Shafer, C. L., Dummer, G. M., Cross, L. K., Deuman, G. W., & Malmberg, S. R. (1988). Prevalence of pathogenic weight-control behaviors among native American women and girls. *International Journal of Eating Disorders, 7*, 807–11.

Rosenberg, F. & Simmons, R. G. (1975). Sex differences in the self-concept in adolescence. *Sex Roles, 1*, 147–59.

Rozee, P. (1988, August). *The effects of fear of rape on working women.* Paper presented at the meeting of the American Psychological Association, Atlanta, GA.

Russo, N. F. (1985). *A women's mental health agenda.* Washington, DC: American Psychological Association.

Schur, E. M. (1983). *Labeling women deviant: Gender, stigma, and social control.* Philadelphia: Temple University Press.

Seligman, M. E. P. (1975). *Helplessness: On depression, development, and death.* San Francisco: Freeman.

Shilling, C. (1993). *The body and social theory*. London: Sage.

Silber, T. J. (1986). Anorexia nervosa in Blacks and Hispanics. *International Journal of Eating Disorders, 5*, 121–28.

Silberstein, L. R., Striegel-Moore, R., & Rodin, J. (1987). Feeling fat: A woman's shame. In H. B. Lewis (Ed.), *The role of shame in symptom formation* (pp. 89–108). Hillsdale, NJ: Lawrence Erlbaum.

Simmons, R. G. & Rosenberg, F. (1975). Sex, sex-roles and self-image. *Journal of Youth and Adolescence, 4*, 229–58.

Simmons, R. G., Blyth, D. A., Cleave, E. F. V., & Bush, D. M. (1979). Entry into early adolescence: The impact of school structure, puberty, and early dating on self-esteem. *American Sociological Review, 44*, 948–67.

Singh, D. (1993). Adaptive significance of female physical attractiveness: Role of waist-to-hip ratio. *Journal of Personality and Social Psychology, 65*, 293–307.

Snow, J. T. & Harris, M. B. (1985). Maintenance of weight loss: Demographic, behavioral and attitudinal correlates. *Journal of Obesity and Weight Regulation, 4*, 234–55.

Soley, L. C. & Kurzbard, G. (1986). Sex in advertising: A comparison of 1964 and 1984 magazine advertisements. *Journal of Advertising, 15*, 46–64.

Stapley, J. C. & Haviland, J. M. (1989). Beyond depression: Gender dif-

ferences in normal adolescents' emotional experiences. *Sex Roles, 20*, 295–308.
Steiner-Adair, C. (1990). The body politic: Normal female adolescent development and the development of eating disorders. In C. Gilligan, N. P. Lyons, & T. J. Hanmer (Eds.), *Making connections: The relational worlds of adolescent girls at Emma Willard School* (pp. 162–82). Cambridge, MA: Harvard University Press.
Stoltenberg, J. (1989). *Refusing to be a man.* New York: Penguin.
Tevlin, H. E. & Leiblum, S. R. (1983). Sex role stereotypes and female sexual dysfunction. In V. Franks & E. D. Rothblum (Eds.), *The stereotyping of women: Its effects on mental health* (pp. 129–50). New York: Springer.
Thornberry, O. T., Wilson, R. W., & Golden, P. (1986). Health promotion and disease prevention provisional data from the National Health Interview Survey: United States, January–June, 1985. *Vital and Health Statistics of the National Center for Health Statistics, 119*, 1–16.
Thorne, B. (1993). *Gender play: Girls and boys in school.* New Brunswick, NJ: Rutgers University Press.
Trickett, A. K. & Putnam, F. W. (1993). Impact of child sexual abuse on females: Toward a developmental psychobiological integration. *Psychological Science, 4*, 81–87.
Umiker-Sebeok, J. (1981). The seven ages of women: A view from American magazine advertisements. In C. Mayo & N. M. Henley (Eds.), *Gender and non-verbal behavior* (pp. 209–52). New York: Springer-Verlag.
Unger, R. K. (1979). *Female and male.* New York: Harper and Row.
Ussher, J. M. (1989). *The psychology of the female body.* London: Routledge.
Van Zoonen, L. (1994). *Feminist media studies.* London: Sage.
Wallston, B. S. & O'Leary, V. (1981). Sex makes a difference: Differential perceptions of women and men. In L. Wheeler (Ed.), *Review of personality and social psychology*, Vol. 2 (pp. 9–41). Beverly Hills, CA: Sage.
Walster, E., Aronson, E., Abrahams, D., & Rottman, L. (1966). Importance of physical attractiveness in dating behavior. *Journal of Personality and Social Psychology, 4*, 508–16.
Wernick, A. (1991). *Promotional culture: Advertising, ideology and symbolic expression.* London: Sage.
Westkott, M. (1986). *The feminist legacy of Karen Horney.* New Haven: Yale University Press.
Wincze, J. P., Hoon, E. F., & Hoon, P. W. (1976). Physiological responsivity of normal and sexually dysfunctional women during erotic stimulus exposure. *Journal of Psychosomatic Research, 20*, 445–51.
Wolf, N. (1991). *The beauty myth: How images of beauty are used against women.* New York: Anchor Books.
Wooley, O. W., Wooley, S. C., & Dyrenforth, S. R. (1979). Obesity and women: A neglected feminist topic. *Women's Studies International Quarterly, 2*, 81–92.
Wooley, S. C. & Wooley, O. W. (1980). Eating disorders: Anorexia and

obesity. In A. M. Brodsky & R. Hare-Mustin (Eds.), *Women and psychotherapy* (pp. 135–58). New York: Guilford Press.

Young, I. M. (1990). *Throwing like a girl and other essays in feminist philosophy and social theory*. Bloomington: Indiana University Press.

Zegman, M. A. (1983). Women, weight and health. In V. Franks & E. D. Rothblum (Eds.), *The stereotyping of women: Its effects on mental health* (pp. 172–200). New York: Springer.

7 Women and Weight: Gendered Messages on Magazine Covers

AMY R. MALKIN

KIMBERLIE WORNIAN

JOAN C. CHRISLER

In this content analysis, the covers of 21 popular women's and men's magazines were examined for gendered messages related to bodily appearance. Magazine covers were divided according to gender of readers and each cover was reviewed using a checklist designed to analyze visual images and text as well as the placement of each on the covers. Analyses showed that 78% of the covers of the women's magazines contained a message regarding bodily appearance, whereas none of the covers of the men's magazines did so. Twenty-five percent of the women's magazine covers contained conflicting messages regarding weight loss and dietary habits. In addition, the positioning of weight-related messages on the covers often implied that losing weight may lead to a better life. Men's magazines focus on providing entertainment and expanding knowledge, hobbies, and activities; women's magazines continue to focus on improving one's life by changing one's appearance.

Feminist researchers have repeatedly reported on the significant role that the media play in the construction of the "beauty ideal" that society holds up to women (Faludi, 1991; Freedman, 1986; Wolf, 1991). For the majority of women this ideal is impossible to attain and may lead to feelings of inadequacy. Feelings of inadequacy are also likely to be fed by cosmetic manufacturers and weight management programs whose ad campaigns focus on convincing women that they can ameliorate their bodily flaws and imperfections only by purchasing their products or taking part in their programs (Freedman, 1986).

The messages sent out by the media regarding bodily appearance are quite different for women and men. A strong emphasis has been placed on the bodily appearance of women that equates a thin body to beauty, sexuality, and social status; less focus has been placed on the bodily appearance of men (Freedman, 1986). These gendered messages can clearly be seen in magazine articles and advertisements. For example, Anderson and DiDomenico (1992) examined the 20 most popular magazines read by women and men to see if the number of articles that focused on dieting and body shape would reflect the actual prevalence rates of eating disorders in the general population. The results indicated that the 10 magazines most frequently read by women contained significantly more diet articles and advertisements than the 10 magazines most frequently read by men. The ratio of diet articles in men's and women's magazines was 1:10, which is identical to the actual ratio of eating disorders in men and women in the general population. The authors noted that when the men's magazines focused on bodily appearance the articles and advertisements centered on changes in body shape (i.e., "bulking up"), whereas the women's magazines focused on changes in body weight (i.e., "slimming down"). Anderson and DiDomenico suggested that "Instead of simply reflecting the weight and shape ideals of our society, popular media may be, to some extent, imposing gender-related norms, which then lead to sex-related differences in the frequency of critical behaviors" (Anderson & DiDomenico, 1992, p. 286).

Nemeroff, Stein, Diehl, and Smilack (1994) also examined women's and men's magazines to see if different types of magazines contained discrepant messages for men and women and whether this has changed over time. They looked at articles that focused on the behavioral means used to achieve physical ideals, which they placed into four categories: weight loss, beauty, fitness, and health. Based on previous work in the area, Nemeroff et al. chose to examine three categories of general interest magazines (i.e., traditional magazines, fashion magazines, and modern magazines), and they picked magazines with broad circulation and longevity of publication to represent each of the categories over a 12 year duration. They found that, overall, the women's magazines contained far more body-oriented articles than did the magazines that targeted male readers. However, the frequency of weight loss articles increased over the time period for men, but decreased for women, which indicated a gender-related change in trends. In addition, when they compared analyses of gender by magazine category, it appeared that over time the frequency of health articles seemed to increase in men's fashion magazines but not in women's fashion magazines. The authors concluded that at least some concern with the body was now being portrayed in men's fashion magazines. Finally, in comparing the different types of magazines, the researchers noted that fashion magazines were the most body oriented, modern magazines the least so, and traditional magazines fell somewhere in-between.

The purpose of the present study was to examine gendered messages regarding weight and bodily appearance on the covers of popular magazines. We chose to examine magazine covers because often it is the cover that initially attracts the reader to the magazine. Titles, catch phrases, and pictures displayed on magazine covers are usually all that the reader has time to look at in a store. Frequently it is these items that influence the reader to buy the magazine, as is reflected in the following statement by a corporate circulation director in the marketing industry. "The cover is primarily a sales tool . . . the images selected and the way we describe the contents must be provocative, hard-hitting and full of elements that sell—not feature oriented" (Lee, 1998, p.1). For this reason, it is important to explore the messages that are being presented to readers on the covers of popular magazines.

It was hypothesized that, overall, covers of women's magazines would be more likely to contain a message about bodily appearance than covers of magazines targeted at men. We were interested in examining conflicting messages (i.e., message with opposite meanings placed in close proximity to each other) that were displayed on magazine covers. It was hypothesized that covers of women's magazines would also be more likely to contain conflicting messages about bodily appearance than would covers of men's magazines.

Method

Materials Twenty-one magazines were chosen for the present analysis (see Table 1). Of these, 18 were chosen based on the results of the 1987 Simmon's Study of Media and Markets, which rated magazines on the basis of readership by gender and age. These magazines were essentially the same ones used by Anderson and DiDomenico (1992), however two were eliminated (i.e., *Playboy* and *Penthouse*) because they were not available in public libraries, where the rest of the magazines were obtained. Three additional magazines (i.e., *Vogue, Ms*, and *Esquire*) were chosen based on suggestions from other members of the authors' research team. These magazines were included because it was believed that they were frequently-read magazines that were not included on the Simmon's list.

For each magazine title, six monthly issues were reviewed from different seasons throughout the year of 1996. At least one issue from

TABLE 1 Magazines Used in this Analysis

Women's Magazines		
Traditional	Fashion	Modern
Better Homes and Gardens	*Cosmopolitan*	*Ms.*
Family Circle	*Glamour*	
Good Housekeeping	*Seventeen*	
Ladies' Home Journal	*Vogue*	
McCall's		
Redbook		
Women's Day		
Men's Magazines		
Traditional	Fashion	Entertainment
Life	*Esquire*	*Field and Stream*
National Geographic	*Gentlemen's Quarterly*	*Jet*
Newsweek		*Rolling Stone*
		Sports Illustrated

each season was included to account for seasonal variability in topical articles. For one magazine (i.e., *Ms*) only three issues were obtainable. In total, 69 covers of women's magazines and 54 covers of men's magazines were examined.

Procedure A checklist was designed to examine the magazine covers; it concerned the content of the visual images and text on the covers, as well as the placement of each. The content of the text was analyzed to determine whether it contained a diet message (e.g., "Cut 100 Calories a Meal and Lose 10 Pounds"), an exercise message (e.g., "Walk Your Way to Thin"), a message regarding cosmetic surgery to change the size of the body (e.g., "I Love My New Thighs: Diary of a Liposuction"), or a general message about weight loss with no specifications about how to lose the weight (e.g., "5 Ways to Lose 5 Pounds"). The position of messages was examined to determine if conflicting messages were placed next to each other (e.g., a message about losing weight next to a cookie recipe), if the conflicting messages were separated on the page, and if there were articles about appearance and romance placed adjacent to each other. Magazines were divided by gender of readers, and percentages for each item of the checklist were obtained for each magazine category. Percentages for each magazine category were calculated by dividing the number of magazine issues that contained each checklist item by the total number of magazine issues for that magazine category.

Each cover was examined by two of the authors together as they completed each checklist. It was determined beforehand that differences between the authors on which section a message fell into (i.e., diet, exercise, cosmetic surgery, other) would be discussed until an agreement was reached. No differences arose, however, and all messages clearly fit into only one section of the checklist.

Results/Discussion

Table 2 displays the percentages of each type of message related to bodily appearance found in women's and men's magazines. Of the 12 magazines most frequently read by women, 54 of the 69 covers (78%) contained some message about bodily appearance, whereas none of the 53 covers of men's magazines contained such messages, χ^2 (1, $N = 123$) = 49.62, $p < .005$. Therefore, consistent with previous research (Anderson & DiDomenico, 1992; Nemeroff *et al.*, 1994), the analysis showed that women's magazines were more likely to contain messages about diet, exercise, and cosmetic surgery to change body size than were men's magazines. Although the majority of the most popular women's magazines focused on changing and improving one's self, most of the popular men's magazines focused on the outside world, news, politics, hobbies, and activities.

An examination of the body types displayed on magazine covers revealed that 94% of the covers of women's magazines showed a thin female model or celebrity in excellent shape, whereas only about 3%

TABLE 2 Percentages of Each Message Type on Magazine Covers, by Gender[a]

Type of Message	Women (n = 69) n (%)	Men (n = 54) n (%)	χ^2
Diet	23 (33)	0 (0)	
Exercise	16 (23)	0 (0)	
Cosmetic surgery	4 (6)	0 (0)	
Unspecified	11 (16)	0 (0)	
At least one message (any type)	54 (78)	0 (0)	49.62[b]
Conflicting message	18 (26)	0 (0)	8.59[b]

[a]Percentages may sum to more than 100 because some magazine covers contained more than one type of message.
[b]p < .005.

showed a male on the cover. Of the covers of men's magazines, however, 28% showed a male model or celebrity, whereas women appeared almost 50% of the time. Again, most women were young, thin, and wore revealing clothing. Overall it seems that visual images on both men's and women's magazine covers tend to portray what women should look like and what men should look for. There is minimal focus on the male body.

In addition to examining weight loss messages on magazine covers, visual images and text related to food were also examined to determine the prevalence of conflicting messages about weight loss. Eighteen of the 69 covers of women's magazines contained some type of conflicting message (26%), whereas none of the covers of men's magazines contained such messages, χ^2 (1, $N = 123$) = 8.59, $p < .005$. Therefore, the hypothesis that women's magazines would contain more conflicting messages than men's was supported. It is interesting that the majority of these conflicting messages (61%) were positioned right next to one another. For example, a magazine might show a picture of an ice-cream cake with a message that says "Ice-cream Extravaganza!" next to an exercise message that says "Trim Your Thighs in 3 Weeks." Recent research (Nemeroff *et al.*, 1994) has suggested that there has been a decrease in the emphasis on weight loss in women's magazines over the last decade, however it is apparent from this study that women are still receiving gendered messages from magazines regarding weight and bodily appearance at a fairly high rate.

Because articles on weight loss do not consistently appear in the most popular men's magazines, the rest of this report will focus on the messages displayed in women's magazines. Magazine covers in popular women's magazines were further separated into three magazine categories: Modern magazines (e.g., *Ms.*), Traditional magazines (e.g., *Family Circle*), and Fashion magazines (e.g., *Cosmopolitan*). Table 3 displays the percent-

TABLE 3 Percentages of Each Message Type on Women's Magazine Covers, by Magazine Category[a]

Type of Message	Traditional (n = 42) n (%)	Fashion (n = 24) n (%)	Modern (n = 3) n (%)
Diet	19 (45)	5 (21)	0 (0)
Exercise	11 (26)	5 (21)	0 (0)
Cosmetic surgery	0 (0)	4 (17)	0 (0)
Unspecified	10 (24)	4 (17)	0 (0)
At least one message (any type)	40 (95)	14 (58)	0 (0)

[a]Percentages may sum to more than 100 because some magazine covers contained more than one type of message.

TABLE 4 Examples of Message Positioning that Implies that Changing Bodily Appearance Will Lead to a Better Life

Text next to	Text
"Get the Body You Really Want"	"How to Get Your Husband to Really Listen"
"Tighten Your Butt"	"Habits of Confident Women"
"Drop 8 Pounds this Month"	"25 Ways to Make your Marriage Hot Again"
"Get a Really Firm Body in 30 Days"	"5 Ways to Keep Your Husband Faithful"
"Lose 10 Pounds"	"Ways to Make Your Life Easier, Happier, and Better"
"Stay Skinny"	"What Men Want Most"

ages of each type of message for each magazine category. Although no statistical analyses were calculated, a comparison of the frequencies of messages about weight loss and bodily appearance in each category of magazine revealed a trend in which traditional magazines contained the most messages regarding weight loss and bodily appearance (58%) and contained all of the conflicting messages involving weight loss and fattening foods. Fashion magazines contained a smaller percentage of messages (20%). Finally, modern magazines did not contain any messages related to weight or bodily appearance. Similarly, Nemeroff *et al.* (1994) found that modern magazines contained the least amount of messages related to bodily appearance, however their results suggested that fashion magazines were more body-oriented than traditional magazines. It is interesting that many of the same magazines were used in both studies.

Perhaps the most alarming finding in this study was the position of weight-related messages in relation to other messages on the magazine covers. By their positioning of messages on magazine covers, magazines may imply that losing weight or changing the shape of one's body will lead to a better life (see Table 4). For example, messages such as "Get the Body You Want" placed next to "How to Get Your Husband to Really Listen" and "Lose 10 Pounds" placed next to "Ways to Make Your Life Easier, Happier, and Better" may give women the false idea that changing the appearance of their bodies will lead to better relationships, stronger friendships, and happier lives.

It is possible that different results may have been found if other types of magazines (i.e., men's body-building magazines or health magazines) had been included in this study. However, the magazines in this study were chosen on the basis of popularity and not on specific magazine theme or content. Magazines specifically associated with fitness, health, or appearance were not purposefully chosen for women or men. Instead, magazines that were reported as "frequently read" were selected. One limitation of this study is the sample of magazines chosen. As the authors did not have access to a more recent Simmon's Study of Media and Markets, the 1987 list was used to determine which magazines were most frequently read by women and men in this study. Many new magazines have been introduced in the 1990s, and it is possible that the magazines examined in this study may no longer be the most frequently read. We also used three additional magazines that were perceived to be "popular" but were not on the Simmon's 1987 list. Perhaps it would have been better to use a recent list and not add additional magazines. However, many of the magazines selected in this study have been used in previous research on messages related to bodily appearance (i.e., Anderson & Di-Domenico, 1992; Nemeroff *et al.*, 1994). Because the present study builds on this prior work, we believe that the results from the magazines used in this study are meaningful. Finally, it is not our intention to suggest that magazines such as *Newsweek, Life*, or *National Geographic* are exclusively "men's magazines" and that women do not read them. The categories of "women's" and "men's" magazines in this study were based entirely on the outcomes of the 1987 Simmon's Study.

In conclusion, it seems that in men's popular magazines the focus is on providing entertainment and improving one's life by expanding knowledge, hobbies, and activities. Women's magazines, however, seem to focus on improving one's life by changing one's appearance, especially by losing weight. It is implied through both images and text that being thin means being happier, sexier, and more lovable. Women's magazines also contain conflicting messages about weight loss strategies and eating behaviors, including the placement of weight loss prescriptions next to recipes and pictures of foods that are extremely high in fat content. The findings from this analysis suggest that women are not only being told that they should focus on obtaining an impossible body shape through dieting and exercising, but they are also being told that they should be able to do so while eating, or at least preparing for others, foods that are high in fat content. These fattening foods, obviously not typical diet foods, may make women think that it is even more impossible for them to obtain the thin ideal that is being presented to them or the ideal life that goes with it. The consequences of striving for these unrealistic ideals may be that an increasing number of women take aggressive means to control and reduce their weight (Wadden, Brown, Foster, & Linowitz, 1991). These dieting efforts can have serious implications, including inadequate nutrition, fatigue, weakness, irritability, depression, social withdrawal, loss of sexual desire, and even sudden death from cardiac arrhythmia (Ciliska, 1990). In addition, dietary restraint increases the likelihood of binge eating, which may initiate the cycle of bulimia in individuals at risk for developing eating disorders (Polivy & Herman, 1985). In short, dieting should never be considered a risk-free activity (Chrisler, 1994). Perhaps editors of popular women's magazines need to be more aware of the implications of gendered messages on magazine covers and the physical and psychological consequences they may have for women.

References

Anderson, A. E., & DiDomenico, L. (1992). Diet vs. shape content of popular male and female magazines: A dose-response relationship to the incidence of eating disorders? *International Journal of Eating Disorders, 11*, 283–287.

Chrisler, J. C. (1994). Reframing women's weight: Does thin equal healthy? In A. Dan (Ed.), *Reframing women's health: Multidisciplinary research and practice*. Newbury Park, CA: Sage.

Ciliska, D. (1990). *Beyond dieting: Psychoeducational interventions for chronically obese women-a non dieting approach.* New York: Brunner/Mazel.

Faludi, S. (1991). *Backlash: The undeclared war against American women.* New York: Crown.

Freedman, T. (1986). *Beauty bound.* Lexington, MA: D. C. Heath.

Lee, D. (1998). Make the cover a sales tool. *Folio: The Magazine for Magazine Management.* [On-line]. Available: http://web.lexis-nexis.com/universe/docum . . . 5a3&_md5=6c7c5c4598976a0df9b148028bbd3c87.

Nemeroff, C. J., Stein, R. I., Diehl, N. S., & Smilack, K. M. (1994). From the Cleavers to the Clintons: Role choices and body orientation as reflected in magazine article content. *International Journal of Eating Disorders, 16*, 167–176.

Polivy, J., & Herman, C. P. (1985). Dieting and bingeing: A causal analysis. *American Psychologist, 40*, 193–201.

Simmon's study of media and markets. (1987). New York: Simmon's Market Research Bureau, Inc.

Wadden, T. A., Brown, G., Foster, G. D., & Linowitz, J. R. (1991). Salience of weight-related worries in adolescent males and females. *International Journal of Eating Disorders, 10*, 407–414.

Wolf, N. (1991). *The beauty myth: How images of beauty are used against women.* New York: William Morrow.

8 Throwing Like a Girl

IRIS MARION YOUNG

In discussing the fundamental significance of lateral space, which is one of the unique spatial dimensions generated by the human upright posture, Erwin Straus pauses at "the remarkable difference in the manner of throwing of the two sexes"[1] (p. 157). Citing a study and photographs of young boys and girls, he describes the difference as follows:

> The girl of five does not make any use of lateral space. She does not stretch her arm sideward; she does not twist her trunk; she does not move her legs, which remain side by side. All she does in preparation for throwing is to lift her right arm forward to the horizontal and to bend the forearm backward in a pronate position. . . . The ball is released without force, speed, or accurate aim. . . . A boy of the same age, when preparing to throw, stretches his right arm sideward and backward; supinates the forearm; twists, turns and bends his trunk; and moves his right foot backward. From this stance, he can support his throwing almost with the full strength of his total motorium. . . . The ball leaves the hand with considerable acceleration; it moves toward its goal in a long flat curve. (p. 157–60)[2]

Though he does not stop to trouble himself with the problem for long, Straus makes a few remarks in the attempt to explain this "remarkable difference." Since the difference is observed at such an early age, he says, it seems to be "the manifestation of a biological, not an acquired, difference" (p. 157). He is somewhat at a loss, however, to specify the source of the difference. Since the feminine style of throwing is observed in young children, it cannot result from the development of the breast. Straus provides further evidence against the breast by pointing out that "it seems certain" that the Amazons, who cut off their right breasts, "threw a ball just like our Betty's, Mary's and Susan's" (p. 158). Having thus dismissed the breast, Straus considers the weaker muscle power of the girl as an explanation of the difference, but concludes that the girl should be expected to compensate for such relative weakness with the added preparation of reaching around and back. Straus explains the difference in style of throwing by referring to a "feminine attitude" in relation to the world and to space. The difference for him is biologically based, but he denies that it is specifically anatomical. Girls throw in a way different from boys because girls are "feminine."

What is even more amazing than this "explanation" is the fact that a perspective that takes body comportment and movement as definitive for the structure and meaning of human lived experience devotes no more than an incidental page to such a "remarkable difference" between masculine and feminine body comportment and style of movement, for throwing is by no means the only activity in which such a difference can be observed. If there are indeed typically "feminine" styles of body comportment and movement, this should generate for the existential phenomenologist a concern to specify such a differentiation of the modalities of the lived body. Yet Straus is by no means alone in his failure to describe the modalities, meaning, and implications of the difference between "masculine" and "feminine" body comportment and movement.

A virtue of Straus's account of the typical difference of the sexes in throwing is that he does not explain this difference on the basis of physical attributes. Straus is convinced, however, that the early age at which the difference appears shows that it is not an acquired difference, and thus he is forced back onto a mysterious "feminine essence" in order to explain it. The feminist denial that the real differences in behavior and psychology between men and woman can be attributed to some natural and eternal feminine essence is perhaps most thoroughly and systematically expressed by Beauvoir. Every human existence is defined by its *situation*; the particular existence of the female person is no less defined by the historical, cultural, social, and economic limits of her situation. We reduce women's condition simply to unintelligibility if we "explain" it by appeal to some natural and ahistorical feminine essence. In denying such a feminine essence, however, we should not fall into that "nominalism" that denies the real differences in the behavior and experiences of men and women. Even though there is no eternal feminine essence, there is "a common basis which underlies every individual female existence in the present state of education and custom."[3] The situation of women within a given sociohistorical set of circumstances, despite the individual variation in each woman's experience, opportunities, and possibilities, has a unity that can be described and made intelligible. It should be emphasized, however, that this unity is specific to a particular social formation during a particular epoch.

Beauvoir proceeds to give such an account of the situation of women with remarkable depth, clarity, and ingenuity. Yet she also, to a large extent fails to give a place to the status and orientation of the woman's body as relating to its surroundings in living action. When Beauvoir does talk about the woman's bodily being and her physical relation to her surroundings, she tends to focus on the more evident facts of a woman's physiology. She discusses how women experience the body as a burden, how the hormonal and physiological changes the body undergoes at puberty, during menstruation and pregnancy, are felt to be fearful and mysterious, and claims that these phenomena weigh down the woman's existence by tying her to nature, immanence, and the requirements of the species at the expense of her own individuality.[4] By largely ignoring the situatedness of the woman's actual bodily movement and orientation to its surroundings and its world, Beauvoir tends to create the impression that it is woman's anatomy and physiology *as such* that at least in part determine her unfree status.[5]

This essay seeks to begin to fill a gap that thus exist both in existential phenomenology and feminist theory. It traces in a provisional way some of the basic modalities of feminine body comportment, manner of moving, and relation in space. It brings intelligibility and significance to certain observable and rather ordinary ways in which women in our society typically comport themselves and move differently from the ways that men do. In accordance with the existentialist concern with the situatedness of human experience, I make no claim to the universality of this typicality of the bodily comportment of women and the phenomenological description based on it. The account developed here claims only to describe the modalities of feminine bodily existence for women situated in contemporary advanced industrial, urban, and commercial society. Elements of the account developed here may or may not apply to the situation of woman in other societies and other epochs, but it is not the concern of this essay to determine to which, if any, other social circumstances this account applies.

The scope of bodily existence and movement with which I am concerned here is also limited. I concentrate primarily on those sorts of bodily activities that relate to the comportment or orientation of the body as a whole, that entail gross movement, or that require the enlistment of strength and the confrontation of the body's capacities and possibilities with the resistance and malleability of things. The kind of movement I am primarily concerned with is movement in which the body aims to accomplish of a definite purpose or task. There are thus many aspects of feminine bodily existence that I leave out of this account. Most notable of these is the body in its sexual being. Another aspect of bodily existence, among others, that I leave unconsidered is structured body movement that does not have a particular aim—for example, dancing. . . .

Before entering the analysis, I should clarify what I mean here by "feminine" existence. In accordance with Beauvoir's understanding, I take "femininity" to designate not a mysterious quality or essence that all women have by virtue of their being biologically female. It is, rather, a set of structures and conditions that delimit the typical *situation* of being a woman in a particular society, as well as the typical way in which this situation is lived by the women themselves. Defined as such, it is not necessary that *any* women be "feminine"—that is, it is not necessary that there be distinctive structures and behavior typical of the situation of women.[6] This understanding of "feminine" existence makes it possible to say that some women escape or transcend the typical situation and definition of women in various degrees and respects. I mention this primarily to indicate that the account offered here of the modalities of feminine bodily existence is not to be falsified by referring to some individual women to whom aspects of the account do not apply, or even to some individual men to whom they do. . . .

As a framework for developing these modalities, I rely on Beauvoir's account of woman's existence in patriarchal society as defined by a basic tension between immanence and transcendence.[7] The culture and society in which the female person dwells defines woman as Other, as the inessential correlate to man, as mere object and immanence. Woman is thereby both culturally and socially denied by the subjectivity, autonomy, and creativity that are definitive of being human and that in patriarchal society are accorded the man. At the same time, however, because she is a human existence, the female person necessarily is a subjectivity and transcendence, and she knows herself to be. The female person who enacts the existence of women in patriarchal society must therefore live a contradiction: as human she is a free subject who participates in transcendence, but her situation as a woman denies her that subjectivity and transcendence. My suggestion is that the modalities of feminine bodily comportment, motility, and spatiality exhibit this same tension between transcendence and immanence, between subjectivity and being a mere object. . . .

The basic difference that Straus observes between the way boys and girls throw is that girls do not bring their whole bodies into the motion as much as the boys do. They do not reach back, twist, move backward, step, and lean forward. Rather, the girls tend to remain relatively immobile except for their arms, and even the arms are not extended as far as they could be. Throwing is not the only movement in which there is a typical difference in the way men and women use their bodies. Reflection on feminine comportment and body movement in other physical activities reveals that these also are frequently characterized, much as in the throwing case, by a failure to make full use of the body's spatial and lateral potentialities.

Even in the most simple body orientations of men and women as they sit, stand, and walk, one can observe a typical difference in body style and extension. Women generally are not as open with their bodies as are men in their gait and stride. Typically, the masculine stride is longer proportional to a man's body than is the feminine stride to a woman's. The man typically swings his arms in a more open and loose fashion than does a woman and typically has more up and down rhythm in his step. Though we now wear pants more than we used to and consequently do not have to restrict our sitting postures because of dress, women still tend to sit with their legs relatively close together and their arms across their bodies. When simply standing or leaning, men tend to keep their feet farther apart than do women, and we also tend more to keep our hands and arms touching or shielding our bodies. A final indicative difference is the way each carries books or parcels; girls and women most often carry books embraced to their chests, while boys and men swing them along their sides.

The approach that people of each sex take to the performance of physical tasks that require force, strength, and muscular coordination is frequently different. There are indeed real physical differences between men and women in the kind and limit of their physical strength. Many of the observed differences between men and women in the performance of tasks requiring coordinated strength, however, are due not so much to brute muscular strength as to the way each sex *uses* the body in approaching tasks. Women often do not perceive themselves as capable of lifting and carrying heavy things, pushing and shoving with significant force, pulling, squeezing, grasping, or twisting with force. When we attempt such tasks, we frequently fail to summon the full possibilities of our muscular coordination, position, poise, and bearing. Women tend not to put their whole bodies into engagement in a physical task with the same ease and naturalness as men. For example, in attempting to lift something, women more often than men fail to plant themselves firmly and make their thighs bear the greatest proportion of the weight. Instead, we tend to concentrate our effort on those parts of the body most immediately connected to the task—the arms and shoulders—rarely bringing the power of the legs to the task at all. When turning or twisting something, to take another example, we frequently concentrate effort in the hand and wrist, not bringing to the task the power of the shoulder, which is necessary for its efficient performance.[8]

The previously cited throwing example can be extended to a great deal of athletic activity. Now, most men are by no means superior athletes, and their sporting efforts more often display bravado than genuine skill and coordination. The relatively untrained man nevertheless engages in sport generally with more free motion and open reach than does his female counterpart. Not only is there a typical style of throwing like a girl, but there is a more or less typical style of running like a girl, climbing like a girl, swinging like a girl, hitting like a girl. They have in common first that the whole body is not put into fluid and directed motion, but rather, in swinging and hitting, for example, the motion is concentrated in one body part; and second that the woman's motion tends not to reach, extend, lean, stretch, and follow through in the direction of her intention.

For many women as they move in sport, a space surrounds us in imagination that we are not free to move beyond; the space available to our movement is a constricted space. Thus, for example, in softball or volleyball women tend to remain in one place more often than men do, neither jumping to reach nor running to approach the ball. Men more often move out toward a ball in flight and confront it with their own countermotion. Women tend to wait for and then *react* to its approach, rather than going forth to meet it. We frequently respond to the motion of a ball coming toward us as though it were coming *at* us, and our immediate bodily impulse is to flee, duck, or otherwise protect ourselves from its flight. Less often than men, moreover, do women give self-conscious direction and placement to their motion in sport. Rather than aiming at a certain place where we wish to hit a ball, for example, we tend to hit it in a "general" direction.

Women often approach a physical engagement with things with timidity, uncertainty, and hesitancy. Typically, we lack an entire trust in our bodies to carry us to our aims. There is, I suggest, a double hesitation here. On the one hand, we often lack confidence that we have the capacity to do what must be done. Many times I have slowed a hiking party in which the men bounded across a harmless stream while I stood on the other side warily testing my footing on various stones, holding on to overhanging branches. Though the others crossed with ease, I do not believe it is easy for *me*, even though once I take a committed step I am across in a flash. The other side of this tentativeness is, I suggest, a fear of getting hurt, which is greater in women than in men. Our attention is often divided between the aim to be realized in motion and the body that must accomplish it, while at the same time saving itself from harm. We often experience our bodies as a fragile encumbrance, rather than the media for the enactment of our aims. We feel as though we must have our attention directed upon our bodies to make sure they are doing what we wish them to do, rather than paying attention to what we want to do *through* our bodies.

All the above factors operate to produce in many women a greater or lesser feeling of incapacity, frustration, and self-consciousness. We have more of a tendency than men do to greatly underestimate our bodily capacity.[9] We decide beforehand—usually mistakenly—that the task is beyond us, and thus give it less than our full effort. At such a halfhearted level, of course, we cannot perform the tasks, become frustrated, and fulfill our own prophecy. In entering a task we frequently are self-conscious about appearing awkward and at the same time do not wish to appear too strong. Both worries contribute to our awkwardness and frustration. If we should finally release ourselves from this spiral and really give a physical task our best effort, we are greatly surprised indeed at what our bodies can accomplish. It has been found that women more often than men underestimate the level of achievement they have reached.[10]

None of the observations that have been made thus far about the way women typically move and comport their bodies applies to all women all of the time. Nor do those women who manifest some aspect of this typicality do so in the same degree. There is no inherent, mysterious connection between these sorts of typical comportments and being a female person. . . .

. . . [T]he modalities of feminine bodily existence have their root in the fact that feminine existence experiences the body as a mere thing—a fragile thing, which must be picked up and coaxed into movement, a thing that exists as *looked at and acted upon*. To be sure, any lived body exists as a material thing as well as a transcending subject. For feminine bodily existence, however, the body is often lived as a thing that is other than it, a thing like other things in the world. To the extent that a woman lives her body as a thing, she remains rooted in immanence, is inhibited, and retains a distance from her body as transcending movement and from engagement in the world's possibilities.

Women in sexist society are physically handicapped. Insofar as we learn to live out our existence in accordance with the definition that patriarchal culture assigns to us, we are physically inhibited, confined, positioned, and objectified. As lived bodies we are not open and unambiguous transcendences that move out to master a world that belongs to us, a world constituted by our own intentions and projections. To be sure, there are actual women in contemporary society to whom all or part of the above description does not apply. Where these modalities are not manifest in or determinative of the existence of a particular woman, however, they are definitive in a negative mode—as that which she has escaped, through accident or good fortune, or, more often, as that which she has had to overcome.

One of the sources of the modalities of feminine bodily existence is too obvious to dwell upon at length. For the most part, girls and women are not given the opportunity to use their full bodily capacities in free and open engagement with the world, nor are they encouraged as much as boys are to develop specific bodily skills.[11] Girls' play is often more sedentary and enclosing than the play of boys. In school and after-school activities girls are not encouraged to engage in sport, in the controlled use of their bodies in achieving well-defined goals. Girls, moreover, get little practice at "tinkering" with things and thus at developing spatial skill. Finally, girls are not often asked to perform tasks demanding physical effort and strength, while as the boys grow older they are asked to do so more and more.[12]

The modalities of feminine bodily existence are not merely privative, however, and thus their source is not merely in lack of practice, though this is certainly an important element. There is a specific positive style of feminine body comportment and movement, which is learned as the girl comes to understand that she is a girl. The young girl acquires many subtle habits of feminine body comportment—walking like a girl, tilting her head like a girl, standing and sitting like a girl, gesturing like a girl, and so on. The girl learns actively to hamper her movements. She is told that she must be careful not to get hurt, not to get dirty, not to tear her clothes, that the things she desires to do are dangerous for her. Thus she develops a bodily timidity that increases with age. In assuming herself to be a girl, she takes herself to be fragile. Studies have found that young children of both sexes categorically assert that girls are more likely to get hurt than boys are,[13] and that girls ought to remain close to home, while boys can roam and explore.[14] The more a girl assumes her status as feminine, the more she takes herself to be fragile and immobile and the more she actively enacts her own body inhibition. When I was about thirteen, I spent hours practicing a "feminine" walk, which was stiff and closed, and rotated from side to side.

Studies that record observations of sex differences in spatial perception, spatial problem-solving, and motor skills have also found that these differences tend to increase with age. While very young children show virtually no differences in motor skills, movement, spatial perception, etc., differences seem to appear in elementary school and increase with adolescence. If these findings are accurate, they would seem to support the conclusion that it is in the process of growing up as a girl that the modalities of feminine bodily comportment, motility, and spatiality make their appearance.[15]

There is, however, a further source of the modalities of feminine bodily existence that is perhaps even more profound than these. At the root of those modalities, I have stated in the previous section, is the fact that the woman lives her body as *object* as well as subject. The source of this is that patriarchal society defines woman as object, as a mere body, and that in sexist society women are in fact frequently regarded by others as objects and mere bodies. An essential part of the situation of being a woman is that of living the ever-present possibility that one will be gazed upon as a mere body, as shape and flesh that presents itself as the potential object of another subject's intentions and manipulations, rather than as a living manifestation of action and intention.[16] The source of this objectified bodily existence is in the attitude of others regarding her, but the woman herself often actively takes up her body as a mere thing. She gazes at it in the mirror, worries about how it looks to others, prunes it, shapes it, molds and decorates it.

This objectified bodily existence accounts for the self-consciousness of the feminine relation to her body and resulting distance she takes from her body. As human, she is a transcendence and subjectivity, and cannot live herself as mere bodily object. Thus, to the degree that she does live herself as mere body, she cannot be in unity with herself, but must take a distance from and exist in discontinuity with her body. The objectifying regard that "keeps her in her place" can also account for the spatial modality of being positioned and for why women frequently tend not to move openly, keeping their limbs closed around themselves. To open her body in free, active, open extension and bold outward-directedness is for a woman to invite objectification.

The threat of being seen is, however, not the only threat of objectification that the woman lives. She also lives the threat of invasion of her body space. The most extreme form of such spatial and bodily invasion is the threat of rape. But we daily are subject to the possibility of bodily invasion in many far more subtle ways as well. It is acceptable, for example, for women to be touched in ways and under circumstances that it is not acceptable for men to be touched, and by persons—i.e., men—whom it is not acceptable for them to touch.[17] I would suggest that the enclosed space that has been described as a modality of feminine spatiality is in part a defense against such invasion. Women tend to project an existential barrier closed around them and discontinuous with the "over there" in order to keep the other at a distance. The woman lives her space as confined and closed around her, at least in part as projecting some small area in which she can exist as a free subject.

This essay is a prolegomenon to the study of aspects of women's experience and situation that have not received the treatment they warrant. I would like to close with some questions that require further thought and research. This essay has concentrated its attention upon the sorts of physical tasks and body orientation that involve the whole body in gross movement. Further investigation into woman's bodily existence would require looking at activities that do not involve the whole body and finer movement. If we are going to develop an account of the woman's body experience in situation, moreover, we must reflect on the modalities of a woman's experience of her body in its sexual being, as well as upon less task-oriented body activities, such as dancing. Another question that arises is whether the description given here would apply equally well to any sort of physical task. Might the kind of task, and specifically whether it is a task or movement that is sex-typed, have some effect on the modalities of feminine bodily existence? A further question is to what degree we can develop a theoretical account of the connection between the modalities of the bodily existence of women and other aspects of our existence and experience. For example, I have an intuition that the general lack of confidence that we frequently have about our cognitive or leadership abilities is traceable in part to an original doubt of our body's capacity. None of these questions can be dealt with properly, however, without first performing the kind of guided observation and data collection that my reading has concluded, to a large degree, is yet to be performed.

Notes

1. Erwin W. Straus, "The Upright Posture," *Phenomenological Psychology* (New York: Basic Books, 1966), pp. 137–65. References to particular pages are indicated in the text.

2. Studies continue to be performed that arrive at similar observations. See, for example, Lolas E. Kalverson, Mary Ann Robertson, M. Joanne Safrit, and Thomas W. Roberts, "Effect of Guided Practice on Overhand Throw Ball Velocities of Kindergarten Children," *Research Quarterly* (American Alliance for Health, Physical Education and Recreation) 48 (May 1977); pp. 311–18. The study found that boys achieved significantly greater velocities than girls did.
See also F. J. J. Buytendijk's remarks in *Woman: A Contemporary View* (New York: Newman Press, 1968), pp. 144–45. In raising the example of throwing, Buytendijk is concerned to stress, as am I in this essay, that the important thing to investigate is not the strictly physical phenomenon, but rather the manner in which each sex projects her or his Being-in-the-world through movement.

3. Simone de Beauvoir, *The Second Sex* (New York: Vintage Books, 1974), p. xxxv. See also Buytendijk, p. 175–76.

4. See Beauvoir, *The Second Sex*, chapter 1, "The Data of Biology."

5. Firestone claims that Beauvoir's account served as the basis of her own thesis that the oppression of women is rooted in nature and thus requires the transcendence of nature itself to be overcome. See *The Dialectic of Sex* (New York: Bantam Books, 1970). Beauvoir would claim that Firestone is guilty of desituating woman's situation by pinning a source on nature as such. That Firestone would find inspiration for her thesis in Beauvoir, however, indicates that perhaps de Beauvoir has not steered away from causes in "nature" as much as is desirable.

6. It is not impossible, moreover, for men to be "feminine" in at least some respects, according to the above definition.

7. See Beauvoir, *The Second Sex*, chapter 21, "Woman's Situation and Character."

8. It should be noted that this is probably typical only of women in advanced industrial societies, where the model of the bourgeois woman has been extended to most women. It would not apply to those societies, for example, where most people, including woman, do heavy physical work. Nor does this particular observation, of course, hold true in our own society for women who do heavy physical work.

9. See A. M. Gross, "Estimated Versus Actual Physical Strength in Three Ethnic Groups," *Child Development* 39 (1968), pp. 283–90. In a test of children at several different ages, at all but the youngest age level, girls rated themselves lower than boys rated themselves on self-estimates of strength, and as the girls grow older, their self-estimates of strength become even lower.
10. See Marguerite A. Cifton and Hope M. Smith, "Comparison of Expressed Self-Concept of Highly Skilled Males and Females Concerning Motor Performance," *Perceptual and Motor Skills* 16 (1963), pp. 199–201. Women consistently underestimated their level of achievement in skills such as running and jumping far more often than men did.
11. Nor are girls provided with example of girls and women being physically active. See Mary E. Duquin, "Differential Sex Role Socialization Toward Amplitude Appropriation," *Research Quarterly* (American Alliance for Health, Physical Education and Recreation) 48 (1977), pp. 188–92. A survey of textbooks for young children revealed that children are thirteen times more likely to see a vigorously active man than a vigorously active woman and three times more likely to see a relatively active man than a relatively active woman.
12. Sherman (see note 18) argues that it is the differential socialization of boys and girls in being encouraged to "tinker," explore, etc., that accounts for the difference between the two in spatial ability.
13. See L. Kolberg, "A Cognitive-Developmental Analysis of Children's Sex-Role Concepts and Attitudes," in E. E. Maccoby, ed., *The Development of Sex Differences* (Palo Alto, Calif.: Stanford University Press, 1966), p. 101.
14. Lenore J. Weitzman, "Sex Role Socialization," in Jo Freeman, ed., *Woman: A Feminist Perspective* (Palo Alto, Calif.: Mayfield Publishing Co., 1975), pp. 111–12.
15. Maccoby and Jacklin, *The Psychology of Sex Differences*, pp. 93–94.
16. The manner in which women are objectified by the gaze of the Other is not the same phenomenon as the objectification by the Other that is a condition of self-consciousness in Sartre's account. See *Being and Nothingness*, trans., Hazel E. Barnes (New York: Philosophical Library, 1956), part three. While the basic ontological category of being for others is an objectified for itself, the objectification that women are subject to is being regarded as a mere in itself. On the particular dynamic of sexual objectification, see Sandra Bartky, "Psychological Oppression," in Sharon Bishop and Marjories Weinzweig, ed., *Philosophy and Women* (Belmont, Calif.: Wadsworth Publishing Co., 1979), pp. 33–41.
17. See Nancy Henley and Jo Freeman, "The Sexual Politics of Interpersonal Behavior," in Freeman, ed., *Woman: A Feminist Perspective*, pp. 391–401.

CHAPTER THREE

Sexuality

The papers in this section explore both the meanings and personal experiences of female sexuality. Actually, a better term would be "women's *sexualities,*" because women's sexual identities and experiences vary widely and are influenced by many social factors such as ethnicity, age, and religion. Included are papers that span a wide range of approaches to this topic, from cultural representations of women's bodies, to feminist views of women's sexual personae and lesbianism, to the work on the relationship between physiological and subjective sexual arousal. Of course, they represent only the smallest window into the multiply-determined phenomena associated with women's sexual lives.

The first piece in this section, I realize, is shocking for its title. However, my students have asked for some years that we read Muscio's ideas in class, and I have agreed. There is much to discuss in this work, whether you find it offensive or inspiring. The first sentence reads: "'Cunt' is very arguably the most powerful negative word in the American English language." Do you agree? Why do you think so, and what does this say about societal attitudes toward women's sexual selves? Muscio argues that this word is ours to do with what we want. What she wants is to re-examine it and the contexts in which it is used, and for women, to reconcile themselves with it. Words are powerful determiners of experience, and in taking back the word "cunt," Muscio believes women will take back their bodily, sexual selves.

You might contemplate the ways in which Muscio's work is decidedly *third wave* feminist, and compare it, for example, to a work by Gloria Steinem (e.g., "If Men Could Menstruate" in Chapter 4) who represents *second wave* feminism. How do their perspectives differ and what do they share?

The second article in this section, by Deborah Tolman, is a qualitative piece exploring adolescent female sexual desire, and like Inga Muscio, argues that the ways we *speak* about sexuality are crucial in shaping how women actually understand and experience their own sexual selves. Her argument is that girls' knowledge and experiences of their bodies and of their sexual desires are undermined by the stories that are available in our culture about female relationships and sexuality. These stories inevitably have a "Harlequin romance" feel: good girls don't want sex; they want love. Sexual desire is masculine. There are few, if any, stories available of normal girls who feel and act on their own sexual desires.

Tolman interviews one girl—Isabel—to see if she can uncover an "erotic voice" in her narrative about her subjective experiences of her sexuality. This case-study methodology is a fascinating one that gives us a very close look at Isabel's own voice and at the complexities of her self-understanding. How does this way of approaching the question of women's sexuality provide us with different insight than a more quantitative approach (for example, a questionnaire distributed to many adolescent girls) might? You may wish to explore Chapter 10, on research methodology, in the context of this article, to identify the ways in which Tolman's approach is decidedly feminist, and rejects many of the assumptions of objectivity and control that are central to much of traditional social-scientific research.

Next we read a piece by Carla Golden, "Diversity and Variability in Women's Sexual Identities," in which she posits that the relationship between sexual behavior and sexual identity may be particularly fluid and dynamic in women. She comes to this conclusion through qualitative interviews with college-aged women who define themselves as lesbian (their avowed sexual "identity"), despite the fact that their current or previous sexual experiences were heterosexual (their sexual behaviors).

In this context, what, she asks, is a lesbian? Feminists before Golden, such as Adrienne Rich, have suggested that one way to understand lesbianism is with a "lesbian continuum," which represents the great range of women-identified experiences, from genital sexual experience to emotional bonding. What do you think of this notion? The novel, *Fried Green Tomatoes at the Whistle Stop Café*, by Fannie Flagg is a lovely exploration of this very notion of the range of intensity between women.

Golden argues not only that women's sexual identities may not be predictable based on their sexual behavior, but that the societal emphasis placed on striving for congruence between our sexual feelings, behaviors, and identities may be inhumane. Fluidity may be more achievable than permanent congruence. The feminist movement has enabled women to see that the category "woman" does not automatically mean members prefer certain roles or activities; it belies the diversity of interests, attitudes, and identities that real women embody. So too, Golden concludes, sexual feelings and activities are not always accurately described in either/or terms, nor do they map perfectly on to our sexual identities. By thinking in terms of women's sexual fluidity, we can perhaps enable women to move beyond the dichotomous limitations that partriarchal, heterosexist social attitudes construct.[1]

The final piece in this section is an interview conducted by Natalie Angier for the *New York Times* with researcher Ellen Laan. Laan performs ground-breaking research on the determinants of women's sexual arousal, with innovative laboratory paradigms. For centuries, "medical" understanding of women's sexual functioning has been murky at best, due in part to the appalling lack of real knowledge about their sexual physiology. Women have been variously described as "furnaces of carnality" (Shorter, 1984), capable of leading righteous men to sexual depravity (the predominant view in the Middle Ages), to completely ignorant maidens who had to be wooed by men in order for any sexual feelings at all to be awakened (the main view in Victorian times). It was not until the mid-1960s that researchers Masters and Johnson studied and carefully described bodily sexual arousal in women. Unfortunately, their research left the question of women's subjective sexual experience completely out. Lenore Tiefer (1991) has criticized the Masters and Johnson studies for their exclusive emphasis on physiology, largely a reflection, she argues, of a male-bias toward penile-vaginal intercourse as the paradigm for understanding women's sexual functioning.

This lack of understanding regarding the relationship between physiological arousal and the subjective *experience* of sexual arousal is what Laan and her colleagues have sought to redress in their research in Amsterdam, Holland. One of their main findings is a fairly simple yet, I think, profound one: genital arousal appears to be a less important factor in subjective sexual arousal for women than for men. For women, external contextual cues contribute greatly to feelings of sexuality. One hypothesis that comes from this is that women's appraisal of a "sexual" situation will account for a greater part of their subjective experience of sexual arousal than will "objective" bodily genital sensations. The experiment referred to in this article was one of many testing this idea.

Laan points out that until very recently, the erotic film industry was run almost exclusively by male producers and directors, whose products could hardly be called "woman friendly." The study compared women's physiological and subjective sexual arousal in response to two types of erotic films: a traditional "man-made," man-focused film versus a woman-made film focusing on the sexual pleasure of the female actor. You will find the results fascinating and perhaps surprising. What distinctions does Laan make about the types of arousal, and how do they help us understand how she arrives at her basic conclusion: if you want to know whether a woman wants to have sex, ask her. Think of the reduction in the rates of acquaintance rape on college campuses, for example, if such advice were heeded.

Note

1. In her book *Myths of Gender,* Anne Fausto-Sterling does a wonderful job of critiquing the rather unconvincing research on "the homosexual brain," and all the hype that has come from it. Among the points she makes is that *no* research has been done on the brains of lesbians. "Perhaps for once," she points out, "women should be grateful for the persistent neglect with which science has treated female sexuality"! (p. 249)

References

Fausto-Sterling, A. (1992). *Myths of gender* (revised edition). New York: Basic Books.

Shorter, E. (1984). *A history of women's bodies*. Bungay: Pelican Books.

Tiefer, L. (1991). Historical, scientific, clinical and feminist criticisms of "The Human Sexual Response Cycle" model. *Annual Review of Sex Research, 2,* 1–23.

9 Cunt: A Declaration of Independence

INGA MUSCIO

"Cunt" is very arguably the most powerful negative word in the American English language. "Cunt" is the ultimate one-syllable covert verbal weapon any streetwise six-year-old or passing motorist can use against a woman. "Cunt" refers almost exclusively to women, and expresses the utmost rancor. There's a general feeling of accord on this.

Except for some friends . . . , no one calls me a "cunt" to communicate what a cool and sublime human being they think I am. Up until a certain time in my life, I never employed "cunt" to express respect or admiration.

I qualify these statements because my relationship with "cunt" is no longer what it once was.

One day I came home from third grade and asked my pops, "What's a wetback?"

With resignation and a sigh, Dad elucidated a brief history of "wetback." He concluded, "Don't you *ever* say it."

A list of words I was similarly not to utter was forthcoming: nigger, beaner, kike, wop, jap, injun, spic. The only formal cuss word included on his roster was "cunt."

Coming as I did from a family where us kids were allowed to strew profanities like rice at a wedding, I was mighty affected by all this. Why, in my father's way of thinking, could I call someone an asshole but not a wetback nigger cunt?

The foreshadowings of a mystery.

In my childhood home, the 1965 Random House Dictionary was as much a part of dinnertime as laughter, arguments 'n wanton table manners. Throughout dinner, my siblings and I were required to spell and define new vocabulary words. It was a custom I enjoyed very much.

I was raised to appreciate the power of words.

Little did I know that when I grew up, out of the billion and one words in the 1965 Random House Dictionary and beyond, there would exist no word that I could use to adequately describe myself.

This wouldn't be much of a problem except that there are millions of me's: articulate, strong, talented, raging, brilliant, grooving, sexy, expressive, dancing, singing, laughing women in America, of all shapes, hues, ethnicities, sizes, sexual orientations and dispositions.

We are everywhere.

But what are we.

The only dimly representational, identifying term that advocates truly authentic recognition for the actual realities of women in this world is "feminism." This is a relatively youthful word. Our actual realities, on the other hand, are rooted deep. We are born with them in our hearts.

Inherited them from our mothers.

Grandmothers.

Under the influence of this dilemma, I've asked myself if there might be a word as old, as universal and as deeply rooted as women's actual realities in patriarchal society. Hidden somewhere in the English language, could there be a word with power steeped in our history, a word which truly conveyed the rage and hope of *all women*?

And lo and behold, I return to the one formal cuss word on Pop's roster:

cunt.

This is about my reconciliation with
the word
and

the anatomical jewel.

. . . I assert that the context in which "cunt" is presently perceived does not serve women, and should therefore be thoroughly re-examined.

English is considered the "universal language" because it represents the victors of history's present telling. Seizing this language and manipulating it to serve your community is a very powerful thing to do, and—based on a variety of specific elements, such as ethnicity, musical tastes, credit limits and/or sexuality—it is done a lot in America. Creating a general, woman-centered version of the English language, however, is just insanely difficult.

Womankind is varied and vast.

But we all have cunts.

While one word maketh not a woman-centered language, "cunt" is certainly a mighty potent and versatile contribution. Not to mention how *deliciously satisfying* it is to *totally snag* a reviled word and elevate it to a status which all women should rightfully experience in this society.

When viewed as a positive force in the language of women—as well as a reference to the power of the anatomical jewel which unites us all—the negative power of "cunt" falls in upon itself, and we are suddenly equipped with a word that describes all women, regardless of race, age, class, religion or the degree of lesbianism we enjoy.

. . . Our cunts bleed and have weird, unpredictable orgasms. The birthing process is painful and messy. Lordisa knows what our cunts are up to. Generally speaking, we don't understand them, we don't like them and we often think they're ugly.

A different, more sublime way of looking at this is that our cunts are the symbolic and physical zenith of our existence.

When our cunts bleed, *we* are *bleeding people.* Clairvoyant dreams visit our sleepytime heads. Sometimes, the swaggering braggadocio of human males causes our wombs to clench up in spasms of pain. When cunts have stupendous orgasms, we may reel for days, and have a fetching smile for every person we meet when we're walkin' down the street. When cunts get filled up with sperm, women sometimes get pregnant and experience either the trauma of aborting, or the courageous and under-appreciated tribulation of devoting *the rest of our lives* to another human being. When men fuck our cunts against our will, we often feel like a diarrhea shit has been offed upon the very essence of our soul, and may live *the rest of our days* cleaning it off in whatever way we see fit.

An aisle in all American grocery stores is devoted to various commercial products, dreamed up by corporations owned and operated by men, which are designed to "care for" and deodorize cunts. An entire branch of Western medicine, male style, exists because of the infernal, confounding magic of cunts. Doctors who treat cunts have special names.

Famous cunts in history have caused empires to rise and fall.

Sex industries throughout the world enjoy exorbitant profit margins because of the wonderful things cunts do and represent.

When women endure cultural customs such as clitoridectomies, chastity belts, Mississippi Appendectomies (i.e., forced sterilization), infibulation, forced prostitution, slavery and rape, cunts are where? Why, in the spotlight, of course.

Yes, though they often play supporting roles to cocks, cunts deserve star billing in the marquee of every woman's life.

Cunts are very important.

Unfortunately, cunts are important to all the wrong people for all the wrong reasons.

Cunts are not important to women because they are the very fount of our power, genius and beauty. Rather, cunts are important to men because they generate profits and episodes of ejaculation, and represent the precise point of vulnerability for keeping women divided and thus, conquered.

History, the media, economic structures and justice systems have led women to the understanding that delighting in a love affair with our cunts will get us no further than Sitting Bull, had he opted to have a passionate love affair with the Seventh Cavalry.

Which, of course, he did not.

Why should Sitting Bull love the Seventh Cavalry? The Seventh Cavalry consistently represented the undoing of his people.

Why should women love our cunts? They, too, consistently represent the undoing of our people.

The main contention here, of course, is that the Seventh Cavalry did not reside between Sitting Bull's legs.

. . . The fact that women learn to dislike an actual, undeniable, unavoidable physical region of ourselves results in a crappy Sisyphean situation, warranting an intense focus of attention. . . .

My cunt is *mine*.

In order to re-establish a close relationship with my cunt, I must take responsibility not only for what it is to me today, but for everything it has become due to the seemingly endless throng of spin doctors, past and present. My cunt serves me in ways *cavernously* unrelated to generating profits, procuring episodes of ejaculation in males and representing the precise point of vulnerability for keeping women divided and thus, conquered. It is therefore my responsibility to insure this reality resides at the forefront of humanity's consciousness when history is rewritten once again.

We women have a lot of responsibilities.

Here are a few:

Seizing a vocabulary for ourselves.

Actively teaching ourselves to perceive cunts—ours and others'—in a manner generating understanding and empathy.

Taking this knowledge out into the community.

Learning self-protection.

Seeking out and supporting cuntlovin' artists, businesses, media and role models.

Using our power as consumers.

Keeping our money in a community of cuntlovin' women.

We arrive at reconciliation by confronting learned, internalized misogyny and re-educating ourselves on our terms. Three of the most important aspects of reconciliation involve fighting with our minds, art and money to create a cultural consciousness that supports and respects all women. . . .

Women are blue-black as the ocean's deepest knowledge, creamy-white 'n lacy blue-veined, freshly ground–cinnamon brown. Women are Christian motorcycle dykes, militantly hetero Muslim theological scholars, Jewish-Chinese bisexual macrobiotic ballerinas and Chippewa shawomen who fuck not just lovers, but Time and Silence too.

Women are drug addicts, anti-abortion activists and volunteers for Meals on Wheels. Women have AIDS, big fancy houses, post-traumatic stress disorder and cockroach-infested hovels. Women are rock stars, Whores, mothers, lawyers, taxidermists, welders, supermodels, scientists, belly dancers, cops, filmmakers, athletes and nurses.

There are not many things which unite *all women*. I have found "cunt," the word and the anatomical jewel, to be a venerable ally in my war against my own oppression. Besides global subjugation, our cunts are the only common denominator I can think of that *all women* irrefutably share.

We are divided from the word.

We are divided from the anatomical jewel.

I seek reconciliation.

On the choice occasions popes and politicians directly refer to female genitalia, the term "vagina" is discreetly engaged.

If you will be so kind, say "vagina" out loud a few times. Strip away the meaning and listen solely to the phonetic sound. It resonates from the roof of your mouth.

A "vagina" could be an economy car:

"That's right, Wanda! Come within five hundred dollars of the actual sticker price, and you'll win this! A brand new *Chrysler Vagina*!"

Or a rodent:

"Next on *Prairie Safari*, you'll see a wily little silver-tailed vagina outwit a voracious pair of ospreys."

Say "cunt" out loud, again stripping away the meaning. The word resonates from the depths of your gut. It *sounds* like something you definitely don't want to tangle with in a drunken brawl in a dark alley.

A "cunt" could be a serious weather condition:

"Next on *Nightline*, an exclusive report on the devastation in Kansas when last night's thunder cunt, with winds exceeding 122 miles an hour, ripped through the state."

Or a monster truck:

"The City Arena is proud to present the Coors Crush 'Em Demolition Round-Up competition, where Randy Sam's *Beast of Burden* will challenge Mike Price's undefeated *Raging Cunt* in the 666 barrel jump."

Moving from phonetics to etymology, "vagina" originates from a word meaning sheath for a sword.

Ain't got no vagina.

I came across the power of "cunt" quite accidentally. After writing an article for a newspaper, I typed in "word count," but left out the "o." My editor laughingly pointed out the mistake. I looked at the two words together and decided "Word Cunt" seemed like a nice title for a woman writer. As a kind of intraoffice byline, I started typing "Word Cunt" instead of "word count" on all my articles.

The handful of people who saw hard copies of my work reacted strongly and asked why I chose to put these two words on my articles. After explaining my reasoning to editorial assistants, production magis, proofreaders and receptionists, I started wondering about the actual, decontextualized power of "cunt."

I looked up "cunt" in Barbara G. Walker's twenty-five-year research opus, *The Women's Encyclopedia of Myths and Secrets*, and found it was indeed a title, back in the day. "Cunt" is related to words from India, China, Ireland, Rome and Egypt. Such words were either titles of respect for women, priestesses and witches, or derivatives of the names of various goddesses:

> In ancient writings, the word for "cunt" was synonymous with "woman," though not in the insulting modern sense. An Egyptologist was shocked to find the maxims of Ptah-Hotep "used for 'woman' a term that was more than blunt," though its indelicacy was not in the eye of the ancient beholder, only in that of the modern scholar. (Walker, 1983, 197)

The words "bitch" and "whore" have also shared a similar fate in our language. This seemed rather fishy to me. Three words which convey negative meanings about women, specifically, all happen to have once had totally positive associations about women, specifically.

Of the three, "cunt" garners the most powerful negative reaction.

How come?

This was obviously a loaded question to be asking myself, 'cause the answer evolved into quite the life-consuming project.

According to every woman-centered historical reference I have read—from M. Esther Harding to bell hooks—the containment of woman's sexuality was a huge priority to emerging patrifocal religious and economic systems.

Cunts were anathema to forefather types. Literally and metaphorically, the word and anatomical jewel presided at the very nexus of many earlier religions which impeded phallic power worship. In Western civilization, forefather types practiced savior-centered religions, such as Catholicism. Springing forth from a very real, very fiscal fear of women and our power, eventually evolving into sexual retardation and womb envy, a philosophy and social system based on destruction was culled to thriving life. One of the more well-documented instances of this destruction-oriented consciousness is something called the Inquisition. It lasted for over *five hundred years*. That is how long it took the Inquisition to rend serious damage to the collective spirit of non-savior-centered religious worshippers.

The Inquisition justified the—usually sadistic—murder, enslavement or rape of every woman, child and man who practiced any form of spiritual belief which did not honor savior-centered phallic power worship.

Since the beginning of time, most cultures honored forces which were tangible, such as the moon, earth, sun, water, birth, death and life. A spirituality which was undetectable to any of the human senses was considered incomprehensible.

One imagines victims of the Inquisition were not hard to come by. Women who owned anything more than the clothes on their backs and a few pots to piss in were religiously targeted by the Inquisition because all of women's resources and possessions became property of the famously cuntfearing Catholic Church. Out of this, the practice of sending "missionaries" into societies bereft of savior-centered spiritualities evolved.

Negative reactions to "cunt" resonate from a learned fear of ancient yet contemporary, inherent yet lost, reviled yet redemptive cuntpower.

Eradicating a tried and true, stentorian-assed word from a language is like rendering null the Goddess Herself.

It's impossible.

Ancient, woman-centered words and beliefs never, like, *fall off the planet.* Having long done taken on a life of their own, they—like womankind—evolve, and survive.

Chameleon style.

For women this has involved making many, many concessions, such as allowing our selves, goddesses, priestesses and words to be defined and presented by men.

Many words found in woman-centered religions, such as cunt, bitch, whore, dog, ass, puta, skag and hag, along with the names of just about all goddesses—over time—assimilated bad connotations. As matrifocal lifestyles became less and less acceptable, "cunt" survived, *necessarily* carrying a negative meaning on into the next millennium.

Words outlive people, institutions, civilizations. Words spur images, associations, memories, inspirations and synapse pulsations. Words send off physical resonations of thought into the nethersphere. Words hurt, soothe, inspire, demean, demand, incite, pacify, teach, romance, pervert, unite, divide.

Words be powerful.

Grown-ups and children are not readily encouraged to unearth the power of words. Adults are repeatedly assured a picture is worth a thousand of them, while the playground response to almost any verbal taunt is "Sticks and stones may break my bones, but words will never hurt me."

I don't beg so much as command to differ.

For young girls in this society, coming into the power we are born with is no easy task. As children, our power is not culled out of us as it is for boys. Still, culling power is—above and beyond all social conditioning—a very surmountable *task* to which womankind collectively rises higher each day.

But we need a language.

A means of communication demands and precedes change.

I posit that we're free to seize a word that was kidnapped and coopted in a pain-filled, distant past, with a ransom that cost our grandmother's freedom, children, traditions, pride and land. I figure we've paid the ransom, but now, everybody long done forgot "cunt" was ours in the first place. . . .

Since everybody already knows that the diabolization of "cunt" is an absolute reality of our language, nobody has to waste time and energy defending its honour.

A cunt by any other name is still a cunt.

"Cunt" is a highly satisfying word to utter on a regular basis.

Every girl and lady who is strong and fighting and powerful, who thrives in this world in a way that serves her, is a rockin', cuntlovin' babe doing her part to goad the post-patriarchal age into fruition.

"Cunt" is the crusty, disgusting bottle in the city dump pile that is bejewelled underneath and has a beautiful genie inside.

Here is a nice story about the transformation of destructive negative, crap-ola into constructive, positive brilliantiana.

Once upon a time, civil rights activist Dick Gregory went into a restaurant and ordered some chicken. Three or four men who wore pointy white hoods for their nighttime fashion statement presently came into the restaurant and said, (I'm paraphrasing here) "Yo, boy. Anything y'do tah dat chicken, we're gone do tah yoo."

Mr. Gregory looked at the chicken on the plate before him and was silent.

The men repeated, "Anything y'do tah dat chicken, boy, we're gone do tah yoo."

Everybody in the restaurant stopped what they were doing and stared.

Mr. Gregory sighed, picked up the chicken and gave it a big ol', sweet ol' kiss.

Perhaps, as some "historians may have it, I fabricated the historic considerations in reassessing the way we presently perceive "cunt."

Even if "cunt" were simply four spontaneous letters someone strung together one day 'cause his wife didn't have dinner on the table when he got home from a hard day's labor offing witches or indigenous peoples, it is still *our word*. Demographically, the women who have *no chance* of negatively being called "cunts" throughout life can be found in totally cloistered nunneries and maybe Amish communities.

Based on the criteria that "cunt" can be neither co-opted nor spin-doctored into having a negative meaning, venerable history or not, it's ours to do with what we want. And thanks to the versatility and user-friendliness of the English language, "cunt" can be used as an all new woman-centered, cuntlovin' noun, adjective or verb.

I, personally, am in love with the idea.

10 Object Lessons: Romance, Violation, and Female Adolescent Sexual Desire

DEBORAH L. TOLMAN

Good girls don't want sex; what they really want is love. Even in an era of teen magazines offering girls tips on how to hone their sexual skills (Ussher, 1997), there remains an assumption that the sexual part of adolescent sexuality is the domain and desire of boys. The familiar story which organizes "normal" female adolescent sexuality is a romance narrative (Kirkman, Rosenthal, & Smith, 1998) in which a (good) girl, who is on a quest for love (Thompson, 1992), does not feel sexual desire—strong, embodied, passionate feelings of sexual wanting. In this story, sexual desire is male; it is intractable, uncontrollable, and victimizing. There continues to be no readily available image or story of a normal girl who has and responds to her own sexual desire (Tolman, 1994b). The romance narrative positions girls as more and less willing sexual objects, rendering their sexual subjectivity difficult at best (Carpenter, 1998). Michelle Fine observed that, "[T]rained through and into positions of passivity and victimization, young women are currently educated away from positions of sexual self-interest." (Fine, 1988, p. 42).

The problem is, however, that if sexual desire is part of the human condition, then being able to know and feel one's sexual desire is an important component of one's lived experience. Sexual desire provides us with potent information, an embodied compass, about ourselves and our relationships. However, rather than investigate the sentient body, girls' sexuality has been reduced to their sexual and reproductive parts: investigations of how the emergence of secondary sexual characteristics (breast and pubic hair development) and menarche relate to personality traits and social behaviors (i.e., Petersen, Leffert, & Graham, 1995) abound, in essence re-enacting the sexualized objectification of young women that pervades our society. Research on girls' sexuality has been defined as sexual behavior rather than sexual feelings, which is almost always categorized as a "deviant" behavior (Tolman, 1996). To construct sexual desire as a normative feature of female adolescence, then, is to challenge psychology's covert but persistent collusion with a culture that alternately denies and denigrates girls' sexual feelings (Fine, 1988; Tolman, 1994a).

In my research, I began with a radical assumption: that a normative expectation for adolescent girls is that they can and should experience sexual desire—not that they should or will necessarily act on these feelings, but that they should be able to recognize and acknowledge what is a part of the self. In analyzing (that is, listening to) the narratives of 30 midadolescent (aged 15–18) girls who attended urban and suburban public high schools, I heard girls from diverse racial, class, and ethnic backgrounds struggling, by themselves, out of relationship with other girls or women, with the following question: How can I know my powerful erotic bodily feelings and respond to them, in relationship with myself and with others, in the context of a dominant culture that tells me, in a range of ways, that sexual desire is not normal for adolescent girls? Understandably, I have found that for these girls, feeling and responding to sexual desire—knowing, listening to and taking into account their own bodily sexual feelings—poses a dilemma (Tolman, 1994a, 1994b, 1996; Tolman & Higgins, 1996). For these girls, feeling desire meant that either they were at odds with cultural context(s) that discourage them from living full-bodied lives, or they were at odds with or dissociated from their own feelings.

Following a social constructivist perspective (Gergen, 1985), the ways in which we do and do not "story" sexuality into being are definitive in how we make meaning out of our bodies and our relationships, and so the ways in which we do and do not speak about sexuality are crucial (Reinholtz, Muehlenhard, Phelps, & Satterfield, 1995). This perspective also suggests that providing critiques and alternatives to sanctioned stories can be a crucial intervention.

This paper examines the stories that are available to one girl for understanding her sexuality and portraying the tensions, revelations, and challenges in the interplay between these stories and her experiences. Central to this endeavor is the use of a method of narrative analysis called *The Listening Guide* (Brown, Tappan, Gilligan, Miller, & Argyris, 1989) that I have utilized to develop an understanding of adolescent girls' sexuality in terms of their own desire. I present a case from my current exploration of how girls' knowledge and experiences of their bodies and of their desire is shaped, enabled, and undermined by stories available in the culture about female intimate relationships and sexuality. In this case, I listened to a White, middle-class, 17-year-old girl, Isabel, who described this part of her life in a 2-hour clinical interview with me. The fact that she is White and middle-class matters, because the ways that we talk about girls' sexuality are largely determined by their race and their class. White, middle-class girls tend to be rendered asexual, whereas poor girls and girls of color are often sexualized (Tolman, 1996). . . .

Object Lessons of the Romance Narrative

After my interview with Isabel, I was sitting in a small, wood-paneled room, arranged with the bright orange furniture that was popular in the '70s when community organizations like the one in which I find myself were funded. I felt like I needed to come up for air; the interview was not what I had expected. Statuesque and pretty, Isabel literally regaled me with an unexpected barrage of cultural convention. As a White, middle-class girl, I know Isabel has had to deal with an image of herself as not having or acting on any of her own sexual feelings if she is to be considered good. As a smart girl (like I was), it is likely that Isabel is thought of as a "brain"—that is, without a body and thus without the ability or interest to be sexual. I know Isabel to be a self-declared feminist. I heard these contradictory constructions of herself in her interview, as she voiced what amounts to a struggle and wish to feel desire and to be sexual in her body—something she thinks about and writes about in her journal a lot, but something that she spoke about for the first time in this interview and has in fact experienced very little.

When I look at Isabel's interview, I notice two things. The erotic voice surfaced very rarely during this 2-hour inquiry about her experiences of sexual pleasure, sexual desire, feeling sexy, sexual fantasy—her subjective experiences of her sexuality. In contrast, the voice of the body is prevalent. This pattern makes me wonder about what Isabel is saying about her body, if it is not in sync with an erotic voice (a more common pattern in other interviews). What can I learn about girls' experience of sexuality by the absence of an erotic voice in how Isabel spoke about her body, her experiences, her knowledge, and her fantasies?

The first clue is that Isabel interrupted my opening questions to tell me about an association she was having to my general questions about girls' sexuality. It is one of the few times in this interview that an erotic voice appeared.

> Every time you say sexuality I think of um, I think it was *The Color Purple* . . . it just, she had to discover her, like she was totally sealed off from her whole body and um, because people kept telling her you know, not to look down there, yeah, I guess it was *The Color Purple*, um, like not to look down there and um, and just (clears throat) concentrate instead on like getting your work done. And then she was raped by her father or something and then, and she just gave her life and her body and everything over to this man who she had to marry. And then all of a sudden one day she sort of like broke the bonds just by, I mean broke um, this whole uh fear that she had of herself, just by looking, she had like a mirror and she was looking at her vagina, and just broke everything. And, and she was all, all of a sudden like a new person, with a really deep and um, and understanding of herself, and it seemed not only she became so much more connected and at one with herself, but also so much more of a sexual person, just because she knew who she was, and then she knew that there was this other guy there. And then there, you know, she knew that they could come together because she was so sure of herself.

As a set piece for our interview, Isabel introduced a story about the transformation that brings together an erotic voice and a voice of the body for a woman who had been "totally sealed off from her whole body," who had learned not to know her own body and who had experienced sexual violation. From the many experiences that the main character, an African-American woman named Celie, has in learning about her own sexuality in this powerful novel (Walker, 1982), Isabel chose to recount here how Celie is able to "come together" with a man she loves. Isabel links Celie's overcoming being "raped" and "giving her body . . . over to a man who she had to marry" and her ability to enter an authentic sexual relationship to her having become "more connected and at one with herself" through knowing her own body. I hear Isabel telling me that she knows the possibility of an erotic connection, to self, through one's own body, and to others—knowledge and experience that makes a woman "so sure of herself." (Au. Note: The selection Isabel made from *The Color Purple* refers to Celie's initial experience with masturbation.

Later in the interview, I asked Isabel about her own experiences with masturbation. She reported that she has "tried it before and it really doesn't give me any pleasure at all . . . and I've stopped doing it. I've maybe done it like 5 times?" Her lack of response to these attempts keeps afloat the questions of her being "extremely asexual," since she has "heard" that "it gives you so much pleasure that you just shouldn't do it at all. And anyway, it didn't give me any pleasure." Yet it is important to point out that Isabel's reports about not finding masturbation pleasurable resonate with virtually all of the 50 adolescent girls whom I've interviewed. Only a handful of girls report even trying masturbation, with most of them responding by looking at me quizzically, noting that it did not make any sense to them, because "no one else is there.")

I understand Isabel's early interruption of my protocol as a way of tipping me off in several ways to help me hear her, to know about and, I think, join her in shaping and pursuing her own query about herself, her body, and her thoughts, hopes, and fantasies about relationships. In fact, Isabel has had very little direct experience in exploring her sexuality with others. She prepared me to hear that she, too, feels "sealed off from her whole body" in relationships. I also heard her telling me that she knows about how women's oppression is accomplished in part through suppression, or maybe possession, of women's sexuality, as well as the empowering effect of a woman gaining "a really deep . . . understanding of herself" through knowing and owning her own body. Celie's sense of self seems to Isabel to stand in contrast to how she and (she says) adolescent girls feel about themselves: "It's so hard to be at one with yourself when you don't know who you are . . . you have these biological hormones going and so it's, it, it doesn't always get together, like the sexuality part."

Framing this interview with her knowledge of an erotic voice, this voice then quickly disappeared as Isabel told me about her sexuality; she voiced it as a wish rather than an experience as she divulged to me the contours of her fantasies and experiences. What sets Isabel apart from most other girls is that the question of her own desire matters to her. Isabel notices, talks about, questions, and worries about the absence of sexual feelings in her life. I attribute this insight to her feminist perspective. However, when Isabel spoke explicitly about sexual desire, contradictions abounded. One the one hand, she tells me she is worried that she is "asexual" because she has not felt a "sexual urge."

> Maybe I'd go to a college campus just to hunt out the guys, and and they're just not there. And maybe it's because I don't know them, but

> nothing's like striking a chord. Um, and then I, I guess in the past like month, or I mean it's been going on for awhile, but I just starting to get really scared, like, 'Oh my God, I'm asexual,' (laughs) you know, I'm like nothing's happening. I'm not finding anybody and when I fantasize, I don't fantasize about having sex. And, and I don't think that I'm a lesbian which would be fine with me if I were, but I just don't think I am. And I don't think um, I mean I'm pretty sure that I'm like heterosexual, but there's no sexual urge there. And I keep like checking, like, you know, like, um, tracing my birthday back, and like, I'm only 16. So maybe it's coming next year. Like, it better hurry, cause you know, there's just like no impetus there for like, losing virginity.

In listening to Isabel tell me about her search for a boyfriend, I heard an echo of my inquiry in her questions about herself. For her, the search for a boyfriend also seems to be a search for herself, for a sign that will tell her something about who she is. I heard Isabel exerting a lot of energy in trying to figure out why she is not experiencing desire. In part, I heard Isabel wondering what, in fact, desire is. Is it something associated with age, so that being "only 16" might explain her silent body, the absence of a "sexual urge"? Perhaps she is confused about the object of her desire, her sexual identity—she considers and rejects this possibility. Isabel said that the absence of desire is making her "scared"; knowing about her desire is, in part, a way of knowing herself that Isabel actually misses. Notable also is Isabel's conception of her own desire as the "impetus" for having sex; this sense of entitlement to her own feelings, this refusal to engage in a romance narrative in which she has the privilege of trading sex for love, sets Isabel apart from other girls' descriptions of curiosity, fear of losing a boyfriend, having a certain amount of time elapse in a relationship, or desire to fit in as the impetus for having sex (Billy, Brewster, & Grady, 1994; Thompson, 1990; Tolman, 1994a).

While Isabel has a belief in her desire as a source of strength, why is it so hard for Isabel to know about her desire, to connect with an erotic voice within herself? I note several interrelated possibilities as I read our interview. She spoke frequently about her body. Her reflections give me some possibilities about the absence of an erotic voice in her life. Isabel does not actually have very much real-life experience with her body in sexual relationships; in the few examples that she offered of what "society defines as sexual pleasure"—which I regard as her reference to what is put forth in the culture as being normative sexual experiences for girls—she narrated a very few experiences colored by disappointment and violation. I wonder whether Isabel simply has not had any opportunity to explore such relationships (she says that she hasn't found anyone in her high school whom she wants to date), or whether she keeps herself from having such experiences. But she chose to respond often and at great length to my questions about her relationship with her body and her struggle and desire to know her body better and to feel her embodied feelings. Her interest in this topic was noticeably more intense than that of other girls with whom I've spoken. Her interest in feminism has provoked her own inquiry.

In attending to how Isabel spoke about her body, I realize that while speaking about her body often, she referred to her body as if she was looking at it rather than feeling it—even in response to my direct questions about what her body feels like. In such descriptions, there is no evidence of an erotic voice: her body is an object that she examines, evaluates, and judges; breaks into parts; and about which she fantasizes in other shapes and sizes as well. Evidence of having been socialized into objectifying her own body (Bartky, 1990; Bordo, 1993) abounds. A striking example is when I asked her to talk about what her body feels like in a fantasy that is ephemeral and spiritual but distinctly disembodied. This question was meant to be interruptive on my part, to invite her to speak the unspeakable, that is, voice her body, as well as to encourage her to explore the question of a sealed-off body that she herself has raised. "What does your body feel like?" I asked her.

> Like, in, in the fantasy? Oh, just I feel wonder—I mean, it's like the same kind of feeling that I was telling you, oh gosh I really wish I were like really, really eloquent, because then I could make this so good, cause I have really good pictures in my mind, but it's the same picture that um, like when I'm walking down like, and Sam's brother was um, staring at me and I was like, 'Wow, I'm so gorgeous,' and when I looked back at that later I was like crazy, cause I knew I wasn't, but it's that same kind of feeling, where all over you, you know like your leg is just absolutely perfect, and your feet are not too big, and and your shoulders are just like, you're actually standing up straight for once, um, and you're just gorgeous, and your bones, like are sticking out at the right places (laughs), you know cause you're, like you're, you're so, like you're um, your throat bones, are just like pushing out a little bit because . . . your cheekbones are like all high up and, and your hair is like radiating.

Tolman: "You are giving me this amazing image of what you look like. But I want to get a sense of what it feels like. What, how does this feel, in your body?"

> I don't, I guess I don't understand. I mean, I feel wonderful. And I feel absolutely like I love myself and like everybody that I'm walking past is staring at me, and that this guy that I'm with is like, 'Wow, I have the best of everything, cause she's really smart and she's really beautiful.' Which are two (clears throat) things that I'm constantly trying to connect. Um, like think about the connection between myself, but um, is that what you mean, like those kinds of things?

When I asked her to tell me about feeling sexy, she described the experience of looking sexy; she equated "knowing that I look beautiful" with "yeah, I'm so sexy." When I persisted in asking her about the feeling, she persisted in describing looking sexy. In fact, this may make her feel sexy, but she voiced her thoughts about her looks, the image she projects as a desirable object. So I asked her, "What's it feel like, feeling sexy?"

> Oh, it's so wonderful. And sometimes, like once in awhile, on a really good day, when I'm in a very good mood, it happens in real life, where I just feel sexy, and, and I know that everybody must be just looking at me like, 'Oh wow, she's like so beautiful.' Or like, 'Oh my gosh, she must have 30 boyfriends outside of school.' (laughs) Um, or, or just like, 'Wow she looks just so um, amazing. I really wish I looked like her.'

I encouraged her to continue.

> Like the girls would say that, and the boys were like, 'Oh, maybe I should ask her out,' you know? Those things. Or actually, the boys wouldn't even say that, because the boys would say, and this has to do with I don't know what, but um, the boys would say, 'Wow, she's so beautiful she doesn't even look like she belongs in high school cause she looks so much older,' and things like that. Um, but yeah, I mean, the whole like notion of feeling sexy is an integral part of my life (laughs).

In Isabel's world, sexy is neither about her body or about her desire; it is about being rather than feeling. Isabel is so accustomed to experiencing her body as something that she watches and manipulates that she has difficulty knowing whether she is really experiencing an embodied feeling, whether her body's voice is authentic or just something she is imagining.

> Sometimes when somebody um touches me, just like putting a hand on a shoulder, or stands really close, that also can happen, um, yeah like um, yeah. But it's, I'm more aware of it because when somebody,

> I mean I'm, it's just a little confusing because when somebody like really gorgeous comes close um, and I'm thinking, I think to my—and, and that same kind of like really inner peace, like warmness happens, I think, 'Oh, that's just because you're, you want this to happen right now' . . . because they're standing close and they're really cute so you start to do this, um, so I don't know if that's me telling my body to do it or if it just happening. Oh my gosh, I wish it would just happen because I mean, like I'm progressing somewhere (laughs).

In listening to Isabel talk about her experiences, I heard how well Isabel has learned to objectify her body. An object has no feelings of its own, no sense of agency, an absence of subjectivity (Tolman & Debold, 1993). I also heard how Isabel is engaged in a struggle to be embodied, to know herself as a sexual person with sexual feelings; she finds it "confusing" when someone she finds "gorgeous comes close," and when her body responds with "warmness," she is not sure if it is "me telling my body to do it or if it is just happening." I understand Isabel to wonder whether she is convincing herself that she is having the response she believes in her mind is appropriate or "normal," or whether she is having an authentic response. Her difficulty in knowing her own body's feelings was underscored, and perhaps in part explained, by her descriptions of feeling vulnerable when being objectified by men and also the anger she feels as she finds herself joining them in their appraisal of her body, worrying that:

> I should look more beautiful right now, so you know I try to stand a little bit straighter, even though I'm so angry, at, in one sense at this guy um, and like if my hair's parted down the middle maybe I'll like part it down the side and stuff so I don't look like a geek or anything like that, but just all these things that um, that are going on. And they're very conflicting, and it's very frustrating. I feel very vulnerable then, um, because I'm not in control.

Isabel told of the power of having been socialized into knowing and relating to her own body as an object. She voiced an experience that many feminist women have and keep to themselves: despite our conscious sense of outrage and anger at this violation, we have been well trained to be the best objects we can be, even at the very moment of violation—which is a moment of consumption as well. Isabel has the strength to be able to know and voice the contradictory nature of her response.

Isabel's descriptions of experiencing her own body as an object were explicitly associated with situations that she calls "romantic" or potentially sexual. The romance narrative posits a man who woos a woman, and then conquers her—sometimes construed as her giving herself to him, being the object of his sexual desire, being a woman who is a body yet who has no embodied feelings of her own (Moore & Rosenthal, 1992). In the romance narrative, the normative path of development demands girls' dissociation from their own agency and embodied feelings, that they become good (hetero) sexual objects for the sexual gaze and conquest of men (Ramazanoglu & Holland, 1993). Feminist analyses of the romance narrative delineate how it disempowers women by positing them as objects rather than subjects in their relationships and in their own lives, keeping them out of touch with the knowledge they gain through their own embodied experience (i.e., Tolman & Debold, 1993). The romance narrative codifies the objectification of women into bodies rather than embodied persons; it does not acknowledge female sexual desire as something that figures in the experience of the girl who ultimately is swept off her feet by a handsome beau (Christian-Smith, 1990).

It is not inconsequential, then, that the primary theme in Isabel's descriptions of her sexual fantasies is romance. The simplicity and clarity in her discussion of Celie's coming into an authentic heterosexual relationship through her ability to be connected with her body disappeared when Isabel talked about her wishes for relationship. Isabel invoked the romance narrative over and over again in describing girls' sexuality. The organization of her thoughts and few experiences according to the romance narrative is a possible explanation for how rarely an erotic voice appeared in her stories, as well as the extent to which the voice of her body is relentlessly objectified.

> I have this little fantasy world where um, where everything's just totally romantic and I like wanted to meet this guy who's in college, who's just absolutely gorgeous, and he's just going to be incredible, and he's like, he knows, like he's memorized a hundred selected poems by ee cummings, you know, and he just, but he knows like all these other poets, too. He plays the guitar, which is a must, and, and he would like make picnics for me, and we'd just go out and um, and have this wonderful time, and, and we'd just lie close together, but we wouldn't do anything. We would just like lie close together and um, and it would just be so romantic, and I'd feel like I was deeply connected to him. But it never goes beyond that. It never goes like, and then we'd strip off our clothes or something. I mean, maybe we would, but it wouldn't be like, as in any kind of sexual, any like, a deeply sexual connotation, like we were going to have intercourse.

When speaking within the confines of the romance narrative, Isabel seemed to lose access to speaking about, maybe even knowing, what she has told me she knows by relaying Celie's experience—that her body can and should have an erotic voice. Yet perhaps because Isabel has access to an alternative story about herself, her body, and her sexuality, because she knows to have questions and wishes about her own sexual desire, I heard her interrupting the construction of herself as an object through contradictions. When Isabel told me these stories in which I noticed an absence of an erotic voice and her objectification of her own body, I interrupted to ask her about her bodily feelings. It is in these interruptions that I gleaned the way in which she has learned to relate to her body as an object of another's desire rather than as a subject of her own feelings, yielding no erotic voice. In that sense, the romance narrative effects a particularly insidious form of violation.

Her Body Speaks

In addition to constituting a form of violation, the objectification that is produced through the romance narrative leads inevitably to violations. Isabel has had her share of experiences of violation. Rather than label and then discard or disregard Isabel's stories as the not-surprising outcome of an experience of abuse, Isabel's stories of violation are common and expected, a kind of everyday or normalized violation that most women have encountered. The interplay between the romance narrative and these violations, which construct and cement Isabel's status as a sexual object for others to acquire or use rather than a person whose body is her own to experience, is of critical importance in understanding girls' experiences with their own sexual desire. In a stunning description of dissociation, Isabel recounted a time when she was molested as an 8-year-old girl by an adolescent boy.

> It must have been like when I was 8 and we were watching fireworks. We had um, we (clears throat) lived in this apartment building in South Boston, and it was um, we had the whole roof, and we'd always watch fireworks on the roof, like with this big blanket, and this guy came, he must, oh I have no idea how old he was, maybe 15, 16, 17, 18, but he was much older than I was. And um, and his parents were there, and I was under the blanket because I was really cold. And all of a sudden like I felt his fingers like walking up my leg, and um, and he got like really close to me. I don't remember what happened, um, I

> mean it was nothing like really terrible, but it just made me very uncomfortable, and I remember I kept, and this happened before when we, I mean I do this when I'm under like extreme stress . . . When I was lying under this blanket I would imagine that um, my father had said that I should go down the stairs to bed because it was way past my bedtime, and I was in bed. Like it, wrapped up in my bunk bed, and and um, then I'd wake up and find out I was still under this blanket and this guy had his like nasty fingers all over me. And then I kept thinking, um, um, and it's like one of those really painful like dream-like states where you're like *Chariots of Fire* song, and you know, very slowly, and and you just remember your mother telling you like, 'All you have to do is just say no whenever someone comes.' And I remember I kept thinking like No! No! and and thinking, 'Oh, this is so vivid,' just thinking, um, that I would yell at the top of my lungs, 'Do you know what you're doing?' and like 'Do you know where your hand is?' so everyone would just look at him. He would be humiliated, like die, and melt like the wicked witch and things like that. And, and I just wanted to keep yelling like, 'No!' or like 'Get your hands off me!' and all I did, I mean after all these like really wonderfully like terrible aggressive things I could have done like verbally um, terrible things, all I did was just pee on him (laughs) which was, which was fine, I guess, but um, because I was just so nervous, and, and I woke up and I realized like my legs were all wet but his hand was still there . . . Oh, gosh, I just kept dreaming, like drifting off to sleep and waking up, you know like pretending I was in my bunk bed and finally waking up, and being like, oh, and um, I guess I finally fell asleep, and they carried me down to bed, and he left . . . that didn't give me any kind of sexual pleasure.

Knowing what she wants to say but not able to say it, rendered voiceless, Isabel's body made its objection by urinating on the offender, who ignored the protesting voice of her body and continued. Isabel explained that she did not decide to urinate on him, that she wanted to speak but could not; she was in a dissociated state when she urinated. She attributes what I interpret to be a self-protective act to being "nervous." I hear how powerless she must have felt and how her body was struggling to assert what her voice was unable to say. Isabel told this story in response to my question about a time when she experienced sexual pleasure. I wonder if "sexual" and "pleasure" haven't been inappropriately (though understandably) fused for Isabel; while this experience involved someone doing sexual things to her—which she supposes should be associated with pleasure—they were in fact a violation and use of her body that were not in the least pleasurable. Isabel has had little opportunity to work through this experience and to separate out the possibility or indicators of sexual pleasure from the effects of sexual violation, because such discourse is neither common nor necessarily acceptable among most girls and women.

This is not the only experience of having her body objectified and then violated that Isabel described. When she was in the 6th grade, she was solicited by an adult man.

> I was wearing this miniskirt that I usually never wear, and this guy pulled up and he rolled down his window, and he's like, 'Come over here,' so I went up (snorts) and, and I was like, and he said, 'How much?' and I said, 'What?' And and goes 'Well how much is it for the night?' And I was like, 'What are you talking about?' because I was so naive, I had no idea what was going on . . . He was like 25 or something, maybe 30, and um, and he goes, 'Well, if you want to spend the night with me, how much do I have to pay?' and I was like, 'Well I don't know, but I think I have to go catch my bus.' And, and I didn't realize until like when I was over my friend's the next day, what that meant, but I felt very vulnerable anyway, just because I knew that it probably had some kind of sexual connotation to it.

As I listened to these stories of feeling and being vulnerable, which are both associated with "some kind of sexual connotation" and also have at their heart being treated like an object rather than a person, I heard the interplay of Isabel's romance fantasies which leave out her sexual desire, her feeling unable to find a boyfriend, and her own and others' objectification of her body. In fact, Isabel herself makes these connections: "And that's what makes me really afraid um, that all experiences will be like that. And that's why I keep having these like extreme, pathetic, desperate fantasies with um, (laughs) like um, like true pleasure, um, where I just skip over the whole sexual kind of stuff."

Perhaps Isabel is drawn to a sexless romance fantasy, and wary of actual romantic and sexual relationships, because it is a lot safer and more pleasant than the memory of violation and dissociation that is associated for her with the concept of sexual pleasure. Because it is idealized, the romance narrative is attractive; coupled with the vulnerability that can feel paramount in connecting with one's body and erotic voice in explicitly sexual situations, it is not surprising that becoming a good sexual object has a certain appeal. Yet the romance narrative has pitfalls of its own for adolescent girls. This narrative undermines the embodiment or sexual agency of Isabel and other young women, to encourage them to connect the powerful feelings in their own bodies, "to be more connected and at one with yourself" that Isabel knows is possible and also deeply desirable.

Listening to (Some)body: Isabel's Erotic Voice

Despite Isabel's inculcation into the romance narrative, she does in fact have access to her body as a source of powerful feeling and information about relationships. On the heels of telling me about a disappointing experience being kissed by a boy, which she found "disgusting" but associated with "society's definition of sexual pleasure," she offered a description filled with an erotic voice interplaying with the voice of her body. I was taken aback when she suddenly began recounting a potent experience of embodied pleasure, revealing a close knowledge of the voice of her body and of an erotic voice—in fact, the two voices seemed to blend into one as she spoke about a feeling that could, she seems to wonder, be called sexual pleasure:

> If sexual pleasure is what gives you like this really inner sense of like peace and relaxation and just like thinking that's everything's okay and like, and um, and like when you really can start to feel like your um like your juices or like your blood flowing throughout you, and like everything just becomes relaxed and light, and this is the weirdest thing in the world, but when somebody I really respect, and it either can be male or female, um, but I really think it's beautiful, and, and to be beautiful in my little world of beauty you don't have to be like um gorgeous in a physical sense, you can be just like really mature, and self-assured and powerful, that's what makes um, somebody beautiful. If they start to talk, and, and if they're talking they have to be talking for like more than a minute, obviously, but if they start to talk, and I'm just totally absorbed in what they're saying and their voice, and like the flux of their voice, and they can just be reading poetry, or or just talking about like biology, or you know, like chemistry, or something, I mean, my chemistry teacher doesn't do that for me, but, but they can just be talking about the most blasé or mundane subject and um, and I just get totally immersed in what they're saying . . . And I have no idea, this is like the one thing that gives me the most pleasure, so I'm just associating sexual pleasure, cause I guess that's, I mean sexual pleasure is supposed to give you a lot of pleasure too, so, but . . .

Tolman: "Is there something about your body that gets involved with that?"

> Yeah, it's um, it's everything gets really loose . . . and um, and sort of like very warm, and I just, and like I have just this great sense of being one, like being connected when that happens, um, just hearing this person speak, like the words flow right through me, but I can like totally, I mean just crystal clear in my mind like what they're saying, and but, but everything gets involved in what they're saying, and I'm just sitting there like, 'Oh, you know, just speak forever, it's just wonderful.'

With the exception of the poetry reading, this story has no elements of the romantic narrative. Isabel revealed a deep knowledge of profound pleasure and intense bodily feeling in connection with another person—"just hearing this person speak, like the words flow right through me"—that is not socially constructed as either romantic or sexual, but which she experiences as a profoundly embodied and erotic. I was struck that Isabel experiences a powerful connection to herself and to other people only in situations that she does not construe as sexual.

Conclusions

So what is keeping Isabel out of relationship with her body in sexual situations? What is keeping her out of sexual situations? It is surely over determined. She has little lived experience with sexual relationships, perhaps in part because she avoids them due to her experiences of violation and vulnerability. It is also in these situations, as opposed to her description of listening to someone, that she is conscious of her body as an object. She experiences her body explicitly as an object in situations that are socially labeled sexual. Indeed, her body has been treated as an object, out of her control and certainly as if she did not have her own desire.

What sets Isabel apart from many other adolescent girls who have learned to know their bodies as objects rather than as sexual subjects is that she also knows that desire, empowerment, and self-actualization are accessible to her through her own body. In her access to an alternative narrative through the experiences of Celie, I hear Isabel wondering about her own desire, initiating a process of resisting her internalized objectification, and coming into her body by asking questions about who she is, about her sexuality, that have the potential to interrupt the silencing of her sexuality produced by the romance narrative and her experiences of violation. A key piece of information that resonates with what other girls have told me is that Isabel has not had an opportunity to speak to other girls or to adult women about her experiences, her fantasies, or her questions. This silence, which shrouds active, passionate female adolescent sexuality, is both cause for concern and opportunity for change (Thompson, 1992; Tolman & Szalacha, 1999).

When educating girls about sexual health, not only are we obliged to teach them about the physical and emotional risks of sexuality, but also of the ways in which our sexuality can make us more resilient and more alive and about our entitlement to an erotic voice. By cultivating an erotic voice, we are not going to turn girls into sex fiends. However, we will challenge a system that depends on the erotic silence of many girls—the lynchpin of our current construction of adolescent sexuality. If girls can know and incorporate their own erotic voices into their relationships and sexual choices, they are no longer "dependable" for bearing the responsibility to control boys' "raging hormones."

When we acknowledge girls' desire, boys' accountability will become more acute and harder to deny, and everyday violations will become harder to overlook or normalize. By speaking to girls and boys about girls' entitlement to their sexual desire, we demand a rewrite of the romance narrative in which girls will be sexual subjects rather than sexual objects.

References

Bartky, S. L. (1990). *Femininity and domination: Studies in the phenomenology of oppression.* New York: Routledge.

Billy, J. O. G., Brewster, K. L., & Grady, W. R. (1994). Contextual effects on the sexual behavior of adolescent women. *Journal of Marriage and the Family, 56*, 387–404.

Bordo, S. (1993). *Unbearable weight: Feminism, western culture, and the body.* Berkely, CA: University of California Press.

Brown, L. M. (In press). White working class girls, femininities and the paradox of resistance. In D. Tolman & M. Brydon-Miller, (Eds.), *From subjects to subjectivities: A handbook of interpretive and participatory methods.* New York: New York University Press.

Brown, L. M., & Gilligan, C. (1992). *Meeting at the crossroads: Women's psychology and girls' development.* Cambridge, MA: Harvard University Press.

Brown, L. M., Tappan, M. B., Gilligan, C., Miller, B. A., & Argyris, D. E. (1989). Reading for self and moral voice: A method for interpreting narratives of real-life moral conflict and choice. In M. J. Packer & R. B. Addison (Eds.), *Entering the circle: Hermeneutic investigation in psychology* (pp. 141–164). Albany, NY: State University of New York Press.

Carpenter, L. (1998). From girls into women: Scripts for sexuality and romance in Seventeen Magazine, 1974–1994. *The Journal of Sex Research, 35*(2), 158–168.

Christian-Smith, L. K. (1990). *Becoming a woman through romance.* New York: Routledge.

Debold, E. W., M.; Malave, I. (1993). *Mother daughter revolution: From betrayal to power.* Reading, MA: Addison-Wesley Publications.

Fine, M. (1988). Sexuality, schooling, and adolescent females: The missing discourse of desire. *Harvard Educational Review, 58*(1), 29–53.

Gergen, K. J. (1985). The social constructionist movement in modern psychology. *American Psychologist, 40*(3), 266–275.

Kirkman, M., Rosenthal, D., & Smith, A. M. A. (1998). Adolescent sex and the romantic narrative: Why some young heterosexuals use condoms to prevent pregnancy, but not disease. *Psychology, Health and Medicine, 3*(4), 355–370.

Moore, S., & Rosenthal, D. (1992). The social context of adolescent sexuality: Safe sex implications. *Journal of Adolescence, 15*(4), 415–435.

Petersen, A. C., Leffert, N., & Graham, B. L. (1995). Adolescent development and the emergence of sexuality. *Suicide and Life-Threatening Behavior, 25* (Supplement), 4–17.

Ramazanoglu, C., & Holland, J. (1993). Women's sexuality and men's appropriation of desire. In C. Ramazanoglu (Ed.), *Up against Foulcault* (pp. 239–264). New York: Routledge.

Reinholtz, R. K., Muehlenhard, C. L., Phelps, J. L., & Satterfield, A. T. (1995). Sexual discourse and sexual intercourse: How the way we communicate affects the way we think about sexual coercion. In P. J. Kalbfleisch & M. J. Cody (Eds.), *Gender, power, and communication in human relationships* (pp. 141–188). Hillsdale, NJ: Lawrence Erlbaum Associates, Publishers.

Thompson, S. (1990). Putting a big thing into a little hole: Teenage girls' accounts of sexual initiation. *Journal of Sex Research, 27*(3), 341–361.

Thompson, S. (1992). Search for tomorrow: On feminism and the reconstruction of teen romance. In C. S. Vance (Ed.), *Pleasure and danger: Exploring female sexuality* (pp. 350–384). London: Pandora Press.

Tolman, D. L. (1994a). Daring to desire: Culture and the bodies of adolescent girls. In J. Irvine (Ed.), *Sexual cultures: Adolescents, communities and the construction of identity.* Philadelphia: Temple University Press.

Tolman, D. L. (1994b). Doing desire: Adolescent girls' struggles for/with sexuality. *Gender and Society, 8*(3), 324–342.

Tolman, D. L. (1996). Adolescent girls' sexuality: Debunking the myth of the urban girl. In B. J. R. Leadbeater & N. Way (Eds.), *Urban girls: Resisting stereotypes, creating identities* (pp. 255–271). New York: New York University Press.

Tolman, D. L., & Debold, E. (1993). Conflicts of body and image: Female adolescents, desire, and the no-body body. In P. Fallon, M. Katzman, & S. Wooley (Eds.), *Feminist perspectives on eating disorders* (pp. 301–317). New York: Guilford Press.

Tolman, D. L., & Higgins, T. (1996). How being a good girl can be bad for girls. In N. B. Maglin & D. Perry (Eds.), *Good girls/bad girls: Women, sex, violence and power in the 1990s*. New Brunswick, NJ: Rutgers University Press.

Tolman, D. L., & Szalacha, L. A. (1999). Dimensions of desire: Bridging qualitative and quantitative methods in a study of female adolescent sexuality. *Psychology of Women Quarterly*, *23*(2), 7–39.

Ussher, J. M. (1997). *Fantasies of femininity: Reframing the boundaries of sex*. New Brunswick, NJ: Rutgers University Press.

Walker, A. (1982). *The Color Purple*. New York: Washington Square Press.

Way, N. (In press). Using feminist research methods to explore boys' relationships. In D. Tolman & M. Brydon-Miller, (Eds.), *From subjects to subjectivities: A handbook of interpretive and participatory methods*. New York: New York University Press.

11 Diversity and Variability in Women's Sexual Identities

CARLA GOLDEN

Psychologists and feminists alike tend to assume that most persons can be neatly categorized according to membership in one of four groups: heterosexual, homosexual, bisexual, or asexual (celibate). Furthermore, they tend to accept uncritically the notion that when a person's behavior fits into one of those four sexual preference categories, that person adopts a corresponding sexual identity to match the behavior. If such beliefs are not questioned, it seems logical to assume that a person whose sexual behavior is exclusively heterosexual would also assume a heterosexual identity, and conversely, that a person with a heterosexual identity would only engage in heterosexual behavior. The same connection between sexual behavior and sexual identity would be assumed of homosexuality as well.

The relation between sexual behavior and sexual identity may not be so clear-cut, however. For women, sexuality may be an aspect of identity that is fluid and dynamic as opposed to fixed and invariant. I came to think of women's sexuality in this way as a function of interviews and more general discussions with young college women who were exploring their sexuality. Many of these women were defining themselves as lesbians despite the fact that their current or previous sexual experience was heterosexual. I was confused by this, because I had tended to think of sex between women as rather central to the definition of lesbianism. However, as I read more feminist literature on sexuality and spoke with women who were feminists and/or lesbians, I came to see that the definition of a lesbian is both problematic and far from unambiguous. As a psychologist, I am primarily interested in how women subjectively experience their identities, and how they react when their personally constructed identities are not concordant with social definitions. Exploring these issues led me to a new view of women's sexuality.

I will review here some of the controversial definitional issues that have been identified in the feminist sexuality literature, and then will present the findings from interviews with college women. These interviews suggest that there is enormous diversity and variability in women's self-defined sexual identities, and that these identities are often at odds with social definitions. Finally, I will discuss how the exploration of sexuality from the perspective of a "deviant" group (i.e., lesbians) sheds some important light on the nature of women's sexuality in general.

How do feminist theorists interested in women's sexuality define lesbianism? Adrienne Rich's conception of the lesbian continuum provides an interesting introduction to the problematic nature of the term.[1] Instead of using the word *lesbianism*, which for her has connotations both clinical and pejorative, Rich suggests thinking in terms of a lesbian continuum. She notes that across history and cultures, women have in a variety of ways been primarily committed to other women, and she uses the term *lesbian continuum* to refer to the range of such women-identified experiences. That a woman has actually had, or has consciously desired, genital sexual experience with another woman is but one point on the lesbian continuum. By conceiving of lesbianism in these terms, Rich suggests that many more forms of primary intensity between and among women (including emotional bonding) can be included than would be possible with a narrower definition based solely on sexual behavior. Furthermore, according to Rich's definition, a woman need not identify herself as a lesbian in order to be considered one. By defining lesbianism in terms of primary intensity between women, she allows for women from previous historical periods to be considered as lesbians, even though at the time when they lived there may have been no cultural conception of lesbianism. . . .

Ann Ferguson has argued that defining lesbianism in such a manner incorrectly downplays the importance of sexual feelings and behavior.[2] Such a definition in effect unsexes lesbianism and makes it more agreeable to some people by diminishing what is undeniably a significant difference.

Furthermore, Ferguson argues that it isn't meaningful to talk about a woman as a lesbian if she doesn't acknowledge herself to be one. She suggests that, because before the twentieth century there was no cultural conception of lesbianism, one cannot and should not attempt to consider women lesbians who did not consider themselves to be such. As an alternative, Ferguson offers the following definition: "A lesbian is a woman who has sexual and erotic-emotional ties primarily with women or who sees herself as centrally involved with a community of self-identified lesbians whose sexual and erotic-emotional ties are primarily with women *and* who is herself a self-identified lesbian."[3] Without de-emphasizing the role of sexual behavior, this definition includes both celibate and bisexual women as lesbians, as long as they identify themselves as such. . . .

Some have argued that attempts to define who is and who is not a lesbian will only be divisive, and it seems undeniable that to a certain extent it has been. Jacquelyn Zita has aptly referred to this judging and weighing of who does and does not qualify for membership as the "Lesbian Olympics."[4] However, it does seem both intellectually important and socially useful for groups to define themselves. It is critical for any minority or oppressed group to break free from the confining definitions of the dominant culture and to create their own. In collectively resisting oppression, minority groups need to foster not only a positive group identity, but also a sense of the cohesiveness of the group based at least partially on shared characteristics and self-definitions.

While acknowledging that it is important for minority groups to define themselves (as opposed to being defined by the dominant group), it must be recognized that it is a sociopolitical task to do so, and that there are certain limitations inherent in such an enterprise. That is, to construct a definition is to identify a set of criteria according to which individual women can be considered to fit or not. Describing a social group is quite different from the psychological task of understanding what it means to any particular woman to identify as a member of that group. In fact, the construction of a categorical definition of lesbian is bound to obscure the personal and variable meanings of lesbian identity as it is experienced by real women. I say this because sexual feelings, attractions, and behavior are not necessarily fixed and invariant with regard to the sex of the person toward whom they are directed. When definitions of lesbian are conceptualized with primary reference to sexual feelings and activities, it may be difficult (if one wishes to allow for the complexity of lived experience) to construct unambiguous criteria that would specify who does and does not belong in the category *lesbian*.

A precise definition of lesbian that establishes unchanging sexual criteria according to which individual women can be judged as legitimate members of the category may not have the flexibility to account for the diversity and variability in subjectively experienced lesbian identities. One serious problem that results is that individual women may find their experience of themselves at odds with the socially constructed category, even when it emanates from the lesbian community. At this point in history when so many women are self-consciously asking who they are and how they can understand their place in society, it is possible to explore these issues with them directly.

Between 1977 and 1983, I taught at a northeastern women's college, where I served, albeit unofficially, as a counsellor to young women exploring their sexual and personal identities. For many of the women I spoke with over the years, these were times of change and transition, and among the most prominent changes were those in their sexual feelings, activities, and identities, and in their sense of possibilities for the future. Although many of these young women had been sexual (in varying degrees and with different sexual object choices) before coming to college, several features of their new environment converged to make the issue of sexuality in general, and their own sexuality in particular, more salient than it had been in their high school years.

One important aspect of their new environment was that they were away from their parents and had the option of engaging in sexual relations without having to be overly concerned about their parents' discovery of their behavior. Second, they were in an all-women's environment where close connections between women were valued, and where they were free to develop in ways not often matched in coeducational environments. In women's colleges, relationships between women can and do flourish; women have the opportunity to live, love, learn, work, and grow together. Although such environments are special in any historic time period, there was something unique about their atmosphere in the last ten years. As a result of the women's movement, the visibility of a small but dedicated number of feminist faculty, and the presence in the curriculum of women's studies courses, a certain self-consciousness about being women existed among a majority of the students. This consciousness gave rise to both self-exploration and a broader consideration of women's lives and possibilities, including the variety of vocational choices and sexual life-styles available to women. Added to this was a highly visible and active Lesbian Alliance on campus. At a time when many students were having to deal with themselves as sexual beings, they were also being exposed to "out" lesbians, many of whom were in more than a few respects indistinguishable from themselves. Workshops conducted by the Lesbian Alliance did a tremendous job in raising consciousness, and they also served, for some students, to heighten questions and thinking about their own sexuality. . . .

. . . I had extensive contact with students who were active members of the Lesbian Alliance (and who were thus viewed as "the lesbian community" on campus), as well as with students who were not publicly affiliated with the Alliance. I will articulate as well as I can from their perspective some of the ways in which these young women were defining themselves, and how they made sense of their pasts, their present, and their futures.

One major distinction that emerged from interviews with women who defined themselves as lesbian was between those who felt their lesbianism was essentially beyond their control and those who felt it was self-consciously chosen. Some of these women had from an earlier age (usually between six and twelve) considered themselves to be different from other girls. Whether or not they had a label for it, they experienced themselves as different in that they felt sexually attracted to and oriented toward other girls or women. Their feelings could be independent of actual sexual experiences. In other words, they may or may not have had lesbian relationships, and they may even have had heterosexual ones, but regardless, they felt themselves to be different in that they were attracted to females. Furthermore, this was experienced either at the time, or in retrospect, as something beyond their control; these women had not chosen to be attracted to women, they just were. Some of these women offered comments to the effect that they were "born" lesbians and would spontaneously contrast themselves with women who described their lesbianism as resulting from a conscious decision. Following a distinction made by Barbara Ponse in her study of a southern lesbian community, I have characterized these women as primary lesbians; that is, women who from an early age have a conscious sense of difference based on sexual attraction toward members of the same sex, and who do not perceive this difference to be based on any kind of conscious choice.[5]

In contrast to primary lesbians were women who could be characterized, again following the distinction made by Ponse, as elective lesbians. For these women, their lesbian identity is perceived as consciously chosen. This is not to imply that it is strictly a political choice; for the majority it is experienced as an erotic choice as well. Unlike primary lesbians, these women did not have a conscious sense of being different from other girls at a younger age. But in similarity with primary lesbians, their sense of identity was independent of their actual sexual history. As girls, some of these elective lesbians had crushes on other girls; they may even have engaged in sexual play and exchanges with other girls. Despite such lesbian-like experiences, they did not think of themselves as different.

No one had ever labeled their behavior as deviant, and it had not occurred to them that others might consider it to be.

These women usually had some heterosexual experience as they got older, and even when they had not, they had heterosexual identities. However, regardless of their actual sexual experience, they never thought of themselves as different from the "average" female in terms of their sexual orientation. Although they may never have explicitly called themselves heterosexuals, neither did they consider the possibility that they were anything else (much in the manner of white people who never give much explicit thought to their race). I have characterized as elective lesbians women who perceive of their lesbianism as a conscious choice, and who do not have a history of thinking of themselves as different from other females in the realm of sexual inclinations.

Among elective lesbians, I found two distinctive sub-patterns that suggested another salient dimension of lesbian identity. Some of these women viewed their sexual attraction to women as a central, basic, and unchanging aspect of who they were, and it seemed to me that this was not merely a political stance but a strongly experienced subjective feeling about their essential natures. In light of this sense of themselves, their past heterosexual behavior and identity presented an inconsistency. Unwilling to accept this apparent discontinuity and given their belief in the stability and enduring quality of their sexual orientation, they repeatedly expressed the view that there was something "unreal" about their previous heterosexuality. This was reflected in their tendency to reinterpret their past history to suggest a continuity between past and present senses of self. As one woman put it, "In high school when I had a steady boyfriend, the real me, the lesbian, was suppressed. I just wasn't my real self back then." For other women, their less-than-satisfactory heterosexual experiences confirmed that they had really been lesbians all along. Still others pointed to their intense friendships with girlfriends as suggestive of their true lesbian identities. Sexual feelings and behaviors were central to the lesbian identities of these women, and they believed in the essentiality of their lesbianism.

Other elective lesbians did not view their lesbianism as an essential and enduring aspect of who they were. They did not show any tendency to reinterpret their past history, and did not experience dissonance or contradiction in describing themselves as lesbians with heterosexual pasts. As one woman put it quite simply, "Then I was heterosexual, and now I'm a lesbian." These women expressed the view that there was nothing inconsistent or in need of explanation about their present identity and the one they had assumed in the past. Some of these women revealed, upon questioning, that they had engaged in childhood sexual play with other girls or had had strong attachments to camp counsellors and teachers, but had never thought of these as lesbian feelings. Although they currently identified themselves as lesbians, they saw no reason to reconstruct their pasts as implicitly lesbian. Unlike the elective lesbians previously described, they did not view sexual attraction to women as an essential and unchanging aspect of who they were, although they strongly believed they would continue to have their primary (if not all) relationships with women. Some women said they considered themselves to be lesbians whose sexual feelings could be most accurately characterized as bisexual, or just sexual; however, these comments tended to be private as opposed to publicly stated. Other lesbians in this subgroup defined themselves as lesbian and let its essentiality be assumed, while privately they experienced their sexuality as fluid, or potentially so.

To summarize, in the sample of college women with whom I worked, one major difference that emerged was in whether their lesbianism was experienced as determined (i.e., primary) or self-consciously chosen (i.e., elective). Another major difference had to do with whether their lesbianism was experienced as a central and enduring aspect of who they were, or whether it was experienced as more fluid and dynamic in nature. These two dimensions of difference were not entirely independent of one another. Among those lesbians whose identity was a chosen one, some experienced their sexuality as essential, others as fluid; among those lesbians whose identity felt determined, sexuality was experienced as essential by definition.

With respect to these dimensions of sexuality, there appear to be some interesting age differences. I have spoken with elective lesbians in their late twenties, thirties, and forties who described shifts in their thinking about the nature of their lesbianism. Some had at an earlier age experienced their sexuality as essential and fixed, that is, invariantly focused on women, but later in the development of their lesbian identity had come to feel that their sexuality was in fact more fluid. For a few, this shift resulted from bisexual experiences later in life. Others who felt this way had continued to have relationships only with women. They attributed their earlier position to their more adamant lesbian feminist politics or to what they thought was a developmental phase many lesbians go through.

Alternatively, some elective lesbians felt that in their younger years, when they were engaged in sexual exploration and discovery, their sexuality was more fluid, but that in the context of lesbian culture and relationships they had developed a very explicit preference for women. These women thought of their sexuality as having become more fixed as they got older. Whereas the college women with whom I worked characterized their sexuality as either fixed or fluid, some older women had experienced shifts over the life-cycle in this aspect of their sexuality.

It seems that as lesbians engage in the continuing process of self-definition, their sense of the essentiality or fluidity of their sexuality may change. In contrast, the distinction between primary and elective lesbianism seems to remain more dichotomous over the course of development. Women of all ages with whom I have spoken made reference to such a distinction; they tended to identify as one or the other, and experienced this identification as one that was stable.

Let me return to my discussion of these differing dimensions of lesbian identity as they were experienced by the students with whom I spoke. Because among themselves some of these students discussed lesbianism and their differing experiences of it, they were often aware that not all lesbians described themselves similarly. Sometimes they had distinct opinions about themselves in relation to other lesbians who described themselves differently. For example, some women whom I have characterized as primary lesbians referred to themselves as "born" or "real" lesbians with the implicit designation of elective lesbians as "fake."

It was not uncommon for an elective lesbian to express to me privately her speculations about whether she was "really" a lesbian. At times she wondered whether she wasn't "really" bisexual, or even heterosexual. While some primary lesbians interpret such uncertainty as difficulty in coming out, unwillingness to give up heterosexual privilege, or internalized homophobia, it seems to me that at least some of the elective lesbian's uncertainty can be traced back to the belief within the campus lesbian community that women who choose to be lesbians are somehow less real, or legitimate, than those who felt they had no choice about it.

Despite this belief, there did seem to me to be a tolerance within the community for differences based on primary, compared with elective, lesbianism. In contrast, the issue of whether sexuality was thought of as essential or fluid was a much more sensitive one. For example, there was a noteworthy asymmetry in the application of the concept of the fluidity of sexual attractions when discussed in relation to lesbian and heterosexual women. I spoke with more than a few lesbians who were quite intolerant of (some) heterosexual women's insistence that they simply were not sexually attracted to women and that they couldn't imagine ever feeling differently. Implied in their intolerance was the belief that, despite heavy socialization pressures, sexual attraction is never so fixed and unmalleable as to be irrevocably focused just on persons of one sex. Yet some of these same women were equally intolerant of the opposite stance, that sexual feelings could exist toward persons of either sex, when expressed by a lesbian.

The assumption was often made about lesbians who were unwilling to state that they were (forever) uninterested sexually in men, that they must be having difficulty coming out, or were unwilling to accept a stigmatized identity. Sometimes they were assumed to be going through a bisexual phase, or worse yet, to be male-identified and operating under a false consciousness. The assumption that bisexuality is simply a phase in the coming-out process of lesbians, and that those who call themselves bisexuals are really lesbians unwilling to call themselves that, has been countered by the contention from self-proclaimed bisexuals that their lesbianism was a phase in their coming out as bisexuals.[6]

The problem with all of these assumptions is that one person or set of persons presumes an attitude of knowing and understanding the meaning of another person's experience better than the person who is herself experiencing it. In this climate, individual women may have a difficult time finding their own voices and defining their own experiences. To the extent that lesbianism is very narrowly defined, the categories will restrict, rather than give full expression to, the diversity among women who subjectively define themselves as lesbian.

The question of sexual identity and how it is formed is not well understood, but some of our psychological conceptions do not do justice to the complexity of the process. We have often simplistically assumed that people have sexual attractions to persons of one or the other sex (but not both), that they act on those exclusive attractions, and that they eventually come to adopt the identity appropriate to their sexual activities, although there may be resistance when that identity is a stigmatized one. It appears to be the case, however, that sexual feelings and activities change; they can be fluid and dynamic. And furthermore, the reality is that feelings, activities, and self-conscious identities may not at all times be congruent. It has been suggested by social psychologists that people strive for congruence between their thoughts and feelings,[7] and that with respect to sexual identity in particular, we are motivated to achieve congruence between our feelings, activities, and self-proclaimed identities.[8] This suggestion, however, does not accord with what I observed during my six-and-a-half years at a women's college in the late seventies and early eighties.

What particularly struck me, among this select sample of college women, was the diversity in self-definitions and the degree of incongruence between their sexual activities and their sexual identities (as expressed both publicly and privately). Every possible permutation of feelings and activities existed within each sexual identification category. Further, I was impressed by the way in which these young women were able to tolerate the ambiguity without significant internal distress.

Let me elaborate on the observation that every possible permutation existed. Among women who identified themselves to me as lesbians, there were some whose sexual behavior was explicitly and exclusively lesbian, and some whose behavior was exclusively heterosexual or bisexual (these latter also described themselves as "political lesbians"). In addition, I spoke with sexually inexperienced women who considered themselves to be lesbians. Although no student ever self-consciously identified herself as a celibate lesbian, this is a distinct possibility and has been described by Susan Yarborough.[9] Thus, among women who call themselves lesbians, a wide range of sexual behavior is evident.

Far fewer women described themselves to me as having a bisexual identity, and those who did made it quite clear that this was a confidential disclosure. The small number of self-identified bisexuals was particularly interesting in light of the findings from a survey of sexual behavior and attitudes taken in a psychology of women class I taught. The survey was constructed by students in the class and administered in such a way as to insure complete anonymity. In response to the question of how they would label their sexuality to themselves, regardless of their actual sexual experiences, 65 percent (of 95 students) identified as heterosexual, 26 percent identified as bisexual, and 9 percent identified as lesbian. When asked what their actual sexual experiences were, the responses were as follows: 72 percent heterosexual, 20 percent bisexual, 4 percent lesbian, and 4 percent lacking sexual experience. Two things are interesting about these figures. First, they reveal that the way in which women sexually identify themselves does not always coincide with their actual sexual experience. Second, although three times as many women privately considered themselves to be bisexual as contrasted with lesbian, their concerns were never publicly raised, nor were their bisexual identities ever acknowledged in class. In comparison, lesbian concerns and identities were much more visible in the classroom. It began to occur to me that acknowledging one's bisexuality, or raising such issues publicly, was as stigmatized as discussing lesbianism, if not more so.

To return to the question of the various permutations of sexual activity and identity: Among those interviewed women who identified themselves to me as bisexual, some were engaged in exclusively lesbian activity, some were engaged in exclusively heterosexual activity, while others actually had bisexual experience. Some women who were sexually inexperienced considered themselves on the basis of their potential sexual behavior to be bisexual.

Finally, to complete consideration of the various permutations, consider women who identified themselves to me as heterosexual. Here too, I found women whose current sexual behavior was exclusively lesbian (of the "I just love Mindy; I'm not a lesbian" variety) as well as those whose sexual behavior was exclusively heterosexual. A few women considered themselves to be basically heterosexual even though they had had bisexual experience. And again, some women who were sexually inexperienced nevertheless asserted that they knew they were heterosexual.

The point I wish to make by describing these combinations is not simply that one's sexual identity is not always predictable on the basis of one's sexual behavior, but rather that the assumption that we inherently strive for congruence between our sexual feelings, activities, and identities may not be warranted, and that given the fluidity of sexual feelings, permanent congruence may not be an achievable state. The women with whom I spoke were not personally distressed by the fact of discrepancies between sexual behavior and sexual identity. For example, women who identified as lesbians but found themselves to be occasionally sexually attracted to men were made more uncomfortable by the thought of what other lesbians might think than by their own fluid and changing attractions. These were women who wanted to be considered legitimate members of the lesbian community, but who often felt that they were not welcome, or that if they were, they were not trusted. Although very often they felt compelled to identify themselves publicly and unequivically as lesbians whose sexuality was stable and enduring and exclusively focused on women, they privately experienced their sexuality in a more fluid and dynamic manner. The pressure to be congruent and to proclaim an identity that was in line with their sexual activities was often more externally than internally motivated.

These women are real, not hypothetical. Although the kind of lesbian they represent did not constitute a majority of the self-defined lesbians with whom I spoke, I think that the way they experienced their identities and their relation to the community has implications for how psychologists talk about sexuality and sexual identity.

Identity is constructed both societally and psychologically; it is both a social and a personal process. The process of psychological self-definition takes place within the context of existing dominant culture definitions as well as those that emanate from within the minority community itself. Not only are lesbians a stigmatized and oppressed group, with the result that many have internalized negative images of self, but they are also a group whose central characteristic is debatable and not altogether invariant. Hence its boundaries are more permeable than those of other minority groups. Unlike one's sex or race, which is typically both highly visible and unchanging, one's sexuality (like one's class) is less visible and not so static over the course of a lifetime. Thus, the process of lesbian identity formation is complicated not only because of homophobia, but also because of the nature of sexuality itself.

When counselling women who are engaged in the act of sexual self-definition, therapists need to be aware of the variations in the process of identity formation. On the basis of the findings presented here, it is suggested that psychologists need to take a more serious look at the assumptions inherent in the phrase "coming out." It is not uncommon to hear clinicians talk about women who are in the process of coming out, or who have difficulty with coming out, as if they know what the "right" result looks like. We should begin to question not only whether there is a "right" way to come out, but also whether there is some static end point at all. Liberal teachers and clinicians often think their appropriate role with lesbians is to help them deal with coming out, but I would urge us to think seriously about the relationship between coming out and self-definition. It seems to me that the aim ought to be to encourage each woman as she struggles to define herself. This may mean facilitating her search for authenticity rather than assuming a fixed sexuality that the therapist will help her discover. If being authentic entails accepting the fluidity of one's sexual feelings and activities and identifying as a lesbian, therapists should support this rather than convey the impression that the woman is confused or unwilling to accept a stigmatized identity.

These interviews suggest that sexuality is experienced by some women (both heterosexual and lesbian) as an aspect of identity that may change over the course of their lives. Although there has not been research on this issue with male homosexuals, from reading gay male literature, speaking with a small sample of gay men, and exchanging views with therapists who work with them, my sense is that gay men do not experience their sexuality in the fluid manner that some lesbian and heterosexual women do. I have no strong data on this, but I suspect that very few gay men could be characterized as elective homosexuals. Although this observation might at first seem puzzling and lead one to wonder why the nature of sexuality would be different for women and for men, I think it becomes more understandable with reference to psychoanalytic theories of mothering that place emphasis on the primary human need for social relationship and then examine the expression of that need in terms of the infant's first love object: its mother. Specifically, object relations theory can provide the framework for understanding how the conditions of early infancy might lead women to have greater bisexual potential than men. Dorothy Dinnerstein has discussed how the first relationship with a woman establishes a homoerotic potential in women,[10] and Nancy Chodorow has elaborated on the early psychic foundations of women's homoemotional needs and capacities.[11] The writings of both of these authors can provide the basis for formulation of a new question: Why do so many women become exclusively heterosexual as opposed to bisexual or lesbian?

One of the most important insights of both feminist psychology and the women's movement is that our being born female does not mean that we automatically and naturally prefer certain roles and activities. We have recognized that the category *woman* has been socially constructed, and that societal definitions notwithstanding, women are a diverse group with interests, attitudes, and identities that do not always conform to what is traditionally considered feminine. We have long been told that we are not "real" women unless we are wives and mothers, and to counter this, feminists have been forceful and articulate in asserting that one's sex is not related in any inevitable or natural way to one's sexual preference or societal role. In a similar vein I suggest, on the basis of my discussions with a select sample of college women, that sexual feelings and activities are not always accurately described in either/or terms, nor do they exist in a simple one-to-one relation to our sexual identities. Just as we have protested the constricting social definition of what a real woman is, precisely because it has served to oppress women and to limit the expression of our diverse potentials, so too must we be careful in our social construction of sexuality not to construct categories that are so rigid and inflexible that women's self-definitions put them at odds with the social definitions. To do so only limits the expression of the diversities and variabilities in women's sexual identities.

Notes

1. Adrienne Rich, "Compulsory Heterosexuality and Lesbian Existence," *Signs* 5 (Summer 1980): 631–60.
2. Ann Ferguson, "Compulsory Heterosexuality and Lesbian Existence: Defining the Issues," *Signs* 7 (Autumn 1981): 158–72.
3. Ferguson, "Compulsory Heterosexuality," 166.
4. Jacquelyn Zita, "Compulsory Heterosexuality and Lesbian Existence: Defining the Issues," *Signs* 7 (Autumn 1981): 172–87.

5. Barbara Ponse, *Identities in the Lesbian World* (Westport, Conn.: Greenwood Press, 1978).
6. Lisa Orlando, "Loving Whom We Choose: Bisexuality and the Lesbian/Gay Community," *Gay Community News*, Feb. 25, 1984.
7. Leon Festinger, *A Theory of Cognitive Dissonance* (Evanston, Ill.: Row, Peterson, 1957).
8. Vivienne Cass, "Homosexual Identity Formation: A Theoretical Model," *Journal of Homosexuality* 4 (Fall 1979): 219–35.
9. Susan Yarborough, "Lesbian Celibacy," *Sinister Wisdom* 11 (Fall 1979): 24–29.
10. Dorothy Dinnerstein, *The Mermaid and the Minotaur: Sexual Arrangements and Human Malaise* (New York: Harper & Row, 1976).
11. Nancy Chodorow, *The Reproduction of Mothering: Psychoanalysis and the Sociology of Gender* (Berkeley: University of California Press, 1978).

12 What Women Really Want

NATALIE ANGIER

We've had J's sensuous woman, Nancy Friday's secret garden, Mars and Venus in the bedroom, Kinsey and every issue of Cosmo, yet the old Freudian query persists: What do women really want? Or, more bluntly, what turns them on?

Ellen T. M. Laan, a psychologist at the University of Amsterdam, is doing the sort of work that few American scientists, in these starchy times, are given the financial support to pursue. She is studying the fundamental elements of female sexuality, taking both a psychological and physiological approach. In one recent study, she found that there is a sharp divergence between a woman's physiological and subjective assessment of sexual arousal—that is, between whether a woman says she is sexually stimulated, and how her body is actually responding.

Showing a group of 47 women two explicit pornographic film clips, one made by a male director for the standard male porno consumer, the other directed by a woman and given a female-friendly spin, Dr. Laan found that her subjects reported being annoyed, repulsed, disgusted and decidedly not turned on by the man-made film; while they said they were excited, amused and aroused by the woman-made film. None of the subjects knew anything about who made these films. However, a measurement of their physical arousal, as indicated by a rise in genital blood flow, showed that the women responded equally—and powerfully—to both clips. Dr. Laan talked about the meaning of these results as well as her other explorations of female sexuality.

Q. What was the motivation for doing this study?
A. We wanted to know, what is it that women are reporting when they say they are sexually aroused? There were some indications in the scientific literature that what women say they feel, and how their bodies are responding don't correspond, while in men they do. Men listen to their bodies to determine if they're sexually aroused; they say, oh, I have an erection, I must be aroused. But for women, it wasn't supposed to be that simple.

Something Different

We thought one of the problems with past studies is the type of erotica used. Most pornography movies portray women in ways that women don't find very appealing. We wanted to try something different, but we didn't know where to turn. Then, in reading an issue of Dutch Playgirl magazine, we found out about this New Yorker, Candida Royalle. She'd been a porn actress but was very unhappy with what the end results of the films were, and how they portrayed women, so she decided to make her own films.

To find the comparison man-made film was easy. We went to a video store and asked them for the porno film with the highest rental rate.

Q. What was the difference between the two clips?
A. They were similar in the types of sexual activities shown, but very different in other respects. In the woman-made film, a man and woman meet in an elevator, the woman takes the initiative, and she is clearly the one who is enjoying everything that is happening. She's making sure she gets what she wants. Also, she's a normal-looking woman, not a perfect blonde with an impossibly beautiful body.

It's quite the opposite in the other film, which is a very typical, corny thing. It takes place in a brothel-like environment, the woman is the stimulus, she does a lot of work, but she doesn't seem to enjoy it.

Our results were that there was no difference in physiological arousal. As soon as you turn on an erotic film clip, you immediately see an increase in vaginal blood flow. But the women's responses to questions about the films were very different. They reported positive emotions and sexual arousal about the woman-made film, but quite the opposite for the man-made film.

Q. What do these results tell us?

A. They tell us that a woman's sexual arousal, unlike a man's, is not based on her assessment of physiological cues. Instead, she relies on environmental cues. Our subjects were telling us they were aroused by a film when they liked the film. The sexual arousal they reported was due mostly to how they appreciated the situation.

Apparently, for both men and women, when you show them a sexual cue, the body responds to it. It's an automatic response, it's probably hard-wired, and it's probably a good mechanism for the survival of the species. But it doesn't mean that women who respond physiologically necessarily want to have sex. I always tell men if you want to know whether a woman wants to have sex with you, you have to ask.

Rape Fantasy

These results could also explain why women, when they are raped, sometimes respond by getting lubricated. Rape victims often feel guilty about this, they think maybe on an unconscious level they led the guy on. But this means nothing of the sort. Getting wet is an automatic, physiological thing. Incidentally, if women didn't have this automatic response, there would be a lot more physical harm to them from the rape.

Q. But don't women have fantasies about being raped?

A. I think the term rape fantasy is completely wrong. What happens in these fantasies is what I would call being overwhelmed. The woman is so desired, so wanted, that the other character has to do what he has to do, and of course it's very arousing being wanted that much. But ultimately women do have control in the fantasy, which in rape you do not.

Q. Do these results tell us anything about whether women and men have different sex drives?

A. The results suggest that they have more or less equal potential for sexual arousal. But there's an evolutionary rationale for why women might be more discriminating, and why they might screen the situation before taking action. Women are, after all, the ones who get pregnant from sex. I also believe there are many more cues in the environment that are likely to stimulate men than women. Just look at advertising, and the way women's bodies are everywhere exposed.

Q. Many men have the assumption that underneath it all, women don't like sex. Can you address that issue from this work at all?

A. Well, I didn't have any trouble finding subjects for this research. I think women do like sex, but a lot of women don't like the sex that's going on in the bedroom. They still don't dictate the terms of it or the pace of it. For example, women feel there is something wrong with them if they don't have orgasms through intercourse. But only one-third of women report having regular orgasms through intercourse. Should "normal" be defined as what happens to one-third of women, or to two-thirds?

CHAPTER FOUR

Reproductive Health

Menstruation: One of the bodily events that distinguishes all women from all men. About one-quarter of women's lives are spent menstruating, and yet monthly bleeding is not a topic of public conversation. I am always amazed by the eagerness with which my students approach this topic. They are starved for the opportunity simply to talk about their periods! Nearly all of them say that they've never had the chance to discuss menstruation, to share stories and ask questions, in a classroom before.

I have occasionally had my students in psychology of women participate in a consciousness-raising exercise that invariably generates strong emotions.[1] I bring to class a container of red ribbons with small safety pins. I tell each student to take a ribbon and (only if they want to, of course) wear it pinned to their clothes when they have their period. It is up to them to answer questions from others about what the ribbon is for and then to share their stories about explaining the ribbon with the class. The shock of this "assignment" often causes protests at first. "What?! You can't be serious!" But I find that by the end of the semester, nearly every student has worn their red ribbon for at least one period, and many for a few, and most come to class with delightful stories about explaining the ribbon's significance to curious passers-by. (Incidentally, I ask men as well as post-menopausal and pregnant women in the class to take a ribbon too, and to "shadow" a significant woman in their life. That is, they are to wear the ribbon when their girlfriend, friend, or sister is menstruating.) The majority of students find the experience of publicly acknowledging their cycles quite liberating. Many say that they find themselves far less embarrassed about the ribbon than are those whom they inform about its meaning. The exercise is one of the most powerful ways to demonstrate the culture's "conspiracy of silence" surrounding menstruation.

The first two articles in this section explore not only the physiological reality of menstruation, but also its *meaning* in the culture. In the first article, Sharon Golub explores the event of menarche, or the first menstrual period. First she discusses the physiological components of menarche, including its relationship to other pubertal events, hypotheses about its biological triggering mechanisms, and the role of hormones. These processes are in turn influenced by genetics, nutrition, exercise, climate, and illness, which may accelerate or slow the onset of the first period. Golub then discusses research on the psychosocial aspects of menarche, including expectations, reactions, changes in body image, maturational timing, relationships with parents, and effects on sexual behavior. Since feelings about menarche are so ambivalent, and research shows that girls want to know more about menstruation as a personal event, Golub suggests that both daughters and mothers need better preparation for the first period—preparation that not only emphasizes the physical aspects of menstruation, but more importantly its social and emotional meanings and implications.

In Gloria Steinem's whimsical but eye-opening piece, "If Men Could Menstruate," she turns the tables and ponders how differently the culture would view menstruation if it happened to the more powerful sex. In doing so, she reveals how deeply rooted are the taboos surrounding women's monthly cycling. It's almost hard for one's side-splitting laughter at "He's a three-pad man" and "menses-envy" not to turn into bittersweet tears. For what the essay really leaves one with is a sense of sadness that we are all somehow co-conspirators in this culture of silence and shame about a bodily event that *could* be construed completely differently.

In 1920 Margaret Sanger wrote, "No woman can call herself free who does not own and control her body. No woman can call herself free until she can choose conscientiously whether she will or will not be a mother." Fortunately today, unlike seventy-five years ago when Sanger was leading the birth control movement, women have many choices related to pregnancy and childbearing. I often remind my women students that our ability to decide for ourselves whether and when we will become pregnant has made our relationship to the world quite different from our grandmothers' and, perhaps, literally enabled us to sit together in the classroom and pursue our educational goals.

Pregnancy and motherhood are still choices that are made by the vast majority of women in this country. Images and stereotypes abound to describe these experiences. Women's ability to gestate, give birth to, and nurture life has been both glorified and demonized. Women are idealized as natural and even instinctive caregivers of children at the same time that they are devalued for fulfilling this role. The next two papers in this section represent a beginning in terms of understanding and appreciating the complexities of women's relationships with their pregnancies and their children.

Joy Harjo writes about "Three Generations of Native American Women's Birth Experience." In this moving portrait, she recalls the story of her own birth, describes the very different births of her two children, and completes the circle with the description of her daughter's experience of labor and delivery. In the span of these three generations, there is both commonality of experience and eventual change. Sadly, what is shared is a sense of victimization by a medical system that treated these Native American women as statistics, viewing them as ignorant and unknowledgable about their own bodies and babies. What fortunately changes is support from within the community. Whereas both she and her own mother endured labor alone, her daughter was surrounded by relatives and friends. Harjo, a professor of creative writing, writes that her work is about reclaiming the history of her people, stolen by the U.S. government when they were dispossessed from their land. Here in this piece, particularly with the birth of her granddaughter, she begins to reclaim the history of the *women* of her family—strong mothers all—despite their mistreatment by a system that fails to recognize what she calls the "sacredness" of their birth experiences.

In "Natural Born Mothers," Sarah Blaffer Hrdy, a biological anthropologist and feminist debunks many myths of motherhood with biological evidence from an evolutionary framework. The human mammal, she points out, is "iteroparous." That is, we have the opportunity to breed more than once over a breeding career that in our particular species may last over twenty-five years (as opposed to "semelparous," breeding only once, then dying). One of the "arts," as Hrdy puts it, of iteroparity is to survive poor conditions (bodily or environmental) to breed again under better ones. Until recently, biological and evolutionary frameworks have tended to provide fodder for essentialist views of human motherhood, supporting such concepts as the "maternal instinct," which argues that human females, like their mammalian relatives, are uniquely suited and have an instinctive drive to care for young. Of course such frameworks have lended themselves well to conservative political agendas by, for example, promoting the view that abortion or daycare are demonic *unnatural* aberrations from "true," "natural" motherhood.

But Hrdy and other new scholars of animal behavior now recognize the importance of *context* to the biological understanding of mammals like us. True, mother mammals (humans included) *do* tend to nurse, carry, and generally nurture their young, particularly in environmentally friendly contexts (e.g., plentiful food and shelter, friendly and helpful neighbors, a mate who sticks around or at least keeps other hostile males away). But very different "motherly" behavior can also occur under stressful conditions, as female mammals (our own species included) weigh the costs of "babies in hand" against their own survival and well-being and the possibility of breeding again later under more conducive circumstances. Such maternal choices can range from giving up one's own baby and hiring oneself out as a wet-nurse, to thwarting one's own pregnancy, to even infanticide. Overpopulation, social oppression, and resource scarcity are among the threatening conditions that can lead either to any number of "natural" birth control phenomena, such as delayed egg implantation or suppression of ovulation, or to chosen strategies, such as abortion or abandonment. All of these "strategies" buy females time and allow for the possibility of breeding in the future under better conditions.

Hrdy's work in sociobiology challenges us. Feminists have been suspicious of sociobiological views of gender because they have tended to justify the status quo. They often provide supportive "evidence" for men's dominance and the subordination of women on the grounds of biological inevitability ("they can't help it!"). Indeed, sociobiology has been characterized as the psychology of sex, violence, and oppression (Scarr, 1989). But Hrdy's research proves that evolutionary and feminist perspectives are not necessarily incompatible. Biological frameworks need not be essentialist, for a true understanding of evolution necessitates an *interactionist* perspective. That is, evolution operates to allow creatures to adapt their biology to particular environments. By exploring the ways environmental contexts impact mothering, Hrdy brings our understanding of the biology of motherhood to new and fascinating heights. As she puts it, in her bold last sentence, "Far from invalidating biological bases for material behavior, the extraordinary flexibility in what it means to be a mother should merely remind us that the physiological and motivational underpinnings of an archetypically prochoice mammal are scarcely new."

Note

1. Credit goes to the late Juanita Williams for this wonderful consciousness-raising exercise.

References

Sanger, M. (1920). *Woman and the new race.* New York: Truth, p. 94.

Scarr, S. (1989). Sociobiology: The psychology of sex, violence, and oppression? *Contemporary Psychology, 34*, 440–43.

13 Menarche: The Beginning of Menstrual Life

SHARON GOLUB

In "The Curse of an Aching Heart," playwright William Alfred captures the significance of menarche in a woman's life. One of the characters, a woman in her sixties, recalls being frightened and embarrassed when she got her first period. She awoke with stained bed clothes and sheets and didn't understand what was happening to her. Confused, she ran out of the house and after walking for awhile she happened upon a neighbor who recognized that she was upset and invited her in for a cup of tea. The neighbor explained menstruation to the girl and then, in honor of the occasion, the woman gave the girl a brooch. In the play, memory of this event was poignantly related to another woman more than forty years later.

Is this vignette a fluke, a bit of sentimental whimsy? Probably not. Psychological research confirms the dramatist's intuition that menarche is an important developmental event. In a study of recollections of menarche, Golub and Catalano (1983) found that almost all of the 137 women studied, ranging in age from 18 to 45, remembered their first menstruation. And a majority could describe in detail where they were when it happened, what they were doing, and whom they told. How many events in our lives are so vividly recalled?

It is surprising, therefore, that menarche has received so little research attention until quite recently. Now scientists have begun to look at both the physical and psychological aspects of menarche and at the ways in which they are inextricably linked. It is acknowledged that the changes of puberty do not occur in a psychosocial vacuum. Body changes affect a person psychologically and socially, and the person's life experiences influence the biological processes as well. Nowhere is this seen more clearly than at menarche. For example, what is the relationship between exercise and the onset of menarche? Do menarcheal experiences affect the later development of menstrual distress? What determines whether menarche is a stressful time for girls? What does the menarcheal experience mean to the pubertal girl? How does it affect the way she sees herself? And how soon after menarche is a young woman fertile? Although there is a great deal that we still do not know, this paper will address these questions and will review the highlights of what is known about the physiological and psychosocial aspects of menarche.

Physiological Aspects of Menarche

Sequence of Pubertal Development

Menarche is preceded by characteristic body changes that occur some time between the ages of 9 and 16. Breast development usually, but not always, occurs first. There is an increase in body hair and there is also a weight gain, growth spurt, and a change in body proportions with the hips becoming fuller. Sweat glands become more active and a body odor develops that is thought to be related to an increase in sex hormone secretions from the adrenal gland. The skin becomes oilier, sometimes giving rise to skin problems. And while these external changes are going on there are concomitant changes occurring within the body: the uterus and vagina are growing (Grumbach, Grave, & Mayer, 1974; Katchadourian, 1977).

As noted above, breast development is usually the first sign of puberty with breast buds beginning to form around the age of 11. Breast development is influenced by the secretion of estrogen, particularly estradiol from the ovary, and probably by the secretion of prolactin from the anterior pituitary gland as well (Warren, 1983). There is a slight enlargement of the areolar and elevation of the breast as a small mound. Soon after, pubic hair begins to develop, usually at about age 11½. Axillary hair generally appears about two years after the beginning of pubic hair development.

On the average, menarche occurs between 12.8 and 13.2 years. (For photographs and a detailed description of the stages of breast and pubic hair growth during puberty see Tanner, 1978.)

Pubertal development may be fast or slow. Some girls pass rapidly through the stages of breast and pubic hair development while others move slowly. On the average, the total time for the overall process of physical transformation from child to adult is about four years (Tanner, 1978). However, some girls may take only 1½ years to pass through all the stages while the slower developers may take as long as five years to do so. For those working or living with girls in this age group it is important to keep in mind that there can be great variation in the normal time of onset and completion of pubertal development. It is perfectly normal for a girl to begin to menstruate any time between the ages of 9 and 16 and age mates may be at very different stages of sexual maturation—one 12 year old can look like a woman, another very much like a child.

There is a close relationship between menarche and the pubertal spurt in height. Girls start to menstruate after the growth spurt has peaked, when the rate of increase in height (height velocity) is falling. The growth spurt is nearly over at the time of menarche, with girls on the average growing only about two more inches after the onset of menstruation. However, some girls do grow as much as four inches or more (Tanner, 1978).

Menarche marks a mature stage of uterine development but not reproductive maturity. Early cycles are often irregular and between 55 and 82 percent of menstrual cycles during the first two postmenarcheal years are anovulatory. Regular menstruation may not occur for several years. However, it is important to remember that despite the apparent absence of regular monthly ovulation, any individual cycle may be ovulatory and is potentially fertile (Brennock, 1982) as indicated by the fact that there were 30,000 pregnancies among girls under the age of 15 in the United States between 1973 and 1978. These teenagers are at high risk for pregnancy complications such as low birthweight, high infant mortality, and pregnancy induced hypertension (Leppert, 1983), in addition to the stressful social and psychological consequences of having a baby at 13 or 14 years of age.

What Triggers Menarche?

There is some controversy about what triggers menarche. Currently there are two hypotheses which relate menarcheal age to physical growth: one focusing on skeletal growth and the other on the accumulation of fat. The skeletal growth hypothesis is based on the idea that the premenarcheal girl must reach an appropriate stage of skeletal development in order to reproduce and, therefore, the age at which she reaches this structural status (mature height and pelvic dimensions) is closely correlated with menarcheal age (Tanner, 1978). The importance of skeletal maturity is related to the need for a body, specifically a pelvis, that is adequate in size to bear a child. And there is some data to support the idea that pelvic dimensions—an average biiliac diameter of 26.2 cms.—are significantly correlated with menarcheal age (Ellison, 1982). Thus menarcheal age is closely related to skeletal development and bone age can be used as an appropriate measure of developmental age in predicting when menarche will occur (Tanner, 1978). This view attributes the decline in average age at menarche during the last century (referred to in the literature as the secular trend) to the acceleration of skeletal growth during this time, presumably related to better nutrition and health. In contrast, slow skeletal growth, resulting from poor nutrition or high altitude, leads to delay in the onset of menstruation.

An alternative hypothesis, proposed by Frisch (1980), suggests that the onset of menstruation is contingent upon the accumulation of fat and that a critical minimum weight for height is necessary to trigger and maintain ovulation and menstruation. Frisch's explanation of the secular trend in menarcheal age is that girls reach 101 to 103 pounds, the average weight at menarche, sooner now, and therefore menstruation begins earlier. She points out that a late menarche is associated with slower increases in body weight such as that seen in cases of malnutrition, or among twins, because they grow more slowly. Frisch notes that the greatest change during the adolescent growth spurt up to the time of menarche is a 120 percent increase in body fat. At menarche, girls' bodies average about 24 percent fat, not much different from the 28 percent fat found in the average 18 year old woman. In contrast, boys at about 18 years of age are much leaner with 14 percent fat. Frisch theorizes that reproduction requires energy and the function of the stored fat is to provide readily accessible energy should it be needed for pregnancy and lactation.

In a recent study entitled, "Skeletal Growth, Fatness, and Menarcheal Age," Ellison (1982) compared the two hypotheses using factor analysis of longitudinal growth data on 67 middle-class white girls born in 1928 and 1919 and drawn from the Berkeley Guidance Study. Ellison found that height velocity prior to menarche was the strongest independent correlate of menarcheal age, accounting for over 50 percent of the variance. The weight factor made the second largest contribution, accounting for 18 percent of the variance in menarcheal age. Thus while there seems to be a strong relationship between adolescent weight and menarcheal age, its effect is apparently less than that of the skeletal development. Ellison makes the point that since skeletal growth tends to cease soon after menarche, natural selection would delay menarche until the pelvis could handle reproduction.

Hormones

Although incompletely understood, significant hormonal changes occur at puberty. The gonadal, adrenal, and hypothalamic-hypophyseal hormones are of major importance. It is the interrelationship of these hormones that later controls the female reproductive cycle. However, endocrinologists now believe that the hormonal changes associated with sexual maturation actually begin at the time of conception. By the third trimester of pregnancy, the negative feedback system is established. (See Figure 1.) During infancy the hypothalamic gonadotropin regulating mechanism is "set" at a low level and remains there until around the time of puberty when there is an increase in the secretion of follicle stimulating hormone (FSH) and luteinizing hormone (LH) and a decrease in hypothalamic sensitivity. Put another way, the hypothalamic set point increases inducing a subsequent increase in the secretion of FSH, LH, and gonadal hormones (Petersen & Taylor, 1980).

The adolescent growth spurt is a result of the joint action of androgens and growth hormone (Tanner, 1978). A progressive increase in plasma dehydroepiandosterone and dehydroepiandosterone sulfate, which are weak androgens, begins at about eight years of age and continues through ages 13 to 15. These hormones, thought to originate from the adrenal gland, are the earliest hormonal changes to take place at puberty (Warren, 1983). They and the more potent androgens—testosterone and dihydrotestosterone—increase significantly as pubertal development progresses (Dupon & Bingel, 1980). Increased secretion of gonadotropins from the pituitary (FSH and LH) and sex steroids from the gonads follow (Warren, 1983).

The main female sex hormone secreted by the ovaries is estradiol which is present in relatively small amounts in the blood until about age eight or nine when it begins to rise. This increase in blood levels of estradiol causes growth of the breasts, uterus, vagina, and parts of the pelvis. When menstruation begins, estradiol levels fluctuate with the various phases of the cycle and are controlled by pituitary FSH (Tanner, 1978).

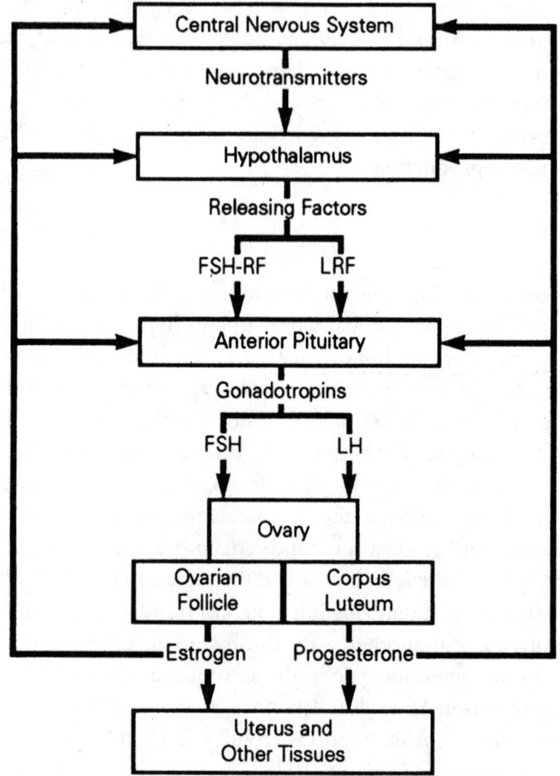

FIGURE 1 Menstrual cycle hormone feedback system.

The two pituitary gonadotropins, follicle stimulating hormone (FSH) and luteinizing hormone (LH), are both secreted in small amounts during childhood and increase at puberty. The pubertal rise is first seen as pulses of LH that are released during sleep. This sleep-associated rise in LH is not seen in either the prepubertal child or the adult (Warren, 1983). Gradually LH is released during the daytime too.

Menstruation, as well as earlier pubertal development, is thought to begin with a signal to the hypothalamus from the central nervous system. As noted above, a hypothalamic feedback system does exist before puberty, but the hypothalamus is responsive to low levels of LH in the prepubertal girl. Then around the time of menarche, a gradual change occurs making the hypothalamus less sensitive. Higher levels of estrogen are needed. The hypothalamus then secretes more FSH-releasing hormone. This neurohormone stimulates the pituitary gland to release FSH, which, in turn, triggers the growth of the ovarian follicle. As the follicles grow they secrete estrogen which causes growth of the cells lining the uterus (the endometrium). Increasing levels of estrogen in the blood also signal the pituitary to reduce FSH and secrete LH. LH triggers the release of the ovum from the follicle which then evolves into the corpus luteum and secretes progesterone and a little estrogen. If the ovum is not fertilized, the pituitary stops production of LH, levels of both estrogen and progesterone drop, menstruation begins, and the cycle starts again. (See Figure 1.)

Other Factors Affecting Pubertal Development

Genetics Genetic factors play an important role in determining rate of growth, pubertal development, and age at menarche. Studies of monozygotic twin sisters growing up together indicate that they reach menarche about two months apart, with the first born twin—for some unknown reason—more likely to menstruate first (Shields, 1962). Dizygotic twins differ by about 12 months (Tanner, 1978). Mother-daughter and sister-sister correlations have also been reported to be significant (Chern, Gatewood, & Anderson, 1980). Kantero and Widholm (1971) found other menstrual similarities between mothers and daughters: significant correlations were found between mothers' and daughters' length of cycle, duration of menstrual flow, and symptoms of dysmenorrhea and premenstrual tension. It is thought that both mother and father exert an equal influence on rate of growth and maturation. Thus a late-maturing girl is as likely to have a late-maturing father as a later-maturing mother (Tanner, 1978).

Nutrition There is a well documented link between nutrition and fertility. Famine amenorrhea was reported in both world wars (Menkin, Watkins, & Trussell, Note 1). Young women who are undernourished because of excessive dieting or those with anorexia nervosa often do not have menstrual periods. And it is well known that malnutrition retards growth and will delay menarche (Tanner, 1978). The fall in age at menarche that has occurred between 1830 and 1960 coincides with the increased availability of protein in the diet of developed countries during this time. In some countries, where nutrition has remained inadequate, age of menarche is comparatively high. For example, in contrast with the average age of menarche in the United States, which is now 12.8 years, in Bangladesh it is just under 16, and among certain New Guinea tribes, it is about 18 (Menkin, Watkins, & Trussell, Note 1). A recent study by Goodman, Grove, and Gilbert (1983) in which no differences in age at menarche were found among Caucasian, Japanese, and Chinese women living in Hawaii, suggests that nutrition and environmental factors are responsible for population differences. Tanner (1978) has noted that children in urban, as opposed to rural, areas are more likely to have more rapid growth and an earlier menarche that is probably attributable to better nutrition, health, and sanitation.

Exercise Exercise also affects menstruation. Women who experience high energy outputs, such as ballet dancers and athletes who train intensively, have a later age at menarche and a high incidence of amenorrhea. This is particularly true when intensive training begins at an early premenarcheal age (Frisch, 1980; Frisch et al., 1981; Frisch, 1983). It is not known whether an altered lean-fat ratio is responsible for the delay in menarche in young athletes, as proposed by Frisch, or if the delay occurs through the direct effects of exercise on hormonal secretion and metabolism (Rebar & Cumming, 1981). Some investigators have questioned whether delays in the age of menarche in athletes occur at all (Malina, 1982). Others have expressed concern about the short-term and long-term effects of exercise on reproductive function (Rebar & Cumming, 1981). Also at this time it is not known whether it is disadvantageous to have a later menarche rather than an early one. However, the consensus seems to be that exercise-related alterations in reproductive function are not serious and are readily reversible.

Climatic and seasonal effects Climate has no more than a very minor effect on age at menarche. In fact, contrary to earlier beliefs, people who live in tropical countries are somewhat more likely to have a *late* menarche. This is thought to be related to nutrition rather than a climate because children in the higher socioeconomic groups in these countries experience menarche at about the same time as children living in temperate zones.

Season of the year does influence growth velocity, with peak growth seen between March and July, and girls are most likely to have their first menstruation in the late fall or early winter (Science News, 1980; Tanner, 1978).

Acute and chronic illness There are some conditions where menstruation will not occur. For example, a child with Turner's Syndrome, a chromosomal anomaly in which the second X chromosome is absent, will not menstruate because she lacks ovaries. Ehrhardt and Meyer-Bahlberg (1975) advise that sex hormone administration is crucial in order for these girls to attain psychosocial and psychosexual maturity. Administration of estrogen will cause the breasts to grow and an artificial menstrual cycle may be produced by giving estrogen for three weeks followed by a week without treatment. This is important because these girls want to look, develop, and be treated like normal female adolescents.

Other illnesses can delay menarche, probably because of their effects on nutrition. This is most likely to be true in cases of uremia, regional enteritis, ulcerative colitis, congenital heart disease, cystic fibrosis, and diabetes mellitus. The timing of the onset of the illness as well as the illness per se seem to be important. For example, if diabetes develops during the initial pubertal period, menarche is delayed, whereas if it develops later, menarche may be unaffected (Warren, 1983).

Conversely, some conditions will advance the age of menarche. These include hypothyroidism, central nervous system tumors, encephalitis, head trauma, and some virilizing disorders. Inactive, retarded, or bedridden children also reach menarche at an earlier age than their more active counterparts. And blind children have a younger age at menarche that may be related in part to their limited activity (Warren, 1983).

Thus menarche occurs after a series of changes in hormone secretion and somatic growth. These processes are in turn influenced by genetic and environmental factors such as nutrition, exercise, and illness which may accelerate or retard the onset of menstruation. We now turn to the psychosocial aspects of menarche and its meaning to the adolescent girl and those around her.

Psychosocial Aspects of Menarche

Effects of Menarche on the Early Adolescent Girl

Much of the early writing about the psychology of menarche presented it as a traumatic experience. For example, early psychoanalytic theory postulated a marked increase in sex drive at puberty and an inevitable period of anxiety, worry about impulse control, and increased lability as "a relatively strong id confronts a relatively weak ego" (A. Freud, 1946). Benedek (1959) believed that menarche might evoke fears associated with the anticipation of pain during intercourse and childbirth. Current psychoanalytic views are much more positive. Notman (1983) and others suggest that meeting the developmental tasks of adolescence need not be as tumultuous as was previously believed. True, the early adolescent needs to modify her attachment to her parents and develop the capacity to form relationships with peers; and eventually she must establish her identity as a woman and develop the capacity for intimacy with another person. However, this need not happen overnight and the process should not cause turmoil or disintegration.

Menarche can have an organizing effect for the adolescent girl, helping her to clarify her perception of her own genitals, particularly confirming the existence of the vagina and correcting the confusion she may have had about the female genita lia. Kestenberg (1965) suggests that menarche may serve as a reference point around which girls can organize their pubertal experiences; it is a landmark for feminine identification. This is in keeping with the greater awareness of sexual differentiation between males and females among postmenarcheal girls demonstrated by Koff, Rierdan, and Silverstone (1978).

Knowledge, Attitudes, and Expectations in Anticipation of Menarche

What do the girls themselves say? Whisnant and Zegans (1975) interviewed 35 white middle class pre- and postmenarcheal girls at a summer camp. The girls had learned about menstruation from friends, commercial booklets, school, and their parents—especially their mothers. They perceived themselves as being knowledgeable about menstruation and used the appropriate terms. However, when questioned further the interviewer found that they really did not have a good conception of what the internal organs were like or how they functioned and they were even more inept at describing the external genitalia. Thus, despite their access to information about menstruation, they had not assimilated it particularly well. The girls were most concerned about what to do when they got their periods and many had mentally rehearsed what they would do in a variety of situations.

Brooks-Gunn and Ruble (1980) found that both boys and girls in the seventh and eighth grades have similar and mostly negative beliefs about menstruation. For example, most believed that menstruation is accompanied by physical discomfort, increased emotionality, and a disruption of activities. Only a third thought that the onset of menstruation was something to be happy about.

Williams (1983) found more positive attitudes toward menstruation in a group of 9- to 12-year-old girls, most of whom were premenarcheal. These girls generally equated menstruation with growing up and being normal. However, about a third of these subjects also believed menstruation to be embarrassing, 28 percent thought it a nuisance, 27 percent found it disgusting, and 23 percent disliked the idea that it is not controllable. The girls in this sample also believed some of the popular menstrual taboos. About half the subjects thought a girl should not swim when menstruating and 22 percent believed she should not be active in sports. Many were influenced by concealment taboos with a majority expressing concern about concealing sanitary pads and menstrual odor. A striking 85 percent thought that a girl should not talk about menstruation to boys and 40 percent did not even think that it was all right to discuss menstruation with their fathers. And, as in the Brooks-Gunn and Ruble study noted above, most believed that girls are more emotional when they menstruate.

Reactions to Menarche

What do girls actually experience at the time of menarche? In several studies menarche has been found to be an anxiety producing or negative event (Brooks-Gunn & Ruble, 1980; Golub & Catalano, 1983; Koff, Rierdan, & Jacobson, 1981; Whisnant & Zegans, 1975) and mixed feelings such a being "excited but scared" or "happy and embarrassed" are common (Petersen, 1983; Woods, Dery, & Most, 1983). Most of these data were collected using interviews and questionnaires, and sometimes were based on recollection of older subjects.

Petersen (1983) in looking at menarche as one part of her study of 400 middle-class suburban boys and girls in the 6th, 7th, and 8th grades, found that the adolescents were remarkably inarticulate in describing their feelings about their changing bodies. Therefore, she decided that projective measures might be more useful than direct questions in exploring girls' feelings about menstruation. The girls were presented with an incomplete story about menarche adapted from Judy Blume's book, *Are You There, God? It's Me, Margaret.* For example:

> "Mom—hey, Mom—come quick!" When Nancy's mother got to the bathroom she said: "What is it? What's the matter?" "I got it," Nancy told her. "Got what?" said her mother.

The girls were then asked, "What happened next?" Some of the girls responded that, "She told her Mom that she had gotten her period;" others said that Mom explained or helped. They were then asked "How did Nancy feel?" About a third gave negative or fearful responses, about half were positive or pleased, and another five percent were ambivalent.

Maxine Kumin (1982) in a short story entitled "Facts of Life" differentiates between the expectations about menarche and its actual occurrence. She describes a group of twelve-year-old girls as longing to begin to menstruate. "An eager band of little girls, itchy with the work of sprouting, sits expectant. The old reticences, embarrassments, and complaints have given way to progress. Now we have sex education, cartoon films of the reproductive tract, a beltless sanitary napkin, a slender, virginal tampon" (p. 11). Yet, when the first blood does indeed come the girl is described as both terribly happy and terribly sad as mother and daughter celebrate together.

Changes in Body Image

Changes in body image are among the most dramatic reactions to menarche. Although the body changes associated with puberty occur gradually, girls do expect to act differently after menarche and they also see themselves differently. In a clever study of seventh grade girls, Koff (1983) asked the subjects to draw male and female human figures on two occasions, approximately six months apart. Of the 87 girls sampled, 34 were premenarcheal on both test occasions, 23 were postmenarcheal, and 30 changed menarcheal status between the two test sessions. The findings were striking. Postmenarcheal girls produced drawings that were significantly more sexually differentiated than those of their premenarcheal peers and a greater percentage of the postmenarcheal girls drew their own sex first. Most notable was the difference in the drawings done by the girls whose menarcheal status changed during the course of the study. There was a significant increase in the sexual differentiation of their drawings at the time of the second testing with the postmenarcheal girls drawing womanly females with breasts and curves in contrast to their earlier, more childlike, premenarcheal drawings. (Examples of these drawings may be seen in Koff, 1983.)

To further explore girls' beliefs about the change menarche would have on them, Koff, Rierdan, and Jacobson (1981) gave a sentence completion task to seventh and eighth grade girls. In response to the cue sentence "Ann just got her period for the first time," the girls said such things as, "She saw herself in a different way," and "She felt very grown up." In response to another item, "Ann regarded her body as . . . ," postmenarcheal girls were more likely than premenarcheal girls to describe a change in body image. For example, Ann's body was "a woman's body" and "more mature than it was."

These studies clearly demonstrate that girls do experience menarche as a turning point in their development and they apparently reorganize their body images in the direction of "greater sexual maturity and feminine differentiation" (Koff, 1983). Postmenarcheal girls are more aware of sexual differentiation between males and females and of themselves as women than are premenarcheal girls of the same age.

The Early Maturing Girl

The age at which a girl experiences menarche does seem to affect her reaction to it. Peterson (1983) found that girls who experience menarche early, in the sixth grade or before, seem to have more difficulty with it. Some of the girls denied that they had begun to menstruate and when Petersen questioned the mothers of her early maturing subjects, over 70 percent of the mothers reported that menarche was very difficult for their daughters. The mothers of five of the six girls who denied having gotten their periods reported the negative aspects of the experience for them. Notman (1983) has suggested that the denial of menstruation may be related to conflicts about accepting the female role or to an attempt to delay adulthood. Certainly one of the girls in Petersen's sample who denied menstruating lends support to that view. In response to a Thematic Apperception Test card showing a middle-aged woman with a girl holding a doll, this subject described the girl in the picture as scared about growing up and asking her mother when she was going to get her period.

Unlike boys who are eager for their growth spurt and physical signs of maturity, girls would prefer to mature at the same time as everyone else. This may be because of the age difference between the sexes in the onset of puberty—boys normally start later than girls. Girls' attitudes about early development may also be related to the changes in their lives that occur when they develop the breasts and curves characteristic of a woman. There is some evidence that sixth and seventh grade girls who are already pubertal are more likely to be dating and, somewhat paradoxically, these girls also have lower self-esteem, lower school achievement, and more behavioral problems than comparable boys and non-pubertal girls (Simmons, Blyth, Van Cleave, & Bush, 1979). In this study pubertal development per se had little effect on the girls' self-esteem. However, the early maturing girls who had also begun dating were most likely to indicate low self-esteem (50 percent as opposed to 36–40 percent of the other girls). It is interesting that while early dating behavior is disadvantageous for girls, it has no statistically significant impact on boys.

Thus girls' self-esteem was negatively affected by their own physiology (early menarche) and social relationships, while boys' self-esteem was not. Simons et al. (1979) suggest some reason why this may be so. First, the sexes develop different value systems at this age. For girls, appearance and sociability assume priority, while for boys these values remain secondary. When asked to rank the importance of popularity, competence, and independence, seventh grade girls were more likely to rank popularity first. This places a great deal of importance on other people's opinions of oneself. These girls also placed a high value on looks. Moreover, the changes in body image may be qualitatively different for girls than for boys. Pubertal boys are generally happy with their new height and muscle development. Pubertal girls are not sure whether their new figures make them better or worse looking than their peers. Further, pubertal girls' negative reactions to dating may be a result of sexual pressures from their male partners for which these girls are not prepared. In interviews with some of these girls the researchers found them likely to express dislike for "guys trying to touch me." One subject said, "I don't really like to be kissed." It looks as if some of these girls were vulnerable, with their emotional maturity lagging well behind their physical development, causing confusion and contributing to their feelings of low self-esteem. This is in keeping with data from the California Adolescent Study which show that it is the girl with accelerated growth and maturation who is at a disadvantage (Jones, 1958; Jones & Mussen, 1959). However, social class may also play a role. Clausen (1975) found that for middle-class girls early maturation was positively related to self-confidence, whereas working class girls experienced a negative effect. In contrast to early maturation, late maturation, although quite disturbing for boys, does not seem to have the same degree of negative consequences for girls, perhaps because a childlike appearance is part of femininity for some adult women (Friedman, Note 2).

Relationships with Parents

In view of the changes that go on in girls' perceptions of themselves it seems reasonable to ask if menarche affects girls' relationships with other people, particularly family members. On the basis of limited data, the answer seems to be a qualified yes. Danza (1983) compared 48 pre- and postmenarcheal girls in the sixth and seventh grades. She found that although they were no different in age than their premenarcheal peers, the postmenarcheal girls were more likely to wear make-up or a bra, to shave their legs, and to date. They also slept less on school nights, moving from nine or more hours a night toward the more usual adult eight hour sleep cycle. The postmenarcheal girls were also significantly more uncomfortable in discussing emotionally charged topics such as love, sex, drugs, and alcohol with their parents, and they reported having more conflict with their parents than the premenarcheal girls did.

Effects on Sexual Behavior

Because it marks the onset of reproductive potential, menarche is important to a girl's family and community as well as to herself. This is seen in other cultures when one looks at the different tribal rituals celebrating menarche and at customs, such as purdah, veiling, and virginity tests, which guard girls' reproductive potential. Economics comes into play too. Paige (1983) has suggested that there is a relationship between various methods of controlling girls' chastity and the economic resources of a particular culture. In societies where marriage bargains are important, chastity is crucial to the girl's marriageability and is rigorously controlled.

This is not seen in our culture today. Rather, in the United States the physical transformation from girl to woman and the onset of menstruation are accompanied by changes in social and sexual behavior. And the timing of menarche is important. Several researchers have reported that girls with an early menarche were more likely to date and pet at an earlier age than their later maturing peers (Gagnon, 1983; Presser, 1978; Simons et al., 1979; Udry, 1979). And there is data indicating that women with early menarche begin premarital coitus earlier as well (Gagnon, 1983; Presser, 1978; Udry, 1979). In an extensive study of black and white low income women in 16 American cities, Udry (1979) found that girls with early menarche, as compared to those with late menarche, were more than twice as likely to have had intercourse by age 16. Udy and Cliquet (1982) also examined the relationship between ages at menarche, marriage, and first birth among women in four widely diverse countries (United States, Malay, Belgium, and Pakistan) and concluded that there was a clear behavioral sequence relating age at menarche to age at first intercourse and first birth. Menarche seems to initiate a chain of events. In the United States the pattern is one of dating and other sexual behavior that increase the probability of early intercourse and early childbearing.

Whether this sequence is more readily attributable to hormonal or sociocultural factors is a difficult question to answer. Gagnon (1983) found no significant relationship between the onset of menarche and masturbatory experience. Similarly, in their studies of children with the problem of precocious puberty (beginning at six to eight years of age), Ehrhardt and Meyer-Bahlberg (1975) have found that early puberty does not automatically trigger an early sex life. Masturbation and sex play in childhood did not appear to be enhanced and premarital intercourse did not occur earlier than normally expected. Thus at this time it seems reasonable to conclude that the timing of puberty influences when the girl, her parents, and her peers perceive of her as being someone for whom dating and heterosexual relationships are appropriate and this in turn affects her socio-sexual behavior.

Preparation of Menarche

In view of the ambivalent feelings about menarche expressed by so many adolescent girls and the difficulties experienced by the early maturing girl, it seems reasonable to ask if adequate preparation makes any difference? It probably does. Both Rierdan (1983) and Golub and Catalano (1983) found that subjects who report being adequately prepared have a more positive initial experience with menstruation. There are other studies indicating a need for more and better menstrual education. For example, Logan (1980), in a study of 95 women from 23 foreign countries, found that 28 percent complained about not having enough information. Similarly, in a large study of American women, 39 percent reported that their preparation was inadequate (Weideger, 1976), and Brooks-Gunn and Ruble (1980) reported that the adolescent girls they tested said they had sufficient prior knowledge about menstruation but still felt unprepared for menarche.

What do girls want to know? Rierdan (1983), in a study of 97 college women's recollections of menarche, found that the young women wanted to know about menstrual physiology and menstrual hygiene—the facts that are usually included in menstrual education materials—but they also wanted information about menstruation as a personal event. Subjects said that girls need to know about the normality of menstruation and it must be distinguished from disease, injury, and uncleanliness. They suggested that the feelings of fright and embarrassment girls experience at menarche be acknowledged as normal and the negative aspects of the menstrual experience need to be discussed in order to provide a balanced view of menstruation. The college women emphasized that girls need support and reassurance at the time of menarche and Rierdan says, "Many referred specifically to the importance of an informed, understanding, accepting mother" (Rierdan, 1983). Unfortunately, however, interviews with mothers of adolescent girls indicate that the mothers themselves are not prepared to fill this role, suggesting a need to prepare mothers as well as daughters for menarche.

In Support of a New Tradition

Some researchers have suggested that we need a "contemporary tradition for menarche" in order to overcome some of the negative connotations associated with it (Logan, Calder, & Cohen, 1980). They believe that currently we address the physical needs of the menarcheal girl, teaching her how to take care of herself, but leaving her without the social and emotional support that she needs at this time. In order to explore what the appropriate ritual might be, Logan et al. designed five short stories describing possible responses to a girl's first period and gave them to girls between the ages of eight and seventeen, mothers of girls in this age group, and women psychologists. The most popular response of the mothers and daughters to being told about the onset of menstruation was "Congratulations, our little girl is growing up." However, the psychologists preferred, "Something special has happened," apparently acknowledging the ambivalent and even negative emotions that a girl may have about the beginning of menstruation. As for symbolic gestures, the most popular among the mothers was a toast to the girl from her mother and father, or a meal in her honor. But the daughters had reservations about this, fearing an invasion of privacy and reinforcing feelings that "everyone is watching her." The daughters preferred a hug or a kiss and a material token such as a gift or flowers. It seems dramatists often capture in a few lines what scientists seek in reams of data: William Alfred was right on target with the gift of a brooch.

Notes

1. Menkin, J., Watkins, S. C., & Trussell, J. Nutrition, health, and fertility. Report prepared for The Ford Foundation, December 1980.
2. Freedman, R. Personal Communication, December 1983.

References

Benedek, T. Sexual functions in women and their disturbance. In S. Arieti (Ed.) *American handbook of psychiatry*. New York: Basic Books, 1959.

Blume, J. *Are you there, God? It's me, Margaret.* New York: Dell, 1970.

Brennock, W. E. Fertility at menarche. *Medical Aspects of Human Sexuality.* 1982, *16*, 21–30.

Brooks-Gunn, J., & Ruble, D. Menarche. In A. J. Dan, E. A. Graham, & C. P. Beecher (Eds.) *The menstrual cycle, Vol. 1.* New York: Springer, 1980.

Chern, M. M., Gatewood, L. C., & Anderson, V. E. The inheritance of menstrual traits. In A. J. Dan, E. A. Graham, & C. P. Beecher (Eds.) *The menstrual cycle, Vol. 1.* New York: Springer, 1980.

Clausen, J. A. The social meaning of differential physical and sexual maturation. In S. E. Dragastin, & G. H. Elder, Jr. (Eds.) *Adolescence in the life cycle.* New York: Halsted, 1975.

Danza, R. Menarche: Its effects on mother-daughter and father-daughter interactions. In S. Golub (Ed.) *Menarche.* Lexington, Massachusetts: D. C. Heath, 1983.

Dupon, C. & Bingel, A. S. Endocrinologic changes associated with puberty in girls. In A. J. Dan, E. A. Gramham, & C. P. Beecher (Eds.) *The menstrual cycle, Vol. 1.* New York: Springer, 1980.

Ehrhardt, A. E., & Meyer-Bahlberg, H. F. I. Psychological correlates of abnormal pubertal development. *Clinics in Endocrinology and Metabolism.* 1975, *4*, 207–222.

Ellison, P. T. Skeletal growth, fatness, and menarcheal age: A comparison of two hypotheses. *Human Biology*, 1982, *54*, 269–281.

Freud, A. *The ego and the mechanisms of defense.* New York: International Universities Press, 1946.

Frisch, R. E. Fatness, puberty and fertility. *Natural History*, 1980, *89*, 16–27.

Frisch, R. E. What's below the surface. *New England Journal of Medicine*, 1981, *305*, 1019–1020.

Frisch, R. E., Gotz-Welbergon, A. V., McArthur, J. W., Albright, T., Witscht, J., Bullen, B., Birnholz, J., Reed, R. B., & Hermann, H. Delayed menarche and amenorrhea of college athletes in relation to age of onset of training. *Journal of the American Medical Association*, 1981, *246*, 1559–1563.

Frisch, R. E. Fatness, menarche, and fertility. In S. Golub (Ed.) *Menarche*, Lexington, Massachusetts: D. C. Heath, 1983.

Gagnon, J. H. Age at menarche and sexual conduct in adolescence and young adulthood. In S. Golub (Ed.) *Menarche.* Lexington, Massachusetts: D. C. Heath, 1983.

Golub, S., & Catalano, J. Recollections of menarche and women's subsequent experiences with menstruation. *Women & Health*, 1983, *8*, 49–61.

Goodman, M. J., Grove, J. S., & Gilbert, R. I. Age at menarche and year of birth in relation to adult height and weight among Caucasian, Japanese and Chinese women living in Hawaii. In S. Golub (Ed.) *Menarche.* Lexington, Massachusetts, D. C. Heath, 1983.

Grumbach, M. M., Grave, G. D., & Mayer, F. E. (Eds.) *Control of the onset of puberty.* New York: Wiley, 1974.

Jones, M. C. A study of socialization patterns at the high school level. *Journal of Genetic Psychology*, 1958, *93*, 87–111.

Jones, M. C., & Mussen, P. H. Self conceptions, motivations, and interpersonal attitudes of early and late maturing girls. *Child Development*, 1958, *29*, 491–501.

Kantero, R. L., & Widhelm, O. Correlation of menstrual traits between adolescent girls and their mothers. *Acta Obstetricia et Gynecologica Scandinavica, Supplement,* 1971, *14,* 30–36.
Katchadourian, H. The biology of adolescence. San Francisco: W. H. Freeman & Co., 1977.
Kestenberg, J. S. Menarche. In S. Lorand, & H. Schneer (Eds.) *Adolescents.* New York: Dell, 1965.
Koff, E., Rierdan, J., & Silverstone, E. Changes in representation of body image as a function of menarcheal status. *Developmental Psychology,* 1978, *14,* 635–642.
Koff, E., Rierdan, J., & Jacobson, S. The personal and interpersonal significance of menarche. *Journal of the American Academy of Child Psychiatry,* 1981, *20,* 148–158.
Koff, E. Through the looking glass of menarche: What the adolescent girl sees. In S. Golub (Ed.) *Menarche.* Lexington, Massachusetts, D. C. Heath, 1983.
Kumin, M. *Why can't we live together like civilized human beings?* New York: Viking Press, 1982.
Leppert, P. Menarche and adolescent pregnancy. In S. Golub (Ed.) *Menarche.* Lexington, Massachusetts: D. C. Heath, 1983.
Logan, D. D. The menarche experience in twenty-three foreign countries. *Adolescence,* 1980, *15,* 247–256.
Malina, R. M. Delayed age of menarche of athletes. *Journal of the American Medical Association,* 1982, *247,* 3312.
Notman, M. Menarche: A psychoanalytic perspective. In S. Golub (Ed.) *Menarche.* Lexington, Massachusetts: D. C. Heath, 1983.
Paige, K. E. Virginity rituals and chastity control during puberty: Cross-cultural patterns. In S. Golub (Ed.) *Menarche.* Lexington, Massachusetts: D. C. Heath, 1983.
Petersen, A. C., & Taylor, B. The biological approach to adolescence. In J. Adelson (Ed.) *Handbook of adolescent psychology.* New York: Wiley, 1980.
Petersen, A. E. Menarche: Meaning of measures and measuring meaning. In S. Goloub (Ed.) *Menarche.* Lexington, Massachusetts: D. C. Heath, 1983.
Presser, H. B. Age at menarche, socio-sexual behavior, and fertility. *Social Biology,* 1978, *25,* 94–101.
Rebar, R. W., & Cumming, D. C. Reproductive function in women athletes. *Journal of the American Medical Association,* 1981, *246,* 1590.
Rierdan, J. Variations in the experience of menarche as a function of preparedness. In S. Golub (Ed.) *Menarche.* Lexington, Massachusetts: D. C. Heath, 1983.
Rosenbaum, M. B. The changing body image of the adolescent girl. In M. Sugar (Ed.) *Female adolescent development.* New York: Brunner/Mazel, 1979.
Shields, J. *Monozygotic twins.* London: Oxford University Press, 1962.

Simmons, R. G., Blyth, D. A., Van Cleave, E. F., & Bush, D. M. Entry into early adolescence: The impact of school structure, puberty, and early dating on self esteem. *American Sociological Review*, 1979, *44*, 948–967.

Tanner, J. M. *Foetus into man.* Cambridge, Massachusetts: Harvard University Press, 1978. To everything there is a season. *Science News*, 1980, *118*, 150.

Udry, J. R. Age at menarche, at first intercourse, and at first pregnancy. *Journal of Biosocial Science*, 1979, *11*, 433–441.

Udry, J. R., & Cliquet, R. L. A cross-cultural examination of the relationship between ages at menarche, marriage, and first birth. *Demography*, 1982, *19*, 53–63.

Warren, M. P. Clinical aspects of menarche: Normal variations and common disorders. In S. Golub (Ed.) *Menarche.* Lexington, Massachusetts: D. C. Heath, 1983.

Weideger, P. *Menstruation and menopause.* New York: Knopf, 1976.

Whisnant, L., & Zegans, L. A study of attitudes toward menarche in white middle class American adolescent girls. *American Journal of Psychiatry*, 1975, *132*, 809–814.

Williams, L. R. Beliefs and attitudes of young girls regarding menstruation. In S. Golub (Ed.) *Menarche.* Lexington, Massachusetts: D. C. Heath, 1983.

Woods, N. F., Dery, G. K., & Most, A. Recollections of menarche, current menstrual attitudes, and perimenstrual symptoms. In S. Golub (Ed.) *Menarche.* Lexington, Massachusetts: D. C. Heath, 1983.

14 If Men Could Menstruate

GLORIA STEINEM

Living in India made me understand that a white minority of the world has spent centuries conning us into thinking a white skin makes people superior, even though the only thing it really does is make them more subject to ultraviolet rays and wrinkles.

Reading Freud made me just as skeptical about penis envy. The power of giving birth makes "womb envy" more logical, and an organ as external and unprotected as the penis makes men very vulnerable indeed.

But listening recently to a woman describe the unexpected arrival of her menstrual period (a red stain had spread on her dress as she argued heatedly on the public stage) still made me cringe with embarrassment. That is, until she explained that, when finally informed in whispers of the obvious event, she had said to the all-male audience, "and you should be *proud* to have a menstruating woman on your stage. It's probably the first real thing that's happened to this group in years!"

Laughter. Relief. She had turned a negative into a positive. Somehow her story merged with India and Freud to make me finally understand the power of positive thinking. Whatever a "superior" group has will be used to justify its superiority, and whatever an "inferior" group has will be used to justify its plight. Black men were given poorly paid jobs because they were said to be "stronger" than white men, while all women were relegated to poorly paid jobs because they were said to be "weaker." As the little boy said when asked if he wanted to be a lawyer like his mother, "Oh no, that's women's work." Logic has nothing to do with oppression.

So what would happen if suddenly, magically, men could menstruate and women could not?

Clearly, menstruation would become an enviable, boastworthy, masculine event:

Men would brag about how long and how much.

Young boys would talk about it as the envied beginning of manhood. Gifts, religious ceremonies, family dinners, and stag parties would mark the day.

To prevent monthly work loss among the powerful, Congress would fund a National Institute of Dysmenorrhea. Doctors would research little about heart attacks, from which men were hormonally protected, but everything about cramps.

Sanitary supplies would be federally funded and free. Of course, some men would still pay for the prestige of such commercial brands as Paul Newman Tampons, Muhammad Ali's Rope-a-Dope Pads, John Wayne Maxi Pads, and Joe Namath Jock Shields—"For Those Light Bachelor Days."

Statistical surveys would show that men did better in sports and won more Olympic medals during their periods.

Generals, right-wing politicians, and religious fundamentalists would cite menstruation ("*men*-struation") as proof that only men could serve God and country in combat ("You have to give blood to take blood"), occupy high political office ("Can women be properly fierce without a monthly cycle governed by the planet Mars?"), be priests, ministers, God Himself ("He gave this blood for our sins"), or rabbis ("Without a monthly purge of impurities, women are unclean").

Male liberals or radicals, however, would insist that women are equal, just different; and that any woman could join their ranks if only she were willing to recognize the primacy of menstrual rights ("Everything else is a single issue") or self-inflict a major wound every month ("You *must* give blood for the revolution").

Street guys would invent slang ("He's a three-pad man") and "give fives" on the corner with some exchange like, "Man, you lookin' *good!*"

"Yeah man, I'm on the rag!"

TV shows would treat the subject openly. (*Happy Days:* Richie and Potsie try to convince Fonzie that he is still "The Fonz," though he has missed two periods in a row. *Hill Street Blues:* The whole precinct hits the same cycle.) So would newspapers. (SUMMER SHARK SCARE THREATENS MENSTRUATING MEN. JUDGE CITES MONTHLIES IN PARDONING RAPIST.) And so would movies. (Newman and Redford in *Blood Brothers!*)

Men would convince women that sex was *more* pleasurable at "that time of the month." Lesbians would be said to fear blood and therefore life itself, though all they needed was a good menstruating man.

Medical schools would limit women's entry ("they might faint at the sight of blood").

Of course, intellectuals would offer the most moral and logical arguments. Without that biological gift for measuring the cycles of the moon and planets, how could a woman master any discipline that demanded a sense of time, space, mathematics—or the ability to measure anything at all? In philosophy and religion, how could women compensate for being disconnected from the rhythm of the universe? Or for their lack of symbolic death and resurrection every month?

Menopause would be celebrated as a positive event, the symbol that men had accumulated enough years of cyclical wisdom to need no more.

Liberal males in every field would try to be kind. The fact that "these people" have no gift for measuring life, the liberals would explain, should be punishment enough.

And how would women be trained to react? One can imagine right-wing women agreeing to all these arguments with a staunch and smiling masochism. ("The ERA would force housewives to wound themselves every month": Phyllis Schlafly. "Your husband's blood is as sacred as that of Jesus—and so sexy, too!": Marabel Morgan.) Reformers and Queen Bees would adjust their lives to the cycles of the men around them. Feminists would explain endlessly that men, too, needed to be liberated from the false idea of Martian aggressiveness, just as women needed to escape the bonds of "menses-envy." Radical feminists would add that the oppression of the nonmenstrual was the pattern for all other oppressions. ("Vampires were our first freedom fighters!") Cultural feminists would exalt a female bloodless imagery in art and literature. Socialist feminists would insist that, once capitalism and imperialism were overthrown, women would menstruate, too. ("If women aren't yet menstruating in Russia," they would explain, "it's only because true socialism can't exist within capitalist encirclement.")

In short, we would discover, as we should already guess, that logic is in the eye of the logician. (For instance, here's an idea for theorists and logicians: If women are supposed to be less rational and more emotional at the beginning of our menstrual cycle when the female hormone is at its lowest level, then why isn't it logical to say that, in those few days, women behave the most like the way men behave all month long? I leave further improvisations up to you.)

The truth is that, if men could menstruate, the power justifications would go on and on.

If we let them.

15 Three Generations of Native American Women's Birth Experience

JOY HARJO

It was still dark when I awakened in the stuffed back room of my mother-in-law's small rented house with what felt like hard cramps. At 17 years of age I had read everything I could from the Tahlequah Public Library about pregnancy and giving birth. But nothing prepared me for what was coming. I awakened my child's father and then ironed him a shirt before we walked the four blocks to the Indian hospital because we had no car and no money for a taxi. He had been working with another Cherokee artist silk-screening signs for specials at the supermarket and making $5 a day, and had to leave me alone at the hospital because he had to go to work. We didn't awaken his mother. She had to get up soon enough to fix breakfast for her daughter and granddaughter before leaving for her job at the nursing home. I knew my life was balanced at the edge of great, precarious change and I felt alone and cheated. Where was the circle of women to acknowledge and honor this birth?

It was still dark as we walked through the cold morning, under oaks that symbolized the stubbornness and endurance of the Cherokee people who had made Tahlequah their capital in the new lands. I looked for handholds in the misty gray sky, for a voice announcing this impending miracle. I wanted to change everything; I wanted to go back to a place before childhood, before our tribe's removal to Oklahoma. What kind of life was I bringing this child into? I was a poor, mixed-blood woman heavy with a child who would suffer the struggle of poverty, the legacy of loss, for the second time in my life I felt the sharp tug of my own birth cord still connected to my mother. I believe it never pulls away, until death, and even then it becomes a streak in the sky symbolizing that most important warrior road. In my teens I had fought my mother's weaknesses with all my might, and here I was at 17, becoming as my mother, who was in Tulsa, cooking breakfasts and preparing for the lunch shift at a factory cafeteria as I walked to the hospital to give birth. I should be with her; instead, I was far from her house, in the house of a mother-in-law who later would try to use witchcraft to destroy me.

After my son's father left me I was prepped for birth. This meant my pubic area was shaved completely and then I endured the humiliation of an enema, all at the hands of strangers. I was left alone in a room painted government green. An overwhelming antiseptic smell emphasized the sterility of the hospital, a hospital built because of the U.S. government's treaty and responsibility to provide health care to Indian people.

I intellectually understood the stages of labor, the place of transition, of birth—but it was difficult to bear the actuality of it, and to bear it alone. Yet in some ways I wasn't alone, for history surrounded me. It was with the birth of children that history is given form and voice. Birth is one of the most sacred acts we take part in and witness in our lives. But sacredness seemed to be far from my lonely labor room in the Indian hospital. I heard a woman screaming in the next room with her pain, and I wanted to comfort her. The nurse used her as a bad example to the rest of us who were struggling to keep our suffering silent.

The doctor was a military man who had signed on this watch not for the love of healing or out of awe at the miracle of birth, but to fulfill a contract for medical school payments. I was another statistic to him; he touched me as if he were moving equipment from one place to another. During my last visit I was given the option of being sterilized. He explained to me that the moment of birth was the best time to do it. I was handed the form but chose not to sign it, and am amazed now that I didn't think too much of it at the time. Later I would learn that many Indian women who weren't fluent in English signed, thinking it was a form giving consent for the doctor to deliver their babies. Others were sterilized without even the formality of signing. My light skin had probably saved me from such a fate. It wouldn't be the first time in my life.

When my son was finally born I had been deadened with a needle in my spine. He was shown to me—the incredible miracle nothing prepared me for—then taken from me in the name of medical progress. I fell asleep with the weight of chemicals and awoke yearning for the child I had suffered for, had anticipated in the months proceeding from his unexpected genesis when I was still 16 and a student at Indian school. I was not allowed to sit up or walk because of the possibility of paralysis (one of the drug's side effects), and when I finally got to hold him, the nurse stood guard as if I would hurt him. I felt enmeshed in a system in which the wisdom that had carried my people from generation to generation was ignored. In that place I felt ashamed I was an Indian woman. But I was also proud of what my body had accomplished despite the rape by the bureaucracy's machinery, and I got us out of there as soon as possible. My son would flourish on beans and fry bread, and on the dreams and stories we fed him.

My daughter was born four years later, while I was an art student at the University of New Mexico. Since my son's birth I had waitressed, cleaned hospital rooms, filled cars with gas (while wearing a miniskirt), worked as a nursing assistant, and led dance classes at a health spa. I knew I didn't want to cook and waitress all my life, as my mother had done. I had watched the varicose veins grow branches on her legs, and as they grew, her zest for dancing and sports dissolved into utter tiredness. She had been born with a caul over her face, the sign of a gifted visionary.

My earliest memories are of my mother writing songs on an ancient Underwood typewriter after she had washed and waxed the kitchen floor on her hands and knees. She too had wanted something different for her life. She had left an impoverished existence at age 17, bound for the big city of Tulsa. She was shamed in a time in which to be even part Indian was to be an outcast in the great U.S. system. Half her relatives were Cherokee full-bloods from near Jay, Oklahoma, who for the most part had nothing to do with white people. The other half were musically inclined "white trash" addicted to country-western music and Holy Roller fervor. She thought she could disappear in the city; no one would know her family, where she came from. She had dreams of singing and had once been offered a job singing on the radio but turned it down because she was shy. Later one of her songs would be stolen before she could copyright it and would make someone else rich. She would quit writing songs. She and my father would divorce and she would be forced to work for money to feed and clothe four children, all born within two years of each other.

As a child growing up in Oklahoma, I liked to be told the story of my birth. I would beg for it while my mother cleaned and ironed. "You almost killed me," she would say. "We almost died." That I could kill my mother filled me with remorse and shame. And I imagined the push-pull of my life, which is a legacy I deal with even now when I am twice as old as my mother was at my birth. I loved to hear the story of my warrior fight for my breath. The way it was told, it had been my decision to live. When I got older, I realized we were both nearly causalities of the system, the same system flourishing in the Indian hospital where later my son Phil would be born.

My parents felt lucky to have insurance, to be able to have their children in the hospital. My father came from a fairly prominent Muscogee Creek family. *His* mother was a full-blood who in the early 1920s got her degree in art. She was a painter. She gave birth to him in a private hospital in Oklahoma City; at least that's what I think he told me before he died at age 53. It was something of which they were proud.

This experience was much different from my mother's own birth. She and five of her six brothers were born at home, with no medical assistance. The only time a doctor was called was when someone was dying. When she was born her mother named her Wynema, a Cherokee name my mother says means beautiful woman, and Jewell, for a can of shortening stored in the room where she was born.

I wanted something different for my life, for my son, and for my daughter, who later was born in a university hospital in Albuquerque. It was a bright summer morning when she was ready to begin her journey. I still had no car, but I had enough money saved for a taxi for a ride to the hospital. She was born "naturally," without drugs. I could look out the hospital window while I was in labor at the bluest sky in the world. I had support. Her father was present in the delivery room—though after her birth he disappeared on a drinking binge. I understood his despair, but did not agree with the painful means to describe it. A few days later Rainy Dawn was presented to the sun at her father's pueblo and given a name so that she will always be recognized as a part of the people, as a child of the sun.

That's not to say that my experience in the hospital reached perfection. The clang of metal against metal in the delivery room had the effect of a tuning fork reverberating fear in my pelvis. After giving birth I held my daughter, but they took her from me for "processing." I refused to lie down to be wheeled to my room after giving birth; I wanted to walk out of there to find my daughter. We reached a compromise and I rode in a wheelchair. When we reached the room I stood up and walked to the nursery and demanded my daughter. I knew she needed me. That began my war with the nursery staff, who deemed me unknowledgeable because I was Indian and poor. Once again I felt the brushfire of shame, but I'd learned to put it out much more quickly, and I demanded early release so I could take care of my baby without the judgment of strangers.

I wanted something different for Rainy, and as she grew up I worked hard to prove that I could make "something" of my life. I obtained two degrees as a single mother. I wrote poetry, screenplays, became a professor, and tried to live a life that would be a positive influence for both of my children. My work in this life has to do with reclaiming the memory stolen from our peoples when we were dispossessed from our lands east of the Mississippi; it has to do with restoring us. I am proud of our history, a history so powerful that it both destroyed my father and guarded him. It's a history that claims my mother as she lives not far from the place her mother was born, names her as she cooks in the cafeteria of a small college in Oklahoma.

When my daughter told me she was pregnant, I wasn't surprised. I had known it before she did, or at least before she would admit it to me. I felt despair, as if nothing had changed or ever would. She had run away from Indian school with her boyfriend and they had been living in the streets of Gallup, a border town notorious for the suicides and deaths of Indian peoples. I brought her and her boyfriend with me because it was the only way I could bring her home. At age 16, she was fighting me just as I had so fiercely fought my mother. She was making the same mistakes. I felt as if everything I had accomplished had been in vain. Yet I felt strangely empowered, too, at this repetition of history, this continuance, by a new possibility of life and love, and I steadfastly stood by my daughter.

I had a university job, so I had insurance that covered my daughter. She saw an obstetrician in town who was reputed to be one of the best. She had the choice of a birthing room. She had the finest care. Despite this, I once again battled with a system in which physicians are taught the art of healing by dissecting cadavers. My daughter went into labor a month early. We both knew intuitively the baby was ready, but how to explain that to a system in which numbers and statistics provide the base of understanding? My daughter would have her labor interrupted; her blood pressure would rise because of the drug given to her to stop the labor. She would be given an unneeded amniocentesis and would have her labor induced—after having it artificially stopped! I was warned that if I took her out of the hospital so her labor could occur naturally my insurance would cover nothing.

My daughter's induced labor was unnatural and difficult, monitored by machines, not by touch. I was shocked. I felt as if I'd come full circle, as if I were watching my mother's labor and the struggle of my own birth. But I was there in the hospital room with her, as neither my mother had been for me, nor her mother for her. My daughter and I went through the labor and birth together.

And when Krista Rae was born she was born to her family. Her father was there for her, as were both her grandmothers and my friend who had flown in to be with us. Her paternal great-grandparents and aunts and uncles had also arrived from the Navajo Reservation to honor her. Something *had* changed.

Four days later, I took my granddaughter to the Saguaro forest before dawn and gave her the name I had dreamed for her just before her birth. Her name looks like clouds of mist settling around a sacred mountain as it begins to speak. A female ancestor approaches on a horse. We are all together.

16 Natural-born Mothers

SARAH BLAFFER HRDY

On the day that the eleventh-century Italian saint Peter Damian was born, his mother was ready to call it quits. According to the saint's biography, written by his associate John of Lodi, his mother was "worn out by childbearing" and further disheartened by the reproach of an adolescent son who took her to task for bringing into the world yet another mouth to feed and one more son to add to her already existing "throng of heirs." In despair, the mother refused to nurse. The fledgling saint was on the verge of starvation when a neighbor, the kindly concubine of a local priest, intervened, reminding her that even a savage beast, a tigress or a mother lion, would suckle her own young. Could a Christian woman do less?

Five hundred years later, Italian poet Luigi Tansillo echoed similar sentiments in response to the widespread use of wet nurses—the main alternative to maternal breast-feeding in the days before the baby bottle. In a poem entitled "La Balia" (The Nurse), Tansillo wrote, "What fury, hostile to our common kind, / First led from nature's path the female mind . . . [resulting in] a babe denied its mother's breast?" In the following centuries, tens of thousands of babies in Europe were deposited in foundling homes or shipped to middlemen who contracted for a lactating woman to suckle them. In urban centers like Paris, the majority of babies were suckled by strangers. This traffic in babies led to staggering rates of infant mortality.

Reaction against wet-nursing reached a peak during the Enlightenment. In 1793, the French National Convention decreed that only mothers who nursed their own children would be eligible for state aid. The writings of Jean Jacques Rousseau inspired many reformers (although the great philosopher sent his own five children to foundling homes). Almost always, reformers invoked "natural laws," encouraging mothers to follow their instinctive urges to nurture their babies. "Look to the animals for your example," French physician and moralist Jean Emmanuel Gilibert admonished his patients. "Even though the mothers have their stomachs torn open. . . . Even though their offspring have been the cause of all their woes, their first care makes them forget all they have suffered. . . . They forget themselves, little concerned with their own happiness. . . . Woman, like all animals, is under the sway of this instinct."

For further support of their beliefs, reformers could turn to Carolus Linnaeus, the father of modern taxonomy. A physician and the father of seven children, Linnaeus was an ardent advocate of maternal breastfeeding. In 1752 he set down his views in *Nutrix noverca* (Step-Nurse), a widely read denunciation of commercial wet-nursing (which Gilibert translated from Latin into French). In the 1758 edition of his opus *Systema Naturae*, Linnaeus subsumed all warm-blooded, hairy, viviparous vertebrates into a single group—the class Mammalia—identified with the milk-secreting glands of the female. (The Latin term for breasts, *mammae*, derives from the plaintive cry "mama," spontaneously uttered by young children from widely divergent linguistic groups and often conveying a single, urgent message, "suckle me.")

Linnaeus's nomenclature underscored a natural role for women based on a salient homology between women and other animals that nursed their young. Mother mammals are alchemists able to transform available fodder—grass, insects, even toxic leaves—into biological white gold. Lactation allows a mother to stockpile resources while they are available, repackage them in digestible form, and then parcel them out to growing infants at her own pace. Able to rely on its mother for food, an immature can stay safe either attached to the mother or stashed in hiding places she chooses, buffered from the vagaries and hazards of foraging in the wide world.

But motherhood is not as straightforward a matter as just turning on the milk. Mothers have to factor in recurring food shortages, predators, and social exploitation by members of their own species. Faced with poor conditions, a mother must weigh babies in hand against her own well-being, long-term survival, and—most important—the possibility of breeding again under better circumstances. Behavioral ecologists are only beginning to understand how mother mammals respond to such natural dilemmas, called fitness trade-offs.

Most mammals are iteroparous: breeding more than once, they produce offspring, either singly or in litters, over a breeding career that may last several years—twenty-five or more in the case of a woman. (A very few mammals—primarily some marsupial mice—are semelparous, breeding in one fecund burst followed by death.) In an evolutionary sense, the bottom line for iteroparous females is not the success of any particular birth but reproductive output over a lifetime. The art of iteroparity, therefore, is generally to survive poor conditions and breed again under better ones. By drawing on help from others, however, some mothers manage to breed under circumstances that would otherwise be impossible.

Consider the case of the cotton-top tamarins. Although the birth of twins is rare among primates, the pint-sized tamarins and marmosets of South America are exceptions. Adapted for fluctuating habitats, these monkeys have the potential to breed at a staggering pace, sometimes giving birth as often as twice a year to twins whose combined weight totals up to 20 percent of the mother's. Only the help of other group members—fathers, older offspring, and transient adults—makes the mother's feat of fecundity possible. Helpers carry the offspring most of the time, except when the mother is suckling. Near weaning, helpers also provide infants with crickets and other tidbits.

Working with captive cotton-tops, Lorna Johnson, of the New England Primate Center, revealed how important helpers can be. (This species is endangered in the wild but is still well represented in research colonies.) In her analysis of breeding records over an eighteen-year period, Johnson focused on experienced parents that had already successfully reared offspring. She found that among these veterans, fully 57 percent of parents without help abandoned their young, nearly five times the rate at which parents with helpers voted "no-go."

Among marmosets and tamarins, it is usual for only one female in the group to reproduce during a breeding season. A similar situation prevails among the communally breeding dwarf mongooses of the Serengeti. Studying what keeps the other females from breeding, Purdue University biologist Scott Creel discovered that estrogen levels of these nonbreeders remained only one-third as high as in the breeding female, below that necessary for ovulation. Creel speculates that in species producing large litters, heavy young, or young designed to grow rapidly after birth, the cost of gestation and lactation is just too high for any but the most advantaged female to hazard giving birth. Often harassed and less well fed, a subordinate has such a slim chance of producing young that survive to weaning that she is better off deferring reproduction, helping instead to rear the offspring of her kin—occasionally even suckling them—and generally doing her best to be tolerated in the group and to stay alive until she can become a breeder in her own right.

While studying a closely related subspecies of dwarf mongoose, O. Anne E. Rasa, of Bonn University, learned that subordinate females have an even more pressing reason to postpone reproduction. The dominant female may destroy the pups of any rival that does breed. Earlier this year, Duke University's Leslie Digby reported that there appears to be the same pattern among wild common marmosets in Brazil. In a rare instance when a subordinate female gave birth, one of her infants was killed; the other disappeared at about the same time. For marmosets and dwarf mongooses, then, most subordinate females make the best of a grim lot by temporarily shutting down their ovaries. With luck, their time to breed does come.

Suppression of ovulation is only one of the many means for mothers to adjust the timing of their reproductive effort. In a diverse array of mammals—including bats, skunks, minks, and armadillos—ovulation occurs, but implantation of the fertilized egg in the uterine wall is delayed so as to insure birth of the offspring at the optimal season. As soon as a kangaroo mother ceases to suckle one joey, levels in her blood of the nursing hormone prolactin fall. At this signal, a tiny blastocyst (a nearly hollow globe of cells, produced by the fertilized egg, inside of which the embryo will develop) emerges from diapause (a period of developmental dormancy) and begins to grow again. In the European badger, this blastocyst-in-waiting continues to grow, but ever so slowly. Embryonic slowdown or diapause can persist for days in rodents or even months in large mammals, until some cue signals the embryo to attach to the uterine wall and resume development. American black bears breed from May to July, but not until the female repairs to her den for winter does implantation occur, so that birth takes place to a lethargic mother in the snug safety of her winter refuge. Yet if the berry crop that year had failed, and the mother, as a result, was not in good condition, implantation might well have failed, too.

Planned parenthood primate style revolves around breast-feeding. In almost all monkeys and apes, as well as in people still living in traditional settings where infants enjoy nearly continuous contact with their mothers, babies nurse on demand. Emory University anthropologists Mel Konner and Carol Worthman report that the !Kung San of the Kalahari suckle their babies for two minutes or so as often as four times every hour, even while they sleep at night.

Throughout most of human evolution, mothers suckled their children on demand from infancy to the age of three or four—in some circumstances, even longer. A series of studies of hunter-gatherers from Central Africa, Botswana, and New Guinea, as well as of housewives in New England, have documented the dynamic interaction between a woman's nutritional status, her workload, and her fertility—what Harvard anthropologist Peter Ellison likes to call the ecology of the ovaries. Nipple stimulation from nearly continuous "Pleistocene style" suckling causes the pituitary to secrete more prolactin, the body's "work order" for more milk production. Through a complex and as yet poorly understood series of mediating effects involving the hypothalamus, ovulation is somehow inhibited when prolactin levels are high. The result is birth intervals as long as five years in long-suckling people like the !Kung. According to Ellison, the link between the intensity of suckling and postpartum infertility prevents a nursing mother, already energetically burdened by metabolizing for two, from being saddled with another pregnancy and the even more daunting task of metabolizing for three. (Unless, that is, she happens to be particularly well fed. Worthman and others have recently discovered that among well-nourished mothers, the inhibition of ovulation by suckling is less effective.)

Like delayed implantation, lactational suppression of ovulation provides made-to-order birth control. No system is foolproof, however. Saddled with an inopportune conception, a mother mammal may resort to remedies that although unmotherly to modern tastes, are nonetheless utterly natural. Possible options depend on what type of mammal she is. Untimely fetuses may be reabsorbed, spontaneously aborted, abandoned after birth, or under some circumstances, killed and even eaten.

Golden hamsters, for instance, are highly flexible breeders adapted to the irregular rainfall and erratic food supplies in their native habitat in the arid regions of the Middle East. In addition to building a nest, licking their pups clean, protecting and suckling them—all pleasantly conventional maternal pursuits—these hamster moms may also recoup maternal resources otherwise lost in the production of pups by eating a few.

For hamsters, to quote Canadian psychologist Corinne Day and Bennett Galef, cannibalizing pups is an "organized part of normal maternal behavior which allows an individual female to adjust her litter size in accord with her capacity to rear young in the environmental conditions prevailing at the time of her parturition." Quality control can also be an issue. Among mice (but not hamsters), pups below median weight are the ones most likely to be rejected when mothers cull very large litters.

Another "rule of paw" might read: abort poor prospects sooner rather than later and, if possible, recoup resources. Recall how the mother bear's body factors in the latest update on food supplies before either canceling implantation or committing to gestation. The cues mothers respond to may derive from prevailing conditions or their own internal state. Biologist John Hoogland spent sixteen years monitoring a population of black-tailed prairie dogs in South Dakota. Mothers attempt to rear 91 percent of all litters produced: the rest of the time, they abandon their pups at birth and allow other group members to eat them, sometimes even joining in. Under closer examination, Hoogland found that the mothers that gave up on their litters weighed less. He speculated that abandonment was an adaptive response to poor body condition.

Deteriorating social conditions can also alter maternal commitment. Across a broad spectrum of animals from mice to lions, the appearance of strange males on the horizon can present a danger to unweaned infants sired by other, rival males. By killing these infants, the newcomers subvert the mother's control over the timing of her own reproduction. To minimize her loss, she breeds again sooner than she would have if she had continued to suckle her babies. Although this revised schedule of breeding is detrimental to the mother (not to mention her babies), she may ovulate again while the killer is still in the vicinity. Had the killer waited until her infants were weaned, his own window of opportunity might have long since shut, for he too is bound to be replaced by another male.

Among the strains of house mice studied by Frederick vom Saal, at the University of Missouri, and by Robert Elwood, at Queen's University in Belfast, Northern Ireland, roving males that have failed to mate in the preceding seven weeks (equivalent to a three-week pregnancy, followed by four weeks of lactation) attack babies in any nest they bump into. By contrast, males that have mated during that crucial period are statistically more likely to behave "paternally," retrieving pups that have slipped out of the nest, keeping them warm, and licking them clean. Some behavioral switch accompanying ejaculation (especially if he remains near the female) transforms this potential killer into a kinder, gentler rodent. This transformation (Elwood calls it a "switch in time") saves the male from mistakenly destroying his own progeny (although, depending on circumstances, it may occasionally lead him to tolerate offspring of another male).

Male mice can also have a devastating effect on unborn young, for a pregnant mouse that encounters a strange male may reabsorb her budding embryos. This form of early abortion avoids the even greater misfortune of losing a full-term litter later on. It has become known as "the Bruce effect," after biologist Hilda Bruce, who first reported the phenomenon for laboratory mice in 1959 (at the time, its function was unclear). The Bruce effect has since been reported for deer mice, collared lemmings, and several species of voles. Elwood and others have shown that pregnant mice are especially likely to block pregnancies when confronted with males known to be infanticidal.

From the female's point of view, losing a pregnancy is scarcely an ideal strategy. Rather, her body is making the best of dismal circumstances. As bizarre as it may seem, when a mammal mother thwarts her pregnancy, she is behaving—in strictly biological terms—just like a mother. For she may soon conceive again, perhaps with a male who will stick around to help or at least keep other males away. Bruce had discovered a natural, spontaneous form of energy-conserving, early-stage abortion.

Mice are not the only animals that have to cope with infanticidal males. Among the lean and graceful langur monkeys that I studied at Mount Abu, Rajasthan, India, males pose serious threats to infants. My colleagues S. M. Mohnot and Volker Sommer, whose team has monitored the langur population at nearby Jodhpur for more than twenty years, learned that one-third of all infants born are killed by males coming into the group. Mothers initially avoid such usurpers or even fight back, but once a new male becomes ensconced in the group, he has the advantage of being able to try to kill the babies again and again, day after day.

Confronted with discouraging odds, a mother may try to deposit a nearly weaned infant with former resident males, now ousted and roving about the vicinity. This strategy rarely works. The infant will usually wend its way back to its mother, placing itself right back in harm's way. Especially if she is young with many fertile years ahead of her, a mother under persistent assault may simply stop defending her infant, leaving more intrepid kin—usually old females that have not reproduced for years—to intervene. And so it was that I once observed an aged and stiff twenty-pound female, assisted by another older female, wrest a wounded infant from the sharp-toothed jaws of a forty-pound male. The far stronger and healthier young mother watched from the sidelines. Just days before, the same young mother had made no effort to intervene when her infant fell from a jacaranda tree branch and was grabbed up by the male. Again, it was the old female who rushed to the rescue.

In the last weeks of pregnancy, langurs may respond to a usurping male by aborting rather than continuing to expend energy on a reproductive venture so unlikely to end well. Similar late-pregnancy variations on the Bruce effect have been reported for an odd assortment of large mammals, including wild horses. University of Nevada's Joel Berger, an animal behaviorist who studied wild horses in the Great Basin, watched what happens when one stallion successfully challenges another for possession of his harem. During the disruption following the changeover, 82 percent of the mares that had been impregnated in the last six months by the deposed stallion aborted their fetuses.

Infanticide, abortion, cannibalism, these are altogether natural lapses from imagined "natural laws." Why is it only in the last two decades that researchers have begun to view such behaviors as other than aberrations? Opinions, even scientific ones, are often influenced by received wisdom. As late as the 1960s, when animal behaviorists set up labs to study the maternal activities of rats, monkeys, and dogs, the categories devised to describe their behavior took for granted that mothers were instinctively nurturing. In her pioneering studies of dogs, for example, comparative psychologist Harriet Rheingold separated mothers and their pups from all other animals and then recorded behaviors that fell into her preconceived protocol of maternal activities: contact, nursing, licking, play, and so forth.

Indeed, much of the time mother mammals do carry, groom, and suckle their young. The types of maternal activities Rheingold and others investigated were those that insured that mothers passed on their genes to future generations—the primary focus of the time. Such a view of what it means to be a mother could fairly be classified as essentialist.

But the study of animal behavior has changed. With the emergence of sociobiology in the 1970s, researchers began to focus on individuals and the idiosyncratic social and environmental circumstances of each. With this new perspective, it not only became clear that one mother is not the same as another but also that not all females would be mothers. Far from essentialist or biologically determinist, most biologists today think context is critically important. Researchers like Scott Creel and Carol Worthman combine fieldwork with laboratory measures to search for the cues—inside and out—that prompt a female to opt for one reproductive strategy rather than another.

Across her life course, both a mother and her circumstances are constantly changing—as she ages, finds a new mate, loses a potential helper, stockpiles fat. In a world of leisure, plenty, and supportive social groups or in realms where offspring cost their parents little to rear, trade-offs fade from view. In contrast, overpopulation, social oppression, scarcity, bad times—none of these have ever been conducive to the development of the sort of mother characterized in Marge Piercy's poem "Magic mama" as "an aphid enrolled to sweeten the lives of others. The woman who puts down her work like knitting the moment you speak."

Real mamas must not only be magic but also multifaceted. Motherhood is more than all the licking, tending, suckling, and awe-inspiring protectiveness for which mother mammals are so justly famous. Such indeed is the art—and the tragedy—of iteroparity: offspring born at one time may be more costly to a mother or less viable than offspring born at another. Far from invalidating biological bases for maternal behavior, the extraordinary flexibility in what it means to be a mother should merely remind us that the physiological and motivational underpinnings of an archetypically prochoice mammal are scarcely new.

PART TWO

Women in Society

CHAPTER FIVE

Women's Relationships

The importance of relationships in women's lives is explored in this section, with articles on women's friendships and heterosexual and lesbian love relationships. Many feminist theorists have argued that interpersonal connections are more central to the lives of women than of men. Girls are socialized from a very young age to develop personality characteristics that lend themselves particularly well to relationship building and maintenance. Empathy, nurturance, emotional expressiveness, vulnerability, sensitivity—all of these traits are clearly important to the quality of our relationships with others. Indeed theorists such as Carol Gilligan and Nancy Chodorow argue that the ethic of *caring*, more highly developed in women out of the bond shared by mothers and daughters, is the main psychological distinction between the genders.

Women are more likely than men to have very close, intimate, long-lasting same-sex friendships. And women tend to find their friendships with other women to be very supportive. Some data even show that women find the end of a close same-sex friendship to be more devastating than the break-up of a romantic relationship (Pierce, Smith, & Akert, 1984). It has always been puzzling to me, therefore, that as a culture we seem to have relatively few "female buddy" stories, compared to stories about male-male pals. Women are often portrayed instead in our media either as sidekicks to men, or as pitted against one another in the battle for male attention (e.g., "Don't hate me because I'm beautiful"). But perhaps this is changing. Recently, more and more television programs and movies, such as *Thelma and Louise* and *The Gilmore Girls*, celebrate women's friendships with one another. Let's hope this is a trend that continues.

From the time we first become interested in Barbie, women are taught to invest themselves deeply in romance. In our culture, which is saturated with heterosexuality, women are expected to groom themselves for the romantic love of a man and to work hard to keep it. An afternoon of watching talk shows or browsing through the self-help section of any bookstore ought to convince anyone that this is the case. But is women's reputation of being the more hopelessly romantic sex deserved? Do women actually benefit as much as is popularly believed from their investment in romantic relationships?

In their article "Women and Men in Love: Gender Differences in Close Heterosexual Relationships," Letitia Anne Peplau and Steven Gordon explore these and other interesting questions about heterosexual romance. They actually report several counter-intuitive findings from the research literature in this area. For example, in terms of believing in romantic ideology (e.g., "true love lasts forever") and of falling in love quickly, men, not women, appear to be the more romantic sex. Women, on the other hand, appear to be more pragmatic in their approach to love. Also, quite contrary to popular stereotypes, marriage appears to contribute more to the psychological health and well-being of husbands than of wives. Some other, less surprising findings are that women are more expressive and facilitative of communication than are men in heterosexual relationships, that women perform the vast majority of the domestic work in marriages (regardless of whether or not they are employed outside the home), and that men and women use different power strategies to influence one another in relationships. The authors explore many fascinating reasons for these various differences, but for the most part, many questions about causality still remain. Important to consider is the difference in social status and power between men and women, which appears to have a significant impact on the way each gender experiences and interacts in heterosexual relationships.

What about women's experiences in lesbian love relationships? In the next piece, Letitia Anne Peplau and Hortensia Amaro review the available research on lesbian relationships. They begin by arguing that there is no such thing as the "typical lesbian couple," and emphasize throughout their review the diversity and complexity of such relationships. However, studies do provide some interesting general themes regarding the stability of lesbian relationships, the degree of intimacy and expressiveness among lesbians, and the values of equality in the relationship.

The final piece in this section takes a very different kind of look at female relationality, exploring its underbelly: adolescent relational aggression. This topic has not been explored much until recently. One reason for this is researchers' heavy focus on girls' ethic of caring, nurturance, and empathy. The popularization of such research perhaps blinded many in the field of psychology to the fact that girls can and do behave in aggressive ways toward one another. In her article "Mean Girls," Margaret Talbot presents research on girls' aggressive behavior, as well as intervention efforts to curb girls' "meanness" toward one another. What is fascinating here is the fact that it is precisely their fluency in the world of social interaction and emotion that enables some girls to wage battles aimed at damaging relationships and reputations. These battles are typically fought with words, not fists—secret-telling, exclusions, and manipulations.

Despite the negative image it paints of some girls, I like to think of this new research on female relational aggression as enabling us to view girls and women in a more complex, human way. To simplify our understanding of gender into "Venus and Mars" or "women are caring while men are aggressive" is to fall into the many traps that stereotyping lays. Research shows that even benevolent stereotypes are harmful in the long run; they help support and sustain the status quo of power inequity between the genders. So women may indeed be caring, but to view them as exclusively so is to blind ourselves to the fact that they, like men, can also be aggressive. Where gender appears to play a big role is in the *kind* and *quality* of that aggression: more physical for males, and more interpersonal for females.

The articles in this section represent the great variety of relationships in which girls and women invest their time and energy. Not all those relations are harmonious and happy. However, one thing seems indisputable: it is largely in the relational domain that women experience the drama of their lives. Women make excellent friends, lovers, and enemies.

Women provide the lion's share of social support to others, and this seems to be both good and bad for them. I can't help but think that the negative consequences of "relational work" for women are due in large measure to the fact that our society still expects far less of such work to be done by men. As a woman, I can only hope that the future will allow men to share more in the life-work of acknowledging, caring for, and nurturing others' emotional needs, for their own sake as well as ours.

References

Pierce, K., Smith, H., & Akert, R. M. (1984, April). Terminating adult same-sex friendships: The role of gender and decision to terminate in the break-up process. Paper presented at the meeting of the Eastern Psychological Association, Baltimore, MD.

17 Women and Men in Love: Gender Differences in Close Heterosexual Relationships

LETITIA ANNE PEPLAU

STEVEN L. GORDON

. . . This chapter takes stock of research findings about gender differences in heterosexual love relationships. Much of the existing research has been descriptive, aimed at documenting male-female differences. Explanations about the causes of these sex-linked patterns have often been offered *post hoc.* Where possible, we have speculated about the origins of observed sex differences. Our belief is that future research should move beyond mere description and focus explicitly on explaining sex differences in close relationships. . . .

What Women and Men Want in Relationships

The experiences of women and men in close relationships are shaped by their attitudes and values. Most Americans value love relationships highly. Although stereotypes depict men as more resistant to marriage and "settling down" than women, actual gender differences in expectations about marriage are very small. For example, a study of college students (Hill, Rubin & Peplau, 1976; Rubin, Peplau & Hill, unpublished data) asked men and women about the likelihood that they would eventually get married. Among students currently in a steady dating relationship, only 3% of the men and 1% of the women said they would "definitely" never marry. Among students not currently "going with" one partner, 5% of the men and none of the women said they would definitely never marry. Intimacy and its institutionalized expression in marriage are major goals for most heterosexual women and men.

Men have somewhat more traditional attitudes about relations between the sexes than do women. When asked about such matters as whether the husband should be the primary wage earner for the family and whether the wife should have major responsibility for homemaking and childcare, men consistently endorse more traditional male-female role differentiation (e.g., Osmond & Martin, 1975; Parelman, 1983; Peplau, 1976; Scanzoni & Fox, 1980; Spence & Helmreich, 1978; Tomeh, 1978). For example, one survey (Astin, King & Richardson, 1980) asked students entering college in the fall of 1980 whether "women's activities should be confined to the home." About 35% of the men agreed with this statement, compared to only 19% of the women. In any particular dating or marital relationship, partners tend to be relatively similar in their sex-role attitudes. For example, in a sample of college dating couples, Peplau (1976) reported a significant correlation of .48 between partners' scores on a 10-item sex-role attitude scale. Traditionalists are usually matched with traditionists and feminists with feminists. Nonetheless, there is also likely to be a small but consistent difference in the relative traditionalism of partners, with women being more pro-feminist than their male partners.

Relationship values are also reflected in people's goals for dating or for marriage. Much commonality has been found in men's and women's relationship priorities. For example, one study of dating couples (Rubin, Peplau & Hill, unpublished data) asked college students to rate the importance of six goals as a reason for entering their current dating relationship. Both sexes gave the greatest importance to a desire "to have a good time with someone" and "to have a friend of the opposite sex." Men and women both gave the lowest priority to the desire "to find a marriage partner" or "to have a guaranteed date," and intermediate importance to the desire "for sexual activity" and "to fall in love." However, whereas men rated sex more important than love, women rated love more important than sex.

Several studies have asked husbands and wives to rank the importance of various marriage goals. Levinger (1964) found that the overall ranking of nine goals was, in the order of their importance: affection, companionship, happy children, personal development, religion, economic security, attractive home, wise financial planning, and a place in the community. Levinger found few sex differences: Both sexes emphasized affection and companionship and gave low priority to task-oriented goals about the standard of living. There is also some evidence that the ranking of such goals is affected by social class (Farber, 1957). Across all social classes, women rank affection high, but men vary. Levinger has suggested that "The more a couple is assured of economic security and occupational stability, the more likely it is that the husband will share the wife's concern with socio-emotional matters" (1964, p. 442). Working-class men, on the other hand, may put less emphasis on companionship than do their wives (e.g., Rubin, 1976).

More recent studies have attempted to go beyond the ranking of fairly global goals in order to identify more precisely those specific features of relationships that are most important to women and to men. Cochran and Peplau (in press) asked college students to rate the importance of 22 features of love relationships, such as partners having similar attitudes, sharing many activities, sexual exclusivity, and disclosing intimate feelings. A factor analysis of responses indicated that values clustered around two themes. "Dyadic attachment" values concerned a desire for a close and relatively secure love relationship, and were reflected in an emphasis on seeking permanence in a relationship, wanting to reveal personal feelings, sharing many activities with the partner, and valuing sexual exclusivity. "Egalitarian autonomy" values indicated a concern with maintaining one's independence. This theme was reflected in wanting to have separate interests and friends apart from the dating relationship, and wanting to preserve one's independence within the relationship by dividing decision-making and finances in an egalitarian manner. Men and women did not differ significantly in their ratings of dyadic attachment issues; both sexes were equally likely to value—or to devalue—these more traditional features of close relationships. Students' attachment values were unrelated to their general sex-role attitudes. In contrast, the sexes did not differ in their ratings of personal autonomy values. Women were more likely than men to emphasize the importance of independence and equality. In addition, students with pro-feminist attitudes gave greater value to maintaining separate interests outside the relationship and to equality within the relationship. (When the effects of sex-role attitudes were controlled, women continued to score higher on autonomy values.) It should be emphasized, however, that although significant sex differences in autonomy were found, their magnitude was small. There was much overlap in the expressed values of both sexes. Indeed, the relative ranking of specific values was highly similar for both women and men.

Also pertinent are findings from a study of young married couples by Parelman (1983). She examined spouses' ideals of marital closeness—what each considered to be the important ingredients of an ideal marriage. Women gave greater importance to feeling emotionally involved with the spouse and to verbal self-disclosure. Women also gave greater importance to partners' being independent and self-reliant. Men gave greater emphasis to themes of "sacrifice and dependency"—feeling responsible for the partner's well-being, spending time with the spouse, putting the spouse's needs first. Parelman concluded that "in this sample, women were more concerned with maintaining their separate activities and interests and with accommodating less to their spouse." Parelman noted, however, that the similarities between men and women were much greater than the differences. Further, she found that gender was not as good a predictor of relationship values as were measures of sex-role attitudes. For both sexes, profeminist attitudes were associated with wanting less sacrifice and dependency, greater independence, less similarity, fewer traditional role divisions, and greater verbal expressiveness.

People's preferences about relationships can also be seen in the traits they seek in a partner. Not surprisingly, there is much commonality in the qualities desired by men and women. Both sexes seek a partner who is affectionate, understanding, and has the right "personality" (e.g., Laner, 1977; Pietropinto & Simenauer, 1981; Wakil, 1973). Nonetheless, small but consistent gender differences do emerge. American culture encourages sex-linked asymmetries in the characteristics of dating and marriage partners (Bernard, 1972; Peplau, 1976). Women are traditionally taught to seek a man who is taller, older, more "worldly," more occupationally successful—someone to be a protector and provider. Men are traditionally taught to desire a woman who is an attractive companion and will be a good mother and homemaker. Empirical evidence (Burchinal, 1964; Hundson & Henze, 1969) indicates that people's personal preferences often reflect these cultural norms.

Several studies reveal that men put greater importance on a partner's physical attractiveness and sex appeal than do women (Hudson & Henze, 1969; Huston & Levinger, 1978; Pietropinto & Simenauer, 1981). In one study (Laner, 1977), 48% of heterosexual college men rated "good looks" as very important in a "permanent partner," compared to only 16% of college women. Women often give greater emphasis to a partner's intelligence and occupational attainment (e.g., Burchinal, 1964; Hudson & Henze, 1969; Langhorne & Secord, 1955). In Laner's (1977) study, 70% of the women ranked being "intelligent" as very important, compared with 53% of the men. The comments of a husband and wife interviewed by Pietropinto and Simenauer (1981) illustrate these common gender differences:

> Husband: She was attractive, vivacious, and interesting. I thought she would prove to be a loving companion, a wonderful wife and mother.
>
> Wife: We were in love. . . . He went out of his way to make me happy. I felt he could be a good provider and give me financial security (p. 43).

Studies of actual mate selection suggest that these sex-linked preferences are not always translated into action. In general, dating partners and spouses tend to be reasonably similar in social characteristics (Leslie, 1976). For instance, Hill et al. (1976) found that college dating couples were significantly matched in age, height, physical attractiveness (as rated from photos by a panel of judges), educational aspirations, and SAT scores. When asymmetries do occur, however, it is more often the boyfriend or husband who is older, has more education, and is higher in occupational attainment (Bernard, 1972; Leslie, 1976; Rubin, 1968). This phenomenon, called the "marriage gradient," has led sociologists to speculate that the pool of "eligible" partners may be smallest for high-status, occupationally successful women and for low-status, occupationally less successful men. . . .

Our understanding of sex roles in close heterosexual relationships benefits from these examinations of what men and women want in relationships. But existing research leaves many unanswered questions. We do not know how well most people are able to articulate their personal values and goals. Such issues may not be very salient for some people, whose answers to researchers may be heavily influenced by stereotypes and social desirability pressures. We do not know whether the sexes interpret values such as "affection" and "companionship" in similar ways. It is possible that when men think of companionship they imagine joint activities such as hiking or going to a movie, whereas women think of intimate conversations (Caldwell & Peplau, 1982). We know little about how relationship values affect people's actual selection of partners and behavior in relationships. An especially important question may be whether sex differences in values lead to conflict and problems in heterosexual relationships. Finally, we can profitably ask how young people's relationship values are affected by the changing roles of men and women in American society.

Falling in Love

Is one sex more "romantic," or prone to falling in love more easily? The answer depends a good deal on terminology (Gordon, 1981). We find it useful to distinguish people's ideology or beliefs about the nature of love from their subjective experiences in a close relationship.

Love Ideologies

A distinction has frequently been made between romantic versus pragmatic beliefs about love (e.g., Hobart, 1958; Knox & Sporakowski, 1968). The romantic person believes that true love lasts forever, comes but once, is strange and incomprehensible, and conquers barriers of custom or social class. The pragmatist rejects these ideals, knowing that we can each love many people, that economic security is more important than passion, and that some disillusionment surely accompanies marriage.

By these criteria, men are apparently more romantic than women. Several studies (e.g., Fengler, 1974; Hobart, 1958; Knox & Sporakowski, 1968; Rubin, 1970; Rubin, Peplau, & Hill, 1981) have found small but consistent sex differences on various romanticism scales. Further evidence comes from responses to questions about the importance of love as a basis for marriage. For example, Kephart (1967) asked students, "If a boy (girl) had all the other qualities you desired, would you marry this person if you were not in love with him/her?" Most of the men (65%) said no, compared to only 24% of the women. Finally, recent research developing a typology of six styles or orientations to love (e.g., Hatkoff & Lasswell, 1979; Lasswell & Lobsenz, 1980; Lee, 1977) further corroborates this picture. Hatkoff and Lasswell (1979) found that women were more likely than men to adopt "logical" or "best friends" approaches to love. Men were more likely to be "romantics" who believed in love at first sight, or "game players" who enjoyed flirtation.

Intrigued by these findings, social scientists have freely speculated about the reasons for men's greater romanticism. The most common explanation concerns the social and economic context of mate selection. As Waller (1938) explained, "A man, when he marries, chooses a companion and perhaps a helpmate, but a woman chooses a companion and at the same time a standard of living. It is necessary for a woman to be mercenary" (p. 243). Men, it seems, can afford to be more frivolous in love. Other explanations (see Rubin et al., 1981) have emphasized women's presumed lesser emotional dependence on men, or have cited the greater stigma of spinsterhood as a reason for women's willingness to marry regardless of love (Knox & Sporakowski, 1968). Whether social changes increasing women's financial independence and making singlehood more acceptable will alter these sex differences remains to be seen.

The Experience of Love

Another research tradition has investigated sex differences in the intensity of a person's feelings toward his or her partner. Rubin (1970, 1973) argued that love and liking are qualitatively distinct attitudes toward another person, and he developed separate scales to assess each. The 9-item Liking Scale measures feelings or respect and affection toward another. The 9-item Love Scale assesses feelings of attachment, caring, and intimacy. Rubin found that, on the average, boyfriends and girlfriends love each other equally yet girlfriends reported greater liking for their dating partner. . . .

The Symptoms of Romantic Love Although the sexes may not differ in global assessments of their love for each other, other aspects of the love experience do distinguish men and women. In dating relationships, women are more likely than men to report various emotional symptoms of love. In one study (Kanin, Davidson & Scheck, 1970), women were more likely to report that they were "floating on a cloud," "wanted to run, jump or scream," had "trouble concentrating," "felt giddy and carefree," and had a general sense of well-being. Dion and Dion (1973, 1975) also found greater feelings of euphoria among women. Whether these results represent actual sex differences in the experience of love, or simply women's greater willingness to disclose intimate feelings is unclear.

Speed of Falling in Love Rubin, Peplau, and Hill (1981) have reviewed evidence that men tend to fall in love more readily than women. For example, men report that they recognize feelings of love earlier in the development of a relationship than do women (Burgess & Wallin, 1953; Cate & Huston, 1980; Kanin et al., 1970). In a computer dating study (Coombs & Kenkel, 1966), men reported greater "romantic attraction" to their randomly assigned partner than did women. In another study (Kephart, 1967), twice as many men as women said they were "very easily attracted" to opposite-sex partners. And, among college dating couples, Rubin (1970) found that in short-term relationships, men scored higher on his Love Scale than did their girlfriends; no sex differences were found among longer-term couples. These differences may be tied to men's greater romanticism, but they may also result from men's greater emphasis on physical attractiveness in a partner—a characteristic that is easily ascertained. The man's role as initiator in dating relationships may also contribute to his higher level of initial attraction.

Which sex is more romantic? Discussions of this matter will benefit from greater precision in terminology. Among young adults, men are stronger proponents of a romantic love ideology than are women, and men report falling in love earlier in the development of a relationship. But women report more emotional and euphoric symptoms of love. The origins of these sex differences, like the romantic's conception of love, remains mysterious.

Communication

Are women the expressive or socio-emotional leaders in close relationships? The discussion of this issue has often suffered from vagueness in defining the central concept. We focus specifically on research about gender differences in self-disclosure and interactional style.

Self-Disclosure

The sharing of intimate feelings is often considered the hallmark of a close relationship (Jourard, 1959). Yet folk wisdom, suggests that men are often less expressive than women. A working class couple interviewed by Lillian Rubin illustrates this pattern:

> Wife: He doesn't ever think there's anything to talk about. I'm the one who has to nag him to talk always, and then I get disgusted.
>
> Husband: I'm pretty tight-lipped about most things most of the time, especially personal things. I don't express what I think or feel. She keeps trying to get me to, but, you know, it's hard (cited in L. B. Rubin, 1976, p. 124).

Just how common are the sex differences in disclosure found in this couple? The clearest evidence of sex differences comes from studies of same-sex friendship. Throughout adult life, women often disclose more personal information to friends than do men (Cozby, 1973), and are more likely to say that they have an intimate, same-sex confidant (Booth, 1972; Booth & Hess, 1974; Lowenthal & Haven, 1968). Women are also more likely to enjoy "just talking" with their same-sex friends, and to say that talking helped form the basis of their relationship (Caldwell & Peplau, 1982).

Studies of heterosexual couples present a more complex picture. In general, people disclose more to their spouse than to anyone else (Jourard & Lasakow, 1958; Rosenfeld, Civikly, & Heron, 1979). A norm of reciprocity in self-disclosure generally encourages similar levels of disclosure between partners. Nonetheless, wives sometimes disclose more than their husbands do (Burke, Weir & Harrison, 1976; Hendrick, 1981; Jourard, 1971; Komarovsky, 1967; Levinger & Senn, 1967). This sex difference has been observed in both working-class and middle-class couples. For example, in *Blue Collar Marriage* (1967), Komarovsky reported diverse patterns of self-disclosure: 35% of the couples interviewed had equal and full disclosure by both spouses, 10% had equal and moderate disclosure, and 24% had equal but meager disclosure. In 21% of the couples, the wife disclosed more; in 10% the husband disclosed more. Education and social class often have dramatic efforts on the general level of self-disclosure by both husbands and wives. Komarovsky found that only 35% of men with less than a high school education disclosed fully to their wives, compared with 61% of those men who had completed high school. In Komarovsky's view, the less educated working-class man is the prototype of the inexpressive male.

Komarovsky argues that when there is low disclosure in a marriage, it is typically the husband who blocks communication. This would be consistent with the notion that men generally prefer lower levels of verbal communication. Burke and Weir (1977) examined how spouses react to stress. They found that wives were more willing to tell their husbands when they were feeling tense and to try to explain their feelings. In general, women may be more likely than men to seek emotional support from other people when they are feeling stressed or depressed (e.g., DeBurger, 1967; Funkabiki, Bologna, Pepping & Fitzgerald, 1980; Pearlin & Schooler, 1978).

Some studies of college students (e.g., Komarovsky, 1976; Rubin, Hill, Peplau & Dunkel-Schetter, 1980) suggest that younger, more educated couples may be moving away from the traditional pattern of silent men and talkative women toward a pattern of more equal and intimate disclosure by both sexes. For example, a study of college dating couples (Rubin et al., 1980) found that high proportions of both men and women reported having disclosed their thoughts and feelings "fully" to their partners in almost all domains. Disclosure was higher among men and women who had egalitarian sex-role attitudes than among more traditional couples. A few small sex differences were found. When students perceived unequal disclosure in their relationships, it was more often the man who was considered less revealing. Men revealed less than women on specific topics, such as their greatest fears. Overall, however, disclosure tended to be quite symmetrical. Taken together, self-disclosure research shows that women are sometimes—but not always—more verbally expressive than men. The extent to which this pattern is influenced by social class, education, and changing cultural values is an important topic for future research. . . .

Power and Decision-Making

Power is a basic element in all relationships, yet it has proved frustratingly difficult for researchers to investigate in close relationships. Research on power in dating and marital relationships has encountered knotty conceptual and methodological problems (see Cromwell & Olson, 1975; Huston, 1983; Safilios-Rothschild, 1970). We consider three aspects of power: sex-typing in domains of decision-making, the balance of power in a relationship, and power tactics.

Decision-Making: His and Hers

Although most American couples say that many of their decisions are "mutual," partners usually do have sex-typed areas of influence. Boyfriends may have greater say about recreational activities, making decisions about how a couple spends their leisure time together; girlfriends may have more say about progress toward sexual intimacy in the relationship (Peplau, 1984). In marriage, husbands typically make decisions about their own job, the family car, and insurance. Wives typically decide about meals, home decorating, and the family doctor (cf., Blood & Wolfe, 1960; Centers, Raven & Rodrigues, 1971). The division of labor between the sexes includes not only who does which tasks, but also who makes various decisions.

The Balance of Power

Is the general power structure of American heterosexual relationships male-dominant or egalitarian? Unfortunately, research provides no definitive answer to this deceptively simple question.

A common approach to assessing marital power (e.g., Blood & Wolfe, 1960; Centers et al., 1971) is to ask one spouse to indicate which partner typically makes each of several types of decisions (e.g., about insurance and home decorating). These are summed to arrive at an overall index indicating whether one spouse makes more decisions than the other. Studies using this method have often concluded that American marriages are usually egalitarian. For example, Centers et al. (1971) reported that only about 10% of marriages were husband-dominant, 4% were wife-dominant, and the rest were relatively egalitarian (i.e., decisions were either shared or divided equally). The interpretation of these and similar findings is, however, controversial (see discussion by Safilios-Rothschild, 1970).

In these decision-making studies, researchers decide a priori which family decisions are important and determine how to combine these decisions into an overall index of family power. In a widely cited study, Blood and Wolfe (1960) deliberately included four "masculine" areas and four "feminine" areas, weighted each type of decision equally, and then concluded that most couples are egalitarian. The assumptions implicit in this research strategy are questionable: Whether the husband's decision to move the family to a new city in order to advance his career is equivalent to the wife's decision to serve the family pot roast is open to debate. Of equal concern is that participants in a relationship may perceive and evaluate power differently than observers (Olson, 1977). The wife who appears to outsiders to make most of the family's decisions may actually cater scrupulously to her husband's wishes and see herself as implementing his ideas. In addition, partners may differ from each other in their views about the balance of power in their relationship (Hill, Peplau & Rubin, 1981; Peplau, 1984).

One alternative approach has been to ask individuals about their perceptions of power in the relationship. For example, one study (Peplau, 1984) asked members of college dating couples, "Who do you think has more of a say about what you and your partner do together—your partner or you?" Only about 45% of the young adults thought that their relationship was "exactly equal" in power. When the relationship was unequal, students said it was usually the man who had more say (40%) rather than the woman (15%). The high proportion of students reporting greater male power is all the more striking given that most students rejected a patriarchal model for relationships. When asked which partner should ideally have more say, 95% of women and 87% of men said that both partners should ideally have exactly equal say.

The analysis of factors that tip the balance of power in favor of one partner rather than the other has been a topic of sustained research interest (e.g., Cromwell & Olson, 1975; Peplau, 1984; Rollins & Bahr, 1976). Three factors seem important. First, social convention has long given men greater status and authority in male-female relations (cf., Bernard,

1972). The belief that the husband should be the "head" of the family, or that the boyfriend has the right to be "leader" can give men a power advantage in heterosexual relationships. Second, consistent with social exchange theory (Blau, 1964; Thibaut & Kelley, 1959), the balance of power is influenced by the relative resources of the partners, such as education or income. For example, in Peplau's (1984) study of college couples, the woman's educational and career goals were an important predictor of power. If the girlfriend aspired to less than a bachelor's degree, 87% of the students reported that the man had greater power; if the girlfriend planned to pursue an advanced degree, only 30% reported that the man had greater power. There is also evidence (e.g., Heer, 1958) that paid employment increases wives' relative power in marriage. Kidder et al. (1981) have suggested that the prospects for an egalitarian relationship are further enhanced when both partners contribute and receive similar rewards from a relationship. A third factor influencing power is the relative involvement or dependency of the two partners. As social exchange theory predicts, when there is an imbalance of involvement in a relationship, the partner who is less involved often has greater influence. Dependency on a relationship can be based on many factors, including both attraction to the partner, and the lack of alternative opportunities. Traditional marital roles have put wives at a power disadvantage, as Bernard (1972) colorfully notes:

> Take a young woman who has been trained for feminine dependencies, who wants to "look up" to the man she marries. Put her at a disadvantage in the labor market. Then marry her to a man who has a slight initial advantage over her in age, income, and education, shored up by an ideology with a male bias. . . . Then expect an egalitarian relationship? (p. 146)

The effects of contemporary changes in sex roles on power in male-female relationships are an important topic for future research.

Power Strategies

Another facet of power in close relationships concerns the tactics that individuals use to try to influence one another. Only a few studies of power strategies have explicitly focused on dating and marital relationships (Falbo & Peplau, 1980; Frieze, 1979; Kaplan, 1975; McCormick & Jesser, 1983; Raven, Centers, & Rodrigues, 1975; Raush, Barry, Hertel, & Swain, 1974; Raven, Centers, & Rodrigues, 1975). Although it is too early to draw firm conclusions about sex differences in power tactics, the available data are provocative.

In one study (Raven et al., 1975), wives were more likely to attribute "expert" power to their husbands than vice versa. Husbands indicated that their wives more often used "referent" power, appealing to the fact that they were all part of the same family and should see eye to eye. In a study of interaction in dating couples, Kaplan (1975) found that boyfriends offered information more often than their girlfriends did. Girlfriends were more likely to disagree with an idea or contradict information given by their boyfriend. Kaplan suggested that whereas men take an assertive stance, women derive power from resisting male initiatives. Kaplan viewed this as consistent with a traditional pattern in which the man "proposes" and the woman "opposes."

In another study of college dating relationships, Falbo and Peplau (1980) found that men were more likely to report using direct and mutual power strategies, such as bargaining or logical arguments, than were women. In contrast, women were more likely to report using indirect and unilateral strategies, such as becoming silent and withdrawn, or pouting. Women's strategies were similar to those of individuals (regardless of sex) who perceived themselves as relatively less powerful than their partner.

Somewhat similar results were found in Raush et al.'s (1974) study of newlyweds. In role-playing conflictual interactions, husbands more often attempted to resolve the conflict and restore harmony; wives more often were cold and rejecting, or used appeals to fairness or guilt induction. The researchers suggested that "women, as a low power group, may learn a diplomacy of psychological pressure to influence male partners' behavior" (p. 153). In a more recent study, Gottman (1979) examined the behavior of spouses in structured situations varying in degrees of conflict. In low conflict situations, the husband responded to the wife's negative behavior in a positive way more often. In the high conflict situations, however, it was the wife who was agreeable and expressed positive affect in response to the husband's complaints. Gottman concluded that "in our culture, it appears to be the wife's responsibility to keep negative affect from escalating in high conflict situations" (p. 210).

Another perspective on the complex matter of how men and women respond in conflict situations is provided by Kelley and his associates (1978). They investigated what young couples say and do during naturally occurring conflicts. Both sexes expected the woman to cry and sulk, and to criticize the boyfriend for his insensitivity to her feelings. The man was expected (again, by both sexes) to show anger, to reject the woman's tears, to call for a logical and less emotional approach to the problem, and to give reasons for delaying the discussion. Partners in actual dating relationships reported that their conflict interactions were consistent with these stereotypes. Kelley et al. interpreted this pattern as reflecting gender differences in people's general orientation to conflict. The man is a conflict-avoidant person who finds the display of emotions uncomfortable or upsetting. The woman is a conflict-confronting person, who is frustrated by avoidance and asks that the problem be discussed and that feelings be considered. Kelley et al. further suggested that the placating behavior seen in the husbands studied by Rausch et al. (1974) reveals how a conflict-avoidant person behaves when he or she cannot escape dealing with an issue. Kelley et al. proposed that these sex differences in the approach to conflict stem from the socialization of women as socioemotional specialists, and the socialization of men as task specialists. It seems equally plausible to us that different orientations to conflict reflect the current power structure of a relationship. If men have greater power in a relationship, they may have nothing to gain by discussing problems with their partner and may benefit from avoidance. If women have lesser power, they may see confrontation as the only way to protect or to enhance their own position.

Finally, although Americans like to think of close relationships in sentimental terms, it is important to recognize that physical coercion can and does occur. In survey studies of marital power tactics (e.g., Raven et al., 1975), few spouses reported the use of coercion of any kind. But, as Frieze (1979) has pointed out, these data may be affected by social desirability biases. In a study using in-depth interviews, Frieze (1979) found higher rates of reported coercive tactics. It is likely that physical force is most often used as a last resort when other influence strategies appear ineffective. Nonetheless, researchers (e.g., Steinmetz, 1978) estimate that about 3.3 million American wives and over a quarter million husbands have experienced severe beatings from their spouses. Although we do not have precise information on how frequently physical coercion is used as an influence strategy, it appears that this tactic is predominantly used by men against women.

In summary, research suggests that men and women do use somewhat different power tactics to influence one another. These differences may reflect three interrelated factors. First, as a result of sex-role socialization, men and women may learn somewhat different influence strategies or approaches to interpersonal conflict. It is difficult, for example, to imagine a traditional American husband using tears as a power tactic. Second, men and women may have characteristically different goals in interpersonal interactions. Kelley et al. (1978) linked conflict behavior to preferences for avoiding versus confronting conflict. In another context, McCormick (1979) demonstrated that sex differences in influence tactics used in sexual encounters are closely tied to men's goal of persuading a partner to have sex, and women's desire to resist sexual advances. Third, both power tactics and interpersonal goals may reflect, in some measure, the general power structure of heterosexual relationships. To the extent that partners have different resources in terms of skills, physical strength, expertise, money, and the like, they may be disposed to use different power strategies.

Satisfaction and Well-Being

Cultural stereotypes often depict marriage as a crowning achievement for women, who "finally trap a man," and something of a defeat for men, who are forced to abandon the "carefree" life of a bachelor. These images might lead us to believe that women are more satisfied with their love relationships than are men. Yet research examining subjective satisfaction with relationships, and the impact of relationships on psychological well-being find few sex differences. If anything, marriage may be more beneficial to men than to women (Bernard, 1972).

Satisfaction

Much research has examined partners' evaluations of their satisfaction or happiness in a relationship, especially marriage. Despite both methodological and conceptual problems with this literature (discussed by Aldous, Osmond, & Hick, 1979; Laws, 1971; Lewis & Spanier, 1979; McNamara & Bahr, 1980), several general trends can be identified.

No consistent sex differences have been found in global ratings of personal satisfaction with dating relationships or marriage. In dating relationships, boyfriends and girlfriends usually report equal and high levels of satisfaction and closeness (e.g., Cochran & Peplau, in press; Risman, Hill, Rubin, & Peplau, 1981). Presumably, most dating relationships that are not mutually gratifying are short-lived.

Studies of marital satisfaction are more numerous and complex (see reviews by Aldous et al., 1979; Hicks & Platt, 1970; Lewis & Spanier, 1979). In general, most husbands and wives report that their marriage is satisfying, and spouses' happiness ratings are positively correlated. Differences between the sexes, when they do emerge, are small. The results from three large surveys investigating the quality of life in many domains are illustrative. Gurin, Veroff, and Feld (1960) asked Americans to rate the quality of their marriage. Similar proportions of men and women rated their marriage as "very happy" (45% of the women and 48% of the men), and as "not at all happy" (3% of the women, 2% of the men). In another large-scale study (Bradburn, 1969), about 60% of wives and husbands rated their marriage as "very happy." The exception to this pattern occurred among those in the lower socio-economic group, where only 49% of wives compared to 59% of husbands rated their marriage as "very happy." In a more recent survey by Campbell, Converse, and Rodgers (1976), 56% of wives and 60% of husbands indicated that they were "completely" satisfied with their marriage. Asked if they had ever wished they had married someone else, 70% of the women and 72% of the men said they had "never" wished for a different spouse.

The marriage and family literature contains many smaller-scale investigations of marital satisfaction that have produced inconsistent sex differences. Several studies have found that husbands report higher marital satisfaction than wives (e.g., Burr, 1970; Komarovsky, 1967; Renne, 1970). A few studies (e.g., Spanier, Lewis & Cole, 1975) have found that at certain times in the life cycle, women report greater marital satisfaction. Other studies have found no sex differences (e.g., Gilford & Bengtson, 1979; Rollins & Cannon, 1974). We conclude that there are probably no appreciable differences in the reported marital satisfaction of most American husbands and wives, although, small sex differences may occur in specific subpopulations.

Although global assessments of marital satisfaction are quite similar for men and women, it is useful to examine the ways in which gender and sex roles may influence marital quality for both spouses. We turn now to a consideration of sex differences in the correlates of marital satisfaction, and to an examination of the impact of role differentiation, role consensus, paid employment, and the balance of power on satisfaction.

Gender Differences in the Correlates of Satisfaction Global assessments of martial satisfaction may have somewhat different determinants for women and for men. For example, Levinger (1964) found that global marital satisfaction was related to expressions of affection and supportiveness for both sexes (see also Hendrick, 1981). However, sexual satisfaction was more strongly related to overall marital satisfaction for husbands than for wives, and communication was of greater importance to wives than to husbands. A more recent study (Wills, Weiss & Patterson, 1974) found that for husbands (but not wives), marital satisfaction was related to the frequency of pleasurable instrumental activities in the relationship. For wives (but not for husbands), marital satisfaction was associated with the frequency of pleasurable affectional activities. An examination of the factors that contribute to marital satisfaction for both sexes is an important direction for future research.

Role Differentiation Is marital satisfaction linked to the overall degree of sex-role differentiation—whether husband and wife have rigidly distinct versus shared roles? Two different views on this matter can be identified (Aldous et al., 1979). Some (e.g., Parsons, 1955) have argued that the existence of clear-cut and complementary roles is beneficial to marriage and to the spouses' happiness. in contrast, others such as Komarovsky (1967) have proposed that the "separate worlds of the sexes" in traditional marriage set the stage for marital discontent.

Empirical evidence about the impact of role differentiation on marital happiness is mixed. In a study of British couples, Bott (1971) found no relationship between marital satisfaction and the degree of role segregation. Similar results were obtained in a study of middle-class American families (Rainwater, 1965). But some evidence has been found linking role-sharing in marriage to greater enjoyment of couple activities (Rapoport, Rapoport & Thiessen, 1974), and to reporting fewer serious problems in marriage (Rainwater, 1965). In a study of blue collar marriages, Komarovsky (1967) found that the divergent interests of the sexes contributed to dissatisfaction with marital communication. One reason for these mixed findings may be that people's global assessments of marital satisfaction are based not only on their actual experiences, but also on their aspirations (Komarovsky, 1967). Couples with rigid differentiation of husband—wife roles may expect little interaction or sharing between spouses, and judge their marriage on that basis. More generally, traditional and nontraditional couples may use different yardsticks in assessing marital success.

Role Consensus The specific pattern of interaction that a couple adopts is probably less important to satisfaction than whether the partners agree about the pattern. Several studies (reviewed in Hicks & Platt, 1970; Lewis & Spanier, 1979) document the importance of "role fit" or consensus between the marital role expectations and behavior of spouses (e.g., Chadwick, Albrecht & Kunz, 1976). It seems almost a truism that an ardent feminist who desires shared roles in marriage will be happier with a partner who supports these views than with a staunch traditionalist (cf. Bahr & Day, 1978). Disagreement between spouses about marital roles is a major source of potential conflict and dissatisfaction.

Several older studies (reviewed in Hicks & Platt, 1970; Laws, 1971) found that marital satisfaction was significantly linked to the wife's ability to perceive her husband as he perceives himself, and to conform to his expectations—but not vice versa. Laws (1971) referred to this as the norm of wife-accommodation, and explained that "an accommodative (or empathic, or considerate) spouse contributes to *anyone's* marital satisfaction, . . . and the social norms decree that it shall be the wife's role" (p. 501). This pattern may occur because husbands and wives share a stereotype of masculinity and perceive the husband as enacting it. The opposite pattern has not been found; marital satisfaction is not related to the husband's ability to perceive the wife as she sees herself. New research on this issue would be useful.

Paid Employment Many studies have found that the greater the husband's occupational success and income, the greater the marital satisfaction of both spouses (Lewis & Spanier, 1979). Recently, Aldous et al. (1979) suggested that this relationship may actually be curvilinear, with extremely low and high occupational success by the husband detracting from the enjoyment of marriage. The impact of the wife's employment status on marital satisfaction is more controversial.

Some family theorists such as Parsons (1955) have viewed role differentiation as essential to marital success and so emphasized the hazards of wives' venturing into the occupational domain. Early studies (reviewed in Hicks & Platt, 1970) seemed to show that marriages were often less happy when wives were employed fulltime, rather than being fulltime homemakers or working for pay only parttime. More recent studies (e.g., Booth, 1979; Staines, Pleck, Shepard, & O'Connor, 1978) cast doubt on this conclusion, however, and suggest that the impact of wives' employment on marital satisfaction is complex. Research is beginning to identify factors that influence the impact of wives' employment on marital satisfaction—such as social class, the woman's choice of employment, and the husband's attitudes about his wife's employment. In thinking about this issue, it seems essential to distinguish wives who enjoy paid employment and have supportive husbands from wives who prefer to stay home, or whose husbands object to their employment.

Several studies show that paid employment can have beneficial effects for wives. For example, Burke and Weir (1976) found that employed wives were happier and had higher self-esteem than did fulltime homemakers. The impact of the wife's employment on her husband's marital satisfaction has been a recent topic for inquiry. Burke and Weir reported that husbands were more satisfied with their marriage and were healthier when their wives did not work fulltime for pay. But studies with larger samples and better controls (e.g., Booth, 1979; Staines et al., 1978) have not replicated this pattern. Rather, no relationship has been found between the wife's employment status and her husband's marital happiness, experience of stress, or personal health. We agree with Lewis and Spanier (1979) that overall marital satisfaction is probably highest when both partners are satisfied with the wife's employment status.

The Balance of Power Satisfaction in heterosexual relationships is significantly associated with the balance of power or decision-making. One study (Peplau, 1984) examined the balance of power in college-age dating couples. No differences were found between equal-power and male-dominant couples on measures of satisfaction, closeness, or staying together versus breaking up over a two-year period. In contrast, however, both boyfriends and girlfriends reported less satisfaction in relationships where the woman had greater say. Studies of married couples (e.g., Blood & Wolfe, 1960; Centers et al., 1971; Lu, 1952; Rainwater, 1965) have generally found high levels of satisfaction among both egalitarian and male-dominant marriages, and lesser satisfaction among female-dominant marriages. Illustrative findings come from a study by Centers et al. (1971). Over 70% of individuals in husband-dominant and egalitarian marriages reported being "very satisfied," compared to only 20% of those in wife-dominant relationships. Minor variations have been found across studies in whether greater satisfaction is found among egalitarian or male-dominant couples; no clear conclusion emerges on this point. It is usually more comfortable, however, to adhere to traditional patterns of male dominance or newer patterns of egalitarianism than to experience female dominance.

Psychological Well-Being

Although husbands and wives typically report roughly equal satisfaction—or dissatisfaction—with their marriage, evidence suggests that marriage provides greater health benefits to men than to women. In general, married individuals enjoy better mental and physical health, report greater happiness and psychological well-being, and experience fewer symptoms of psychological distress than do the single, divorced, or widowed. But evidence also indicates that the positive effects of marital status are greater for men than for women (Bernard, 1972; Dohrenwend & Dohrenwend, 1976; Gove, 1972; Knupfer, Clark & Room, 1966; Lynch, 1977; Pearlin & Johnson, 1977). Gove (1979) concluded that "marriage is more beneficial to men than women, whereas being single is if anything more stressful for men than for women" (p. 57). A common pattern is for married men to score highest on measures of psychological well-being, married and single women to score moderately, and single men to receive the lowest scores. For example, Perlman, Gerson and Spinner (1978) found that widowed men were significantly lonelier than married men; among women, no significant difference was found in loneliness between those who were married and those who were widowed. Although some contradictory evidence has been reported (e.g., Warheit, Holzer, Bell, & Arey, 1976), the bulk of existing research suggests that husbands often enjoy better mental health than wives.

The reasons for the differential effects of marriage for women and men are not well understood, but several possible explanations have been offered (e.g., Bernard, 1972; Peplau, Bikson, Rook, & Goodchilds, 1982). Although response biases and differential selection into marriage for women and men may contribute to this pattern (Bernard, 1972), they do not offer a complete explanation (Gove, 1979). Several researchers have suggested that the traditional homemaker's role is less rewarding than the breadwinner's role. Housework is seen as unstructured, frustrating, and low in prestige (Gove, 1979). For employed wives, there may also be problems of role overload, since husbands do not typically share fully in homemaking and childcare (e.g., Robinson, et al., 1977). Power differences favoring husbands may also contribute in some cases. In short, it has been proposed that asymmetries in the roles of husbands and wives, and inequities in the family division of labor may put women at a disadvantage.

Others have suggested that men benefit from marriage in part because wives serve as important social and emotional resources for their husbands. For example, it is often wives who initiate and maintain relations with friends and relatives. Knupfer, Clark, and Room (1966) speculated that the "man's lesser ability to form and maintain personal relationships creates a need for a wife, as the expressive expert, to perform this function for him" (p. 848). As a result, unmarried men experience an "expressive hardship." The caring functions of the wife may extend into nursing the husband when he is ill and encouraging him to take care of his own health (Troll & Turner, 1979).

At present, the reasons why marriage contributes more to the psychological health of husbands than of wives remain an intriguing puzzle. Speculations abound, but are typically post hoc and unsubstantiated by solid research. Equally puzzling is the discrepancy between findings for marital happiness and psychological well-being. Even though wives exhibit more psychological distress than husbands, both groups report roughly equal marital satisfaction. A better understanding of the social and psychological factors that determine satisfaction with relationships is needed. We know little about the psychological algebra that people use in arriving at overall assessments of their relationships, and whether such processes differ by gender or sex role. . . .

Building Successful Relationships

A concern with relationships (and their dissolution) raises questions about how to create gratifying relationships. Feminist psychologists have challenged traditional psychological prescriptions. At the level of personality, it was once believed that healthy adults had to have a clearcut and secure sense of their "masculinity" or "femininity" (see Pleck, 1981b). Today, psychologists are suggesting that greater sex-role flexibility, whether it is called androgyny or sex-role transcendence (e.g., Garnets & Pleck, 1979) is beneficial to individual functioning. At the dyadic level, a similar shift is occurring. Family sociologists (e.g., Parsons, 1955) used to emphasize the benefits of highly differentiated male-female roles in marriage. Such patterns were believed to increase efficiency, decrease competition and conflict, foster mutual dependency, and encourage marital stability. Today, all of these assumptions have been questioned (see Peplau, 1983). It is argued instead that traditional male-female roles often prevent partners from being the kind of companion each wants (e.g., Friedland, 1982). There is a growing belief that role sharing and flexibility may be more beneficial to heterosexual relationships.

It should be emphasized, of course, that research demonstrating the benefits of egalitarian relationships is very limited. Nonetheless, examples of the inhibiting effects of traditional sex differences are readily found. Rubin (1976) has described one marriage:

> When they try to talk, she relies on the only tools she has. . . . She becomes progressively more emotional and expressive. He falls back on the only tools he has; he gets progressively more rational—determinedly reasonable. She cries for him to attend to her feelings. . . . He tells her it's silly to feel that way. . . . [His] clench-teeth reasonableness invalidates her feelings (p. 117).

Clinical discussions emphasize similar problems. For instance, Napier (1978) has described a "rejection-intrusion" pattern in distressed couples. One partner, typically the woman, seeks closeness and reassurance while the other, typically the man, desires greater separateness and independence. When the woman's bids for affection are rebuffed, she feels hurt, rejected and misunderstood. As a result of the wife's attempts at closeness, the husband feels intruded upon and engulfed. Whether socialization for sex-role similarity and the building of relationships based on equality would reduce such problems is an intriguing question.

A Social Psychology of Close Relationships

Social psychology has been criticized from time to time (e.g., Pepitone, 1981) for an overemphasis on individual processes such as impression formation or social cognition, and for a neglect of interpersonal processes in dyads and groups. The renewed interest of recent years in close relationships promises to move research on couples more squarely into the mainstream of American social psychology (Kelley et al., 1983). We welcome this change in the field.

As social psychologists seek to broaden their understanding of social relationships, the impact of gender and culturally-based sex roles cannot be ignored. Symons (1979) has argued that "the comparison of males and females is perhaps the most powerful available means of ordering the bewildering diversity of data on human sexuality" (p. 4). This argument can be extended to many aspects of social interactions; gender differences are a common feature of heterosexual relationships in contemporary society. Bernard's (1972) notion that in every marriage (and we would add in every heterosexual relationship) there are really two relationships—his and hers—which are experienced differently and which have distinct personal consequences for each sex is compelling. No examination of close relationships can be wholly complete or wholly accurate unless it recognizes differences in the experiences and behaviors of women and men. The careful description and causal analysis of gender differences in relationships is a major avenue for understanding basic processes of interaction in close relationships.

References

Aldous, J., Osmond, M. W., & Hicks, M. W. (1979). Men's work and men's families. In W. R. Burr, R. Hill, F. I. Nye & I. L. Reiss (Eds.), *Contemporary theories about the family* (Vol. 1). New York: Free Press.

Allgeier, E. R., & McCormick, N. B. (Eds.) (1983). *Changing boundaries: Gender roles and sexual behavior.* Palo Alto, Calif.: Mayfield.

Aronoff, J., & Crano, W. D. (1975). A re-examination of the cross-cultural principles of task segregation and sex role differentiation in the family. *American Sociological Review, 40*, 12–20.

Astin, A. W., King, M., & Richardson, G. T. (1980). *The American freshman: National norms for fall 1980.* Los Angeles: American Council on Education.

Bahr, S. J., & Day, R. D. (1978). Sex role attitudes, female employment, and marital satisfaction. *Journal of Comparative Family Studies, 9*, 55–65.

Beckman, L. J., & Houser, B. B. (1979). The more you have, the more you do: The relationships between wife's employment, sex-role attitudes and household behavior. *Psychology of Women Quarterly, 4*(2), 160–174.
Berk, R. A., & Berk, S. F. (1979). *Labor and leisure at home: Content and organization of the household day.* Beverly Hills, Calif.: Sage.
Berk, S. F. (Ed.) (1980). *Women and household labor.* Beverly Hills, Calif: Sage.
Bernard, J. (1972). *The future of marriage.* New York: Bantam Books.
Berscheid, E., & Walster, E. H. (1978). *Interpersonal attraction* (2nd ed.). Menlo Park, Calif: Addison-Wesley.
Blau, P. M. (1964). *Exchange and power in social life.* New York: Wiley.
Blood, R. O., & Wolfe, D. M. (1960). *Husbands and wives: The dynamics of married living.* New York: Free Press.
Booth, A. (1972). Sex and social participation. *American Sociological Review, 37,* 183–193.
Booth, A. (1979). Does wives' employment cause stress for husbands? *The Family Coordinator, 28*(4), 445–449.
Booth, A., & Hess, E. (1974). Cross-sex friendship. *Journal of Marriage and the Family, 36,* 38–47.
Bott, E. (1971). *Family and social network* (2nd ed). New York: Free Press.
Bradburn, N. (1969). *The structure of psychological well-being.* Chicago: Aldine.
Bryson, R. B., Bryson, J. B., Licht, M. H., & Licht, B. G. (1976). The professional pair: Husband and wife psychologists. *American Psychologist, 31*(1), 10–16.
Burchinal, L. G. (1964). The premarital dyad and love involvement. In H. T. Christensen (Ed.), *Handbook of marriage and the family.* Chicago: Rand McNally.
Burgess, E. W., & Locke, H. J. (1960). *The family: From institution to companionship* (2nd ed.). New York: American.
Burgess, E. W., & Wallin, P. (1953). *Engagement and marriage.* Philadelphia: Lippincott.
Burgess, R. L., & Huston, T. L. (Eds.) (1979). *Social exchange in developing relationships.* New York: Academic Press.
Burke, R. J., & Weir, T. (1976). Relationship of wives' employment status to husband, wife and pair satisfaction and performance. *Journal of Marriage and the Family, 38,* 279–287.
Burke, R. J., & Weir, T. (1977). Husband-wife helping relationships: The "mental hygiene" function in marriage. *Psychological Reports, 40,* 911–925.
Burke, R. J., Weir, T., & Harrison, D. (1976). Disclosure of problems and tensions experienced by marital partners. *Psychological Reports, 38,* 531–542.
Burr, W. R. (1970). Satisfaction with various aspects of marriage over the life cycle. *Journal of Marriage and the Family, 32,* 29–37.
Byrne, D., & Griffitt, W. (1973). Interpersonal attraction. In P. H. Mussen & M. R. Rosenzweig (Eds.), *Annual Review of psychology.* Palo Alto, Calif.: Annual Review.

Caldwell, M. A., & Peplau, L. A. (1982). Sex differences in same-sex friendship.*Sex Roles, 8*(7), 721–732.

Campbell, A., Converse, P. E., & Rodgers, W. L. (1976). *The quality of American life.* New York: Russell Sage Foundation.

Cate, R. M., & Huston, T. L. (1980). *The growth of premarital relationships: Toward a typology of pathways to marriage.* Unpublished manuscript, Oregon State University.

Centers, R., Raven, B. H., & Rodrigues, A. (1971). Conjugal power structure: A re-examination. *American Sociological Review, 36*, 264–278.

Chadwick, B. A., Albrecht, S. L., & Kunz, P. R. (1976). Marital and family role satisfaction. *Journal of Marriage and the Family, 38*(3), 431–450.

Cochran, S. D., & Peplau, L. A. (in press). Value orientations in heterosexual relationships. *Psychology of Women Quarterly.*

Cook, M., & Wilson, G. (Eds.) (1979). *Love and attraction.* Oxford, England: Pergamon.

Coombs, R. H., & Kenkel, W. F. (1966). Sex differences in dating aspirations and satisfaction with computer-selected partners. *Journal of Marriage and the Family, 28*, 62–66.

Cozby, P. C. (1973). Self-disclosure: A literature review. *Psychological Bulletin, 79*, 73–91.

Cromwell, R. E., & Olson, D. H. (Eds.) (1975). *Power in families.* New York: Wiley.

DeBurger, J. E. (1967). Marital problems, help-seeking, and emotional orientation as revealed in help-request letters. *Journal of Marriage and the Family, 29*, 712–721.

Degler, C. N. (1980). *At odds: Women and the family in America from the revolution to the present.* New York: Oxford University Press.

Derlega, V. J., Durham, B., Gockel, B., & Sholis, D. (1981). Sex differences in self-disclosure: Effects of topic content, friendship and partner's sex. *Sex Roles,* 7(4), 433–447.

Dion, K. K., & Dion, K. L. (1975). Self-esteem and romantic love. *Journal of Personality, 43*, 39–57.

Dion, K. L., & Dion, K. K. (1973). Correlates of romantic love. *Journal of Consulting and Clinical Psychology, 41*, 51–56.

Dohrenwend, B. P., & Dohrenwend, B. S. (1976). Sex differences in psychiatric disorders. *American Journal of Sociology, 81*, 1447–1454.

Duck, S., & Gilmour, R. (1981). *Personal relationships 1: Studying personal relationships.* London: Academic Press.

Falbo, T., & Peplau, L. A. (1980). Power strategies in intimate relationships. *Journal of Personality and Social Psychology, 38*(4), 618–628.

Farber, B. (1957). An index of marital integration. *Sociometry, 20*, 117–118.

Farkas, G. (1976). Education, wage rates, and the division of labor between husband and wife. *Journal of Marriage and the Family, 38*(3), 473–483.

Fengler, A. P. (1974). Romantic love in courtships: Divergent paths of male and female students. *Journal of Comparative Family Studies, 5*(1), 134–139.

Festinger, L., Schachter, S., & Back, K. (1950). *Social pressures in informal groups: A study of human factors in housing.* Stanford, Calif.: Stanford University Press.

Fishman, P. M. (1978). Interaction: The work women do. *Social Problems, 25*(4), 397–406.

Friedland, R. F. (1982). *Men's and women's satisfying and frustrating experiences in close relationship interactions.* Unpublished doctoral dissertation, University of California, Los Angeles.

Frieze, I. H. (1979, April). *Power and influence in violent and nonviolent marriages.* Paper presented at the annual meeting of the Eastern Psychological Association, Philadelphia.

Funabiki, D., Bologna, N. C., Pepping, M., & Fitzgerald, K. C. (1980). Revisiting sex differences in the expression of depression. *Journal of Abnormal Psychology, 89,* 194–202.

Garnets, L., & Pleck, J. H. (1979). Sex-role identity, androgyny, and sex-role transcendence: A sex-role strain analysis. *Psychology of Women Quarterly, 3*(3), 270–283.

Gilford, R., & Bengtson, V. (1979). Measuring marital satisfaction in three generations: Positive and negative dimensions. *Journal of Marriage and the Family, 41*(2), 387–398.

Gordon, S. L. (1981). The sociology of sentiments and emotion. In M. Rosenberg & R. H. Turner (Eds.), *Social psychology: Sociological perspectives.* New York: Basic Books.

Gottman, J. M. (1979). *Marital interaction: Experimental investigations.* New York: Academic Press.

Gove, W. (1972). The relationships between sex roles, mental illness, and marital status. *Social Forces, 51,* 34–44.

Gove, W. (1979). Sex differences in the epidemiology of mental disorder: Evidence and explanations. In E. S. Gomberg & V. Franks (Eds.), *Gender and disordered behavior.* New York: Bruner-Mazel.

Gurin, G., Veroff, J., & Feld, S. (1960). *Americans view their mental health.* New York: Basic Books.

Hacker, H. M. (1961). Blabbermouths and clams: Sex differences in self-disclosure in same-sex and cross-sex friendship dyads. *Psychology of Women Quarterly, 5*(3), 385–401.

Harris, L., & Associates. (1971). *The Harris survey yearbook of public opinion 1970.* New York: Louis Harris.

Harvey, J., Christensen, A., & McClintock, E. (1983). Research methods in studying close relationships. In H. H. Kelley et al., *Close relationships.* New York: Freeman.

Hatkoff, T. S., & Lasswell, T. E. (1979). Male/female similarities and differences in conceptualizating love. In M. Cook & G. Wilson (Eds.), *Love and attraction.* London: Pergamon.

Heer, D. M. (1958). Dominance and the working life. *Social Forces, 35,* 341–347.

Hendrick, S. S. (1981). Self-disclosure and marital satisfaction. *Journal of Personality and Social Psychology, 40*(6), 1150–1159.

Henley, N. M. (1977). *Body politics: Power, sex and nonverbal communication.* Englewood Cliffs, N.J.: Prentice-Hall.

Hicks, M. W., & Platt, M. (1970). Marital happiness and stability: A review of the research in the sixties. *Journal of Marriage and the Family, 32*, 553–574.

Hill, C. T. (1981, September). *Statistical analysis of dyadic data: Similarity, agreement, and reciprocity.* Unpublished manuscript, University of Washington.

Hill, C. T., Peplau, L. A., & Rubin, Z. (1981). Differing perceptions in dating couples: Sex roles vs. alternative explanations. *Psychology of Women Quarterly, 5*(3), 418–434.

Hill, C. T., Rubin, Z., & Peplau, L. A. (1976). Breakups before marriage: The end of 13 affairs. *Journal of Social Issues, 32*(1), 147–168.

Hill, C. T., Rubin, Z., Peplau, L. A., & Willard, S. G. (1979). The volunteer couple: Sex differences, couple commitment, and participation in research on interpersonal relationships. *Social Psychology Quarterly, 4*, 415–420.

Hinde, R. A. (1979). *Towards understanding relationships.* London: Academic Press.

Hobart, C. W. (1958). The incidence of romanticism during courtship. *Social Forces, 36*, 362–367.

Horner, M. S. (1970). Femininity and successful achievement: A basic inconsistency. In J. M. Bardwick, E. Douvan, M. S. Horner, & D. Guttmann (Eds.), *Feminine personality and conflict.* Belmont, Calif.: Brooks-Cole, 1970.

Hudson, J. W., & Henze, L. F. (1969). Campus values and mate selection: A replication. *Journal of Marriage and the Family, 31*, 772–775.

Huston, T. L. (1983). Power. In H. H. Kelley, et al., *Close relationships.* New York: Freeman.

Huston, T. L., & Levinger, G. (1978). Interpersonal attraction and relationships. *Annual Review of Psychology, 29*, 115–156.

Jourard, S. M. (1959). *The transparent self.* New York: Van Nostrand.

Jourard, S. M. (1971). *Self-disclosure: An experimental analysis of the transparent self.* New York: Wiley-Interscience.

Jourard, S. M., & Lasakow, P. (1958). Some factors in self-disclosure. *Journal of Abnormal and Social Psychology, 56*, 91–98.

Kanin, E. J., Davidson, K. R., & Scheck, S. R. (1970). A research note on male-female differentials in the experience of heterosexual love. *Journal of Sex Research, 6*(1), 64–72.

Kaplan, S. L. (1975). *The exercise of power in dating couples.* Unpublished doctoral dissertation, Harvard University.

Kelley, H. H. (1979). *Personal relationships: Their structures and processes.* Hillsdale, N.J.: Lawrence Erlbaum Associates.

Kelley, H. H., Berscheid, E., Christensen, A., Harvey, J. H., Huston, T. L., Levinger, G., McClintock, E., Peplau, L. A., & Peterson, D. R. (1983). *Close relationships.* New York: Freeman.

Kelley, H. H., Cunningham, J. D., Grisham, J. A., Lefebvre, L. M., Sink, C. R., & Yablon, G. (1978). Sex differences in comments made during conflict within close heterosexual pairs. *Sex Roles, 4*(4), 473–491.

Kephart, W. M. (1967). Some correlates of romantic love. *Journal of Marriage and the Family, 29,* 470–474.

Kidder, L. H., Fagan, M. A., & Cohn, E. S. (1981). Giving and receiving: Social justice in close relationships. In M. J. Lerner & S. C. Lerner (Eds.), *The justice motive in social behavior.* New York: Plenum.

Knox, D. H., & Sporakowski, M. J. (1968). Attitudes of college students toward love. *Journal of Marriage and the Family, 30,* 638–642.

Knupfer, G., Clark, W., & Room, R. (1966). The mental health of the unmarried. *American Journal of Psychiatry, 122,* 841–851.

Komarovsky, M. (1967). *Blue-collar marriage.* New York: Random House.

Komarovsky, M. (1976). *Dilemmas of masculinity.* New York: Norton.

Lakoff, R. (1975). *Language and woman's place.* New York: Harper & Row.

Laner, M. R. (1977). Permanent partner priorities: Gay and straight. *Journal of Homosexuality, 3,* 12–39.

Langhorne, M. C., & Secord, P. F. (1955). Variations in marital needs with age, sex, marital status, and regional locations. *Journal of Social Psychology, 41,* 19–38.

Lasswell, M., & Lobsenz, N. M. (1980). *Styles of loving.* New York: Ballantine Books.

Laws, J. L. (1971). A feminist review of the marital adjustment literature: The rape of the Locke. *Journal of Marriage and the Family, 33*(3), 483–516.

Lee, J. A. (1977). *The colors of love.* New York: Bantam.

Leik, R. K. (1963). Instrumentality and emotionally in family interaction. *Sociometry, 26,* 131–145.

Leslie, G. R. (1976). *The family in social context* (3rd ed.). New York: Oxford University Press.

Levinger, G. (1964). Task and social behavior in marriage. *Sociometry, 27*(4), 433–448.

Levinger, G., & Raush, H. L. (Eds.) (1977). *Close relationships: Perspectives on the meaning of intimacy.* Amherst: University of Massachusetts Press.

Levinger, G., & Senn, D. J. (1967). Disclosure of feelings in marriage. *Merrill-Palmer Quarterly, 13,* 237–249.

Lewis, R. A., & Spanier, G. B. (1979). Theorizing about the quality and stability of marriage. In W. R. Burr, R. Hill, R. I. Nye, & I. L. Reiss (Eds.), *Contemporary theories about the family* (Vol. 1). New York: Free Press.

Lloyd, C. B. (Ed.) (1975). *Sex, discrimination and the division of labor.* New York: Columbia University Press.

Lowenthal, M. F., & Haven, C. (1968). Interaction and adaptation: Intimacy as a critical variable. *American Sociological Review, 33,* 20–30.

Lu, Y. C. (1952). Marital roles and marriage adjustment. *Sociology and Social Research, 36*, 364–368.

Lynch, J. J. (1977). *The broken heart: The medical consequences of loneliness.* New York: Basic Books.

Mason, K. O., Czajka, J. L., & Arber, S. (1976). Change in U.S. women's sex-role attitudes, 1964–1974. *American Sociological Review, 41*(4), 573–596.

McCormick, N. B. (1979). Come-ons and put-offs: Unmarried students' strategies for having and avoiding sexual intercourse. *Psychology of Women Quarterly, 4*, 194–211.

McCormick, N. B., & Jesser, C. J. (1983). The courtship game: Power in the sexual encounter. In E. R. Allgeier & N. B. McCormick (Eds.), *Changing boundaries: Gender roles and sexual behavior.* Palo Alto, Calif.: Mayfield.

McNamara, M. L. L., & Bahr, H. M. (1980). The dimensionality of marital role satisfaction. *Journal of Marriage and the Family, 42*, 45–55.

Murstein, B. I. (1976). *Who will marry whom?* New York: Springer.

Napier, A. Y. (1978). The rejection-intrusion pattern: A central family dynamic. *Journal of Marriage and Family Counseling, 4*, 5–12.

Newcomb, T. M. (1981). *The acquaintance process.* New York: Holt, Rinehart, & Winston.

Olson, D. H. (1977). Insiders' and outsiders' views of relationships: Research strategies. In G. Levinger & H. L. Raush (Eds.), *Close relationships: Perspectives on the meaning of intimacy.* Amherst: University of Massachusetts Press.

Osmond, M. W., & Martin, P. Y. (1975). Sex and sexism: A comparison of male and female sex-role attitudes. *Journal of Marriage and the Family, 37*, 744–758.

Paloma, M. M., & Garland, T. N. (1971). The married professional woman: A study in the tolerance of domestication. *Journal of Marriage and the Family, 33*, 531–540.

Parelman, A. (1983). *Emotional intimacy in marriage: A sex-roles perspective.* Ann Arbor, Mich.: UMI Research Press.

Parsons, T. (1955). The American family: Its relations to personality and to the social structure. In T. Parsons & R. F. Bales, *Family: Socialization and interaction process.* Glencoe, Ill.: Free Press.

Pearlin, L., & Johnson, J. (1977). Marital status, life-strains, and depression. *American Sociological Review, 42*, 704–715.

Pearlin, L., & Schooler, C. (1978). The structure of coping. *Journal of Health and Social Behavior, 19*, 2–21.

Pepitone, A. (1981). Lessons from the history of social psychology. *American Psychologist, 36*, 972–985.

Peplau, L. A. (1976). Impact of fear of success and sex-role attitudes on women's competitive achievement. *Journal of Personality and Social Psychology, 34*, 561–568.

Peplau, L. A. (1983). Roles and gender. In H. H. Kelley et al., *Close relationships*. New York: Freeman.

Peplau, L. A. (1984). Power in dating relationships. In J. Freeman (Ed.), *Women: A feminist perspective* (3rd ed.). Palo Alto, Calif.: Mayfield.

Peplau, L. A., Bikson, T. K., Rook, K., & Goodchilds, J. D. (1982). Being old and living alone. In L. A. Peplau & D. Perlman (Eds.), *Loneliness: A sourcebook of current theory, research and therapy*. New York: Wiley-Interscience.

Peplau, L. A., & Rook, K. (1978, April). *Dual-career relationships: The college couple perspective*. Paper presented at the annual meeting of the Western Psychological Association, San Francisco.

Perlman, D., Gerson, A. C., & Spinner, B. (1978). Loneliness among senior citizens: An empirical report. *Essence, 2*(4), 239–248.

Perrucci, C. C., Potter, H. R., & Rhoads, D. L. (1978). Determinants of male family-role performance. *Psychology of Women Quarterly, 3*(1), 53–66.

Pietropinto, A., & Simenauer, J. (1981). *Husbands and wives*. New York: Berkeley Books.

Pifer, A. (1978). Women working toward a new society. *The Urban and Social Change Review, 11*, 3–11.

Pleck, J. H. (1975, November). *Men's role in the family: A new look*. Paper presented at the World Family Sociology Conference, Merrill-Palmer Institute, Detroit.

Pleck, J. H. (1976). The male sex role: Definitions, problems and sources of change. *Journal of Social Issues, 32*(3), 155–164.

Pleck, J. H. (1981a, August). *Changing patterns of work and family roles*. Paper presented at the annual meeting of the American Psychological Association, Los Angeles.

Pleck, J. H. (1981b). *The myth of masculinity*. Cambridge, Mass.: MIT Press.

Pleck, J. H., & Rustad, M. (1980). *Husbands' and wives' time in family work and paid employment in the 1975–1976 Study of Time Use*. Wellesley, Mass.: Wellesley College Center for Research on Women.

Rainwater, L. (1965). *Family design*. Chicago: Aldine.

Rapoport, R., Rapoport, R., & Thiessen, V. (1974). Couple symmetry and enjoyment. *Journal of Marriage and the Family, 36*(3), 588–591.

Raush, H. L., Barry, W. A., Hertel, R. K., & Swain, M. A. (1974). *Communication, conflict and marriage*. San Francisco: Jossey-Bass.

Raven, B. H., Centers, R., & Rodrigues, A. (1975). The bases of conjugal power. In R. E. Cromwell & D. H. Olson (Eds.), *Power in families*. New York: Wiley.

Renne, K. (1970). Correlates of dissatisfaction in marriage. *Journal of Marriage and the Family, 32*, 54–67.

Risman, B. J., Hill, C. T., Rubin, Z., & Peplau, L. A. (1981). Living together in college: Implications for courtship. *Journal of Marriage and the Family, 43*, 77–83.

Robinson, J. P. (1977). *How Americans use time.* New York: Praeger.

Robinson, J. P., Yerby, J., Fieweger, M., & Somerick, N. (1977). Sex-role differences in time use. *Sex roles, 3*(5), 443–458.

Rollins, B. C., & Bahr, S. J. (1976). A theory of power relationships in marriage. *Journal of Marriage and the Family, 38*, 619–627.

Rollins, B. C., & Cannon, K. L. (1974). Marital satisfaction over the family life cycle: A reevaluation. *Journal of Marriage and the Family, 36*, 271–282.

Rosenfeld, L. B., Civikly, J. M., & Herron, J. R. (1979). Anatomical and psychological differences. In G. J. Chelune et al. (Eds.), *Self-disclosure.* San Francisco, Calif.: Jossey-Bass.

Rubin, L. B. (1976). *Worlds of pain.* New York: Basic Books.

Rubin, Z. (1968). Do American women marry up? *American Sociological Review, 33*(5), 750–760.

Rubin, Z. (1970). Measurement of romantic love. *Journal of Personality and Social Psychology, 16*, 265–273.

Rubin, Z. (1973). *Liking and loving: An invitation to social psychology.* New York: Holt, Rinehart, & Winston.

Rubin, Z., Hill, C. T., Peplau, L. A., & Dunkel-Schetter, C. (1980). Self-disclosure in dating couples: Sex roles and the ethic of openness. *Journal of Marriage and the Family, 42*(2), 305–318.

Rubin, Z., Peplau, L. A., & Hill, C. T. (1981). Loving and leaving: Sex differences in romantic attachments. *Sex Roles,* 7, 821–835.

Rubin, Z., Peplau, L. A., & Hill, C. T. *Unpublished data from the Boston Couples Study.*

Safilios-Rothschild, C. (1970). The study of family power structure: A review 1960–1969. *Journal of Marriage and the Family, 32*, 539–552.

Scanzoni, J., & Fox, G. L. (1980). Sex roles, family, and society: The seventies and beyond. *Journal of Marriage and the Family, 42*, 743–756.

Scanzoni, L., & Scanzoni, J. (1976). *Men, women, and change: A sociology of marriage and the family.* New York: McGraw-Hill.

Soskin, W. M., & John, V. (1963). The study of spontaneous talk. In R. Barker (Ed.), *The stream of behavior.* New York: Appleton-Century-Crofts.

Spanier, G. B., Lewis, R. A., & Cole, C. L. (1975). Marital adjustment over the family life cycle: The issue of curvilinearity. *Journal of Marriage and the Family, 37*(2), 263–275.

Spence, J. T., & Helmreich, R. L. (1978). *Masculinity and femininity: Their psychological dimensions, correlates and antecedents.* Austin: University of Texas Press.

Staines, G., Pleck, J., Shepard, L., & O'Connor, P. (1978). Wives' employment status and marital adjustment. *Psychology of Women Quarterly, 3*, 90–120.

Thibaut, J. W., & Kelley, H. H. (1959). *The social psychology of groups.* New York: Wiley.

Tomeh, A. K. (1978). Sex-role orientation: An analysis of structure and attitudinal predictors. *Journal of Marriage and the Family, 40*, 341–354.

Troll, L. E., & Turner, B. F. (1979). Sex differences in problems of aging. In E. S. Gomberg & V. Franks (Eds.), *Gender and disordered behavior: Sex differences in psychopathology*. New York: Brunner-Mazel.

Wakil, S. P. (1973). Campus mate selection preferences. A cross-national comparison. *Social Forces, 51*, 471–476.

Walker, K. (1970). Time spent by husbands in household work. *Family Economics Review, 3*, 8–11.

Walker, K., & Woods, M. (1976). *Time use: A measure of household production of family goods and services*. Washington, D.C.: Home Economics Association.

Waller, W. (1938). *The family: A dynamic interpretation*. New York: Dryden.

Warheit, G. J., Holzer, C. E., Bell, R. A., & Arey, S. A. (1976). Sex, marital status, and mental health: A reappraisal. *Social Forces, 55*(2), 459–470.

Wills, T. A., Weiss, R. L., & Patterson, G. R. (1974). A behavioral analysis of the determinants of marital satisfaction. *Journal of Consulting and Clinical Psychology, 42*(6), 802–811.

Yankelovich, D. (1974). *The new morality: A profile of Americans in the 70s*. New York: McGraw-Hill.

18 Understanding Lesbian Relationships

LETITIA ANNE PEPLAU

HORTENSIA AMARO

Although love may not "make the world go 'round," the lives of most adults are powerfully affected by their experiences in intimate relationships. It is commonly believed that the psychologically healthy adult must have the capacity for work and love. The importance of intimate relationships is no less great for lesbians than for heterosexuals. Yet, whereas heterosexual women can readily find information about the joys and problems of relationships with men in advice columns, scholarly books, and college courses on marriage and family, lesbians have few comparable sources of accurate information. For anyone interested in understanding lesbian lifestyles, factual information is essential.

In this chapter we review scientific knowledge about lesbian love relationships. Although fiction, biographies, the impressions of therapists, and other sources (e.g., Berzon & Leighton, 1979; Vida, 1978) can provide useful insights into lesbian relationships, we have restricted our review to empirical research. We are acutely aware of the methodological problems of conducting research in the gay community—or among members of any partially hidden group (Morin, 1977; see Gonsiorek's introduction, Chapter 5). The most serious problem in this area has been the impossibility of obtaining representative samples of lesbians. As a result, it is imperative that research results be interpreted cautiously.

In attempting to portray lesbian relationships, it is important to curb the impulse to oversimplify the complexities of women's experiences. There is no such thing as the "typical lesbian couple." Most empirical research has concentrated on a limited segment of the lesbian population: Typical respondents have been younger, educated, middle-class white women. Unfortunately, very little is known about lesbians from other backgrounds. Existing research contributes little to our understanding of the role of such factors as age, education, social class, religion, ethnicity and culture in lesbian relationships.

With these cautions in mind, we reviewed the available empirical research. We began with the question of how many lesbians are currently involved in steady relationships. Seven studies[1] provide information on this issue. Among these studies, the proportion of women who were currently in a steady relationship ranged from 45 to 80 percent. In most studies, the proportion of women in ongoing relationships was close to 75 percent. Furthermore, the same studies indicate that many lesbians are living with their partners; estimates range from 42 to 63 percent of all lesbians surveyed living with their partners.

Although these figures should not be taken as representative of all lesbians, they do suggest that at any particular point in time many lesbians are involved in an intimate relationship. What these statistics do not tell us, of course, is what these relationships are like—whether or not lesbian couples are happy, loving, or committed. Later in the chapter we probe more deeply into the quality of lesbian relationships. It is important to recognize that those lesbians who are *not* currently in a steady relationship are a diverse group. They include women who have recently ended a relationship through breakup or through the death of a partner, women who are eager to begin a new relationship, and others who do not want a steady relationship.

A related question concerns the average length of lesbian relationships. Do most lesbians have fairly short-lived affairs or longer-term relationships? This is a difficult question to answer. For an adolescent—whether lesbian or heterosexual—a relationship of three months may seem "long"; for a 50-year-old person, a relationship of 15 years may be long. In other words, a person's age determines to some extent the length of time that a relationship can have endured and subjective perceptions of whether or not a relationship has lasted a "long" time.

A recent study by Bell and Weinberg (1978) of 283 lesbians living in San Francisco inquired about the length of the women's *first* lesbian relationship. On the average, women in this sample were 22 years old when they had their first "relatively steady relationship." Nearly 90 percent said they had been "in love" with this first partner, and the typical first relationship lasted for a median of one to three years. For less than 8 percent of the women did this first relationship end in three months or less. This pattern of establishing relatively enduring relationships characterizes not only lesbians' first intimate relationships but also their subsequent relationships.

Several studies[2] have asked lesbians to describe the length of their current love relationship. In these studies, most participants have been young lesbians in their 20s. The typical length of their relationships was two to three years. Studies of older lesbians would be especially useful in understanding the length of relationships, but such research is strikingly absent from the existing literature. Studies that have included small numbers of older lesbians[3] document that relationships of 20 years or more are not unusual.

The relative stability of most lesbians' relationships is further reflected in data on the total number of different partners lesbians have had. In the Bell and Weinberg (1978) study, in which nearly half the white lesbians sampled were over age 35, the majority of women had had fewer than 10 different lesbian sexual partners during their lifetimes. One-time or brief sexual liaisons occurred but were uncommon.

Thus, the picture that tentatively emerges from these statistics is that the majority of lesbians experience relatively stable, long-term relationships. Important exceptions to this pattern should be noted, however. A minority of lesbians have shorter relationships and a greater number of different partners. For example, in two studies (Bell & Weinberg, 1978; Jay & Young, 1977), 15 percent of respondents reported that they had had sexual relations with 25 or more lesbian partners. It seems likely that for some lesbians this reflects a pattern of choice—a rejection of committed relationships as a personal goal. For other lesbians, casual sexual affairs may occur concurrently with a committed relationship. For still others, a pattern of many partners may reflect difficulties in establishing intimate bonds; such problems might be based on the internalization and acting out of the culture's rejection of lesbian relationships and of stereotypes that lesbians are unable to develop long-term relationships (compare Ettorre, 1980).

Having seen that most lesbians spend much of their adult lives in intimate love relationships, we next turn to findings about the nature of lesbian relationships. We begin with an examination of lesbians' attitudes and values about relationships, and look at issues of commitment and permanence in lesbian couples. In a later section we investigate role-playing in lesbian relationships and present findings debunking the myth that lesbian couples adopt characteristically "masculine" and "feminine" roles. This is followed by a discussion of research on power in lesbian relationships and an examination of the sexual lives of lesbian couples.

Attitudes About Relationships

For most lesbians, love relationships are important. Bell and Weinberg (1978) asked lesbians how important it was to them to have a "permanent living arrangement with a homosexual partner." One-quarter of lesbians said that this was "the most important thing in life" and another 35 percent said it was "very important." Less than one woman in four said that a permanent living arrangement was not important to her. So, again, we see a range of views, with a couple orientation being most common.[4]

It has frequently been speculated that lesbian relationships are more "romantic" than those of heterosexuals. For example, Hyde and Rosenberg (1976) suggest that "homosexual women live almost an idyllic love relationship with their partner, with more intense emotion and imagination than the typical heterosexual relationship" (p. 176). Only one study has examined this issue empirically. Peplau et al. (1978) administered a six-item romanticism scale to a sample of 127 lesbians in Los Angeles. Items assessed adherence to the belief that "love conquers all." Included were statements about true love lasting forever and love overcoming barriers of race, religion, and economics. As a whole, lesbians in this sample were not strongly romantic in their beliefs. Further, when lesbians' romanticism scores were compared to those of matched samples of heterosexual women, gay men, and heterosexual men, no significant differences were found among any of the groups (Cochran & Peplau, 1979). So, while some lesbians may indeed have a highly romanticized or idealized view of love relationships, this orientation does not appear to be any more common among lesbians than among other adults.

Given that most lesbians want a steady relationship, what are the characteristics they seek in such partnerships? The single most consistent theme to emerge from empirical research is the strong importance most lesbians place on emotional intimacy and expressiveness. In this regard, lesbians are quite similar to heterosexual women. For example, Ramsey, Latham and Lindquist (1978) asked members of lesbian and heterosexual couples to rank the importance of 11 possible relationship goals. Lesbians ranked the sharing of affection as most important, with personal development and companionship next. The same three goals topped the list of heterosexual women. Further, women in both groups gave least importance to economic security, community standing, and religious sharing. In another study (Peplau et al., 1978; Cochran & Peplau, 1979), 127 lesbians rated the importance they personally gave to 16 features of love relationships. Again, lesbians gave greatest importance to "being able to talk about my most intimate feelings" and "laughing easily with each other." These same features were also given greatest importance by a matched group of heterosexual women.

A second theme that recurs is the value lesbians place on equality in relationships. In one study (Peplau et al., 1978), lesbians strongly endorsed the importance of "having an egalitarian (equal-power) relationship" and strongly rejected the idea of "having more influence than my partner in our joint decision-making." Similar findings have been reported in ethnographic studies of lesbian communities in California (Wolf, 1979) and Oregon (Barnhart, 1975). For many lesbians, an emphasis on egalitarianism is linked to a more general endorsement of feminist values. Feminist lesbians may be more conscious of the power dimension in close relationships and more concerned about equality as a goal than are nonfeminist lesbians.

There is more diversity of opinion among lesbians about the desirability of other features of love relationships. Two important dimensions along which the relationship values of lesbians differ have been identified by Peplau et al. (1978). A dimension of "dyadic attachment" concerns the importance women give to having a close-knit, exclusive, relatively permanent relationship. Some women are strong proponents of attachment who want to spend most of their free time with their partner, share many activities, preserve sexual exclusivity, and know that the relationship will endure. Other women reject many of these goals, preferring instead to have a lesser degree of togetherness in their relationship. A second dimension, "personal autonomy," concerns boundaries between the individual and her relationship. While some individuals prefer to immerse themselves in a relationship to the exclusion of outside interests and activities, other women prefer to maintain greater personal independence.

Lesbians' attitudes about relationships are affected not only by their personal histories but also by the social context in which they live. Ethnographic studies of particular lesbian communities illustrate how group norms can affect relationship values. For example, in the early 1970s Barnhart (1975) studied intensively a counterculture community of lesbian women in Oregon. Among women in this group, an ideology had developed emphasizing that the individual's first loyalty should be to the community; couple relationships should be secondary. The community further encouraged women to reject the idea of sexual exclusivity because, in their analysis, it conflicted with norms of equality and sisterhood. As Barnhart points out, many women experienced some difficulty in reconciling their preexisting beliefs about monogamous relationships with the newer attitudes endorsed by their social group. Further research on variations among different lesbian groups and communities in relationship values would be useful.

Satisfaction, Love, and Commitment Given that many lesbians would like to establish a satisfying, close relationship, how successful are they in achieving this goal? Unfortunately, information about satisfaction, love, and commitment in lesbian relationships comes from a few studies based on fairly small samples and using self-report measures. So the following results are presented cautiously. They suggest that most lesbians find their relationships to be highly satisfying.

One study (Cardell, Finn, & Marecek, in press) compared a small Pennsylvania sample of lesbians, gay men, and heterosexuals on a measure of couple adjustment. They found that lesbians did not differ from the other two groups in adjustment; most couples were very satisfied with their relationship. Another recent study (Ramsey et al., 1978) compared 26 lesbian couples to 27 gay male couples and 25 heterosexual couples. All couples had lived together for at least six months; the average length of cohabitation for lesbian couples was over six years. Relationship satisfaction was measured by the widely used Locke-Wallace marital adjustment scale. The lesbian couples scored in the "well-adjusted" range and did not differ significantly from couples in the other two groups.

Only recently have social psychologists attempted to measure love systematically, spurred by Zick Rubin's development of scales to measure "love" and "liking" for a romantic partner. Cochran and Peplau (1979) compared matched samples of younger lesbians, gay men, and heterosexuals, all of whom were in steady relationships. On Rubin's measures, lesbians reported high love for their partner, indicating strong feelings of attachment, caring, and intimacy. They also scored high on the liking scale, reflecting feelings of respect and affection toward the partner. On other measures, lesbians rated their current relationship as highly satisfying and very close. When comparisons were made among lesbians, gay men, and heterosexuals on these measures, no significant differences were found. Also included in this research were open-ended questions asking participants to describe in their own words the "best things" and "worst things" about their current relationship. Systematic analyses (Cochran, 1978) found no significant differences in the responses of lesbians, gay men, and heterosexuals, all of whom reported similar types of joys and problems. To examine the possibility that more subtle differences existed among groups that were not captured by the coding scheme, the statements were typed on cards in a standard format with information about gender and sexual orientation removed. Panels of judges were asked to sort the cards, separating men and women and heterosexuals and homosexuals. Judges were not able to distinguish correctly the responses of lesbians from those of heterosexual women, heterosexual men, or gay men.

Taken together, these findings suggest that many lesbian relationships are highly satisfying. Lesbian couples appear, on standardized measures, to be as well-adjusted as heterosexual couples. This does not, of course, mean that lesbians have no difficulties in their relationships. They undoubtedly have some of the same problems as heterosexuals—for example, in coordinating joint goals and resolving interpersonal conflicts. Lesbian couples may also have special problems arising from the hostile and rejecting attitudes of many people toward lesbians. Overall, however, existing research suggests that lesbian relationships are as likely to be personally satisfying as are heterosexual ones.

Correlates of Satisfaction Researchers are only beginning to examine factors that promote personal feelings of love and satisfaction in lesbian relationships. A study by Peplau, Padesky, and Hamilton (1982) is a first step in this direction. They found that among a group of relatively young lesbians from Los Angeles, satisfaction was strongly related to equality of involvement in the relationship. Those relationships in which partners were equally committed and equally "in love" tended to be the happiest. In contrast, lopsided relationships in which one partner was much more involved than the other were less satisfying. This pattern is quite similar to results of studies of heterosexual relationships (e.g., Hill, Rubin, & Peplau, 1976).

A second factor contributing to satisfaction in the lesbian relationships in this study was equality of power. We saw earlier that most lesbians are strong proponents of egalitarianism in relationships. Perhaps not surprisingly, those women who perceived their current relationship as egalitarian were significantly more satisfied than were women who thought their relationship was not. Third, evidence was also found indicating that similarity of attitudes and backgrounds facilitated successful relationships. This is consistent with the widely replicated finding among heterosexuals that similarity increases attraction.

It is also interesting to note factors that were *not* related to satisfaction in lesbian relationships. In the Peplau, Padesky, and Hamilton (1982) study, satisfaction was not related to the extent of involvement in lesbian or feminist groups and activities; nor was it related to the degree to which women were open versus closeted about being lesbian. Finally, the three studies that have examined satisfaction have looked for age-related differences. Results indicated, however, that older and younger lesbians are equally likely to have satisfying relationships. . . .

Role-Playing

A false stereotype of lesbian relationships is that they mimic traditional sex-typed heterosexual patterns, with one partner adopting a "masculine" role and the other a "feminine" role. Such role-playing is supposedly manifested in the division of household tasks, style of dress, patterns of dominance-submission, and preferences about sexual behavior. In popular thinking, such role-playing is seen as reflecting a desire by some lesbians to be men. Research clearly discredits all of these common beliefs.

Research indicates that sex-typed role-playing is rare in contemporary lesbian life. Most lesbians say they dislike such categories as "butch" and "femme," and reject the idea of role-playing (Barnhart, 1975; Jay & Young, 1977; Tanner, 1978). For example, one lesbian wrote:

> I strive to eliminate all vestiges of role-playing in my relationship with women, as the opportunity to do so is one of the major reasons I am a lesbian. My lover and I have constantly shifting roles . . . depending on the needs of the moment. If ever I felt we were getting locked into any roles, especially those of butch/femme, I would run . . . to escape from this relationship [Jay & Young, 1977, p. 320].

The theme reflected in this quotation and in other anecdotal accounts is that lesbian relationships permit women to avoid limitations imposed by traditional male-female role-playing that occurs in many heterosexual relationships.

Several studies[5] have examined role-playing patterns in the division of household tasks, style of dress, and sexual conduct of lesbians. The consistent finding is that most lesbians do *not* conform to rigid masculine-feminine roles. Instead, role shifting and role flexibility are the predominant pattern. A reasonable estimate would be that only about 10 percent of lesbians today engage in clear-cut role-playing. One lesbian explained her participation in role-playing:

> When I am with a younger girl, I like to . . . protect her, and I like it very much if she lets me buy drinks, etc. . . . What I like best about the "male" or "butch" role is the protective angle, even though I realize intellectually that this is a lot of sexist shit [Jay & Young, 1977, p. 322].

It appears that role-playing was more prevalent in the "old gay life" (Wolf, 1979), a period before the 1950s evolution of homophile organizations and the more recent effects of feminism in the lesbian community. Cultural stereotypes about lesbian role-playing may have developed during this earlier period, when the straight community's knowledge of lesbian life was largely derived from behavioral patterns observed in gay bars. We do not know how prevalent role-playing used to be, since most research is of recent vintage. Two studies based on data collected before 1969 (Bass-Hass, 1968; Jensen, 1974) reported that a majority of respondents engaged in role-playing. Ethnographic accounts (e.g., Wolf, 1979) contain descriptions by lesbians of the old bar scene in major cities. It appears that there has been a historical decline in role-playing among American lesbians.

Nevertheless, let us examine factors that may foster the adoption of these sex-typed patterns. Four possibilities are suggested by existing studies. First, role-playing may be more common among older women who were or continue to be part of the old gay life. Second, role-playing may be more common among lesbians from lower socioeconomic levels (Gagnon & Simon, 1973; Wolf, 1979). Although virtually no data exist on blue-collar and working-class lesbians, research has suggested that lower-income heterosexuals have more sex-typed behavior patterns than do higher-income heterosexuals (e.g., Komarovsky, 1967). It may be that stronger adherence to masculine-feminine roles is found among women who have traditional values, perhaps based on religious and cultural socialization. Third, role-playing may be related to the coming-out experiences of some lesbians (Gagnon & Simon, 1973; Saghir & Robins, 1973). For example, a young woman who is new to the lesbian community may initially dress in a stereotypically butch manner in order to be more easily identified as lesbian and to conform to her perception of group expectations about behavior. Fourth, in some cases, role-playing may result from temporary situational factors. Saghir and Robins (1973) found that 12 percent of their lesbian respondents had engaged in role-playing; the majority had developed such roles because one partner was temporarily unemployed or attending school.

In summary, masculine-feminine role-playing is another area in which variations among lesbians have been found. While the great majority of lesbians rejects role-playing, a minority continues to behave in sex-typed ways. What should be remembered, of course, is that the greatest amount of role-playing has always been and continues to be found among heterosexual couples.

Power

In the earlier discussion of lesbians' attitudes about relationships, we saw that most gay women consider equality an important relationship goal. How successful are women in achieving this egalitarian ideal? There has been only one empirical investigation of power in lesbian relationships (Caldwell & Peplau, in press), based on questionnaire responses from a sample of 77 younger Los Angeles lesbians who were in a steady relationship. When asked directly who they thought should have more power in their relationship, 97 percent of these women said that both partners should have "exactly equal" say in their relationship. Not all women believed that their relationship attained this ideal, however. When asked to describe the overall balance of power in their current relationship, 64 percent reported equal power, but a sizable 36 percent minority reported that one partner had greater influence than the other.

Caldwell and Peplau investigated factors that tip the balance of power away from equality in lesbian relationships. Some years ago sociologist Willard Waller (1938) proposed the "principle of least interest"—suggesting that when one partner in a relationship is relatively less interested or committed, she/he will have greater power. Clear evidence was found for such a link between imbalances of involvement and imbalances of power in lesbian relationships. Social psychological theory also suggests that power is likely to accrue to the partner who has greater personal resources, in terms of greater education or income or other desirable characteristics. In this study, women who had relatively greater income and education than their partner tended to have relatively greater power. Thus, both relative dependency and personal resources affected the balance of power. Further research is needed to confirm these findings about power in lesbian relationships.

Sexual Behavior

A cultural stereotype depicts lesbians as highly sexual people. Perhaps because of this myth, much of the research on lesbians has investigated their sexuality. Yet research suggests many commonalities—and a few differences—between the sexual attitudes and experiences of lesbians and of heterosexual women.

Studies of physiological aspects of sexuality (Kinsey et al., 1953; Masters & Johnson, 1979) have found no differences in the pattern of sexual response of lesbians and heterosexual women. It is hardly surprising that the physiological mechanics of sexual arousal and orgasm are similar for all women, regardless of sexual orientation.

It may also be useful in this context to recognize that the majority of lesbians have had sexual relations with men as well as with women. In one study of 151 lesbians (Schaefer, 1976), 55 percent of respondents had had heterosexual coitus prior to their first lesbian experience. Studies[6] suggest that close to 80 percent of lesbians have had sex with men at some point in their lives. For many lesbians, these heterosexual experiences occurred in the context of dating or marital relationships. One study found that a majority of lesbians had dated men (Peplau et al., 1978). A significant minority of lesbians (perhaps 25 percent) has been heterosexually married.[7]

Lesbians' evaluations of their sexual relationships with men vary considerably. Jay and Young (1977) found that 23 percent of lesbians rated their past heterosexual experiences as positive, 21 percent as neutral, and 55 percent as negative. One factor contributing to this may be that for some lesbians, sexual activities with men did not lead to orgasm (e.g., for 33 percent of lesbians in Bell and Weinberg's study). Equally important, however, may be differences in the emotional tone of sexual experiences with female and male partners. Schaefer (1976) asked the 57 lesbians in her sample who had had sexual relations during the past year with both women and men to compare these experiences. Major differences were reported. Most women said that compared to sex with men, sex with women was more tender (94 percent), intimate (91 percent), considerate (88 percent), partner-related (73 percent), exciting (66 percent), diversified (52 percent), and less aggressive (71 percent).

Studies of lesbians' sexual experiences with women have identified two patterns. First, for many lesbians, sex and love are closely linked. In a survey of 962 lesbians (Jay & Young, 1977), 97 percent of women said that emotional involvement was important to sex, and 92 percent said that in their own personal experiences, emotional involvement always or very frequently accompanied sex. Consistent with this emphasis on affection, Bell and Weinberg (1978) found that 62 percent of lesbians had never had sex with a stranger, and 81 percent said that they had felt affection toward most of their sexual partners. Gundlach and Reiss (1968) found that equal proportions of lesbians and heterosexual women—64 percent—said they could have sex only if they were in love with the partner. So, whereas a minority of lesbians enjoys casual or "recreational" sex, the majority prefers to limit sexual activities to partners toward whom they feel at least affection. Given this pattern, it is not surprising that many lesbians draw their sexual partners from people they already know as friends (Peplau et al., 1978; Schaefer, 1977; Tanner, 1978), and that the incidence of cruising—meeting casual partners in bars and other settings—is quite low (Jay & Young, 1977).

Research also shows that most lesbians find their sexual interactions with women highly satisfying. Lesbian love-making typically leads to orgasm.[8] For example, lesbians in one study said that they seldom had difficulty achieving orgasm during sex (Jay & Young, 1977). Only 4 percent said they never had an orgasm and 5 percent said they had orgasms infrequently. Comparative studies suggest that lesbians achieve orgasm more often during love-making than do heterosexual women. Kinsey et al. (1953) compared heterosexual women who had been married for five years with lesbians who had been sexually active for an equal number of years. Among these women, 17 percent of the heterosexuals compared to only 7 percent of the lesbians never had an orgasm. And only 40 percent of heterosexuals had orgasm easily (i.e., 90–100 percent of the time they had sex), compared to 68 percent of lesbians. These differences may, as Kinsey suggested, reflect differences in the knowledge and sexual techniques of women's partners. But differences in the emotional quality of sexual experiences may be equally important.

Studies examining sexual behavior in steady lesbian relationships find that for most women, sex is an enjoyable part of such relationships. In one study (Peplau et al., 1978), three-quarters of lesbians said that sex with their steady partner was "extremely satisfying," and only 4 percent said that it was not at all satisfying.

Available data[9] suggest that lesbian couples have sex about as often as do heterosexual couples. Among the younger lesbians typically studied by researchers, the average frequency of sex is about two to three times per week. This figure varies widely from couple to couple, however. Among the lesbians studied by Jay and Young, only 5 percent reported having sex daily. Most women (57 percent) had sex two to five times per week, 25 percent had sex once a week, and 8 percent had sex less often with their partner. Little is known about the factors that influence the actual or desired frequency of sex in lesbian relationships.

Sexual exclusivity is a controversial issue for many American couples, both lesbian and heterosexual, as discussed above. The predominant pattern reported in available studies[10] of lesbians is serial monogamy—women participate in a series of sexually exclusive relationships. But other patterns are also common. Commenting on sexual openness, a lesbian explained, "I have sex outside the relationship, and we talk about it openly. So far it has had a positive effect. We both agree to be nonmonogamous" (Jay &

Young, 1977, p. 326). One study (Peplau et al., 1978) found that sexual openness was not related to dissatisfaction within women's primary relationship. Women in sexually open relationships were just as satisfied with their steady partner as were women in monogamous relationships. More needs to be known about how different lesbian couples handle this contemporary issue.

Finally, it is important to note that although many lesbians are happy with sex in their relationships, some lesbians do have sexual difficulties. The myth that all lesbians have perfect sex can be quite harmful to women who experience problems. No systematic research exists on sexual difficulties faced by lesbians, but observations by clinicians offer a few speculative clues. Toder (1978) suggested that lesbians share some of the same sexual problems as heterosexual women, including orgasmic dysfunction and differences in the desired sexual frequency of partners. But lesbians may also have some special problems, such as discomfort in taking the initiative in making love to a partner or sexual inhibitions about such activities as oral sex. More research on lesbian sexuality is needed to understand this aspect of lesbian relationships, and to provide information for counselors who seek to help lesbian clients.

Conclusions

Our review of research on lesbian relationships has found wide variations in the experiences of individual lesbians. For every general pattern that can be identified, there are many exceptions.

When possible, we have compared the attitudes and experiences of lesbians and heterosexual women. It is important to understand why such comparisons are useful. We do *not* assume that heterosexuality or heterosexual marriage is an ideal pattern to be used as the standard in analyses of lesbian relationships. Rather, such comparisons highlight similarities in the values and experiences of all women. For example, childhood socialization experiences of girls in this culture often emphasize emotional expressiveness and love as central to close relationships, and these themes can be seen in the adult relationships of both lesbians and heterosexuals (Cochran & Peplau, 1979; Gagnon & Simon, 1973; Schaefer, 1976; for similar issues in male homosexuality, see Peplau & Gordon, in press). Second, comparisons of lesbian and heterosexual relationships point to basic issues that confront all intimate couples, regardless of sexual orientation. For instance, imbalances of dependency can tip the balance of power away from equality in lesbian and heterosexual relationships alike. Finally, such comparisons help to identify those unique qualities of lesbian relationships that make them a positive and desirable lifestyle for women.

There is a long list of needed research about lesbian relationships. Because virtually all of the research we have reviewed is based on white women (exceptions are Bell & Weinberg, 1978 and Hidalgo & Hidalgo-Christensen, 1976), findings cannot be generalized to ethnic lesbians. Existing research says little about the impact of cultural, ethnic, economic, and religious factors on values and behavior in lesbian relationships. Yet it is obvious that relationships reflect both the personal experiences of the partners and the social context in which the relationship exists. The nature of satisfaction, commitment, sexuality, or power may differ for a Hispanic couple living in the barrio, a Black professional couple, a first-generation Asian couple, and the white respondents typically studied in previous research. Ethnic lesbians find themselves part of two minorities, each of which may reject the other. In ethnic communities, traditional values often result in hostility toward lesbian relationships (Hidalgo & Hidalgo-Christensen, 1976; Mays, 1980). Similarly, within the lesbian community, cultural insensitivity—or worse, racism—may lead to the exclusion of ethnic couples. Clearly, investigations of the relationships of minority lesbians are needed (Mays, 1980).

Many questions about lesbian relationships remain unanswered. For example, what impact do children have on lesbian relationships? How do the social support networks of lesbians affect the development of love relationships, and how do these networks respond when relationships end? What role do family ties play in lesbian relationships, especially for women from cultures where familial bonds are strong? What issues arise in lesbian couples where partners differ in race, religion, class, or age? What impact does social oppression have on lesbian relationships? What factors foster happiness and commitment in lesbian couples?

Most studies of lesbians have not focused specifically on relationships, and so we have had to gather relevant pieces of information as best we could. Research directly investigating lesbian relationships would be useful to lesbians themselves, and to relatives, friends, counselors, and others who want to understand lesbians' lives. We hope this review will soon become outdated as better research provides a more complete picture of the diversity of lesbian relationships.

Notes

1. The percentage of lesbians currently in a steady relationship varies across studies: Bell and Weinberg (1978), 72 percent; Cotton (1975), 83 percent; Jay and Young (1977), 80 percent; Oberstone and Sukoneck

(1977), 80 percent; Peplau et al. (1978), 61 percent; Raphael and Robinson (1980), 45 percent; and Schaefer (1976), 72 percent. These variations reflect differences in the wording of questions, the sampling procedures, the date of the research, and the lesbian populations themselves.

2. The average or median length of lesbians' current relationship varies across studies: Bell and Weinberg (1978), 1–3 years; Oberstone and Sukoneck (1977), 22 months; Peplau et al. (1978), 2.5 years; and Gundlach and Reiss (1968), 1–9 years.

3. Several studies have included a small proportion of older lesbians (Bell & Weinberg, 1978; Jay & Young, 1977; Saghir & Robins, 1973). Only one study (Raphael & Robinson, 1980) has explicitly focused on older lesbians.

4. An emphasis on emotional bonds in relationships is described by Bell and Weinberg (1978), Cotton (1975), Hidalgo and Hidalgo-Christensen (1976), Peplau et al. (1978), and Ramsey et al. (1978).

5. Studies investigating role-playing include Bass-Hass (1968), Bell and Weinberg (1978), Caldwell and Peplau (in press), Cardell et al. (in press), Cotton (1975), Gagnon and Simon (1973), Jay and Young (1977), Jensen (1974), Ponse (1980), Saghir and Robins (1973), Tanner (1978), and Wolf (1979).

6. Studies of sexual behavior include Bell and Weinberg (1978), Jay and Young (1977), Gundlach and Reiss (1968), Peplau et al. (1978), and Schaefer (1976).

7. The proportion of lesbians who have been heterosexually married varies across studies: Bell and Weinberg (1978), 35 percent; Gundlach and Reiss (1968), 29 percent; Saghir and Robins (1973), 25 percent; Schaefer (1976), 14 percent.

8. Data on orgasms are found in Bell and Weinberg (1978), Gundlach and Reiss (1968), Jay and Young (1977), Kinsey et al. (1953), and Masters and Johnson (1979).

9. Data on sexual frequency in lesbian relationships are found in Jay and Young (1977), Peplau et al. (1978), and Schaefer (1976).

10. Serial monogamy has been described by Cotton (1975), Peplau et al. (1978), Saghir and Robins (1973), Tanner (1978), and Wolf (1979). Exceptions to this pattern are discussed by Barnhart (1975), Bell and Weinberg (1978), Ettorre (1980), Jay and Young (1977), and Peplau et al. (1978).

19 Girls Just Want to Be Mean

MARGARET TALBOT

Today is Apologies Day in Rosalind Wiseman's class—so, naturally, when class lets out, the girls are crying. Not all 12 of them, but a good half. They stand around in the corridor, snuffling quietly but persistently, interrogating one another. "Why didn't you apologize to *me*?" one girl demands. "Are you stressed right now?" says another. "I am *so* stressed." Inside the classroom, which is at the National Cathedral School, a private girls' school in Washington, Wiseman is locked in conversation with one of the sixth graders who has stayed behind to discuss why her newly popular best friend is now scorning her.

"You've got to let her go through this," Wiseman instructs. "You can't make someone be your best friend. And it's gonna be hard for her too, because if she doesn't do what they want her to do, the popular girls are gonna chuck her out, and they're gonna spread rumors about her or tell people stuff she told them." The girl's ponytail bobs as she nods and thanks Wiseman, but her expression is baleful.

Wiseman's class is about gossip and cliques and ostracism and just plain meanness among girls. But perhaps the simplest way to describe its goals would be to say that it tries to make middle-school girls be nice to one another. This is a far trickier project than you might imagine, and

Apologies Day is a case in point. The girls whom Wiseman variously calls the Alpha Girls, the R.M.G.'s (Really Mean Girls) or the Queen Bees are the ones who are supposed to own up to having back-stabbed or dumped a friend, but they are also the most resistant to the exercise and the most self-justifying. The girls who are their habitual victims or hangers-on—the Wannabes and Messengers in Wiseman's lingo—are always apologizing anyway.

But Wiseman, who runs a nonprofit organization called the Empower Program, is a cheerfully unyielding presence. And in the end, her students usually do what she wants: they take out their gel pens or their glittery feather-topped pens and write something, fold it over and over again into origami and then hide behind their hair when it's read aloud. Often as not, it contains a hidden or a not-so-hidden barb. To wit: "I used to be best friends with two girls. We weren't popular, we weren't that pretty, but we had fun together. When we came to this school, we were placed in different classes. I stopped being friends with them and left them to be popular. They despise me now, and I'm sorry for what I did. I haven't apologized because I don't really want to be friends any longer and am afraid if I apologize, then that's how it will result. We are now in completely different leagues." Or: "Dear B. I'm sorry for excluding you and ignoring you. Also, I have said a bunch of bad things about you. I have also run away from you just because I didn't like you. A." Then there are the apologies that rehash the original offense in a way sure to embarrass the offended party all over again, as in: "I'm sorry I told everybody you had an American Girl doll. It really burned your reputation." Or: "Dear 'Friend,' I'm sorry that I talked about you behind your back. I once even compared your forehead/face to a minefield (only 2, 1 person though.) I'm really sorry I said these things even though I might still believe them."

Wiseman, who is 32 and hip and girlish herself, has taught this class at many different schools, and it is fair to say that although she loves girls, she does not cling to sentimental notions about them. She is a feminist, but not the sort likely to ascribe greater inherent compassion to women or girls as a group than to men or boys. More her style is the analysis of the feminist historian Elizabeth Fox-Genovese, who has observed that "those who have experienced dismissal by the junior-high-school girls' clique could hardly, with a straight face, claim generosity and nurture as a natural attribute of women." Together, Wiseman and I once watched the movie "Heathers," the 1989 black comedy about a triad of vicious Queen Bees who get their comeuppance, and she found it "pretty true to life." The line uttered by Winona Ryder as Veronica, the disaffected non-Heather of the group, struck her as particularly apt: "I don't really like my friends. It's just like they're people I work with and our job is being popular."

Wiseman's reaction to the crying girls is accordingly complex. "I hate to make girls cry," she says. "I really do hate it when their faces get all splotchy, and everyone in gym class or whatever knows they've been crying." At the same time, she notes: "The tears are a funny thing. Because it's not usually the *victims* who cry; it's the aggressors, the girls who have something to apologize for. And sometimes, yes, it's relief on their part, but it's also somewhat manipulative, because if they've done something crappy, the person they've done it to can't get that mad at them if they're crying. Plus, a lot of the time they're using the apology to dump on somebody all over again."

Is dumping on a friend really such a serious problem? Do mean girls wield that much power? Wiseman thinks so. In May, Crown will publish her book-length analysis of girl-on-girl nastiness, "Queen Bees and Wannabes: Helping Your Daughter Survive Cliques, Gossip, Boyfriends and other Realities of Adolescence." And her seminars, which she teaches in schools around the country, are ambitious attempts to tame what some psychologists are now calling "relational aggression"—by which they mean the constellation of "Heathers"-like manipulations and exclusions and gossip-mongering that most of us remember from middle school and through which girls, more often than boys, tend to channel their hostilities.

"My life is full of these ridiculous little slips of paper," says Wiseman, pointing to the basket of apologies and questions at her feet. "I have read thousands of these slips of paper. And 95 percent of them are the same. 'Why are these girls being mean to me?' 'Why am I being excluded?' 'I don't want to be part of this popular group anymore. I don't like what they're doing.' There are lots of girls out there who are getting this incredible lesson that they are not inherently worthy, and from someone—a friend, another girl—who was so intimately bonded with them. To a large extent, their definitions of intimacy are going to be based on the stuff they're going through in sixth and seventh grade. And that stuff isn't pretty."

This focus on the cruelty of girls is, of course, something new. For years, psychologists who studied aggression among schoolchildren looked only at its physical and overt manifestations and concluded that girls were less aggressive than boys. That consensus began to change in the early 90's, after a team of researchers led by a Finnish professor named Kaj Bjorkqvist started interviewing 11- and 12-year-old girls about their behavior toward one another. The team's conclusion was that girls were, in fact, just as aggressive as boys, though in a different way. They were not as likely to engage in physical fights, for example, but their superior social intelligence enabled them to wage complicated battles with other girls aimed at damaging relationships or reputations—leaving nasty messages by cellphone or spreading scurrilous rumors by e-mail, making friends with one girl as revenge against another, gossiping about someone just loudly enough to be overheard. Turning the notion of women's greater empathy on its head, Bjorkqvist focused on the destructive uses to which such emotional attunement could be put. "Girls can better understand how other girls feel," as he puts it, "so they know better how to harm them."

Researchers following in Bjorkqvist's footsteps noted that up to the age of four girls tend to be aggressive at the same rates and in the same ways as boys—grabbing toys, pushing, hitting. Later on, however, social expectations force their hostilities underground, where their assaults on one another are more indirect, less physical and less visible to adults. Secrets they share in one context, for example, can sometimes be used against them in another. As Marion Underwood, a professor of psychology at the University of Texas at Dallas, puts it: "Girls very much value intimacy, which makes them excellent friends and terrible enemies. They share so much information when they are friends that they never run out of ammunition if they turn on one another."

In the last few years, a group of young psychologists, including Underwood and Nicki Crick at the University of Minnesota, has pushed this work much further, observing girls in "naturalistic" settings, exploring the psychological foundations for nastiness and asking adults to take relational aggression—especially in the sixth and seventh grades, when it tends to be worst—as seriously as they do more familiar forms of bullying. While some of these researchers have emphasized bonding as a motivation, others have seen something closer to a hunger for power, even a Darwinian drive. One Australian researcher, Laurence Owens, found that the 15-year-old girls he interviewed about their girl-pack predation were bestirred primarily by its entertainment value. The girls treated their own lives like the soaps, hoarding drama, constantly rehashing trivia. Owens's studies contain some of the more vivid anecdotes in the earnest academic literature on relational aggression. His subjects tell him about ingenious tactics like leaving the following message on a girl's answering machine—"Hello, it's me. Have you gotten your pregnancy test back yet?"—knowing that her parents will be the first to hear it. They talk about standing in "huddles" and giving other girls "deaths"—stares of withering condescension—and of calling one another "dyke," "slut" and "fat" and of enlisting boys to do their dirty work.

Relational aggression is finding its chroniclers among more popular writers, too. In addition to Wiseman's book, this spring will bring Rachel Simmons's "Odd Girl Out: The Hidden Culture of Aggression in Girls," Emily White's "Fast Girls: Teenage Tribes and the Myth of the Slut" and Phyllis Chesler's "Woman's Inhumanity to Woman."

In her book, the 27-year-old Simmons offers a plaintive definition of relational aggression: "Unlike boys, who tend to bully acquaintances or strangers, girls frequently attack within tightly knit friendship networks, making aggression harder to identify and intensifying the damage to the victims. Within the hidden culture of aggression, girls fight with body language and relationships instead of fists and knives. In this world, friendship is a weapon, and the sting of a shout pales in comparison to a day of someone's silence. There is no gesture more devastating than the back turning away." Now, Simmons insists, is the time to pull up the rock and really look at this seething underside of American girlhood. "Beneath a facade of female intimacy," she writes, "lies a terrain traveled in secret, marked with anguish and nourished by silence."

Not so much silence, anymore, actually. For many school principals and counselors across the country, relational aggression is becoming a certified social problem and the need to curb it an accepted mandate. A small industry of interveners has grown up to meet the demand. In Austin, Tex., an organization called GENaustin now sends counselors into schools to teach a course on relational aggression called Girls as Friends, Girls as Foes. In Erie, Pa., the Ophelia Project offers a similar curriculum, taught by high-school-aged mentors, that explores "how girls hurt each other" and how they can stop. A private Catholic school in Akron, Ohio, and a public-school district near Portland, Ore., have introduced programs aimed at rooting out girl meanness. And Wiseman and her Empower Program colleagues have taught their Owning Up class at 60 schools. "We are currently looking at relational aggression like domestic violence 20 years ago," says Holly Nishimura, the assistant director of the Ophelia Project. "Though it's not on the same scale, we believe that with relational aggression, the trajectory of awareness, knowledge and demand for change will follow the same track."

Whether this new hypervigilance about a phenomenon that has existed for as long as most of us can remember will actually do anything to squelch it is, of course, another question. Should adults be paying as much attention to this stuff as kids do or will we just get hopelessly tangled up in it ourselves? Are we approaching frothy adolescent bitchery with undue gravity or just giving it its due in girls' lives? On the one hand, it is kind of satisfying to think that girls might be, after their own fashion, as aggressive as boys. It's an idea that offers some relief from the specter of the meek and mopey, "silenced" and self-loathing girl the popular psychology of girlhood has given us in recent years. But it is also true that the new attention to girls as relational aggressors may well take us into a different intellectual cul-de-sac, where it becomes too easy to assume that girls do not use their fists (some do), that all girls are covert in their cruelties, that all girls care deeply about the ways of the clique—and that what they do in their "relational" lives takes precedence over all other aspects of their emerging selves.

After her class at the National Cathedral School, Wiseman and I chat for a while in her car. She has to turn down the India Arie CD that's blaring on her stereo so we can hear each other. The girl she had stayed to talk with after class is still on her mind, partly because she represents the social type for whom Wiseman seems to feel the profoundest sympathy: the girl left behind by a newly popular, newly dismissive friend. "See, at a certain point it becomes cool to be boy crazy," she explains. "That happens in sixth grade, and it gives you so much social status, particularly in an all-girls school, if you can go up and talk to boys.

"But often, an Alpha Girl has an old friend, the best-friend-forever elementary-school friend, who is left behind because she's not boy crazy yet," Wiseman goes on, pressing the accelerator with her red snakeskin boot. "And what she can't figure out is: why does my old friend want to be better friends with a girl who talks behind her back and is mean to her than with me, who is a good friend and who wouldn't do that?"

The subtlety of the maneuvers still amazes Wiseman, though she has seen them time and again. "What happens," she goes on, "is that the newly popular girl—let's call her Darcy—is hanging out with Molly and some other Alpha Girls in the back courtyard, and the old friend, let's call her Kristin, comes up to them. And what's going to happen is Molly's going to throw her arms around Darcy and talk about things that Kristin doesn't know anything about and be totally physically affectionate with Darcy so that she looks like the shining jewel. And Kristin is, like, I don't exist. She doesn't want to be friends with the new version of Darcy—she wants the old one back, but it's too late for that."

So to whom, I ask Wiseman, does Kristin turn in her loneliness? Wiseman heaves a sigh as though she's sorry to be the one to tell me an obvious but unpleasant truth. "The other girls can be like sharks—it's like blood in the water, and they see it and they go, 'Now I can be closer to Kristin because she's being dumped by Darcy.' When I say stuff like this, I know I sound horrible, I know it. But it's what they do."

Hanging out with Wiseman, you get used to this kind of disquisition on the craftiness of middle-school girls, but I'll admit that when my mind balks at something she has told me, when I can't quite believe girls have thought up some scheme or another, I devise little tests for her—I ask her to pick out seventh-grade Queen Bees in a crowd outside a school or to predict what the girls in the class will say about someone who isn't there that day or to guess which boys a preening group of girls is preening for. I have yet to catch her out.

Once, Wiseman mentions a girl she knows whose clique of seven is governed by actual, enumerated rules and suggests I talk with this girl to get a sense of what reformers like her are up against. Jessica Travis, explains Wiseman, shaking her head in aggravated bemusement at the mere thought of her, is a junior at a suburban Maryland high school and a member of the Girls' Advisory Board that is part of Wiseman's organization. She is also, it occurs to me when I meet her, a curious but not atypical social type—an amalgam of old-style Queen Bee-ism and new-style girl's empowerment, brimming over with righteous self-esteem and cheerful cattiness. Tall and strapping, with long russet hair and blue eye shadow, she's like a Powerpuff Girl come to life.

When I ask Jessica to explain the rules her clique lives by, she doesn't hesitate. "O.K.," she says happily. "No 1: clothes. You cannot wear jeans any day but Friday, and you cannot wear a ponytail or sneakers more than once a week. Monday is fancy day—like black pants or maybe you bust out with a skirt. You want to remind people how cute you are in case they forgot over the weekend. O.K., 2: parties. Of course, we sit down together and discuss which ones we're going to go to, because there's no point in getting all dressed up for a party that's going to be lame. No getting smacked at a party, because how would it look for the rest of us if you're drunk and acting like a total fool? And if you do hook up with somebody at the party, please try to limit it to one. Otherwise you look like a slut and that reflects badly on all of us. Kids are not that smart; they're not going to make the distinctions between us. And the rules apply to all of us—you can't be like, 'Oh, I'm having my period; I'm wearing jeans all week.'"

She pauses for a millisecond. "Like, we had a lot of problems with this one girl. She came to school on a Monday in jeans. So I asked her, 'Why you wearing jeans today?' She said, 'Because I felt like it.' 'Because you felt like it? Did you forget it was a Monday?' 'No.' She says she just doesn't like the confinement. She doesn't want to do this anymore. She's the rebel of the group, and we had to suspend her a couple of times; she wasn't allowed to sit with us at lunch. On that first Monday, she didn't even try; she didn't even catch my eye—she knew better. But eventually she came back to us, and she was, like, 'I know, I deserved it.'

Each member of Jessica's group is allowed to invite an outside person to sit at their table in the lunch room several times a month, but they have to meet at the lockers to O.K. it with the other members first, and they cannot exceed their limit. "We don't want other people at our table more than a couple of times a week because we want to bond, and the bonding is endless," Jessica says. "Besides, let's say you want to tell your girls about some total fool thing you did, like locking your hair in the car door. I mean, my God, you're not going to tell some stranger *that.*"

For all their policing of their borders, they are fiercely loyal to those who stay within them. If a boy treats one of them badly, they all snub him. And Jessica offers another example: "One day, another friend came to school in this skirt from Express—ugliest skirt I've ever seen—red and brown plaid, O.K.? But she felt really fabulous. She was like, Isn't this skirt cute? And she's my friend, so of course I'm like, Damn straight, sister! Lookin' good! But then, this other girl who was in the group for a while comes up and she says to her: 'Oh, my God, you look so stupid! You look like a giant argyle sock!' I was like, 'What is wrong with you?'"

Jessica gets good grades, belongs to the B'nai B'rith Youth Organization and would like, for no particular reason, to go to Temple University. She plays polo and figure-skates, has a standing appointment for a once-a-month massage and "cried from the beginning of 'Pearl Harbor' till I got home that night." She lives alone with her 52-year-old mother, who was until January a consultant for Oracle. She is lively and loquacious and she has, as she puts it, "the highest self-esteem in the world." Maybe that's why she finds it so easy to issue dictums like: "You cannot go out with an underclassman. You just *cannot*—end of story." I keep thinking, when I listen to Jessica talk about her clique, that she must be doing some kind of self-conscious parody. But I'm fairly sure she's not.

On a bleary December afternoon, I attend one of Wiseman's after-school classes in the Maryland suburbs. A public middle school called William H. Farquhar has requested the services of the Empower Program. Soon after joining the class, I ask the students about a practice Wiseman has told me about that I find a little hard to fathom or even to believe. She had mentioned it in passing—"You know how the girls use three-way calling"—and when I professed puzzlement, explained: "O.K., so Alison and Kathy call up Mary, but only Kathy talks and Alison is just lurking there quietly so Mary doesn't know she's on the line. And Kathy says to Mary, 'So what do you think of Alison?' And of course there's some reason at the moment why Mary doesn't like Alison, and she says, Oh, my God, all these nasty things about Alison—you know, 'I can't believe how she throws herself at guys, she thinks she's all that, blah, blah, blah.' And Alison hears all this."

Not for the first time with Wiseman, I came up with one of my lame comparisons with adult life: "But under normal circumstances, repeating nasty gossip about one friend to another is not actually going to get you that far with your friends."

"Yeah, but in Girl World, that's currency," Wiseman responded. "It's like: Ooh, I have a dollar and now I'm more powerful and I can use this if I want to. I can further myself in the social hierarchy and bond with the girl being gossiped about by setting up the conference call so she can know about it, by telling her about the gossip and then delivering the proof."

In the classroom at Farquhar, eight girls are sitting in a circle, eating chips and drinking sodas. All of them have heard about the class and chosen to come. There's Jordi Kauffman, who is wearing glasses, a fleece vest and sneakers and who displays considerable scorn for socially ambitious girls acting "all slutty in tight clothes or all snotty." Jordi is an honor student whose mother is a teacher and whose father is the P.T.A. president. She's the only one in the class with a moderately sarcastic take on the culture of American girlhood. "You're in a bad mood one day, and you say you feel fat," she remarks, "and adults are like, 'Oh-oh, she's got poor self-esteem, she's depressed, get her help!'"

Next to Jordi is her friend Jackie, who is winsome and giggly and very pretty. Jackie seems more genuinely troubled by the loss of a onetime friend who has been twisting herself into an Alpha Girl. She will later tell us that when she wrote a heartfelt e-mail message to this former friend, asking her why she was "locking her out," the girl's response was to print it out and show it around at school.

On the other side of the room are Lauren and Daniela, who've got boys on the brain, big time. They happily identify with Wiseman's negative portrayal of "Fruit-Cup Girl," one who feigns helplessness—in Wiseman's example, by pretending to need a guy to open her pull-top can of fruit cocktail—to attract male attention. There's Courtney, who will later say, when asked to write a letter to herself about how she's doing socially, that she can't, because she "never says anything to myself about myself." And there's Kimberly, who will write such a letter professing admiration for her own "natural beauty."

They have all heard of the kind of three-way call Wiseman had told me about; all but two have done it or had it done to them. I ask if they found the experience useful. "Not always," Jordi says, "because sometimes there's something you want to hear but you don't hear. You want to hear, 'Oh, she's such a good person' or whatever, but instead you hear, 'Oh, my God, she's such a bitch.'"

I ask if boys ever put together three-way calls like that. "Nah," Jackie says. "I don't think they're smart enough."

Once the class gets going, the discussion turns, as it often does, to Jackie's former friend, the one who's been clawing her way into the Alpha Girl clique. In a strange twist, this girl has, as Daniela puts it, "given up her religion" and brought a witch's spell book to school.

"That's weird," Wiseman says, "because usually what happens is that the girls who are attracted to that are more outside-the-box types—you know, the depressed girls with the black fingernails who are always writing poetry—because it gives them some amount of power. The girl you're describing sounds unconfident; maybe she's looking for something that makes her seem mysterious and powerful. If you have enough social status, you can be a little bit different. And that's where she's trying to go with this—like, I am *so* in the box that I'm defining a new box."

Jackie interjects, blushing, with another memory of her lost friend. "I used to tell her everything," she laments, "and now she just blackmails me with my secrets."

"Sounds like she's a Banker," Wiseman says. "That means that she collects information and uses it later to her advantage."

"Nobody really likes her," chimes in Jordi. "She's like a shadow of her new best friend, a total Wannabe. Her new crowd's probably gonna be like, 'Take her back, pulleeze!'"

"What really hurts," Jackie persists, "is that it's like you can't just drop a friend. You have to dump on them, too."

"Yeah, it's true," Jordi agrees matter-of-factly. "You have to make them really miserable before you leave."

After class, when I concede that Wiseman was right about the three-way calling, she laughs. "Haven't I told you girls are crafty?" she asks. "Haven't I told you girls are *evil*?" . . .

A little over a month after the last class at Farquhar, I go back to the school to have lunch with Jordi and Jackie. I want to know what they've remembered from the class, how it might have affected their lives. Wiseman has told me that she will sometimes get e-mail messages from girls at schools where she has taught complaining of recidivism:

"Help, you have to come back! We're all being mean again"—that kind of thing.

The lunchroom at Farquhar is low-ceilinged, crowded and loud and smells like frying food and damp sweaters. The two teachers on duty are communicating through walkie-talkies. I join Jordi in line, where she selects for her lunch a small plate of fried potato discs and nothing to drink. Lunch lasts from 11:28 to 11:55, and Jordi always sits at the same table with Jackie (who bounds in late today, holding the little bag of popcorn that is her lunch) and several other girls.

I ask Jackie what she remembers best about Wiseman's class, and she smiles fondly and says it was the "in and out of the box thing—who's cool and who's not and why."

I ask Jordi if she thought she would use a technique Wiseman had recommended for confronting a friend who had weaseled out of plans with her in favor of a more popular girl's invitation. Wiseman had suggested sitting the old friend down alone at some later date, "affirming" the friendship and telling her clearly what she wanted from her. Jordi had loved it when the class acted out the scene, everybody hooting and booing at the behavior of the diva-girl as she dissed her social inferiors in a showdown at the food court. But now, she tells me that she found the exercise "kind of corny." She explains: "Not many people at my school would do it that way. We'd be more likely just to battle it out on the Internet when we got home." (Most of her friends feverishly instant-message after school each afternoon.) Both girls agree that the class was fun, though, and had taught them a lot about popularity.

Which, unfortunately, wasn't exactly the point. Wiseman told me once that one hazard of her trade is that girls will occasionally go home and tell their moms that they were in a class where they learned how to be popular. "I think they're smarter than that, and they must just be telling their moms that," she said. "But they're such concrete thinkers at this age that some could get confused."

I think Wiseman's right—most girls do understand what she's getting at. But it is also true that in paying such close attention to the cliques, in taking Queen Bees so very seriously, the relational-aggression movement seems to grant them a legitimacy and a stature they did not have when they ruled a world that was beneath adult radar.

Nowadays, adults, particularly in the upper middle classes, are less laissez-faire about children's social lives. They are more vigilant, more likely to have read books about surviving the popularity wars of middle school or dealing with cliques, more likely to have heard a talk or gone to a workshop on those topics. Not long ago, I found myself at a lecture by the best-selling author Michael Thompson on "Understanding the Social Lives of our Children." It was held inside the National Cathedral on a chilly Tuesday evening in January, and there were hundreds of people in attendance—attractive late-40's mothers in cashmere turtlenecks and interesting scarves and expensive haircuts, and graying but fit fathers—all taking notes and lining up to ask eager, anxious questions about how best to ensure their children's social happiness. "As long as education is mandatory," Thompson said from the pulpit, "we have a huge obligation to make it socially safe," and heads nodded all around me. He made a list of "the top three reasons for a fourth-grade girl to be popular," and parents in my pew wrote it down in handsome little leather notebooks or on the inside cover of Thompson's latest book, "Best Friends, Worst Enemies." A red-haired woman with a fervent, tremulous voice and an elegant navy blue suit said that she worried our children were socially handicapped by "a lack of opportunities for unstructured cooperative play" and mentioned that she had her 2-year-old in a science class. A serious-looking woman took the microphone to say that she was troubled by the fact that her daughter liked a girl "who is mean and controlling and once wrote the word murder on the bathroom mirror—and this is in a private school!"

I would never counsel blithe ignorance on such matters—some children are truly miserable at school for social reasons, truly persecuted and friendless and in need of adult help. But sometimes we do seem in danger of micromanaging children's social lives, peering a little too closely. Priding ourselves on honesty in our relationships, as baby-boomer parents often do, we expect to know everything about our children's friendships, to be hip to their social travails in a way our own parents, we thought, were not. But maybe this attention to the details can backfire, giving children the impression that the transient social anxieties and allegiances of middle school are weightier and more immutable than they really are. And if that is the result, it seems particularly unfortunate for girls, who are already more mired in the minutiae of relationships than boys are, who may already lack, as Christopher Lasch once put it, "any sense of an impersonal order that exists independently of their wishes and anxieties" and of the "vicissitudes of relationships."

I think I would have found it dismaying if my middle school had offered a class that taught us about the wiles of Marcie and Tracie: if adults studied their folkways, maybe they were more important than I thought, or hoped. For me, the best antidote to the caste system of middle school was the premonition that adults did not usually play by the same rigid and peculiar rules—and that someday, somewhere, I would find a whole different mattering map, a whole crowd of people who read the same books I did and wouldn't shun me if I didn't have a particular brand of shoes. When I went to college, I found it, and I have never really looked back.

And the Queen Bees? Well, some grow out of their girly sense of entitlement on their own, surely; some channel it in more productive directions. Martha Stewart must have been a Q.B. Same with Madonna. At least one of the Q.B.'s from my youth—albeit the nicest and smartest one—has become a pediatrician on the faculty of a prominent medical school, I noticed when I looked her up the other day. And some Queen Bees have people who love them—dare I say it?—just as they are, a truth that would have astounded me in my own school days but that seems perfectly natural now.

On a Sunday afternoon, I have lunch with Jessica Travis and her mother, Robin, who turns out to be an outgoing, transplanted New Yorker—"born in Brighton Beach, raised in Sheepshead Bay." Over white pizza, pasta, cannoli and Diet Cokes, I ask Robin what Jessica was like as a child.

"I was fabulous," Jessica says.

"She was," her mother agrees. "She was blond, extremely happy, endlessly curious and always the leader of the pack. She didn't sleep because she didn't want to miss anything. She was just a bright, shiny kid. She's still a bright, shiny kid."

After Jessica takes a call on her pumpkin-colored cellphone, we talk for a while about Jessica's room, which they both describe as magnificent. "I have lived in apartments smaller than her majesty's two-bedroom suite," Robin snorts. "Not many single parents can do for their children what I have done for this one. This is a child who asked for a pony and got two. I tell her this is the top of the food chain. The only place you can go from here is the royal family."

I ask if anything about Jessica's clique bothers her. She says no—because what she calls "Jess's band of merry men" doesn't "define itself by its opponents. They're not a threat to anyone. Besides, it's not like they're an A-list clique."

"Uh, Mom," Jessica corrects. "We are definitely an A-list clique. We are totally A-list. You are giving out incorrect information."

"Soooorry," Robin says. "I'd fire myself, but there's no one else lining up for the job of being your mom."

Jessica spends a little time bringing her mother and me up to date on the elaborate social structure at her high school. The cheerleaders' clique, it seems, is not the same as the pom-pom girls' clique, though both are A-list. All sports cliques are A-list, in fact, except—"of course"—the swimmers. There is a separate A-list clique for cute preppy girls who "could play sports but don't." There is "the white people who pretend to be black clique" and the drama clique, which would be "C-list," except that, as Jessica puts it, "they're not even on the list."

"So what you are saying is that your high school is littered with all these groups that have their own separate physical and mental space?" Robin says, shaking her head in wonderment.

When they think about it, Jessica and her mom agree that the business with the rules—what you can wear on a given day of the week and all that—comes from Jessica's fondness for structure. As a child, her mom says she made up games with "such elaborate rules I'd be lost halfway through her explanation of them." Besides, there was a good deal of upheaval in her early life. Robin left her "goofy artist husband" when Jessica was 3, and after that they moved a lot. And when Robin went to work for Oracle, she "was traveling all the time, getting home late. When I was on the road, I'd call her every night at 8 and say: 'Sweet Dreams. I love you. Good Night.'"

"Always in that order," Jessica says. "*Always* at 8. I don't like a lot of change."

Toward the end of our lunch, Jessica's mother—who says she herself was more a nerd than a Queen Bee in school—returns to the subject of cliques. She wants, it seems, to put something to rest. "You know I realize there are people who stay with the same friends, the same kind of people, all their life, who never look beyond that," she says. "I wouldn't want that for my daughter. I want my daughter to be one of those people who lives in the world. I know she's got these kind of narrow rules in her personal life right now. But I still think, I really believe, that she will be a bigger person, a person who spends her life in the world." Jessica's mother smiles. Then she gives her daughter's hair an urgent little tug, as if it were the rip cord of a parachute and Jessica were about to float away from her.

CHAPTER SIX

Women and Work

Despite many stereotypes and a good deal of popular press regarding differences in the abilities and achievements of men and women, research in this area has consistently shown very few meaningful gender differences. Where gender differences have been shown (as, for example, in the areas of spatial reasoning and mathematics problem solving, where males appear to excel), research has tended to show very little evidence for "innate" or biological explanations. Rather, socialization practices and experience appear to better explain male-female differences in these abilities. In other words, many studies show that changes in gender-role socialization practices, or opportunities for training in a particular ability area, dramatically reduce any gender difference.

What is clear from research in the area of women's achievement, however, is that there is a great disparity between the generally high, school achievements of girls and their eventual career and power attainments in the adult world of work. Theorists have argued that there are two factors that help explain this discrepancy (e.g., Basow, 1992; Hyde, 1991). The first are *internal* or intra-psychic barriers to achievement. For example, studies have shown that girls and women show lower achievement motivation in competitive situations, and tend to set lower expectations for their own success. The second are *external* barriers to achievement, such as job discrimination, tokenism, the stress of multiple roles, or the lack of cultural support.

The papers in this section explore a number of questions regarding women's experience of work. One of my favorite bumper stickers reads, "EVERY woman is a working woman." The majority of American women work outside the home for pay, and of course do lots of work inside the home for no pay, and too many do both. The three papers in this section deal with the work women do and present sobering examples of some of the "external barriers" to women's attainment of equity in and satisfaction from their work.

Recent statistics show that women now make about 70 cents for every dollar earned by men (National Committee on Pay Equity, 1998). Unfortunately, the pay gap is unlikely to close very soon. One of the main reasons for this is the sex segregation of the labor market. That is, the majority of jobs in the United States are performed almost exclusively by one sex or the other. Garbage collectors are mostly male, day care workers are mostly female. And guess who earns more? To make matters even worse, research shows that once a significant number of women move into a traditionally male occupation, it shifts and becomes a female-dominated job (these jobs are often referred to as "pink collar") and wages fall. And what of jobs that are performed by both men and women? In the case of waiting tables for example, men will tend to be employed by fancier, higher paying restaurants and women by coffeeshops. I can remember when I was in graduate school I studied and worked in the four-story psychology building. Different subdisciplines of psychology resided on each floor, and sure enough, the floors were almost entirely sex segregated—with women on the first and second floors, where social, personality and developmental psychology professors worked, and men on the third and fourth floors, with cognitive and physiological psychology and neuroscience. After graduate school, of course, those with "harder science" Ph.D.s within psychology tend to earn more.

In other words, as unbelievable as it often is to my optimistic students soon to enter the job market themselves, the pay gap between men and women is likely to stay around. This is not because employers pay women less than men for the same job (hopefully that illegal practice is disappearing), but rather for more subtle reasons related to the sex segregation of the labor market. If you think about it, Barrie Thorne's research on the sex segregation of children in elementary school (Chapter 1) paints a remarkably similar picture. It seems that the business of childhood (play) is merely practice for the business of adulthood (work), where males and females exist in largely separate spheres and hold different status and power.

The pay gap between women and men holds for every level of education. Obviously many of you are getting a college education at least in part to increase your lifetime earnings. But unfortunately, statistics show that the financial payoff from college is greater for men. Women college gradutates (or all races) can expect to earn about $13,000 less annually than college-educated white men (National Committee on Pay Equity, 1998). In "Living in McJobdom," Michelle Sidler, a young, "Generation X" graduate student, reflects with pessimism on the harsh economic realities she faces in the new millennium. She argues that young women today face different economic concerns than did their foremothers and that these must be acknowledged if third-wave feminists are to develop a sound agenda for economic equity between the sexes. Secondly, she points out that gender equality, which is increasing in the workforce, does not necessarily bring economic progress to women.

Many of the difficult decisions faced by women of the second-wave feminist movement (e.g., family versus work) are no longer applicable to young women. Higher education is quickly becoming a necessity in an increasingly technologically-based economy. Decisions to have children are increasingly complicated by college tuition debt. Young women can no longer depend on the security of a husband's income, and this makes work a necessity, not a political choice.

Are you concerned about being trapped in a "McJob"—a low-prestige, part-time, or temporary position with no benefits and little hope for advancement? If not, this article may be a wake-up call. Sidler argues that McJobdom is a sutble condition, fueled by global capitalism, which is overtaking many of the social structures that women of previous generations operated within. Young women have been given the opportunity to enter the workforce, in large part due to the hard, political work of second-wave feminists who came before. Now, however, young women need to create their own economic agenda, incorporating the changing realities of technology, debt, and globalization, if they are to find satisfying work that pays well enough to live a good life.

For women who work in jobs that are high-status, rather than "pink collar" or McJob-like *tokenism* can be a significant external barrier to their work satisfaction. Minority women are especially likely to experience the stresses of being the "only," the "odd," the sole representative in a workplace of their "group." Tokens suffer in the workplace because they are highly visible and therefore often experience extreme performance pressure. They lack mentors and role models. In "Career Patterns of Women and Men in the Sciences," a piece published in *American Scientist*, Gerhard Sonnert and Gerald Holton discuss tokenism as one of several obstacles to women's advancement in the sciences. These authors provide data from an extensive questionnaire and interview study of nearly 900 people. Among their findings was that out-and-out exclusion or blatant prejudice did not occur often enough to account for the large gender gap in the sciences. Instead, more subtle exclusions and marginalizations appear to be at work here.

You may wish to discuss the interesting and subtle forms of discrimination against women in the sciences that these authors document. Do you think things like "style," "perfectionism," and "access to great chances" are also likely barriers to women's advancement in areas other than just science? Perhaps these subtle areas of bias are important to remember as you enter the world of work?

The bumper sticker I referred to earlier is funny because it plays upon the idea that a woman does not really *work* unless she is *paid* for what she does. A great deal of work women do is *unpaid*, and this represents yet another external barrier for women. In her book *The Second Shift*, Arlie Hochschild (1989) reports that women work an extra month of twenty-four-hour days each year. Whew! As a "working mom" of two children, I can definitely say it sure feels that way. Of course the work Hochschild is referring to consists of domestic responsibilities: housework and childcare. Full-time homemakers suffer the culture's general lack of appreciation for the complexity, difficulty, and import of their work (witness the phrase, "No she doesn't work, she's just a housewife."). They perform their duties in relative isolation, with no salary, no benefits, and no vacation. Furthermore, research shows that whether or not a woman is employed outside the home for pay, she is still responsible for these domestic tasks. This *double burden* that many working women have is not only a strain in terms of the number of hours it means they are putting in each day, but it also disadvantages them in terms of equal treatment in the workplace. Professional careers especially are designed for people who do not have domestic responsibilities such as housework and childcare (or for people who have someone at home to take care of those things). Of course this means that single working women, particularly those with children, are enormously disadvantaged.

Without more sharing of domestic responsibility, women's second-class status in the workforce is likely to remain. "The Politics of Housework," by Pat Mainardi, is now a classic feminist treatise. Written in 1970, this humorous essay puts a spotlight on housework as a major source of women's oppression by illustrating one liberated husband's varied methods of avoiding having to share it. Although much of its language reveals that this essay is quite dated, it's clear that the inequity Mainardi discusses is as much a part of women's lives today as it was more than thirty years ago.

It is clear that there are still many obstacles to women's work satisfaction and achievement. Social and political action to improve women's opportunities for achievement, and the satisfaction that comes from it, must recognize both long-standing gender inequities in the workplace and at home, as well as changing economic realities.

References

Basow, S. A. (1992). *Gender stereotypes and roles*, 3rd ed. Pacific Grove, CA: Brooks/Cole Publishing Co.

Hochshchild, A. (1989). *The second shift: Working parents and the revolution at home.* New York: Viking.

Hyde, J. S. (1991). *Half the human experience: The psychology of women*, 4th ed. Lexington, MA: D. C. Heath and Company.

National Commiuttee on Pay Equity (1998, Fall). *Newsnotes.* Washington, D.C.

20 Living in McJobdom: Third Wave Feminism and Class Inequity

MICHELLE SIDLER

I recently read *Changing Subjects: The Making of Feminist Literary Criticism* (Greene and Kahn 1993), a collection of essays by women who were leaders in second wave feminism—literary scholars and teachers who came of age in the 1960s and 1970s. Many of the essays were personal and reflective, recounting the difficulties of working in departments as the first and only woman professor. These feminists defied blatant sexism and existing cultural norms against working women to fulfill their potential as intelligent, independent people. I was moved by the dedication to literary studies that initially led so many of the women to attend graduate school, where they often faced an unreceptive academia dominated by male scholars.

It occurred to me that when I entered graduate school in 1991, I did not anticipate gender barriers, partially because of my own naïveté, but also because of an undergraduate experience within an English department almost exclusively made up of women. It was at this moment that I realized to the fullest my indebtedness to second wave feminism—all of the female instructors of undergraduates whose brilliance and support fostered my eventual career in English studies were part of the second wave feminist movement. If not for the vital social and political work of these women, I might not have been in a position to consider even the possibility of obtaining a doctoral degree.

But looking closer at my reason for entering graduate school directly after receiving my bachelor's degree, I must confess that my decision had less to do with an overwhelming desire to study Milton or Joyce or even Welty than with my fear of facing a bleak job market holding, as I did, few technical skills and a liberal arts degree. Too many friends before me had fallen into McJobs,[1] working in part-time or temporary positions with no benefits and no hope of advancement. If I can just make it through graduate school, I thought, I will have it all—job security, benefits, great working hours, and an academic position that will allow me to engage in two of my favorite activities, teaching and writing. In a time when temporary employment agencies such as Manpower are among the most prosperous American companies, such economic concerns loom large.[2] My choices were discouragingly simple: either survive graduate school and work in academia, or risk being swallowed up into the black hole of McJobdom and losing the security and prospects of my middle-class upbringing. Indeed, going to graduate school seemed the only foreseeable alternative to what Jeff Giles in *Newsweek* magazine called, "for newly minted grads, arguably the worst job market since World War II" (1994, 65).

Many second wave feminists were faced with an either/or dilemma also: either get (or stay) married and sacrifice their own professional ambitions, or follow their desires as self-sustaining, intelligent women. Rachel Blau DuPlessis writes of the mixed messages she received at college in the 1960s: "A major contradiction lay between the culture's incessant (and our internalized) demand for instantly ratifying engagement and marriage, and any sense of independence, self-definition, autonomy, social commitment" (1993, 98). She, like other second wave feminists, found herself torn between two conflicting messages: raise a family or be economically self-sufficient. Second wave feminists, driven by a sense of independence and a need for equality, struggled to break down that either/or dilemma.

For many young women now, the choice whether or not to work is no longer an either/or proposition. Most twentysomething women do not question the possibility of work, and not necessarily because we feel particularly empowered or independent. With stagnant wages in many fields, women often must work just to stay afloat, even if they are married to working husbands. Generally, women no longer feel trapped into housekeeping and motherhood; on average, we are waiting later and later to have children. Since women's liberation, more women than ever are entering the professional workplace. According to Robert Reich in *Rolling Stone*, "In 1973, 57 percent of women in their 20's were in the workforce. Twenty years later, the figure had climbed to 73 percent" (1994, 119). However, many young women do not view this new presence in the workforce as an opportunity. Many, like myself, feel trapped by lower wages for all workers and know that even for married couples, two incomes are quickly becoming a necessity.

Second wave feminism helped bring about professional self-sufficiency for women, and their work paved the way for new feminisms, such as that being constructed by young women of the post-baby boom generation. But postmodernism and the new global economy have brought on concerns about the homogeneity of the so-called bourgeois white feminism of the second wave. Who has reaped the benefits of the women's movement of the 1960s and 1970s? To what extent did second wave feminism help the rise of women in *all* classes, including those outside privileged classes, and to what extent must feminism revamp itself in the wake of the new global economy? What can we learn from second wave feminism as we face an economy driven by profits, with workers edged out by technology and global competition?

The rise of women in the workplace sounds like bright news, but it begins to take on a new face when I consider again my own shaky job dilemma. Like many other twentysomethings, I feel job security slipping out from under me. Economic restructuring has destabilized employment for both men and women. Women can no longer depend on the security of a husband's income (or their own, for that matter). Nor can they assume that jobs are available; often women just have not had access to them. Even young working men are finding more McJobs and lower salaries. Third wave feminism will have to face these harsh economic conditions.

Academia itself poses an excellent example of this new destabilization. Women (and men) in academia have less encouraging economic prospects than did second wave feminists. Since my entrance into graduate school, I have found that most of the academic perks I once looked forward to are not guaranteed. Due to budget crunching and an overabundance of out-of-work academics, many universities have turned to hiring professors part-time or temporarily, thus eliminating higher salaries, benefits, and the security of tenure. In the new restructuring of faculty, many professors are paid by each course hour they teach, prompting them to teach heavy loads and leaving little time for professional development. The shortage of positions was a minor problem when most second wave feminists looked for their first academic appointments. As second waver Elizabeth

Ermath writes. "When I began looking for a tenure-track job in 1969–70 the job market was just beginning to get pinched" (1993, 227). After twenty-five years, that pinch has become a painful squeeze. Doctoral students feel the economic pressure even before they graduate. While they pursue degrees, most endure their own versions of McJobs—teaching assistantships with salaries so low (and often few benefits) that many are forced to take out even more student loans, thus increasing their postdoctoral debt.

I am not alone in my pessimism about the economy. Many young Americans, so-called Generation Xers, have continued to list the economy as a concern; from *Time* magazine's groundbreaking feature on twentysomethings by David Gross and Sophfronia Scott in 1990 to *Newsweek*'s 1994 cover story by Giles, the economy continues to haunt postboomers. These two articles frame what has become a confusing and controversial discussion about exactly what Generation X is. Many of the initial media characterizations of twentysomethings have been proven inaccurate, such as the claims that they are "slackers" or "whiners." Some polls, in fact, show that Generation Xers work as hard as, and moan less than, members of older generations (Giles 1994, 65; Aley 1994). However, young workers are having an increasingly difficult time grappling with their economic conditions. . . .

. . . Among the countries represented at the March 1994 G7 conference (excepting only Germany), the jobless rate for people under twenty-five was worse than that for older workers.[3] In America, youth joblessness is not as bad as it is in most countries, but the employment available for twentysomethings in the United States is "often ill-paid or temporary or both" (Generation 1994, 27). This trend will only continue in the future, as new technologies and overseas job competition remain threats for working people. And we cannot rely on technological fields to create new jobs, because the number of jobs created by these fields is a fraction of what is needed to relieve U.S. and global unemployment (Rifkin 1995, xvii). Jeremy Rifkin notes that the future of many U.S. workers may be dire because of technology: "more than 90 million jobs in a labor force of 124 million are potentially vulnerable to replacement by machines" (1995, 5). In the specialized world of technologies, there are simply not enough jobs for all of these workers, and educated young Americans are already feeling the effects. According to the Bureau of Statistics, "Approximately 25% of under-35 college graduates have jobs that do not require college degrees" (Lane 1995, 106). Many of these twentysomethings work in temporary, part-time, and low-wage jobs. Temporary jobs alone employ 8.1 million Americans (Thurow 1996, 165).

These statistics have been proved in my personal life: I have seen many of my college friends (most of whom have four-year degrees) bounce from one McJob to another. And the financial situation continues to look as grim for women as it did in the past. According to Giles's statistics, women between twenty-five and thirty-four are still making an average salary only 82 percent that of their male counterparts. In *Working Woman*, Pamela Krueger notes that for college-educated women, future finances are even more complicated by the desire to have a family (1994, 62). The best-educated and most-skilled young women are demanding flexibility in the workplace. This goal will be difficult, if not impossible, to achieve, even for professionally prepared women, in the current economic instability. . . .

Annette Fuentes and Barbara Ehrenreich recognize the motivating force behind the worldwide employment crisis—multinational corporations guided by the "profit motive" (1983, 57). They argue that we must create a global network among working women for support and recognition. Although such a goal is an essential first step, much more needs to be done, and soon. Women, men, and feminism must redirect the profit motive, confront the widening gap between the wealthy and the underclasses, and produce options beyond the present corporate model. To prepare for such a challenge, women of all classes must familiarize themselves with economics as an integral part of feminism and of their daily lives. This need has never been greater or clearer than it is now in my generation. We can expect little improvement in these economic conditions as long as corporations value profit more than workers.

Marxist feminists argue that the union of capitalism and patriarchy leads to the domestic oppression of women.[4] These feminists have exposed the oppression of women, through domestic labor, as the reproducers of the capital workforce. However, the image of women as domestic servants to patriarchy first and capitalism second is quickly becoming outdated. Many families cannot afford the traditional family structure of the domestic mother when one-third of all men from twenty-five to thirty-four years of age earn less than what is needed to keep a family of four out of poverty (Thurow 1996, 31). Men do not have the luxury of an unemployed wife. Most women of my generation must work, whether we have families or not, to survive economically. Feminism can use the experience of resisting the oppressive yet ingrained patriarchal system to fight capitalism, but we must begin to move away from viewing patriarchy as the immediate cause of oppression and try to combat the even larger threat of American and worldwide economic hardship.

Without a new economic theory and political mission, feminism risks alienating this new generation of women, many of whom experience economic instability and, in some cases, a drop in class status. With the added insecurity of McJobs comes the decline of raw salary figures: between 1973 and 1992, real wages dropped for people at all levels of income except those in the top 20 percent (Rifkin 1995, 23). If this trend continues (and it most certainly will with the rising of corporate downsizing and global job competition), only women in the top 20 percent will have a choice about working. Material feminists must change their priorities from fighting the patriarchy first and capitalism second. Women's oppression must be seen as, first, a function of wage earning and, second, a result of domestic servitude, because soon there will be few homes without working mothers. Second wave feminists did not enter an economic forecast so grim; they had no way of knowing that my generation would need their help to counter the raw face of global profit-driven capitalism.

So how can a new feminist political agenda work to relieve the economic disparity facing twentysomethings? First, we must recognize that gender equality in the workforce does not automatically bring economic progress. Feminism in the 1960s and 1970s worked toward giving women the same economic opportunities as men. Now, however, there will be fewer economic opportunities for either gender, so we have to broaden our concerns to include issues previously viewed as gender neutral. In "The Long Goodbye," Linda Kauffman calls for a renewed sense of a feminist project that will readdress the current state of affairs, with its list of injustices that goes beyond those tackled by second wave feminism. She proposes a women's movement that addresses "injustices that might not normally be regarded as specifically feminist concerns because it is precisely the interconnection of feminist issues with other injustices that urgently needs our attention in the '90's" (1993, 141). This interconnection involves not just recognizing the plight of others but also learning how all injustices are an integral part of feminism itself.

Feminism can begin interconnecting by addressing at least three areas: academics, the media, and technology. These structures function broadly on economic, social, and cultural levels, and they have all been important in the progression of feminism. They also work on a personal level for me, as a teacher of using computers for writing. In my experience, academics, the media, and technology usually exist as contradictory forces. Feminists have been actively trying to usurp these structures as places of empowerment and change for women. But these areas have proved detrimental to twentysomethings, women, and workers. In many ways academics, the media, and technology are complicit in the workings of corporate oppression and the profit motive. . . .

The economic adversity of young workers can also be transformed on political and social levels, particularly through the media. The women's movement of second wave feminism learned hard lessons that can aid in this struggle. One way is to stop the cycle of blame on twentysomethings. As Susan Faludi spells out so effectively in *Backlash* (1991), feminism was reflected back onto the women's movement when much popular press in the 1980s claimed that feminism was its own worst enemy. A similar backlash has begun in response to reports of the economic plight of twentysomethings. Exploiting the false stereotypes about my generation, some members of the popular press blame young workers for their financial problems. David Martin, for example, labels twentysomethings "the Whiny Generation" and argues, "Instead of blaming everyone for this state of [economic] affairs, the Whiners should acquire more skills, education and specialized knowledge for the careers of the 21st century" (1993). Of course, Martin is mistaken about the possibilities for careers of the next century; with fewer jobs even for the educated, many skilled workers will be underemployed. In addition, as technology speeds up the progression of the market, many skills acquired now by young people will be obsolete soon.

Further, Martin's statement presents a problem facing twentysomethings that feminism also faces. Martin blames young workers themselves for their dissatisfaction, asserting that they were spoiled by privileged childhoods with high standards of living and economic prosperity. Ignoring for the moment Martin's obvious overgeneralizations about the standards of living for all postboomer youth, his blame tactics echo those chronicled in Faludi's book. Such reports targeted the "triumph of women's equality" as the cause of reports of increased stress and unhappiness among women (Faludi 1991, xiii). Feminism learned valuable lessons from this type of conservative media reaction, lessons that could now be used to counter backlash in the popular press concerning economic inequality for young men and women. Such lesson sharing is a realization of the interconnectedness between feminism and other movements that Kauffman identifies. . . .

This brings the discussion back to the personal level, to my stake in this economic inequity as a member of the twentysomething workforce. I am looking for a new feminism that tackles the issue of affording an education that will lead to economic prosperity, a struggle that parallels the employment equality sought by second wave feminists. I am personally invested in this problem not only as a student in higher education but also as a teacher in higher education. As a student, I have had to contend with the rising cost of my studies, at both the undergraduate and the graduate levels. I have already superseded the average $35,000 debt incurred by students seeking graduate degrees (Heilemann 1993, 42). And I am not alone—as of the 1991–92 school year, student loans overtook grants as the largest source of federal educational funds that college and graduate students receive (Financial 1993). This is no surprise as I consider my college classmates, some of whom graduated from our private, four-year university with debts totaling $5,000, $20,000, even $40,000. And with direct student loan dispersal (through increased technology, students can receive their checks as soon as seventy-two hours after applying), this trend will no doubt continue to rise (Wilkinson 1994).

Whereas many women in second wave feminism faced difficult decisions between family or school, or family or work, twentysomethings have little choice in these matters. First, higher education is quickly becoming a necessity; we are told there is no longer a job for us on the factory floor, so we must incur heavy debt to obtain a degree. Second, we must put off decisions such as having children for five, ten, maybe even twenty years because of the financial burden left by our education. This too is a feminist concern. Young women may not feel as much pressure to have children as did the previous generation of women, but their decision has become even more complicated by debt.

As an instructor in academia, I bring these concerns to my classroom and discuss them with my students. Teaching technical writing to seniors, I empathize with them as they surf the Internet desperately for the job that will take them out of this debt cycle. Some succeed; many do not. And my students are the ones on "the right path," obtaining the technical degrees touted as the promise of the twenty-first century. What of those students, like me, who did not choose "the right path," who obtained liberal arts degrees not for the money expected after graduation but for the desire to learn, to teach, and, in my case, to write? As I watch my students, I often wonder, if I had the chance to go back, would I choose a different direction, perhaps one with a more promising economic outlook?

And so I return again to those undergraduate English professors who supplied me with strong female role models in academic positions of power, juggling families and careers so skillfully. Their stories echo those told in *Changing Subjects* (Greene and Kahn 1993), as many of those women also came to grips with their own sexuality, independence, and social power through second wave feminism. But even with the professional and personal barriers they overcame, there were lessons that my professors did not know to teach me, struggles they had not faced as women pursuing careers. Mass job shortage was not a hardship they had needed to overcome; neither was oppressive, lingering debt. These conditions must be concerns of a third wave feminism. Yet we can learn from the struggles fought by second wavers against oppression, transforming the aggressor from patriarchy to capitalism.

Many boomer feminists found that patriarchy could be fought not on a mass level (the bitter defeat of the Equal Rights Amendment attests to that), but in smaller, more localized ways over a long period of time. Whereas their activism took the shape of hard work in positions that pushed on the glass ceiling, a third wave activism might take the form of denying or resisting corporate America by starting worker-friendly businesses or by helping employees unite to buy out their companies, thus returning the wealth and capital of the company to those who fostered it. Whereas second wave feminists strove for equality with men, third wave feminists cannot reasonably expect equality from capitalism. But we can fight to preserve basic rights and decent working conditions for people.

Another concern—another connection and contradiction—will be the importance placed on technology. Who will benefit from a feminism that finds its economic (as well as social and political) answers in the power of or power over technology? Personal computers and instant information did not influence the economy for second wave feminists as it does now. Whereas my undergraduate professors completed their dissertations on typewriters, I am learning the Internet in graduate school and submitting papers through E-mail. Although a new feminist agenda must keep up with the changes in technology, we must not lose sight of the economic privilege required and sustained by these machines. Technologies are, after all, the master's tools, created by men for the advancement of capitalism. Haraway argues that we must usurp those tools and use them for our benefit, but I am more skeptical about our chances. The Internet, for example, should be a place for open, global discussion and organization, much along the lines that Fuentes and Ehrenreich describe (1983). However, it is quickly becoming a place of commodification, a quick and easy instrument for corporations. We cannot turn our backs on this powerful medium, but we must understand its contradictions and limitations as well.

The McJobdom inhabited by so many twentysomethings is but a local manifestation of a growing economic condition. The condition is so subtle and pervasive that women and men of my generation do not know how to fight it. We have to recognize that global capitalism is overtaking many of the social structures under which second wave feminists operated. Academia is no longer a place of support for critically conscious scholars, media representations of the underprivileged and marginalized are often suspect, and technology is as much a hindrance to women and workers as it is an empowering tool. Leaving domestic roles to pursue a career is no longer a political statement either; it is a necessity that does not constitute activism for twentysomething women. A new, third wave feminism must combine our forces in the areas of academia, the media, and technology, constructing alliances against the profit motive and looking for the interconnection Kauffman describes. Such connections now supersede the traditional academic/popular, male/female binaries, providing the opportunity to explore injustice and inequity in new ways. But we also have to understand the contradictions inherent in many of the areas available for connection. We have to create an agenda with skepticism, looking closely and critically at the avenues we choose. Second wave feminism's identity politics gave twentysomething women the opportunity to enter the workforce and empowered us to create our own agenda, but with the rise of class instability we face a new playing field complicated by factors such as unemployment, debt, and technology. In short, third wave feminism needs a new economy.

Notes

1. Douglas Coupland describes "McJobs" as "Low pay, low prestige, low benefits, low future" (1991, 5).
2. Jeremy Rifkin describes the magnitude of Manpower: "Manpower, the nation's largest temp agency, is now the country's single largest employer, with 560,000 workers" (1995, 190).
3. The G7 conference is an annual summit of labor and finance leaders from the "Group of Seven," seven countries with some of the largest economies in the world, Italy, France, Canada, Britain, Japan, Germany, and the United States. The conference is primarily a chance to exchange information and discuss possible economic strategies. It is also known for producing a lot of talk but little action. For more information about the 1995 G7 conference, see "The G7 Summit: A Modest Proposal" (1995).
4. Barbara Hartmann provides an excellent discussion of the theoretical bases for the primacy of patriarchy (1981).

References

Aley, James. 1994. "Slacker Myths." *Fortune*, 21 February, 24.

Coupland, Douglas. 1991. *Generation X: Tales for an Accelerated Culture*. New York: St. Martin's.

Derrida, Jacques. 1994. *Specters of Marx*. Translated by Peggy Kamuf. New York: Routledge.
DuPlessis, Rachel Blau. 1993. "Reader, I Married Me: A Polygynous Memoir." In *Changing Subjects: The Making of Feminist Literary Criticism*, edited by Gayle Greene and Coppelia Kahn, 97–111. London: Routledge.
Ermath, Elizabeth. 1993. "On Having a Personal Voice." In *Changing Subjects: The Making of Feminist Literary Criticism*, edited by Gayle Greene and Coppelia Kahn, 226–39. London: Routledge.
Faludi, Susan. 1991. *Backlash*. New York: Crown.
"Financial Need and Loans Soar." 1993. *USA Today*, April, 10.
Fuentes, Annette, and Barbara Ehrenreich. 1983. *Women in the Global Factory*. Boston: South End.
"The G7 Summit: A Modest Proposal." 1995. *Economist*, 10 June, 19–21.
Generation X-onomics. 1994. *Economist*, 19 March, 27–28.
Giles, Jeff. 1994. "Generalizations X." *Newsweek*, 6 June, 62–72.
Greene, Gayle, and Coppelia Kahn, eds. 1993. *Changing Subjects: The Making of Feminist Literary Criticism*. London: Routledge.
Gross, David M., and Sophfronia Scott. 1990. "Proceeding with Caution." *Time*, 16 July, 56–62.
Haraway, Donna. 1990. "A Manifesto for Cyborgs." In *Feminism/Postmodernism*, edited by Linda J. Nicholson, 190–231. London: Routledge.
Hartmann, Barbara. 1981. "The Unhappy Marriage of Marxism and Feminism." In *Women and Revolution: A Discussion of the Unhappy Marriage of Marxism and Feminism*, edited by Lydia Sargent, 1–41. Boston: South End.
Heilemann, John. 1993. "Debt 101." *Washington Monthly*, March, 42–44.
Kauffman, Linda S. 1993. "The Long Goodbye: Against the Personal Testimony or, An Infant Grows Up." In *Changing Subjects: The Making of Feminist Literary Criticism*, edited by Gayle Greene and Coppelia Kahn, 129–46. London: Routledge.
Krueger, Pamela. 1994. "Superwoman's Daughters." *Working Woman*, May.
Lane, Randall. 1995. "Computers Are Our Friends." *Forbes*, 8 May, 102–8.
Mahar, Maggie. 1994. "Why Baby Boomers Aren't Going Bust." *Working Woman*, April, 22.
Martin, David. 1993. "The Whiny Generation." *Newsweek*, 1 November, 10.
Reich, Robert. 1994. "Hire Education." *Rolling Stone*, 20 October, 119–25.
Rifkin, Jeremy. 1995. *The End of Work: The Decline of the Global Labor Force and the Dawn of the Post-Market Era*. New York: Tarcher/Putnam.
Thurow, Lester C. 1996. *The Future of Capitalism: How Today's Economic Forces Shape Tomorrow's World*. New York: Morrow.
Wilkinson, Francis. 1994. "Clinton's Credit: The 72-Hour Student Loan." *Rolling Stone*, 25 August, 53.

21 Career Patterns of Women and Men in the Sciences

GERHARD SONNERT

GERALD HOLTON

The current status of women in science is a blend of decisive advance and unfulfilled promise. For more than two decades, discrimination against women in the sciences (as in other professional fields) has been outlawed in the United States, and consequently the gender gap has shrunk. Nevertheless, disparities remain in several areas and fields. A recent National Science Foundation report on women, minorities and persons with disabilities in science and engineering concluded, "On essentially all variables examined here, women fare less well than men." Whether the glass appears half full or half empty, a gender gap persists.

Why is it so? The explanations that have been advanced in the social-science literature can be categorized under two main headings. One, which we call the *deficit model*, is based on structural explanations of scientific careers. It posits the existence of mechanisms of formal and informal exclusion of women scientists. Women as a group, according to this model, receive fewer chances and opportunities along their career paths, and for this reason they collectively have worse career outcomes. The emphasis is on structural obstacles—legal, political and social—that exist (or that, in their most blatant forms, existed earlier) in the social system of science.

The *difference model*, on the other hand, posits the existence of deeply ingrained differences in behavior, outlook and goals between women and men. In this model the root cause of gender disparities in career achievement is internal to the individual. It is said to lie in gender differences—be they innate, or the result of gender-role socialization or cultural patterns. To a significant degree, the argument goes, these differences shape the behavior of individuals as well as the character of social institutions.

Within the difference model, the literature has discussed the possibility of several types of gender differences, of which we find three particularly relevant. First, females may be more likely than males to be socialized with general orientations and attitudes that serve to reduce the drive for professional success in any field. Second, particular attitudes about science may define it as a male field and thus tend to encourage males to participate while discouraging females. Third, some writers assert that deep-seated epistemological gender differences exist that may make science, as practiced today, not sufficiently compatible with "women's ways of knowing."

These two main explanatory models should not be regarded as mutually exclusive. Elements of both can be reinforcing factors in shaping career outcomes. In its dynamics over time, a scientific career path can be viewed in terms of the "kick-reaction" model developed by Jonathan R. Cole and Burton Singer: It is formed by a sequence of (positive or negative) "kicks" from the environment, followed by reactions to these kicks by the individual. Deficit-model obstacles would roughly correspond to negative "kicks" and difference-model obstacles to inopportune reactions.

A good reason to pay attention to the possibility of interactions between structural impediments and behavioral-attitudinal issues is that it seems no longer possible to explain gender disparities by pointing to a few dramatic and clear-cut career obstacles for women scientists. Blatant barriers have receded, although they have not disappeared, as discrimination has been formally abolished. So one must look closer, considering the possibility that small and subtle disadvantages might accumulate over the course of a woman's career in science, along the lines of Robert K. Merton's concept of the accumulation of advantages and disadvantages.

The Project Access Study

In this article we take such a closer look by reviewing the results of our research project, named Project Access, which studied in detail a sample—the largest of its kind—of female and male scientists, to determine both the degree of gender disparity in the average career outcome and the causes for the disparity. The results of the study suggest that significant differences in outcomes can indeed be found by comparing, in particular, the careers of highly promising women and men in science. The disparities appear to result chiefly from a series of subtle but identifiable (and sometimes counterintuitive) impediments and slight gender differences in socialization.

Project Access focused exclusively on a group of female and male scientists who had the same kind of auspicious starting positions as they began their careers as professional scientists: They had received prestigious postdoctoral fellowships. To illuminate the fine structure of their career paths, we augmented a quantitative research approach with a qualitative one. Our results, described briefly below, are based on 699 replies to a structured questionnaire, as well as on 200 open-ended, face-to-face interviews. The questionnaire responses were obtained from 460 (361 men, 99 women) former awardees of an NSF postdoctoral research fellowship, from the inception of the program in 1952 through 1985, and 239 (147 men, 92 women) former recipients of a National Research Council postdoctoral associateship from the start of the program in 1959 through 1986. We attempted to reach every woman who had received such an NSF or NRC fellowship, as well as a control group of men. In addition to the questionnaire survey, we conducted personal interviews lasting two to three hours with 92 men and 108 women who had received postdoctoral fellowships in the sciences from NSF, NRC or the Bunting Institute of Radcliffe College, or who had been Bunting finalists. Our sample included scientists in all fields as well as mathematicians and engineers; here we shall use the term "scientists" to encompass all these groups.

In focusing on a group of especially promising scientists who had, so to speak, set forth from the same starting line, our study differs from those that concern themselves with samples representing the whole population of scientists. We aimed to complement such studies by providing an in-depth look at an important subgroup. It seemed sensible to try to track and understand the causes for attrition or other disadvantages among that relatively small fraction of women who had stayed in science to the point of gaining prestigious postdoctoral fellowships, if only to find out what became of the heavy investments they and society had made in their scientific careers.

A study of this group, we reasoned, ought also to help sort out the merits of the "glass ceiling" and "threshold" hypotheses. The glass-ceiling hypothesis postulates an invisible but real barrier that impedes women from reaching top positions in their professions. The alternative hypothesis rests on the concept of a threshold. In this view, women who have succeeded in overcoming earlier barriers might have passed a threshold beyond which gender no longer matters in careers.

Women scientists who have been awarded prestigious postdoctoral fellowships should have accumulated significant advantages up to that point, and should be highly qualified and motivated to pursue a successful research career. If these promising women scientists as a group turn out to be less successful than comparable men in attaining high positions, this may indicate the existence of a glass ceiling of gender-specific obstacles in the later stages of their professional careers. On the other hand, if they have overcome certain earlier barriers and passed a threshold beyond which gender no longer matters in careers, one might expect to see less evidence of later professional stratification along gender lines.

Here we shall consider first what our study suggested about the persistence of the gender gap. Then we shall look at factors that may be at play in different ways in different fields of science—at gender-influenced social and professional styles, the self-perceptions of scientists, the interaction of career and family life and the role of serendipity.

Career Outcomes of the Study Group

As we turn now to summarizing a few key results from Project Access (whose findings are presented in detail in two books, Sonnert and Holton 1995a and 1995b), we should emphasize that we did not find monolithic blocks of women scientists on one side and men scientists on the other. Rather, we typically observed great variations within each gender group and a great deal of overlap between them. Yet, as will be shown, some differences between the average experiences are striking, and overall the career outcomes of women in our sample must be regarded as less desirable than those of their male cohorts. For example:

In terms of institutional prestige, the women of our questionnaire sample were well represented at top-rated departments. Twenty-nine percent of the women working in academe, compared with 27 percent of the men, were located at institutions ranked among the top 15 percent in a large national survey (Jones, Lindzey and Coggeshall 1982). But women, as a group, "paid" for prestigious affiliation with disadvantages in rank achievement, whereas men did not experience such a trade-off.

In academic rank achievement, we found substantial variation among academic fields. In biology, our group of women appeared to have passed a threshold. There were no statistical differences in their career progress through the academic ranks, compared with their male cohorts. However, great gender disparities were found in physical sciences, mathematics and engineering (labeled "PSME" in *Figure* 1), even in our elite sample. Among the younger cohort of scientists in these fields, for instance, the women's average academic status was almost one full rank below the men's. Here a glass ceiling became clearly visible. Controlling for the level of productivity in scientific publication, women were still at a disadvantage in rank—again with the exception of biology, where the situation was more favorable for women than in other sciences. (The issue of publication productivity will receive special attention below.)

The attrition rate (the proportion of former fellows who are no longer research scientists) was 10.5 percent for women and 8.5 percent for men in our questionnaire sample. This gender difference did not reach statistical significance. As a group, the female former fellows were remarkably persistent in their pursuit of a science career. A considerable gender difference existed, however, in the reasons given by those who

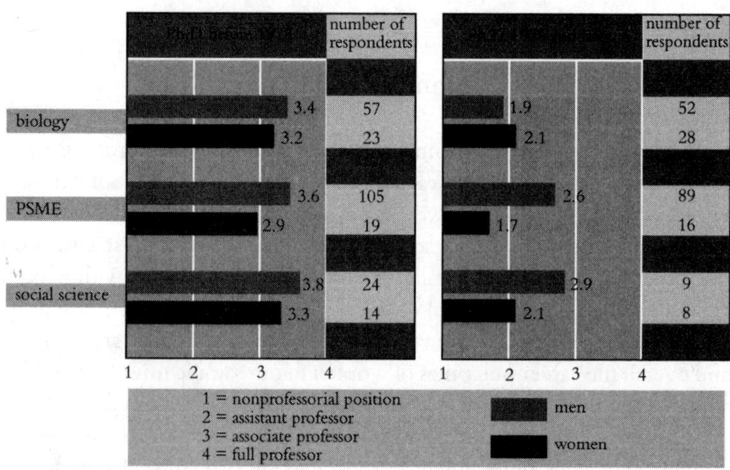

FIGURE 1 Statistical differences between the career outcomes of men and women appeared in the Project Access sample when the academic-rank achievement of the recipients of postdoctoral fellowships was compared. In biology, virtually no differences appeared between the career progress of men and women; however in the physical sciences, mathematics and engineering (lumped together as "PSME" above) a significant gap separated the average academic rank achieved by women and men, particularly among the younger cohort. The disadvantage in PSME persisted when the authors controlled for the level of publication productivity.

had left science. As one might expect, leaving science was more strongly connected with family responsibilities for women than for men.

Discrimination, Exclusion and Tokenism

One of the first questions to be considered in a study such as this is to what extent gender discrimination persists as a structural obstacle to a woman's career in science. Despite the legal prohibitions, 72.8 percent of the women interviewees reported that they had experienced discrimination. Among the men, 12.9 percent said they had been subject to reverse discrimination.

What forms does discrimination take? There were reports of a few egregious cases, such as the denial of jobs and tenure for women who considered themselves well qualified for a positive decision. But in the interviews there were many more accounts of very subtle exclusions and marginalizations. The area of scientific collaboration provides a good example. When we asked about the extent of collaboration in our participants' careers, the women as a group reported a slightly more collaborative research style than the men did when recalling the period before the postdoctoral fellowship—that is, during graduate school. On the other hand, the women collaborated noticeably less than the men both during and after the postdoctoral period.

Thus, compared with men, women on average experienced less collaboration as an equal or senior partner but more collaboration as a junior partner. It has been proposed that it may be harder for women scientists to establish egalitarian, collegial collaborations. Comments in our interviews supported this suggestion. More women than men said that their postdoctoral advisors ignored them or that their advisors treated them as subordinates.

Another structural question deserves special mention. R. M. Kanter has suggested that rare representatives of a social group, called tokens, tend to face particular difficulties in obtaining career success in their fields. This view is consistent with the striking statistical contrast we found between women's career outcomes in biology and those in the other sciences. For women biologists, whose numbers may have reached a "critical mass" some time ago, gender stratification within the discipline seems attenuated. Women have a relatively long and strong tradition of professional participation in biology, as compared with the other natural sciences, and one might speculate that this has contributed to the reduction of the gender gap in career success in this field.

But numbers alone may not be enough to make a difference. In accordance with recent research results (Etzkowitz *et al.* 1994), we found a picture that was partly counterintuitive and certainly more complex than any simple relation between women's numbers (and the resulting availability of mentors and role models) and women's success. Women in our questionnaire sample who had been affiliated with female advisors during their postdoctoral fellowships later left science at a *higher* rate than those who had not (16.7 percent *vs.* 9.7 percent), whereas the reverse was the case for men with female advisors (0 *vs.* 8.7 percent). The small number of respondents with female advisors limits our confidence in this finding, but it was echoed in the comments of a woman interviewee who eventually left science. She indicated that she was deterred, rather than attracted, by the example of her female advisor in college. "The more you got to know her, the more you realized she'd given up all personal life to be a scientist. She had a very lonely and isolated life." On the other hand, reports of the positive influence of female mentors and role models were more common.

Socialization

Socialization is a key issue in discussions of women's career paths. It is often reported that many women are hampered in their careers by a lack of confidence in their own abilities. We found evidence to support this statement: Even our group of women, who had achieved recognition for their accomplishment at the doctoral level, differed on average from their male cohorts in their estimation of their own self-confidence, ambition and related traits.

Substantially more men than women among our interviewees reported that they considered their scientific ability to be above average (men, 69.7 percent; women, 51.5 percent). More women considered their ability to be average (men, 18.0 percent; women, 34.7 percent). And when asked whether they should have handled their career obstacles in a different way, many more women than men thought they should have had more confidence or should have been more assertive (25.3 percent *vs.* 4.6 percent of the men). In addition, more than three times as many women as men (15.9 percent *vs.* 4.4 percent) in our interview sample said they had vague or unclear career aspirations when they started out in science.

These self-assessments can be looked at in two ways. Approaching the evidence using the difference model, one would consider such attitudes to be among the causes that make women scientists, on average, less successful than men in career achievement. But the deficit model also offers an explanation: Women whose careers were impeded by structural obstacles may have adjusted their ambitions and self-expectations downward. Our data cannot determine causality. But they suggest that it is useful to look at whether internal and external processes at work in women's and men's science careers might interact to develop a tendency for gender-specific ways of doing science.

Scientific and Professional Styles

Do men and women "do science" differently? Yes, said many of our interviewees. Somewhat more women than men (60.8 percent *vs.* 49.4 percent) said that they believed in the existence of gender differences in the work of scientists in general.

In addition, substantially more women than men interviewees thought that their own gender influences the way they pursue their work. Of the women interviewed, 51.2 percent thought their gender plays a role in their own professional conduct and interaction with other scientists, whereas 25.6 percent of the men perceived such an influence. Fewer interviewees thought that their gender influenced their choice of research subjects (men, 15.7 percent; women, 40.0 percent) and their ways of thinking in science (men, 20.0 percent; women, 36.0 percent). Still fewer interviewees perceived gender differences on the methods they used in their scientific work (men, 9.9 percent; women, 34.8 percent).

Scientists' perceptions and self-reports are not, of course, necessarily based in reality. Nonetheless, it is worth noting that a sizeable proportion of the scientists in our study considered gender a relevant variable for interpreting the behavior of working scientists.

When the people we interviewed talked about these gender differences in "scientific style," certain themes emerged. Both men and women commonly observed that, in their professional style, men seem to have what one woman called more "entrepreneurial spunk." Male scientists are, in this view, more aggressive, combative and self-promoting in their pursuit of career success, and so they achieve higher visibility. In short, they are better at playing the political game of career advancement.

Some women interviewees reported that men have a way of "showing off" at conferences. The following comment by a female scientist illustrates this observation as well as the relatively greater difficulty experienced by women, on average, in initiating collegial contact with male scientists: "Men . . . stood in the hallways and found the great men and went over and shook their hands or asked them to have a drink with them or something, and women couldn't do that in my day. . . . They took themselves terribly seriously and they said any kind of thing that came to their head. I call it 'professor talk' . . . and I found that a waste of my time."

"Professor talk" may indeed be a waste of time in terms of exchanging research information or gaining scientific insights. But it may be anything but wasteful in terms of its hidden agenda. What other women respondents called a "bull session" or "chatty self-promotion" may have the function of a bonding ritual. And the social bonds thus forged may have beneficial effects on a scientist's research and career.

An important aspect of a career in science is one's choice of a subfield and research problem. A number of our male and female respondents perceived a gender difference here, agreeing with a woman who noticed "fewer women in highly theoretical/mathematical subfields." But gender differences appeared to go beyond differences in mathematics interest or training.

In selecting a problem, many women reported that they had followed a "niche approach," creating their own area of research expertise. One respondent observed that "women may shy away from very competitive projects more than their male counterparts." A good example is a woman who said she liked "to sense that I had my own area, that I wasn't just a cog." Another woman respondent said she was predisposed to selecting research problems that were completely her own because "I very much dislike working on problems that I know other people are working on." Rather than competing with other investigators and research groups in a race toward the solution of the same problem, she carved out a niche for herself. Of course, following a niche approach is not an exclusively female tendency. And as the example of Marie Curie shows, it is not necessarily disadvantageous for career success.

Women's Methodology: Perfectionism

Some scholars have suggested that women's participation in the sciences might be enhanced if an alternative or "non-androcentric" sort of science was developed. Our interviewees, however, hardly ever implied a belief in a feminine methodology or way of thinking. Rather, the overriding theme that emerged from the responses of both men and women who saw gender differences in this area had to do with scientists' ways of applying traditional methodology. Women were considered to be more cautious and careful in their methods, and to pay more attention to details. A woman respondent believed that "women are often more careful in their research and more hesitant to make statements until they feel they can really 'prove' them."

Many women acknowledged that they have a tendency to be perfectionists in their scientific work. Some said they were perfectionists because they wanted to avoid failure or criticism. One stressed women's attention to detail. "Women are more meticulous," she said, " . . . and so I think that does affect how you do science. I don't know why that is; it just seems that for me, and the other women scientists I've dealt with, we tend more to deal in the minute details, fine points."

It does not follow that women scientists exclusively concern themselves with details. On the contrary, along with the theme of greater thoroughness, the interviews also emphasized a tendency among women to look for the broader picture and do work that is more comprehensive. In the words of a woman scientist, "women tend to work longer on individual projects and take on projects that are broader in scope than do men. Women seem to find it more difficult to break projects into small parts."

These results suggest a reinterpretation of the often-observed gap between the genders in publication productivity. We too found a gap in our group of scientists: The male questionnaire respondents who now work in academe produced an average of 2.8 scientific publications per year, as compared with the women's average of 2.3 publications per year. If it is true that women are more thorough and perfectionist, on average, and inclined toward more comprehensive and synthetic work, one would expect that they would produce a smaller number of publications per year. And this fact might have a deleterious effect on career progress whenever the sheer number of publications is taken to indicate excellence—for instance, during a competition for an academic position.

A research scientist's claim that he or she trades off quantity for quality can, of course, be a self-serving explanation of low productivity. However, we found some indirect factual evidence that women scientists may tend to publish articles that contain more substantial or comprehensive work. In a small study using a subsample of 25 former NSF fellows in biology who are now academic scientists, we examined (among other inquiries) the citations in the scientific literature to these biologists' articles. The articles written by women in this small sample received significantly more citations per article, on average, than did men's articles—24.4 *vs.* 14.4 citations (Sonnert 1995). This greater citation impact might indicate that the content of the women's articles, on the whole, was more noteworthy. We cannot place a great deal of confidence in this statement, given the small sample size. But in a study of a large sample of biochemists, J. S. Long found a gender difference in citations per article in the same direction (Long 1992). Such results support current efforts to shift the scientific reward system toward a more qualitative evaluation of publication productivity when important decisions about scientists' careers are made.

The Roots of Scientific Style

In sum, our respondents reported gender differences in scientific style, but the differences were much more in the social aspects of science than in the areas of epistemology and methodology. Rather than being iconoclasts, women tended to uphold to a particularly high degree the traditional methodological standards of science, such as carefulness, replicability and connection to fundamentals. As a group, women, as relative newcomers to science, adopted—or were taught to adhere to—an extra-high measure of conformity to the formal norms of conducting research. All the while, they may still be standing somewhat on the margins in regard to the more informal aspects of social interactions and professional conduct among scientists, but these aspects may be crucial elements in the search for career success.

Differences in the ways women approach science may spring from various roots. Approached from the perspective of the difference model, women might be seen as socialized to be less competitive, so that they choose their own niche rather than enter the fray with numerous competitors working on the same topic. They may be more sensitized to criticism and therefore try harder to produce perfect work that is above any possibility of criticism.

Viewed in terms of the deficit model, the same difference may be thought to arise from a collegial environment particularly hostile to women who deviate from accepted standards. A woman scientist reported that "there's always somebody watching for me to make a mistake." Another woman concurred that women scientists find themselves often "under the magnifying glass." In the view of these scientists, the burden of proof is reversed for women: Whereas male Ph.D.'s are considered competent scientists until proven otherwise, their female counterparts have to demonstrate their competence fully before it is generally accepted.

Obstacles rooted in both the difference model (internal gender differences) and the deficit model (scientific environment) surely apply to different women scientists' careers to different extents. What seems more important than gauging the relative weight of these explanations is realizing that they compound in ways described by the kick-reaction model. If women scientists tend to receive fewer positive and more negative kicks during their careers than do men, and if their reactions to these kicks are less than optimal, those elements combine in bringing about considerably worse overall career outcomes.

Marriage and Parenthood

Many scientists face the challenge of combining a particularly demanding career and a family life. We investigated with our questionnaire sample whether respondents' current marital and parental status were related to some basic career outcomes (employment area, academic rank, publication productivity and whether they had left science). In general, we found that marital and parental status were unrelated to these career outcomes, both for men and (what is more surprising) for women. The overall analysis failed to show any strong relations between the family and career spheres for women scientists, but does this mean there are none? We believe that interactions between family and science career do exist, but that they have become too complex and idiosyncratic to be captured by such broad variables as marital or parental status. If a career in science is considered as a path that takes many turns, it is clear that at certain points family factors do have an effect on the path.

For example, consider the respondents to our survey who took their particular postdoctoral fellowships to be with a spouse. This group of respondents turned out to be less successful in terms of later academic rank than were those who did not give this motivation. Women were far more likely than men to take their postdoctoral fellowship for this reason (24.5 percent *vs.* 8.5 percent). Moreover, in the presence of children, the husband's career assumed a much clearer priority over the wife's career. Women with children were more likely to take the postdoctoral fellowship to be with a spouse than were women without children (30.1 percent *vs.* 22.0 percent), but the opposite effect was observed for men (3.0 percent *vs.* 12.2 percent). Being a parent during the postdoctoral fellowship thus appeared to shift the pattern toward traditional gender roles, with the emphasis on the husband's career.

Most of our interviewees (93.4 percent of men, 86.8 percent of women) were married at some point in their lives, and almost half of these—men and women—said marriage had a positive effect on their careers (men, 45.7 percent; women, 49.4 percent). Only a smaller group mentioned an explicitly negative impact from marriage (men, 14.8 percent; women, 17.6 percent).

A likely scenario for women scientists is to be married to another scientist, often in the same field. In our questionnaire sample, 62.0 percent of the married women, but only 18.9 percent of the married men, had a spouse with a doctorate. Spouses who were also scientists were often described as understanding and supportive of the work-dedicated lifestyle of scientists. Among the drawbacks of marriage, restrictions in mobility figured prominently.

Single women seemed to face particular disadvantages within the social system of science, although the small number of single interviewees in our sample limits generalization. A man reported observing "enormous pressure on an unattached woman scientist to date her colleagues and no pressure for a comparable male scientist."

A similarly complex picture emerged in respect to parenthood. Our interview and questionnaire results suggest that marriage and parenthood might be seen as a set of opportunities and problems for careers. The set is somewhat different for women scientists, who are faced with the dilemma of synchronizing the often- conflicting demands of three clocks: the biological clock, the career clock (as in timetables for tenure) and a spouse's career clock. These complications can be offset, our respondents reported, by the emotional security and financial stability that a husband and family can provide, as well as by the possibility of intellectual support if the spouse is a scientist in the same field. Largely depending on how the problems are resolved and the opportunities are utilized, the effect of marriage and parenthood on women scientists' careers may be positive or negative. Some women's choices turned out to be more fortuitous than others.

Getting and Taking Chances

Any analysis of the factors that impinge on science careers must emphasize the role of luck. Many of the people we interviewed mentioned that they had benefited markedly from luck and serendipity during career decisions, a fact that makes overall statistical conclusions particularly difficult. An overwhelming majority of both men and women acknowledged that good luck had affected their careers (men, 89 percent; women, 85 percent). Bad luck was acknowledged by a higher proportion of women than men (men, 34 percent; women, 49 percent).

Luck in a science career can take various shapes. Both conceiving a creative hypothesis and having that hypothesis quickly corroborated by experiment depend to some degree on luck. Good luck may be being in the right place at the right time, for instance, in a research program or a field that is "hot." Serendipity is also often involved in meeting the right people—leading scholars who inspire a young scientist, powerful figures who make introductions and connections, people who make an impact with personal integrity and kindness, or mentors who teach the young scientists how to play the political career game.

A key problem for career-minded scientists, then, is to recognize and take advantage of serendipitous situations—to realize the potential effects of a "kick" and respond with a proper reaction. In a male interviewee's words, "the way people really succeed is being able to recognize when a good thing has happened, and take advantage of it."

Do women scientists have equal access to such chances, and are there obstacles that keep them from taking advantage of them? The collective outcomes suggest a larger accumulation of disadvantages than of advantages, although gender disparities were not uniform across the board. They were concentrated in the top ranks of achievement and in fields outside of biology. Very large and very obvious gender differences and disparities were absent. But even the women in our specially selected group faced gender-specific career obstacles, particularly in fields where women are greatly underrepresented.

It may now be futile to search for the "big remaining obstacle" to women's career parity in the sciences. Rather, the accumulation of subtle structural disadvantages, as suggested by the deficit model, together with the attitudinal and behavioral disadvantages offered by the difference model, may afford a partial explanation of the glass ceiling where it persists. Policymakers should keep this in mind when trying to influence the social system of science. No single policy can be expected to produce general success. A great variety of targeted efforts may be more advantageous. And in the lives of individual scientists, our study shows that attention paid to career strategies can be important—a lesson of particular use, perhaps, for women who are making their way as strangers through territories of science that are relatively new to their gender.

Bibliography

Belenky, M. F., B. M. Clinchy, N. R. Goldberger and J. M. Tarule. 1986. *Women's Ways of Knowing: The Development of Self, Voice and Mind.* New York: Basic Books.

Brush, S. G. 1991. Women in science and engineering. *American Scientist* 79: 404–419.

Chodorow, N. 1974. Family structure and feminine personality. In *Women, Culture and Society*, ed. M. Z. Rosaldo and L. Lamphere. Stanford, Calif.: Stanford University Press.

Cole, J. R., and B. Singer. 1991. A theory of limited differences: Explaining the productivity puzzle in science. In *The Outer Circle: Women in the Scientific Community*, ed. H. Zuckerman, J. R. Cole and J. T. Bruer. New York: Norton.

Cole, J. R., and H. Zuckerman. 1983. The productivity puzzle: Persistence and change in patterns of publication of men and women scientists. In *Advances in Motivation and Achievement*, ed. M. W. Steinkamp and M. L. Maehr (Vol. 2). Greenwich, Conn.: JAI Press.

Eccles, J. S. 1987. Gender roles and women's achievement-related decisions. *Psychology of Women Quarterly* 11:135–172.

Etzkowitz, H., C. Kemelgor, M. Neuschatz, B. Uzzi and J. Alonzo. 1994. The paradox of critical mass for women in science. *Science* 266:51–54.

Fava, S. F., and K. Deierlein. 1988. Women physicists in the U.S. The career influence of marital status. *Gazette: A Newsletter of the Committee on the Status of Women in Physics of the American Physical Society* 8(2):1–3 (August).

Fox, M. F. 1983. Publication productivity among scientists: A critical review. *Social Studies of Science* 13:285–305.

Jones, L. V., G. Lindzey and P. E. Coggeshall, eds. 1982. *An Assessment of Research-Doctorate Programs in the United States*. Washington, D.C.: National Academy Press.

Long, J. S. 1992. Measures of sex differences in scientific productivity. *Social Forces* 71:159–178.

Kanter, R. M. 1977. Some effects of proportions on group life: Skewed sex ratios and responses to token women. *American Journal of Sociology* 82: 965–990.

Merton, R. K. 1973. *The Sociology of Science: Theoretical and Empirical Investigations*. Chicago: University of Chicago Press.

National Science Foundation. 1994. *Women, Minorities, and Persons with Disabilities in Science and Engineering: 1994*. (NSF 94–333) Arlington, Va.: National Science Foundation.

Reskin, B. F. 1978. Sex differentiation and the social organization of science. In *Sociology of Science*, ed. J. Gaston. San Francisco: Jossey-Bass.

Sonnert, G. 1995. What makes a good scientist? Determinants of peer evaluation among biologists. *Social Studies of Science* 25: 35–55.

Sonnert, G. (with the assistance of Gerald Holton). 1995a. *Gender Differences in Science Careers: The Project Access Study*. New Brunswick, N.J.: Rutgers University Press.

Sonnert, G. (with the assistance of Gerald Holton). 1995b. *Who Succeeds in Science? The Gender Dimension*. New Burnswick, N.J.: Rutgers University Press.

Tannen, D. 1990. *You Just Don't Understand: Women and Men in Conversation*. New York: Ballentine.

Zuckerman, H. 1989. Accumulation of advantage and disadvantage: The theory and its intellectual biography. In *L'Opera di R. K. Merton e la Sociologia Contemporeana*, ed. C. Mongardini and S. Tabboni. Genoa: Edizioni Culturali Internationali Genova.

22 The Politics of Housework

PAT MAINARDI

> Though women do not complain of the power of husbands, each complains of her own husband, or of the husbands of her friends. It is the same in all other cases of servitude; at least in the commencement of the emancipatory movement. The serfs did not at first complain of the power of the lords, but only of their tyranny.
>
> —John Stuart Mill,
> *On the Subjection of Women*

Liberated women—very different from women's liberation! The first signals all kinds of goodies, to warm the hearts (not to mention other parts) of the most radical men. The other signals—*housework.* The first brings sex without marriage, sex before marriage, cozy housekeeping arrangements ("You see, I'm living with this chick") and the self-content of knowing that you're not the kind of man who wants a doormat instead of a woman. That will come later. After all, who wants that old commodity anymore, the Standard American Housewife, all husband, home and kids. The New Commodity, the Liberated Woman, has sex a lot and has a Career, preferably something that can be fitted in with the household chores—like dancing, pottery, or painting.

On the other hand is women's liberation—and housework. What? You say this is all trivial? Wonderful! That's what I thought. It seemed perfectly reasonable. We both had careers, both had to work a couple of days a week to earn enough to live on, so why shouldn't we share the housework? So I suggested it to my mate and he agreed—most men are too hip to turn you down flat. "You're right," he said, "It's only fair."

Then an interesting thing happened. I can only explain it by stating that we women have been brainwashed more than even we can imagine.

Probably too many years of seeing television women in ecstasy over their shiny waxed floors or breaking down over their dirty shirt collars. Men have no such conditioning. They recognize the essential fact of housework right from the very beginning. Which is that it stinks. Here's my list of dirty chores: buying groceries, carting them home and putting them away; cooking meals and washing dishes and pots; doing the laundry, digging out the place when things get out of control; washing floors. The list could go on but the sheer necessities are bad enough. All of us have to do these things, or get someone else to do them for us. The longer my husband contemplated these chores, the more repulsed he became, and so proceeded the change from the normally sweet considerate Dr. Jekyll into the crafty Mr. Hyde who would stop at nothing to avoid the horrors of—*housework*. As he felt himself backed into a corner laden with dirty dishes, brooms, mops, and reeking garbage, his front teeth grew longer and pointier, his fingernails haggled and his eyes grew wild. Housework trivial? Not on your life! Just try to share the burden.

So ensued a dialogue that's been going on for several years. Here are some of the high points:

"I don't mind sharing the housework, but I don't do it very well. We should each do the things we're best at."
Meaning: Unfortunately I'm no good at things like washing dishes or cooking. What I do best is a little light carpentry, changing light bulbs, moving furniture (*how often do you move furniture?*).
Also Meaning: Historically the lower classes (black men and us) have had hundreds of years experience doing menial jobs. It would be a waste of manpower to train someone else to do them now.
Also Meaning: I don't like the dull stupid boring jobs, so you should do them.

"I don't mind sharing the work, but you'll have to show me how to do it."
Meaning: I ask a lot of questions and you'll have to show me everything every time I do it because I don't remember so good. Also don't try to sit down and read while I'm doing my jobs because I'm going to annoy the hell out of you until it's easier to do them yourself.

"We used to be so happy!" (Said whenever it was his turn to do something.)
Meaning: I used to be so happy.
Meaning: Life without housework is bliss. (*No quarrel here. Perfect agreement.*)

"We have different standards, and why should I have to work to your standards. That's unfair."
Meaning: If I begin to get bugged by the dirt and crap I will say "This place sure is a sty" or "How can anyone live like this?" and wait for your reaction. I know that all women have a sore called "Guilt over a messy house" or "Household work is ultimately my responsibility." I know that men have caused that sore—if anyone visits and the place *is* a sty, they're not going to leave and say, "He sure is a lousy housekeeper." You'll take the rap in any case. I can outwait you.
Also Meaning: I can provoke innumerable scenes over the housework issue. Eventually doing all the housework yourself will be less painful to you than trying to get me to do half. Or I'll suggest we get a maid. She will do my share of the work. You will do yours. It's women's work.

"I've got nothing against sharing the housework, but you can't make me do it on your schedule."
Meaning: Passive resistance. I'll do it when I damned well please, if at all. If my job is doing dishes, it's easier to do them once a week. If taking out laundry, once a month. If washing the floors, once a year. If you don't like it, do it yourself oftener, and then I won't do it at all.

"I *hate* it more than you. You don't mind it so much."
Meaning: Housework is garbage work. It's the worst crap I've ever done. It's degrading and humiliating for someone of *my* intelligence to do it. But for someone of *your* intelligence . . .

"Housework is too trivial to even talk about."
Meaning: It's even more trivial to do. Housework is beneath my status. My purpose in life is to deal with matters of significance. Yours is to deal with matters of insignificance. You should do the housework.

"This problem of housework is not a man-woman problem! In any relationship between two people one is going to have a stronger personality and dominate."
Meaning: That stronger personality had better be *me*.

"In animal societies, wolves, for example, the top animal is usually a male even where he is not chosen for brute strength but on the basis of cunning and intelligence. Isn't that interesting?"
Meaning: I have historical, psychological, anthropological, and biological

justification for keeping you down. How can you ask the top wolf to be equal?

"Women's liberation isn't really a political movement."
Meaning: The Revolution is coming too close to home.
Also Meaning: I am only interested in how *I* am oppressed, not how I oppress others. Therefore the war, the draft, and the university are political. Women's liberation is not.

"Man's accomplishments have always depended on getting help from other people, mostly women. What great man would have accomplished what he did if he had to do his own housework?
Meaning: Oppression is built into the System and I, as the white American male receive the benefits of this System. I don't want to give them up.

Postscript

Participatory democracy begins at home. If you are planning to implement your politics, there are certain things to remember.

1. He *is* feeling it more than you. He's losing some leisure and you're gaining it. The measure of your oppression is his resistance.
2. A great many American men are not accustomed to doing monotonous repetitive work which never ushers in any lasting let alone important achievement. This is why they would rather repair a cabinet than wash dishes. If human endeavors are like a pyramid with man's highest achievements at the top, then keeping oneself alive is at the bottom. Men have always had servants (us) to take care of this bottom strata of life while they have confined their efforts to the rarefied upper regions. It is thus ironic when they ask of women—where are your great painters, statesmen, etc? Mme. Matisse ran a millinery shop so he could paint. Mrs. Martin Luther King kept his house and raised his babies. . . .
3. Keep checking up. Periodically consider who's actually *doing* the jobs. These things have a way of backsliding so that a year later once again the woman is doing everything. After a year make a list of jobs the man has rarely if ever done. You will find cleaning pots, toilets, refrigerators and ovens high on the

> list. Use time sheets if necessary. He will accuse you of being petty. He is above that sort of thing—(housework). Bear in mind what the worst jobs are, namely the ones that have to be done every day or several times a day. Also the ones that are dirty—it's more pleasant to pick up books, newspapers etc. than to wash dishes. Alternate the bad jobs. It's the daily grind that gets you down. Also make sure that you don't have the responsibility for the housework with occasional help from him. "I'll cook dinner for you tonight" implies it's really your job and isn't he a nice guy to do some of it for you. . . .

I was just finishing this when my husband came in and asked what I was doing. Writing a paper on housework. Housework? he said, *Housework*? Oh my god how trivial can you get. A paper on housework.

Little Politics of Housework Quiz

The lowest job in the army, used as punishment is: a) working 9–5; b) kitchen duty (K.P.).

When a man lives with his family, his: a) father b) mother does his housework.

When he lives with a woman, a) he b) she does the housework.

A) his son b) his daughter learns in preschool how much fun it is to iron daddy's handkerchief.

From the *New York Times*, 9/21/69: "Former Greek Official George Mylonas pays the penalty for differing with the ruling junta in Athens by performing household chores on the island of Amorgos where he lives in forced exile" (with hilarious photo of a miserable Mylonas carrying his own water). What the *Times* means is that he ought to have a) indoor plumbing b) a maid.

Dr. Spock said (*Redbook* 3/69): "Biologically and temperamentally I believe, women were made to be concerned first and foremost with child care, husband care, and home care." Think about: a) *who* made us b) why? c) what is the effect on their lives d) what is the effect on our lives?

From *Time* 1/5/70, "Like their American counterparts, many housing project housewives are said to suffer from neurosis. And for the first time in Japanese history, many young husbands today complain of being henpecked. Their wives are beginning to demand detailed explanations when they don't come home straight from work and some Japanese males nowadays are even compelled to do housework." According to *Time*, women become neurotic a) when they are forced to do the maintenance work for the male caste all day every day of their lives or b) when they no longer want to do the maintenance work for the male caste all day every day of their lives.

CHAPTER SEVEN

Women's Mental Health and Therapy

In a now-famous study published in 1970 by Inge Broverman and her colleagues, practicing psychologists and psychiatrists were presented with a series of gender-stereotyped personality traits (e.g., aggressive, leader-like, dependent, sensitive). One third of these clinicians were asked to use these traits to describe a "mature, healthy *male*," one third to describe a "mature, healthy *female*," and one third to describe a "mature, healthy *adult*." The results were intriguing, and revealed the *double-bind* women can face with respect to mental health. No measurable differences were found between clinicians' descriptions of mentally healthy "males" and "adults," but there was a difference between descriptions of "females" and "adults." Furthermore, the traits the clinicians tended to assign to males were more socially desirable than the ones assigned to females. In other words, the standards for mental health in human beings are masculine. Feminine-labelled behavior is, in contrast, a more negatively-valenced deviation from that norm.

So women are caught: they can choose to adopt feminine norms of behavior such as submissiveness and dependence, and be considered less than human, or they can adopt desirable *human* traits and be labelled unfeminine and therefore "crazy." The character of Esther Greenwood in Sylvia Plath's *The Bell Jar* faces exactly this double bind. Caught between her wish to be a writer, independent and self-sufficient in the world, and the fear that this will make her unfeminine (and therefore unattractive to men), a "bell jar" of paralyzing depression descends upon her.

Research shows that gender is a reliable predictor of psychological diagnosis. That is, certain disorders are diagnosed predominantly in women (e.g., eating disorders, depression, agoraphobia), while other disorders are diagnosed predominantly in men (e.g., substance abuse, anti-social personality disorder). The question of why this should be so is a fascinating one. Do women actually *experience* more depression than men, or are they simply more likely to label the same underlying state as "depression"?

The answer is, of course, complex. In 1990, the American Psychological Association appointed a Task Force on Women and Depression. What this group of researchers found was that women's vulnerability to depression is very much a function of their social *status* and roles. That is, women's lesser power in the workplace and in relationships is a key risk factor, because it means they have greater exposure to uncontrollable negative events and less access to resources that help them mediate the stress from such events. In an important way, then, the female role (in a sexist culture) is hazardous to one's mental health!

The gender difference in depression appears to emerge during adolescence. Researchers have argued that this may be because of the particular challenges that puberty (not simply as a hormonal, but as a *social* event) can pose for females in a culture that so devalues womanhood. This is the time when, as Carol Gilligan has said, girls begin to lose their once-loud-and-clear voices, when they begin to say "I don't know."

The first piece in this section is a chapter from Dana Crowley Jack's book *Silencing The Self: Women and Depression*. In it she argues that *self-evaluation* lies at the heart of our ability to understand gender differences in the prevalence and dynamics of depression. That is, depressed women appear to suffer from particularly negative self-evaluation characterized by poor self-esteem, anger toward the self, and feelings of worthlessness. These negative feelings toward the self can take on a moral quality. According to Jack, depressed women consistently use words such as "should," "ought," "selfish," and "bad" to describe themselves. What are the beliefs that guide such harsh self-recrimination? Jack outlines certain cultural imperatives, largely impossible for real women to attain, regarding what makes a "good woman." These, she feels, operate as invisible bonds, restricting women's freedom to be active, responsible selves within relationships. Depression is an all-too-common tragic mental health consequence.

Jack's is only one of a wide variety of theories about the causes for women's greater vulnerability to depression. Hers is a socio-cultural framework. Other theories are more bio-behavioral, and one commonly-held set of beliefs centers around women's hormones and hormone fluctuation. There is ample cultural mythology around women's hormones being responsible for their "greater emotionality" and even their vulnerability to certain mental health problems such as depression. Today, on prime-time television, we find advertisements depicting irritable women returned to their smiling, calm selves through prescription medication to help control "Pre-Menstrual Dysphoric Disorder" (the new psychiatric term for "PMS"). The belief that menstruating women are unstable is alive and well, in other words (even though only 3–10 percent of women actually have premenstrual symptoms severe enough to disrupt their lives).

Well, we're damned if we do, and we're damned if we don't, according to the next piece in this chapter, "Who Are You Calling Crazy?" by Priscilla Grant. If you thought menopause might bring relief from so-called "PMS," think again. Now menopause is increasingly viewed as bringing its very own bag full of mental and emotional symptoms to women. But is a new diagnosis for women of "MMS"—Menopausal Mental Syndrome—justified and helpful? Some argue that doing so would enable women who do suffer to discuss their symptoms and seek treatment. But others, such as the author of this piece, worry that such medicalization encourages the idea that women are the sick ones, the hormonally-challenged ones. It is commonly expected that men act out their emotional frustrations. But when women lose control emotionally, our culture offers a psychiatric diagnosis and medication. "Where are the symposiums and research studies and popular books about 'testopause'?" Grant asks ironically.

Gender issues simply abound in mental illness and health. A social-constructivist perspective on mental illness (see Crawford & Unger, 2000) views psychological distress not just as a personal matter, but as a social event. Social norms and prevailing public opinion help to define what traits and behaviors are considered "normal" versus "abnormal." And expectations about women's personalities and bodies obviously play a key role in how we label and treat their mental health concerns.

One cannot help but feel somewhat bleak about the picture that emerges when we look carefully at women's mental health issues. There is hope, however. And feminist theorists and therapists offer what I consider to be the most far-reaching and promising possibilities for change. In the last article in this section, Mary Ballou and Carolyn West offer a wealth of information on how feminist therapeutic approaches are unique. A feminist framework argues that individual pathology cannot be decontextualized. That is, in order to understand why women suffer from any of the psychological disorders, and in order to begin curing them, their social, political, and economic circumstances must be understood. When one adopts this perspective, one realizes that personal change for women is unlikely to come about on a large scale without significant societal transformation.

References

Broverman, I. K., Broverman, D. M., Clarkson, F. E., Rosenkrantz, P. S., & Vogel, S. R. (1970). Sex role stereotypes and clinical judgments of mental health. *Journal of Consulting and Clinical Psychology, 34*, 1–7.

Crawford, M. & Unger, R. K. (2000). *Women and Gender: A Feminist Psychology*, 3rd Ed. New York: McGraw-Hill.

Plath, S. (1971). *The bell jar.* New York: Harper and Row.

23 Silencing the Self: Women and Depression

DANA CROWLEY JACK

> I feel like I did my best in all the areas I could and my marriage didn't work out. So I feel like I'm a failure.
>
> I feel like I'm trash, I really do. I can't face my friends.
>
> I feel like a lost cause, I'm overweight and I don't have enough patience with my family.
>
> I'm always worrying about other people instead of myself—but sometimes when I do something for myself, I feel very guilty.

Depressed women consistently use moral language—words such as "should," "ought," "good," "bad," "selfish"—as they assess themselves and their role in causing the problems in their relationships. Self-judging declarations such as "I don't measure up," "I'm a liar, a cheat, and I'm no good," "I feel like a failure," are also pervasive in their narratives. As we seek to understand women's depression, it is important to uncover the beliefs that guide such harsh self-reproach.

Negative self-evaluation is linked to central aspects of depression. It affects self-perception, self-esteem, anger directed toward the self, and feelings of worthlessness, hopelessness, and paralysis. Among the diagnostic symptoms of major depression, DSM III (1980) lists the effects of negative self-evaluation as follows: "self-reproach, inappropriate guilt, feelings of worthlessness" (p. 214).

Both historically and currently, the fall in self-esteem, basic to depression, has been tied to harsh self-judgment. As early as 1917, Freud observed that the "most outstanding feature" of the clinical picture of melancholia was the patient's "dissatisfaction with the ego on moral grounds" (pp. 247–248). Freud also asserted a difference in superego development and activity between women and men. Yet the illness in which the "superego" is most active—depression—has not been explored in terms of gender difference, or with regard to gender-specific standards women use to evaluate themselves.

In my view, self-evaluation holds the key to understanding gender differences in the prevalence and dynamics of depression. Developmental and psychoanalytic theorists consistently portray differences in the formation and functioning of men's and women's moral concerns. Regardless of theoretical perspective, observers find a female morality attuned to relationships and affection, and a male morality based on abstract principles expressed in laws and rules. Freud, for example, wrote that women are "more often influenced in their [moral] judgments by feelings of affection or hostility" and are consequently "less ethical" than men. While most theorists, including Piaget and Kohlberg, consider with Freud that a relationally oriented morality is less mature, less "independent of its emotional origins as we require it to be in men," the feminist critique has clarified the bias of such evaluations (Freud, 1925, pp. 257–258).

Carol Gilligan (1977, 1982, 1990), tracing the characteristics of women's moral focus, finds its roots in an orientation toward relationships and interdependence. Growing out of the female relational sense of self is a distinct vision of the social world and morality. What Freud and Kohlberg describe as women's less developed ethical sense, Gilligan (1982) reinterprets as a morality attuned to the specific contexts of people's lives that follows an ethic of care with the imperative not to hurt others. Within this framework, responsibility means an extension of self to protect another from hurt, whereas for the separate self, responsibility implies a restraint of aggression. Thus, what is seen from a traditional perspective as women's lack of ego boundaries, dependence, and weak superego, Gilligan reinterprets as a valuable strength, a reflection of a developmental context that values interdependence, empathy, and emotional closeness.

In spite of these longstanding observations of differences in male and female ethical orientations, and the clear tie between self-evaluation and depression, we have not had systematic analysis of the moral themes in depressed women's narratives. Given the sex differences in rates of depressive illness, the increasing rates of depression, and the rapid changes in women's social roles outside the home, it is imperative to explore women's experience of depression through their moral language.

The "Good Me"

The culture contributes powerfully to gender differences in the standards people use to judge the self. By imposing divergent expectations for girls' and boys' behavior, it creates different yardsticks that each gender uses to measure attainment of a "good me." Obviously, some of the characteristics men and women strive to attain do overlap, but many, particularly those associated with intimate behaviors, are gender-specific.

Gender is socially constructed from the moment of birth on. Caretakers attribute different characteristics and qualities to infant boys and girls, and, on the basis of those ascribed attributes, engage with them differently. The infant learns to expect different types of encounters with adult males and females. Brazelton's (1982) videotapes of interactions between three-month-old infants and their mothers and fathers show radically different patterns, with mother-infant interchanges mapped as a smooth, wave-like undulation of initiation, sensitive response, and elaboration. Fathers "jazz up" their babies, often initiating interactions by playfully poking at them. Infants react to their father's arrival with more motor excitement, and the duet moves quickly to more assertive and explosive interchanges, sometimes ending with sensory overload for the infant. Such patterns of interaction, deeply affected by gender, profoundly shape the developing child's sense of self in relationship.

Not only do interactional patterns with parents affect a gendered sense of self in relationship, but the cultural norms that govern male and female "goodness" in relationship also reinforce different behaviors and prerogatives. Boys are allowed and encouraged to express more anger, aggression, and competition; girls, even now, continue to be praised for interpersonal sensitivity, for being "nice" to others. Parents give boys and girls different toys to play with, encourage them in different pursuits, and expect them to respond differently.

Schools reinforce patterns begun at home, with most teachers unaware of their different responsiveness to gender. Teachers give boys more of both positive and negative attention than girls; girls are more likely to be the quiet and invisible classroom members. Boys receive praise for the intellectual quality of their work; girls are more likely to receive praise for the neatness of their work and its compliance with rules of form (Harvey and Stables, 1986; Sadker and Sadker, 1985, 1986). Meanwhile, the media, while powerfully transmitting cultural symbols to the growing child, clearly convey not only sex-role stereotypes but the message that masculine values and traits are more highly regarded than feminine ones. At each stage of development, females and males encounter different expectations, including social norms about what it is to be a good woman or man. All these experiences convey images about who a boy or girl is, and what he or she *should* be like in order to be recognizable in gender and acceptable to others.

The growing child shapes the self into the parents' vision, into a "good me," to gain their love and acceptance. These forms of good behavior, particularly when they fit the outlines prescribed by the wider environment of school, media, and peers, are difficult to challenge. Thus, ingrained in both women and men are gender-specific images of how to be good in relationships in order to be loved. These images guide behavior *and* self-evaluation, and are deeply entwined with understandings of how to achieve intimacy. They include an individual's experience of freedom and compliance within early relationships: how much one was loved "for free" and allowed the leeway to be oneself, and how much one had to comply with the parents' images and develop a "false self" (Winnicott, 1965) in order to be loved.

Images of the "good me," profoundly affected by gender, enter into the story of depression. From the perspective of ego psychology (Bibring, 1953), the low self-esteem and feelings of hopelessness characteristic of depression stem from an impossible gap between the self one would like to be (the ego ideal) and the self one is (the actual self). The greater the discrepancy between these two senses of self, the lower the self-esteem. Despite important theoretical differences, theorists agree that depression results from an early environment where the child learned that, in order to be loved, she or he had to repress authentic feelings and present an outwardly conforming, false self, becoming self-alienated and cut off from emotions in the process.

Since the culture presents women and men with different images from which to create an idealized self, striving to attain these diverging configurations of the ideal affects them in gender-specific ways. Further, if events in the interpersonal sphere are especially critical to the definition and evaluation of women's core sense of self, then analysis of a woman's images of a "good" self in relation is essential for understanding her depression. . . .

The Inner Dialogue of Depression

In the narratives of each depressed woman, a dialogue between two parts of the self becomes apparent as the woman talks about the sources of her sadness and feelings of loss. One hears this dialogue as a woman shifts her self-portrayal from the first-person to the third-person voice. The first-person voice is the self that speaks from experience, that knows from observation. This voice says, "I want, I know, I feel, I see, I think."

The bases for its values and beliefs are empirical; they come from personal experience and observation. In this sense, the first-person voice is authentic; I will call it the "I," the authentic self.

The other voice in the dialogue speaks with a moralistic, "objective," judgmental tone that relentlessly condemns the authentic self. It sounds like a third-person voice, not because it never uses the pronoun "I," but because it speaks *to* the "I." It says "one should, you can't, you ought, I should." It speaks to the self, and like the classical psychoanalytic concept of the superego, it has the feeling of something *over* the "I," which carries the power to judge it. Or like the object-relations notion of the false self, it conforms to outer imperatives and perceived expectations in order to gain approval and protect the true self. I will call this third-person voice the Over-Eye, because of its surveillant, vigilant, definitively moral quality.

The Over-Eye carries a decidedly patriarchal flavor, both in its collective viewpoint about what is "good" and "right" for a woman and in its willingness to condemn her feelings when they depart from expected "shoulds." The Over-Eye persistently pronounces harsh judgment on most aspects of a woman's authentic strivings, including her wish to express herself freely in relationship, her creativity, and her spirituality. Because the judgments of the Over-Eye include a cultural consensus about feminine goodness, truth, and value, they have the power to override the authentic self's viewpoint.

How a woman judges herself and makes choices for her life is critical for an understanding of female depression. The analysis of voices in the inner dialogue provides a framework for hearing how a depressed woman's understanding of herself shifts between the terms of the dominant culture and the reality of her own experience, a personal reality that she often has trouble believing and even conveying. Listening to these inner voices and the shifts in a woman's perspective on her self gives us the possibility of standing with her to comprehend her experience of depression. Attending to the two-voice dialogue also lets us hear how claiming one's authentic perspective on the self and experience, and acting on its values, coincides with a woman's movement out of depression.

In the following interview, we hear the voice of Maya, age 31, who attended college for five years and began a career in teaching. She was married for seven years to a physically abusive man, had two children, and was divorced. Two years later she married again, and then separated from her second husband when she was three months pregnant. At the first interviews, Maya's son was seven and her daughter was three. She was still severely depressed a year and three months later, when reinterviewed. At that time, she was divorced from her second husband, was on welfare, and had a third child, an eight-month-old daughter. Approximately two and one half years after the first interview, Maya had emerged from her serious depression. The excerpts come from the transcript of Maya's first interview. After Maya's own words, I paraphrase the negative judgments implicit in what she says so as to clearly convey the cultural imperatives carried by the Over-Eye.

In the columns below, Maya's two voices reflect disparate points of view from which she sees and evaluates herself and her relationships. The authentic self, based on her own experiences and feelings, is at odds with the "right" or conventional way to think about how relationships should be and what is a good woman. These two perspectives result in a central disparity between what Maya in fact sees and knows from her own experience and what she thinks she *should* think, influenced by role expectations, family history, and cultural norms for women.

Authentic "I"	*Over-Eye*
	I have an inferiority complex, I suppose. (Judgment: *You are inferior.*)
I'm going to start crying. I don't know why I do this, every time, I start crying.	
	It's the idea of having been divorced twice. It bothers me something terribly and I don't know . . . I think it's just because I was raised . . . you know, you marry and you live happily ever after. A lot of my friends have been divorced once and that seems more acceptable than the fact of making the mistake twice. I think maybe because when I was growing up I always felt divorce was wrong and I've always felt that when people got a divorce, it was the woman's fault. (Judgment: *Divorce is wrong; the divorces are your fault: you are responsible for the failures of relationship.*)
But I don't know how it could be the woman's fault. I don't know, that doesn't even make sense now that I look at it. I don't know where I came up with that.	
	But it's probably because she didn't please her husband. You know, whether

Authentic "I"	*Over-Eye*
	it's, I have this idea . . . marriage . . . the woman is there to please her husband, just to provide for his needs, physical, sexual, and whatever else, and if he's not satisfied then that would be reason enough for him not to want to be married. (Judgment: *In order to be loved, you must meet a man's needs.*)
And that's what's so difficult because I feel like I did the best in all the areas I could and it didn't work out.	
	So I feel like I'm a failure. (Judgment: *You met men's needs and the relationships still failed; something is wrong with you.*)
I don't know, I can't pinpoint what happened, because I know it wasn't all my fault. I think, "What went wrong?" I don't have any answer for it. Oh, people give me answers, "They were creeps and you shouldn't have married them." But for myself, I don't have answers.	
	That's been a real affliction on my self-esteem and it has been really difficult to build up because I think that if I can't succeed at something that simple, as an everyday thing as marriage, then how can I be successful anywhere else? (Judgment: *You don't know how to keep love while everyone else does; you will never succeed at anything.*)
I want to accept a lot of the new ideas, new thoughts that I have, but something inside is afraid that they're wrong, afraid of being wrong. Unacceptable. Unacceptable to whom I don't know. That doesn't even make sense. I'm afraid of them not being accepted but there's nobody to worry about, I don't know why I'm concerned about that because that's something I'm choosing within myself and it has no reflection or bearing on anyone else. I don't know why there's such a conflict.	

Authentic "I"	*Over-Eye*
	If you please, you're the kind of woman, the kind of wife you should be. And if you don't, then you're not. (Judgment: *You must please in order to be loved/to be good.*)
I know the latter is true, a marriage working if you each have your own degree of freedom and you come together for sharing. It's not realistic and it doesn't work out when marriage is one-sided and it's the woman having to give of herself all the time.	
	I didn't leave because I thought marriage was binding, for life. That boils down to the idea of divorce, I didn't believe in it. I didn't think it was right. I guess because you say a vow before God. It's just not to be broken. (Judgment: *Divorce is emotionally, socially, and morally wrong; you are a failure.*)
But that's not even human, but that's it, anyway.	
	They've [marriages] made me feel like I'm unsuccessful. That I've failed. As a wife and a woman, as a person, I guess. They've made me feel like I really don't count, like I'm a nobody, that I can't achieve the goal that I've set out to. That I'm not competent. (Judgment: *If you fail at relationship, you are morally worthless and incompetent.*)
And yet, they have to be just feelings because I know that what I'm feeling I'm not seeing.	

In these arguments of voice, the Over-Eye pronounces what a woman "should" do in relationships, while the authentic self responds with what Maya knows from her first-hand experiences of relatedness. The conflict of these perspectives about attachments, morality, and responsibility creates more than just a clash of ideas. Maya's different perspectives on her relational experience lead her into confusion about what is "reality." Is it what the "I" observes and feels, or is it what she has been taught she *should* think and feel? As Maya's Over-Eye says, "If you please, you're the kind of woman, the kind of wife you should be. And if you don't, then you're not." This voice goes on to conclude that if you don't please, "you're an unsuccessful woman."

But this construction of feminine goodness was lived out in two marriages in which Maya was physically and emotionally abused, and she has come to doubt its accuracy. She says: "everything is dependent upon what a woman *should* do and if my concept isn't clear about what is reality, then that's the reason why I'm so confused." In other words, Maya's view of the relationship's reality depends on her moral construction, which is divided between what she believes is the "right" way to think, based on personal history and cultural dictates, and her personal convictions, arising as she has tried to live out these imperatives in adulthood.

This inner division makes reality-testing almost impossible, since testing reality requires a mind of one's own which can observe and choose to act on those observations. Not knowing what is real, Maya feels paralyzed about what direction to pursue. The dilemma is critical, because the outcome determines the most important issues of her emotional life: how she will relate to others to attain intimacy, and how she will relate to herself, either to understand, forgive, and change, or harshly to condemn her "failures." It also affects the broader arena of relatedness to her culture: whether she accepts prevailing views of "the way things are" about gender, about conventional morality, about self-expression. Ways of relating dictated by the Over-Eye—trying to please—have failed her in two marriages. She doesn't "have any answers" for why her attempts to make intimate connection with others have been unsuccessful. In Maya's dialogue, each feeling has its opposite, leaving her suspended about what she, in fact, does feel, and how she should judge her feelings.

What is the Over-Eye—the conventional, compliant self—saying to her? It is not a superego that is warning: "If you break this rule or that rule, you will be punished." Rather, it insists: "If you want anyone to love you, this is what you have to do." It is an Over-Eye that has a theory of how to make and maintain relationships (and of who is to blame if they fail). This theory of attachment carries not only Maya's developmental history but also the culture's injunctions to women about relatedness, both to their intimate partners and, more broadly, to the extended world of other adults and to the abstract sphere of ideas and knowledge. So standards held by the Over-Eye include both personal constructs that incorporate the moral "shoulds" and idiosyncratic values of the family, and social norms acquired from the culture. If the family standards and cultural norms reflect and magnify each other, a woman will find them difficult to challenge on the basis of her personal observations.

The threatened punishment for disobeying the requirements of the Over-Eye is loss of love within real relationships. Unlike Freud's superego, this inner authority is not roused into action by the possibility of directing aggression against a hallowed figure, or by repressed sexual wishes directed at unacceptable targets. Rather, the Over-Eye is activated in situations where a woman wants to enter into intimate relationships or wants to be included and accepted by others. This inner oppressor continually demands behavior based on the norms and authority of the culture—that is, its shoulds: how to behave in order to be loved, in order to be included within the community of peers. This voice confuses the authentic self and obscures what it knows from personal experience, discounting such experience with the weight of shoulds, collective judgments, and negative self-evaluation.

When relationships are troubled or fail, the voice of the Over-Eye becomes even louder, pointing out how a woman's own shortcomings caused the problems, and blaming her for whatever went wrong. Rather than being undermined because it did not work, the theory of how to secure love held by the Over-Eye can gain in strength at this point, since the convictions of the authentic self carry less authority than those imposed by the culture and personal history.

When we employ the two-voice analysis, it becomes clear that what women lose in depression is not the whole self but only a part of the self: the "I," the authentic, creative self. When problems or distance arise in relationship, the Over-Eye turns as a condemning accuser against the "I," the person responsible for the problems: the no-good, fraudulent, selfish woman whom nobody should love anyway. The Over-Eye, mouthing moral shoulds directed at women, continually assaults the self-esteem and legitimacy of the "I." In this way, the harsh inner authority reflects outer configurations of relationships—a woman's personal history of relationships, her current attachments, and the larger social hierarchy of gender. Since we know that the relational self is socially constructed, it is not surprising that a woman's inner world reflects power relationships based on gender. . . .

In the interviews with depressed women, the silencing of the "I" corresponds to the loss of self and the despair of depression. This inner dynamic occurs within relationships marked by emotional distance and lack of communication. The ascendance of the first-person voice marks the women's recovery from depression, and corresponds with asserting one's voice within relationship, or with leaving relationships that do not allow such freedom to be authentic.

Maya traces the beginning of her movement out of severe depression by describing, in a literal sense, her recovery of voice:

> One of the first things I learned right after my divorce was that it felt good to get it out. It felt good to cry and laugh and do all those things that I hadn't done. I remember the first time I laughed out loud and it seemed strange to me to hear my own laughter . . . and then I realized that I never laughed in my marriage. I never let anything out, but then I never felt laughter. I sounded so loud—it was really, really frightening to hear that, to hear the sound, the loudness. It really caught me by surprise because it was so loud, and I must have been so quiet all the time. I talked in a very quiet voice, more than I do now, and you could hardly—nobody heard me and I would have to repeat myself. And that was even more frustrating because I would have to repeat myself all the time.

Through voice, we locate ourselves in the world and can be heard and found. When a woman fears the consequences of voicing her own perspective—whether from an abusive husband, a business that expects her to perform just like men, a classroom that negates her orientation, a culture that has devalued her—then she becomes quiet in order not to draw negating attention. . . .

The Development of the Over-Eye

. . . The imperatives of the Over-Eye are not authentic moral strivings, but are aspects of roles defined by a patriarchal culture. However, the imperatives are not experienced as deriving from roles. Instead, they feel like part of the self, a voice that tells a woman to act in certain ways in order to gain approval from others, from the culture, and from herself. As well as these explicit standards, visible in a depressed woman's self-reproaches, the Over-Eye contains diffuse images of relatedness—of how one *should* be or behave in order to be loved. How do these standards and images come to be organized in the Over-Eye, how are they tied to identification with the mother, to gender, and to culture? How are they related to women's notorious "dependence" and lack of ego boundaries? . . .

. . . [D]aughters observe and internalize the ways their mothers interact, both with them and with others, including husbands and other men. Most daughters notice *differences* between the way a mother acts in relation to the male world—of particular men, of ideas, of professions—and the way she acts in the female world of friends, children, and women's groups. If the mother and father have an unequal relationship, the daughter begins to see that her mother usually defers to her father's needs. Through specific behaviors such as these, a mother instructs her daughter in the ways of living in the Fathers' world and gaining approval and love: males are more powerful, please them, put their needs first, adopt their values. These patterns of relating, these rules for how a woman "should" behave in relation to the male world, take on moral value and become part of the standards held by the Over-Eye. In this way, girls learn images and ways of relating to men that differ from their primary experience of intimacy with their mother but that grow out of identification with her. As this feminine identification with the mother and her values continues, the growing girl experiences how maternal authority is overruled and replaced by paternal authority, both literally and metaphorically. Female authority teaches her by feeling, word, and example how to relate to male authority.

Because many of these images and feelings about how to relate to men come from early experiences and are tied, through identification, to the mother's actions in relationship, they are diffuse and unarticulated, and thus difficult to battle consciously and rationally. By the time a girl is old enough to recognize her mother's mode of interaction with men and say "That's not for me," it has already been internalized at a deep level and is resistant to change. Though children seem to reject disliked aspects of their parents as often as they follow them, these elements of how to be a female self in relationship run deep. By the time she consciously notices them, a girl has already imitated them long enough that they have become part of her identity, hard to break and hard to replace because of their tie with critical issues of approval, love, and feminine identity.

In adulthood, a woman is particularly vulnerable to depression if she equates caring for others with self-sacrifice. From what Gilligan (1982) has called the conventional perspective, goodness is understood as conformity to social norms and values, as fulfilling the obligations and functions of the roles one occupies: wife/mother/daughter/woman. At the conventional stage of development, the imperatives attached to the traditional female role converge with the woman's early-formed value on caring and responsibility. The cultural definition of feminine goodness as selfless giving in relationship moves in to restrict and to channel the authentic wish to love and care, and provides a stereotypic conception of the way to do it. This image of goodness as selfless love joins with the deep desire to make and maintain relationships to create a powerful obstacle to self-expression and recognition of anger. In tandem with social conditions that limit women's self-concept and expression, and with stereotypic prescriptions for female behavior, this ideal of goodness renders women particularly vulnerable to loss of self in heterosexual relationship.

Depressed women describe how they were taught throughout childhood to anticipate and react to male needs and how they, in turn, prepare their own daughters for similar interpersonal patterns. For example, Susan discusses her daughter, Jane, now 8:

> A lot of times when he's [her husband] gone, we're all relaxed and happy, we're harmonious, things are so nice. He'll drive up in the driveway and I see Jane start looking around the house thinking, "Now what can we do to make sure that Daddy does not get set off. Is the room picked up, what are we going to have for dinner tonight Mommy, is dinner ready?" I mean, I really am picking up some things like that from her that I'm really concerned about.

Jane has already learned to see her interpersonal context through the father's eyes. Though she and her mother are "relaxed and happy," Jane has learned that her father will not evaluate the domestic scene in the same way. Though maternal authority is present—Jane has her mother's approval, things are harmonious—the paternal world inserts a different authority. Jane has already learned to become a housekeeper of the man's feelings, has learned that her role is to pacify the male, to make things nice for him, to protect him from the disruption of daily life. In her concern that things be right for her father to avoid argument, Jane is already enacting her mother's role and submissive position. When mother authority defers to father authority, a mother hands her daughter over to the patriarchy without teaching her how to resist. Such early learnings make it difficult for women, in adulthood, to bring their own needs and feelings, their *agency*, into heterosexual relationships.

Susan elaborates about her daughter's response:

> She's already the kind of a child that wants to please. She's like how I was when I was little, doesn't want to rock the boat, always wants peace and so when there are arguments, she hates arguments, she hates any raising of voices, so when Harry says something harmful to me or hurtful to me, she wants me to just stay quiet. She just wants me to

> stay quiet. She feels that that's what I should do. She's only seeing that when we're arguing its probably Mom's fault because she said something that really got to Daddy and made him mad.

Beyond learning to be reactive, this daughter has clearly internalized the belief that the man's needs come first, and that the woman's needs and reality are not as important. Also, she has already learned the pattern of self-silencing to avoid the threat of disharmony. . . .

If a girl learns that others' needs come first, then the unspoken (and perhaps unconscious) corollary is: "My needs are less important than those of others and they will never be met, or will be met reciprocally only as I care for others." This childhood learning, passed on through identification between mother and daughter, in tandem with a social structure in which women hold a lesser position, lays the basis for pervasively low self-esteem as well as for repressed anger over unmet needs. Depressed women describe a sense of self-diminution that results from seeing themselves as less important than others in their relationships. Investing a large amount of self into their intimate relationships, they feel a gradual "loss of self" as they continually compromise the expression of their feelings and needs, and as they evaluate themselves as unable to attain intimacy. . . .

The child . . . incorporates statements of moral value and their imperatives in early childhood, but also observes as fact, as "the way things are," the rules that govern her parents' relationship. These "givens" of relationship carry with them moral judgments and values which the child learns along with her ideas of male and female behavior in a marital or intimate relationship. For example, when one parent is not living up to the role expectations of the other, the child will probably hear emotionally laden value statements around the themes of "You should be a better father/mother/husband/provider."

The morality of relatedness the girl internalizes has a critical integrative function in her life. Most important, it integrates the role accorded to women by society with her internal valuing of that role. Thus, the link between the female social role and women's vulnerability to depression lies in a set of moral imperatives that dictate how a woman *should* care for another—that is, how she should relate interpersonally, particularly to the male world. Learned first from the maternal world, care is highly valued as the medium that creates and cements connections to others. Yet, in relation to the male world, care becomes narrowed to a compliant relatedness that excludes significant aspects of the self, and caring becomes a well-marked path leading not to relation and expansion but to loss of self and depression.

The imperatives of feminine goodness, internalized in the Over-Eye, operate as a demanding taskmaster and an inner judge and jury. They require a posture in relationship that is doomed to failure, as well as self-perfection that is impossible to attain—perfect looks, perfect qualities, perfect behavior. Because the dictates of the Over-Eye promise to secure intimacy, a woman can rationalize them as legitimate, positive ways of being in relationship with a man and can overlook fundamental inequities in relationships between the sexes. In this way, the demands of the Over-Eye operate to keep a woman "in her place" both within heterosexual relationship and within the wider society.

In its defensive function, the morality of the "good woman" protects against anxiety: it guides a woman's actions to keep her "safe" from abandonment. Following the dictates of the Over-Eye protects against fear of loss of love, and against the fear that others in the wider social environment will judge her negatively. Thus, deviation from the standards of the Over-Eye feels so frightening to a woman because external and internal imperatives recite in unison the possible consequences—loss of relationship.

The imperatives of the Over-Eye regarding women's goodness in relationships are strengthened by the social reality of women's subordination—the experience of being a target of male violence (including sexual abuse), and the difficulties of financial dependence and poverty. In the world of achievement, conformity to male patterns—dedication to career that excludes a focus on children, norms of competition, detachment, self-promotion—are enforced by clear sanctions if one does not follow the established path.

Measuring Beliefs About Intimacy

Depressed women's images of self, role, and morality create a characteristic model of goodness which directs their behavior in relationships. These underlying beliefs about how to connect intimately with others lead a woman to subordinate her own needs to those of her partner and to believe that acting to get her own needs met is selfish and/or will disrupt relationship. These beliefs about how to make and maintain intimacy lead women to socially supported self-negating behaviors and feelings that erode both their relationships and their sense of self. These core images of relatedness, when activated, are *prior to* and *create* in women what Aaron Beck (1970) describes as the characteristic pattern of thoughts central to depression—a negative view of self, the past, and the future.

The importance of cognitive schemas (patterns of thought by which a person organizes and interprets experience) to clinical depression has been clearly demonstrated by Beck's extensive work. Assuming that cognitive, neurochemical, and affective systems are interrelated, Beck argues that "certain cognitive patterns (schemas) become activated and prepotent in depression and structure the kinds of interpretations [of experience] that are made by the patient. These negative interpretations, consequently, cast their shadow on the patient's mood and motivation" (1984, p. 1113).

The findings of [my] exploratory, long-term study of depressed women provide . . . support for the hypothesis that a certain pattern of beliefs about how women "should" act in relationships in order to secure intimacy is associated with female depression. To allow for more systematic study of how this pattern of beliefs correlates with depression in women, I constructed the Silencing the Self Scale or SSS. Sentences in the scale present the specific images of the self in intimate heterosexual relationships that I heard most often in the narratives of depressed women. Respondents agree or disagree on a five-point scale with thirty-one sentences that carry underlying moral standards. For example, Item 3, "Caring means putting the other person's needs in front of my own," includes an imperative of the traditional female role, a belief about how one should behave in intimate relationships, and a standard used to judge the self. . . .

In order to allow for continuing research concerning the standards depressed individuals use to judge the self, Item 31 of the SSS asks the person to agree or disagree with the statement "I never seem to measure up to the standards I set for myself." For those who answer that they agree or strongly agree, the questionnaire then instructs, "Please list up to three of the standards you feel you don't measure up to." Space is provided for people to write answers in their own words. Examples of standards depressed women use to judge the self have been collected from three diverse populations—63 college women (and a comparison male sample of 38), 140 residents of battered women's shelters, and approximately 175 new mothers who used cocaine during pregnancy. . . .

The standards people feel they don't live up to (as reflected by their responses, formulated in their own words) reveal the imperatives of the culture. Women and men list different standards, but the imperatives sound remarkably the same when they come from women, even women in very different stages of life, socioeconomic groups, and types of relationships.

Residents of battered women's shelters endorse the conventional "good woman" standards at a significantly higher level than the college student women. Battered women's agreement with these imperatives seems poignant when we consider that such moral beliefs constitute one of the factors that lead women to stay in hurtful relationships. Part of the trap of such beliefs stems from the interlocking, multifaceted nature of the imperatives: they include a *vision* of self in relationship, they guide *behavior* within it, they direct self-blaming *judgment* toward the self, they incite *anger* but demand its repression, and they directly affect *self-esteem*.

For example, if a woman believes that "Considering my needs to be as important as those of the people I love is selfish" (Item 4), then that standard directs her vision of the hierarchy of needs within relationship; it directs behavior by dictating how she should choose when her needs conflict with those of others she loves; it provides a standard for harsh self-judgment if she veers from its command. Further, it arouses anger as, following its dictates, she places her needs second to those of others; yet it also commands the repression of anger by purporting a moral basis for the suppression of her own needs. It reinforces a woman's low self-esteem by affirming that she is not as worthy or important as others, and, finally, it legitimizes the historical and still prevalent view of woman's nature as essentially self-sacrificing and maternal.

Thus, in the group of battered women, when a husband uses force and/or emotional cruelty, women blame themselves for not loving enough, or in the right ways. Anger becomes a club that is used against the self, and further entraps a woman in a damaging relationship and in debilitating depression. For example, Subject #7007, age 51, with eighteen years of education, has two teenage children at home and is raising two preschool grandsons. . . . She lists incidents of all three types of abuse: psychological (including threats, humiliation, and isolation), physical (beating, slap, punch), and sexual. Yet, in response to Item 31 (which asks respondents to list, in their own words, standards they fail to meet), this woman states standards of perfection that keep her attention focused on her own failure rather than on an accurate perception of what is happening in the relationship:

> I can never get everything done; I can't seem to keep the peace between family members so that all are happy; I consistently fail to achieve my own goals: weight loss, appearance, business activities, recreation desires, needs, etc.

. . . Subject #1002, age 26, with two children, writes:

> I'm not able to keep up with two kids, a house, and a husband with special problems, and daily tasks as well as I feel I should be able to. I'm not able to deal with my husband's disability in the sense of helping him deal with it, and I don't make myself look my best.

On the abuse history form, this woman listed incidents of psychological and sexual abuse in her current, nine-year marriage.

Finally, evidence of the hopelessness of depression appears in women who have given up on themselves. Subject #6040, age 26, with thirteen years of education and one child: "I've quit setting standards because I feel like nothing." Subject #6028, age 38, with twelve years of education and two children: "No self-confidence, can't keep a job, I feel like a lost cause."

Fifty-four percent (75 of 140) of the battered women's sample agreed with Item 31, "I never seem to measure up to the standards I set for myself," and listed their own standards. The following categories encompass the range of standards they listed: wife/partner, personal appearance/weight, mother/homemaker, employment/finances, personal characteristics, self-esteem/self-assertion, and education. For example, eleven women listed standards that fit the category wife/partner, such as "perfect wife," "loving him, making him happy," "being a good wife," "being a better wife," "making my relationship work," "trying to please my husband," "being married three times." Fifteen women listed failure to live up to standards for personal appearance, such as "poor looking," "I don't feel pretty enough," "be slim, healthy, and 'put together,'" "not able to be beautiful and slim," "don't have slim figure, shiny hair, manicured nails," "overweight," "fat and ugly," "gained weight, eat whatever." Under employment/finances, twenty-eight women listed standards for financial independence and meeting career goals such as "can't earn acceptable salary," "want to be financially stable," "choosing what I want as a career," "don't think I could ever support myself and my children," "can't get better-paying job," "can't make my check last," "I don't make enough money," and more of very similar statements.

The superwoman image appears when women endorse conventional standards for the "good woman" and then also list demands for filling career or work goals. Subject #8009: "I should be able to work an eight-hour job and still be a great Mom." Subject #9002: "Have trouble keeping a job and dealing with family problems/housework/being wife and mother. Not enough energy."

Among cocaine-abusing mothers, a group who are currently under intense public scrutiny and condemnation, the standards sound similar to those battered women use. Most of the standards center on parenting, relationships with partner or husband, personal appearance, drug use, and on improving the self through education and employment. For example, Subject #4853: "I set too high of daily goals, I don't commend myself for what I do accomplish, I set others' goals and let myself down when they don't meet my expectation." Subject #4236: "I try to do things just so and it always fails." Subject #3110: "Being consistent as a mother; giving friendship to others, doing the things that I want to in life." Subject #2738: "Being more understanding of my older children; being the best mom and wife I can; opinion of myself is low and has been for a long time; fat, ugly, etc. But not having the willpower to do anything about it!" Subject #4142: "Should look better, should be able to do more, want to give more of myself." Subject #2901: "To always be there for my son and husband; to work and take care of my son (giving 100% to everything all the time)." Subject #4120: "Not able to keep up my house and other family needs as well as would like to; lost a lot of energy that I would like to use being a more assertive wife and companion to my husband; wish I could have patience with *all* my children." Subject #3498: "Consistency—in housework, childraising; also there are things I want to do like artwork. I'll get started but usually don't finish. I'm discouraged before I get started."

These standards, sounding so similar across different groups of women, channel massive amounts of feminine energy and desire toward illusory goals. They divert women from seeing and accurately naming the impediments to their development and lead them to stay in negating relationships by making them believe the fault lies within themselves. Striving for perfection by trying to fulfill such standards is a quest doomed to failure and frustration. These standards also divert women from reaching the goals of their search: intimate connection and authentic self-development. Women strive for connection, but the *forms* of connection lead to self-defeat and low self-esteem. These forms are supplied by the culture and appear to promise love; yet enacting them leads to the loss of an active, authentic self.

The moral themes in depressed women's narratives reveal internal impediments that prevent women from claiming the authority of their first-person, authentic voices. It is difficult for women to know and to speak what they feel, think, and perceive when to do so challenges a tradition of male authority and female silence. Yearning for connection, a woman adopts the forms of relating she learned from her mother, from her father, and from culture, and ends up self-alienated and paralyzed. Mother authority, with its mythic, powerful connection to creation and life, teaches the daughter to defer to Father authority, with its emphasis on rules, hierarchy, and obedience. In so doing, the maternal world hopes to prepare daughters to live safely and to find love in the paternal world. If a woman tries to defy such authorities, lodged in the Over-Eye, she is assaulted from within by harsh self-condemnation, while she faces the external possibility of rejection or physical assault from males simply because she is female. These inner and outer restraints operate as invisible bonds, restricting a woman's freedom to be an active, responsible self within relationship. As women with the potential for raising daughters and sons, we must ask ourselves and our partners, "Into whose hands are we to deliver our children, who are we training them to obey, and for whose benefit?" (Rich, 1979, p. 218). Mothers fear their daughters will meet with rejection, isolation, and danger if they stray too far outside social norms that govern gender interactions. Trying to save their daughters from a certain kind of pain and loss, mothers unknowingly teach them a way of relating to the male world that leads to a different form of loss.

References

Beck, A.T.N. (1970). The core problem in depression: The cognitive triad. In J. Masseman (Ed.), *Science and psychoanalysis*. New York: Grune and Stratton.

Beck, A.T.N. (1984). Cognition and therapy. Letter to the editor. *Archives of General Psychiatry, 41*, 1112–1114.

Bibring, E. (1953). The mechanisms of depression. In P. Greenachre (Ed.), *Affective disorders: Psychoanalytic contribution to their study*. New York: International Universities Press.

Brazelton, T.B. (1982). Joint regulation of neonate-parent behavior. In E. Tronick (Ed.), *Social interchange in infancy*. Baltimore, MD: University Park Press.

Freud, S. (1917). Mourning and melancholia. In J. Strachey (Ed.), *The standard edition of the complete works of Sigmund Freud*, Vol. 14. London: Hogarth Press, 1957.

Freud, S. (1925). Some psychological consequences of the anatomical distinction between the sexes. In J. Strachey (Ed.), *The standard edition of the complete works of Sigmund Freud*, Vol. 19. London: Hogarth Press, 1961.

Gilligan, C. (1977). In a different voice: Women's conceptions of self and of morality. *Harvard Educational Review, 47*, 481–517.

Gilligan, C. (1982). *In a different voice: Psychological theory and women's development*. Cambridge, MA: Harvard University Press.

Gilligan, C. (1990). Joining the resistance: Psychology, politics, girls and women. *Michigan Quarterly Review, 29*, 501–536.

Harvey, T.J. & Stables, A. (1986). Gender differences in attitudes to science for third year pupils: An argument for single-sex teaching groups in mixed schools. *Research in Science and Technological Education, 4*, 163–170.

Rich, A. (1979). *On secrets, lies and silence: Selected prose, 1966–1978*. New York: W.W. Norton.

Sadker, M. & Sadker, D. (1985). Sexism in the classroom. *Vocational Educational Journal, 60*, 30–32.

Sadker, M. & Sadker, D. (1986). Sexism in the classroom: From grade school to graduate school. *Phi Delta Kappan, 67*, 512–515.

Winnicott, D.W. (1965). *The maturational process and the facilitating environment: Studies in the theory of emotional development*. New York: International Universities Press.

24 Who Are You Calling Crazy?

PRISCILLA GRANT

Imagine going to the gynecologist for your annual checkup. She examines you, asks about your periods, does a Pap smear and then says, "You should know that, after age forty, women may feel like they're losing their minds. But don't worry," she smiles cheerfully, "we can take care of that." She hands you a brochure for "Menopausal Mental Syndrome," or "MMS," that lists its signs—depression, irritability, insomnia, weepiness, anxiety, verbal slips, memory lapses, inability to concentrate, outbursts of anger—and tells you to call her if "it" hits.

Sound far-fetched? Maybe not. If some leading physicians have their way, a definition of "MMS" might be well-established in just a few years. Recently a group of scientists met to discuss the mental changes that some women experience before and during menopause and to advance research into their long-term effects. One of the organizers was Stanley J. Birge, M.D., a prominent geriatrician at Washington University School of Medicine. The group couldn't agree on a definitive list of symptoms, says Birge, nor could they come up with a name for the cluster of mood disorders or cognitive problems some women report, nor could they estimate how many midlife women might be suffering. Yet, they're convinced such a syndrome exists. "We don't have all the science yet," says

Birge, "but the biggest breakthrough is the recognition by the scientific community that there is a problem."

Birge believes that, whatever it's called, something like "MMS" should join the lexicon as a medical condition, along with premenstrual syndrome (PMS), premenstrual dysphoric disorder (PMDD) and postpartum depression. "If you don't have a label," he explains, "it's difficult to talk about." When women in perimenopause go to their doctors, Birge says, they may report irregular periods, but be reluctant to discuss mental or emotional changes. "We have to get this message out. This is normal physiology. Women who experience symptoms are not crazy."

Yet we might wonder if labeling a woman's menopausal passage a medical disorder isn't craziness itself. Remember when PMS was introduced as a diagnosis in the Eighties? It was controversial precisely because it reinforced a negative view of menstruation already prevalent in our culture. It threatened to stereotype all menstruating women as untrustworthy, subject to their "raging hormones." And indeed, the crazy creature with PMS has become a Hallmark staple—even though only 3–10 percent of women have premenstrual symptoms severe enough to disrupt their lives. Do we really want another "hormonal disorder" added to the list of women-only psychiatric ills? Won't such a diagnosis stigmatize midlife women—and there are an estimated 5,000 of us entering menopause every day—as mentally unstable?

Women have cause to be wary. Medicine doesn't have a great track record on this subject. In ancient times, emotionally volatile women were diagnosed with "hysteria" (which, as if by way of explanation, means "uterus"). In the 19th century, physicians would confine sad or unruly menopausal women in insane asylums, treating them with bowel purges, leeches and heavy doses of morphine. Nobody seemed to want to ask them what was going on in their lives that might make them sorrow or rage. In our own time, until 1979, "involutional melancholia"—a.k.a. "menopausal depression"—was listed in the *Diagnostic and Statistical Manual of Mental Disorders* (*DSM*), the bible of the psychiatric profession. Following work by feminist-minded scientists, the diagnosis was expunged, so that in 1989, citing 25 years of research, the *American Journal of Psychiatry* would report that experts now accept that menopausal depression "has become mythical." According to the report, studies showed that depressive symptoms were not any more common during perimenopause than at other ages and seemed more influenced by psychological factors, such as the number of confidantes a woman felt she could count on.

Maggie Scarf, the author of *Unfinished Business* (Doubleday, 1980) and other works on the psychology of women, remembers the effort to erase menopausal depression from the *DSM.* The diagnosis "was total nonsense," she says. Life circumstances that had nothing to do with hormones could make women vulnerable to emotional upheaval in midlife. "To decide that women are more prone to be nutty or depressed at menopause—which occurs over a number of years—is just anti-female prejudice."

But today science appears to be bringing us full circle. In response to recent findings, some researchers and clinicians argue that the drop in estrogen is a crucial factor in the mood swings, depressive symptoms, anxiety, memory problems and cognitive slips that some perimenopausal women experience. Recent books have raised the alarm about the mental perils women face at midlife. . . .

The common thread in all these works? Research that shows that the "female hormone" is crucial to healthy brain function—not only in women, but in men, too. (Men get theirs by converting some testosterone to estrogen, with the curious effect that males in their seventies may have more circulating estrogen than women the same age.) Estrogen improves blood flow to the brain, increases the growth of new neuronal connections and maintains the strength of dendrites, the neuron branches that conduct electrical impulses and release neurotransmitters. Estrogen receptors are found in many areas of the brain, including those that specialize in memory, emotion and decision making.

It seems reasonable to speculate, therefore, that declining estrogen levels—they go down some 70–80 percent by menopause—might have a destabilizing effect. The National Institute of Mental Health acknowledges that a small number of perimenopausal women become clinically depressed and is recruiting women for further studies of mood disorders at this stage of life. Several small studies have shown that estrogen replacement in postmenopausal women can boost memory, attention and even I.Q. For depressed women in perimenopause, estrogen replacement has been shown to enhance the effect of antidepressants. Birge and other scientists speculate that there's a connection between the estrogen loss during perimenopause and later development of Alzheimer's disease (which women suffer at one and a half times the rate of men).

If menopause's mental symptoms earned a name as a medical condition, the argument goes, women who do suffer would be more likely to discuss their symptoms and seek treatment. And getting help early might prove important, since preliminary research suggests that perimenopause may offer the crucial window of opportunity for treatment. "At perimenopause," says Birge, "there's a greater impact [for hormone supplementation] on the brain than we would see five to ten years later. It's similar to bone density—you see a dramatic decline perimenopausally, and if you wait until menopause [i.e., after a woman has had no periods for twelve months] to start hormonal therapy, it won't be as effective."

But if "mental menopause" is triggered by the loss of estrogen (and deserving of a listing in the *DSM*), why don't all midlife women exhibit mental symptoms? The short answer: Nobody knows for sure. Just as nobody knows why some women have hot flashes and others don't, or why women in our society exhibit many more menopausal symptoms overall than do, say, women in Japan. Just as nobody knows what combination of genes, hormones, neurotransmitters, family upbringing and bad movies lead a disaffected 40-something male to pick up a shotgun and mow down his fellow workers.

Calling attention to menopausal women's emotional swings or mental lapses is a loaded proposition. Yes, it could make it easier for the minority whose lives are disrupted and who need medication, but it could also encourage—once again—the idea that women are the sick ones, the not-to-be-trusted, hormonally challenged sex. It's a societal norm that men act out their frustrations, sometimes violently. Yet, when women lose control and rage at their circumstances, our culture offers medication. This year saw the start of a new ad campaign on TV for Sarafem. It's shot in muted tones, signifying gritty reality. Women in various states of distress are shown while their symptoms—"bloating, irritability, sadness"—pop up on screen. One figure grows blurry, shouts, raising her arms overhead, while behind her a man cowers. "Think it's PMS?" asks the ad, ominously. "Think again. It could be PMDD." Not to worry, though: Sarafem—Prozac, repackaged for the hormonally beset—stands ready to restore the female to her calm, smiling, beguiling self.

"Why is it that things we don't understand become psychiatric illnesses?" asks Driscoll, who is against a proposed disease label. "You know, I love men, but I think it's the patriarchal health system at work again. I mean, why don't we have diagnoses like 'semen retention headache'?"

She and others believe that the emotional and mental turmoil that can occur around perimenopause is not purely biological and may even be healthy. Reaching middle age, after all, has a funny way of triggering a need to reassess how happy you are with your career, marriage and the general direction your life might take over the next 30 years. But to attribute alterations in a woman's attitude solely to the hormonal changes of menopause "strips those attitudes of respectability," suggests Germaine Greer in her bracing exploration of *The Change* (Knopf, 1992). "Admitting that unhappiness might be justified would undermine the entire rationale of medicating the mind. There can be no suggestion that feeling tired and disillusioned at fifty might be the appropriate response."

Christiane Northrup, M.D., feminist, physician and author of *The Wisdom of Menopause* (Bantam Books, 2001), does not want to ignore the biological underpinnings of menopause's mental symptoms. But she has qualms about "pathologizing" the emotions of the perimenopausal woman as a disease. She encourages a more holistic (and female-friendly) view of the menopausal transition as a significant chance for a woman to reclaim herself. (Northrup herself went through a divorce in perimenopause.) She believes "the brain catches fire"—triggered by hormonal changes—for a reason. "Say a depression comes on in perimenopause. This is a signal that you need to look at everything—relationships, job, exercise, diet, where you're living. You could be taking an antidepressant or estrogen or whatever, but at the same time ask, 'Why is this happening to me now?' The real power of midlife comes when you trust your own authority more than you ever did."

It is not helpful to promote expectations of a mental disorder, Northrup adds, when "depression is not more common in perimenopause and after menopause—it's less common."

Even Klaiber, who specializes in helping women and men with hormonal disorders, is conflicted over the possibility of declaring menopause a mental condition. On the one hand, he wants a wider understanding that women with mood and cognitive problems can benefit enormously from individualized fine-tuning of hormonal drugs. On the other, he says, "Labels make me nervous, because I do not want to do anything that would have a negative effect on women's gains." What we need to remember, he says, is, "hormones are not gender biased." The latest research, he adds, confirms that both women and men experience hormonal fluctuations that can affect their thinking, behavior, moods and sexuality.

Why, then, isn't there more attention to the midlife male's hormonal transition? Might not his declining hormones lie behind "symptoms" such as alcohol abuse, depression, sexual dysfunction, the new red sports car, the 25-year-old girlfriend? Where are the symposiums and research studies and popular books about "testopause"? "Men go through a whole midlife crisis that's completely underrecognized," says Northrup. . . .

Whether a diagnosis of "MMS" becomes a reality or not, there's no halting the train of research that Birge, Klaiber, Warga and others recommend. Nor should there be. The last ten years have seen incredible advances in neuroscience and brain imagery that are literally illuminating how our mind works. Who wouldn't want to know more? Certainly not women who get help from hormones or a combination of hormones and antidepressants—and who doctors say are tremendously relieved to find they're not "crazy." In raising the profile of mental problems at menopause, the challenge will be to prevent some women's hormonal vulnerability from becoming an excuse for sexism. In her book, *The Pause* (Plume, 2000), psychologist Lonnie Barbach, Ph.D., puts it this way: "The feminist in me is tempted to say that in this regard we are no different from men. But in truth we are. And while many women remain emotionally unaffected by the change in their hormonal balance, others are affected to varying degrees. Certainly this does not mean that we are rendered incompetent at this time in our lives, and denying us opportunities because of potential vulnerability to hormone fluctuations is unwise and unjust."

As we continue to explore the brave new world of hormone and brain research, let's just be sure that everyone remembers this last part.

25 Feminist Therapy Approaches

MARY BALLOU

CAROLYN WEST

Carla is a mixed race adolescent who is referred for therapy following a suicide attempt. She is 14 years old and lives with her Irish immigrant mother and 11-year-old brother in the working class section of a predominantly white, middle-class community. Her Hispanic father left the family after a long history of marital discord. The mother had coped within a controlling and often abusive marital relationship by being quiet and passive, and had been repeatedly encouraged by Carla to stand up for herself. Since the separation, however, Carla has assumed an increasingly blaming attitude toward her mother.

It was shortly after her parents separated that Carla took an overdose of sleeping pills. She currently presents with eating and sleeping problems and repeatedly misses school because of complaints about headaches and stomach problems. She reports demeaning treatment at the time of hospitalization around her suicide attempt; medical professionals consistently tell her that her physical complaints have no physiological basis.

In attempting to gain support at Carla's middle school, her mother reports being told that only 2 percent of the school population is Hispanic and that statistics show that youngsters of Carla's ethnicity rarely complete high school. Carla's mother has no relatives in the United States and Carla is currently estranged from her father's family of origin. This mother does not know where to go for help. She does not know where she and her daughter fit or how to gain an understanding of how the American culture works. This chapter explicates the issues that a feminist therapist would consider as she works with Carla.

. . .

Feminist Therapy Principles

Feminist therapy is remarkable in many regards. While the more traditional and widely used techniques emanate from somewhat imposing and distant theoretical frameworks, feminist therapy asserts its grounding in a model that can be thought of as circular and interactive rather than linear and static. Here, information flows naturally and bidirectionally from theorist and therapist to client, into the culture and back round again. Paraphrasing Marcia Westkott (1979), it is FOR women rather than ABOUT them and it is less a prescription or technique than it is a philosophy of therapy emerging out of the lived experiences of women within a social context. This philosophy, which is potentially mapped onto and informs a range of treatment modalities, is best articulated via a set of clear and consensual principles that have served as the building materials and unifying constructs of theory, practice, and ethics within feminist therapy.

Feminist therapy can be characterized by several key principles:

1. Feminist therapy is unwaveringly rooted in the search for and valuing of ALL women's experiences (Hill & Ballou, 1998). Essential to feminist therapy is the "valuing of the diverse and complex experiences of women from all racial, class, religious, age and sexual orientation groups" (Brown & Brodsky, 1992, p.51). "Considering behavior alone is insufficient to understanding women in patriarchy, nor is it adequate to link women's behavior only to the dominant, male-created ideology" (Westkott, 1979, p. 429). Rather than forcing women's experiences into the ideological frames constructed without attention to their voice and status by in so doing, devaluing and distorting both the experiences and the women themselves, feminist therapy inquires into, listens for, and attempts to understand the experiences of all women as "they have grown up and lived in social contexts that are opposed to their needs as human beings" (Westkott, 1979, p. 424).

2. Feminist therapy recognizes a primary need to consider behaviors and intrapsychic processes as they are embedded within a sociopolitical context. Feminist therapy rests on and respects the notion of "the personal is political," a way of viewing and analyzing experience WITHIN its sociopolitical context which evolved out of the consciousness raising groups of the second wave of the women's movement (Hill & Ballou, 1998). It has as its purpose the exploration of the "inherent contradictions in the prescribed social roles for women" (Espin, 1994, p. 271).
3. Feminist therapy seeks to redress the power imbalance that is typically maintained within the counseling relationship and that mirrors the power imbalance of the larger sociocultural context—a context in which the client has already experienced destructive misuses of power (Hill & Ballou, 1998). Holding issues of power at the forefront of all exchanges, feminist therapists seek to build an egalitarian therapeutic relationship that can empower the client and that models more collaborative ways of being in the world (Hill & Ballou, 1998). This sorting out and reconfiguring of power inequities includes all aspects and exchanges of the therapeutic relationship including such ordinary and at the same time power-laden issues as fees and payment schedules, the use of titles, therapist self-disclosure, touch, and therapist availability between sessions (Brown, 1994).
4. Feminist therapy attends not to issues of gender alone but also recognizes and names additional categories of oppression. At its core, feminist therapy honors and respects the inherent worth and dignity of all human beings while seeking to expose both subtle and overt manifestations of oppression directed toward gender, race, class, religion, age, ethnicity, sexual orientation, disability, and the identities that flow out of belongings anchored in multiple cultural contexts.
5. The goals of feminist therapy are not about achieving a better, a quieter, a more compliant fit within a system that oppresses, but are directed toward helping the individual to recognize the sociopolitical and economic forces, the societal structures and gendered expectations that contribute to pain and discomfort while simultaneously discovering personal resources and healthy resistances as means of empowerment. Feminist therapists deal not only with individuals, but also have an overarching commitment to social change (Morrow & Hawxhurst, 1998; Whalen, 1996).

6. Feminist therapy recognizes and respects a range of methods in its effort to seek out and validate knowledge. Multiple ways of knowing (epistemologies) replace singular, outdated and limiting constructions, and include a deliberate and concerted interdisciplinary effort (Ballou, 1990).
7. Feminist therapy adopts a questioning stance toward the status quo, consistently surveying dominant institutions, theories, practices, and research methods in an effort to expose ideas and practices that fail to include or account for, and are harmful to marginalized peoples. Feminist therapy does not reject science but it does note and mark its limits and continually attempts to locate the questions of research within a sociopolitical context.

These principles serve as an organizing framework for a therapy model that both accepts and seeks diversity. They provide a conceptual framework as issues of feminist assessment, diagnosis, and therapy practice are discussed.

Early feminist therapists were like anthropologists, unearthing and exposing sexist problems, abuses to women, and power politics as these functioned in traditional mental health theory and practice. Brought to light and given voice were issues involving social control, the devaluing and pathologizing of women's roles and coping strategies, and the ignoring of contextual environments and structures. It is interesting to note that many of these early critiques seem to be reemerging within the context of the corporate mental health industry of today. Specifically, feminist therapists criticize mainstream views of women and the associated normative standards that are routinely applied throughout therapy—in assessment, in diagnosis, and in treatment planning. They also critique therapy practices and the very nature of the therapeutic relationship as it exists within traditional therapy. . . .

Feminist Therapy Practiced

So just how does one do therapy that is feminist? Does it really differ from conventional psychotherapeutic practice? If so, in what ways? These are reasonable and important questions. Feminist therapy has evolved substantially over the 25 years since Mander and Rush wrote *Feminism as Therapy*. . . . [I]t differs in both obvious and subtle ways from conventional therapy. It seems important to say that unlike other therapeutic models, there is no single or predominant therapy school that dictates feminist therapy practice and so this presentation is organized around feminist principles as they contribute to a range of feminist therapy techniques and considerations.

Women's Experiences "While feminist therapy is not about therapy with women, it is therapy practiced by feminist women whose insights are profoundly informed by living in diverse female realities" (Brown, 1994, p. 10). One of the central points of feminist therapy is that it is based in the valuing of ALL women's experiences (Ballou, 1995; Brown, 1994; Enns, 1997; Gilbert, 1980; Hill, 1990; Kaschak, 1992; Lerman, 1986, 1992; Worell & Remer, 1992).

This basic tenet holds a number of implications for the practice of feminist therapy. A client's description of her life, her feelings, and areas of concern are heard and believed as her truth. Unlike the custom in conventional therapies, they are not decontextualized and processed into intake histories and data that are later used to develop a diagnosis and treatment plan. Nor are misinterpretation, repression, or other "psychological mechanisms" presumed to distort her perceptions and descriptions. Yet, it seems important to say that while the valuing of women's experience is a central and complex aspect of feminist therapy, all perceptions are not necessarily assumed to be accurate or in full awareness. Thus, the careful process of reflecting, critical questioning, and learning are also essential features of doing feminist therapy.

One difference between feminist and conventional therapies is that in feminist therapy the descriptions of the client are not reinterpreted through some remote theory. Neither are expressions of fear, anxiety, pain, and depression represented in the traditional language of psychological distancing (e.g., "enmeshment," "irrational thought," "codependency"). Feminists consider that social images and messages as well as normative standards and theory emanate from the dominant ideology. Because such sources of information about women and how they ought to be are apt to be contaminated, women's direct experiences are centrally featured in feminist therapy.

Indeed, unless the agency, hospital, or cost management entity requires formal DSM diagnosis, the descriptions of concerns and problems are formulated by the client and counselor together without the distancing and sometimes prejorative labels of formal diagnosis. This collaborative process, perhaps possible only in such venues as a college counseling center, uses ordinary and accessible language and is negotiated in a way that respects both the expert knowledge of the therapist and the lived experiences of the woman. Even when interactions with an insurance company or similar gatekeeping agency is required, feminist therapists seek out creative ways to empower and respect their clients by involving them in such processes as diagnosis and negotiation about the number of sessions. Marcia Hill (1999), for example, describes her practice of talking to the insurance company case manager on a speaker phone while sitting with her client.

Unlike more standard formulations, a feminist therapy frame would consider the devaluation, danger, and difficulties of life alongside cultural and individual coping efforts. In the case of Carla, a feminist therapist would seek to understand Carla's experience of being devalued within her educational setting, of feeling misunderstood and dismissed by medical professionals and of feeling hopeless in the face of a culture that expects her to fail.

The valuing of women's experiences within the feminist therapy model also involves a recognition and honoring of the whole of women's lives and work. Here, in contrast to traditional models, women's lives replace men's as the basis for theory building and understanding. We gain valuable insights into the lived realities across the diversity of women through such descriptions as those provided by Beverly Greene (1994), who tells us about African-American women teaching their children how to cope with racism. Rather than capitulating to the helplessness engendered by the structures of racist oppression, Greene's mothers take a proactive stance. These women acknowledge and name racism and seek to resist its damage by preparing their children for its inevitability.

In a similar fashion, women-based theories such as the Stone Center's relational model (Jordan et al., 1992) and the work of Taylor, Gilligan, and Sullivan (1995) in adolescent girls' development are set squarely in this principle of valuing women's experience. Some of the interventions that have been developed around listening and finding voice demonstrate feminist therapy's clear commitment to valuing all of women's experiences. Feminist therapists evoke voice and experience through such means as bibliotherapy and journal and poetry writing (Rogers, 1993), as well as other expressive arts. All of these tools are used to encourage clients to find avenues of voice and self-expression by providing multiple opportunities to be heard and understood.

Two additional examples are now provided of this essential feature of feminist therapy—the process of listening carefully and of drawing insights from women's lived experiences in all their complexities. In its understanding of each of the following situations, feminist therapy would consider the woman's construction of meaning and her own awareness of possible alternatives.

The first example concerns the experiences of a Cambodian woman who endures physical abuse by her husband. When her experience is contextualized and situated culturally and sociopolitically, a story emerges of a family who has suffered great humiliation in refugee camps. The husband, who formerly maintained a professional status in Cambodia, is now working as a cook in an Asian restaurant. Understandably wary of authorities, given her experiences in Cambodia and in the refugee camps, the woman, in her silence, reflects her culture's constraints around shaming of the family and seeks to retain her family's respect in the Asian-American community.

Here, feminist therapy listens not only to what has happened to this woman, but also seeks to understand her experiences and the complex social, cultural, economic, and structural influences that combine and interweave to influence her decisions. Feminist therapy listens for these often difficult choices as described by the women themselves. A number of authors, including Cole, Espin, and Rothblum (1992), Ho (1990), and Root (1995), have expanded our understanding of the experience of Asian-American women.

A second example comes from the context of a mixed race, bicultural, adolescent female gang member. Gold (1998) reports these girls' experiences often include sex on demand, utilitarian sex devoid of the partners' emotional involvement, and sex used as an initiation rite with multiple gang members. Certainly a white, middle-class feminist may readily classify these experiences as sexual abuse. Yet, in listening to the girls' voices, Gold learns of the significant value placed on their relationships with the boy gang members. To the girls, these relationships involve being listened to in a way that has been glaringly absent from their experience. The coupling, here, of being listened to and of being sexually abused forms a very real contradiction for the feminist therapist. While these stories may be difficult to hear, what is critically important is that the girls' reality is understood in terms of what these relationships have meant to them.

Over the last decade, feminist therapy has made a commitment to understand women's experiences as multiple, diverse, and interactive. This is a basic principle of feminist therapy and occupies a central position within the therapeutic relationship. Feminist therapists are themselves engaged in raising their own consciousness about the multiple realities of various women's lives so as not to replicate and perpetuate the embedded normative notions of monocultural experiences (Barrett, 1998). So while feminist therapists thoughtfully analyze sociocultural contributions to their clients' distress they are, at the same time, committed to an ongoing analysis of their own understandings of diversity and multiple realities.

External Factors and Sociocultural Influences Women's experiences also provide us with compelling examples of sociostructural factors as they impact on individuals (Ballou, 1990, 1995; Ballou & Gabalac, 1985; Brown & Root, 1990; Brown & Ballou, 1992; Brown & Brodsky, 1992; Comas-Diaz & Greene, 1994; Kaschak, 1992; Rawlings & Carter, 1997; Worell & Remer, 1992). For instance, that many single mothers struggle with issues of child care and finances is a reality borne out of women's experience. Yet, it is a reality reflective of the values and patterns that are part of a much larger socioeconomic system. Highlighting this basic tenet of the personal as political, McGrath, Keita, Strickland, and Russo (1990) concluded, in a major American Psychological Association (APA) task force report that gendered politics, are strongly associated with depression. Others have similarly analyzed the relationships between gendered politics and eating disorders and sexual conflicts.

Feminist therapy attempts to deconstruct, with the client, just how her experiences are tied to this sociocultural context and its structural factors. Just as the political context shapes the individual lives of women, so, too, do the specific aspects of individual experience reflect the political. For example, when women work for less pay than men and are also expected to do the unpaid work of child and man care within their families and workspace, their structural second-class position shapes not only the time/demand/resource realities but their self-evaluation as well. Gender stereotypes are not only unenlightened but oppressive and harmful to self-worth. Feminist therapy is directed toward exposing this reciprocal influence of the political and personal to help the client move beyond her overwhelming feelings of guilt and self-blame.

Carla's situation represents a bicultural example of ways in which a family's economic and social status can be radically affected by the loss of a family member due to separation and divorce. While Carla initially encouraged her mother to end the relationship with her father because of the ongoing spousal abuse, the current helplessness of both mother and daughter has resulted in Carla's feelings of guilt, ambivalence, and internalized anger. Aside from the personal and interpersonal complexities of their current situation, there are very clear social, economic, and cultural factors impacting this family.

This process of taking note of the intersection between personal issues (e.g., depression, anxiety, hopelessness) that often bring women into therapy, and their often less obvious sociopolitical context, involves recognizing the trauma, destructiveness, and devaluation that occur through such acts of power as rape, abuse, and domestic violence (Walker,

1999). Broadening our own and our clients' understanding of the damage incurred through such violations is an especially important endeavor. Among the many authors who have written extensively on this topic are Maria Root (1992), who provides sociocultural analyses of insidious trauma. While psychotherapy has traditionally been sought for the traumatic damage done to the individual by these crimes and human rights violations, feminist therapy has brought to the foreground the external causes of individual distress and their impact on the developmental patterns of girls and women.

Cole, Espin, and Rothblum (1992) provide an example of this in their reports of refugee women immigrating into the United States. These women are frequently assigned psychiatric diagnoses and given medication to minimize their "symptoms." Yet, as pointed out by such authors as Adleman and Enguidanos (1996), co-cultural community support, acknowledgement of the women's trauma, credible and understandable explanations of United States' rights and protections, and interventions for the women's physical and security needs both contextualize their problems and provide a socially responsive treatment.

Thus, lucid and thorough bio–psycho–social–cultural–structural analysis is a major aspect of the conduct of feminist therapy.

Egalitarian Relationship Another cornerstone of feminist therapy is its focus on the relationship between the client and therapist and the distribution of power within this relationship. In conventional therapy the therapist implicity holds the institutional, expert and referent-formal power. Feminist therapy, howver, demands that the power be shared between the client and the therapist. Therapeutic relationships that attempt to reduce the power asymmetries (Brown, 1994) and to coordinate the power to name and the right to bargain (Ballou & Gabalac, 1985) are quintessential aspects of the egalitarian relationship principle. In sharing power, feminist therapy engages in an ethic of respect (Hill, 1990) and strives to avoid replication of hierarchical structures which have sometimes wrought damage on the client.

While this tenet is implemented in a variety of ways in feminist therapy, there are some applications that are considered fundamental and consensual. For instance, decisions regarding the frequency and length of treatment, payment amounts and schedules, and treatment modalities are typically decided collaboratively through discussion. Depending on the readiness of the client, she will participate in naming her distress and establishing appropriate outcomes, goals, and areas of work. Consistent with the principle of an egalitarian relationship, some feminist therapists provide information to the client that addresses how to raise concerns about the therapy or the therapeutic relationship in the initial session (Hill & Ballou, 1998). Similarly, issues of progress, termination, respite, and the future availability of the therapist are discussed mutually.

Both the principles and ethics of feminist therapy call on feminist therapists to raise these matters on all levels of complexity and to enter into and consistently maintain an egalitarian relationship that questions and works out the responsibilities of each party.

> An example of the careful decision-making and often subtle issues involved in feminist therapy involves a feminist therapist and her client, Alice, both of whom live and work in a Western rural setting. The therapist is experienced in trauma work through a gender and power abuse perspective; Alice is 18 and the fourth generation to be born into and work on the family ranch. She has a high school education.
>
> Alice comes to therapy for treatment of symptoms related to the trauma of ongoing physical and emotional abuse perpetrated by her uncle, a man who owns one half of the ranch and who wields the power that accompanies this economic, gendered, and sociopolitical status. Alice's family is aware of her situation, but in the context of hierarchical notions gender roles and out of fear of losing the ranch, they minimize Alice's distress and chide her either to toughen up or leave. Alice has limited financial resources and few interpersonal supports outside of her abusive family.
>
> In this context of vulnerability, isolation, and distress, Alice seeks safety and security within the therapeutic relationship and requests frequent sessions and daily contact with the feminist therapist. While mental health resources are very limited in this rural setting, there is a community health center 50 miles away, a center that is known for its psychoanalytic approach and tendency to manage care through hospitalization.
>
> There is no easy answer, here. Conventional guidelines would sanction a referral for Alice to the community health center. Yet, therapeutically, this feminist therapist would note the incompatiblity of the psychobiological medical model with a feminist therapy interpretation of Alice's situation, and may choose instead to discuss with Alice the community treatment center and its perspective vis-a-vis her history and needs. The therapist would provide for Alice a supportive and healing relationship while engaging with her in taking a trauma history and in providing gender role and power analyses. She may work with Alice to expand her identities from that of "a bad person" to that of a daughter/woman/client who is caught in a damaging situation with little means of control or agency. The feminist therapist would attempt

> to assist Alice in making connections between what has happened to her and the broader sociopolitical, economic, and gendered context of her situation.
>
> And the therapist would be challenged to consider and negotiate with Alice regarding the request for and possibilities around frequent contact in terms of Alice's need and the therapist's attention to her own self-care. She would also discuss with Alice financial arrangements that would take into account both Alice's limited ability to pay and the therapist's regard for her own livelihood.

Feminist therapy offers no easy, programmed answers to the complexity of Alice's therapy, either in content or process. What is clear and imperative, however, is that feminist therapy is deeply, fully, and consistently reflective and involves a co-creation with the client around choices and meaning-making. In addition, its commitment to an egalitarian relationship insists that the feminist therapist and client collaboratively consider choices and consequences and arrive at mutual decisions.

Such mutual decision-making is infused into every level of the therapeutic process, including adaptation of standard techniques. For example, some feminist therapists use hypnosis, a practice that may seem antithetical to the mandate for an egalitarian relationship. Yet, from a feminist perspective, the therapist can practice the technique of hypnosis and simultaneously transfer power to the client by asking for explicit permission throughout each step of the process. Other feminist therapists who use hypnosis techniques do so by teaching SELF-hypnosis to their clients (Hill & Ballou, 1998).

The issue of therapist self-disclosure is also viewed differently by the feminist therapist than it is by more conventional therapists. A feminist therapist routinely articulates her own values and world views, for example, as well as her own needs regarding working conditions. Throughout her work, a feminist therapist also carefully considers to what extent self-disclosure regarding their common struggles as women will be of benefit to her client. With the well-being of her client always uppermost in her mind, she may choose to share age-related experiences or to model situations of coping or negotiation.

Indeed, the importance of an appropriate fit with a particular client's needs and unique, yet complex experience, as well as this process of joint negotiation, make the conduct of feminist therapy both tentative and flexible. This is not to be interpreted as anything goes, nor should it be assumed that the process is without standards and limits, for this is clearly not the case. In particular, feminist ethics, discussed in the next section, demand careful and responsible actions within and surrounding feminist therapy.

Perhaps this vigilantly thoughtful and reflective posture of feminist therapists emanates out of the history of feminist therapy, with its transformations of conventional psychology, and its newly developing theory and practices. By their very orientation, feminist therapists have learned to seek out and question the assumptions embedded within the standard workings of the social order and, thus, they also take great care to maintain a relationship with their client which is honest and forthright. It is important for a feminist therapist to share her expert knowledge about psychology, feminist analyses, and the counseling process with her client. She also defines herself in terms of her own questioning stance toward the standards and practices of conventional therapy as well as toward feminist practices that are inconsistent with her own.

The importance of the egalitarian relationship within feminist therapy has evolved beyond its initial efforts to address the power inequities inherent in the therapeutic relationship. In large part through the contributions of the developing Relational Theory model (Jordan et al., 1992), feminist therapy considers the therapist—client relationship to be a primary and valuable means of healing. Through the therapy relationship, feminist therapy can offer empathic connection, which is an essential step in ameliorating the disempowerment, shame, and negative, distorted self-evaluation too often resulting material, psychic, and/or cultural violations.

In addition, the therapeutic relationship itself becomes a means of treatment and healing. This mutually respectful and connected relationship, with its emphasis on health and caring and the clarification and negotiation of values and needs, provides an experience that the client can take out in the world to use in judging and negotiating relationships in her own life and community. And, recursively, it allows therapists to experience some of the further reaches of human connections which they can then infuse into their therapy practice as well as their efforts in community-building, within social action initiatives and in theory-building.

Feminist therapy encourages the building and maintaining of relationships within a dyadic model as well as through groups and communities. The process of connecting and healing in mutually growth enhancing relationships is a major development in feminist therapy. Feminist therapy in group settings is consistent with the notion of building community and also provides healing opportunities for women. Again, we can refer to Carla. She demonstrates feelings of disempowerment and disconnection—from her family, her culture, the institutional forces in her school and, ultimately, from herself. Feminist therapy would begin by providing Carla with a healing relationship that would eventually allow her to reconnect her with herself and with other caring individuals.

As we end the twentieth century, feminist therapy is moving beyond the well-established, traditional boundaries, both in perspective and in space. In addition to the care of individuals and groups in therapy practice, feminist practitioners are promoting health, and differentiated and multiple identities in the lives of girls, women, and other nondominant groups. Indeed, feminists are moving into the very spheres that have been the targets of earlier analyses. If sociopolitical oppression is the issue, then feminist therapy is finding ways to enter the social-political system, identify its oppression, and support healthy and liberating change.

The work of the Stone Center is now extending beyond its model of self-in-relation-to-another to a model of organizational change that speaks to (1) ways in which relational awareness can be made visible in the workplace and (2) how through an analysis of gender, power, and hierarchy, movement toward mutuality and "relational leadership" can be "cultivated as an organizational value" (Wellesley Research Report, 1998). This task is quite obviously monumental within a culture in which business is arranged in an entrenched, competitive hierarchy. Yet it is being addressed in the feminist tradition of women talking to women. A study group formed out of the Jean Baker Miller Training Institute (Wellesley College) is currently holding seminars to examine how to "bring relational awareness to the workplace, how to name and strengthen connections that create effective functioning in an organization and how to develop specific strategies to deal with the 'disappearing' of relational practice or the shaming that occurs around practices that are not valued by the dominant work culture" (Wellesley Research Report, 1998 p. 6).

A second project that speaks to relationship and community-building involves bringing together the mothers of adolescent girls in an effort to name the cultural, sociopolitical, economic, educational, and gender issues that silently, insidiously, and harmfully initiate these young women into the dark sisterhood of oppression (West, 1999). Tapping into "women's creative imagination," the place where "mainstream social science with its insistence on recording behavior" (Westkott, 1979, p. 429) has failed to go, this project and others like it are reminiscent of the consciousness-raising groups of the 70s. It uses a format in which consciousness can be acknowledged and safely given voice and in which what Debold, Wilson, and Malave (1993) call "revolutionary mothering can devise ways to "encourage girls' resistance" (p. 246).

Integrated Analysis of Oppression The integrated analysis of oppression that is at the core of feminist therapy acknowledges the complexity of human experience. Pluralism, which refers to the valuing of differences among people, is critically important to the practice of feminist therapy as it opens up the range of acceptable life scripts. For example, having children or choosing to be childless, pursuing career, family, or some combination, working in the public or underground economy, living life alone, in community, or with one or more partners, are different, certainly, but not more or less right, healthy, or desirable. Instead of bringing the dominant group's rules and values into therapy as standard assessments of risks and benefits, a feminist therapist considers the individual merits of different choices. This obviously demands a therapist with experience and the capacity for self-reflection, and a client with appropriate developmental and life circumstance capabilities.

Feminist practice extends well beyond the analysis of gender to consider the multiple ways in which people have been categorized and evaluated through hierarchies disguised as normative standards. Some of the ways in which humans vary include size, age, race, ethnicity, disability, class, sexual orientation, religion, geographic region, type of work, economic status, cultural traditions, family structure, social organizations, kinds of intelligence, sensitivities, and relationships with power, people, and the earth. These multiple factors interact and overlap and influence individuals, their life conditions, others' evaluations of them, and the opportunities or lack thereof available to them.

Each of these classifications of human variation calls the feminist therapist to awareness and demands particular knowledge and literacy. Also, each aspect of individual identity comprises a complicated web of dimensions of influence, requiring models representing interactions of multiple influences and levels. Feminist therapists consider the multiple factors that are involved in personal, group, and institutional oppression. And as these realities are part of women's experiences, sociopolitical contexts, and power relationships, they are also coming to be addressed in the theory and practice of feminist therapy (Hill & Ballou, 1998): "In perhaps the last ten years, feminist therapy has evolved a more complex analysis of oppression and an awareness that gender cannot be separated from other ways in which a culture stratifies human difference, privileging some at the expense of others" (p. 3).

Hope Landrine (1995), in her introduction to readings of cultural diversity in feminist psychology, provides a compelling example of the intersect of multiple oppressions, external factors, and women's experiences. Landrine tells us that studies conducted in the late 80s and early 90s revealed the prevalence of AIDS to be significantly higher among young Latinas than among other ethnic groups. It was found that this difference could in part be accounted for by the higher incidence of anal intercourse (particularly with intravenous drug users) among young, unmarried, heterosexual Latina women whereas this behavior was relatively infrequent among other heterosexual populations. Without an integrated analysis of oppressive factors, it was easy to assume that these young women simply did not have information regarding the risks of unprotected anal intercourse.

What was missing from this line of reasoning, however, was an understanding of the sociopolitical, cultural, and structural context in which these young women lived their lives. A feminist analysis found that Latinas did *not* hold erroneous beliefs about the transmission of the AIDS virus through unprotected vaginal or anal intercourse. Indeed, they knew it was dangerous and especially dangerous with a partner who was also an intravenous drug user. Nor, Landrine points out, was this pattern representative of a "titillating" ethnic difference or an "exotic" or "primitive" sexual "deviance." Rather, these young women had found a way to satisfy the demands of their boyfriends for intercourse while remaining virgins, a status that was also demanded within their community. Therefore, to understand their behavior, a thoughtful and thorough analysis needed to consider the intersect of culture, gender, age, and class.

As mentioned previously, some feminist therapists approach their work through one of the more conventional models and infuse these models and techniques with the principles and ethics specific to feminist therapy. So, for example, the feminist application of cognitive behavioral techniques standpoint may address multiple oppressions by challenging cognitions based on learned responses to cultural and gender expectations. As used in feminist therapy, cognitive reframing would invite the client to join with the therapist in clarifying the cultural and structural influences of individual beliefs and distress, using such questions as "What do you get out of this?" "What does the other get out of this?" and "Are these equal?" (Hill & Ballou, 1998, p. 12).

Interestingly, while feminist therapy is in the process of expanding pluralistic, multicultural, and antiracist conceptual frameworks (Brown, 1994; Sue, Ivey & Pederson, 1996), multicultural psychology is moving toward feminist therapy's gender and sociopolitical analyses, its critiques of conventional theory and therapy, and its counseling processes, which include critical consciousness-raising, reflection, and social change.

Social Change With its foundation principle of social change, feminist therapy extends out of the office and into the world in a way that moves beyond analysis to action. At first glance, working to create social change seems a necessary but somewhat idealistic goal. Yet the initiation of social change (Worell & Remer, 1992) and the ultimate intention of creating social change (Hill & Ballou, 1998) is an unambiguous and consistent call within most of the feminist therapy literature and practice. Ballou (1990, 1995), Brown (1992, 1994), Enns (1997), Lerman and Porter (1990), Greenspan, (1993), Whalen (1996), Maracek and Kravetz (1998), and others all write of the need for broad social and institutional change. This engagement in social change may occur at a variety of levels.

Simply doing feminist therapy involves clients in gendered reflections on their distress, lives, and the larger sociocultural context. Creating change at any of a variety of levels—individual, relational, community, interpersonal, policy—is certainly a part of feminist therapy. The feminist therapist engages in social change in a variety of ways: by reframing pathology, by discovering coping strategies for oppressive devaluation, discrimination and damage, and by bringing her sex role and power analyses to bear in her work.

Additionally, it may be therapeutically important at particular points for particular clients to encourage them to engage in empowering social change activities. This may take the form of protesting welfare policies that serve to increase poverty and decrease safe child care, or of participation in "Take Back the Night" demonstrations to increase awareness regarding the violence women face in their communities. Social action may also take the form of negotiating healthful decisions and arrangements within relationships, families, and communities, or within the environments of work, school, or social service agencies. Therapist supported client social actions may address power and gender arrangements. They are activities that may be initiated within the context of the feminist therapy relationship and, at the same time, they are political actions which may strengthen the resistance of the client to the forces of the sociocultural context. Resistance, says Laura Brown (1994, p. 25), "means the refusal to merge with dominant cultural norms and to attend to one's own voice and integrity." Fostering and supporting healthy resistance is a primary goal of feminist therapy practiced.

However, to practice feminist therapy is also to be involved in social change within one's own community and sometimes within much broader spheres. The efforts of many feminist therapists to challenge and change mainstream mental health and to influence legal decisions and national policy are at once encouraging and enlightening. A current example of such work can be seen in the ideology and actions of ecofeminists who link personal pain and physical illness (increases in cancer, asthma, and environmental disease) to global damage perpetrated by patriarchal institutions, in particular, the greed of advanced global capitalism. In addition to their advocacy around expanding treatment issues to include the link between spirituality and healing, treatment issues for this group include active and collective resistance to global injustice.

Lenore Walker is an example of a feminist therapist who has been involved in change at multiple levels. She counsels women and has engaged in theory-building and research. She has moved into the legal arena to advocate for battered women and to educate judges. She has worked within professional associations to educate and change policy. And most recently, she has created alliances with other women's and professional groups internationally to name the violence against women and children as a human rights violation. While the extent of this involvement may be unusual, commitment to working toward social change in a variety of local community and professional efforts is an integral part of feminist therapy practiced. . . .

Conclusions

Carla . . . and Alice; the unmarried Latina women; the girl gang members; the refugee women; and the African-American mothers each represent unique cases. Yet in each gender, class, and ethnicity, and values and cultural expectations result in a particular interaction of influences. These multiple identities and complex interactions also meet, and collide with, the often unspoken norms, standards, expectations, and dictates of the dominant culture. Each of these women could be labeled in standard diagnostic terms and treated by traditional mental health interventions. However, feminist therapy would seek to understand them in all of their complexity and would attempt to accept them as they are. Feminist therapy would engage these women in a relationship and would decide with them what actions would be in their best interests. Feminist therapy would further engage in social action efforts to diminish the harmful effects of the external forces that oppress them.

. . . [W]e have tried to give the reader a sense of the wide range of perspectives within feminist therapy—perspectives that are grounded in feminist theory, principles, and ethics. In describing feminist therapy we have tried to note those domains in assessment, diagnosis and practice in which feminist therapy diverges from more traditional models at the same time that it attempts to address the complexity of human existence. At its foundation, feminist therapy represents a consciousness of multiple standpoints, multiple life experiences, multiple cultures, multiple inquiries, and multiple histories that continually challenge and engage those who do its work.

References

Adleman, J., & Enguidanos, G. (Eds.). (1996) *Racism in the lives of women: Testimony, theory, and guides to anti-racist action.* New York: Haworth.

American Psychiatric Association. (1994). *Diagnostic and statistical manual of mental disorders* (4th ed., rev.). Washington, DC: Author.

Ballou, M. (1990). Approaching a feminist-principled paradigm in the construction of personality theory. In L. Brown & M. Root (Eds.), *Diversity and complexity in feminist therapy* (pp. 23–40). New York: Haworth.

Ballou, M. (1995). Women and spirit: Two nonfits in psychology. *Women and Therapy, 16,* 9–20.

Ballou, M., & Gabalac, N. (1985). *A feminist position on mental health.* Springfield, IL: Charles C Thomas.

Barrett, S. (1998). Contextual identity: A model for therapy and social change. *Women and Therapy, 18,* 3/4.

Brown, L. (1994). *Subversive dialogues: Theory in feminist therapy.* New York: Basic Books.

Brown, L. (1995). Cultural diversity in feminist therapy: Theory and Practice. In H. Landrine (Ed.), *Bringing cultural diversity to feminist therapy: Theory, research, and practice* (pp. 143–161). Washington, DC: American Psychological Association.

Brown, L., & Ballou, M. (Eds.). (1992). *Personality and Psychotherapy: feminist reappraisals.* New York: Guilford. Brown, L. & Brodsky, A. (1992). The future of feminist therapy. *Psychotherapy: Theory, Research, Practice, Training, 29,* 51–57.

Brown, L., & Root, M. (Eds.). (1990). *Diversity and complexity in feminist therapy.* New York: Haworth.

Burstone, B. (1992). *Radical feminist therapy: Working in the context of violence.* Newbury Park, CA: Sage.

Chesler, P. (1972). *Women and madness.* Garden City, NY: Doubleday.

Cole, E., Espin, O., & Rothblum, E. (Eds.). (1992). *Refugee women and their mental health.* New York: Haworth.

Comas-Diaz, L., & Greene, B. (Eds.). (1994). *Mental health and women of color.* New York: Guilford.

Debold, E., Wilson, M., & Malave, I. (1993). *Mother–daughter revolution.* Reading, MA: Addison-Wesley.

Enns, C. (1997). *Feminist theories and feminist psychotherapies*. New York: Harrington Park Press.

Espin, O. (1994). Feminist approaches. In L. Comas-Diaz & B. Greene (Eds.), *Women of color: Integrating ethnic and gender identities in psychotherapy* (pp. 265–286). New York: Guilford.

Gilbert, L. (1980). Feminist therapy. In A. Brodsky & R. Hare-Musten (Eds.), *Women and psychotherapy* (pp. 245–265). New York: Guilford.

Gold, J. (1998). *Understanding girls and their involvement in gangs through their stories: A qualitative psychological study*. Unpublished doctoral dissertation. Boston, MA: Northeastern University.

Greene, B. (1994). African american women. In L. Comas-Diaz & B. Greene (Eds.), *Women of color: integrating ethnic and gender identities in psychotherapy* (pp. 10–29). New York: Guilford.

Greenspan, M. (1993). *A new approach to women and therapy*. New York: John Wiley & Sons.

Hill, M. (1990). On creating a theory of feminist therapy. In L. Brown & M. Root (Eds.), *Diversity and complexity in feminist therapy* (pp. 53–66). New York: Haworth.

Hill, M. (March, 1999). Address to Association of Women Psychologists. Providence, Rhode Island.

Hill, M., & Ballou, M. (1998). Making feminist therapy: A practice survey. *Women & Therapy*, *21*, 1–16.

Ho, C. (1990). An analysis of domestic violence in Asian American communities: A multicultural approach to counseling. In L. Brown & M. Root (Eds.), *Diversity and complexity in feminist therapy* (pp. 129–150). New York: Haworth.

Jordan, J., Kaplan, A., Miller, J., Stiver, I., & Surrey, J. (1992). *Women's growth in connection: Writings from the Stone Center*. New York: Guilford.

Kaschak, E. (1992). *Engendered lives: A new psychology of women's experience*. New York: Basic Books.

Kitzinger, C., & Perkins, R. (1993). *Changing our minds: Lesbian feminism and psychology*. New York: New York University Press.

Landrine, H. (Ed.). (1995). *Bringing cultural diversity to feminist psychology*. Washington, DC: American Psychological Association.

Lerman, H. (1986). *A mote in Freud's eye: From psychoanalysis to the psychology of women*. New York: Springer.

Lerman, H. (1992). The limits of phenomenology: A feminist critique of the humanistic personality theories. In L. Brown & M. Ballou (Eds.), *Personality and psychopathology: Feminist reappraisals* (pp. 8–19). New York: Guilford.

Lerman, H. (1996). *Pigeonholing women's misery: A history and critical analysis of the psychodiagnosis of women in the twentieth century*. New York: Basic Books.

Lerman, H., & Porter, N. (Eds.). (1990). *Feminist ethics in psychotherapy*. New York: Springer.

Mander, A., & Rush, A. (1974). *Feminism as therapy.* New York: Random House.

Marecek, J., & Kravetz, D. (1998). Putting politics into practice: Feminist therapy as feminist praxis. *Women & Therapy, 21,* 17–36.

McGrath, E., Keita, G., Strickland, B., & Russo, N. (1990). *Women and depression: Risk factors and treatment issues.* Washington, DC: American Psychological Association.

McLellan, B. (1995). *Beyond Psychoppression: Feminist alternative therapy.* Melbourne, Australia: Scinifex Press Pry Ltd.

Morrow, S., & Hawxhurst, D. (1998). Feminist therapy: Integrating political analysis in counseling and psychotherapy. *Women & Therapy, 21,* 37—50.

Porter, N., & Vasquez, M. (1997). *Covision: Feminist supervision, process and collaboration.* Washington, DC: American Psychological Association.

Rave, E., & Larsen, C. (Eds.). (1995). *Ethical decision making in therapy: Feminist perspectives.* New York: Guilford.

Rawlings, E., & Carter, D. (1997). *Psychotherapy for women: Treatment toward equality.* Springfield, IL: Charles Thomas.

Rogers, A. (1993). Voice, play, and a practice of ordinary courage in girls' and women's lives. *Harvard Educational Review, 63,* 265–295.

Root, M. (1992). Restructuring the impact of trauma on personality. In L. Brown & M. Ballou (Eds.), *Personality and psychopathology: Feminist reappraisals* (pp.229—265) New York: Guilford.

Root, M. (1995). The psychology of Asian American women. In H. Landrine (Ed.), *Bringing cultural diversity to feminist psychology* (pp.265–301). Washington, DC: American Psychological Association.

Santos de Barona, M., & Dutton, M. (1997). Feminist perspectives on assessment. In J. Worell & N. Johnson (Eds.), *Shaping the future of feminist psychology* (pp. 37–56). Washington, DC: American Psychological Association.

Sturdivant, S. (1980). *Therapy with women: A feminist philosophy of treatment.* New York: Springer.

Sue, D., Ivey, A., & Pederson, P. (1996). *A theory of multicultural counseling and psychotherapy.* Pacific Grove, CA: Brooks/Cole.

Szasz, T. (1961). *The myth of mental illness: Foundations of a theory of personal conduct.* New York: Dell.

Taylor, J., Gilligan, C., & Sullivan, A. (1995). *Between voice and silence: Women and girls, race and relationship.* Cambridge, MA: Harvard University Press.

Walker, M. (1999). Dual traumatization: A sociocultural perspective. In Y. Jenkins (Ed.), *Diversity in college settings* (pp.52—65). New York: Routledge.

Wellesley Centers for Women. (1998). *Relational Approaches to workplace change.* Research Report. Wellesley, MA: Author.

West, C. (1999). *Strengthening the resistance: An exploration of how mothers can ally with and support their adolescent daughters.* Unpublished doctoral dissertation. Boston, MA: Northeastern University.

Westkott, M. (1979). Feminist criticism of the social sciences. *Harvard Educational Review, 49*, 422–430.

Whalen, M. (1996). *Counseling to end violence against women: A subversive model.* Thousand Oaks, CA: Sage.

Worell, J., & Johnson, N. (Eds.). (1997). *Shaping the future of feminist psychology.* Washington, DC: American Psychological Association.

Worell, J., & Remer, P. (1992). *Feminist perspectives in therapy: An empowerment model for women.* New York: Wiley.

CHAPTER EIGHT

Violence Against Women

If it were between countries, we'd call it a war. If it were a disease, we'd call it an epidemic. If it were an oil spill, we'd call it a disaster. But it is happening to women, and it's just an everyday affair. It is violence against women.

—*Beginning manifesto of the White Ribbon Campaign*

When one considers the scope and range of violence committed against women across the globe, it's hard not to get seriously angry, or seriously depressed. In this chapter, we focus on the vicimization of women through rape and sexual harassment. An in-depth discussion of all the forms of violence committed against women and girls simply because of their gender (e.g., infanticide, clitoridectomy and infibulation, battery, incest, pornography) is beyond what can be covered in one chapter. But I encourage you to think about and discuss the ideas engendered by these three readings with respect to all victimization of females.

The women's movement of the 1970's brought violence against women into the public sphere. But still, it has not seemed to be a terribly urgent matter on the national or international agenda. What does this tell us about patriarchy? The American Psychological Association's Task Force on Violence Against Women conceptualized the many forms of men's violence against women along a continuum of ever increasing physical force (Goodman, Koss, Fitzgerald, Russo & Keita, 1993). That is, at one end are the most dramatic and physically extreme forms, such as rape. At the other end are coercive actions, often supported by threats of the loss of something valuable to a woman, such as her children or her job. The Task Force's report gives a chilling sense of the "everyday affair" quality of violence against women, and illuminates the tremendous mental health, economic, and social costs of the continuum of aggression against women and girls.

The first piece in this chapter, by Robin Warshaw, comes from a *Ms.* magazine report entitled "I Never Called it Rape," and discusses the brutal reality of acquaintance rape. Acquaintance rape occurs when the victim and assailant know one another, and, contrary to much popular belief (about "strangers" being the most common rapists), it accounts for the great majority of sexual assaults. Acquaintance rape is also called "hidden rape" because it is less likely to be reported, and less likely to result in conviction if reported. Over the years, I have found more than a few young women in my classes squirming in their seats when we discuss the information in this piece. This, of course, is one of the reasons I assign it. I have often wondered whether these students may be among the close to 30% of women whose sexual assault met the legal definition of rape, but who have never thought of themselves as rape victims. Because we are all raised in a culture that endorses the rape myths Warshaw outlines, we all covertly conspire in supporting the sense that men have difficulty controlling their sexual urges and ought not to be held responsible for them, and that women generally cannot be trusted to relay accurate accounts of sexual assaults. Campus movements like "Take Back the Night" are efforts to raise awareness about acquaintance rape and to debunk the myths that keep it hidden.

The next piece, by Phoebe Morgan, presents straightforward and sobering facts about sexual harassment in the workplace. Sadly, although 97% of all employing and educational institutions in the U.S. have policies prohibiting sexual harassment, this pernicious form of violence against women continues to be a problem in our country. What would you define as sexually harassing behavior? This piece helps to clarify the legal definitions of such behaviors, and gives eye-opening facts regarding the ways sexual harassment amounts to sex discrimination against women in the workplace. Who do you think harasses, and who is likely to be harassed? Again, this piece offers some fascinating, and at times surprising, answers to this question. What is difficult to unravel, and what I hope you discuss in your classrooms, is why the problem of sexual harassment appears to be so resistant to efforts to eliminate it. As Morgan writes, sexual harassment occurs in the places in our culture precisely where economic and sexual power overlap. Failing to acknowledge that sexual harassment is the wielding of *power*, and persisting in the belief that it is benign and occurs only privately between "deranged" men and "weak" women, keeps this destructive form of violence alive.

I often start class on the day we are to begin discussion of violence against women with the following question to the male students: "What did you do yesterday to insure your personal safety?" I am sometimes met with a blank stare to this question. I ask any of the men to specify actions they took to feel safe. Sometimes I hear, "I locked my door." But mostly this is a hard question for them to answer. Then I turn the same question to the women, and am typically barraged with activities they engaged in—during the course of one, average day—to insure their safety. They locked doors, and checked the locks on doors. They carried their keys in between their fingers, or carried pepper-spray. They took a longer, well-lit route home from the library as opposed to the shorter, darker one. They avoided eye-contact with strangers. They didn't go for a jog when they wanted to, because it was too late. The list, of course, goes on and on.

Finally, we turn to one of very few male voices in this book. Tim Beneke wrote *Men on Rape* in 1982, and frankly it was about time. The fact that his insights about how women's lives are impacted by the threat of rape, how women's lives are fundamentally different from men's in this way, are still fresh and challenging, it is a grave testament to the resilience of our "rape prone culture" (Griffin, 1972) to change. I think his piece has a way of bringing together women and men to have a difficult conversation, and I have it in this book to encourage you to do just that. Just like the men in my classroom listening to women's long lists of self-preserving activities performed daily and nearly always without question or complaint, Beneke opens his eyes to the details of the "everyday affair" that the threat of violence means for women. He is angry about this arrangement—angry for what it means for the women he cares about—but also angry for himself and other men, who have been taught to think of sex as achievement of a valued commodity or aggressive degradation. The piece asks you to think carefully about an irony. The irony is that rape and other forms of violence against women are typically not the products of men's feelings of security, power, and manliness. Instead, they are the consequence of insecurity, the need for control, and the urge to assert manliness within a cultural context that says "boys will be boys," that condones sexual violence. What do you make of this? And what does it suggest about cultural solutions to rape?

In closing the introduction to what is sure to be a difficult set of readings, I'd like to point toward the positive. I believe that feminism offers us a framework for understanding violence against women, and also a vision for putting an end to it. But we must keep in mind the following:

> Social movements, feminism included, move toward a vision; they cannot operate solely on fear. It is not enough to move women away from danger and oppression; it is necessary to move toward something: toward pleasure, agency, self-definition. Feminism must increase women's pleasure and joy, not just decrease our misery (Vance, 1984, p. 24).

And we must ask men to join us in this movement. The White Ribbon Campaign, a movement of men working to end violence against women in Canada, is an excellent role model. Research shows that the more men defy gender stereotypes and rape myths (e.g., "no harm was done;" "she really wanted it") the less likely they are to aggress against women. And the more women defy such stereotypes the less likely they are to be victims of such aggression. Deep change, therefore, requires deep rethinking of how men and women relate, and how we can most humanely answer both the call to power and influence, as well as to care and community. As feminists have long said, the humanization of men is directly linked to the social empowerment of women.

References

Goodman, L. A., Koss, M. P., Fitzgerald, L. F., Russo, N. F., & Keita, G. P. (1993). Male violence against women: Current research and future directions. *American Psychologist, 48,* 1054–1058.

Griffin, S. (1971). Rape: The All-American crime. *Ramparts, 10,* 26–35.

The White Ribbon Campaign: Men working to end violence against women. 365 Bloor St. East, Suite 203, Toronto, Ontario, Canada M4W 3L4. *http://www.whiteribbon.ca/*

Vance, C. S. (1984). *Pleasure and danger: Exploring female sexuality.* Boston: Routledge and Kegan Paul.

26 The Reality of Acquaintance Rape

ROBIN WARSHAW

I never heard of anybody having that happen to them.
—*Lori, raped at 19 by a date*

Women raped by men they know—acquaintance rape—is not an aberrant quirk of male-female relations. If you are a woman, your risk of being raped by someone you know is *four times greater* than your risk of being raped by a stranger.

A recent scientific study of acquaintance rape on 32 college campuses conducted by *Ms.* magazine and psychologist Mary P. Koss showed that significant numbers of women are raped on dates or by acquaintances, although most victims never report their attacks.

Ms. survey stats

- 1 in 4 women surveyed were victims of rape or attempted rape.
- 84 percent of those raped knew their attacker.
- 57 percent of the rapes happened on dates.

Those figures make acquaintance rape and date rape more common than left-handedness or heart attacks or alcoholism. These rapes are no recent campus fad or the fantasy of a few jilted females. They are real. And they are happening all around us.

The Extent of "Hidden" Rape

Most states define rape as sexual assault in which a man uses his penis to commit vaginal penetration of a victim against her will, by force or threats of force or when she is physically or mentally unable to give her consent. Many states now also include unwanted anal and oral intercourse in that definition and some have removed gender-specific language to broaden the applicability of rape laws.

In acquaintance rape, the rapist and victim may know each other casually—having met through a common activity, mutual friend, at a party, as neighbors, as students in the same class, at work, on a blind date, or while traveling. Or they may have a closer relationship—as steady dates or former sexual partners. Although largely a hidden phenomenon because it's the least reported type of rape (and rape, in general, is the most underreported crime against a person), many organizations, counselors, and social researchers agree that acquaintance rape is the most prevalent rape crime today.

. . . Government estimates find that anywhere from three to ten rapes are committed for every one rape reported. And while rapes by strangers are still underreported, rapes by acquaintances are virtually nonreported. Yet, based on intake observations made by staff at various rape-counseling centers (where victims come for treatment, but do not have to file police reports), 70 to 80 percent of all rape crimes are acquaintance rapes.

Those rapes are happening in a social environment in which sexual aggression occurs regularly. Indeed, less than half the college women questioned in the *Ms.* survey reported that they had experienced *no* sexual victimization in their lives thus far (the average age of respondents was 21). Many had experienced more than one episode of unwanted sexual touching, coercion, attempted rape, or rape. Using the data collected in the study, . . . the following profile can be drawn of what happens in just one year of "social life" on America's college campuses:

Ms. survey stats

- In one year 3,187 women reported suffering:
- 328 rapes (as defined by law)
- 534 attempted rapes (as defined by law)
- 837 episodes of sexual coercion (sexual intercourse obtained through the aggressor's continual arguments or pressure)
- 2,024 experiences of unwanted sexual contact (fondling, kissing, or petting committed against the woman's will)

. . .

In 1984, 20 percent of the female students questioned in a study at the University of South Dakota in Vermillion, South Dakota, said they had been physically forced to have intercourse while on a date. At Brown University in Providence, Rhode Island, 16 percent of the women surveyed reported they were raped by an acquaintance and 11 percent of the men said they had forced sexual intercourse on a woman. And another study coauthored by Auburn's Burkhart showed 15 percent of the male respondents reporting having raped a date.

That same year, the study of acquaintance rape moved beyond the serenity of leafy college quadrangles into the hard reality of the "dangerous" outside world. A random sample survey of 930 women living in San Francisco, conducted by researcher Diana Russell, showed that 44 percent of the women questioned had been victims of rape or attempted rape—and that 88 percent of the rape victims knew their attackers. A Massachusetts Department of Public Health study, released in 1986, showed that two-thirds of the rapes reported at crisis centers were committed by acquaintances.

These numbers stand in stark contrast to what most people think of as rape: that is, a stranger (usually a black, Hispanic, or other minority) jumping out of the bushes at an unsuspecting female, brandishing a weapon, and assaulting her. The truth about rape—that it usually happens between people who know each other and is often committed by "regular" guys—is difficult to accept.

Most people never learn the truth until rape affects them or someone they care about. And many women are so confused by the dichotomy between their acquaintance-rape experience and what they thought rape really was that they are left with an awful new reality: Where once they feared strange men as they were taught to, they now fear strange men *and* all the men they know.

Lori's Story

How can a date be a rape?

The pairing of the word "date," which conjures up an image of fun shared by two companions, with the word "rape," which evokes the total loss of control by one person to the will of another, results in the creation of a new phrase that is nearly impossible for most people to comprehend. To understand how date rape happens, let's look at a classic case.

The Setup It was natural. Normal. Lori's friend Amy wanted to go out with Paul, but felt awkward and shy about going out with him alone. So when Paul's roommate, Eric, suggested that he and Lori join Amy and Paul for a double date, it made sense. "I didn't feel anything for Eric except as a friend," Lori says of her reaction to the plan. "I said, 'Okay, maybe it will make Amy feel better.'"

Agreeing to go out with Eric was no great act of charity on Lori's part. He *was* attractive—tall, good-looking, in his mid-20s and from a wealthy family. Lori, who was 19 at the time, knew Eric and Paul as frequent customers at the popular Tampa Bay restaurant where she worked as a waitress when she was between college semesters.

On the day of the date, Eric called several times to change their plans. Finally, he phoned to say that they would be having a barbecue with several of his friends at the house he and Paul shared. Lori agreed.

> We went to his house and I mentioned something about Paul and Amy and he kind of threw it off, like, "Yeah, yeah." I didn't think anything of it. There we are, fixing steaks, and he was saying, "Well, this is obviously something to help Amy."
>
> He kept making drinks all night long. He kept saying, "Here, have a drink," "Here, drink this." I didn't because I didn't want it. He was just downing them right and left.

The Attack Unknown to Lori, Amy had canceled her plans to see Paul the day before. Paul told Eric, but Eric never told Lori. As the barbecue party progressed and her friend failed to show up, Lori questioned Eric again. He then lied, telling her that Paul had just called to say he and Amy weren't coming.

> I was thinking to myself, "Well, okay." Not in my wildest dreams would I have thought he was plotting something. Then all of his friends started leaving. I began to think, "Something is wrong, something is going on," but I've been known to overreact to things, so I ignored it.
>
> After his friends left, we're sitting on the couch and he leans over and he kisses me and I'm thinking, "It's a date, it's no big deal." So then we started kissing a little bit more and I'm thinking, "I'm starting to enjoy this, maybe this isn't so bad." Then the phone rang and when he came back I was standing up. He grabbed me from behind and picked me up. He had his hands over my eyes and we were walking through his house. It was really dark and I didn't know where on earth he was taking me. I had never actually walked through his house.
>
> He laid me down [on a bed] and kissed me. . . . He starts taking off my clothes and I said, "Wait—time out! This is not what I want, you know," and he said to me something like this is what I owed him because he made me dinner.

> I said, "This is wrong, don't do this. I didn't go out with you with this intent."
>
> He said, "What do you call that on the couch?"
>
> I said, "I call it a kiss, period."
>
> And he said, "Well, I don't."

The two struggled until Eric rolled off her momentarily. Lori jumped up and went into the bathroom. Her plan was to come out in a few minutes and tell him it was time to take her home.

> The whole time I'm thinking, "I don't believe this is happening to me." I didn't even have time to walk fully out of the bathroom door when he grabbed me and threw me on the bed and started taking my clothes off. I'm yelling and hitting and pushing on him and he just liked that. He says, "I know you must like this because a lot of women like this kind of thing." Then he says, "This is the adult world. Maybe you ought to grow up some."
>
> I finally got to the point where there was nothing I could do.

Eric pushed his penis into her and, after a few minutes, ejaculated. Lori had had only one other experience with sexual intercourse, about a year before with a longtime boyfriend.

> Then Eric just rolled over and I started to get my clothes together. He said, "Don't tell me you didn't like that." I looked at him and said, "No," and by this time I'm crying because I don't know what else to do. I never heard of anybody having that happen to them.

The Aftermath Finally, Eric took her home.

> In the car he said, "Can I call you tomorrow? Can I see you next weekend?" I just looked at him and he just looked at me and started laughing.
>
> My mom had gone out and I just laid on my bed with the covers up. Everything I could possibly put on I think I put on that night—leg warmers, thermal underwear—everything imaginable in the middle of summer I put on my body. That night I dreamed it was all happening again. I dreamed I was standing there watching him do it.
>
> For two weeks I couldn't talk. People would talk to me and I felt nothing. I felt like a zombie. I couldn't cry, I couldn't smile, I couldn't eat. My mom said, "What's wrong with you? Is something going on?" I said, "Nothing's wrong."
>
> I thought it was my fault. What did I do to make him think he

> could do something like that? Was I wrong in kissing him? Was I wrong to go out with him, to go over to his house?

After two weeks, she told her mother what happened and they talked about what to do. Lori decided not to report it to the police for fear Eric would blame her. Eric continued to frequent the restaurant where she worked. Several weeks after their date, he cornered her in a hallway near the kitchen.

> He touched me and I said, "Get your hands off me." At first, he thought it was funny. He said, "What's wrong?" then he started pulling me, trying to hug me. I pushed him and said, "Leave me alone," and I was starting to get a little loud. As I was walking away, he said, "Oh, I guess you didn't get enough."
>
> I walked in the kitchen and I picked up this tray full of food. I don't know how it happened, I just dropped the whole tray and it went everywhere. My friend, another waitress, went to the manager and said, "She's not going to be much good to you tonight," so they sent me home.

Lori decided to move to a town about 150 miles away to avoid continued encounters with Eric. There she found work as an office assistant and cashier and enrolled for a few classes at a new college.

Sitting in a darkened restaurant on her lunch break one year after the rape, Lori is still looking for answers.

> When I moved here, nobody knew about it. I just figured, this only happened to me. Then my roommate told me it happened to her in Ohio. We talked about it once and that was it. It just upset me too much to talk about it anymore. I mean, she understood, it upset her a lot, too, so we just don't bring it up.
>
> How do other women handle it? I work two jobs and I go to school because I don't want to have to deal with the situation of having somebody ask me on a date. If I go out with a guy, I'm wondering, is he thinking dinner means "I'll get you into bed"?
>
> I'm not going to be stupid enough to put myself in that situation again. I grew out of being naive just like that. This experience grew me up in about two weeks.

The Myths About Acquaintance Rape

Like most women with date-rape or acquaintance-rape experiences, Lori did not report the incident to police and did not, at first, even understand it to be rape. Instead, she felt almost totally isolated and blamed herself for what happened. She changed her life in order to feel physically safe from her attacker. She is now filled with doubts about her own judgment, fears socializing with men, and despairs about her ability to have a "normal" relationship.

But ask a group of college students what they think of a story like Lori's and they might tell you:

- "She deserved it."
- "What did she expect? After all, she went to his house."
- "That's not rape. Rape is when a guy you don't know grabs you and holds a gun to your head."
- "She wasn't a virgin, so no harm was done."
- "He bought her dinner. She owed him."
- "She liked kissing him. What's the big deal if he went farther?"
- "She just 'cried rape' later because she felt guilty about having sex."

Those are the kinds of comments heard recently on all kinds of campuses—Ivy League, state universities, small schools—when date rape was discussed by both male and female undergraduates. But let's not blame college students alone for their views: Their parents, indeed most of our society, would agree with one or more of those statements.

These are the myths that have formed what we believe to be the truth about women who are raped by men they know. But the actual truth is different indeed. Here are several of the most common myths about acquaintance rape juxtaposed with the reality:

Myth	*Reality*
Rape is committed by crazed strangers.	Most women are raped by "normal" acquaintances.
A woman who gets raped deserves it, especially if she agreed to go to the man's house or ride in his car.	No one, male or female, deserves to be raped. Being in a man's house or car does not mean a woman has agreed to have sex with him.
Women who don't fight back haven't been raped.	You have been raped when you are forced to have sex against your will, whether you fight back or not.

Myth	*Reality*
If there's no gun or knife, you haven't been raped.	It's rape whether the rapist uses a weapon or his fists, verbal threats, drugs or alcohol, physical isolation, your own diminished physical or mental state, or simply the weight of his body to overcome you.
It's not really rape if the victim isn't a virgin.	Rape is rape, even if the woman isn't a virgin, even if she willingly had sex with the man before.
If a woman lets a man buy her dinner or pay for a movie or drinks, she owes him sex.	No one owes sex as a payment to anyone else, no matter how expensive the date.
Agreeing to kiss or neck or pet with a man means that a woman has agreed to have intercourse with him.	Everyone has the right to say "no" to sexual activity, regardless of what has preceded it, and to have that "no" respected.
When men are sexually aroused, they need to have sex or they will get "blue balls." Also, once they get turned on, men can't help themselves from forcing sex on a woman.	Men don't physically need to have sex after becoming aroused any more than women do. Moreover, men are still able to control themselves even after becoming sexually excited.
Women lie about being raped, especially when they accuse men they date or other acquaintances.	Rape really happens—to people you know, by people you know.

Like most of our beliefs, we absorb these myths as we grow up: from the people around us, from the books we read, from the movies and television programs we watch, even from the way products are sold to us in advertisements.

Because of the myths, the reality of acquaintance rape is largely ignored. On college campuses, when a woman is raped in a dormitory or fraternity house by another student, university officials announce new plans for better lighting in the parking lots and expanded hours for escort services—positive safety precautions that have nothing to do with stopping acquaintance rape. The few women who report their date rapes (and whose cases are accepted for prosecution) are usually met with skepticism and disbelief from jurors and judges when they testify about being raped by a man they knew or chose to be with in a social setting.

No wonder that while many rape-prevention activists would like to see more prosecutions for acquaintance-rape cases, many admit privately that they counsel women not to press charges because of the difficulty of convincing jurors—whose views are shaped by the myths—that a rape has really taken place. . . .

Ms. survey stat

- 1 in 12 of the male students surveyed had committed acts that met the legal definitions of rape or attempted rape.

Blaming the Acquaintance-Rape Victim

Without question, many date rapes and acquaintance rapes could have been prevented by the woman—if she hadn't trusted a seemingly nice guy, if she hadn't gotten drunk, if she had acted earlier on the "bad feeling" that many victims later report they felt but ignored because they didn't want to seem rude, unfriendly, or immature. But acknowledging that in some cases the woman might have prevented the rape by making a different decision does not make her responsible for the crime. Says a counselor for an Oregon rape-crisis agency: "We have a saying here: 'Bad judgment is not a rapeable offense.'"

As a society, we don't blame the victims of most crimes as we do acquaintance-rape survivors. A mugging victim is not believed to "deserve it" for wearing a watch or carrying a pocketbook on the street. Likewise, a company is not "asking for it" when its profits are embezzled; a store owner is not to blame for handing over the cash drawer when threatened. These crimes occur because the perpetrator decides to commit them.

Acquaintance rape is no different. There are ways to reduce the odds, but, like all crimes, there is no way to be certain that it will not happen to you.

Yet acquaintance-rape victims are seen as responsible for the attacks, often more responsible than their assailants. "Date rape threatens the assumption that if you're good, good things happen to you. Most of us believe that bad things don't happen out of the blue," says psychologist Koss, chief investigator of the *Ms.* study, now affiliated with the department of psychiatry at the University of Arizona Medical School in Tucson, Arizona. Society, in general, is so disturbed by the idea that a "regular guy" could do such a thing—and, to be sure, many "regular guys" are made uncomfortable by a concept that views their actions as a crime—that they would rather believe that something is wrong with the woman making such an outlandish claim: She is lying, she has emotional problems, she hates men, she is covering up her own promiscuous behavior. In fact, the research in the *Ms.* survey shows that women who have been raped by men they know are not appreciably different in any personal traits or behaviors than women who are not raped.

Should we ask women not to trust men who seem perfectly nice? Should we tell them not to go to parties or on dates? Should we tell them not to drink? Should we tell them not to feel sexual? Certainly not. *It is not the victim who causes the rape. . . .*

Date Rape and Acquaintance Rape on College Campuses

Despite philosophical and political changes brought about by the women's movement, dating relationships between men and women are still often marked by passivity on the woman's part and aggression on the man's. Nowhere are these two seen in stronger contrast than among teenagers and young adults who often, out of their own fears, insecurity, and ignorance, adopt the worst sex-role stereotypes. Such an environment fosters a continuum of sexual victimization—from unwanted sexual touching to psychologically coerced sex to rape—that is tolerated as normal. "Because sexually coercive behavior is so common in our male-female interactions, rape by an acquaintance may not be perceived as rape," says Py Bateman, director of Alternatives to Fear, a Seattle rape-education organization.

Indeed, we speak of "the battle of the sexes" and, for many, it is just that. In their teens, many boys are counseled by their friends and older males to practice the "4Fs" when dealing with women: "Find 'em; feel 'em; fuck 'em; forget 'em." On the other hand, many girls, who have been admonished to "save it" for Mr. Right, want sexual intercourse to take place in the context of a relationship with some continuity attached to it. Kurt Weis and Sandra S. Borges, researchers at the University of California at Berkeley, pointed out in a 1973 paper that dating places individuals with these highly socialized but differing expectations into an ambiguous situation in which there is maximum privacy.

That is, dating can easily lead to rape.

Not surprising, then, that the risk of rape is four times higher for women aged 16 to 24, the prime dating age, than for any other population group. Approximately half of all men arrested for rape are also 24 years old or younger. Since 26 percent of all 18- to 24-year-olds in the United States attend college, those institutions have become focal points for studying date rape and acquaintance rape, such as the *Ms.* research.

> *Ms.* survey stat
> • For both men and women, the average age when a rape incident occurred (either as perpetrator or victim) was 18½ years old.

Going to college often means going away from home, out from under parental control and protection and into a world of seemingly unlimited freedoms. The imperative to party and date, although strong in high school, burgeons in this environment. Alcohol is readily available and often used in stultifying amounts, encouraged by a college world that practically demands heavy drinking as proof of having fun. Marijuana, cocaine, LSD, methamphetamines, and other drugs are also often easy to obtain.

Up until the 1970s, colleges adopted a "substitute parent" attitude toward their students, complete with curfews (often more strict for females than males), liquor bans, and stringent disciplinary punishments. In that era, students were punished for violating the three-feet-on-the-floor rules during coed visiting hours in dormitories or for being caught with alcohol on college property. Although those regulations did not prevent acquaintance rape, they undoubtedly kept down the number of incidents by making women's dorms havens of no-men-allowed safety.

Such regulations were swept out of most schools during the Vietnam War era. Today, many campuses have coed dorms, with men and women often housed in alternating rooms on the same floor, with socializing unchecked by curfews or meaningful controls on alcohol and drugs. Yet, say campus crisis counselors, many parents still believe that they have properly prepared their children for college by helping them open local bank accounts and making sure they have enough underwear to last until the first trip home. By ignoring the realities of social pressures at college on male and female students—and the often catastrophic effects of those pressures—parents help perpetuate the awareness vacuum in which date rape and acquaintance rape continue to happen with regularity.

"What's changed for females is the illusion that they have control and they don't," says Claire P. Walsh, program director of the Sexual Assault Recovery Service at the University of Florida in Gainesville.

"They know that they can go into chemical engineering or medical school and they've got their whole life planned, they're on a roll. They transfer that feeling of control into social situations and that's the illusion."

When looking at the statistical results of the *Ms.* survey, it's important to remember that many of these young people still have years of socializing and dating ahead of them, years in which they may encounter still more acquaintance rape. Students, parents of college students, and college administrators should be concerned. But many are not, lulled by the same myths that pervade our society at large: Rape is not committed by people you know, against "good" girls, in "safe" places like university campuses.

The Other Victims of Acquaintance Rape

Date rape and acquaintance rape aren't confined to the college population, however. Interviews conducted across the country showed that women both younger and older than university students are frequently acquaintance-rape victims as well.

A significant number of teenage girls suffer date rape as their first or nearly first experience of sexual intercourse (see Chapter 8, page 115) and most tell no one about their attacks. Consider Nora, a high school junior, who was raped by a date as they watched TV in his parents' house or Jenny, 16, who was raped after she drank too much at a party. Even before a girl officially begins dating, she may be raped by a schoolmate or friend.

Then there are the older women, the "hidden" population of "hidden" rape victims—women who are over 30 years old when their rapes occur. Most are socially experienced, yet unprepared for their attacks nonetheless. Many are recently divorced and just beginning to try the dating waters again; some are married; others have never married. They include women like Helene, a Colorado woman who was 37 and the mother of a 10-year-old when she was raped by a man on their third date, and Rae, who was 45 when she was raped by a man she knew after inviting him to her Oklahoma home for coffee.

"I Never Called It Rape"

Ms. survey stat

- Only 27 percent of the women whose sexual assault met the legal definition of rape thought of themselves as rape victims.

Because of her personal relationship with the attacker, however casual, it often takes a woman longer to perceive an action as rape when it involves a man she knows than it does when a stranger assaults her. For her to acknowledge her experience as rape would be to recognize the extent to which her trust was violated and her ability to control her own life destroyed.

Indeed, regardless of their age or background, many women interviewed . . . told no one about their rapes, never confronted their attackers, and never named their assaults as rape until months or years later.

27 Sexual Harassment: Violence Against Women at Work

PHOEBE MORGAN

Nearly a century ago, Louisa Mae Alcott (1874) published a moving account of a brief career in waged domestic work. According to Alcott, although the physical demands of house care took their toll, it was the uninvited sexual attention of her employer, the Reverend Joseph, that made her job intolerable. Fortunately for her—and for consumers of great literature—Alcott found the means to leave the Reverend's employ, quit domestic service altogether, and become one of America's most prolific novelists. The other working women of her day, however, were not so lucky.

At the turn of the last century, women whose only means of support was waged labor had little choice but to take work where toleration of sexualized aggression was part of the job. Like Alcott, those who complained about it or who confronted their harassers were punished with either demotion or the assignment of exceptionally harsh duty. Sadly, those who succumbed to seduction were deemed no better than whores by their family and friends and treated accordingly. In either case—those who confronted their harassers, as well as those who capitulated—sexually harassed women were nearly always dismissed. Those who lost their jobs to sexual harassment lost their reputations both as workers and as virtuous women. Deemed unfit for either marriage or reputable work, many sexual harassment victims joined the ranks of the poor and destitute (Bularzik, 1978).

Today, 97% of all employing and educational institutions in the United States have policies that expressly prohibit sexual harassment, and 84% of those who work and learn in these places are aware of the consequences for violating the rules ("Sexual Harassment," 1999). Steady increases in the number of reports made to state and federal agencies since 1991 suggest that a growing number of women are no longer tolerating such behavior (Bureau of National Affairs, 1994; U.S. Equal Employment Opportunity Commission, 1999). Despite these changes, sexual harassment continues to be one of American society's most pernicious forms of violence against women (National Council for Research on Women, 1992).

. . . What exactly is sexual harassment? Who is at risk of becoming a sexual harassment victim? How does this type of victimization affect those who endure it? The following pages pursue answers to these questions through a synthesis of legal theory, social science research, government data, and firsthand accounts of victims and complainants.

What Is Sexual Harassment?

Although sexual harassment has been practiced since the advent of waged labor, it has only been in recent years that women have had a name for their experiences of it. A name is no small thing, for without one, victims cannot take the next step—to assign blame for their plights—much less lay claim to redress (Felstiner, Abel, & Sarat, 1980–1981). So, until there was language for articulating their experiences in a way that allowed authorities to hear their pain and meaningfully act on it, victims of sexual harassment suffered in silence. In the early 1970s, the phrase *sexual harassment* was first used (Farley, 1978). Since that time, millions of women and men around the world have added it to their daily lexicon.

In the early 1980s, the Equal Employment Opportunity Commission (EEOC) and the Office of Civil Rights (OCR) put the sex discrimination theory to the test by adding sexual harassment to their list of discriminatory behaviors. The U.S. Supreme Court has consistently upheld and therefore legitimized the actionability of sexual harassment claims under Titles VII and IX. As a result of these actions, early sexual harassment claims laid the foundation for more recent attempts to conceptualize violence against women as a civil rights issue.

The EEOC defines sexual harassment as any form of uninvited sexual attention that either explicitly or implicitly becomes a condition of one's work (U.S. EEOC, 1999). Along the same lines, the OCR conceptualizes it as a form of unwanted sexual attention that becomes a condition of one's educational experience (U.S. Office of Civil Rights, 1999). The types of behaviors that fit EEOC and OCR definitions include but are not limited to unwanted talk about sex, jokes about sex or sexualized horseplay, uninvited physical contact, requests for sexual favors, pressures for dates or sex, sexual abuse, and sexual assault. A substantial body of case law now supports the labeling of such behaviors as illegal and organizes them into two types of discrimination claims: quid pro quo and hostile environment.

Some Sexual Harassment Is Sexual Blackmail The Latin phrase *quid pro quo* refers to the trading of favors. With respect to sexual harassment, it references the exchange of sexual favors for special employment treatment. In a quid pro quo situation, going on a date, providing sexual services, or simply enduring sexual touching or talk is rewarded with a decision to hire, to promote, or to deliver job-related perks (i.e., better office space, a new computer, the mobilization of travel stipends, etc.). Those who appear to renege or fail to deliver sexual favors risk punishment in the form of demotion, dismissal, or the denial of basic necessities for doing their jobs. Thus, as was so vividly illustrated by the plot of the highly controversial movie, *Disclosure*, quid pro quo harassment operates as a form of on-the-job blackmail.

Only those individuals with sufficient organizational authority to affect the condition of another person's employment have the power to perpetrate this type of sexual harassment. For this reason, the vast majority of quid pro quo complaints involve harassment of a subordinate by a person with the power to hire, promote, or assign benefits (Benson & Thomson, 1982).

Most Sexual Harassment Is a Manifestation of Hostility The first wave of sexual harassment litigation almost exclusively involved complaints of quid pro quo harassment, and in fact, until the late 1980s, only those cases involving the loss of employment were deemed worthy of legal action. But in 1985, the U.S. Supreme Court broke new conceptual ground by declaring actionable a claim in which there was no evidence of the exchange of favors, nor was there any suggestion that the victim was punished for her intolerance (see *Meritor Savings Bank v. Mechele Vinson*, 1985). Their opinion legitimated a second category of perpetration, now commonly referred to as "hostile environment" harassment.

Hostile environment is a far more common form of harassment than sexual blackmail. In a study of graduate women, for example, 80% of the respondents who experienced harassment reported hostile environment experiences. Since *Meritor vs. Vinson*, the number of sexual harassment claims filed has grown almost exponentially (Bureau of National Affairs, 1994).

Hostile environments are created when sexualized talk and behavior is experienced by some as demeaning or humiliating. They occur when acts of sexual harassment are both the products and the precipitators of sexist thinking and misogynistic attitudes (Cook & Stambaugh, 1997). Hostile climates are nurtured in any organization where values supporting gender inequality are legitimated and hostility against women is permitted. They thrive in workplaces and classrooms where masculinity is conflated with success and femininity is associated with failure (Messerschmidt, 1993). As a result, many hostile environment complaints have been filed by women attempting to work in occupations where masculinity is an implicit job requirement—oil rigging (Holcombe & Wellington, 1992), coal mining (Yount, 1991), policing (Martin, 1994), corrections (Jurik, 1985), automobile manufacturing (Gruber & Bjorn, 1982), and the military (U.S. Department of Defense, 1993)—to name only a few.

Sexual Harassment Is Part of the Larger Continuum Of Violence Against Women In a number of important ways, sexual harassment is more like than different from other forms of violence against women (National Council for Research on Women, 1992). Sexual harassment is a form of woman control. As with rape, incest, and battering, the locus of control is sex (MacKinnon, 1979, 1995). Sexual harassment sustains male dominance and women's subordination by privileging the sexual desires of men over the needs of women.

As in other forms of violence against women, secrecy shrouds the face of sexual harassment victimization (Fitzgerald & Ormerod, 1991). Sexual harassment is practiced in public at many workplaces and inside classrooms. It is common; yet, talk of the experience is taboo. Women have been socialized to keep the details of their victimization private. Thus, the pain that sexual harassment brings often goes unnoticed, and the suffering of its victims is greatly underestimated.

Mythology about the "true" sexual natures of men and women mystifies the motivations of sexual harassers and the responses of the women they target. Too often, men who impose talk about sex or sexual behavior onto women are forgiven for "just being a guy" or "acting like a man." When a woman questions the naturalness of such impositions, it is her own credibility and reasonableness—not the actions of her harasser, nor those of the organization that permitted it—that are suspect (Estrich, 1991).

Sexual Harassment Is a Form of Sex Discrimination Whereas 44% to 85% of American women will experience sexual harassment at some point in their lifetime (National Council for Research on Women, 1992), less than 19% of men report being sexually harassed (U.S. Merit Systems Protection Board, 1981, 1988). Thus, a disproportionate number of women contend with this type of behavior and, therefore, are unfairly burdened by its effects (MacKinnon, 1979).

The practice of sexual harassment supports the institutionalization of gender inequality in all its forms. Even those women who manage to avoid firsthand experience with it are negatively affected by its practice (MacKinnon, 1979). Too often, the decision to hire or promote a woman depends on the degree to which she appears capable of provoking, resisting, or simply surviving sexual harassment. Because so many women have no other recourse but to handle their sexual harassment problems by quitting or changing jobs, sexual harassment is a significant factor in women's job turnover and slower career advancement; therefore, it sustains the gender gap in pay.

For a lot of women, the term *sexual harassment* effectively summarizes a core experience associated with work or school. But for many, the term is an inadequate reference for their violation. For example, for lesbians, there is no specialized term to articulate the added dimension that being homosexual adds to their experience of being sexually harassed by a man (Schneider, 1982). For women of color, the experience of being harassed by white men does not fit neatly into the rubrics of either sexism or racism (Defour, 1990). As a consequence, for these women, evoking the term can mystify rather than clarify the ways in which homophobia and racism carve unique contours into an otherwise common experience (Winston, 1991).

Who Is at Risk of Becoming a Victim of Sexual Harassment?

In a highly hierarchical society such as ours, women and men work and attend school within complex interlocking systems of oppression (Collins, 1990). As a consequence, risk of sexual harassment victimization varies within the social strata. Certainly, the greatest risk factor is being female, as 44% to 85% of American women will experience sexual harassment during their academic or working lives (National Council for Research on Women, 1992). Although the risk of victimization for men is significantly smaller (12% to 19%), they are not immune, and the proportion of men reporting sexual harassment appears to be growing over time (U.S. EEOC, 1999; U.S. Merit Systems Protection Board, 1992).

The amount of risk a woman assumes varies according to the type of environment in which she performs her work or attends school. Women who work in highly sexualized environments experience more harassment than those who do not (Loe, 1996). Those who work in male-dominated workplaces or who assume masculine occupations report more harassment than those who perform jobs associated with women's work (Gruber, 1998). Especially vulnerable are those who depend on men for job security or career advancement (Defour, 1990).

The Sexualization of Work Promotes Sexually Harassing Behavior It is not possible, nor even desirable, for students, teachers, workers, and their supervisors to check their sexual desires at the classroom or office door. However, when talk about sex and sexual behavior is part of a work group's routine, sexual harassment is likely to be, as well. Some lines of work invite sexualization more than others do, and as a result, they carry a higher risk of sexual harassment as well. Sexualization of work relieves the stress of danger and even boredom. Once sexual behavior becomes routine, it becomes difficult for workers to imagine doing their jobs without it.

For example, in her participant observational study of underground coal mining, Yount (1991) noticed that male miners reduce stress and build solidarity by sharing especially crude jokes and engaging in highly sexualized horseplay. Those who are unwilling or unable to play along become easy targets for derision. As a consequence, most of the women coal miners became the butts of their coworkers' jokes.

In addition, those who have jobs where sex is commodified, or where it is performed as a service, endure more sexual harassment than those who do not. Waitresses, for example, who are required to wear sexually seductive uniforms, or who have been trained to flirt with their customers as part of the job, encounter sexual harassment from their supervisors and customers (Loe, 1996). An occupational hazard of the sex trades is sexualized violence, and sexual harassment by customers is endemic (Pettiway, 1996). Even those sex trade workers who provide services deemed legal assume a much greater risk but receive less protection than other types of service workers (Ronai & Ellis, 1989).

Male Domination Is a Primary Risk Factor The vast majority of sexual harassers are men. One study, for example, found that only 1% of the female and 35% of the male respondents experienced harassment by a woman (Dubois, Knapp, Farley, & Kustis, 1998). Thus, next to being a woman, working or learning in close proximity to men increases one's risk of sexual harassment victimization more than any other factor.

Few areas of employment are more male-dominated than the armed forces. The majority of military personnel are men. In addition, the majority of jobs in the military continue to be viewed as "men's work." As the number of women inside military academies and on bases has grown, so have the number of sexual harassment complaints made by them (Moss, 1997). In fact, one survey by *The New York Times* ("Two Out of Three," 1991) found that two out of every three military women experience at least one form of sexual harassment. Although male domination in the armed forces is more visible than in other areas of the workforce, there are other masculine domains where sexual harassment is common. For example, sexual harassment is equally pervasive in such male-dominated occupations as criminology (Stanko, 1992) and criminal justice work (Martin & Jurik, 1996).

Women Who Depend on Men for Employment Are Especially Vulnerable Despite significant advances within the last two decades, a disproportionate number of women perform low prestige jobs where their work is organized and evaluated by men (Kelly, 1989). Women who depend on men for their job security or for career advancement are especially vulnerable to on-the-job sexual blackmail—or, quid pro quo harassment.

Some women are more dependent on men for employment and educational opportunities than others, and as a result, their risk is especially high (DeCoster, Estes, & Mueller, 1999). Women who depend solely on their own wages to support themselves and their families are unlikely to take risks at work. Their reluctance to either confront or complain makes them easy prey for sexual harassers (Stambaugh, 1997). Single mothers—especially those unable to obtain child support—are in greatest need of employment and therefore have the least leverage for a direct confrontation (Morgan, 1999). It is no wonder that victimization rates are significantly higher among young, single, and divorced women than among older married women (U.S. Merit Systems Protection Board, 1988).

In addition, women building careers in male-dominated workplaces and professions have little choice but to depend on men for their training and mentoring. Thus, in workplaces where interactions have become sexualized and harassment is common, a woman's ability to obtain her own organizational authority rests on her efforts to manage not only harassment by male coworkers and supervisors but also harassment by her male subordinates. Those who complain about sexualized hazing or who protest sexualized epithets risk being branded as unduly sensitive or too brusque and are then passed over for promotion. For this reason, ambitious women whose careers are on the rise are likely to encounter more sexual harassment than the complacent (DeCoster et al., 1999).

Far more women of color than white women depend on men for job security and career advancement. With the exception of Asian women, women of color earn significantly less than either white women or white men. Because unemployment among men of color is disproportionately high, women of color are more likely than their white counterparts to be the family's breadwinner (Collins, 1990). For these reasons, a larger proportion of women of color support entire families on a single wage, depend on male superiors for job security, and therefore have fewer options for escaping by their harassers (e.g., transferring, quitting, changing jobs). At least among auto workers, black women endure more sexual harassment and experience more severe forms of it than their white counterparts (Gruber & Bjorn, 1982). Perhaps for these reasons, women of color filed a preponderance of the first wave of sexual harassment claims (Winston, 1991).

Few women are more dependent on men that those residing in U.S. prisons. As a consequence, those most vulnerable to sexual harassment in all its forms are incarcerated women who are supervised by male correctional officers ("Patriarchy in Prison," 1997). Lawsuits filed by incarcerated women assert that sexual blackmail is commonplace. In addition, they claim that male correctional officers routinely subject female inmates to unwarranted surveillance and gratuitous pat-downs (Finder, 1998).

Those Who Challenge Male Dominance Are at Greater Risk Than Those Who Comply When routinely practiced, sexual harassment does more than gratify the few individuals who perpetrate it, it also serves to enforce the patriarchal status quo (Wise & Stanley, 1987). Within highly patriarchal institutions, those who question the superiority of a few men, or who resist dominance by them, are likely to be labeled traitors and then treated accordingly. Within the ranks of traitors can be found noncompliant women, unconventional men, and homosexuals.

Women who challenge the superiority of men by acquiring social, economic, or organizational power over them are visible targets for sexualized hostility. In fact, the findings from one study revealed that the more tenure and education a woman possesses, the greater her risk of sexual harassment victimization will be (DeCoster et al., 1999). Thus, the more power a woman acquires, the more she is perceived to be a threat to those in power and the greater her risk of being sexually harassed will be.

Within any patriarchal system, only a few men possess superordinate status. Sexual harassment is one of many tools used by the powerful elite for managing unruly men, as well. Powerful men routinely sexually harass other men as a means to intimidate them into subservience (Messerschmidt, 1993). Men who violate patriarchal norms by doing women's work, being feminine, or questioning the superiority of men are at a greater risk than are those who accept their place without question.

Because heterosexuality as it has been traditionally practiced serves to normalize male dominance and female subordination, the acceptance of homosexuality poses a formidable challenge to the patriarchal status quo. Thus, inside organizations where the heterosexual mandate is especially strong, lesbians and gays who are out (as well as heterosexuals who are erroneously labeled as such) can become the lightning rods of homophobic hostility. Such homophobia is often expressed in the form of sexual harassment (Brienza, 1996; Bull, 1997). Crude jokes about homosexual acts, homophobic slurs (dyke, queer, homo, for example), negative commentary about the gay lifestyle, and even malicious gossip about a person's sexual orientation are all forms of sexual harassment that serve to punish those who fail to conform to heterosexual norms. In the armed forces, for example, regardless of their true sexual orientation, women who resist sexual blackmail or who complain about sexualized hostilities are labeled lesbians, and their fitness to serve is called into question (Moss, 1997).

How Does Sexual Harassment Affect Those Who Experience It?

There is no singular sexual harassment experience. The effects of sexual harassment are as varied and complex as the women who endure it. A history of victimization is a significant factor in how a person interprets and responds to sexual harassment. Specifically, past experience of other forms of violence against women—rape, battering, abuse, and incest, for example—may heighten the feeling of being violated (Fitzgerald, 1993).

In addition, a person's values about gender, sex, work, and relationships can color the experience. Those with feminist orientations, for example, are more likely to define unwanted sexual attention as harassing (Ryan & Kenig, 1991). Specifically, women who value gender equality, who believe that women should have the right to pursue careers, and who believe that working women can be good mothers are more offended by unwanted sexual attention at work than those who hold more traditional views.

The nature of the relationship between a woman and her harasser is important as well. The greater the power disparity, the more distressing the experience is likely to be (Benson & Thomson, 1982). Feelings of violation are particularly strong when women are harassed by authorities entrusted with their care. Sexual harassment is especially traumatic when coaches, mentors, therapists, doctors, or clergy commit it (Rutter, 1989).

As previously mentioned, both the sexual and racial identities of the harasser make a difference, as well. Harassment by someone of a different orientation or race is more offensive than if the harasser and victim are of the same background (Defour, 1990; Schneider, 1982).

Even though no two sexual harassment experiences are alike, analysis of women's talk about how sexual harassment feels and its effect on their lives has uncovered a few salient themes. For most, loss is a core experience. Coping with the negative effects of sexual harassment is emotionally distressing as well as physically exhausting. Those who manage to survive the experience gain strength and wisdom from their adversity (Stambaugh, 1997).

A Core Experience Among the Sexually Harassed Is Loss It is difficult for the sexually harassed to talk about their experiences without mentioning a loss. When victims share their stories, talk of job loss and the fear of losing one's job often dominate the conversation (Morgan, 1999; Stambaugh, 1997). Such fears are not unfounded, as 60% to 70% of victims who contact government agencies for assistance are unemployed (Coles, 1982; New York Governor's Task Force on Sexual Harassment, 1993; Welsh & Gruber, 1999). In filing formal claims, victims usually seek monetary compensation for lost promotions, wages, and benefits. But, beneath these more tangible losses lie less obvious but no less traumatizing sacrifices. Regardless of the circumstances, recipients of unwanted sexual attention commonly feel a loss of personal dignity. Being sexually harassed is an embarrassing, if not humiliating experience. The pressure to exchange sexual favors for employment is demeaning, as is being the butt of a sexualized joke or gag. A consequence is the erosion of trust in others, especially men (Rutter, 1989). For example, in a recent study, 53% of the victims who experienced quid pro quo harassment lost confidence in themselves, 45% lost their confidence in others, and 44% experienced a loss of trust in men (Van Roosmalen & McDaniel, 1998).

The act of filing a report or complaint incurs additional loss of dignity and trust in others. Those who are accused often vilify those who blow the whistle on them or on institutions that harbor them; complainants are also ostracized by those who support sexual harassment (Dandekar, 1990). As a result, the cost of complaint can be the loss of one's reputation, along with collegiality and the support of co-workers.

For Most, Sexual Harassment Is a Distressing Experience The *Diagnostic and Statistical Manual (DSM-IV)* (American Psychiatric Association, 1994) lists sexual harassment as a significant psychosocial stressor, and a growing number of clinicians rate its effects on their patients as severe to extreme (Charney & Russell, 1994). Nearly all (90%) of those who seek help report at least some degree of emotional distress (Crull, 1981). Because sexual harassment is a humiliating experience, most victims experience intense anger. Without the means to fully express it, depression and self-destructive behavior can result. Ironically, the strategies most women employ to control their anger (e.g., escape and avoidance) lead to social isolation, which in turn exacerbates feelings of helplessness and hopelessness (Koss, 1993).

The stress of coping with sexual harassment victimization undermines physical health, as well. Nearly 63% of the women who sought assistance from the Working Women's Institute associated physical illness with being sexually harassed (Crull, 1981). Among them, nausea, headaches, and exhaustion were the most commonly reported forms of physical distress. In one study, a significant minority of victims reported sexual inhibition (Van Roosmalen & McDaniel, 1998).

In many cases, the emotional and physical distress of being sexually harassed lingers long after the violation ends. Without proper treatment, the physical manifestations of suppressed anger and feelings of loss can develop into chronic health conditions. For example, the experience of being sexually harassed can trigger the onset of eating disorders. Thus, in those cases where the harassment was severe, or when it was perpetrated over an extended period of time, it can take years to fully heal (Koss, 1993).

Finally, sexual harassment erodes feelings of satisfaction. Surveys of university and corporate employees document significant differences in job satisfaction between victims and nonvictims (Klein, 1988; Stambaugh, 1993). Those who manage to keep their jobs can become apathetic about work and disaffected with administration (Morgan, 1999). The experience for students is similar. Victims often cite a change in attitude toward school, and some experience a sharp decline in their ability to perform in class (Benson & Thomson, 1982; Van Roosmalen & McDaniel, 1998).

Reporting Is Rarely Satisfying and Can Be Traumatic Despite the fact that mechanisms for reporting sexual harassment abound, the vast majority of those who could benefit from engaging them choose not to do so. Only about 24% of victims who participated in the last U.S. Merit Systems Protection Board (1992) told anyone of their plight, and less than 12% took formal action. Instead, sexually harassed women tend to handle their sexual harassment problems via escape or avoidance (Gruber, 1989). Students escape harassers by dropping courses or changing their programs of study. Workers often seek relief by transferring to a different office or shift, or by quitting altogether. When asked why they do not seek intervention, victims commonly cite fear of retaliation, of not being believed; they express the suspicion that reporting will "do no good" (Gutek, Groff, & Tsui, 1996).

There is evidence to indicate their fears are well founded. Complaints rarely go unpunished, and litigation is quickly becoming the weapon of choice. Increasingly, those accused of harassment punish their accusers and the institutions that stand by them by filing civil suits, the majority of which never go to trial (Conte, 1996). The victims of counterclaims experience the process of litigation as an additional or secondary harassment. In addition, in most cases, countersuits undermine the ability of an employer to deliver meaningful support to the victims who seek their aid, as they divide the attention and loyalty of complaint handlers and tap already limited resources for aid and resolution (Morgan, 1999).

The vast majority of those who seek legal assistance with their sexual harassment problems are turned away (Morgan, 1999). With respect to government agencies, the size of the budget has not kept pace with the rising caseload. As a result, the number of requests for investigation has outstripped agency resources for conducting them. In some states, the result has been a 1- to 2-year backlog in claim processing (Bureau of National Affairs, 1994). As a consequence, agencies prioritize claims, and only the most egregious, and those with ample documentation, are expeditiously processed. Too often, the remaining complaints are disposed of with personal advice and moral lectures before they can ever become cases (Morgan, 1999).

Likewise, because sexual harassment claims have a reputation for being high-risk cases with low returns on the investment, most attorneys practice caution in taking them. Less than 1% of all sexual harassment claims are heard in court, and only one third of the outcomes favor the plaintiff (Terpestra & Baker, 1988). As a consequence, most of those who seek legal aid fail to obtain it. Rejection by agencies and attorneys becomes one more in a long line of betrayals by those with the authority to intervene (Madigan & Gamble, 1991).

For those fortunate enough to garner government intervention or legal representation, the pursuit of justice takes its toll. Without the benefit of legal protections comparable to rape shield laws, the medical, work, and sexual histories of sexual harassment complainants are open to investigation. Credit histories, medical reports, even adoption papers have been probed for evidence of a complainant's unreasonableness. Along with counterclaims, attempts at discrediting them become a third—and for those who have lost their jobs, a fourth—victimization.

Surviving Sexual Harassment Can Be Empowering The humiliation of being sexually harassed is indeed distressful. To be fired or demoted for confronting or complaining about harassment can be traumatizing. Being disbelieved by supervisors, lectured to by government agents, and then sued by one's harasser pours a significant amount of salt into an already gaping wound. Regardless of the outcome, those who successfully survive their ordeals report intense feelings of empowerment (Stambaugh, 1997). For some, the experience of surviving their harassment, complaint, or litigation experience results in a significant increase in personal pride and sense of self-worth.

In addition to pride, those who pursue formal redress find their knowledge of the law is enhanced. Many victims exit the complaint process with greater understanding of their rights at work, the legal system, and the enforcement of rules. Exercising this new expertise can restore self-confidence eroded by harassment. Survivors draw on their legal knowledge to research potential employers, to assess and respond to their work evaluations, and to negotiate better terms of employment (Morgan, 1999).

Finally, the experience of being sexually exploited and economically coerced can be politicizing. Many survivors put their shoulders to the communal wheel by forming peer support groups, writing or participating in media exposes, organizing protests, and lobbying for change.

Conclusions

Louisa Mae Alcott is not the only woman to write about her experience of sexual harassment. Since her account was first published, millions of women from around the world have shared similar accounts. Although the details of each story differ, the plot lines are painfully similar. With each telling, the silence regarding this endemic social problem is broken, and one of America's greatest shames is once again exposed.

Comparing the current level of public concern about the plight of sexual harassment victims with that of Alcott's day, it appears we have come quite a long way, indeed. In just a few short decades, a practice that was once considered to be the working man's prerogative has been recast as an unconscionable abuse of power. Today, women have a name for their experience, laws that prohibit its practice, and mechanisms for redress and justice. Yet the problem of sexual harassment appears to be exceptionally resistant to current efforts to eliminate it.

Since efforts were first made to document them, rates of victimization, at least in the United States and Canada, have remained remarkably stable. Nationwide, incidence hovers around 42%. Among those working and attending school in male-dominated sectors of society, the rates are much higher. Thus, sexual harassment continues to be a pervasive experience among women, and the number of men suffering from it appears to be in the rise.

Increasingly, clinical studies and survey data portray sexual harassment as an occupational health hazard, the risks of which are disproportionately borne by women. Despite widespread institutionalization of reporting mechanisms, most victims continue to endure the problem in silence.

Less than one quarter of the women who experience legally actionable forms of unwanted sexual attention tell anyone about their plight, and only a handful—12%—ever make the attempt to avail themselves of the opportunities for formal redress. Of those who do, most lose their jobs in the process, some are sued, and only a few exit the process feeling justified.

Today, it is almost impossible to talk of sex, work, rights, and law without evoking the term sexual harassment (Schultz, 1998). Yet there remains considerable confusion about the types of behaviors constituting legal action (Fisher, 1998). It is primarily case law that stakes out the boundary that divides a personal problem from a legally actionable one. With respect to sexual harassment, shifts in politics, ideology, and resources have caused the line to drift. Some of the consequences have been confusion and neglect at the institutional level, inadequate protection and intervention by government agencies, and insufficient advocacy among the legal profession. Given the response (or lack of response) that most victims receive from authorities, it is no wonder that most women prefer to resolve their sexual harassment problems via escape or avoidance.

All male violence against women is political; but few experiences so blatantly connect the personal with the political as that of being sexual harassed at work (Koss et al., 1994). Sexual harassment occurs at those places within the social strata where economic and sexual power overlap (Bularzik, 1978). When political, economic, and sexual power converge, the environment is especially ripe for abuse (Benson & Thomson, 1982). Thus, sexual harassment is a unique manifestation of the struggle between those who possess (and abuse) power and those who seek to reclaim it (Smart, 1987), and any response to the problem that fails to acknowledge that reality will fail to resolve it.

References

Alcott, L. M. (1874, June 4). How I went out to service. *The Independent* (New York).

American Psychiatric Association. (1994). *Diagnostic and statistical manual of mental disorders, 4th edition*. Washington, DC: Author.

Benson, D., & Thomson, G. (1982). Sexual harassment on a university campus: The confluence of authority relations, sexual interest, and gender stratification. *Social Problems, 29*(3), 236–251.

Brienza, J. (1996). No recourse for same-sex harassment. *Trial, 32*(3), 78–80.

Bularzik, M. (1978). *Sexual harassment at the workplace: Historical notes*. Somerville, MA: New England Free Press.

Bull, C. (1997, November 25). Same-sex harassment: Gay men and lesbians being harassed in the workplace are about to have their day in court. *The Advocate*, pp. 30–34.

Bureau of National Affairs. (1994). New charges, backlog rising. *Current Developments, 3*, 616.

Charney, D., & Russell, R. (1994). An overview of sexual harassment. *American Journal of Psychiatry, 151*(1), 10–17.

Coles, F. (1982). Forced to quit: Sexual harassment complaints and agency responses. *Sex Roles, 14*(1/2), 81–95.

Collins, P. (1990). *Black feminist thought*. Boston: Unman & Hyman.

Conte, A. (1996). When the tables are turned: Courts consider suits by alleged harassers. *Trial, 32*(3), 30–37.

Cook, K., & Stambaugh, P. (1997). Tuna memos and pissing contests: Doing gender and male dominance on the Internet. In C. Ronai, B. Zsembik, & J. Feagin (Ed.), *Everyday sexism in the third millennium* (pp. 63–83). New York: Routledge.

Crull, P. (1981). The stress effects of sexual harassment on the job. *American Journal of Orthopsychiatry, 52*, 539–544.

Dandekar, N. (1990). Contrasting consequences: Bringing charges of sexual harassment compared with other cases of whistleblowing. *Journal of Business Ethics, 9*, 151–158.

DeCoster, S., Estes, S. B., & Mueller, C. W. (1999). Routine activities and sexual harassment in the workplace. *Work and Occupations, 26*(1), 21–43.
Defour, D. (1990). The interface of racism and sexism on college campuses. In M. Paludi (Ed.), *The ivory tower: Sexual harassment on campus* (pp. 45–52). Albany: University of New York Press.
Dubois, C., Knapp, D., Farley, R., & Kustis, G. (1998). An empirical examination of same- and other-gender sexual harassment in the workplace. *Sex Roles, 39*(9–10), 731–746.
Estrich, S. (1991). Sex at work. *Stanford Law Review, 43*, 813–844.
Farley, C. (1978). *Sexual shakedown: The sexual harassment of women on the job*. New York: McGraw-Hill.
Felstiner, W., Abel, R., & Sarat, A. (1980–1981). The emergence and transformation of disputes: Naming, blaming, claiming. *Law and Society Review, 15*(3), 631–654.
Finder, A. (1998, November 10). Female inmates sue over "pat frisks" by men. *The New York Times*, p. B-5.
Fisher, A. (1998, January 12). After all this time, why don't people know what sexual harassment means? *Fortune*, pp. 156–157.
Fitzgerald, L. (1993). Violence against women in the workplace. *American Psychologist, 48*, 1070–1076.
Fitzgerald, L., & Ormerod, A. (1991). Perceptions of sexual harassment: The influence of gender and context. *Psychology of Women Quarterly, 15*, 281–294.
Gruber, J. (1989). How women handle sexual harassment. *Social Science Research, 74*(1), 3–7.
Gruber, J. (1998). The impact of male work environments and organizational policies on women's experiences of sexual harassment. *Gender & Society, 12*(3), 301–319.
Gruber, J., & Bjorn, L. (1982). Blue collar blues: The sexual harassment of women autoworkers. *Work and Occupations, 9*(3), 271–298.
Gutek, B., Groff, A., & Tsui, A. (1996). Reactions to perceived sex discrimination. *Human Relations, 49*(6), 791–814.
Holcombe, B., & Wellington, C. (1992). *Search for justice*. Walpole, NH: Stillpoint.
Jurik, N. (1985). An officer and a lady: Organizational barriers to women working in men's prisons. *Social Problems, 32*, 375–388.
Kelly, R. (1989). *The gendered economy*. Newbury Park, CA: Sage.
Klein, F. (1988). *The 1988 working women sexual harassment survey executive report*. Cambridge, MA: Klein & Associates.
Koss, M. (1993). Changed lives. In M. Paludi (Ed.), *Ivory power* (pp. 73–92). New York: SUNY Press.
Koss, M., Goodman, L., Browne, A., Fitzgerald, L., Keita, G., & Russo, N. (1994). *Male violence against women at home, at work and in the community*. Washington, DC: American Psychological Association.

Loe, M. (1996). Working for men—at the intersection of power, gender, and sexuality. *Sociological Inquiry, 66*(4), 399–421.

MacKinnon, C. (1979). *The sexual harassment of working women.* New Haven, CT: Yale University Press.

MacKinnon, C. (1995). Sexual harassment: Its first decade in court. In B. Price & N. Sokoloff (Eds.), *The criminal justice system and women* (pp. 297–311). New York: McGraw-Hill.

Madigan, M., & Gamble, N. (1991). *The second rape: Society's continued betrayal of the victim.* New York: Lexington.

Martin, S. (1994). Outsider within the station house: The impact of race and gender on black women police. *Social Problems, 41,* 383–400.

Martin, S., & Jurik, N. (1996). *Doing justice, doing gender.* Thousand Oaks, CA: Sage.

Meritor Savings Bank v. Mechele Vinson, 477 U.S. 57.65 (1985).

Messerschmidt, J. (1993). *Masculinities and crime.* Lantham, MD: Rowman & Littlefield.

Morgan, P. (1999). Risking relationships: Understanding the litigation choices of sexually harassment women. *Law and Society Review, 33*(1), 67–92.

Moss, J. (1997, February 4). Lesbian baiting in the barracks. *The Advocate,* pp. 36–40.

National Council for Research on Women. (1992). *Sexual harassment: Research and resources.* New York: Author.

New York Governor's Task Force on Sexual Harassment. (1993). *Sexual harassment: Building a consensus for change.* New York: Office of the Governor.

Patriarchy in prison. (1997). *off our backs, 27*(2), 3–4.

Pettiway, L. (1996). *Honey, honey, miss thang: Being black and gay on the streets.* Philadelphia: Temple University Press.

Ronai, C., & Ellis, C. (1989). Turn-ons for money, interactional strategies of the table dancer. *Journal of Contemporary Ethnography, 18*(3), 271–298.

Rutter, P. (1989). *Sex in the forbidden zone: When men in power—therapists, doctors, clergy, teachers, and others—betray women's trust.* New York: Fawcett.

Ryan, J., & Kenig, S. (1991). Risk and ideology in sexual harassment. *Sociological Inquiry, 61*(2), 231–241.

Schneider, B. (1982). Consciousness about sexual harassment among heterosexual and lesbian women workers. *Journal of Social Issues, 38,* 75–97.

Schultz, V. (1998). Reconceptualizing sexual harassment. *Yale Law Journal, 107*(6), 1683–1805.

Sexual harassment charges (and dismissals) escalate. (1999). *HR Focus, 76*(4), 4–5.

Smart, C. (1987). *Feminism and the power of law.* London: Routledge.

Stambaugh, P. M. (1993). *Unwanted sexual attention at Arizona State University.* In the unpublished annual report of The ASU Commission on the Status of Women, Arizona State University, Tempe.

Stambaugh, P. M. (1997). The power of law and the sexual harassment complaints of women. *National Women's Studies Association Journal, 9*(2), 23–42.

Stanko, B. (1992). Sexual harassment in the criminological profession. *Criminologist, 17*(5), 1–3.

Terpestra, D., & Baker, D. (1988). Outcomes of sexual harassment charges. *Academy of Management Journal, 31*(1), 181–190.

Two out of three women in the military study report sexual harassment incidents. (1991, September 12). *New York Times*, p. A-22.

U.S. Department of Defense. (1993). *The Tailhook report.* New York: St. Martin's.

U.S. Equal Employment Opportunity Commission. (1998). *Sexual harassment* [On-line]. Available: www.access.gpo.gov/nara/cfr/waisidx/29cfrl604.html

U.S. Equal Employment Opportunity Commission. (1999). *Sexual harassment charges EEOC and FEPAS combined: FY 1992-FY 1998* [On-line]. Available: www.eeoc.gov/state/harass.html

U.S. Merit Systems Protection Board. (1981). *Sexual harassment in the federal government.* Washington, DC: Author.

U.S. Merit Systems Protection Board. (1988). *Sexual harassment in the federal government: An update.* Washington DC: Author.

U.S. Merit Systems Protection Board. (1992). *Sexual harassment in the federal government workplace.* Washington DC: Author.

U.S. Office of Civil Rights. (1999). *Sexual harassment* [On-line]. Available: www.doc.gov/ocr

Van Roosmalen, E., & McDaniel, S. (1998). Sexual harassment in academia: A hazard to women's health. *Women & Health, 28*(2), 33–55.

Welsh, S., & Gruber, J. (1999). Not taking it any more: Women who report or file complaints of sexual harassment. *Canadian Research Society Association, 4*, 559–583.

Winston, J. (1991). Mirror, mirror on the wall. Title VII, Section 1981, and the intersection of race, gender, and the Civil Rights Act of 1990. *California Law Review, 79*, 775–825.

Wise, S., & Stanley, L. (1987). *Georgie porgie: Sexual harassment in everyday life.* London: Pandora.

Yount, K. (1991). Ladies, flirts, and tomboys: Strategies for handling sexual harassment in an underground mine. *Journal of Contemporary Ethnography, 19*(4), 396–422.

28 Men on Rape

TIMOTHY BENEKE

Rape may be America's fastest growing violent crime; no one can be certain because it is not clear whether more rapes are being committed or reported. It *is* clear that violence against women is widespread and fundamentally alters the meaning of life for women; that sexual violence is encouraged in a variety of ways in American culture; and that women are often blamed for rape.

Consider some statistics:

- In a random sample of 930 women, sociologist Diana Russell found that 44 percent had survived either rape or attempted rape. Rape was defined as sexual intercourse physically forced upon the woman, or coerced by threat of bodily harm, or forced upon the woman when she was helpless (asleep, for example). The survey included rape and attempted rape in marriage in its calculations. (Personal communication)
- In a September 1980 survey conducted by *Cosmopolitan* magazine to which over 106,000 women anonymously responded, 24 percent had been raped at least once. Of those, 51 percent had been raped by friends, 37 percent by strangers, 18 percent

by relatives, and 3 percent by husbands. 10 percent of the women in the survey had been victims of incest. 75 percent of the women had been "bullied into making love." Writer Linda Wolfe, who reported on the survey, wrote in reference to such bullying: "Though such harassment stops short of rape, readers reported that it was nearly as distressing."

- An estimated 2–3 percent of all men who rape outside of marriage go to prison for their crimes.[1]
- The F.B.I. estimates that if current trends continue, one woman in four will be sexually assaulted in her lifetime.[2]
- An estimated 1.8 million women are battered by their spouses each year.[3] In extensive interviews with 430 battered women, clinical psychologist Lenore Walker, author of *The Battered Woman*, found that 59.9 percent had also been raped (defined as above) by their spouses. Given the difficulties many women had in admitting they had been raped, Walker estimates the figure may well be as high as 80 or 85 percent. (Personal communication.) If 59.9 percent of the 1.8 million women battered each year are also raped, then a million women may be raped in marriage each year. And a significant number are raped in marriage without being battered.
- Between one in two and one in ten of all rapes are reported to the police.[4]
- Between 300,000 and 500,000 women are raped each year outside of marriage.[5]

What is often missed when people contemplate statistics on rape is the effect of the *threat* of sexual violence on women. I have asked women repeatedly, "How would your life be different if rape were suddenly to end?" (Men may learn a lot by asking this question of women to whom they are close.) The threat of rape is an assault upon the meaning of the world; it alters the feel of the human condition. Surely any attempt to comprehend the lives of women that fails to take issues of violence against women into account is misguided.

Through talking to women, I learned: *The threat of rape alters the meaning and feel of the night.* Observe how your body feels, how the night feels, when you're in fear. The constriction in your chest, the vigilance in your eyes, the rubber in your legs. What do the stars look like? How does the moon present itself? What is the difference between walking late at night in the dangerous part of a city and walking late at night in the country, or safe suburbs? When I try to imagine what the threat of rape must do to the night, I think of the stalked, adrenalated feeling I get walking late at night in parts of certain American cities. Only, I remind myself, it is a fear different from any I have known, a fear of being raped.

It is night half the time. If the threat of rape alters the meaning of the night, it must alter the meaning and pace of the day, one's relation to the passing and organization of time itself. For some women, the threat of rape at night turns their cars into armored tanks, their solitude into isolation. And what must the space inside a car or an apartment feel like if the space outside is menacing?

I was running late one night with a close woman friend through a path in the woods on the outskirts of a small university town. We had run several miles and were feeling a warm, energized serenity.

"How would you feel if you were alone?" I asked.

"Terrified!" she said instantly.

"Terrified that there might be a man out there?" I asked, pointing to the surrounding moonlit forest, which had suddenly been transformed into a source of terror.

"Yes."

Another woman said, "I know what I can't do and I've completely internalized what I can't do. I've built a viable life that basically involves never leaving my apartment at night unless I'm directly going some place to meet somebody. It's unconsciously built into what it occurs to women to do." When one is raised without freedom, one may not recognize its absence.

The threat of rape alters the meaning and feel of nature. Everyone has felt the psychic nurturance of nature. Many women are being deprived of that nurturance, especially in wooded areas near cities. They are deprived either because they cannot experience nature in solitude because of threat, or because, when they do choose solitude in nature, they must cope with a certain subtle but nettlesome fear.

Women need more money because of rape and the threat of rape makes it harder for women to earn money. It's simple: if you don't feel safe walking at night, or riding public transportation, you need a car. And it is less practicable to live in cheaper, less secure, and thus more dangerous neighborhoods if the ordinary threat of violence that men experience, being mugged, say, is compounded by the threat of rape. By limiting mobility at night, the threat of rape limits where and when one is able to work, thus making it more difficult to earn money. An obvious bind: women need more money because of rape, and have fewer job opportunities because of it.

The threat of rape makes women more dependent on men (or other women).

One woman said: "If there were no rape I wouldn't have to play games with men for their protection." The threat of rape falsifies, mystifies, and confuses relations between men and women. If there were no rape, women would simply not need men as much, wouldn't need them to go places with at night, to feel safe in their homes, for protection in nature.

The threat of rape makes solitude less possible for women. Solitude, drawing strength from being alone, is difficult if being alone means being afraid. To be afraid is to be in need, to experience a lack; the threat of rape creates a lack. Solitude requires relaxation; if you're afraid, you can't relax.

The threat of rape inhibits a woman's expressiveness. "If there were no rape," said one woman, "I could dress the way I wanted and walk the way I wanted and not feel self-conscious about the responses of men. I could be friendly to people. I wouldn't have to wish I was ugly. I wouldn't have to make myself small when I got on the bus. I wouldn't have to respond to verbal abuse from men by remaining silent. I could respond in kind."

If a woman's basic expressiveness is inhibited, her sexuality, creativity, and delight in life must surely be diminished.

The threat of rape inhibits the freedom of the eye. I know a married couple who live in Manhattan. They are both artists, both acutely sensitive and responsive to the visual world. When they walk separately in the city, he has more freedom to look than she does. She must control her eye movements lest they inadvertently meet the glare of some importunate man. What, who, and how she sees are restricted by the threat of rape.

The following exercise is recommended for men.

> Walk down a city street. Pay a lot of attention to your clothing; make sure your pants are zipped, shirt tucked in, buttons done. Look straight ahead. Every time a man walks past you, avert your eyes and make your face expressionless. Most women learn to go through this act each time we leave our houses. It's a way to avoid at least some of the encounters we've all had with strange men who decided we looked available.[6]

To relate aesthetically to the visual world involves a certain playfulness, a spirit of spontaneous exploration. The tense vigilance that accompanies fear inhibits that spontaneity. The world is no longer yours to look at when you're afraid.

I am aware that all culture is, in part, restriction, that there are places in America where hardly anyone is safe (though men are safer than women virtually everywhere), that there are many ways to enjoy life, that some women may not be so restricted, that there exist havens, whether psychic, geographical, economic, or class. But they are *havens*, and as such, defined by threat.

Above all, I trust my experience: no woman could have lived the life I've lived the last few years. If suddenly I were restricted by the threat of rape, I would feel a deep, inexorable depression. And it's not just rape; it's harassment, battery, Peeping Toms, anonymous phone calls, exhibitionism, intrusive stares, fondlings—all contributing to an atmosphere of intimidation in women's lives. And I have only scratched the surface; it would take many carefully crafted short stories to begin to express what I have only hinted at in the last few pages. I have not even touched upon what it might mean for a woman to be sexually assaulted. Only women can speak to that. Nor have I suggested how the threat of rape affects marriage.

Rape and the threat of rape pervade the lives of women, as reflected in some popular images of our culture.

...

"She Asked for It"—Blaming the Victim

Many things may be happening when a man blames a woman for rape. We can now make a few points about what goes on when men (and some women) say, "She asked for it," (or are otherwise insensitive or dismissive) after a woman has been raped. (These points apply repeatedly to many of the interviews that follow.)

First, in all cases where a woman is said to have asked for it, her appearance and behavior are taken as a form of speech. "Actions speak louder than words" is a widely held belief; the woman's actions—her appearance may be taken as action—are given greater emphasis than her words; an interpretation alien to the woman's intentions is given to her actions. A logical extension of "she asked for it" is the idea that she wanted what happened to happen; if she wanted it to happen, she *deserved* for it to happen. Therefore, the man is not to be blamed. "She asked for it" can mean either that she was consenting to have sex and was not really raped, or that she was in fact raped but somehow she really deserved it. "If you ask for it, you deserve it," is a widely held notion. If I ask you to beat me up and you beat me up, I still don't deserve to be beaten up. So even if the notion that women asked to be raped had some basis in reality, which it doesn't, on its own terms it makes no sense.

Second, a mentality exists that says: a woman who assumes freedoms normally restricted to a man (like going out alone at night) and is raped is doing the same thing as a woman who goes out in the rain without an umbrella and catches a cold. Both are considered responsible for what happens to them. That men will rape is taken to be a legitimized given, part of nature, like rain or snow. The view reflects a massive abdication of responsibility for rape on the part of men. It is so much easier to think of rape as natural than to acknowledge one's part in it. So long as rape is regarded as natural, women will be blamed for rape.

A third point. The view that it is natural for men to rape is closely connected to the view of women as commodities. If a woman's body is regarded as a valued commodity by men, then of course, if you leave a valued commodity where it can be taken, it's just human nature for men to take it. If you left your stereo out on the sidewalk, you'd be asking for it to get stolen. Someone will just take it. (And how often men speak of rape as "going out and *taking it*.") If a woman walks the streets at night, she's leaving a valued commodity, her body, where it can be taken. So long as women are regarded as commodities, they will be blamed for rape.

Which brings us to a fourth point. "She asked for it" is inseparable from a more general "psychology of the dupe." If I use bad judgment and fail to read the small print in a contract and later get taken advantage of ("screwed" or "fucked over") then I deserve what I get; bad judgment makes me liable. Analogously, if a woman trusts a man and goes to his apartment, or accepts a ride hitchhiking, or goes out on a date and is raped, she's a dupe and deserves what she gets. "He didn't *really* rape her" goes the mentality—"he merely took advantage of her." And in America it's okay for people to take advantage of each other, even expected and praised. In fact, you're considered dumb and foolish if you don't take advantage of other people's bad judgment. And so, again, by treating them as dupes, rape will be blamed on women.

Fifth, if a woman who is raped is judged attractive by men, and particularly if she dresses to look attractive, then the mentality exists that she attacked him with her weapon so, of course, he counter-attacked with his. The preview to a popular movie states: "She was the victim of her own *provocative beauty*." Provocation: "There is a line which, if crossed, will *set me off* and I will lose control and no longer be responsible for my behavior. If you punch me in the nose then, of course, I will not be responsible for what happens: you will have provoked a fight. If you dress, talk, move, or act a certain way, you will have provoked me to rape. If your appearance *stuns* me, *strikes* me, *ravishes* me, *knocks me out*, etc., then I will not be held responsible for what happens; you will have asked for it." The notion that sexual feeling makes one helpless is part of a cultural abdication of responsibility for sexuality. So long as a woman's appearance is viewed as a weapon and sexual feeling is believed to make one helpless, women will be blamed for rape.

Sixth, I have suggested that men sometimes become obsessed with images of women, that images become a substitute for sexual feeling, that sexual feeling becomes externalized and out of control and is given an undifferentiated identity in the appearance of women's bodies. It is a process of projection in which one blurs one's own desire with her imagined, projected desire. If a woman's attractiveness is taken to signify one's own lust and a woman's lust, then when an "attractive" woman is raped, some men may think she wanted sex. Since they perceive their own lust in part projected onto the woman, they disbelieve women who've been raped. So long as men project their own sexual desires onto women, they will blame women for rape.

And seventh, what are we to make of the contention that women in dating situations say "no" initially to sexual overtures from men as a kind of pose, only to give in later, thus revealing their true intentions? And that men are thus confused and incredulous when women are raped because in their sexual experience women can't be believed? I doubt that this has much to do with men's perceptions of rape. I don't know to what extent women actually "say no and mean yes"; certainly it is a common theme in male folklore. I have spoken to a couple of women who went through periods when they wanted to be sexual but were afraid to be, and often rebuffed initial sexual advances only to give in later. One point is clear: the ambivalence women may feel about having sex is closely tied to the inability of men to fully accept them as sexual beings. Women have been traditionally punished for being openly and freely sexual; men are praised for it. And if many men think of sex as achievement of possession of a valued commodity, or aggressive degradation, then women have every reason to feel and act ambivalent.

. . .

These ideas are illustrated in an interview I conducted with a 23-year-old man who grew up in Pittsburgh, and works as a file clerk in the financial district of San Francisco. Here is what he said:

Where I work it's probably no different from any other major city in the U.S. The women dress up in high heels, and they wear a lot of makeup, and they just look really *hot* and really sexy, and how can somebody who has a healthy sex drive not feel lust for them when you see them? I feel lust for them, but I don't think I could find it in me to overpower someone and rape them. But I definitely get the feeling that I'd like to rape a girl. I don't know if the actual act of rape would be satisfying, but the *feeling* is satisfying.

These women look so good, and they kiss ass of the men in the three-piece suits who are *big* in the corporation, and most of them relate to me like "Who are *you*? Who are *you* to even *look* at?" They're snobby and they condescend to me, and I resent it. It would take me a lot longer to get to first base than it would somebody with a three-piece suit who had money. And to me a lot of the men they go out with are superficial assholes who have no real feelings or substance, and are just trying to get ahead and make a lot of money. Another thing that makes me resent these women is thinking, "How could she want to hang out with somebody like that? What does that make her?"

I'm a file clerk, which makes me feel like a nebbish, a nurd, like I'm not making it, I'm a failure. But I don't really believe I'm a failure because I know it's just a phase, and I'm just doing it for the money, just to make it through this phase. I catch myself feeling like a failure, but I realize that's ridiculous.

What exactly do you go through when you see these sexy, unavailable women?

Let's say I see a woman and she looks really pretty and really clean and sexy, and she's giving off very feminine, sexy vibes. I think, "Wow, I would love to make love to her," but I know she's not really interested. It's a tease. A lot of times a woman knows that she's looking really good and she'll use that and flaunt it, and it makes me feel like she's laughing at me and I feel *degraded.*

I also feel dehumanized, because when I'm being teased I just turn off, I cease to be human. Because if I go with my human emotions I'm going to want to put my arms around her and kiss her, and to do that would be unacceptable. I don't like the feeling that I'm supposed to stand there and take it, and not be able to hug her or kiss her; so I just turn off my emotions. It's a feeling of humiliation, because the woman has forced me to turn off my feelings and react in a way that I really don't want to.

If I were actually desperate enough to rape somebody, it would be from wanting the person, but also it would be a very spiteful thing, just being able to say, "I have power over you and I can do anything I want with you," because really I feel that *they* have power over *me* just by their presence. Just the fact that they can come up to me and just melt me and make me feel like a dummy makes me want revenge. They have power over me so I want power over them. . . .

Society says that you have to have a lot of sex with a lot of different women to be a real man. Well, what happens if you don't? Then what are you? Are you half a man? Are you still a boy? It's ridiculous. You see a whiskey ad with a guy and two women on his arm. The implication is that real men don't have any trouble getting women.

How does it make you feel toward women to see all these sexy women in media and advertising using their looks to try to get you to buy something?

It makes me hate them. As a man you're taught that men are more powerful than women, and that men always have the upper hand, and that it's a man's society; but then you see all these women and it makes you think, "Jesus Christ, if we have all the power how come all the beautiful women are telling us what to buy?" And to be honest, it just makes me hate beautiful women because they're using their power over me. I realize they're being used themselves, and they're doing it for the money. In *Playboy* you see all these beautiful women who look so sexy and they'll be giving you all these looks like they want to have sex so bad; but then in reality you know that except for a few nymphomaniacs, they're doing it for the money; so I hate them for being used and for using their bodies in that way.

In this society, if you ever sit down and realize how manipulated you really are it makes you pissed off—it makes you want to take control. And you've been manipulated by women, and they're a very easy target because they're out walking along the streets, so you can just grab one and say, "Listen, you're going to do what I want you to do," and it's an act of revenge against the way you've been manipulated.

I know a girl who was walking down the street by her house, when this guy jumped her and beat her up and raped her, and she was black and blue and had to go to the hospital. That's beyond me. I can't understand how somebody could do that. If I were going to rape a girl, I wouldn't hurt her. I might *restrain* her, but I wouldn't *hurt* her. . . .

The whole dating game between men and women also makes me feel degraded. I hate being put in the position of having to initiate a relationship. I've been taught that if you're not aggressive with a woman, then you've blown it. She's not going to jump on *you*, so *you've* got to jump on *her*. I've heard all kinds of stories where the woman says, "No! No! No!" and they end up making great love. I get confused as hell if a woman pushes me away. Does it mean she's trying to be a nice girl and wants to put up a good appearance, or does it mean she doesn't want anything to do with you? You don't know. Probably a lot of men think that women don't feel like real women unless a man tries to force himself on her, unless she brings out the "real man," so to speak, and probably too much of it goes on. It goes on in my head that you're complimenting a woman by actually staring at her or by trying to get into her pants. Lately, I'm realizing that when I stare at women lustfully, they often feel more threatened than flattered.

Notes

1. Such estimates recur in the rape literature. See *Sexual Assault* by Nancy Gager and Cathleen Schurr, Grosset and Nunlap, 1976 or *The Price of Coercive Sexuality* by Clark and Lewis, The Woman's Press, 1977.
2. *Uniform Crime Reports*, 1980.
3. See *Behind Closed Doors* by Murray J. Strauss and Richard Gelles, Doubleday, 1979.
4. See Gager and Schurr (above) or virtually any book on the subject.
5. Again, see Gager and Schurr, or Carol V. Horos, *Rape*, Banbury Books, 1981.
6. From "Willamette Bridge" in *Body Politics* by Nancy Henley, Prentice-Hall, 1977, p. 144.

PART THREE

The Developing Science

CHAPTER NINE

Feminist Foundations

This section includes three important foundation articles for the discipline of psychology of women. Current contributors to research and theory in the psychology of women owe a great deal to the pioneering thoughts expressed in these pieces. It should be noted, however, that these pieces represent only a tiny sample of the important feminist foundations in the field.

In the first article, Maxine Bernstein and Nancy Felipe Russo begin by asking their readers to try answering a series of questions. Today you, like their own colleagues back in the early 1970s, will probably have a hard time answering even one of them. In this piece, originally published in *American Psychologist*, Bernstein and Russo argue that the study of psychology of women must include the study of women in psychology. To that end, they provide a brief but fascinating intellectual history of women's contributions to psychology. Twenty years later the article is still sobering, and we would do well to heed the authors' call not only to rediscover our foremothers but also to insure that the contributions of contemporary women in psychology are preserved.

In the next piece, originally a paper presented at the American Studies Association conference in 1968, Naomi Weisstein offers one of the first feminist critiques of American psychology's attempts to describe women's "nature." She argues persuasively that psychology's "scientific" theories about women fit precisely with common stereotypes about them, and that these theories serve the purpose of keeping women economically and socially subordinated to men. Perhaps more profoundly, however, she offers two explanations for the failure of psychological research to say anything at all about what women are really like: 1) many researchers in psychology simply refuse to accept ample empirical evidence refuting stereotypes about women; and 2) too many psychologists assume that people exist free of social context and ignore the tremendously unequal social expectations for men and women that undoubtedly affect their behavior. This clever and often bitterly humorous article can, in many ways, be thought of as the clarion call for the birth of a new field: the psychology of women.

In an enormously important *American Psychologist* article from 1975, Stephanie Shields explores the influence of evolutionary theory on the psychology of women. She argues that three topics were of special importance during the functionalist era in psychology: 1) structural brain differences between males and females, and how these differences influence intelligence and temperament; 2) the hypothesis that males are more "variable" psychologically than females, and how this relates to differences between men and women in social and educational opportunity; and 3) the concept of the "maternal instinct," and its importance in understanding women's "nature." Most fascinating, Shields points out that since the 1930s, these three topics, "where they are politically and socially useful . . . have an uncanny knack of reappearing, albeit in an altered form." Indeed, newer technologies for brain scanning have recently brought about a renewed interest in structural brain differences between males and females, for example. The concept of the "maternal instinct" has also reappeared, in altered form, in the writings of contemporary psychoanalytic feminists such as Nancy Chodorow, who argue that women have a greater capacity than men for relatedness and caring (mothering).

To say that this book is about the "psychology of women" is, of course, to imply that there is such a thing, that "women" are a group clearly enough defined to have a "psychology." But women come in all sorts of colors, sizes, shapes, ages, ethnicities, religions, ability levels, and classes, and they therefore have many psychologies. Unfortunately, until quite recently psychology has been interested in understanding differences between women and men, to the exclusion of understanding differences among women. This has been partly due to the ambivalent relationship between feminism and ethnicism, defined as the movement to promote equality among ethnic and racial groups (Comas-Diaz, 1991). Women of color's often complex dual commitment to gender and race has fortunately begun to be recognized recently, reducing some of the alienation they have felt, and paving the way for their unique and important contributions to the feminist agenda. On this, I strongly recommend an article by Aida Hurtado, "Relating to Privilege: Seduction and Rejection in the Subordination of White Women and Women of Color." Hurtado explores the ways in which ethnic and racial diversity among women shapes the ways in which they are subordinated relative to the culture's dominant class (i.e., white men).

The articles in this section are meant to provide a sample of particularly influential theoretical work in psychology of women. What is perhaps most notable about them is their endurance. Some are now over thirty years old yet continue to offer thought-provoking material for reflection and discussion. Does this mean we have come very far in our thinking about the psychology of women, or that we have hardly moved at all? An open question.

References

Comas-Diaz, L. (1991). Feminism and diversity in psychology. *Psychology of Women Quarterly, 15*, 597–609.

Hurtado, A. (1989). Relating to privilege. *Signs: The Journal of Women in Culture and Society, 14*, 833–855.

29 The History of Psychology Revisited: Or, Up with Our Foremothers

MAXINE D. BERNSTEIN

NANCY FELIPE RUSSO

Test yourself (no peeking):

Q1. Who were the first persons to use the term *projective technique* in print?
Q2. Who was the first person to develop child analysis through play?
Q3. Who developed the Cattell Infant Intelligence Test Scale?
Q4. What do the following have in common?
Bender-Gestalt Test (Bender, 1938); Taylor Manifest Anxiety Scale (Taylor, 1953); Kent-Rosanoff Word Association Test (Kent & Rosanoff, 1910); Thematic Apperception Test (Morgan & Murray, 1935); Sentence Completion Method (Rohde, 1946).
Q5. The following are the last names of individuals who have contributed to the scientific study of human behavior. What else do these names have in common?
Ausubel, Bellak, Brunswick, Buhler, Dennis, Gardner, Gibson, Glueck, Harlow, Hartley, Hoffman, Horowitz, Jones, Kendler, Koch, Lacey, Luchins, Lynd, Murphy, Premack, Rossi, Sears, Sherif, Spence, Staats, Stendler, Whiting, Yarrow.

Now for the answers:

A1. Lois Murphy and Ruth Horowitz (1938).
A2. Hermine von Hug-Hellmuth (1921).
A3. Psyche Cattell (1947).
A4. A woman is either the senior author or the sole author of each work.
A5. They are the surnames of female social scientists.

When these questions were asked of an amicable male colleague, his response was to smile, shrug politely, and answer "That's nice—uh—so what?"

One answer to the question "So what?" can be found in an incident that occurred in the Cornell Psychology Department not so very long ago. Some psychology graduate students were concerned about departmental governance. They circulated a memo demanding that the faculty reevaluate department procedures. Included in the memo was the suggestion that the faculty revise its admission policies in light of the high proportion of women accepted for graduate study in psychology. "After all," it was pointed out, "women just drop out or go on to get married and waste their education. *Besides, what have women ever contributed to psychology, anyway?*"

That graduate students at a prestigious Ivy League school would hold so little respect for the contributions of women to their chosen field demonstrates that the male orientation of psychology goes beyond discrimination in employment (Astin et al., 1972), bias in selection of subjects (Carlson, 1971; Schultz, 1969), overgeneralization of findings from males to all persons (Dan & Beekman, 1972), or the formulation of concepts and theories (Broverman et al., 1972; Chesler, 1972; Weisstein, 1968). Male bias pervades the very essence of the profession—the historical definition of the field of psychology itself.

In addition, the fact that two of the originators of the memo at Cornell were attending a seminar on perceptual development given by Eleanor Gibson shows that this sexist attitude will not be overcome by exposure to one or two famed "exceptions." Change will require a reorientation of the professional socialization process. Psychology must rediscover the contributions of its women and give them equal time and space with those of men.

The benefits of sensitizing psychologists to the contributions of women to the field are many. Two of the most important ones are provision of role models and service as a source of pride and inspiration.

In addition, women's history can refute the stereotypes and myths that often form the foundation for discriminatory practices. If psychologists are taught to acknowledge, appreciate, and respect the contributions of women to the profession, their image of women cannot help but be altered, and behavioral change can thus be facilitated.

The lack of historical insight into the contributions of women psychologists is due to a multiplicity of causes, one of the simplest, and most insidious, being our method of documentation. In some publications only initials are used to indicate first names in bibliographies, while in others initials are used for men and women's names are spelled out in full. This inconsistency leads one to assume that the lack of a first name in a citation indicates that the work was done by a man. Unless they are directly involved in a research area, using original sources, psychologists are dependent on informal means (personal stories, anecdotes, etc.) to tell them that "X" was a woman. Confusion is increased when women marry and change their names, losing continuity of documentation. As the years increase between the time a woman first publishes her research and the current moment in time, there is a decrement in the likelihood that someone will be around who "remembers" that this work was done by a woman.

The tendency to cite research by referring only to surnames carries over to informal conversation. Many people, for example, know Freud (1946) first reported on the defense mechanism of intellectualization, but few realize that in that case Freud's first name was Anna. When there are two psychologists of the same name—one male, one female—and research is cited by use of the last name only, it is often assumed that the work referred to is that of the male. If we begin to discuss the work of the social psychologist, Sherif, for example, how many people think of Carolyn? What a shock it was to go through six years of studying perception and then to find out that Zeigarnik's first name was Bluma.

Without a commitment by the profession to historical research and consciousness raising, the early contributions of women to psychology will be lost. We will probably never know how much work was done by women but credited to men: how many footnotes of appreciation should rightfully have been coauthorship, how many times junior authorship should have been senior authorship, or how many times it was the male coauthor who should have received the footnote. But we can, at least, become sensitive to the contributions that we do have record of and develop a better appreciation of them. Perhaps the question "What have women ever contributed to psychology" would not have been asked at Cornell had the students been aware that it was at this very University that Titchener's first doctoral student, Margaret Floy Washburn (1908), put together a compendium of animal psychology, which not only became a classic in the field, but which provided a partial impetus for the development of behaviorism.

Once one starts looking, contributions of women are found everywhere. Indeed, it is a source of inspiration that despite the discrimination, the hardships, and the restrictions, so many women did so much. Yet their work is not given proper recognition. . . .

The leadership of the American Psychological Association has recently been moving to assess and advance the position of women in the profession. The Task Force on the Status of Women in Psychology has done some very fine work toward these ends and has submitted a report which acknowledges the need for a professional reorientation. It recommends, among other things, that "appropriate subspecialties should inquire in depth into the psychology of women. New courses should be created to explore the psychology of women: e.g., developmental psychology of women, social psychology of women's status [Astin et al., 1977, p. 15]."

We affirm the exigency of such curriculum revision. However, psychologists must not limit themselves to the study of the psychology of women—they must also study the women of psychology. Without historical insight, without an intellectual history ("herstory?") women will never be truly integrated into the profession. The current approach seems to be "let us in." We think the approach should be "recognize that we are here—and we have been here for quite a while. See what we've done despite adverse circumstances and incredible odds. Think of what we could do if we had an equal chance."

So we say, "Up with our foremothers." Teach women in psychology their intellectual history and preserve the contributions of contemporary women. Women have a proud tradition of accomplishment in the profession. Let it be recognized—by both women and men.

References

Adorno, T. W., Frenkel-Brunswik, E., Levinson, D. J., & Sanford, R. N. *The authoritarian personality*. New York: Harper, 1950.

Anastasi, A. *Differential psychology*. New York: Macmillan, 1937.

Arnold, M. B. *Emotion and personality*. New York: Columbia University Press, 1960.

Astin, H. S., Bayton, J. A., Brackbill, Y., David, H. P., Fields, R. M., Kieffer, M. M., Maccoby, E. E., Rubinstein, E. A., McKeachie, W. A., &

Cummings, T. *Report of the Task Force on the Status of Women in Psychology.* Washington, D.C.: American Psychological Association, 1972.

Bandura, A., Ross, D., & Ross, S. Transmission of aggression through imitation of aggressive models. *Journal of Abnormal and Social Psychology,* 1961, 63, 575–582.

Baumrind, D. Some thoughts on ethics of research, after reading Milgram's "Behavioral study of obedience." *American Psychologist,* 1964, 19, 421–423.

Bayley, N. Mental growth during the first three years. *Genetic Psychology Monographs,* 1933, 14, 1–93.

Bender, L. A visual motor gestalt test and its clinical use. *American Orthopsychiatric Association, Research Monographs,* 1938, No. 3.

Benedict, R. *Patterns of culture.* Boston: Houghton Mifflin, 1934.

Benedict, R. Continuities and discontinuities in cultural conditioning. *Psychiatry,* 1938, 1, 161–167.

Berenda, R. W. *The influence of the group on the judgments of children.* New York: King's Crown Press, 1950.

Broverman, I. K., Vogel, S. R., Broverman, E. M., Clarkson, F. E., & Rosenkrantz, P. S. Sex-role stereotypes: A current appraisal. *Journal of Social Issues,* 1972, 28, 59–78.

Bruner, J. S., Goodnow, J., & Austin, G. A., *A study of thinking.* New York: Wiley, 1956.

Buhler, C. *The child and his family.* New York: Harper, 1939.

Burks, B. S., Jensen, D. W., & Terman, L. M. *Genetic studies of genius: The promise of youth.* Stanford: Stanford University Press, 1930.

Carlson, R. Where is the person in personality research? *Psychological Bulletin,* 1971, 75, 203–219.

Cattell, P. *The measurement of intelligence of infants and young children.* New York: Psychological Corporation, 1947.

Chesler, P. *Women and madness.* New York: Doubleday, 1972.

Christie, R., & Geis, F. (Eds.) *Studies in Machiavellianism.* New York: Academic Press, 1958.

Cox, C. M. *Genetic studies of genius: The early mental traits of three hundred geniuses.* Vol. 2. Stanford: Stanford University Press, 1926.

Dan, A. J., & Beekman, S. Male versus female representation in psychological research. *American Psychologist,* 1972, 27, 1078.

Eggan, D. The significance of dreams for anthropological research. *American Anthropologist,* 1949, 51, 171–198.

Fernald, M. R. The diagnosis of mental imagery. *Psychological Monographs,* 1912 14(1, Whole No. 58).

Frenkel-Brunswik, E., Levinson, D. J., & Sanford, R. N. The antidemocratic personality. In E. Maccoby, T. M. Newcomb, & E. L. Hartley (Eds.), *Readings in social psychology.* New York: Holt, 1958.

Freud, A. *The ego and the mechanisms of defense.* New York: International Universities Press, 1946.

Goldman-Eisler, F. Breastfeeding and character formation. In C. Kluckhohn, H. A. Murray, & D. M. Schneider (Eds.), *Personality in nature, society and culture.* New York: Knopf, 1953.

Goodenough, F. L. *Developmental psychology.* New York: Appleton-Century, 1945.

Healy, W., & Fernald, G. Tests for practical mental classification. *Psychological Monographs,* 1910, 13(2, Whole No. 54).

Henle, M. (Ed.) *Documents of Gestalt psychology.* Berkeley: University of California Press, 1961.

Horney, K. *New ways in psychoanalysis.* New York: Norton, 1939.

Horowitz, R. E., & Murphy, L. B. Projective methods in the psychological study of children. *Journal of Experimental Education,* 1938, 7, 133–140.

Hug-Hellmuth, H. On the techniques of child analysis. *International Journal of Psychoanalysis,* 1921, 2, 294–295.

Hurlock, E. B. The use of group rivalry as an incentive. *Journal of Abnormal and Social Psychology,* 1927, 22, 278–290.

Jahoda, M., Deutsch, M., & Cook, S. E. (Eds.) *Research methods in social relations.* New York: Dryden, 1951.

Kent, G., & Rosanoff, A. J. A study in association in insanity. *American Journal of Insanity,* 1910, 67, 37–96.

Klein, M. *Contributions to psychoanalysis, 1921–1945.* London: Hogarth Press, 1948.

Kluckhohn, C., & Leighton, D. *The Navaho.* Cambridge: Harvard University Press, 1946.

Kluckhohn, F., & Strodtbeck, F. *Variations in value orientations.* Evanston, Ill.: Row, Peterson, 1961.

Leighton, D., & Kluckhohn, C. *Children of the people.* Cambridge: Harvard University Press, 1947.

Lord, E. Experimentally induced variations in Rorschach performance. *Psychological Monographs,* 1950, 64(10, Whole No. 316).

Maccoby, E. E., Newcomb, T. M., & Hartley, E. L. *Readings in social psychology.* New York: Holt, 1958.

Mead, M. Adolescence in primitive and modern society. In V. F. Calverton & S. D. Schmallhausen (Eds.), *The new generation.* New York: Macauley, 1930.

Morgan, C. D., & Murray, H. A. A method for investigating fantasies. *Archives Neurology and Psychiatry,* 1935, 34, 289–306.

Murphy, L. B. *Social behavior and child personality.* New York: Columbia University Press, 1937.

Rickers-Ovsiankina, M. *Rorschach psychology.* New York: Wiley, 1960.

Rohde, A. R. Explorations in personality by the sentence-completion method. *Journal of Applied Psychology,* 1946, 30, 169–181.

Rosenthal, R. *Experimenter effects in behavioral research.* New York: Appleton-Century-Crofts, 1966.

Schultz, D. P. The human subject in psychological research. *Psychological Bulletin,* 1969, 72, 214–228.

Sherif, M., & Sherif, C. W. *Groups in harmony and tension.* New York: Harper, 1953.
Shirley, M. M. *The first two years: A study of twenty-five babies.* Vols. 1–3. Minneapolis: University of Minnesota Press, 1933.
Strickland, B. R., & Crowne, D. P. Conformity under conditions of simulated group pressure as a function of the need for social approval. *Journal of Social Psychology*, 1962, 58, 171–181.
Taylor, J. A. A personality scale of manifest anxiety, *Journal of Abnormal and Social Psychology*, 1953, 48, 285–290.
Terman, L. M., & Merrill, M. *Measuring intelligence.* Boston: Houghton Mifflin, 1937.
Tyler, L. E. *The psychology of human differences.* New York: Appleton-Century-Crofts, 1956.
Vernon, M. D. *Visual perception.* New York: Macmillan, 1937.
Washburn, M. F. *The animal mind.* New York: Macmillan, 1908.
Watson, J. B., & Rayner, R. Conditioning emotional reactions. *Journal of Experimental Psychology*, 1920, 3, 1–14.
Weisstein, N. *Kinder, küche, kirche as scientific law: Psychology constructs the female.* Boston: New England Free Press, 1968.
Wolfenstein, M., & Leites, N. *Movies: A psychological study.* Glencoe, Ill.: Free Press, 1950.

30 "Kinder, Küche, Kirche" as Scientific Law: Psychology Constructs the Female

NAOMI WEISSTEIN

It is an implicit assumption that the area of psychology which concerns itself with personality has the onerous but necessary task of describing the limits of human possibility. Thus when we are about to consider the liberation of women, we naturally look to psychology to tell us what "true" liberation would mean: what would give women the freedom to fulfill their own intrinsic natures.

Psychologists have set about describing the true natures of women with an enthusiasm and absolute certainty which is rather disquieting. Bruno Bettelheim of the University of Chicago, tells us that:

> We must start with the realization that, as much as women want to be good scientists or engineers, they want first and foremost to be womanly companions of men and to be mothers.[1]

Erik Erikson of Harvard University, upon noting that young women often ask whether they can "have an identity before they know whom they will marry, and for whom they will make a home," explains somewhat elegiacally that "Much of a young woman's identity is already defined in her kind of attractiveness and in the selectivity of her search for the man (or men) by whom she wishes to be sought. . . ."[2] Mature womanly fulfillment, for Erikson, rests on the fact that a woman's ". . . somatic design harbors an 'inner space' destined to bear the offspring of chosen men, and with it, a biological, psychological, and ethical commitment to take care of human infancy."[3] Some psychiatrists even see the acceptance of woman's role by women as a solution to societal problems. "Woman is nurturance . . . ," writes Joseph Rheingold, a psychiatrist at Harvard Medical School, " . . . Anatomy decrees the life of a woman. . . . When women grow up without dread of their biological functions and without subversion by feminist doctrine, and therefore enter upon motherhood with a sense of fulfillment and altruistic sentiment, we shall attain the goal of a good life and a secure world in which to live it."[4]

These views from men of high prestige reflect a fairly general consensus within psychology: liberation for women will consist first in their attractiveness, so that second, they may obtain the kinds of homes, and the kinds of men, which will allow joyful altruism and nurturance. . . .

It is an interesting but limited exercise to show that psychologists' ideas of women's nature fit so remarkably the common prejudice and serve industry and commerce so well. Just because it's good for business doesn't mean it's wrong. What we will show is that it *is wrong*; that there isn't the tiniest shred of evidence that these fantasies of servitude and childish dependence have anything to do with women's true potential; that the idea of the nature of human possibility which rests on the accidents of individual development or genitalia, on what is possible today because of what happened yesterday, on the fundamentalist myth of sex-organ causality, has strangled and deflected psychology so that it is relatively useless in describing, explaining, or predicting humans and their behavior.

It then goes without saying that present psychology is less than worthless in contributing to a vision which could truly liberate—men as well as women.

My central argument, then, is this. Psychology has nothing to say about what women are really like, what they need and what they want, essentially, because psychology does not know. I want to stress that this failure is not limited to women; rather, the kind of psychology which has addressed itself to how people act and who they are has failed to understand, in the first place, why people act the way they do, and certainly failed to understand what might make them act differently.

The kind of psychology which has addressed itself to these questions has been in large part clinical psychology and psychiatry. Here, the causes of failure are obvious and appalling: Freudians and neo-Freudians, Adlerians and neo-Adlerians, classicists and swingers, clinicians and psychiatrists in general have simply refused to look at the evidence against their theory and their practice, and have used as evidence of their theory and their practice stuff so flimsy and transparently biased as to have absolutely no standing as empirical evidence. But even psychology which conforms to rigorous methodology (academic personality research) has gone about looking at people in such a way as to have limited usefulness. This is because it has been a central assumption for most psychologists of human personality that human behavior rests primarily on an individual and inner dynamic, perhaps fixed in infancy, perhaps fixed by genitalia, perhaps simply arranged in a rather immovable cognitive network. But this assumption is rapidly losing ground as personality psychologists fail again and again to find consistency in the assumed personalities of their subjects[5] and as the evidence demonstrates that what a person does and who he believes himself to be, will in general be a function of what people around him expect him to be, and what the overall situation in which he is acting implies that he is. Compared to the influence of the social context within which a person lives, his or her history and "traits," as well as biological makeup may simply be random variations, "noise" superimposed on the true signal which can predict behavior. To summarize: the first reason for psychology's failure to understand what people are and how they act, is that clinicians and psychiatrists, who are generally the theoreticians on these matters, have essentially made up myths without any evidence to support these myths; the second reason for psychology's failure is that personality theory has looked for inner traits when it should have been looking at social context. . . .

I want to turn now to my second major point, which is that, even when psychological theory is constructed so that it may be tested, and rigorous standards of evidence are used, it has become increasingly clear that in order to understand why people do what they do, and certainly in order to change what people do, psychologists must turn away from the theory of the causal nature of the inner dynamic and look to the social context within which individuals live.

Before examining the relevance of this approach for the question of women, let me first sketch the groundwork for this assertion.

In the first place, it is clear that personality tests never yield consistent predictions; a rigid authoritarian on one measure will be an unauthoritarian on the next.[6] But the reason for this inconsistency is only now becoming clear, and it seems overwhelmingly to have much more to do with the social situation in which the subject finds himself than with the subject himself.

In a series of brilliant experiments, Rosenthal and his co-workers have shown that if one group of experimenters has one hypothesis about what they expect to find, and another group of experimenters has the opposite hypothesis, both groups will in fact obtain results in accord with their hypotheses.[7] The results obtained are not due to mishandling of data by biased experimenters; rather, somehow, the bias of the experimenter creates a changed environment in which subjects actually act differently. For instance, in one experiment, subjects were to assign numbers to pictures of men's faces, with high numbers representing the subject's judgment that the man in the picture was a successful person, and low numbers representing the subject's judgment that the man in the picture was an unsuccessful person. One group of experimenters was told that the subjects tended to rate faces high; another group of experimenters was told that subjects tended to rate the faces low. Each group of experimenters was instructed to follow precisely the same procedure: they were required to read a set of instructions to subjects and to say nothing else. For the 375 subjects run, the results showed clearly that those subjects who performed the task with experimenters who expected high ratings gave high ratings; those subjects who performed the task with experimenters who expected low ratings gave low ratings. (The results would have happened by chance about one in one thousand times.) How did this happen? The experimenters all used the same words; it was something in their conduct which made one group of subjects do one thing, and another group of subjects do another thing.

The concreteness of the changed conditions produced by expectation is a fact, a reality: even with animal subjects, where there can be no verbal communication, in two separate studies[8] those experimenters who were told that rats learning mazes had been especially bred for brightness obtained better learning from their rats than did experimenters believing their rats to have been bred for dullness. In a recent study, Rosenthal and Jacobson extended their analysis to the natural classroom situation. Here, they tested a group of students and reported to the teachers that some among the students tested "showed great promise." Actually, the students so named had been selected on a random basis. Sometime later, the experimenters retested the group of students; those students whose teachers had been told that they were promising showed real and dramatic increments in their I.Q.'s as compared to the rest of the students. Something in the conduct of the teachers towards the "bright" students made them brighter.

Thus, even in carefully controlled experiments, and with no outward or conscious difference in behavior, the hypotheses we start with will influence enormously the behavior of another organism. These studies are extremely important when assessing the validity of psychological studies of women. Since it is fairly safe to say that most of us start with hypotheses as to the nature of men and women, the validity of a number of observations on sex differences is questionable, even when these observations have been taken under carefully controlled conditions. Second, and more importantly, the Rosenthal experiments point quite clearly to the influence of social expectation. In some extremely important ways, people are what you expect them to be, or at least they behave as you expect them to behave. Thus, if women, according to Bruno Bettelheim, want first and foremost to be good wives and mothers, it is extremely likely that that is what Bruno Bettelheim (and the rest of the society) want them to be.

There is another series of social psychological experiments which points to the inescapable, overwhelming weight of social context in an extremely vivid way. These are the obedience experiments of Stanley Milgram,[9] concerned with the extent to which subjects in psychological experiments will obey the orders of unknown experimenters, even when these orders carry with them the distinct possibility that the subject is killing somebody.

In Milgram's experiments a subject is told that he is administering a learning experiment, and that he is to deal out shocks each time the other "subject" (in reality, a confederate of the experimenter) answers incorrectly. The equipment appears to provide graduated shocks ranging upwards from 15 to 450 volts; for each four consecutive voltages there are verbal descriptions such as "mild shock," "danger, severe shock," and finally, for the 435 and 450 volt switches, simply a red XXX marked over the switches. Each time the stooge answers incorrectly the subject is supposed to increase the voltage. As the voltage increases the stooge begins to cry in pain; he demands that the experiment stop; finally, he refuses to answer at all. When he stops responding, the experimenter instructs the subject to continue increasing the voltage; for each shock administered, the stooge shrieks in agony. Under these conditions, about 62.5 percent of the subjects administered shock that they believed to be possibly lethal.

No tested individual differences between subjects predicted which of the subjects would continue to obey, and which would break off the experiment. When forty psychiatrists predicted how many of a group of one hundred subjects would go on to give the maximum shock, their predictions were far below the actual percentages; most expected only one-tenth of 1 percent of the subjects to obey to the end. But even though psychiatrists have no idea of how people are going to behave in this situation (despite the fact that one of the central phenomena of the twentieth century is that people have been made to kill enormous numbers of other people), and even though individual differences do not predict which subjects will obey and which will not, it is easy to predict when subjects will be obedient and when they will be defiant. All the experimenter has to do is change the social situation. In a variant of Milgram's experiment, two stooges were present in addition to the "victim;" these worked along with the subject in administering electric shocks. When these two stooges refused to go on with the experiment, only ten percent continued to the maximum voltage. This is critical for personality theory. It says that the lawful behavior is the behavior that can be predicted from the social situation, not from the individual history. . . .

To summarize: if subjects under quite innocuous and noncoercive social conditions can be made to kill other subjects and under other types of social conditions will positively refuse to do so; . . . if students become intelligent because teachers expect them to be intelligent, and rats run mazes better because experimenters are told that the rats are bright, then it is obvious that a study of human behavior requires first and foremost, a study of the social contexts within which people move, the expectations as to how they will behave, and the authority which tells them who they are and what they are supposed to do.

Two theories of the nature of women, which come not from psychiatric and clinical tradition, but from biology, can be disposed of now with little difficulty. The first argument notices social interaction in primate groups, and observes that females are submissive and passive. Putting aside for a moment the serious problem of experimenter bias,[10] the problem with the argument from primate groups is that the crucial experiment has not been performed. The crucial experiment would manipulate or change the social organization of these groups, and watch the subsequent behavior. Until then, we must conclude that, since primates are at present too stupid to change their social conditions by themselves, the "innateness" and fixedness of the behavior is simply not known. As applied to humans, the argument becomes patently irrelevant, since the most salient feature of human social organization is its variety; and there are a number of cultures where there is at least a rough equality between men and women.[11] Thus, primate arguments tell us very little.

The second theory of sex differences argues that since females and males differ in their sex hormones, and sex hormones enter the brain, there must be innate differences in "nature."[12] But the only thing this argument tells us is that there are differences in physiological state. The problem is whether these differences are at all relevant to behavior. . . .

Schachter and Singer[13] have shown that a particular physiological state can itself lead to a multiplicity of felt emotional states, and outward behavior, depending on the social situation.

In brief, the uselessness of present psychology with regard to women, is simply a special case of the general conclusion: one must understand social expectations about women if one is going to characterize the behavior of women.

How are women characterized in our culture, and in psychology? They are inconsistent, emotionally unstable, lacking in a strong conscience or superego, weaker, "nurturant" rather than productive, "intuitive" rather than intelligent, and, if they are at all "normal," suited to the home and the family. In short, the list adds up to a typical minority group stereotype of inferiority: if they know their place, which is in the home, they are really quite lovable, happy, childlike, loving creatures.[14] In a review of the intellectual differences between little boys and little girls, Eleanor Maccoby[15] has shown that there are no intellectual differences until about high school, or, if there are, girls are slightly ahead of boys. At high school, girls begin to do worse on a few intellectual tasks, such as arithmetic reasoning, and beyond high school, the achievement of women now measured in terms of productivity and accomplishment drops off even more rapidly. There are a number of other, nonintellectual tests which show sex differences; I choose the intellectual differences since it is seen clearly that women start becoming inferior. It is no use to talk about women being different but equal; all of the tests I can think of have a "good" outcome and a "bad" outcome. Women usually end up at the "bad" outcome. In light of social expectations about women, what is surprising is not that women end up where society expects they will; what is surprising is that little girls don't get the message that they are supposed to be stupid until high school; and what is even more remarkable is that some women resist this message even after high school, college, and graduate school.

I began with remarks on the task of discovering the limits of human potential. Until psychologists realize that it is they who are limiting discovery of human potential, by their refusal to accept evidence, if they are clinical psychologists, or, if they are rigorous, by their assumption that people move in a context-free ether, with only their innate dispositions and their individual traits determining what they will do, then psychology will have nothing of substance to offer in this task. I don't know what immutable differences exist between men and women apart from differences in their genitalia; perhaps there are some other unchangeable differences; probably there are a number of irrelevant differences. But it is clear that until social expectations for men and women are equal, until we provide equal respect for both men and women, our answers to this question will simply reflect our prejudices.

Notes

1. Bruno Bettelheim, "The Commitment Required of a Woman Entering a Scientific Profession in Present Day American Society," *Woman and the Scientific Professions*, MIT symposium on American Women in Science and Engineering, 1965.
2. Erik Erikson, "Inner and Outer Space: Reflections on Womanhood." *Daedelus* (93), 1964.
3. *Ibid.*
4. Joseph Rheingold, *The Fear of Being a Woman* (New York: Grune & Stratton, 1964), p. 714.
5. J. Block, "Some Reasons for the Apparent Inconsistency of Personality," *Psychological Bulletin* (70) 1968.
6. J. Block, *op. cit.*
7. R. Rosenthal and L. Jacobson, *Pygmalion in the Classroom: Teacher Expectation and Pupil's Intellectual Development* (New York: Holt, Rinehart & Winston, 1968); R. Rosenthal, *Experimenter Effects in Behavioral Research* (New York: Appleton-Century Crofts, 1966).
8. R. Rosenthal and K. L. Fode, "The Effect of Experimenter Bias on the Performance of the Albino Rat," (Harvard University, 1961); R. Rosenthal and R. Lawson, "A Longitudinal Study of the Effects of Experimenter Bias on the Operant Learning of Laboratory Rats," (Harvard University, 1961).
9. Stanley Milgram, "Liberating Effects of Group Pressure," *Journal of Personality and Social Psychology* (1) 1965.
10. For example, H. F. Harlow, "The Heterosexual Affectional System in Monkeys," *The American Psychologist* (17) 1962. After observing differences between male and female rhesus monkeys, Harlow quotes Lawrence Sterne to the effect that women are silly and trivial, and concludes that "men and women have differed in the past and they will differ in the future."
11. Margaret Mead, *Male and Female: A Study of the Sexes in a Changing World* (New York: Mentor, 1955).
12. D. A. Hamburg and D. T. Lunde, "Sex Hormones in the Development of Sex Differences in Human Behavior," in Maccoby, ed. *The Development of Sex Differences* (Stanford: Stanford University Press, 1966), pp. 1–24.
13. S. Schachter and J. E. Singer, "Cognitive, Social, and Physiological Determinants of Emotional State," *Psychological Review* (69) 1962.
14. H. M. Hacker, "Women as a Minority Group," *Social Forces* (30) 1951.
15. Eleanor E. Maccoby, "Sex Differences in Intellectual Functioning," in Maccoby, *op. cit.*

31 Functionalism, Darwinism, and the Psychology of Women: A Study in Social Myth

STEPHANIE A. SHIELDS

The psychology of women is acquiring the character of an academic entity as witnessed by the proliferation of research on sex differences, the appearance of textbooks devoted to the psychology of women, and the formation of a separate APA division, Psychology of Women. Nevertheless, there is almost universal ignorance of the psychology of women as it existed prior to its incorporation into psychoanalytic theory. If the maxim "A nation without a history is like a man without a memory" can be applied, then it would behoove the amnesiacs interested in female psychology to investigate its pre-Freudian past.

The article focuses on one period of that past (from the latter half of the 19th century to the first third of the 20th) in order to clarify the important issues of the time and trace their development to the position they occupy in current psychological theory. Even a limited overview leads the reader to appreciate Helen Thompson Woolley's (1910) early appraisal of the quality of the research on sex differences:

> There is perhaps no field aspiring to be scientific where flagrant personal bias, logic martyred in the cause of supporting a prejudice, unfounded assertions, and even sentimental rot and drivel, have run riot to such an extent as here. (p. 340)

The Functionalist Milieu

Although the nature of woman had been an academic and social concern of philosopher psychologists throughout the ages, formed psychology (its inception usually dated 1879) was relatively slow to take up the topic of female psychology. The "woman question" was a social one, and social problems did not fall within the sharply defined limits of Wundt's "new" psychology. The business of psychology was the description of the "generalized adult mind," and it is not at all clear whether "adult" was meant to include both sexes. When the students of German psychology did venture outside of the laboratory, however, there is no evidence that they were sympathetic to those defending the equality of male and female ability (cf. Wundt, 1901).

It was the functionalist movement in the United States that fostered academic psychology's study of sex differences and, by extension, a prototypic psychology of women. The incorporation of evolutionary theory into the practice of psychology made the study of the female legitimate, if not imperative. It would be incorrect to assume that the psychology of women existed as a separate specialty within the discipline. The female was discussed only in relation to the male, and the function of the female was thought to be distinctly different from and complementary to the function of the male. The leitmotiv of evolutionary theory as it came to be applied to the social sciences was the evolutionary supremacy of the Caucasian male. The notion of the supplementary, subordinate role of the female was ancillary to the development of that theme.

The influence of evolutionary theory on the psychology of women can be traced along two major conceptual lines: (a) by emphasizing the biological foundations of temperament, evolutionary theory led to serious academic discussion of maternal instinct (as one facet of the general topic of instinct); and (b) by providing a theoretical justification of the study of individual differences, evolutionary theory opened the door to the study of sex differences in sensory, motor, and intellectual abilities. As a whole, the concept of evolution with its concomitant emphasis on biological determinism provided ample "scientific" reason for cataloging the "innate" differences in male and female nature.

This article examines three topics that were of special significance to the psychology of women during the functionalist era: (a) structural differences in the brains of males and females and the implications of these differences for intelligence and temperament, (b) the hypothesis of greater male variability and its relation to social and educational issues, and (c) maternal instinct and its meaning for a psychology of female "nature." As the functionalist paradigm gave way to behaviorism and psychoanalytic theory, the definition and "meaning" of each of these issues changed to fit the times. When issues faded in importance, it was not because they were resolved but because they ceased to serve as viable scientific "myths" in the changing social and scientific milieu. As the times change, so must the myths change.

The Female Brain

The topic of female intelligence came to 19th-century psychology via phrenology and the neuroanatomists. Philosophers of the time (e.g., Hegel, Kant, Schopenhauer) had demonstrated, to their satisfaction, the justice of woman's subordinate social position, and it was left to the men of science to discover the particular physiological determinants of female inadequacy. In earlier periods, woman's inferiority had been defined as a general "state" intimately related to the absence of qualities that would have rendered her a male and to the presence of reproductive equipment that destined her to be female. For centuries the mode of Eve's creation and her greater guilt for the fall from grace had been credited as the cause of woman's imperfect nature, but this was not an adequate explanation in a scientific age. Thus, science sought explanations for female inferiority that were more in keeping with contemporary scientific philosophy.

Although it had long been believed that the brain was the chief organ of the mind, the comparison of male and female mental powers traditionally included only allusions to vague "imperfections" of the female brain. More precise definition of the sites of these imperfections awaited the advancement of the concept of cortical localization of function. Then, as finer distinctions of functional areas were noted, there was a parallel recognition of the differences between those sites as they appeared in each sex.

At the beginning of the 19th century, the slowly increasing interest in the cerebral gyri rapidly gathered momentum with the popularization of phrenology. Introduced by Franz Joseph Gall, "cranioscopy," as he preferred to call it, postulated that the seat of various mental and moral faculties was located in specific areas of the brain's surface such that a surfeit or deficiency could be detected by an external examination of the cranium. Phrenology provided the first objective method for determining the neurological foundation of sex differences in intelligence and temperament that had long been promulgated. Once investigation of brain structure had begun, it was fully anticipated that visible sex differences would be found: Did not the difference between the sexes pervade every other aspect of physique and physiological function? Because physical differences were so obvious in every other organ of the body, it was unthinkable that the brain could have escaped the stamp of sex.

Gall was convinced that he could, from gross anatomical observation, discriminate between male and female brains, claiming that "if there had been presented to him in water, the fresh brains of two adult animals of any species, one male and the other female, he could have distinguished the two sexes" (Walker, 1850, p. 317). Gall's student and colleague, Johann Spurzheim, elaborated on this basic distinction by noting that the frontal lobes were less developed in females, "the organs of the perceptive faculties being commonly larger than those of the reflective powers." Gall also observed sex differences in the nervous tissue itself, "confirming" Malebranche's belief that the female "cerebral fibre" is softer than that of the male, and that it is also "slender and long rather than thick" (Walker, 1850, p. 318). Spurzheim also listed the cerebral "organs" whose appearance differed commonly in males and females: females tended to have the areas devoted to philoprogenetiveness and other "tender" traits most prominent, while in males, areas of aggressiveness and constructiveness dominated. Even though cranioscopy did not survive as a valid system of describing cortical function, the practice of comparing the appearance of all or part of the brain for anatomical evidence of quality of function remained one of the most popular means of providing proof of female mental inferiority. Most comparisons used adult human brains, but with the rise of evolutionary theory, increasing emphasis was placed on the value of developmental and cross-species comparisons. The argument for female mental inferiority took two forms: some argued that quality of intellect was proportional to absolute or relative brain size; others, more in the tradition of cortical localization, contended that the presence of certain mental qualities was dependent upon the development of corresponding brain centers.

The measurement of cranial capacity had long been in vogue as one method of determining intellectual ability. That women had smaller heads than men was taken by some as clear proof of a real disparity between male and female intelligence. The consistently smaller brain size of the female was cited as another anatomical indicator of its functional inferiority. More brain necessarily meant better brain; the exception only proved this rule. Alexander Bain (1875) was among those who believed that the smaller absolute brain size of females accounted for a lesser mental ability. George Romanes (1887) enumerated the "secondary sex characteristics" of mental abilities attributable to brain size. The smaller brain of women was directly responsible for their mental inferiority, which "displays itself most conspicuously in a comparative absence of originality, and this more especially in the higher levels of intellectual work" (p. 655). He, like many, allowed that women were to some degree compensated for intellectual inferiority by a superiority of instinct and perceptual ability. These advantages carried with them the germ of female failure, however, by making women more subject to emotionality. . . .

The Variability Hypothesis

The first systematic treatment of individual differences in intelligence appeared in 1575. Juan Huarte attributed sex differences in intelligence to the different humoral qualities that characterized each sex, a notion that had been popular in Western thought since ancient Greece. Heat and dryness were characteristics of the male principle, while moisture and coolness were female attributes. Because dryness of spirit was necessary for intelligence, males naturally possessed greater "wit." The maintenance of dryness and heat was the function of the testicles, and Huarte (1959) noted that if a man were castrated the effects were the same "as if he had received some notable dammage in his very braine" (p. 279). Because the principles necessary for cleverness were only possessed by males, it behooved parents to conduct their life-style, diet, and sexual intercourse in such a manner as to insure the conception of a male. The humoral theory of sex differences was widely accepted through the 17th century, but with the advent of more sophisticated notions of anatomy and physiology, it was replaced by other, more specific, theories of female mental defect: the lesser size and hypothesized simpleness of the female brain, affectability as the source of inferiority, and complementarity of abilities in male and female. It was the developing evolutionary theory that provided an overall explanation for why these sex differences existed and why they were necessary for the survival of the race.

The theory of evolution as proposed by Darwin had little to say regarding the intellectual capacity of either sex. It was in Francis Galton's (Charles Darwin's cousin) anthropometric laboratory that the investigation of intellectual differences took an empirical form (Galton, 1907). The major conclusion to come from Galton's research was that women tend in all their capacities to be inferior to men. He looked to common experience for confirmation, reasoning that:

> If the sensitivity of women were superior to that of men, the self interest of merchants would lead to their being always employed; but as the

> reverse is the case, the opposite supposition is likely to be the true one. (pp. 20–21)

This form of logic—women have not excelled, therefore they cannot excel—was often used to support arguments denigrating female intellectual ability. The fact of the comparative rarity of female social achievement was also used as "evidence" in what was later to become a widely debated issue concerning the range of female ability.

Prior to the formulation of evolutionary theory, there had been little concern with whether deviation from the average or "normal" occurred more frequently in either sex. One of the first serious discussions of the topic appeared in the early 19th century when the anatomist Meckel concluded on pathological grounds that the human female showed greater variability than the human male. He reasoned that because man is the superior animal and variability a sign of inferiority, this conclusion was justified (in Ellis, 1903, p. 237). The matter was left at that until 1871. At that time Darwin took up the question of variability in *The Descent of Man* while attempting to explain how it could be that in many species males had developed greatly modified secondary sexual characteristics while females of the same species had not. He determined that this was originally caused by the males' greater activity and "stronger passions" that were in turn more likely (he believed) to be transmitted to male offspring. Because the females would prefer to mate with the strong and passionate, sexual selection would insure the survival of those traits. A tendency toward greater variation per se was not thought to be responsible for the appearance of unusual characteristics, but "development of such characters would be much aided, if the males were more liable to vary than the females" (Darwin, 1922, p. 344). To support this hypothesis of greater male variability, he cited recent data obtained by anatomists and biologists that seemed to confirm the relatively more frequent occurrence of physical anomaly among males.

Because variation from the norm was already accepted as the mechanism of evolutionary progress (survival and transmission of adaptive variations) and because it seemed that the male was the more variable sex, it soon was universally concluded that the male is the progressive element in the species. Variation for its own sake took on a positive value because greatness, whether of an individual or a society, could not be achieved without variation. Once deviation from the norm became legitimized by evolutionary theory, the hypothesis of greater male variability became a convenient explanation for a number of observed sex differences, among them the greater frequency with which men achieved "eminence." By the 1890s it was popularly believed that greater male variability was a principle that held true, not only for physical traits but for mental abilities as well:

> That men should have greater cerebral variability and therefore more originality, while women have greater stability and therefore more "common sense," are facts both consistent with the general theory of sex and verifiable in common experience. (Geddes & Thomson, 1890, p. 271)

Havelock Ellis (1894), an influential sexologist and social philosopher, brought the variability hypothesis to the attention of psychologists in the first edition of *Man and Woman.* After examining anatomical and pathological data that indicated a greater male *variational tendency* (Ellis felt this term was less ambiguous than *variability*), he examined the evidence germane to a discussion of range of intellectual ability. After noting that there were more men than women in homes for the mentally deficient, which indicated a higher incidence of retardation among males, and that there were more men than women on the roles of the eminent, which indicated a higher incidence of genius among males, he concluded that greater male variability probably held for all qualities of character and ability. Ellis (1903) particularly emphasized the wide social and educational significance of the phenomenon, claiming that greater male variability was "a fact which has affected the whole of our human civilization" (p. 238), particularly through the production of men of genius. Ellis (1934) was also adamant that the female's tendency toward the average did not necessarily imply inferiority of talent; rather, it simply limited her expertise to "the sphere of concrete practical life" (p. 436). . . .

Women's Education The "appropriate" education for women had been at issue since the Renaissance, and the implications of the variability hypothesis favored those who had been arguing for a separate female education. Late in the 18th century, Mary Wollstonecraft Godwin (1759–1797) questioned the "natural" roles of each sex, contending that for both the ultimate goal was the same: "the first object of laudable ambition is to obtain a character as a human being, regardless of the distinction of sex" (Wollstonecraft, 1955, p. 5). Without education, she felt, women could not contribute to social progress as mature individuals, and this would be a tragic loss to the community. Though not the first to recognize the social restrictions arbitrarily placed on women, she was the first to hold those restrictions as directly responsible for the purported "defective nature" of women. She emphasized that women had never truly been given an equal chance to prove or disprove their merits. Seventy years later, John Stuart Mill (1955) also took up the cause of women's education, seeing it as one positive action to be taken in the direction of correcting the unjust social subordination of women. He felt that what appeared as woman's intellectual inferiority was actually no more than the effort to maintain the passive-dependent role relationship with man, her means of support:

> When we put together three things—first, the natural attraction between the sexes; secondly, the wife's entire dependence on the husband . . . and lastly, that the principal object of human pursuit, consideration, and all objects of social ambition, can in general be sought or obtained by her only through him, it would be a miracle if the object of being attractive to men had not become the polar star of feminine education and formation of character. (pp. 232–233)[1]

Although Mill objected to fostering passivity and dependency in girls, other educators felt that this was precisely their duty. One of the more influential of the 19th century, Hannah More, rejected outright the proposal that women should share the same type of education as men, because "the chief end to be proposed in cultivating the understanding of women" was "to qualify them for the practical purposes of life" (see Smith, 1970, p. 101). To set one's sights on other than harmonious domesticity was to defy the natural order. Her readers were advised to be excellent women rather than indifferent men; to follow the "plain path which Providence has obviously marked out to the sex . . . rather than . . . stray awkwardly, unbecomingly, and unsuccessfully, in a forbidden road (Smith, 1970, pp. 100–101). Her values were consonant with those held by most of the middle class, and so her *Strictures on the Modern System of Female Education* (More, 1800) enjoyed widespread popularity for some time.

By the latter part of the century, the question had turned from whether girls should be educated like boys to how much they should be educated like boys. With the shift in emphasis came the question of coeducation. One of the strongest objections to coeducation in adolescence was the threat it posed to the "normalization" of the menstrual period. G. Stanley Hall (1906) waxed poetic on the issue:

> At a time when her whole future life depends upon normalizing the lunar month, is there not something not only unnatural and unhygienic, but a little monstrous, in daily school associations with boys, where she must suppress and conceal her instincts and feelings, at those times when

> her own promptings suggest withdrawal or stepping a little aside to let Lord Nature do his magnificent work of efflorescence. (p. 590)

Edward Clarke (see Sinclair, 1965, p. 123) had earlier elucidated the physiological reasons for the restraint of girls from exertion in their studies: by forcing their brains to do work at puberty, they would use up blood later needed for menstruation.

Hall proposed an educational system for girls that would not only take into consideration their delicate physical nature but would also be tailored to prepare them for their special role in society. He feared that women's competition with men "in the world" would cause them to neglect their instinctive maternal urges and so bring about "race suicide." Because the glory of the female lay in motherhood, Hall believed that all educational and social institutions should be structured with that end in mind. Domestic arts would therefore be emphasized in special schools for adolescent girls, and disciplines such as philosophy, chemistry, and mathematics would be treated only superficially. If a girl had a notion to stay in the "male" system, she should be able to, but, Hall warned, such a woman selfishly interested in self-fulfillment would also be less likely to bear children and so be confined to an "agamic" life, thus failing to produce those very qualities that made her strong (Hall, 1918).

Throughout Hall's panegyric upon the beauties of female domestic education, there runs an undercurrent of the *real* threat that he perceived in coeducation, and that was the "feminization" of the American male. David Starr Jordan (1902) shared this objection but felt that coeducation would nevertheless make young men more "civilized" and young women less frivolous, tempering their natural pubescent inclinations. He was no champion of female ability though, stressing that women "on the whole, lack originality" (p. 100). The educated woman, he said, "is likely to master technic rather than art; method, rather than substance. She may know a good deal, but she can do nothing" (p. 101). In spite of this, he did assert that their training is just as serious and important as that of men. His position strongly favored the notion that the smaller range of female ability was the cause of lackluster female academic performance.

The issue of education was not easily settled, and even as late as 1935, one finds debates over its relative merits (*Encyclopedia of the Social Sciences*, 1935, pp. 614–617).

The Biological Bases of Sex Differences The variability hypothesis was compatible not only with prevailing attitudes concerning the appropriate form of female education but also with a highly popular theory of the biological complementarity of the sexes. The main tenet of Geddes and

Thomson's (1890) theory was that males are primarily "catabolic," females "anabolic." From this difference in metabolism, all other sex differences in physical, intellectual, and emotional makeup were derived. The male was more agile, creative, and variable; the female was truer to the species type and therefore, in all respects, less variable. The conservatism of the female insured the continuity of the species. The authors stressed the metabolic antecedents of female conservatism and male differentiation rather than variational tendency per se, and also put emphasis on the complementarity of the two natures:

> The feminine passivity is expressed in greater patience, more open-mindedness, greater appreciation of subtle details, and consequently what we call more rapid intuition. The masculine activity lends a greater power of maximum effort, of scientific insight, or cerebral experiment with impressions, and is associated with an unobservant or impatient disregard of minute details, but with a more stronger grasp of generalities. (p. 271)

The presentation of evolutionary theory anchored in yin-yang concepts of function represents the most positive evaluation of the female sex offered by 19th-century science. Whatever woman's shortcomings, they were necessary to complete her nature, which itself was necessary to complete man's: "Man thinks more, woman feels more. He discovers more, but remembers less; she is more receptive, and less forgetful" (Geddes & Thomson, 1890, p. 271).

Variability and the Testing Movement Helen Thompson (later Woolley) put Geddes and Thomson's and other theories of sex differences in ability to what she felt was a crucial experimental test (see Thompson, 1903). Twenty-five men and 25 women participated in nearly 20 hours of individual testing of their intellectual, motor, and sensory abilities. Of more importance than her experimental results (whether men or women can tap a telegraph key more times per minute has lost its significance to psychology) was her discussion of the implications of the resulting negligible differences for current theories of sex differences. She was especially critical of the mass of inconsistencies inherent in contemporary biological theories:

> Women are said to represent concentration, patience, and stability in emotional life. One might logically conclude that prolonged concentration of attention and unbiased generalization would be their intellectual characteristics, but these are the very characteristics assigned to men. (p. 173)

In the face of such contradictions, she was forced to conclude that "if the author's views as to the mental differences of sex had been different, they might as easily have derived a very different set of characteristics" (pp. 173–174). Thompson singled out the variability hypothesis for special criticism, objecting not only to the use of physical variation as evidence for intellectual variation but also to the tendency to minimize environmental influences. She held that training was responsible for sex differences in variation, and to those who countered that it is really a fundamental difference of instincts and characteristics that determines the differences in training, she replied that if this were true, "it would not be necessary to spend so much time and effort in making boys and girls follow the lines of conduct proper to their sex" (p. 181).

Thompson's recommendation to look at environmental factors went unheeded, as more and more evidence of woman's incapability of attaining eminence was amassed. In the surveys of eminent persons that were popular at the turn of the century, more credence was given to nature (à la Hall) than nurture (à la Thompson) for the near absence of eminent women (Cattell, 1903; Ellis, 1904). Cattell (1903) found a ready-made explanation in the variability hypothesis: "Women depart less from the normal than men," ergo "the distribution of women is represented by a narrower bell-shaped curve" (p. 375). Cora Castle's (1913) survey of eminent women was no less critical of women's failure to achieve at the top levels of power and prestige. . . .

A small but persistent minority challenged the validity of the variability hypothesis, and it is not surprising that this minority was composed mainly of women. Although the "woman question" was, to some degree, at issue, the larger dispute was between those who stressed "nature" as the major determinant of ability (and therefore success) and those who rejected nature and its corollary, instead emphasizing the importance of environmental factors. Helen Thompson Woolley, while remaining firmly committed to the investigation of the differential effects of social factors on each sex, did not directly involve herself in the variability controversy. Leta Stetter Hollingworth, . . . at Teachers College of Columbia University, actively investigated the validity of the hypothesis and presented sound objections to it. She argued that there was no real basis for assuming that the distribution of "mental traits" in the population conforms without exception to the Gaussian distribution. The assumption of normality was extremely important to the validity of the variability hypothesis, because only in a normal distribution would a difference in variability indicate a difference in range. It was the greater range of male ability that was used to "prove" the ultimate superiority of male ability. Greater range of male ability was usually verified by citing lists of eminent persons (dominated by men) and the numbers and sex of those in institutions for the feeble-minded (also dominated by men). Hollingworth (1914) saw no reason to resort to biological theory for an explanation of the phenomenon when a more parsimonious one was available in social fact. Statistics reporting a larger number of males among the feebleminded could be explained by the fact that the supporting data had been gathered in institutions, where men were more likely to be admitted than women of an equal degree of retardation. The better ability of feebleminded women to survive outside the institutional setting was simply a function of female social role:

> Women have been and are a dependent and non-competitive class, and when defective can more easily survive outside of institutions, since they do not have to compete *mentally* with normal individuals, as men do, to maintain themselves in the social *milieu*. (Hollingworth, 1914, p. 515)

Women would therefore be more likely to be institutionalized at an older age than men, after they had become too old to be "useful" or self-supporting. A survey of age and sex ratios in New York institutions supported her hypothesis: the ratio of females to males increased with age of the inmates (Hollingworth, 1913). As for the rarity of eminence among women, Hollingworth (1914) argued that because the social role of women was defined in terms of housekeeping and child-rearing functions, "a field where eminence is not possible," and because of concomitant constraints placed on the education and employment of women by law, custom, and the demands of the role, one could not possibly validly compare the achievements of women with those of men who "have followed the greatest possible range of occupations, and have at the same time procreated unhindered" (p. 528). She repeatedly emphasized (Hollingworth, 1914, 1916) that the true potential of woman could only be known when she began to receive social acceptance of her right to choose career, maternity, or both. . . .

Maternal Instinct

The concept of maternal instinct was firmly entrenched in American psychology before American psychology itself existed as an entity. The first book to appear in the United States with "psychology" in its title outlined the psychological sex differences arising from the physical differences between men and women. Differences in structure were assumed to imply differences in function, and therefore differences in abilities, temperament, and intelligence. In each sex a different set of physical systems was thought to predominate: "In man the arterial and cerebral systems prevail, and with them irritability; in woman the venous and ganglion systems and with them plasticity and sensibility" (Rausch, 1841, p. 81). The systems dominant in woman caused her greatest attributes to lie in the moral sphere in the form of love, patience, and chastity. In the intellectual sphere, she was not equally blessed, "and this is not accidental, not because no opportunity has offered itself to their productive genius . . . but because it is their highest happiness to be mothers" (Rausch, 1841, p. 83).[2]

Although there was popular acceptance of a maternal instinct in this country, the primary impetus for its incorporation into psychology came by way of British discussion of social evolution. While the variability hypothesis gained attention because of an argument, the concept of maternal instinct evolved without conflict. There was consistent agreement as to its existence, if not its precise nature or form. Typical of the evolutionary point of view was the notion that woman's emotional nature (including her tendency to nurturance) was a direct consequence of her reproductive physiology. As Herbert Spencer (1891) explained it, the female's energies were directed toward preparation for pregnancy and lactation, reducing the energy available for the development of other qualities. This resulted in a "rather earlier cessation of individual evolution" in the female. Woman was, in essence, a stunted man. Her lower stage of development was evident not only in her interior mental and emotional powers but also in the resulting expression of the parental instinct. Whereas the objectivity of the male caused his concern to be extended "to all the relatively weak who are dependent upon him" (p. 375), the female's propensity to "dwell on the concrete and proximate rather than on the abstract and remote" made her incapable of the generalized protective attitude assumed by the male. Instead, she was primarily responsive to "infantile helplessness." . . .

. . . Edward Thorndike (1911) considered the instincts peculiar to each sex to be the primary source of sex differences: "it appears that if the primary sex characters—the instincts directly related to courtship, love, child-bearing, and nursing—are left out of account, the average man differs from the average woman far less than many men differ from one another" (p. 30). Thorndike taught that the tendency to display maternal concern was universal among women, although social pressures could "complicate or deform" it. He conceded that males share in an instinctive "good will toward children" but other instincts, such as the "hunting instinct," predominated (Thorndike, 1914b). He was so sure of the innate instinctual differences between men and women that it was his contention (Thorndike, 1914b) that even "if we should keep the environment of boys and girls absolutely similar these instincts would produce sure and important differences between the mental and moral activities of boys and girls" (p. 203). The expression of instincts therefore was thought to have far-reaching effects on seemingly unrelated areas of ability and conduct. For example, woman's "nursing instinct," which was most often exhibited in "unreasoning tendencies to pet, coddle, and 'do for' others," was also "the chief source of woman's superiorities in the moral life" (Thorndike, 1914a, p. 203). Another of the female's instinctive tendencies was described as "submission to mastery":

> Women in general are thus by original nature submissive to men in general. Submissive behavior is apparently not annoying when assumed as the instinctive response to its natural stimulus. Indeed, it is perhaps a common satisfier. (Thorndike, 1914b, p. 34)

The existence of such an "instinct" would, of course, validate the social norm of female subservience and dependence. An assertive woman would be acting contrary to instinct and therefore contrary to *nature*. There is a striking similarity between Thorndike's description of female nature and that of the Freudians with their mutual emphasis on woman's passivity, dependency, and masochism. For Thorndike, however, the *cause* of such a female attitude was thought to be something quite different from mutilation fears and penis envy. . . .

The fate of instinct at the hands of the radical behaviorists is a well-known tale. Perhaps the most adamant, as well as notorious, critic of the instinct concept was J. B. Watson (1926). Like those before him who had relied upon observation to prove the existence of maternal instinct, he used observation to confirm its nonexistence:

> We have observed the nursing, handling, bathing, etc. of the first baby of a good many mothers. Certainly there are no new ready-made activities appearing except nursing. The mother is usually as awkward about that as she can well be. The instinctive factors are practically nil. (p. 54)

Watson attributed the appearance of instinctive behavior to the mother's effort to conform to societal expectations of her successful role performance. He, like the 19th-century British associationist Alexander Bain, speculated that not a little of the mother's pleasure in nursing and caring for the infant was due to the sexually stimulating effect of those activities.[3]

Even the most dedicated behaviorists hedged a bit when it came to discarding the idea of instinct altogether. Although the teleology and redundancy of the concept of instinct was sharply criticized, some belief in "instinctive activity" was typically retained (cf. Dunlap, 1919–1920). W. B. Pillsbury (1926), for example, believed that the parental instinct was a "secondary" instinct. Physical attraction to the infant guided the mother's first positive movements toward the infant, but trial and error guided her subsequent care. Instinct was thought of as that quality which set the entire pattern of maternal behavior in motion.

In time instinct was translated into *drive* and *motivation*, refined concepts more in keeping with behavioristic theory. Concomitantly, interest in the maternal instinct of human females gave way to the study of mothering behavior in rodents. The concept of maternal instinct did find a place in psychoanalytic theory, but its definition bore little resemblance to that previously popular. Not only did maternal instinct lose the connotation of protectiveness and gentility that an earlier generation of psychologists had ascribed to it, but it was regarded as basically sexual, masochistic, and even destructive in nature (cf. Rheingold, 1964).

The Ascendancy of Psychoanalytic Theory

The functionalists, because of their emphasis on "nature," were predictably indifferent to the study of social sex roles and cultural concepts of masculine and feminine. The behaviorists, despite their emphasis on "nurture," were slow to recognize those same social forces. During the early 1930s, there was little meaningful ongoing research in female psychology: the point of view taken by the functionalists was no longer a viable one, and the behaviorists with their emphasis on nonsocial topics (i.e., learning and motivation) had no time for serious consideration of sex differences. While the functionalists had defined laws of behavior that mirrored the society of the times, behaviorists concentrated their efforts on defining universal laws that operated in any time, place, or organism. Individual differences in nature were expected during the functionalist era because they were the sine qua non of a Darwinian view of the world and of science. The same individual differences were anathema to early learning-centered psychology because, no longer necessary or expedient, they were a threat to the formulation of universal laws of behavior.

In the hiatus created by the capitulation of functionalism to behaviorism, the study of sex differences and female nature fell within the domain of psychoanalytic theory—the theory purported to have all the answers. Freudian theory (or some form of it) had for some years already served as the basis for a psychology of female physiological function (cf. Benedek & Rubenstein, 1939). The application of principles popular in psychiatry and medicine (and their inescapable identification with pathology) to academic psychology was easily accomplished. Psychoanalytic theory provided psychology with the first comprehensive theoretical explanation of sex difference. Its novelty in that respect aided its assimilation.

Psychology proper, as well as the general public, had been well-prepared for a biological, and frankly sexual, theory of male and female nature. Havelock Ellis, although himself ambivalent and even hostile toward Freudian teachings, had done much through his writing to encourage openness in the discussion of sexuality. He brought a number of hitherto unmentionable issues to open discussion, couching them in the commonly accepted notion of the complementarity of the sexes, thus insuring their popular acceptance. Emphasis on masculinity and femininity as real dimensions of personality appeared in the mid-1930s in the form of the Terman Masculinity-Femininity Scale (Terman & Miles, 1968). Although Lewis Terman himself avoided discussion of whether masculinity and femininity were products of nature or nurture, social determinants of masculinity and femininity were commonly deemphasized in favor of the notion that they were a type of psychological secondary sexual characteristic. Acceptance of social sex role soon came to be perceived as an indicator of one's mental health.

The traps inherent in a purely psychoanalytic concept of female nature were seldom recognized. John Dewey's (1957) observation, made in 1922, merits attention, not only for its accuracy but because its substance can be found in present-day refutations of the adequacy of psychoanalytic theory as an explanation of woman's behavior and "nature":

> The treatment of sex by psycho-analysts is most instructive, for it flagrantly exhibits both the consequences of artificial simplification and the transformation of social results into psychic causes. Writers, usually male, hold forth on the psychology of women, as if they were dealing with a Platonic universal entity, although they habitually treat men as individuals, varying with structure and environment. They treat phenomena which are peculiarly symptoms of civilization of the West at the present time as if they were the necessary effects of fixed nature impulses of human nature. (pp. 143–144)

The identification of the psychology of women with psychoanalytic theory was nearly complete by the mid-1930s and was so successful that many psychologists today, even those most deeply involved in the current movement for a psychology of women, are not aware that there was a psychology of women long before there was a Sigmund Freud. This article has dealt only with a brief period in that history, and then only with the most significant topics of that period. Lesser issues were often just as hotly debated, for example, whether there is an innate difference in the style of handwriting of men and women (cf. Allen, 1927; Downey, 1910).

And what has happened to the issues of brain size, variability, and maternal instinct since the 1930s? Where they are politically and socially useful, they have an uncanny knack of reappearing, albeit in an altered form. For example, the search for central nervous system differences between males and females has continued. Perhaps the most popular form this search has taken is the theory of prenatal hormonal "organization" of the hypothalamus into exclusively male or female patterns of function (Harris & Levine, 1965). The proponents of this theory maintain an Aristotelian view of woman as an incomplete man:

> In the development of the embryo, nature's first choice or primal impulse is to differentiate a female. . . . The principle of differentiation is always that to obtain a male, something must be added. Subtract that something, and the result will be a female. (Money, 1970, p. 428)

The concept of maternal instinct, on the other hand, has recently been taken up and refashioned by a segment of the women's movement. Pregnancy and childbirth are acclaimed as important expressions of womanliness whose satisfactions cannot be truly appreciated by males. The idea that women are burdened with "unreasoning tendencies to pet, coddle, and 'do for' others" has been disposed of by others and replaced by the semiserious proposal that if any "instinctive" component of parental concern exists, it is a peculiarly male attribute (Stannard, 1970). The variability hypothesis is all but absent from contemporary psychological work, but if it ever again promises a viable justification for existing social values, it will be back as strongly as ever. Conditions which would favor its revival include the renaissance of rugged individualism or the "need" to suppress some segment of society, for example, women's aspirations to positions of power. In the first case the hypothesis would serve to reaffirm that there are those "born to lead," and in the latter that there are those "destined to follow."

Of more importance than the issues themselves or their fate in contemporary psychology is the recognition of the role that they have played historically in the psychology of women: the role of social myth. Graves (1968, p. v) included among the functions of mythologizing that of justification of existing social systems. This function was clearly operative throughout the evolutionist-functionalist treatment of the psychology of women: the "discovery" of sex differences in brain structure to correspond to "appropriate" sex differences in brain function; the biological justification (via the variability hypothesis) for the enforcement of woman's subordinate social status; the Victorian weakness and gentility associated with maternity; and pervading each of these themes, the assumption of an innate emotional, sexless, unimaginative female character that played the perfect foil to the Darwinian male. That science played handmaiden to social values cannot be denied. Whether a parallel situation exists in today's study of sex differences is open to question.

Notes

1. One of the severest critics of Mill's defense of women was Sigmund Freud. He felt Mill's propositions were in direct contradiction to woman's "true" nature:

> It is really a stillborn thought to send women into the struggle for existence exactly as men. . . . I believe that all reforming action in law and education would break down in front of the fact that, long before the age at which a man can earn a position in society, Nature has determined woman's destiny through beauty, charm, and sweetness. Law and custom have much to give women that has been withheld from them, but the position of women will surely be what it is: in youth an adored darling and in mature years a loved wife. (quoted in Reeves, 1971, pp. 163–164)

2. This sentiment was echoed by Bruno Bettelheim (1965) over 100 years later: "as much as women want to be good scientists or engineers, they want first and foremost to be womanly companions of men and to be mothers" (p. 15).

3. Bain's (1875) position was similar except that he believed that there *was* an innate tendency to nurture that initiated the entire cycle of positive affect-positive action. The instinct was thought to be a natural "sentiment," which was fostered by the long period of gestation and the "special energies" required of the mother to sustain the infant. The positive affect arising from activity connected with the infant then brought about increased nurturance and increased pleasure. At least part of this pleasure was thought to be physical in nature.

References

Allen, C. N. Studies in sex differences. *Psychological Bulletin*, 1927, *24*, 294–302.

Bain, A. *Mental science*. New York: Appleton, 1875.

Benedek, T., & Rubenstein, B. B. The correlations between ovarian activity and psychodynamic processes. II. The menstrual phase. *Psychosomatic Medicine*, 1939, *1*, 461–485.

Bettelheim B. The commitment required of a woman entering a scientific profession in present-day American society. In J. A. Mattfield & C. G. Van Aken (Eds.), *Women and the scientific professions*. Cambridge, Mass.: M.I.T. Press, 1965.

Burt, C., & Moore, R. C. The mental differences between the sexes. *Journal of Experimental Pedagogy*, 1912, *1*, 355–388.

Calder-Marshall, A. *The sage of sex*. New York: Putnam, 1959.

Calkins, M. W. Community of ideas of men and women. *Psychological Review*, 1896, *3*, 426–430.

Castle, C. A. A statistical study of eminent women. *Columbia Contributions to Philosophy and Psychology*, 1913, *22*(27).

Cattell, J. Mck. A statistical study of eminent men. *Popular Science Monthly*, 1903, *62*, 359–377.

Darwin, C. *The descent of man* (2nd ed.). London: John Murray, 1922. (Originally published, 1871; 2nd edition originally published, 1874.)

Dewey, J. *Human nature and conduct*. New York: Random House, 1957.

Downey, J. E. Judgment on the sex of handwriting. *Psychological Review*, 1910, *17*, 205–216.

Dunlap, J. Are there any instincts? *Journal of Abnormal and Social Psychology*, 1919–1920, *14*, 307–311.

Elliott, H. C. *Textbook of neuroanatomy* (2nd ed.). Philadelphia: Lippincott, 1969.

Ellis, H. *Man and woman: A study of human secondary sexual characters*. London: Walter Scott; New York: Scribner's, 1894.

Ellis, H. Variation in man and woman. *Popular Science Monthly*, 1903, *62*, 237–253.

Ellis, H. *A study of British genius*. London: Hurst & Blackett, 1904.

Ellis, H. *Man and woman, a study of secondary and tertiary sexual characteristics* (8th rev. ed.). London: Heinemann, 1934.

Encyclopedia of the Social Sciences. New York: Macmillan, 1935.

Galton, F. *Inquiries into the human faculty and its development*. London: Dent, 1907.

Geddes, P. & Thompson, J. A. *The evolution of sex*. New York: Scribner & Welford, 1890.

Graves, R. Introduction. In *New Larousse encyclopedia of mythology* (Rev. ed.). London: Paul Hamlyn, 1968.

Hall, G. S. The question of coeducation. *Munsey's Magazine*, 1906, *34*, 588–592.

Hall, G. S. *Youth, its education, regimen and hygiene*. New York: Appleton, 1918.

Halleck, R. *Psychology and psychic culture*. New York: American Book, 1895.

Harris, G. W., & Levine, S. Sexual differentiation of the brain and its experimental control. *Journal of Psychology*, 1965, *181*, 379–400.

Hobhouse, L. *Morals in evolution*. New York: Holt, 1916.

Hollingworth, L. S. The frequency of amentia as related to sex. *Medical Record*, 1913, *84*, 753–756.

Hollingworth, L. S. Variability as related to sex differences in achievement. *American Journal of Sociology*, 1914, *19*, 510–530.

Hollingworth, L. S. Social devices for impelling women to bear and rear children. *American Journal of Sociology*, 1916, *22*, 19–29.

Huarte, J. *The examination of mens wits* (trans. from Spanish to Italian by M. Camilli; trans. from Italian to English by R. Carew). Gainesville, Fla.: Scholars' Facsimiles and Reprints, 1959.

James, W. *The principles of psychology*. New York: Dover, 1950.

Jastrow, J. Note on Calkins' "Community of ideas of men and women." *Psychological Review*, 1896, *3*, 430–431.

Jastrow, J. *Character and temperament*. New York: Appleton, 1915.

Jordan, D. S. The higher education of women. *Popular Science Monthly*, 1902, *62*, 97–107.

Mall, F. P. On several anatomical characters of the human brain, said to vary according to race and sex, with especial reference to the weight of the frontal lobe. *American Journal of Anatomy*, 1909, *9*, 1–32.

McDougall, W. *An introduction to social psychology* (7th ed.). London: Methuen, 1913.

McDougall, Meyer, M. *Psychology of the other-one*. Columbia: Missouri Book, 1921.

Mill, J. S. *The subjection of women*. London: Dent, 1955.

Mobius, P. J. The physiological mental weakness of woman (A. McCorn, Trans.). *Alienist and Neurologist*, 1901, *22*, 624–642.

Money, J. Sexual dimorphism and homosexual gender identity. *Psychological Bulletin*, 1970, *74*, 425–440.

More, H. *Strictures on the modern system of female education. With a view of the principles and conduct prevalent among women of rank and fortune*. Philadelphia, Pa.: Printed by Budd and Bertram for Thomas Dobson, 1800.

Patrick, G. T. W. The psychology of woman. *Popular Science Monthly*, 1895, *47*, 209–225.

Pearson, K. Variation in man and woman. In *The chances of death* (Vol. 1). London: Edward Arnold, 1897.

Pillsbury, W. B. *Education as the psychologist sees it*. New York: Macmillan, 1926.

Porteus, S., & Babcock, M. E. *Temperament and race*. Boston: Gorham Press, 1926.

Rausch, F. A. *Psychology; Or, a view of the human soul including anthropology* (2nd rev. ed.). New York: Dodd, 1841.

Reeves, N. *Womankind*. Chicago: Aldine-Atherton, 1971.

Rheingold, J. *The fear of being a woman*. New York: Grune & Stratton, 1964.

Romanes, G. J. Mental differences between men and women. *Nineteenth Century*, 1887, *21*, 654–672.

Shand, A. F. *The foundations of character*. London: Macmillan, 1920.

Sinclair, A. *The better half: The emancipation of the American woman*. New York: Harper & Row, 1965.

Smith, P. *Daughters of the promised land*. Boston: Little, Brown, 1970.

Spencer, H. *The study of sociology*, New York: Appleton, 1891.

Stannard, U. Adams's rib, or the woman within. *Trans-Action*, 1970, *8*, 24–35.

Sutherland, A. *The origin and growth of the moral instinct* (Vol. 1). London: Longmans, Green, 1898.

Terman, L., & Miles, C. C. *Sex and personality*. New York: Russell and Russell, 1968.

Thompson, H. B. *The mental traits of sex*. Chicago: University of Chicago Press, 1903.

Thorndike, E. L. Sex in education. *The Bookman*, 1906, *23*, 211–214.

Thorndike, E. L. *Educational psychology* (2nd ed.). New York: Teachers College, Columbia University, 1910.

Thorndike, E. L. *Individuality*. Boston: Houghton Mifflin, 1911.

Thorndike, E. L. *Educational psychology* (Vol. 3). New York: Teachers College, Columbia University, 1914. (a)

Thorndike, E. L. *Educational psychology briefer course*. New York: Teachers College, Columbia University, 1914. (b)

Walker, A. *Woman physiologically considered*. New York: J & H. G. Langley, 1850.

Watson, J. B. Studies on the growth of the emotions. In *Psychologies of 1925*. Worcester, Mass.: Clark University Press, 1926.

Weininger, O. *Sex and character* (trans.). London: Heinemann, 1906.

Wissler, C. The correlation of mental and physical tests. *Psychological Review Monograph Supplements*, 1899–1901, *3*(6, Whole No. 16).

Wollstonecraft, M. *A vindication of the rights of woman*. New York: Dutton, 1955.

Woolley, H. T. Psychological literature: A review of the recent literature on the psychology of sex. *Psychological Bulletin*, 1910, 7, 335–342.

Wundt, W. *Ethics*. Vol. 3: *The principles of morality, and the departments of the moral life* (M. F. Washburn, Trans.). London: Sonnenschein, 1901.

CHAPTER TEN

Research Methodology

Conducting research in the psychology of women is the topic of this section. In the first article, Mary Brown Parlee reviews what she sees as four general categories of research in psychology of women: 1) critiques of traditional psychological research on women; 2) empirical research from a feminist perspective; 3) theoretical contributions to mainstream psychology; and 4) theoretical contributions to research on problems typically considered "outside" traditional psychology. The first category of research, she argues, serves the important purpose of "setting the record straight" by critiquing empirical evidence for stereotyped gender differences. However, this sort of research has increasingly been replaced by research from the other three perspectives which steps outside traditional theories and explores questions previously ignored by psychology. Parlee then argues that feminist psychology is not yet integrated into the mainstream, providing evidence that feminist scholarship is both ignored and actively excluded from the major journals. Why does this happen? Her answer takes us back to traditional psychology's commitment to positivist, context-stripping experimental methods as the only ways to understand human experience, which Naomi Weisstein referred to in her article in the previous section. Parlee makes the radical argument that such research benefits those who do not want the socio-political contexts and roles of men and women to be examined, and hence potentially changed. She concludes by issuing a challenge to feminist researchers in psychology to do the dangerous, to make hidden assumptions explicit, to focus on social context, and do research on problems of social significance.

In the next article, Maureen McHugh and her colleagues present a "how-to" manual for conducting nonsexist psychological research. By breaking the social-scientific research process down into its various steps, they identify the many places within it where sexist bias enters. From the biased selection of topics, to the choice of research subjects (often males only, in both human and animal samples!), to the fact that sex differences are more likely to be reported, published, and cited than sex similarities, the psychological research process is rife with problems that affect our ultimate understanding of women and gender. The good news is that there are ways to avoid such bias, and McHugh and her colleagues offer a great variety of creative recommendations.

Whereas McHugh and her colleagues offer the possibility of nonsexist research largely within the bounds of the traditional social scientific method, Mary Gergen offers something quite different. In her article, "Toward a Feminist Metatheory and Methodology in the Social Sciences," she provides a fascinating application of the feminist perspective with her own study of menopause, designed and conducted specifically from a feminist framework on research. Her study is a sobering one for those well-trained in traditional psychological methods, for it challenges dearly held assumptions about what is "right and wrong" in conducting a research study at every turn. In it, Gergen employs five fundamental feminist principles: she rejects the presumption of independence of researcher and subject (she herself is one of the subjects in the study!), she refuses to decontextualize her subject matter socially and historically, she makes explicit the politics of her theory, she recognizes the impossibility of objectivity in a world that requires language to describe it, and she rejects the notion that she, as scientist, is more knowledgeable and competent than her subjects. Gergen reflects that her method limited her ability to achieve certain goals she originally set, since power was shared equally between herself and her participants. In exchange, however, she came to new insights about social change because she was a member of the group.

Ultimately, there is room for both alternatives to traditional methods in conducting research on psychology of women. As Peplau and Conrad (1989) have pointed out, any research method can be used toward feminist goals, just as any can be used in sexist ways. Employing experimental methods with statistical analyses, while guarding against sexist bias, allows for large-sample research that provides more widely generalizable results about women and gender. Using nonexperimental methods provides us with richer, more qualitative information about particular women's real life experiences. Indeed both kinds of information are important to the advancement of our understanding of the psychology of women.

Reference

Peplau, L. A. & Conrad, E. (1989). Beyond nonsexist research: The perils of feminist methods in psychology. *Psychology of Women Quarterly, 13*, 379–400.

32 Psychology and Women

MARY BROWN PARLEE

As a subfield of psychology, the psychology of women is acquiring many of the organizational and substantive characteristics of normal science.[1] Researchers in the field are gaining strength in their professional association. . . .

. . . It is possible to identify four general kinds of work in the psychology of women. All of them pose, in different ways, problems concerning the relationship between feminist psychology and the field as a whole. After describing the four kinds of work very briefly, I will focus on the relationship between feminist psychologists and their "parent" discipline and will suggest that psychology's commitment to the experimental method makes this relationship different from that of feminists in other disciplines. I will suggest that this commitment to method is a problem of more than academic interest as far as women are concerned and will outline one way in which feminist psychologists might be able to contribute to a solution.

Research in the Psychology of Women

Critiques of Traditional Psychological Research on Women The critical examination of empirical evidence for or against the existence of gender differences in some domain where gender differences are popularly believed to exist now has a smaller role in the psychology of women than formerly. Maccoby and Jacklin's *The Psychology of Sex Differences* will undoubtedly stand as the most monumental example of work of this kind.[2] Although there has been a decline in the number of such critiques published in recent years, when they do appear, they are welcome reminders that—at its best—psychology can indeed be a self-correcting enterprise. Critiques of traditional literature on sex differences in influenceability by Eagley and on aggression by Frodi, Macauley, and Thome are recent and very good examples of this kind of work, as is Tiefer's critique of physiological research on female sexuality.[3]

Apart from their intrinsic interest, critiques illustrate an important property of scientific psychology as it is currently conceived, a property which poses a dilemma for feminist psychologists vis-à-vis their field as a whole. Critiques represent a substantive contribution to a field that views itself as cumulative. Critiques set the public record straight on matters that have been the subject of previous research and they provide an indispensable basis for building new and different traditions of research on these subjects. They are not relevant, however, to psychologists who think the body of research being critiqued is conceptually misguided. For example, "influenceability" and (though this is more complicated) "aggression" have traditionally been conceptualized in psychology as properties of persons, as personality traits or dispositions, that predispose individuals to behave in particular ways. Among many psychologists, such trait theories are regarded as having outlived their usefulness, since they do not take into account even aspects of the immediate environment which have been demonstrated to influence behavior. Thus, critiques of research that assume the usefulness of a trait analysis of behavior *are* cumulative in the sense that they clarify issues as they have been formulated in the literature, but they are not relevant to research and thinking which rejects such an analysis. And the latter represents the majority—or at least the most defensible—viewpoint in the field. Some of the topics most important to women—in terms of the way research conclusions may be seen to bear upon public policy—seem to have this character. (Some examples are sex differences in brain function, hormonal influences on behavior, and the effects of maternal "deprivation.") That is, a body of traditional research seems to provide support for popular beliefs about women; critiques of the evidence set the record straight by showing the conclusions to be without empirical support. Yet since the research in question is conceptually irrelevant to the most interesting work in the field, the contribution made by a critique is primarily addressed to the potential (indeed the inevitable) misuse of psychological data against women rather than to the development of the field as its forefront.

So feminist psychologists are faced with something of a dilemma. Should we try to use reason, logic, and evidence to persuade the unenlightened in and outside psychology to abandon their pseudoscientific prejudices? Or should we simply ignore the misstatements about women that flow from psychology into society at large and try instead to advance research on and for women by using the best conceptual and methodological tools the field presently has to offer? Increasingly, feminist psychologists seem to be choosing the latter course, that of stepping outside the cumulative development (including critiques) of traditional bodies of research and theories to work on problems relevant to women that have been ignored by psychologists in the past. The remaining three kinds of work in the psychology of women are basically of this ignore-the-tradition-and-start-afresh sort. Ignore many of the conclusions, questions, and concepts of the past, that is, but keep the basic commitment to a positivist view of the scientific method.

Empirical Research from a Feminist Perspective Another kind of research in the field of the psychology of women is that which generates new data bearing on topics that would only have been studied by someone with a feminist perspective. Sometimes these data are explicitly integrated into an established theoretical framework in psychology, sometimes not. Three examples will be described briefly to illustrate this kind of work.

Porter, Geis, and Walstedt have provided an empirical demonstration of what is to many feminists an obvious truth: women are unlikely to be seen as leaders in a mixed-sex group, even when they sit at the head of the table (a cue which has been found in other research to connote leadership); men are.[4] Women, they found, are identified as leaders only in all-female groups. Likewise, Crosby and Nyquist have demonstrated empirically a phenomenon most feminists might have guessed would be true.[5] Women do, as Robin Lakoff suggested, speak differently from men: women typically use more tentative intonations (a questioning intonation on a declarative statement), more tag questions ("you know?"), and more qualifiers. Using a mock jury to simulate a courtroom, O'Barr and his colleagues found that such "women's language" is less likely to be believed by jury members than is the more assertive speech typical of men.[6] Not surprisingly, Crosby and Nyquist's data suggest that while "women's language" is more characteristic of women than of men, it is also used more by someone (anyone) in a less powerful role when speaking to someone more powerful than they. Similarly, observational studies by Dweck and her colleagues on teachers' evaluations of girls and boys seem to make sense in terms of everyday experience.[7] When teachers give negative evaluations to boys, it is related less to the intellectual aspects of the work than to its form (neatness, instruction following) or to the boy's lack of motivation; negative feedback to girls typically focused on the intellectual quality of the work. Teachers' praise, on the other hand, was more related to the intellectual quality of the work for boys than for girls. These patterns of negative and positive feedback were consistent across the several classrooms studied.

Research of this kind breaks important empirical ground in identifying new and previously neglected areas of research, but its theoretical underpinnings generally remain those of the relevant areas of traditional psychology. (Dweck's work is the most explicitly theoretical of the research mentioned here.) By and large, development of new theories is not a goal of this kind of research, nor is it a product.

Theoretical Contributions to Psychology Arising from Feminist Research A third kind of work in the psychology of women is more concerned than are critiques or empirical demonstrations with the theoretical development of concepts arising from feminist research. Research on androgyny, for example, proceeds apace, and there have been a number of serious efforts to clarify both empirical and theoretical issues surrounding the concept.[8] Perhaps the most interesting of this new work is by Sandra Bem herself,[9] who was motivated to look beyond androgyny as she originally conceptualized it for research purposes because, she says, the concept was too readily incorporated into mainstream psychology. Whether or not this is correct, Bem points to an important criterion for assessing the extent to which a new line of work challenges traditional ways of doing psychology.

Research on female development over the life span, on the psychology of menstruation, on issues relevant to feminist therapy, on the conceptualization of gender[10]—all are other examples of research being carried out with an eye to the development of new theory as well as to the generation of new data on hitherto neglected topics. (As with other categories, this list is illustrative rather than exhaustive.) An important point about this kind of feminist research is that it is not incompatible with basic conceptual frameworks or methodological allegiances in the field as a whole. To take one example, research and theory on psychological development over the life span, even when it is reconceptualized from a feminist perspective, is not outrageously outside the purview of existing theories of development. In fact, feminist work on this topic may be theoretically productive within psychology precisely because it does lie within the purview of an existing set of theories which happen now to be at the forefront of some of the more interesting areas of the field as a whole.

Theoretical Contributions to Problem-centered Research Included in a fourth type of research in the psychology of women are topics such as rape, domestic violence, conversational interaction, behavioral medicine, and environmental effects on the individual.[11] While not easily distinguishable on formal or conceptual grounds from the theoretically oriented work mentioned above, research on such topics rather clearly differs in the extent to which it is carried out in, or is compatible with, traditions of research in mainstream psychology. This fourth category, then, consists of research on problems or topics, important from a feminist perspective, that clearly have a psychological component but which do not begin to be completely comprehended by any of the conceptual or methodological paradigms of traditional psychology. Most of them are not regarded as "in" psychology at all. Speaking from a field so narrowly circumscribed by the academic that it sometimes categorizes people as either "students" or "nonstudents," it is tempting to describe research in this fourth category as "interdisciplinary." A more adequate description would be that it is concerned with phenomena which cannot readily be abstracted, even conceptually, from the complex, rich, and varied world of human experience—phenomena which clearly cannot be simulated in laboratory experiments.

Each of these four kinds of research in the psychology of women stands in a slightly different relationship to the concepts, theories, and methods of the field as a whole. Critiques contribute to the cumulative development of lines of research that are usually not themselves at the cutting edges of the field. Empirical demonstrations of "feminist truths" about social interactions rely upon conceptual frameworks and theories of traditional psychology and do not contribute to their development qua theories. Feminist psychological research with a theoretical focus is potentially able to contribute to the development of particular theories or approaches in psychology by ensuring that traditional theories are broadened or altered to include a feminist perspective. The success of such work in the long run depends both upon the long-range significance of the particular theoretical framework within which the feminist work is done *and* upon the extent to which feminist research and theory is incorporated into mainstream thinking. Research by feminist psychologists on "interdisciplinary" problems is, at present, "outside" the boundaries of mainstream psychology.

The relationship of what I have identified as the third category or research on the psychology of women to the field of psychology as a whole is of particular interest here, in part because it seems to differ from the relationship of feminist scholarship in other disciplines to those fields. Let us look more closely, then, at the way feminist research with a clear theoretical focus is related to the relevant areas of research and theory in the field of psychology as a whole.

How integrated feminist psychology is into the mainstream depends on whom you ask. In recent issues of the newsletter of the Society for the Advancement of Social Psychology, several feminist psychologists surveyed the state of the art in the psychology of women.[12] Their conclusion, with which I agree, is that recent feminist research on sex and gender is among the most exciting new developments in social psychology and that, far from requiring special laws and theories, such work "continues to fit within the conceptual framework of social psychology." So from the point of view of feminists doing the work, major areas of research in the psychology of women are successfully integrated into mainstream psychology. Yet I think the evidence suggests that from the point of view of more traditional psychologists this kind of feminist research has not been integrated—indeed, from their vantage point, it may not even exist.

By and large, feminist research does not appear in the "major" journals, feminist psychologists do not survive at the "major" universities, and when feminist research receives federal funding, after stringent peer review, this external evidence of scientific excellence is disregarded on the grounds that the work is "faddish" or "applied."

Nowhere is it possible to find evidence suggesting that the scientific importance of a feminist perspective is recognized by those in the mainstream. Nowhere, for example, does one see the consequences of delighted discovery: "Developmental studies of middle age *have* been done only on men—let's see what happens to our theories when we include women." Rather, women psychologists work creatively to adapt existing developmental theories to accommodate reality, while male psychologists continue to study men in the usual way. It has been six years since feminist psychologists presented a symposium at the American Psychological Association critically discussing the empirical inadequacy of single-sex experiments and other methodological issues having substantive significance.[13] Evidence is clear and everywhere: mainstream psychologists simply do not hear the reasonable arguments and the potentially creative insights of feminist psychologists, no matter that we would wish to believe otherwise. "Do not hear" is probably too passive a description of psychology's response to feminist research and theories. The evidence is fairly compelling that the feminist perspective is actively excluded from the mainstream: feminist research continues to be seen as falling between the cracks of topic areas covered by major journals, departments do not perceive the need to include the psychology of women in their graduate programs, research on women and publication in journals that will publish it do not "count" in tenure evaluations. No conspiracy theory, no implication of conscious intent on the part of traditional psychologists, is necessary to account for this exclusion; rather, traditional criteria, procedures, and institutions being applied and operating in traditional ways have the effect of screening out from the field perspectives other than the traditional ones.

What is it about feminist research that seems to provoke its exclusion from the field? One reason may be that feminist research at its best poses a challenge to the basic methodological commitment by which scientific psychology has traditionally defined itself. Feminism is not the only perspective from which this challenge has been raised, but I think feminists' reasons for doing so are slightly different.

One hallmark of feminist research in any field seems to be the investigator's continual testing of the plausibility of the work against her own experience. The historian, for example, asks what it was like to be a woman and what were women doing at that place and time, and then proceeds to find out—using her own experience both as a guide to formulating questions and as a preliminary way of evaluating the completeness of the results. The usual scholarly principles of reliability, consistency, logical inference, and the like are also used to evaluate the results, but the additional criterion of how does it accord with my own experience does enter into the work process. And similarly in other disciplines, including psychology. Feminist psychologists thus have as a priority finding the best possible version of the truth about the subject matter rather than adhering strictly to a particular method. And this, I think, poses a serious challenge to traditional psychology, a challenge it has attempted to meet simply by suppressing it.

While the underlying reasons may differ, the challenge raised by feminist psychologists is just one of many. Mainstream psychology is under continuing and increasing criticism from many quarters for its unquestioning adherence to a positivist view of science and its reliance upon the experimental method as the best way of arriving at an understanding of human behavior and experience. As one observer has noted, mainstream psychologists appear to suffer from "physics envy,"[14] and constantly strive, in what they wrongly believe to be the manner of the physical sciences, to have ever-"harder" data and ever-firmer "control" over their material. . . .

Mishler[15] characterizes psychology's preferred methodology—the experimental method (supported by the ideology that it is "the" scientific method)—as "context stripping." Concepts, environments, social interactions are all simplified by methods which lift them out of their contexts, stripping them of the very complexity that characterizes them in the real world. Thus, concepts are operationally defined by procedures which are intended to exclude "surplus meaning" ("intelligence is what an intelligence test measures" period), psychological processes are studied in laboratory simulations to avoid the "noise" and "contamination" of real life, and manipulations are performed which vary only one factor at a time regardless of whether it can or does function independently under normal circumstances. Not all psychological research, of course, involves context-stripping methods in their purest form—the laboratory experiment—but nonexperimental, nonlaboratory research is regarded in the field as less than ideal, as "soft." (The arbiters of methodological purity do not quite characterize nonexperimental methods as "effeminate" but one sometimes senses it hovering in the background.)

Despite the logic, vigor, and persuasiveness of the criticisms that have been made of psychology's traditional commitment to context-stripping methods, the criticisms have not promoted significant change in the field. To understand why this commitment in psychology is so resistant to change, we need to explore one further question: Who benefits from the current state of affairs? What function, in other words, is served by psychology's unswerving commitment to a particular method as defining the field? . . .

In some sense psychology's commitment to context-stripping methods is a commitment to making the political personal—the very opposite of what women realize when they become feminists. And there are of course other grounds than feminist ones for rejecting psychology's efforts to portray the individual as an isolated private entity. The commitment to the experimental method which characterizes mainstream psychology not only functions to exclude feminist research, it also serves to obscure the connections between individual experience and social roles and institutions. To the extent that psychology is used to develop or justify public policy, the strained relationship between feminist psychology and the field as a whole is merely symptomatic of a more general problem affecting all women.

Feminists can perhaps contribute something to the solution of this problem. I take the strength of psychology's resistance to feminist insights to be a measure of the "danger" such insights represent to the view that the individual must and can be understood out of context. We could make it considerably more dangerous, I think, if we clarified certain concepts widely used in the psychology of women. I will briefly discuss only one example: the notion of "sex roles" or "gender roles."[16] Is one's sex or gender a "role" any more than one's age or race is? Probably not. What is usually meant by, for example, the "female gender role" or "women's roles" are the roles of wife and mother. But what, exactly, is meant by the role of "wife?" Housework? Financial support by the husband? If so, let us be more accurate and say precisely what we mean—rather than perpetuate hidden assumptions *which it is in our interest to make explicit.* The role of mother is similarly vague, since the activities associated with it depend largely upon the structure of the family and other social groups in the particular society being discussed. Explicitly stating the conditions under which a role exists is not only more precise, it makes the availability of alternatives clearer. I think it is in our interest to use "role" in the technical sense that sociologists use it—to refer to a set of rights, duties, privileges, and obligations vis-à-vis others in the context of particular institutions. Feminists need to have accurate accounts of social reality, and psychologists can contribute to it in a small way only insofar as they are able to clarify their thinking about crucial concepts. My own view is that the last thing wanted by traditional psychologists is clear thinking—focusing on context—about problems of social significance.

So let's do it.

Notes

1. The "psychology of women" here refers to psychological research and theory that is *for* women (see M. B. Parlee, "Psychology: Review Essay," *Signs: Journal of Women in Culture and Society* 1 [1975]: 119–38). Sexist research on women is of course still being done, but its creators do not identify themselves as being in the field of the psychology of women. Feminist psychologists' power to define and name their own field has evidently prevailed, and the psychology of women now denotes and connotes research that is feminist in some very broad (perhaps arguably so) sense of the term. Psychologists who do not want to be associated with this perspective no longer use the label for their work, even if their research is about women.

2. E. E. Maccoby and C. N. Jacklin. *The Psychology of Sex Differences* (Stanford, Calif.: Stanford University Press, 1974).

3. A. H. Eagley, "Sex Differences in Influencibility," *Psychological Bulletin* 85 (1978): 86–116; A. Frodi, J. Macauley, and P. R. Thome, "Are Women Always Less Aggressive than Men?" *Psychological Bulletin* 84 (1977): 634–60; L. Tiefer, "What We Don't Know about the Physiology of Female Sexual-

ity" (paper presented at the Association of Women in Psychology, Dallas, 1979).

4. N. P. Porter, F. L. Geis, and J. J. Walstedt, "The Woman at the Head of the Table—or Is It the Foot?" Xeroxed (University of Delaware, Department of Psychology, 1978).

5. F. Crosby and L. Nyquist, "The Female Register: An Empirical Study of Lakoff's Hypothesis," *Language in Society* 6 (1977): 313–22.

6. W. M. O'Barr and B. K. Atkins, "Women's Language, or 'Powerless Language'?" Duke University Law and Language Project, Research Report 19, 1978; E. A. Lind et al., "Social Attribution and Conversation Style in Trial Testimony," *Journal of Personality and Social Psychology* 36 (1978): 1558–67.

7. C. S. Dweck and T. F. Goetz, "Attribution and Learned Helplessness," in *New Directions in Attribution Research*, ed. J. H. Harvey, W. Ickes, and R. F. Kidd (Hillsdale, N.J.: Lawrence Erlbaum Associates, 1978), vol. 2.

8. W. H. Jones, M. E. O'C. Chernovetz, and R. O. Hansson, "The Enigma of Androgyny: Differential Implications for Males and Females?" *Journal of Consulting and Clinical Psychology* 46 (1978): 298–313; A. G. Kaplan, guest ed., *Psychology of Women Quarterly*, vol. 3 (1979), *Psychological Androgyny: Further Considerations.*

9. S. Bem, "Beyond Androgyny: Some Thoughts on the Cognitive Processes Mediating Sex-Typing and Androgyny" (keynote address, annual meeting of the Association of Women in Psychology, Pittsburgh, March 1978).

10. R. Barnett and G. Baruch, "Women in the Middle Years: A Critique of Research and Theory," *Psychology of Women Quarterly* 3 (1978): 187–97; Dan et al.; A. G. Kaplan, chair, "Women and Anger in the Therapeutic Relationship" (symposium presented at the annual meeting of the American Psychological Association, San Francisco, 1977); Unger.

11. R. S. Albin, "Psychological Studies of Rape: A Review Essay," *Signs: Journal of Women in Culture and Society* 3, no. 2 (1977): 423–35; P. M. Fishman, "What Do Couples Talk about When They're Alone?" in *Women's Language and Style*, ed. D. Buttarff (Akron, Ohio: University of Akron, 1978); I. H. Frieze. "Self-Perceptions of the Battered Woman" (paper presented at the annual meeting of the American Women in Psychology, Pittsburgh, March 1978, as part of a symposium, "Researching Problems of Battered Women"); S. Saegert and G. Winkel, "The Home: A Critical Problem for Changing Sex-Roles" (paper presented at the annual meeting of the American Psychological Association, San Francisco, 1978); S. E. Taylor and S. Levin, "The Psychological Impact of Breast Cancer: Theory and Practice," in *Psychological Aspects of Breast Cancer*, ed. H. Enlow (London: Oxford University Press, 1977); I. Waldron, "Why Do Women Live Longer than Men?" *Journal of Human Stress*, pt. 1 (March 1976), pp. 2–13; I. Waldron and S. Johnston, ibid., pt. 2 (June), pp. 19–29; C. West and D. H. Zimmerman; "Strangers When They Met: A Study of Same-Sex

and Cross-Sex Conversations between Unacquainted Persons" (paper delivered at the American Sociological Association annual meeting, San Francisco, September 4–8, 1978); *Women and Language News* (Linguistics Department, Stanford University, Stanford, California 94305).

12. R. K. Unger, B. S. Wallston, and V. E. O'Leary, "Women, Gender and Social Psychology," *Society for the Advancement of Social Psychology (SASP) Newsletter* 4, no. 4 (May 1978): 1–13. For information, write V. E. O'Leary, Department of Psychology, Oakland University, Rochester, Michigan 48063.

13. R. K. Unger, chair, "Sex Differences or Sex Bias?" (symposium presented at the eighty-second annual meeting of the American Psychological Association, New Orleans, 1974).

14. Interview with Robert Hogar, *APA Monitor* 10, no. 4 (April 1979): 4–5.

15. E. G. Mishler, "Meaning in Context: Is There Any Other Kind?" *Harvard Educational Review* 49 (1979): 1–19.

16. For additional examples, see M. B. Parlee, "The Psychology of Gender" (preliminary statement prepared for the Social Sciences Research Council Meeting on Gender and Society, February 10–11, 1979).

33 Issues to Consider in Conducting Nonsexist Psychological Research: A Guide for Researchers

MAUREEN C. MCHUGH

RANDI DAIMON KOESKE

IRENE HANSON FRIEZE

Many historians, researchers, and philosophers of science (e.g., Buss, 1978; Koch, 1981; Sampson, 1978; Smith, 1979; Unger, 1981; Wittig, 1985) claim that science reflects the social values and concerns of dominant societal groups. There is often a close connection between the capacity to break out of established conceptions and personal experience with social change or marginal social status (Coan, 1979; Samelson, 1978; Sampson, 1978). Creative tension between alternative perspectives can clarify the assumptions held within each group. To the extent that the dominant male group's view is imposed on nonmembers, the potential for breakthrough conceptualizations is decreased, and the creative tension between experiential perspectives is lost. A goal of this article is to explicate the "outsider's" (i.e., male) interpretive framework that has colored much of psychology's accumulated knowledge about women. The dominant group's perspective is one form of sexist bias in psychology.

Psychology is sexist to the extent that its theorizing does not have equal relevance to individuals of both sexes, and greater attention is given to life experiences of one sex. The inadvertent introduction of bias into the research process has resulted in social and scientific costs. Psychologists' untested assumptions about the sexes have impacted on the policies and practices within society. For example, the variability hypothesis of sex differences in intelligence subscribed to by Thorndike (1903) and others was used as an argument against admitting women to institutions of higher learning. The refutation of sexist theories and conclusions has also required extensive use of personpower that might have been spent investigating other human problems. Hollingworth (1914, 1916, 1918) spent a substantial amount of time collecting empirical evidence to refute the variability hypothesis.

Hollingworth's work is representative of one way in which the entry of women into the discipline of psychology has resulted in a challenging of "accepted" psychological principles and practices. Early women psychologists challenged the boundaries of psychology, exploring new content areas and new approaches to social problems (cf. Rosenberg, 1982).

The descriptions of sexist practices and the recommendations to minimize sexist bias in psychology offered here are intended to foster increased awareness of and debate concerning the operation of sexism in research. Biases of the sort described in this article need not be introduced into research intentionally or consciously. Rather, bias routinely occurs because it represents the accumulated "common experience" of being a member of a particular group. Perhaps one of the most difficult tasks of a scientist is to become disengaged from "everyday" shared assumptions about the nature of reality and to generate alternative, testable conceptualizations of reality. Experience as a nonmember or as a marginal member of a group can contribute to the individual's ability to view reality from an alternative perspective (Mayo, 1982).

In this article, an attempt is made to look at the operation of sexism in all areas of psychological research, from broad conceptual issues to more narrow methodological concerns. The article deals with the conceptualization of science and psychological research in general, conceptual models of sex-related differences and conceptualization and operationalization of terms and constructs.

Some issues relevant to the development of a nonsexist psychology are not directly touched upon in these guidelines. For example, sexism in language and sex bias in testing are not explicitly covered. For more information on these topics, see Martyna (1980) and Moulton, Robinson, and Elias (1978) or Wise and Rafferty (1982) on language bias, and Diamond (1976) and Harway (1980) on testing bias.

Excessive Confidence in Traditional Methods of Research

Widely shared beliefs and values, including those about the sexes, may enter the research process even when careful efforts are made to adhere to established research procedures and methodological principles (Buss, 1978; Carlson, 1972; Crawford, 1978; Gilligan, 1979; Koeske, 1978; Laws, 1976; Lipman-Blumen & Tickamyer, 1975; McKenna & Kessler, 1977; Sampson, 1978; Sherif, 1980, 1981; Unger, 1981, 1982; Wallston, 1983). Researchers wishing to avoid sexism need to question more thoroughly the ways they ask questions and gather data. More thorough and systematic efforts to solicit disconfirming information and to encourage professional debate of assumptions, values, and methods have been proposed as ways to improve psychology. Important steps in this process of questioning will be highlighted.

Preference for Objectivity

Although it is widely recognized that all measures contain error, many psychologists make a clear distinction between objective and subjective measures. This distinction rests on the equation of objectivity with value-free, repeatable methods of data collection and on the belief in the generalizability of objective data. In contrast, subjectivity is viewed as being value laden and unrepeatable, based on private events, and focused on unique experiences that cannot be generalized (Koeske, 1978; Sherif, 1979; Wallston, 1983; Wittig, 1985).

This distinction between objectivity and subjectivity provides a rationale for many scientific practices. Various procedural safeguards, such as using behavioral (vs. self-report) measures, minimizing interaction with research participants, concealing the true purpose of the study, and standardizing research procedures are recommended to assure research objectivity. By using such safeguards, the potential biases deriving from the "insider" perspective (such as the respondent's striving for a positive self-presentation or the researcher's hope of achieving predicted results) are thought to be minimized.

Social scientists concerned with eliminating sexism from psychological research question the value of these experimental controls and of being uninvolved or disinterested (cf. Graham & Rawlings, 1980; Koeske, 1978; Reinharz, 1981; Sherif, 1979; Unger, 1981; Wallston, 1981). They have suggested that eliciting subjective viewpoints may be one way to "get behind" the inequality and the limited self-presentation potentially inherent in all researcher–participant interactions. Both the appropriateness and the scientific utility of the experimenter's being neutral, disinterested, and nondisclosing have been challenged, especially when the experimenter desires to have participants behave naturally and honestly. There are dangers in excluding respondents from participation in making decisions about research applications that affect them, in failing to inform or support respondents seeking advice, and in failing to explicate assumptions and misgivings about the research for professional audiences for fear of appearing "subjective" (Graham & Rawlings, 1980; Millman & Kanter, 1975).

Although many psychologists would agree that both objective and subjective methods have advantages and disadvantages, alternative (subjective) methods are often evaluated by comparison to traditional (objective) methods. This practice suggests that we continue to subscribe to the claims that traditional methods can produce more valid, value-free knowledge (Coan, 1979, Wallston, 1983).

Overemphasis on Experimenter Control

Ideally, the choice of data collection procedures and setting is dictated by the goals of the research project. Researchers concerned with avoiding sexism in psychology have suggested that most research designs, particularly the more highly regarded experimental designs, may affect respondents in undesirable ways. Such control of the research situation may inhibit participants' self-disclosure, may make the setting less "real," or may result in participants displaying high levels of conventional behavior. Behavior that is exhibited in an unfamiliar setting and entails little self-involvement and often no prior social relationship with other participants may also be unrepresentative of "real life" behavior. Given these prior constraints, it may become difficult to elicit truly honest responses during a postexperimental interview or debriefing (cf. Graham & Rawlings, 1980; Sherif, 1979; Wallston, 1981).

The inequality between the researcher and the research participants is especially clear and problematic when the experimenter is male and the participants are female. Here the research setting most clearly reflects and reinforces the imposition of male definitions of reality on females. Such a situation may be viewed as an extension of the insider–outsider problem referred to earlier. To the extent that researchers enter a research project with set hypotheses or assumptions, they will remain outsiders who fail to elicit critical insider information or to recognize the potential harm in their approach. Data collection techniques and research review procedures that encourage respondents to participate in the formulation of goals and hypotheses represent one frequently suggested approach to resolving the dilemma of researcher control (Boukydis, 1981; Brannon, 1974; Glaser & Strauss, 1967; Graham & Rawlings, 1980; Reinharz, 1981).

Assumption of the Validity of Established Findings

Even well-established findings can harbor unsuspected sexism in content or method (cf. Caplan, MacPherson, & Tobin, 1985; Gilligan, 1979; Jacobson, 1980). Therefore, researchers undertaking literature reviews or engaging in meta-analyses need to carefully examine primary sources, noting evidence of sexist assumptions and unwarranted generalizations. The persistence of generalizations based on past research may be unjustified if narrowly defined measures (cf. McKenna & Kessler, 1977) or procedures are inappropriate to women (cf. Frieze, Parsons, Johnson, Ruble, & Zellman, 1978) were employed. Researchers should be especially cautious about using a box-score approach in tallying statistically significant findings, because the publishability of results is often influenced by factors other than methodological soundness. Weak or methodologically questionable findings may be published and cited repeatedly as evidence for a generalization when they are consistent with prevailing paradigms about human behavior, whereas important counterevidence may go unpublished or uncited. For example, Parlee (1973) noted that frequent references had been made to one very small, methodologically flawed study showing more airplane crashes for menstruating female pilots. Similarly, Caplan, MacPherson, and Tobin (1985) questioned the continuing belief that males are superior to females in spatial abilities in spite of small samples and inconsistencies in supportive research.

Convergence and divergence across studies and techniques may provide important information about the validity and context-dependence of particular findings. Researchers undertaking literature reviews should make more thoughtful use of convergent and divergent information, noting to what extent findings stand up under widely divergent data collection procedures (cf. Frodi, Macaulay, & Thome, 1977, on sex-related difference in aggression, or Eagly, 1983, on influenceability). The failure of particular researchers or bodies of research to define concepts unambiguously, to confine conclusions to available data, and to provide sex-fair tests of hypotheses should be noted in reviews and should be considered when deciding whether to publish. Although it may not be possible to ignore a large body of findings because of its failure to avoid sexism, thorough discussion of possible sources of bias in studies reporting "established" findings is needed if fresh perspectives are to be developed. Researchers should also consider historical factors and gender-relevant role changes that may make established findings irrelevant to the prediction or explanation of behavior in current research settings (cf. Gergen, 1973,

1976). A summary of ways to avoid overconfidence in traditional research methods is presented in Appendix A (page 519).

Bias in Explanatory Systems

Multiple and Imprecise Use of Terminology

Researchers use the term *sex* in a variety of contexts (Gould & Kern-Daniels, 1977). They may use it when describing behaviors or events that covary with the biological sex of the research participants, without specifically indicating which causal factors might account for such covariations or discussing the generalizability of the covariations (e.g., "sex differences in puzzle-solving ability," "responses did not differ by sex"). The term sex is also used to imply the operation of underlying physiological processes correlated with or necessitated by genetic sex (e.g., "sex hormones," "sexual differentiation of the brain"). In other contexts, sex is used to refer to any of the many social or situational factors that are linked to biological sex through the processes of social learning and social differentiation (e.g., "sex roles," "sex typing") although *gender* is the preferred term for issues related to socialization. Finally, researchers may use the term sex to refer to expressions of physical intimacy or affection (e.g., "sexual behavior," "oral sex," "sexual preference"). Similar examples of multiple usage could be offered for such related terms as *masculine* and *feminine* or *male* and *female*.

In publishing their results, researchers must clearly define the terms they use. Imprecise use of the term sex may create the impression that each of the dimensions of "sex" discussed above is influenced by the same causal factors. There is often an implicit or explicit assumption of biological causation associated with the term *sex differences*. Researchers should clarify whether their results provide evidence of covariation or causal linkage with biological sex. When discussing covariations involving biological sex or when speaking descriptively, researchers should consider the adoption of a more neutral term like *sex-related* to convey the causal ambiguity or complexity of the observed results. Suggestions for appropriate terminology have been offered by others (cf. Unger, 1979a; Vaughter, 1976).

Developing Precise Explanatory Models

Models attempting to explain sex-related behaviors must be specific as to the mechanism and processes involved. A general reference to hormones or social learning is almost always inadequate as an explanation for sex-related behavior (cf. Frieze et al., 1978). Among the many factors to be considered as possible explanations for sex-related behavior are the following: biological factors (e.g., genetic, hormonal, or other physiological factors), sociocultural factors (e.g., familial, peer, economic), and situational factors (e.g., immediate cues or symbols operative in a particular context). Ideally, researchers seeking to explain sex-related behavior should consider all possible explanatory factors, even if all were not explicitly investigated. Even though some factors may be implausible and others may be difficult to measure, the possible role of all these explanatory factors should be carefully reviewed when making inferences, especially as theory is being developed or refined.

Explanations or interpretations that focus on sex as a causal factor usually have very different connotations and implications than those that focus causally on gender. The inappropriate labeling of sex differences is particularly problematic because genetic sex and its physical markers represent socially significant symbols that are used as the basis for social differentiation (cf. Eagley, 1983; Henley, 1977; Unger, 1978). Any of these social correlates may contribute to observed sex-related behavioral differences (Eagley, 1983; Petersen, 1976; Unger, 1979b; Waber, 1976). Because sex covaries with physiological and sociocultural factors simultaneously, both factors represent plausible causes of a single phenomenon. Even if the researcher is not interested in both types of factors, ignoring one set can lead to inaccurate or incomplete inferences. Ultimately, when two conflicting models can explain the same set of results, tests that differentiate between the two explanations are needed.

Awareness of Interactions Between Variables and the Scope of a Variable's Influence

A simple model of biology versus culture should not be assumed in efforts to explain sex-related behavior (Parsons, 1980; Petersen, 1984; Shields, 1975). Most present-day researchers believe that sex-related behavior originates and is maintained in a context of interactions. It is important for researchers to clarify the form of interaction with which they are dealing, because many forms of interaction are possible (cf. Newcomb, 1980).

Physiological factors may exert direct effects on behavior or produce indirect effects that are either physiologically or socially mediated (e.g., hormonal changes associated with the menstrual cycle may affect mood, or the social meaning of menstruation and womanhood may affect mood). Similarly, sociocultural factors may provide relatively constant long-term effects, or their influence may depend on changing cues present only during certain life periods or in certain situations (e.g., morphological sex probably exerts a lifelong effect, but sexual attractiveness changes with age, social relationship, and social setting). Sociocultural factors may themselves affect physiology, directly or indirectly (e.g., gender role affects health through diet and exercise as well as through physical contact and exposure to various health risks). The cues or symbols that exert significant effects on behavior may be imposed by others (e.g., parents' clothing choices for their children) or self-regulated (e.g., adult clothing and makeup choices), and their presence may be socially detectable or private (e.g., makeup versus reconstructive surgery). Each of these distinctions differs in the causal factors it postulates and the behavior it seeks to explain and should be explored carefully by the researcher if oversimplification and imprecision are to be avoided.

Biological variables are sometimes treated as having relatively irreversible and pervasive effects on subsequent behavior, whereas the effects of other variables are viewed as more transient or circumscribed (Unger, 1981). Such a view fails to account for interactions of social and biological factors and the fact that there is little long-term stability in any human behavior (Kagan, 1969). Researchers should be careful not to make assumptions about the stability or the scope of variable effects. Longitudinal research and training studies have been suggested as appropriate ways to investigate these questions (e.g., Wittig, 1979).

Providing Adequate Tests And Useful Dialogue

Researchers eager to argue for the importance of one set of factors often examine available data with an eye to the construction of a convincing case rather than to establishing scientific validity (cf. Bartley, 1964; Weimer, 1975). This partisan stance becomes problematic when unacknowledged by the researcher or when accepted uncritically by others. Both physiological and sociocultural model builders are susceptible to this tendency.

Because proponents of different explanatory models often use different research tools and publish in different journals, dialogue between competing perspectives is often limited. When such theorists do take on the research of a competing model, they may resort to one or more self-justificatory practices. For example, they may fail to specify their own model sufficiently for competing approaches to provide either confirmatory or disconfirmatory data, or they may compile supportive research studies about whose methodological weaknesses they are uncritical.

Practices that encourage dialogue about competing explanatory models involving sex-related behavior are needed. Researchers interested in such models should attempt to develop common terminologies and propose models that clearly specify relationships among sex and gender and both physiological and sociocultural variables. More elaborate efforts are needed to test competing models, not just argue for their plausibility as explanations.

Such efforts are especially important for animal research, which so often relies on an evolutionary perspective to understand sex differentiation. Evolutionary advantages are assumed to attach to characteristics that differentiate each species or each sex within a species. This perspective can be circular and result in sexism when (a) it is used to justify all differences found between the sexes as adaptive and thus necessary, or (b) it is used as the basis for viewing all such differences as biologically rather than culturally determined. Natural selection and environmental adaptation are exceedingly complex processes, and many different solutions to the same problems are possible (cf. Bleier, 1984; Crawford, 1978). Moreover, controversy currently exists about which characteristics are incidental to survival and which are essential. Some characteristics may survive even though they are not wholly adaptive because nonbiological mechanisms (e.g., cultural, medical, or sociopolitical arrangements) render them less of a liability. Claims about the survival value of particular traits or qualities should be tempered by an awareness of the complexity of the factors involved. Researchers who wish to avoid sexism should avoid the circularity of assuming that what exists is adaptive or that what has proven adaptive in the past will remain so as environmental factors change.

When using animal models to examine processes of relevance to humans (e.g., aggression, sexuality, social organization, reactions to stress), researchers should exercise caution about inferring that innate or biological mechanisms underlie human phenomena, even those bearing similarity to behaviors observed in animals. Differences in cognitive and symbolic capacity always make direct cross-species comparisons difficult. Similarities in ecology and social learning, rather than biology, may account for observed similarities (cf. Crawford, 1978; Leibowitz, 1979). Moreover, much animal research requires maintaining animals in unnatural settings in order to systematically observe their behavior. These unnatural settings may produce behaviors that, although infrequent in the natural habitat, come to be viewed as innate by the researcher unfamiliar with the animals' behavior in other settings (cf. Leibowitz, 1979; Rowell, 1972).

Researchers should also be wary of using anthropomorphic concepts (e.g., dominance) instead of operational measures (e.g., mounting), when stating conclusions about animal behavior. Observed animal behaviors may have more circumscribed or different meanings within the animal groupings to which they apply than do the more general human behavioral correlates.

Testing and Reporting Sex Differences

The emphasis on sex differences in the literature seems to imply that differences between the sexes are more frequent, more interesting, or more important than similarities between the sexes (Wallston & Grady, 1985). To the extent that a difference model is accepted by researchers and editors, studies demonstrating sex-related differences are more likely to be reported, published, cited, and used as the basis for public policy than studies demonstrating sex similarities (Frieze et al., 1978; Maccoby & Jacklin, 1974). Researchers and editors should be careful not to accept such a difference model on the basis of stereotypic assumptions. Equal attention should be paid to gender similarities.

Sex-related differences that have not been replicated or have not been predicted by or grounded in a theoretical model may not be appropriate content for published research. Avoiding publication of serendipitous findings by requesting replication before publication may help to limit both the publication of unreliable findings and post-hoc explanations that draw on popular stereotypes (Signorella, Vegega, & Mitchell, 1981). The percentage of variance accounted for when "significant" sex differences are found should also be carefully noted to ensure that the difference is a meaningful one (Sohn, 1982; Wallston & Grady, 1985).

Many researchers may wish to test for sex-related differences as a general strategy, even though such data may not be immediately published. When found, such differences may signal the need to examine the theory, sample, context and research methods for gender bias. Suggestions for avoiding bias in explanatory models are presented in Appendix A.

Inappropriate Conceptualization and Operationalization

Labeling of Individuals and Behavior

Terminology represents one way in which cultural ideologies about sex and gender can influence psychological research and theory. Specifically, judgments concerning the appropriateness of male and female behaviors and traits can influence the labels applied to individuals and their behavior, the definition of terms, and the operationalization of constructs in research. The implicit identification of the male with normative and positively valued traits and behavior is sexist and should be avoided.

The Nontraditionalism of Behavior It is sexist to use negatively toned labels to describe nontraditional role behaviors when the maladaptiveness or undesirability of these behaviors is assumed rather than documented, or when the significance or prevalence of both traditional and nontraditional behaviors is unknown (e.g., doll playing by males labeled as gender-identity confusion or career dedication in a female labeled as a masculinity complex). Instead, descriptive rather than prescriptive labels should be used, and attention should be directed to possible positive consequences of the behavior. The conventionality or social desirability of behavior should not be confused with its incidence.

Sex-Related Differences in Behavior Some labels imply that female behaviors are generally or inherently less valued than the male behaviors from which they supposedly differ. Such labeling of sex-related differences is sexist if no data on the effectiveness or desirability of particular behaviors are available, or if the effectiveness of a behavior depends on its context but this qualification is not made. For example, it is sexist to label females' attentiveness to the context of behavior as "dependence," because this label implies inadequacy (given the general evaluative connotation of the term). Alternatively, "field dependent" behavior might be viewed as an adaptive response to subordinate social status (cf. Kaplan, 1983; Riley & Denmark, 1974). Thorough consideration of the context in which behavior occurs is helpful. Terminology that reflects tolerance of differences rather than implies an absolute preferred standard should be developed.

A Presumed Male–Female Continuum of Behavior A label is sexist when it implies that male–female differences, when found, are to be thought of as bipolar opposites on a single continuum, especially when such an interpretation places the behavior of one gender in a negative light, distorts the complexity of the behavior involved, and is discrepant from the subjective meaning of the behavior to the actor (e.g., a woman's "emotional" behavior is contrasted with a man's "rationality").

Kaplan (1983) has provided some lively examples of the pitfalls of this bipolarity in her critique of DSM-III diagnostic categories (American Psychiatric Association, 1980). Her fictitious diagnostic criteria for Independent Personality Disorder and Restricted Personality Disorder alert us to the fact that the label "dependent" is not routinely applied to men who rely on others to cook, clean, or raise children for them. Some men's inability to write thank you notes or openly express concern for others is also not routinely viewed as an emotional deficit. Researchers (and clinicians) hoping to avoid sexism should use precise behavioral descriptions rather than global trait designations whenever possible.

Generalization of Results

The choice or conceptualization of a research problem may be sexist if the stated generality of the phenomenon or the generalizability of the results differs according to the respondents' biological sex. For example, achievement motivation is presented as a general theory although it is based largely on male behaviors (cf. Mednick, Tangri, & Hoffman, 1975), whereas models of achievement behavior based on female samples have often been viewed as "special cases." In general, studies based on males are more often generalized to both sexes even when such generalization may be inappropriate (Reardon & Prescott, 1977; Schwabacher, 1972).

Choosing Research Topics and Participants

The selection of research topics and the choice of participants represent two related areas in which sexism may operate. Published critiques such as those referred to below have cited sexism in topic and participant selection more frequently than in any other aspect of the research process.

Topic Selection

Topics of primary interest to women (e.g., female alcoholism, victimization by rape and abuse) have either been ignored or have received less research attention than topics that are especially relevant to men (e.g., male alcoholism, male to male aggression; see Denmark, 1983; Lott, 1985; Wallston & Grady, 1985). Moreover, topics of general interest (e.g., power, health) have drawn on examples that are more male- than female-identified (e.g., leadership rather than maternal roles or Type A personality rather than pregnancy and lactation). One factor contributing to this differential attention is the underrepresentation of females in the discipline, especially in research positions. However, the funding priorities of granting agencies may also contribute to this problem. The emphasis on particular paradigms and approaches to psychological research may also limit the study of content areas of special interest to women. For example, the preference for researcher-defined problems and settings may limit attention to the private sphere as an arena for power, thus restricting the number and characteristics of women (and other minorities) who could serve as suitable research participants.

All too often, research conducted in content areas of particular relevance for women has been accorded less status within the discipline than research conducted on topics of particular interest to males. The tendency to characterize topics as either basic/nonclinical or applied/clinical is sexist to the extent that male-oriented topics are viewed as basic, whereas women's issues are seen as applied or clinical. For example, theories or research on male behaviors in a competitive context are more likely to be included in a general text or leading professional journal than theory or research on the menstrual cycle, or childbirth.

In general, topics of interest to women should be accorded the status of resources given those relevant to men. Judgments of the importance of particular topics or their classification as basic or applied should not depend on the sex of the respondents used or the presumed gender relevance of the topic.

Sample Selection

Even when topic selection is sex fair, subject selection and the choice of control groups may reflect sexist biases (Parlee, 1981; Prescott, 1978; Wallston & Grady, 1985). Normative considerations implicit in the choice of typical or atypical samples of each sex may reflect sexist assumptions and may lead to findings that can be better interpreted by reference to an uncontrolled third variable. For example, using employed men and unemployed women as representative of men and women generally may turn up apparent sex-related differences in behavior that are equally attributable to employment status. Failure to carefully consider the gender representativeness of a particular sample may foster sexism if results are inappropriately generalized to all members of the sex sampled (e.g., studies of menstrual difficulties in a sample of female patients are discussed in terms of processes like cycles, phases, or hormonal levels that affect all women).

Factors in addition to sex would be expected to differentiate most research samples, because research generally involves the comparison of accidental groups, that is, individuals who happen to be present or available for testing at a particular time or in a particular context. Accidental groups are not likely to be comparable on all important dimensions and do not reveal much about the "natural" or "inevitable" differences between the sexes (Parlee, 1981).

Comparisons between male and female samples may be complicated by the fact that males and females may differ in life-span activities. Thus, comparing samples where age is similar would not ensure that life activities or priorities are comparable, and comparisons of samples of individuals who are engaged in equivalent life activities may be influenced by age differences. For example, how should males and females be compared in terms of career orientation if men are most involved in their careers at age 30, and women are most career-oriented at age 40 (Parlee, 1981)? Or, are differences in parenting styles between fathers and mothers of a first child due to sex differences or to the relative ages of the fathers and mothers?

Single Sex Samples The frequent use of single-sex samples limits the explanatory robustness of psychology. Historically, researchers have demonstrated a preference for male subjects (Carlson & Carlson, 1961; Etaugh & Spandikow, 1979; Reardon & Prescott, 1976; Smart, 1966). When demonstrated consistently within the discipline or within a particular research area, this preference can result in the construction of theories and models of behavior that have little or no relevance for females.

In one report of psychologists' decision-making practices, researchers reported that they limited subjects to one sex as a way of "controlling" this variable (Prescott, 1978). Although exclusion of females is a frequently used and convenient way to limit experimental complexity and to cut down on research costs, it places a serious limitation on the ability of psychology to develop adequate models of human behavior. For example, Kahn and Gaeddert (1985) discussed how the inclusion of female participants in equity studies has resulted in the questioning of equity as the universal rule of justice, and Gilligan's (1979) work on women's moral reasoning has questioned the completeness of Kohlberg's model of morality.

Some psychological researchers have used single-sex samples out of an erroneous belief that certain topics are only relevant to one sex (cf. McKenna & Kessler, 1977; Signorella et al., 1981). For example, research on aggression has been largely limited to males (cf. Frodi et al., 1977), whereas research on social influence has relied heavily on female participants (cf. Eagly, 1978). Signorella and Vegega (1984) have demonstrated that potential research participants also view certain topics as feminine or masculine, and their tendency to volunteer for various experiments is affected by such perceptions. Assumptions made by either the researchers or the participants about the gender relevance of research topics should be closely examined. Theoretical frameworks should attempt to define problems so that they are relevant to both sexes and should be evaluated on the basis of results derived from both men and women.

Operationalization Problems

Sex-Typing of Experimental Stimuli Differential socialization and past experience may result in males and females differing in their present cognitions about and responses to particular situations in which the individuals are functioning. Various aspects of the current situation may differ in their *salience, familiarity, relevance*, and *meaning* to male and female research participants. Thus, although most studies attempt to control for situational factors by making the external situation the same for males and females, researchers have often ignored the fact that "objectively" identical situations may be psychologically very different for males and females. There is considerable research evidence that contexts are sex-typed and sex-segregated in our culture from an early age (cf. Frieze, et al., 1978; O'Leary, 1977; Unger, 1979b).

In constructing the experimental situation, the researcher may fail to realize that the task or problem utilized in the study may be viewed as more appropriate or relevant to members of one sex or may be more familiar to participants of one sex. For example, Sistrunk and McDavid (1971) concluded that the previous generalizations regarding sex differences in conformity may have been partly due to a greater use of male-related tasks in the research. Other researchers have demonstrated that labeling or presenting the tasks as relevant for a particular sex affects the expectancies, aspiration level, performance, and attributions of the participant and the evaluations and attributions of an observer.

A complex form of sexism occurs when a construct is operationalized differently depending on the sex of the participants. Tasks used in research are more likely to be passive when women rather than men are the participants in the research (cf. Frodi, et al., 1977; McKenna & Kessler, 1977) and when "feminine" rather than "masculine" topics are being studied (Signorella et al., 1981).

Response categories for dependent variables should allow for a variety of responses. As Bart (1971) pointed out, allowing women to describe their sexual role as "passive," "responsive," "aggressive," "deviant," or "other" does not allow for such responses as "playful," "active," or any of a number of other types of sexual responses.

Sex of the Experimenter and Others Many elements of the research context, such as the sex and presence of others, may provide gender role cues that are irrelevant to the question the investigator is asking and yet may affect the research in systematic ways. For example, research has demonstrated that the sex of the experimenter affects the problem-solving performance of females (e.g., Pedersen, Shinedling, & Johnson, 1968).

In another study, participants gave more positive ratings to experimenters of the opposite sex than to those of the same sex (Barnes & Rosenthal, 1985). Despite the evidence that the sex of the experimenter can have differential effects on the responses of male and female participants (Harris, 1971), surveys of psychological journals have consistently demonstrated that authors often fail to specify the sex of the experimenter (e.g., Carlson & Carlson, 1961; Reardon & Prescott, 1977).

Sex composition of the group and sex of other (participants or confederates) are other important contextual variables that can influence the results of studies. In several studies, the mere presence of certain proportions of males and females affected the responses of members of the group (e.g., Ruble & Higgins, 1976; Taylor & Fiske, 1978). The practice of employing single-sex groups as a way of controlling for sex (e.g., equity studies) may result in a confounding of sex-related behaviors with sex composition effects (Kahn, Nelson, & Gaeddert, 1980). In addition, the responses and behaviors of males and females may differ depending on the public versus private nature of the behavior. Thus, the presence, number, and sex of others (including the experimenter and confederates) may differentially influence the behavior of participants.

A related problem is the failure to report the sex composition of the sample, even when this information may be relevant to the generalizability of results and conclusions. This problem has been noted consistently in reports of journal surveys (Carlson, 1971; Carlson & Carlson, 1961; Etaugh & Spandikow, 1979; Reardon & Prescott, 1977; Schwabacher, 1972; Smart, 1966). Failure to thoroughly describe the sample may reflect the author's implicit assumption that gender is irrelevant to the topic or that gender played no important role in the results obtained. It also denies the audience the information needed to make inferences about the generality of results and conclusions. In general, researchers should exercise care in generalizing their results to other subjects or contexts.

Choice of Context In both laboratory and field research, the researcher may have selected a situation or context in which sex-typed behaviors are especially likely to occur. For example, one study found that although girls cried more than boys in one situation, boys cried as much as girls in a second situation (Jacklin, Maccoby, & Dick, 1973). In another study, often-reported sex-related differences in group task performance did not occur when the content of the tasks was selected so as not to favor the interests of one sex over the other (Wood, Polek, & Aiken, 1985). Failure to include multiple contexts in which to investigate behavior may result in an inappropriate conclusion. Misinterpretation of sex of subject effects may also occur in observational research, if the researcher fails to realize that males and females may be differentially distributed across situations and subsequently interprets situational differences as sex-related differences (Grady, 1981). The researcher who finds and reports a "sex difference" in a single situation that cannot be grounded empirically in either differential physiological functioning or identifiably different past experiences may be indicating ignorance of person–environment interactions. Research has demonstrated that sex by situation interactions are more the rule than the exception, being found more frequently than main effects for sex (Deaux, 1976). Suggestions for avoiding sexism in the conduct and interpretation of research are presented in Appendix A (*included here page 519*).

Conclusions

A series of recommendations have been offered to help eliminate sexist bias in psychological research. The recommendations may be characterized as general and idealistic. These characteristics may be both weaknesses and strengths. It is recognized that it is difficult to apply and satisfy all the recommendations in a specific research project. At the same time, it is important to us that the principles we suggest can endure in a constantly changing discipline and can give that discipline some direction for further growth.

These or other recommendations for sex-fair research can be utilized in a variety of ways (McHugh, 1982). They may be used in the training of new researchers so that each new generation of psychologists produces less sexist psychology. They may be useful as guides in the reviewing of grant proposals and paper submissions (Grady, 1982). They may also help policymakers in their evaluation of and in their use of existing psychological research (Burt, 1982).

The primary purpose of these recommendations, however, is to stimulate critical discussion of common practices in the field that either encourage or fail to challenge sexist bias. It is hoped that professional publications and meetings, standards for promotion and leadership, styles of professional communication and collaboration, graduate training, funding incentives, and ultimately, the routine practice of research will come, in time, to reflect whatever new awarenesses emerge from an ongoing debate about bias in psychology. Because scientific findings and approaches can influence societal solutions to problems of living, these new awarenesses should also have the potential to have a positive impact on women's lives. It is to this future vision of psychology that these guidelines are dedicated.

These recommendations are designed to limit gender bias in psychological research, as a means of generating sex-fair research. Sex-fair research is only one goal of feminist psychologists. Feminist psychologists might also be concerned that females not be excluded from training or research opportunities and be given sufficient credit and pay for their contributions. Their goals may also include the selection of research topics and strategies that will benefit women, and making an attempt to provide relevant materials to the women's community. Sex-fair research as encouraged here does not discriminate against women; feminist research works actively for the benefit or advancement of women.

References

American Psychiatric Association (1980). *Diagnostic and statistical manual of mental disorders* (3rd ed.). Washington, DC.

Barnes, M. L., & Rosenthal, R. (1985). Interpersonal effects of experimenter attractiveness, attire, and gender. *Journal of Personality and Social Psychology, 48*, 435–446.

Bart, P. B. (1971). Sexism and social science: From the gilded cage to the iron cage, or, the perils of Pauline. *Journal of Marriage and the Family, 33*, 734–735.

Bartley, W. W. (1964). Rationality vs. the theory of rationality. In M. Bunge (Ed.), *The critical approach to science and philosophy* (pp. 3–31). New York: Free Press.

Bleier, R. (1984). *Science and gender: A critique of biology and its theories on women*. New York: Pergamon.

Boukydis, K. (1981, March). *Existential/phenomenology: A philosophical base for a feminist psychology*. Paper presented at the National Conference of the Association for Women in Psychology, Boston.

Brannon, R. (1974, August). *Feminist ideology and hard nosed methodology*. Paper presented at the meeting of the American Psychological Association, New Orleans.

Burt, M. (1982, August). *Guidelines for nonsexist research: Implications for policy and policy research*. Paper presented at the annual meeting of the American Psychological Association, New York.

Buss, A. R. (1978). The structure of psychological revolutions. *Journal of the History of the Behavioral Sciences, 14*, 57–64.

Caplan, P. J., MacPherson, G. M., & Tobin, P. (1985). Do sex-related differences in spatial abilities exist? A multilevel critique with new data. *American Psychologist, 40*, 786–799.

Carlson, R. (1971). Where is the person in personality research? *Psychological Bulletin, 75*, 203–219.

Carlson, R. (1972). Understanding women: Implications for personality theory and research. *Journal of Social Issues, 28*, 17–32.

Carlson, E. R., & Carlson, R. (1961). Male and female subjects in personality research. *Journal of Abnormal and Social Psychology, 61*, 482–483.

Coan, R. W. (1979). *Psychologists: Personal and theoretical pathways.* New York: Irvington.

Crawford, M. (1978). "Evolution made me do it": Women, men and animal behavior. *International Journal of Women's Studies, 1*, 533–543.

Deaux, K. (1976). *The behavior of women and men.* Monterey, CA: Brooks/Cole.

Denmark, F. L. (1983). Integrating the psychology of women into introductory psychology. *G. Stanley Hall Lecture Series, 3*, 33–71.

Diamond, E. E. (1976). Testing: The baby and the bath water are still with us. *Proceedings of the E.T.S. Invitational Conference*, 31–44.

Eagly, A. H. (1978). Sex differences in influenceability. *Psychological Bulletin, 85*, 86–116.

Eagly, A. H. (1983). Gender and social influence: A social psychological analysis. *American Psychologist, 38*, 971–982.

Etaugh, C., & Spandikow, D. B. (1979). Attention to sex in psychological research as related to journal policy and author sex. *Psychology of Women Quarterly, 4*, 175–184.

Frieze, I. H., Parsons, J. E., Johnson, P., Ruble, D. N., & Zellman, G. (1978). *Women and sex roles: A social psychological perspective.* New York: Norton.

Frodi, A., Macaulay, J., & Thome, P. R. (1977). Are women always less aggressive than men? A review of the experimental literature. *Psychological Bulletin, 84*, 634–660.

Gergen, K. L. (1973). Social psychology as history. *Journal of Personality and Social Psychology, 26*, 309–320.

Gergen, K. J. (1976). Social psychology, science & history. *Personality and Social Psychology Bulletin, 2*(4), 373–383.

Gilligan, C. (1979). Women's place in man's life cycle. *Harvard Educational Review, 49*, 431–446.

Glaser, B. G., & Strauss, A. L. (1967). *The discovery of grounded theory.* Chicago: Aldine.

Gould, M., & Kern-Daniels, R. (1977). Toward a sociological theory of gender and sex. *American Psychologist, 12*, 182–189.

Grady, K. E. (1981). Sex bias in research design. *Psychology of Women Quarterly, 5*, 628–638.

Grady, K. E. (1982, August). *Guidelines for nonsexist research: Implications for journal editorial policies.* Paper presented at the annual meeting of the American Psychological Association, New York.

Graham, D. L. R., & Rawlings, E. I. (1980, June). *Teaching an emerging feminist research methodology*. Paper presented at the annual meeting of the National Women's Studies Association, Bloomington, IN.

Harris, S. (1971). Influence of subject and experimenter in sex in psychological research. *Journal of Consulting and Clinical Psychology, 37*, 291–294.

Harway, M. (1980). Sex bias in educational-vocational counseling. *Psychology of Women, 4*, 412–423.

Henley, N. M. (1977). *Body politics*. Englewood Cliffs, NJ: Prentice-Hall.

Hollingworth, L. S. (1914). Variability as related to sex differences in achievement. *American Journal of Sociology, 19*, 510–530.

Hollingworth, L. S. (1916). Sex differences in mental traits. *Psychological Bulletin, 13*, 377–385.

Hollingworth, L. S. (1918). Comparison of the sexes in mental traits. *Psychological Bulletin, 25*, 427–432.

Jacklin, C. N., Maccoby, E. E., & Dick, A. E. (1973). Barrier behavior and toy preference: Sex differences (and their absence) in the year old child. *Child Development, 44*, 196–200.

Jacobson, M. B. (1980). A nonsexist look at the shift to risk. *Sex Roles, 6*, 481–487.

Kagan, J. (1969). The three faces of continuity in human development. In D. A. Goslin (Ed.), *Handbook of socialization theory and research*. Chicago: Rand-McNally.

Kahn, A., & Gaeddert, W. P. (1985). From theories of equity to theories of justice: The liberating consequences of studying women. In V. E. O'Leary, R. K. Unger, & B. S. Wallston (Eds.), *Women, gender and social psychology* (pp. 129–149). Hillsdale, NJ: Erlbaum.

Kahn, A., Nelson, R. E., & Gaeddert, W. P. (1980). Sex of subject and sex composition of the group as determinants of reward allocations. *Journal of Personality and Social Psychology, 38*, 737–750.

Kaplan, M. (1983). A woman's view of DSM-III. *American Psychologist, 38*, 786–792.

Koch, S. (1981). The nature and limits of psychological knowledge: Lessons of a century qua "science." *American Psychologist, 36*, 257–269.

Koeske, R. D. (1978, March). *Menstrual cycle research: Challenge or chuckle?* Paper presented at the panel, "Politics of menstrual cycle research," Association of Women in Psychology Conference, Pittsburgh, PA.

Laws, J. L. (1976). *Patriarchy as paradigm: The challenge from feminist scholarship*. Paper presented at the annual meeting of the American Sociological Association, New York.

Leibowitz, L. (1979). "Universals" and male dominance among primates: A critical examination. In R. Hubbard & M. Lowe (Eds.), *Genes and gender II: Pitfalls in research on sex and gender* (pp. 35–48). Staten Island, NY: Gordian Press.

Lipman-Blumen, J., & Tickamyer, A. (1975). Sex roles in transition: A ten year perspective. *Annual Review of Sociology, 15*, 297–337.

Lott, B. (1985). The potential enrichment of social/personality research through feminist research and visa versa. *American Psychologist, 40*, 155–164.

Maccoby, E. E., & Jacklin, C. N. (1974). *Psychology of sex differences*. Stanford, CA: Stanford University Press.

Martyna, W. (1980). Beyond the "he/man" approach. The case for nonsexist language. *Signs, 5*, 482–493.

Mayo, C. (1982). Training for positive marginality. *Applied Social Psychology Annual, 3*, 57–73.

McHugh, M. C. (1982, August). *Implementing the Guidelines for Non-sexist Research*. Symposium presented at the annual meeting of the American Psychological Association, New York.

McKenna, W., & Kessler, S. J. (1977). Experimental design as a source of sex bias in social psychology. *Sex Roles, 3*, 117–128.

Mednick, M. T. S., Tangri, S., & Hoffman, L. (Eds.). (1975). *Women and achievement: Social and motivational analysis*. Washington, DC: Hemisphere.

Millman, M., & Kanter, R. M. (Eds.). (1975). *Another voice: Feminist perspectives on social life and social science*. New York: Anchor Books.

Moulton, J., Robinson, G. M., & Elias, C. (1978). Sex bias in language use: Neutral pronouns that aren't. *American Psychologist, 33*, 1032–1036.

Newcomb, N. (1980). Beyond nature and nurture. *Contemporary Psychology, 25*, 807–808.

O'Leary, V. E. (1977). *On understanding women*. Monterey, CA: Brooks/Cole.

Parlee, M. B. (1973). The premenstrual syndrome. *Psychological Bulletin, 80*, 454–465.

Parlee, M. B. (1981). Appropriate control groups in feminist research. *Psychology of Women Quarterly, 5*, 637–644.

Parsons, J. E. (Ed.). (1980). *The psychobiology of sex differences and sex roles*. New York: McGraw-Hill.

Pedersen, D. M., Shinedling, M. M., & Johnson, D. L. (1968). Effects of sex of examiner and subject on children's quantitative test performance. *Journal of Personality and Social Psychology, 10*, 251–254.

Petersen, A. C. (1976). Physical androgyny and cognitive functioning in adolescents. *Developmental Psychology, 12*, 524–533.

Petersen, A. C. (1984, August). *Biology and the psychology of women: What's new and so what?* Invited address for Division 35 at the annual meeting of the American Psychological Association, Toronto, Canada.

Prescott, S. (1978). Why researchers don't study women: The responses of 62 researchers. *Sex Roles, 4*, 899–905.

Reardon, P., & Prescott, S. (1976). Reexamination of male vs. female representation in psychological research. *Clinical and Social Development in Psychology, 6*, 38.

Reardon, P., & Prescott, S. (1977). Sex as reported in a recent sample of psychological research. *Psychology of Women Quarterly, 2*, 157–161.

Reinharz, S. (1981, August). *Dimensions of the feminist research methodology debate: Impetus, definitions, dilemmas and stances.* Paper presented at the annual meeting of the American Psychological Association, Los Angeles.

Riley, T., & Denmark, L. (1974). Field independence and measures of intelligence: Some reconsiderations. *Social Behavior and Personality, 2*(1), 25–29.

Rosenberg, R. (1982). *Beyond separate spheres: Intellectual roots of modern feminism.* New Haven: Yale University Press.

Rowell, T. (1972). *The social behavior of monkeys.* Harmondsworth, England: Penguin Books.

Ruble, D. N., & Higgins, E. T. (1976). Effects of group sex composition on self presentation and sex-typing. *Journal of Social Issues, 32,* 125–132.

Samelson, F. (1978). From "race psychology" to "studies in prejudice": Some observations on the thematic reversal in social psychology. *Journal of the History of the Behavioral Sciences, 14,* 265–278.

Sampson, E. E. (1978). Scientific paradigms and social values: Wanted—a scientific revolution. *Journal of Personality and Social Psychology, 36,* 1332–1343.

Schwabacher, S. (1972). Male vs. female representation in psychological research: An examination of the *Journal of Personality and Social Psychology,* 1970, 1971. *JSAS: Catalog of Selected Documents in Psychology, 2,* 20–21.

Sherif, C. W. (1979). Bias in psychology. In J. A. Sherman & E. T. Beck (Eds.), *The prism of sex: Essays in the sociology of knowledge* (pp. 93–133). Madison: University of Wisconsin Press.

Sherif, C. W. (1980). A social psychological perspective on the menstrual cycle. In J. E. Parsons (Ed.), *The psychobiology of sex differences and sex roles* (pp. 245–266). New York: McGraw-Hill.

Sherif, C. W. (1981). Needed concepts in the study of gender identity. Presidential address to Division 35 of the American Psychological Association. *Psychology of Women Quarterly, 6,* 375–398.

Shields, S. A. (1975). Functionalism, Darwinism and the psychology of women: A study of social myth. *American Psychologist, 30,* 739–754.

Signorella, M. L., & Vegega, M. E. (1984). A note on gender stereotyping of research topics. *Personality and Social Psychology Bulletin, 10*(1), 107–111.

Signorella, M. L., Vegega, M. E., & Mitchell, M. E. (1981). Subject selection and analyses for sex-related differences: 1968–1970 and 1975–1977. *American Psychologist, 36,* 988–990.

Sistrunk, F., & McDavid, J. W. (1971). Sex variable in conforming behavior. *Journal of Personality and Social Psychology, 17*(1), 200–207.

Smart, R. G. (1966). Subject selection bias in psychological research. *Canadian Psychologist, 7a,* 115–121.

Smith, D. E. (1979). A sociology for women: In J. Sherman & E. T. Beck (Eds.), *The prism of sex: Essays in the sociology of knowledge.* Madison: University of Wisconsin Press.

Sohn, D. (1982). Sex differences in achievement self-attributions: An effect size analysis. *Sex Roles, 8*(4), 345–358.

Taylor, S. E., & Fiske, S. T. (1978). Salience, attention and attribution: Top of the head phenomena. In L. Berkowitz (Ed.), *Advances in experimental social psychology* (Vol. 2, pp. 250–283). New York: Academic Press.

Thorndike, E. L. (1903). *Heredity, correlation and sex differences in ability: Vol. 11. Columbia University Contributions to Philosophy, Psychology, and Education.* New York: Columbia University Press.

Unger, R. K. (1978). The politics of gender: A review of relevant literature. In J. Sherman & F. Denmark (Eds.), *The psychology of women: New directions of research.* New York: Psychological Dimensions.

Unger, R. K. (1979a). Toward a redefinition of sex and gender. *American Psychologist, 34,* 1085–1094.

Unger, R. K. (1979b). *Female and male: Psychological perspectives.* New York: Harper & Row.

Unger, R. K. (1981). Sex as a social reality: Field and laboratory research. *Psychology of Women Quarterly, 5,* 645–653.

Unger, R. K. (1982). Advocacy versus scholarship revisited: Issues in the psychology of women. *Psychology of Women Quarterly,* 7, 5–17.

Vaughter, R. H. (1976). Review essay: Psychology. *Signs, 2,* 120–146.

Waber, D. P. (1976). Sex differences in cognition: A function of maturation rate? *Science, 192,* 572–574.

Wallston, B. S. (1981, August). What are the questions in psychology of women? A feminist approach to research. Presidential address for Division 35. *Psychology of Women Quarterly, 5,* 597–617.

Wallston, B. S. (1983). Overview of research methods in sex roles and social change. In J. Wirtenberg & B. L. Richardson (Eds.), *Methodological issues in sex roles and social change* (pp. 51–76). New York: Praeger.

Wallston, B. S., & Grady, K. E. (1985). Integrating the feminist critique and the crisis in social psychology: Another look at research methods. In V. E. O'Leary, R. K. Unger, & B. S. Wallston (Eds.), *Women, gender and social psychology* (pp. 7–33). Hillsdale, NJ: Erlbaum.

Weimer, W. B. (1975). The psychology of inference and expectation: Some preliminary remarks. In G. Maxwell & R. M. Anderson (Eds.), *Induction, probability and confirmation* (pp. 430–486). Minneapolis: University of Minnesota Press.

Wise, E., & Rafferty, J. (1982). Sex bias and language. *Sex Roles, 8,* 1189–1196.

Wittig, M. A. (1979). Genetic influences on sex-related differences in intellectual performance. Theoretical and methodological issues. In M. A. Wittig & A. C. Petersen (Eds.), *Sex-related differences in cognitive functioning: Developmental issues* (pp. 21–65). New York: Academic Press.

Wittig, M. A. (1985). Metatheoretical dilemmas in the psychology of gender. *American Psychologist, 40,* 800–811.

Wood, W., Polek, D., & Aiken, C. (1985). Sex differences in group task performance. *Journal of Personality and Social Psychology, 48,* 63–71.

Appendix A: Suggestions for Sex-Fair Research

Avoiding Excessive Confidence in Traditional Methods

1. Carefully examine the underlying values and assumptions in all research and state them explicitly.
2. Encourage the use of alternative and nonexperimental research methodologies directed toward exploration, detailed description, and theory generation as well as experimental and quasi-experimental approaches designed for hypothesis testing.
3. Engage in ongoing debate about the strengths and weaknesses of all research techniques, focusing attention on the capacities and limitations of experimental and nonexperimental research as procedures for studying processes and systems and for permitting generalizations to particular contexts.
4. When undertaking literature reviews, examine past research for both methodological rigor and unexamined sexism in procedure or interpretation.
   a. Be aware of factors other than methodological soundness that may influence the publishability or distribution of results.
   b. Remember that the convergence of established findings with experience and the convergence of results based on different methods adds to their credibility; divergence should prompt renewed study.

Examining Explanatory Models

1. Exercise care in the terminology employed to describe or explain results in order to avoid (a) confusing sex with gender, (b) confusing description with explanation, and (c) reducing complex or interactionist explanations to overly simple ones.
2. Consider all possible explanations for sex-related phenomena including social–cultural, biological, and situational factors.
   a. Consider alternative explanations even if they have not been investigated.
   b. Recognize that many consistently demonstrated sex-related behaviors may result from either consistent and pervasive cultural factors or biological factors. Often empirical tests differentiating competing explanations are unavailable.

3. Become aware of, consider, and devise studies of alternative and more complex models of causation.
   a. More detailed models that incorporate and specify relationships involving both physiological and sociocultural variables are needed.
   b. Increased effort should be directed toward developing common terminologies and providing more elaborate tests of competing explanatory models.
4. Avoid concluding or implying that a covariation between biology and behavior constitutes evidence for physiological causation if information on alternative theoretical or methodological interpretations is unavailable.
5. Take care in distinguishing between a general construct and the specific measures meant to operationalize it.
   a. Be careful to appropriately delimit the meaning of a concept before operationalizing it.
   b. Avoid operationalizing or defining constructs in a manner that is circular or that does not allow specific tests of expected linkages to sex or gender.
6. Any discussions of sex-related differences should avoid language that (a) implies biological or social causation not demonstrated in the research, (b) implies that the characteristic under study is possessed exclusively by one sex, (c) implies dispositional differences when situational factors may explain the result, or (d) inappropriately implies that men's and women's responses fall on opposite ends of a single continuum.
7. Avoid errors in interpretation of data such as inferring the presence of a significant sex-related difference without conducting direct statistical comparisons or considering results of tests for sex-related differences without consideration of the magnitude of the effect or the degree of overlap between distributions.
8. Perform analyses for sex-related differences whenever such analyses are justified by the theoretical or conceptual framework of the study.
9. Journal editors should discourage the publication of studies in which the only significant finding is an unexpected "sex difference" and should insist instead on the replication of such findings.
10. Equal emphasis in publication should be given to findings of "sex similarities," rather than biasing journal policy toward findings of "sex differences."

Interpreting Without Bias

1. Carefully consider both the basis and the implications of the labels applied to individual traits and behaviors.
2. Do not label behaviors or traits as dysfunctional without any empirical demonstration of their dysfunctionality.
    a. Devote some attention to examining the positive consequences of behaviors that deviate from the status quo or from traditional gender roles.
    b. Specify the context or subpopulation appropriate to the interpretation of normative labels or statements.
3. Psychological analyses require not only the measurement of some pattern of behavior and/or cognition, but also descriptions and analysis of the situational context and the environment.
    a. Complete an analysis of the social context of the study in order to determine if overt or subtle forms of sex bias are present.
    b. Carefully consider the possible differential salience, familiarity, relevance, and/or meaning of the research task, stimuli, and/or dependent measures to male and female participants.
    c. Once the research plan is completed, learn from the research participants how they evaluated and interpreted the research contexts, and how they felt as events transpired.
4. Base conclusions regarding the behaviors and responses of males and females on research in multiple contexts in an attempt to understand situational influences on behavior. Exercise care in drawing conclusions from research based on limited contexts.
5. Consider the role(s) of the experimenter, confederate, target, and others present, as they impact on the response, performance, or behavior of the participants.
    a. When appropriate, incorporate multiple experimenters (confederates and targets) to allow for analysis of experimenter effects and/or counterbalancing.
    b. Vary the sex composition of the group to allow for analysis or counterbalancing of possible effects.
6. Make sure that the theoretical frameworks that form the body of psychological research are relevant to members of both sexes.
7. If a theory is to be generalized to both sexes, generate empirical support for the theory from samples that include both sexes.

8. Try to ensure that topics of interest to women are given the resources and status accorded to topics of interest to men.
   a. Do not limit the content areas of psychological research by the degree to which they can be studied under a single paradigm.
   b. Try to make sure that the extent to which particular research topics are judged as basic versus applied, or nonclinical versus clinical, does not depend on the sex of the respondent used or the judged gender relevance of the topic.
9. Carefully examine the normative assumptions implicit in the choice of typical and atypical samples of males and females and avoid (a) inappropriately generalizing to all members of a sex, (b) unintentionally introducing uncontrolled variables into male–female comparisons, and (c) unwittingly comparing typical samples of one sex with atypical samples of the other.

34 Toward a Feminist Metatheory and Methodology in the Social Sciences

MARY M. GERGEN

In the past decade, feminist intellectual endeavors have blossomed. . . . [However,] while growth and development have occurred in theory and teaching, less has been accomplished in the practice of scholarly research within the university setting. The implications of feminist theory and metatheory for methodology has not been spelled out. For example, within the social sciences, a fountainhead of feminist theory, many scholars who align themselves with feminist causes continue to practice within a traditional methodological framework (cf. Bem 1974; Deaux 1985; Eagly and Carli 1981; Spence and Helmreich 1978). That no well-articulated alternatives have been formulated within conventional academic circles is a matter of grave concern because methods are often considered the true hallmark of the practitioner. New theories may be allowed into a discipline, but methods that deviate markedly from the old ones or that challenge or ignore traditional assumptions are strongly suspect. Thus many so-called feminist social scientists continue to practice their sciences in forms that violate the precepts of an enlightened feminist perspective.

But if the challenges of feminism are to be taken seriously, feminist social scientists need to develop new methods, ones that support the feminist metatheories. We must reject many of the traditional methods of economics, psychology, political science, and sociology, for example, as violations of our feminist beliefs. This leads to the problem of trying to ascertain what a feminist methodology might be. How might a feminist science be created? What means fulfill the evaluative and intellectual demands of feminism? There may be several modes for reaching this goal; my effort in this chapter is to spell out some of the central goals of a feminist methodology, and to illustrate these with one pilot study designed for this purpose. . . .

Empiricist Shortcomings and the Feminist Alternative

There are several major criticisms of the empiricist paradigm in psychology that are relevant to a feminist appraisal of the social sciences. Within each of these criticisms the elements for an alternative metatheory and attendant methodology are suggested. Of critical interest is the relationship of the scientist to the subject matter. At issue is nothing less than the nature of scientific objectivity. Six aspects of this issue will be treated below.

Independence of Scientist and Subject Matter

Psychologists have traditionally supported the necessity of maintaining objectivity in their research (Alexander 1982; Coser 1975; Giddens 1974; Polkinghorne 1983). To achieve this goal the scientist ideally is an independent observer who minimizes any relationship between him/herself and the subject of study (Alexander 1982). It is thought that as long as the scientist is distant, uninvolved, and neutral, subjects will not be influenced by the scientist, and reliable data will be collected. If there is any form of personal relationship between the scientist and the subject this interaction will, as it is said, "contaminate the findings."

Many feminist writers have criticized this perspective (Chodorow 1978; Gilligan 1982; Harding 1986; Keller 1982). They have suggested that for various reasons this view is limited and androcentric. For example, Nancy Chodorow (1978) has argued that men develop a personal identity by separation and differentiation from their mothering agents. This pattern of separation encourages the development of a more general preference for separateness over interdependence. Many feminists believe that what many scientists consider the proper method for organizing social reality is merely an outgrowth of male developmental history. Of course, the irony in the traditional argument is that any form of relationship, distant or close, between the scientist and the subject, constitutes a message of relatedness, regardless of the content, to the subject. It is not possible for humans to simply have "objective" contact within the scientific process, or anywhere else.

The alternative possibility, one that is perhaps more in harmony with female development, is one that admits the interconnectedness of persons. In this view the most feasible approach to scientific investigation is to recognize this bond between people in social contexts, and to construct scientific methods on these grounds (Becker 1986; Oakley 1981; Stanley and Wise 1983). A feminist metatheory and methodology would thus incorporate the tenet that the investigator and the subject are interdependent.

Decontextualization of Phenomenon

Traditional empiricist psychology attempts to establish general laws of human functioning. This means that any given phenomenon is viewed as an expression of universal law. The major problem for the scientist is to determine these laws by testing the relationship among isolated entities. In order to clarify the relationships of the entities under study the scientist typically removes the analytical units of interest from their cultural and historical context. Such context stripping often involves moving the entities into the laboratory—so that they may be studied in isolation from all of their "contaminants" (Reason and Rowan 1981; Weinreich 1977). For example, the complex problem of when to help in an emergency becomes codified into a simple choice of informing an experimenter of a possible emergency in a tidy laboratory setting.

A second form of decontextualization involves the removal of the study from the life circumstances of the scientist (Heron 1981). For example, scientists do not normally report the extent to which the research was inspired because of a certain personal problem or by pressure from department chairpersons to publish. The research is made to seem freestanding, without regard to institutional interests of sponsors or the personal gain that might accrue to the investigator.

The objections of feminists to the decontextualization process have often centered on the consequences that have accrued to women-as-subjects. Decontextualized women subjects are often studied in isolation from their personal circumstances. Frequently scientists attribute women's personal traits, which may stem from their position as an oppressed group, to their "natural dispositions." A tendency to be depressed, for example, might be attributed to a biological cause rather than to difficult social conditions. Often these theories support androcentric biases (Marshall 1986). This decontextualized type of science overlooks important social and cultural factors that influence the lives of women (Bernard 1973; Mednick and Tangri 1972; Minton 1986; Parlee 1979; Sampson 1978; Sherif 1979; Snyder 1979; Vaughter 1976). In accord with the argument for interdependence of researcher and subject, feminist thinking suggests that subjects of research often depend on their context to provide their identity. It is not possible to decontextualize a phenomenon without changing its significance. Thus research should be conducted insofar as possible without violating the social embeddedness of the subject. In addition scientists should consider the historical contingency of the phenomena and the extent to which research aims and outcomes are dependent on the personal circumstances of the scientist.

The Possibility of Value-Free Theory and Practice

A third questionable assumption in the traditional paradigm is that the scientist can and should produce research in a value-free mode. Personal prejudices, ethical principles, and other evaluative concerns should not influence the research endeavor, its outcomes or conclusions. The bad scientist is one who allows scientific conclusions, to become tainted by personal values. In contrast, feminist scholars refute the assumption that knowledge and its creation can be value-free. Instead it is assumed that all work must be value-laden. The claim that science is value-free is a self-deception or an attempt to deceive others.

In *Feminist Philosophers*, Jean Crimshaw illustrated how values are embedded in a supposedly value-free theoretical exposition. She wrote, "A theory like behaviorism, for example, implies that human beings and human behavior can be thought of as material to be 'modified,' and the term 'behavior modification' is often given to programmes which offer to apply behaviorist theory in order to effect changes in human behavior. Such programmes . . . imply a sharp distinction between 'controllers' and 'controlled' and are intrinsically and profoundly anti-democratic" (1986, p. 91). Sociologist Shulamit Reinharz has summarized the feminist position on value-free science: "The feminist critique of social science supports the view that since interest-free knowledge is logically impossible, we should feel free to substitute explicit interest for implicit ones. Feminism challenges us to articulate our values and, on the basis of these, to develop new theories and formulate new research practices" (1985, p. 163).

Many feminists have suggested how women might benefit from the explicit, self-conscious application of values within scientific practice. For example, Vaughter (1976) has advocated that scientists create research that advances the status of women and adds to the quality of their lives; Gilligan (1982) has supported the need for new theoretical formulations about women that enlarge their potentials. Young-Eisendrath (this volume) has discussed how women might redefine personal qualities that have been made negative through male-dominated theorizing. Others have argued for an emancipatory psychology that will liberate men as well as women from the ideological constraints of gender stereotyping (Minton 1986; Pleck 1981).

The Possibility of Brute Facts

A fourth assumption of the traditional paradigm is that facts are independent of the scientist who establishes them. That is, the world is assumed to be as it is, independent of the observer. It is the task of the scientist to reflect that world in his/her theories. In addition, all persons using proper scientific methods should come to the same conclusion regarding the nature of the world.

Feminist critics of the social sciences disagree with this view of objectivity. Rather a feminist perspective holds that all aspects of the scientific method require acts of interpretation. Interpretations are required to select or create a relevant vocabulary and a theoretical framework, to make distinctions among objects, to formulate explanatory systems and to summarize findings. Thus, what becomes established fact is not reflective of the world as it is, but the world as subjected to an a priori linguistic framework.

In this light, feminist thinkers are particularly critical of the ways in which scientific language has been shaped to produce an androcentric world of "facts" that often give men advantage over women. The ongoing conflict between feminist psychologists and defenders of the *Diagnostic and Statistical Manual for Mental Disorders III*, is illustrative. The thrust of the feminist arguments is that male-dominated groups have fashioned categories of mental illness that apply only to women and are discriminatory against them. The contention that languages are tools of male domination has been made by many feminist writers (cf. Daly 1978; Spender 1980). Efforts to recreate language in forms more suitable to women are in progress.

The problem of how language shapes scientific work is particularly central to feminist methodological concerns. Often important concepts are based on preexisting assumptions concerning gender relations. For example, to study "sex-typed behavior" is to accept the notion that males and females have very different patterns of social behavior and to perpetuate this idea by writing about it (See Morawski's chapter in this volume for further reflections on feminist linguistic issues). Even the metaphors in scientific work reflect androcentric assumptions. Pauline Bart (1971) has illustrated the use of the adjectives "hard" and "soft" in the sciences. She wrote: "We speak of hard data as being better than soft data, hard science better than soft science, hard money better than soft money. . . . This is of course a male metaphor, so since discovering this, I have substituted a metaphor based on female sexual experience and refer to wet and dry data" (p. 1).

The Superiority of Science and the Scientist

An empiricist theory of science holds that the only way to establish valid knowledge is through scientific procedure. Thus, all other claims to knowledge are by definition inferior. This assumption of the superiority of science manifests itself among scientists in a variety of common methodological practices.

For one, the researcher is assumed to be more knowledgeable and competent than the subject. As a result the researcher tends not to be interested in finding out what subjects know or are capable of doing, except in the predetermined area mapped out in the design of the study. Second, the researcher expects to have complete control over the way in which the study proceeds. The context, methods, procedures, analyses, outcomes, and recommendations for application are all regulated by the psychologist, and the subject is indeed subjugated. Third, the scientist never shares his/her views with subjects prior to the research because such sharing would supposedly "contaminate" the results.

As feminist thinkers maintain, presumptions of experimenter superiority and the subjugation of the research subject recapitulates the traditional patterns of gender relationships in the culture. . . . In effect, scientific dominance is simply another manifestation of sexual dominance. As an alternative, feminists argue for the enhanced voice of research participants. Rather than considering subjects' views as inherently inferior, the scientist should respect the potential value of the subjects' ideas and be maximally sensitive to the perspectives of the subjects and their experiences. Subjects should also become participants with status equal to the scientist in the research effort (Freire 1976; Mearns and McLeod 1984). Feminists' views would favor research that placed the investigator's orienting presumptions and modes of practice at risk (Elden 1981).

In summary, feminist thinkers reject the following traditional empiricist methodological principles:

1. The independence of scientist and subject;
2. the decontextualization of the subject matter from the field in which it is embedded, physically and historically;
3. value-neutral theory and practice;
4. the independence of "facts" from the scientist;
5. the superiority of the scientist over other people.

Feminist-inspired research would endeavor to recognize that scientists, subjects, and "facts" are all interconnected, involved in reciprocal influences, and subject to interpretation and linguistic constraints. In addition, scientific endeavors would be treated as value-laden and would be formed with specific value orientations in mind. This research approach would treat scientists as participants in the research project along with the subjects of the research and not as superior beings who maintain a knowledge monopoly among themselves.

A Study of Menopause: An Application

. . .

Background of the Study What follows is a brief description of a study I designed specifically with feminist criteria in mind. The topic centered on women's construction of menopause and their related image of themselves as women in their forties. I chose this topic because I had been distressed in reading psychological and popular literature concerned with middle-aged women. The general theme of such material is that during this period women suffer a steady decline in a variety of valued human traits such as beauty, strength, worth as a human being, function, and intelligence. As a result, it seemed, women over forty might be vulnerable to many negative side effects, for example, depression, anomie, and over-compensation. The major impact of such theorizing seemed to me the creation of a cultural expectation that women after forty experience a sharp decline in important human capacities and life satisfaction. A belief in the expectation might further serve to produce some of the very effects that are predicted. (Interestingly we do not find such dire predictions in the literature for men from forty to sixty, and we do not have cultural expectations that such degenerative events must occur to them.)

My goal for this study was to present to a group of my peers through a dialogical procedure the notion that middle age marked a new era in a woman's life during which she could become freer, more self-actualized, and more satisfied with life than in her preceding years. I chose to focus on menopause as the topic under discussion because this process encompasses the major negative stages associated with the passage of women through middle age. Because I wanted to emphasize my role as equal participant, I did not attempt to lead the discussion group in a forceful way. I also invited the other group members to share in the development of the research project and its outcomes.

Method of Exploration The research event took place in my home in June 1985. Seven women, all familiar with each other, primarily through playing tennis together, were invited to participate with me in "a discussion group about the lives of women between forty and sixty." At the time of the study these women were all married, living with their husbands, and mothers. They ranged in age from forty-one to forty-eight. Most had worked at least part-time in the previous year, although only two were then involved in full-time careers. They were all upper-middle-class suburban homeowners. One woman was Australian, living temporarily in the United States while her husband was on a job rotation with an American corporation.

Upon arrival, each woman privately filled out several questionnaires, including an attitudinal measure about menopause and a self-image scale. . . . My goal for the discussion was to influence these women to feel more positively about themselves and their futures as a result of their participation in the experience. Additional questionnaires were thus given to the participants to take home so that they could fill them out the morning following the session, and then mail them back to me. In addition, the postsession questionnaires included a comment sheet on which participants could describe reactions to the session, any new ideas they had been exposed to about menopause, and any suggestions for future research. In being given the opportunity to make suggestions for further research endeavors they were given the opportunity to be coplanners in this project.

A one-and-one-half-hour tape-recorded discussion was the major event of the research session. As the discussion facilitator, I introduced topics at various times. The first hour was devoted to the exploration of beliefs and feelings about the process of menopause and the lives of women in middle age. In the last half hour, I spoke briefly about my views about menopause and women in middle age. I tried to emphasize the socially constructed nature of developmental events such as menopause, and how no one formulation was necessarily true. I argued that it would be possible to see menopause as coordinated with a transition to a new, very positive period of life. I encouraged comments about this perspective and tried to pursue the exposition of this view with the group. The participants included this issue in their discussion during the last portion of the session.

An Analysis of the Discussion The major underlying supposition of the study was that through the interaction of the group and exposure to a social constructionist view of menopause and middle age the participants would alter their attitudes about these issues in what I would consider a more positive direction. The presuppositions of the study included the assumptions that most women are aware of the negative images of middle-aged women in the culture, feel personally concerned about the process of menopause, feel negative about its impact on their lives, and dislike being middle-aged themselves.

The discussion proved enlightening and broadened my understanding of the dimensions of the topic greatly. As the conversation revealed, in general the participants resisted thinking about menopause and their identity as "middle-aged women." Their sense of what it means to be in their forties seems to be in a transition from an older vision of decline to a newer one of freedom, health, and prosperity. I think the discussion brought out some of their shared concerns, especially centered on the process and signification of menopause, and helped to redefine these concerns again as peripheral to their plans and goals in life. The discussion seemed therapeutic in that certain fear-provoking and dismal ideas were shared and perhaps reduced in power by their exposure.

The emancipatory framework of this study was designed so that the participants would be exposed to a model of menopause that emphasized menopause as part of a role transition to a positive new form of womanhood. The social construction of menopause as a medical problem, with negative physical and psychological consequences, was to be abandoned. I wanted to encourage these women to consider the possibility that all concepts of social life are social constructs, which are open to negotiation of meaning, particularly by the members of the affected groups. The discussion group did seem to negotiate new meanings for the menopausal time of life, achieving a synthesis of my intended outcomes and the participants' original opinions. In terms of reorganizing the thoughts of the participants to accept that events such as menopause are not "real," but socially constructed, I was generally unsuccessful. While discussants seemed willing to accept a variety of interpretations of what menopause might include, they did not focus on the social negotiation aspects of the construct itself. In philosophical terms, my coparticipants tended to be naive realists. The major social strategy I saw emerging from the discussion was that of "beating the old system." By this I mean that participants plan to rely on exceptional personal resources to cope with menopause, rather than to change the social construction itself. Let me expand briefly.

The tendency I noted in our group was implicitly to support the medical model as long as one did not suffer personally from it. So, for example, the need to look young and fertile is not questioned. However, keeping eternally young is a goal that many upper middle-class women can pursue quite successfully. As long as it works, the need to bring new value and new attributes to the image of the aging woman is not essential. In fact, to renegotiate the standards of what it means to be attractive so as to give aging women a more positive position would serve to negate the efforts of certain women to evade the role. If having bodily fat, wrinkles, and grey hair is acceptable for a fifty-year-old woman, then why struggle with diet and exercise regimes?

Yet, it was also clear as the discussion developed that the participants saw many very positive aspects to life in the period from forty to sixty. These women became very supportive of the idea that life might even be better than it had been when they were in their twenties and thirties. Many mentioned ways in which they felt freer, more competent, more powerful, and less frustrated by obligations to family. In this respect they were able to see the potential to construe for themselves a life different from what is currently part of the medical/psychiatric model, in which women grieve over their empty nests and lost youth. While it is impossible to judge how much the group as a whole changed to become more positive toward middle age during the discussion, it seemed clear that the tendency for making these more positive comments did occur after I brought up the possibility of middle age being a time for growth and change. Thus, I believe that my goal of improving perceptions of women in mid-life was met in the study, if only to a small extent.

Analysis of Questionnaires

Analyses indicated that the discussion had an influence on participants' attitudes as judged by the difference scores between questionnaires filled out before and after the group discussion. In general the participants became less committed to the medical/psychiatric model of the ill-effects of menopause following the discussion. Participants disagreed more strongly with the view that "Most women would rather continue to menstruate than not," ($X = 2.63$ prediscussion and 1.88 postdiscussion, with $1 =$ strongly disagree and $5 =$ strongly agree) and "feel negative about their loss of fertility" (X = 3.13 prediscussion and X = 2.13 postdiscussion). In fact most women in this study indicated that the freedom from worry about pregnancy is one of the chief gains of menopause. Discussants were also more likely to disagree that women "keep menopause a secret, as something shameful" (X = 2.63 prediscussion and X = 2.25 postdiscussion) and that women "become less attractive after menopause" (X = 2.38 prediscussion and X = 2.0 postdiscussion). Participants also disagreed more with the statement that "Women usually get emotionally more unstable after menopause" (X = 2.38 prediscussion and X = 2.25 postdiscussion) and "less interested in sex" (X = 2.88 prediscussion and X = 2.25 postdiscussion). The means are presented here to indicate the general tendency for the participants to reject these ideas, not to illustrate statistically significant changes.

Comparing the self-image scales, I noted the changes in discrepancies the group found between being a younger women and being a fifty-year-old (the average age of menopause) both before and after the discussion group. As the results showed, the group tended to project a positive self-image into the fifties even at the beginning of the study. Thus there was little room for positive change. The only area in which substantial enhancement did occur was in the trait *strength* (X = 3.75 prediscussion and X = 2.57 postdiscussion). As a result of the discussion, the participants rated strength as increasing in the fiftieth year. Overall the group characterized themselves at fifty as being active, attractive, dominant, sexual, intelligent, logical, outgoing, practical, relaxed, stable, and successful, as well as strong. In these respects the panel chose to describe themselves in ways that fit my vision of what the new middle-aged woman could be.

Conclusion

As mentioned this research was merely a preliminary attempt to put feminist metatheory into action in a research design. In its inception the design of the study tried to respect the interdependency of myself, as the manager of the study, and the other participants. In many respects I endeavored to take an equal place with the others in the discussion. I chose for my panel social peers who knew very little about my professional career. The topic of research was one that interested me personally and was relevant to my future. I attempted to conduct the research in a setting that would be similar to other situations in which women exchange confidences (on my back porch, for lunch). The research was organized in such a way that the values I espouse were to be advanced. In addition, it was intended to support a social constructionist metatheory of science. While these abstract goals directed and informed my efforts, the realizations were not without flaw.

While it seemed that there were some effects that resulted from the dialogical approach to attitude change, the method was not by any means perfect in its form. There are many ways in which this research could have been improved. In future research one might want a greater range of participants, of scientist-facilitators, and of analytical tools. The participants frequently suggested that it would have been worthwhile to have had the comments of women who had already been through menopause. One could imagine other groups of participants who could contribute unique perspectives to the topic. The study might have been more in keeping with feminist goals if the participants had been involved in planning the study from its inception (cf. Elden 1981). However, as a result of all participants having equal access within the discussion group, the control of the outcomes was decentralized and the processes of social negotiation enhanced. It is sobering to recognize that giving the power away means that certain of one's perceived goals for organizing a study are less directly achievable. At the same time, I acquired new ideas about social change as a result of being a member of this group. I recognized that the women I talked with had developed a strategy for evading the traps of becoming middle-aged. This would not have been possible if I had controlled and manipulated most of the process and proceedings. Lastly, I might have tried to incorporate into the study more outcomes that would have been immediately and directly useful to the participants.

For the future, I am enthusiastic about the opportunities for exploring new methodologies, for socially negotiating new realities, and for finding new ways of creating challenging situations that have an impact on the social realities of people. I believe that the feminist perspectives on knowledge will help promulgate fruitful new modes of social science. What is necessary is that communities of scholars and other interested people take up the challenge to create together concrete instantiations of abstract ideals.

References

Alexander, J. (1982). *Theoretical logic in sociology: Positivism, presuppositions, and current controversies*. Berkeley: University of California Press.

Apfelbaum, E., and Lubek, I. (1976). "Resolution vs. revolution? The theory of conflicts in question." In L. Strickland, F. E. Aboud, and K. J. Gergen (Eds.). *Social psychology in transition*. New York: Plenum.

Bart, P. (1971). "Sexism in social science: From the iron cage to the gilded cage, or the perils of Pauline." *Journal of Marriage and the Family* 33:742.

Becker, C. S. (1986). "Interviewing in human science research." *Methods* 1:101–24.

Bem, S. (1974). "The measurement of psychological androgyny." *Journal of Consulting and Clinical Psychology* 42:155–62.

Berg, D. N., and Smith, K. K. (Eds.). (1985). *Exploring clinical methods for social research*. Beverly Hills: Sage.

Bernard, J. (1973). "My four revolutions: An autobiographical history of the American Sociological Association." *American Journal of Sociology* 78: 773–91.

Chodorow, N. (1978). *The reproduction of mothering: Psychoanalysis and the sociology of gender*. Berkeley: University of California Press.

Coser, L. (1975). "Presidential address: Two methods in search of a substance." *American Sociological Review* 40:691–700.

Crimshaw, J. (1986). *Feminist philosophers: Women's perspectives on philosophical traditions*. Brighton, England: Wheatsheaf Books.

Daly, M. (1978). *Gyn/ecology: The Metaethics of radical feminism*. Boston: Beacon Press.

Deaux, K. (1985). "Sex and gender." *Annual Review of Psychology* 36:49–81.

DuBois, E. C., et al. (1985). *Feminist scholarship, Kindling in the groves of the academe*. Urbana: University of Illinois Press.

Eagly, A., and Carli, I. I. (1981). "Sex of researchers and sex-typed communications as determinants of sex differences in influenceability: A meta-analysis of social influence studies." *Psychological Bulletin* 90:1–20.

Elden, M. (1981). "Sharing the research work: Participative research and its role demands." In P. Reason and J. Rowan (Eds.). *Human inquiry: A sourcebook of new paradigm research*. London: Wiley.

Evans, J., et al. (1986). *Feminism and political theory*. Beverly Hills: Sage.

Flax, J. (1983). "Political philosophy and the patriarchal unconscious: A psychoanalytic perspective on epistemology and metaphysics." In S. Harding and M. B. Hintikka (Eds.). *Discovering reality*. Dordrecht: Reidel.

Freire, P. (1976). *Education: The practice of freedom*. London: Writers and Readers Publishing.

Gergen, K. J. (1985). "The social constructionist movement in modern psychology." *American Psychologist* 40:266–75.

Giddens, A. (1974). *Positivism and sociology*. Portsmouth, N.H.: Heinemann.

Gilligan, C. (1982). *In a different voice*. Cambridge: Harvard University Press.

Gould, C. (Ed.). (1984). *Beyond domination: New perspectives on women and philosophy*. Totowa, N.J.: Rowman and Allenheld.

Habermas, J. (1971). *Knowledge and human interests*. Boston: Beacon Press.

Harding, S. (1986). *The science question in feminism.* Ithaca: Cornell University Press.

Harre,, R., and Secord, P. F. (1972). *The explanation of social behaviour.* Oxford: Blackwell and Mott.

Henriques, J., et al. (1984). *Changing the subject.* London: Methuen.

Heron, J. (1981). "Philosophical basis for a new paradigm." In P. Reason and J. Rowan (Eds.). *Human inquiry.* New York: Wiley.

Israel, J., and Tajfel, H. (Eds.). (1972). *The context of social psychology: A critical assessment.* New York: Academic Press.

Jaggar, A. (1983). *Feminist politics and human nature.* Totowa, N.J.: Rowman and Allenheld.

Jay, M. (1973). *The dialectic imagination.* London: Heinmann.

Keller, E. F. (1982). "Science and gender." *Signs: Journal of Women in Culture and Society* 7:589–602.

Kelly, J. (1984). *Women, history and theory: The essays of Joan Kelly.* Chicago: University of Chicago Press.

Marshall, J. (1986). "Exploring the experiences of women managers: Toward rigour in qualitative methods." In S. Wilkinson (Ed.). *Feminist social psychology.* Milton Keynes, England: Open University Press.

Mearns, D. J., and McLeod, J. A. (1984). "A person-centered approach to research." In R. F. Levant and J. Shilen (Eds.). *Client-centered therapy and the person-centered approach: New directions in theory, research and practice.* New York: Praeger.

Mednick, M. S., and Tangri, S. S. (1972). "New social psychological perspectives on women." *Journal of Social Issues* 28:1–16.

Miller, J. B. (1976). *Toward a new psychology of women.* Harmondsworth, England: Penguin.

Minton, H. L. (1986). "Emancipatory social psychology as a paradigm for the study of minority groups." In K. S. Larsen (Ed.). *Dialectics and ideology in psychology.* Norwood, N.J.: ABLEX.

Morgan, G. (Ed.). (1983). *Beyond method: Strategies for social research.* Beverly Hills: Sage.

Oakley, A. (1981). "Interviewing women: A contradiction in terms." In H. Roberts (Ed.). *Doing feminist research.* London: Routledge and Kegan Paul.

Parlee, M. B. (1979). "Psychology and women." *Signs: Journal of Women in Culture and Society* 5:121–33.

Pleck, J. H. (1981). *The myth of masculinity.* Cambridge: MIT Press.

Polkinghorne, D. (1983). *Methodology for the human sciences.* Albany: SUNY Press.

Reason, P., and Rowan, J. (Eds.). (1981). *Human inquiry: A sourcebook of new paradigm research.* New York: Wiley.

Reinharz, S. (1985). "Feminist distrust. Problems of context and content in sociological work." In D. Berg and K. Smith (Eds.). *Exploring clinical methods for social research.* Beverly Hills: Sage.

Roberts, H. (1981). *Doing feminist research.* London: Routledge and Kegan Paul.

Sampson, E. E. (1978). "Scientific paradigms and social values: Wanted-A scientific revolution." *Journal of Personality and Social Psychology* 36:1332–43.

Sherif, C. W. (1979). "Bias in psychology." In J. A. Sherman and E. T. Beck (Eds.). *The prism of sex: Essays in the sociology of knowledge.* Madison: University of Wisconsin Press.

Shotter, J. (1975). *Images of man in psychological research.* London: Methuen.

Snyder, E. C. (1979). "That half of 'mankind' called women: An introduction to women's studies." In E. G. Snyder (Ed.). *The study of women: Enlarging perspectives of social reality.* New York: Harper and Row.

Spence, J., and Helmreich, R. (1978). *Masculinity and femininity: Their psychological dimensions, correlates and antecedents.* Austin: University of Texas Press.

Spender, D. (1978). "Notes on the organization of women's studies." *Women's Studies International Quarterly* 1:255–75.

———. (1980). *Man made language.* London: Routledge and Kegan Paul.

———. (Ed.). (1981). *Men's studies modified.* New York: Pergamon.

Stanley, L., and Wise, S. (1983). *Breaking out: Feminist consciousness and feminist research.* London: Routledge and Kegan Paul.

Strickland, L. H., Aboud, F. E., and Gergen, K. J. (Eds.). (1976). *Social psychology in transition.* New York: Plenum.

Taylor, C. (1971). "Interpretation and the sciences of man." *Review of metaphysics* 25 (1).

Vaughter, R. (1976). "Psychology: Review essay." *Signs: Journal of Women in Culture and Society* 2:120–46.

Weinreich, H. (1977). "What future for the female subject? Some implications of the women's movement for psychological research." *Human Relations* 30:535–43.

Wetherell, M. (1986). "Linguistic repertoires and literary criticism: New directions for a social psychology of gender." In S. Wilkinson (Ed.). *Feminist social psychology.* Milton Keynes, England: Open University Press.

Wilkinson, S. (Ed.). (1986). *Feminist social psychology.* Milton Keynes, England: Open University Press.

CHAPTER ELEVEN

Theoretical Perspectives on Gender Differentiation

The following four papers represent theoretical approaches to understanding women's behavior and personality and to differences in personality between the genders. In the first, we encounter one of Sigmund Freud's few writings specifically on the psychology of women, published in 1925. Freud was the founder of psychoanalysis, an enormously influential theory of the human psyche and its development. Psychoanalytic theory proposes that gender identity emerges as the child develops through a series of psychosexual stages, so named because of Freud's belief that sexual energy becomes focused in various regions of the body during development from infancy to young adulthood. In this paper, Freud attempts to explain what happens to girls during the important "phallic stage" (a stage he had heretofore explicated only in terms of boys' development). Here he introduces the notion that girls view themselves as castrated boys, and experience "penis envy." These facts, he asserts, have far-reaching psychological consequences. One of these consequences is jealousy, which he argues characterizes women's personalities more than men's. A second is that women never develop a superego

(Freud's concept of moral conscience) as fully as do men, evidence he said in their greater emotionality and poorer sense of justice.

Freud's ideas presented here certainly seem outlandish to us today, and indeed Freudian theory has attracted countless critics almost from its beginnings. No scientific proof has ever been given for penis envy in women, nor for its supposed psychical consequences. Why study Freud then? Because of the incredible influence psychoanalytic theory has had on our culture's views of women's psychology and gender differences. Most importantly, these concepts have been used, and continue to be used, in the therapeutic practice of psychoanalysis.

Some of the most articulate critiques of Freudian psychoanalysis have come, it should be no surprise, from feminists. However, there are several important theorists today whose frameworks are *simultaneously* psychoanalytic and feminist. One of the most influential is Nancy Chodorow (e.g., 1974), whose work deserves mentioning here because she has influenced the thinking of many not only within psychological theory and practice, but also within other disciplines, such as literary criticism. Chodorow's developmental theory of gendered personality focuses on the fact that pre-Oedipal infants grow up in the arms of caring, self-sacrificing women. Indeed, the infant's needs are so well met by its mother that it is psychologically merged with her, unable to distinguish between itself and her. The key element of the Oedipal crisis for both girls and boys, then, involves some distancing or breaking of this intense infantile bond with the mother.

For Chodorow, a girl does not make this break as completely as a boy. The development of her gender identity, after all, ultimately involves identification with her mother, the person with whom she has had her earliest and most loving relationship. Therefore, she argues, females remain for life more *relationally* oriented, even having problems experiencing themselves as separate from others with autonomous identities. Boys, on the other hand, have the harder task. They must break fully their intense dependence on the mother in order to establish their masculine, non-feminine, identity. Accomplishing this differentiation involves the devaluation of all things feminine, all reminders of dependence and attachment and relationship. The cycle therefore repeats itself, because girls grow up to be women who seek to meet their relational needs in having children, and boys grow up to be men who, devaluing such needs, dominate women and move out into the world of work. Many feminists have further explored the meaning of this idea that women are more relationally orientated than men.

After Freud's essay, we move to a completely different sort of theory about gender differentiation: evolutionary psychology. Evolutionary theorists believe that underneath all the variation in human behavior lie some regularities that are attributable to our evolutionary past as a species. Furthermore, for our purposes, such theorists argue that certain basic differences in male and female behavior and personality are attributable to the forces of natural selection operating differently on the sexes, based on their differing reproductive biology. In the excerpt from his book *The Moral Animal*, Robert Wright discusses the evolutionary theory of sexual selection and presents the theory of parental investment, which argues that because of women's greater investment in offspring (pregnancy, lactation), they are the "choosier" sex when it comes to mate selection. Researchers who work within this framework point to the fact that diverse cultures across the globe, from industrialized to tribal, all show similar "basic" gender differences in behavior and temperament. This, they believe, lends support to an evolutionary explanation.

Both psychodynamic and evolutionary explanations for gender differentiation invoke distal causes for women's and men's behavior (early childhood conflicts, natural selection of the species). Feminists have been critical of both, arguing that they are difficult to test, and are deterministic, leaving little room for choice or individual variation. However, each of these theories regarding gender and behavior may not be wrong so much as they are incomplete explanations that fail to address humans as cultural beings, embedded in powerful, present-day social contexts. Most of us cannot remember having had an Oedipal conflict or penis envy. It is equally difficult to imagine that some primordial drive to spread our genes is basically what motivates our behavior. However it is easy to recall the toys, teachers, television shows, and role models of our childhood that affected our gendered sense of self.

Several theories of gender differentiation based on the more proximate forces of socialization have been developed within psychology. In the next article in this section, "Gender Schema Theory and Its Implications for Child Development: Raising Gender-aschematic Children in a Gender-schematic Society," Sandra Lipsitz Bem first presents two such socialization-based theories of gender development: social-learning theory and cognitive-developmental theory. She then offers her own theory, "gender schema theory," and presents details of its premises.

Gender schema theory provides a way of understanding the developmental course of gender typing and, most importantly, why there are fascinating individual differences in the outcomes of this process (that is, some of us are highly feminine, some highly masculine, some quite androgynous). Bem begins with the fact that as girls and boys develop, they inevitably learn their society's definitions of femaleness and maleness, and these definitions are very broad, covering myriad aspects of the culture. Furthermore, children learn to evaluate and assimilate new information into this gender dichotomy network. They learn, in other words, to organize information in terms of an evolving gender "schema," and come to understand and socialize themselves within it. Bem, a feminist, then argues that it is possible to be "gender-aschematic in a gender-schematic society" if one employs alternative schemata and therefore "builds up resistance" to the lessons of the dominant culture. She even provides suggestions for feminist parents interested in raising gender-aschematic children.

The final article presents a gender theory that emphasizes not the *developmental* process through which children acquire gender, but rather the *socio-cultural* structures that support and maintain the differences between the genders. Researchers and theorists within this framework argue that gender differences in behavior and personality are really a reflection of the status and power differences between men and women that exist in most cultures. That is, males, as dominant members of society, are rewarded for and hence behave in more "dominant" ways (for example, aggressive, leader-like, self-confident). Females, on the other hand, as subordinate members of society, are rewarded for and hence behave in more "submissive" ways (for example, dependent, emotional, sensitive).

Within this "socio-cultural" framework, Nancy Henley and Marianne LaFrance review research on gender differences in nonverbal communication. Empirical studies have shown gender differences in the areas of facial expression, sensitivity to others' nonverbal cues, use of personal space, and touch. While presenting the evidence for differences in each of these areas, Henley and LaFrance assert that the *explanation* for gender differences should not be built into the *observation* of gender differences. For example, the finding that women appear to occupy smaller space zones than men could be explained any number of ways. Perhaps women are dispositionally more sociable and affiliative (for either biological or socialized reasons), or perhaps women's spaces are seen by others as more "invadable" than men's spaces. The authors' conclusion is that women's smiling, greater attentiveness and responsiveness to others' cues, smaller personal space, and less-frequent touching are all reflective of their subordinate *status* in the social order. Furthermore, any group that is inferior within a culture to other groups (e.g., racial minorities) should be expected to behave similarly—more submissive, more "sensitive." According to this socio-cultural perspective on gender, then, if women and men had equal status many so-called gender distinctions would disappear.

The papers in this section are meant to provide a broad picture of some of the theories that have been brought to bear on the question of why there are differences between the genders. Each theory emphasizes differentially the power of early childhood relationships, evolutionary forces, environmental shaping, cognitive processes, and societal status distinctions in forming and reinforcing women's (and men's) personalities. For the purposes of our understanding the psychology of women, each theory, therefore, undoubtedly provides just a piece of the whole complex puzzle of how it is that a newborn girl becomes a woman in human society.

Reference

Chodorow, N. (1974). Family structure and feminine personality. In M. Z. Rosaldo & L. Lamphere, eds. *Woman, Culture, and Society*, (pp. 43–66). Stanford, CA: Stanford University Press.

35 Some Psychological Consequences of the Anatomical Distinction between the Sexes

SIGMUND FREUD

In my own writings and in those of my followers more and more stress is laid upon the necessity for carrying the analyses of neurotics back into the remotest period of their childhood, the time of the early efflorescence of sexual life. It is only by examining the first manifestations of the patient's innate instinctual constitution and the effects of his earliest experiences that we can accurately gauge the motive forces that have led to his neurosis and can be secure against the errors into which we might be tempted by the degree to which they have become remodelled and overlaid in adult life. This requirement is not only of theoretical but also of practical importance, for it distinguishes our efforts from the work of those physicians whose interests are focussed exclusively upon therapeutic results and who employ analytic methods, but only up to a certain point. An analysis of early childhood such as we are considering is tedious and laborious and makes demands both upon the physician and upon the patient which cannot always be met. Moreover it leads us into dark regions where there are as yet no sign-posts. Indeed, analysts may feel reassured, I think, that there is no risk of their work becoming mechanical, and so of losing its interest, during the next few decades.

In the following pages I bring forward some findings of analytical research which would be of great importance if they could be proved to apply universally. Why do I not postpone publication of them until further experience has given me the necessary proof, if such proof is obtainable? Because the conditions under which I work have undergone a change, with implications which I cannot disguise. Formerly, I was never one of those who are unable to hold back what seems to be a new discovery until it has been either confirmed or corrected. My *Interpretation of Dreams* [1900], and my 'Fragment of an Analysis of a Case of Hysteria' [1905*c*] (the case of Dora) were suppressed by me—if not for the nine years enjoined by Horace—at all events for four or five years before I allowed them to be published. But in those days I had unlimited time before me and material poured in upon me in such quantities that fresh experiences were hardly to be escaped. Moreover, I was the only worker in a new field, so that my reticence involved no danger to myself and no risk of loss to others.

But now everything has changed. The time before me is limited. The whole of it is no longer spent in working, so that my opportunities for making fresh observations are not so numerous. If I think I see something new, I am uncertain whether I can wait for it to be confirmed. And further, everything that is to be seen upon the surface has already been exhausted; what remains has to be slowly and laboriously dragged up from the depths. Finally, I am no longer alone. An eager crowd of fellow-workers is ready to make use of what is unfinished or doubtful, and I can leave to them that part of the work which I should otherwise have done myself. On this occasion, therefore, I feel justified in publishing something which stands in urgent need of confirmation before its value or lack of value can be decided.

In examining the earliest mental shapes assumed by the sexual life of children we have been in the habit of taking as the subject of our investigations the male child, the little boy. With little girls, so we have supposed, things must be similar, though in some way or other they must nevertheless be different. The point in development at which this difference lay could not clearly be determined.

In boys the situation of the Oedipus complex is the first stage that can be recognized with certainty. It is easy to understand, because at that stage a child retains the same object which he previously cathected with his pregenital libido during the preceding period while he was being suckled and nursed. The further fact that in this situation he regards his father as a disturbing rival and would like to get rid of him and take his place is a straightforward consequence of the actual state of affairs. I have shown elsewhere (1924*b*) how the Oedipus attitude in little boys belongs to the phallic phase, and how it succumbs to the fear of castration, that is, to narcissistic interest in their own genitals. The matter is made more difficult to grasp by the complicating circumstance that even in boys the Oedipus complex has a double orientation, active and passive, in accordance with their bisexual constitutions; a boy also wants to take his *mother's* place as the love-object of his *father*—a fact which we describe as the feminine attitude.

As regards the prehistory of the Oedipus complex in boys we are far from complete clarity. We know that that period includes an identification of an affectionate sort with the boy's father, an identification which is still free from any sense of rivalry in regard to his mother. Another element of that stage is invariably, I believe, a masturbatory stimulation of the genitals, the masturbation of early childhood, the more or less violent suppression of which by the persons in charge of the child sets the castration complex in action. It is to be assumed that this masturbation is attached to the Oedipus complex and serves as a discharge for the sexual excitation belonging to it. It is, however, uncertain whether the masturbation has this character from the first, or whether on the contrary it makes its first appearance spontaneously as an activity of a bodily organ and is only brought into relation with the Oedipus complex at some later date; this second possibility is by far the more probable. Another doubtful question is the part played by bed-wetting and by the breaking of that habit through the intervention of training measures. We are inclined to adopt the simple generalization that continued bed-wetting is a result of masturbation and that its suppression is regarded by boys as an inhibition of their genital activity, that is, as having the meaning of a threat of castration; but whether we are always right in supposing this remains to be seen. Finally, analysis shows us in a shadowy way how the fact of a child at a very early age listening to his parents copulating may set up his first sexual excitation, and how that event may, owing to its after-effects, act as a starting-point for the child's whole sexual development. Masturbation, as well as the two attitudes in the Oedipus complex, later on become attached to this early experience, the child having subsequently interpreted its meaning. It is impossible, however, to suppose that these observations of coitus are of universal occurrence, so that at this point we are faced with the problem of 'primal phantasies.' Thus the prehistory of the Oedipus complex, even in boys, raises all of these questions for sifting and explanation; and there is the further problem of whether we are to suppose that the process invariably follows the same course, or whether a great variety of different preliminary stages may not converge upon the same terminal situation.

In little girls the Oedipus complex raises one problem more than in boys. In both cases the mother is the original object; and there is no cause for surprise that boys retain that object in the Oedipus complex. But how does it happen that girls abandon it and instead take their father as an object? In pursuing this question I have been able to reach some conclusions which may throw light upon the prehistory of the Oedipus relation in girls.

Every analyst has come across certain women who cling with especial intensity and tenacity to the bond with their father and to the wish in which it culminates of having a child by him. We have good reason to suppose that the same wishful phantasy was also the motive force of their infantile masturbation, and it is easy to form an impression that at this point we have been brought up against an elementary and unanalysable fact of infantile sexual life. But a thorough analysis of these very cases brings something different to light, namely, that here the Oedipus complex has a long prehistory and is in some respects a secondary formation.

The old paediatrician Lindner [1879] once remarked that a child discovers the genital zones (the penis or the clitoris) as a source of pleasure while indulging in sensual sucking (thumb-sucking). I shall leave it an open question whether it is really true that the child takes the newly found source of pleasure in exchange for the recent loss of the mother's nipple—a possibility to which later phantasies (fellatio) seem to point. Be that as it may, the genital zone is discovered at some time or other, and there seems no justification for attributing any psychical content to its first stimulations. But the first step in the phallic phase which begins in this way is not the linking-up of the masturbation with the object-cathexes of the Oedipus situation, but a momentous discovery which little girls are destined to make. They notice the penis of a brother or playmate, strikingly visible and of large proportions, at once recognize it as the superior counterpart of their own small and inconspicuous organ, and from that time forward fall a victim to envy for the penis.

There is an interesting contrast between the behaviour of the two sexes. In the analogous situation, when a little boy first catches sight of a girl's genital region, he begins by showing irresolution and lack of interest; he sees nothing or disowns what he has seen, he softens it down or looks about for expedients for bringing it into line with his expectations. It is not until later, when some threat of castration has obtained a hold upon him, that the observation becomes important to him: if he then recollects or repeats it, it arouses a terrible storm of emotion in him and forces him to believe in the reality of the threat which he has hitherto laughed at. This combination of circumstances leads to two reactions, which may become fixed and will in that case, whether separately or together or in conjunction with other factors, permanently determine the boy's relations to women: horror of the mutilated creature or triumphant contempt for her. These developments, however, belong to the future, though not to a very remote one.

A little girl behaves differently. She makes her judgement and her decision in a flash. She has seen it and knows that she is without it and wants to have it.[1]

From this point there branches off what has been named the masculinity complex of women, which may put great difficulties in the way of their regular development towards femininity, if it cannot be got over soon enough. The hope of some day obtaining a penis in spite of everything and so of becoming like a man may persist to an incredibly late age and may become a motive for the strangest and otherwise unaccountable actions. Or again, a process may set in which might be described as a 'denial,' a process which in the mental life of children seems neither uncommon nor very dangerous but which in an adult would mean the beginning of a psychosis. Thus a girl may refuse to accept the fact of being castrated, may harden herself in the conviction that she *does* possess a penis and may subsequently be compelled to behave as though she were a man.

The psychical consequences of penis-envy, in so far as it does not become absorbed in the reaction-formation of the masculinity complex, are various and far-reaching. After a woman has become aware of the wound to her narcissism, she develops, like a scar, a sense of inferiority. When she has passed beyond her first attempt at explaining her lack of a penis as being a punishment personal to herself and has realized that that sexual character is a universal one, she begins to share the contempt felt by men for a sex which is the lesser in so important a respect, and, at least in the holding of that opinion, insists upon being like a man.[2]

Even after penis-envy has abandoned its true object, it continues to exist: by an easy displacement it persists in the character-trait of *jealousy*. Of course, jealousy is not limited to one sex and has a wider foundation than this, but I am of opinion that it plays a far larger part in the mental life of women than of men and that that is because it is enormously reinforced from the direction of displaced penis-envy. While I was still unaware of this source of jealousy and was considering the phantasy 'A Child is Being Beaten' (1919), which occurs so commonly in girls, I constructed a first phase for it in which its meaning was that another child, a rival of whom the subject was jealous, was to be beaten. This phantasy seems to be a relic of the phallic period in girls. The peculiar rigidity which struck me so much in the monotonous formula 'a child is being beaten' can probably be interpreted in a special way. The child which is being beaten (or caressed) may at bottom be nothing more nor less than the clitoris itself, so that at its very lowest level the statement will contain a confession of masturbation, which has remained attached to the content of the formula from its beginning in the phallic phase up to the present time.

A third consequence of penis-envy seems to be a loosening of the girl's relation with her mother as a love-object. The situation as a whole is not very clear, but it can be seen that in the end the girl's mother, who sent her into the world so insufficiently equipped, is almost always held responsible for her lack of a penis. The way in which this comes about historically is often that soon after the girl has discovered that her genitals are unsatisfactory she begins to show jealousy of another child on the ground that her mother is fonder of it than her, which serves as a reason for her giving up her affectionate relation to her mother. It will fit in with this if the child which has been preferred by her mother is made into the first object of the beating-phantasy which ends in masturbation.

There is yet another surprising effect of penis-envy, or of the discovery of the inferiority of the clitoris, which is undoubtedly the most important of all. In the past I had often formed an impression that in general women tolerate masturbation worse than men, that they more frequently fight against it and that they are unable to make use of it in circumstances in which a man would seize upon it as a way of escape without any hesitation. Experience would no doubt elicit innumerable exceptions to this statement, if we attempted to turn it into a rule. The reactions of human individuals of both sexes are of course made up of masculine and feminine traits. But it appeared to me nevertheless as though masturbation were further removed from the nature of women than of men, and the solution of the problem could be assisted by the reflection that masturbation, at all events of the clitoris, is a masculine activity and that the elimination of clitoridal sexuality is a necessary pre-condition for the development of femininity. Analyses of the remote phallic period have now taught me that in girls, soon after the first signs of penis-envy, an intense current of feeling against masturbation makes its appearance, which cannot be attributed exclusively to the educational influence of those in charge of the child. This impulse is clearly a forerunner of the wave of repression which at puberty will do away with a large amount of the girl's masculine sexuality in order to make room for the development of her femininity. It may happen that this first opposition to auto-erotic stimulation fails to attain its end. And this was in fact the case in the instances which I analysed. The conflict continued, and both then and later the girl did everything she could to free herself from the compulsion to masturbate. Many of the later manifestations of sexual life in women remain unintelligible unless this powerful motive is recognized.

I cannot explain the opposition which is raised in this way by little girls to phallic masturbation except by supposing that there is some concurrent factor which turns her violently against that pleasurable activity. Such a factor lies close at hand in the narcissistic sense of humiliation which is bound up with penis-envy, the girl's reflection that after all this is a point of which she cannot compete with boys and that it would therefore be best for her to give up the idea of doing so. Thus the little girl's recognition of the anatomical distinction between the sexes forces her away from masculinity and masculine masturbation on to new lines which lead to the development of femininity.

So far there has been no question of the Oedipus complex, nor has it up to this point played any part. But now the girl's libido slips into a new position by means—there is no other way of putting it—of the equation 'penis = child.' She gives up her wish for a penis and puts in place of it a wish for a child: and *with this purpose in view* she takes her father as a love-object. Her mother becomes the object of her jealousy. The girl has turned into a little woman. If I am to credit a single exaggerated analytic instance, this new situation can give rise to physical sensations which would have to be regarded as a premature awakening of the female genital apparatus. If the girl's attachment to her father comes to grief later on and has to be abandoned, it may give place to an identification with him and the girl may thus return to her masculinity complex and perhaps remain fixated in it.

I have now said the essence of what I had to say: I will stop, therefore, and cast an eye over our findings. We have gained some insight into the prehistory of the Oedipus complex in girls. The corresponding period in boys is more or less unknown. In girls the Oedipus complex is a secondary formation. The operations of the castration complex precede it and prepare for it. As regards the relation between the Oedipus and castration complexes there is a fundamental contrast between the two sexes. *Whereas in boys the Oedipus complex succumbs to the castration complex, in girls it is made possible and led up to by the castration complex.* This contradiction is cleared up if we reflect that the castration complex always operates in the sense dictated by its subject-matter: it inhibits and limits masculinity and encourages femininity. The difference between the sexual development of males and females at the stage we have been considering is an intelligible consequence of the anatomical distinction between their genitals and of the psychical situation involved in it; it corresponds to the difference between a castration that has been carried out and one that has merely been threatened. In their essentials, therefore, our findings are self-evident and it should have been possible to foresee them.

The Oedipus complex, however, is such an important thing that the manner in which one enters and leaves it cannot be without its effects. In boys (as I have shown at length in the paper to which I have just referred and to which all of my present remarks are closely related) the complex is not simply repressed, it is literally smashed to pieces by the shock of threatened castration. Its libidinal cathexes are abandoned, desexualized and in part sublimated; its objects are incorporated into the ego, where they form the nucleus of the super-ego and give that new structure its characteristic qualities. In normal, or rather in ideal cases, the Oedipus complex exists no longer, even in the unconscious; the super-ego has become its heir. Since the penis (to follow Ferenczi) owes its extraordinarily high narcissistic cathexis to its organic significance for the propagation of the species, the catastrophe of the Oedipus complex (the abandonment of incest and the institution of conscience and morality) may be regarded as a victory of the race over the individual. This is an interesting point of view when one considers that neurosis is based upon a struggle of the ego against the demands of the sexual function. But to leave the standpoint of individual psychology is not likely to be of any immediate help in clarifying this complicated situation.

In girls the motive for the destruction of the Oedipus complex is lacking. Castration has already had its effect, which was to force the child into the situation of the Oedipus complex. Thus the Oedipus complex escapes the fate which it meets with in boys: it may either be slowly abandoned or got rid of by repression, or its effects may persist far into women's normal mental life. I cannot escape the notion (though I hesitate to give it expression) that for women the level of what is ethically normal is different from what it is in men. Their super-ego is never so inexorable, so impersonal, so independent of its emotional origins as we require it to be in men. Character-traits which critics of every epoch have brought up against women—that they show less sense of justice than men, that they are less ready to submit to the great necessities of life, that they are more often influenced in their judgments by feelings of affection or hostility—all these would be amply accounted for by the modification in the formation of their super-ego which we have already inferred. We must not allow ourselves to be deflected from such conclusions by the denials of the feminists, who are anxious to force us to regard the two sexes as completely equal in position and worth; but we shall, of course, willingly agree that the majority of men are also far behind the masculine ideal and that all human individuals, as a result of their bisexual disposition and of cross-inheritance, combine in themselves both masculine and feminine characteristics, so that pure masculinity and femininity remain theoretical constructions of uncertain content.

I am inclined to set some value on the considerations I have brought forward upon the psychological consequences of the anatomical distinction between the sexes. I am aware, however, that this opinion can only be maintained if my findings, which are based on a handful of cases, turn out to have general validity and to be typical. If not, they would remain no more than a contribution of our knowledge of the different paths along which sexual life develops.

In the valuable and comprehensive studies upon the masculinity and castration complex in women by Abraham (1921), Horney (1923) and Helene Deutsch (1925) there is much that touches closely upon what I have written but nothing that coincides with it completely, so that here again I feel justified in publishing this paper.

Notes

1. This is an opportunity for correcting a statement which I made many years ago. [Freud, 1905*b* (English Translation, 1949, 72).] I believed that the sexual interest of children, unlike that of pubescents, was aroused, not by the difference between the sexes, but by the problem of where babies come from. We now see that, at all events with girls, this is certainly not the case. With boys it may no doubt happen sometimes one way and sometimes the other; or with both sexes chance experiences may determine the event.
2. In my first critical account of the 'History of the Psycho-Analytic Movement,' written in 1914 (*Collected Papers*, 1, 287), I recognized that this fact represents the core of truth contained in Adler's theory. That theory has no hesitation in explaining the whole world by this single point ('organ inferiority,' 'the masculine protest,' breaking away from the 'the feminine line') and prides itself upon having in this way robbed sexuality of its importance and put the desire for power in its place. Thus the only organ which could claim to be called 'inferior' without any ambiguity would be the clitoris. On the other hand, one hears of analysts who boast

that, though they have worked for dozens of years, they have never found a sign of the existence of a castration complex. We must bow our heads in recognition of the greatness of this achievement, even though it is only a negative one, a piece of virtuosity in the art of overlooking and mistaking. The two theories form an interesting pair of opposites—in one of them not a trace of a castration complex, in the other nothing at all but its effects.

36 The Moral Animal

ROBERT WRIGHT

In the most distinct classes of the animal kingdom, with mammals, birds, reptiles, fishes, insects, and even crustaceans, the differences between the sexes follow almost exactly the same rules; the males are almost always the wooers. . . .

—*The Descent of Man (1871)*[1]

Darwin was wrong about sex.

He wasn't wrong about the males being the wooers. His reading of the basic characters of the two sexes holds up well today. "The female, . . . with the rarest exception, is less eager than the male. . . . [S]he is coy, and may often be seen endeavouring for a long time to escape from the male. Every one who has attended to the habits of animals will be able to call to mind instances of this kind. . . . The exertion of some choice on the part of the female seems almost as general a law as the eagerness of the male."[2]

Nor was Darwin wrong about the *consequences* of this asymmetrical interest. He saw that female reticence left males competing with one another for scarce reproductive opportunities, and thus explained why males so often have built-in weapons—the horns of stags, the hornlike mandibles of stag beetles, the fierce canines of chimpanzees. Males not hereditarily equipped for combat with other males have been excluded from sex, and their traits have thus been discarded by natural selection.

Darwin also saw that the choosiness of females gives great moment to their choices. If they prefer to mate with particular kinds of males, those kinds will proliferate. Hence the ornamentation of so many male animals—a lizard's inflatable throat sack, brightly colored during the mating season; the immense, cumbersome tail of the peacock; and, again, the stag's horns, which seem more elaborate than the needs of combat alone would dictate. These decorations have evolved not because they aid in daily survival—if anything, they complicate it—but because they can so charm a female as to outweigh the everyday burdens they bring. . . .

Both of these variants of natural selection—combat among males and discernment by females—Darwin called "sexual selection." He took great pride in the idea, and justifiably so. Sexual selection is a nonobvious extension of his general theory that accounts for seeming exceptions to it (like garish colors that virtually say "Kill me" to predators), and that has not just endured over time but grown in scope.

What Darwin was wrong about was the evolutionary *cause* of female coyness and male eagerness. He saw that this imbalance of interest creates competition among males for precious reproductive slots, and he saw the consequences of this competition; but he didn't see what had created the imbalance. His attempt late in life to explain the phenomenon was unsuccessful. And, in fairness to him, whole generations of biologists would do no better.

Now that there is a consensus on the solution, the long failure to find it seems puzzling. It's a very simple solution. In this sense, sex is typical of many behaviors illuminated by natural selection; though the illumination has gotten truly powerful only within the last three decades, it could in principle have done so a century earlier, so plainly does it follow from Darwin's view of life. There is some subtle logic involved, so Darwin can be forgiven for not having seen the full scope of his theory. Still, if he were around today to hear evolutionary biologists talk about sex, he might well sink into one of his self-effacing funks, exclaiming at his obtuseness in not getting the picture sooner.

Playing God

The first step toward understanding the basic imbalance of the sexes is to assume hypothetically the role natural selection plays in designing a species. Take the human species, for example. Suppose you're in charge of installing, in the minds of human (or prehuman) beings, rules of behavior that will guide them through life, the object of the game being to maximize each person's genetic legacy. To oversimplify a bit: you're supposed to make each person behave in such a way that he or she is likely to have lots of offspring—offspring, moreover, who themselves have lots of offspring.

Obviously, this isn't to say natural selection actually works. It doesn't consciously design organisms. It doesn't consciously do anything. It blindly preserves hereditary traits that happen to enhance survival and reproduction. Still, natural selection works *as if* it were consciously designing organisms, so pretending you're in charge of organism design is a legitimate way to figure out which tendencies evolution is likely to have ingrained in people and other animals. In fact, this is what evolutionary biologists spend a good deal of time doing: looking at a trait—mental or otherwise—and figuring out what, if any, engineering challenge it is a solution to.

When playing the Administrator of Evolution, and trying to maximize genetic legacy, you quickly discover that this goal implies different tendencies for men and women. Men can reproduce hundreds of times a year, assuming they can persuade enough women to cooperate, and assuming that there aren't any laws against polygamy—which there assuredly weren't in the environment where much of our evolution took place. Women, on the other hand, can't reproduce more often than once a year. The asymmetry lies partly in the high price of eggs; in all species they're bigger and rarer than minuscule, mass-produced sperm. (That, in fact, is biology's official definition of a female: the one with the larger sex cells.) But the asymmetry is exaggerated by the details of mammalian reproduction; the egg's lengthy conversion into an organism happens inside the female, and she can't handle many projects at once.

So, while there are various reasons why it could make Darwinian sense for a woman to mate with more than one man (maybe the first man was infertile, for example), there comes a time when having more sex just isn't worth the trouble. Better to get some rest or grab a bite to eat. For a man, unless he's really on the brink of collapse or starvation, that time never comes. Each new partner offers a very real chance to get more genes into the next generation—a much more valuable prospect, in the Darwinian calculus, than a nap or a meal. As the evolutionary psychologists Martin Daly and Margo Wilson have succinctly put it: for males "there is always the possibility of doing better."[3]

There's a sense in which a female can do better, too, but it has to do with quality, not quantity. Giving birth to a child involves a huge commitment of time, not to mention energy, and nature has put a low ceiling on how many such enterprises she can undertake. So each child, from her (genetic) point of view, is an extremely precious gene machine. Its ability to survive and then, in turn, produce its own young gene machines is of mammoth importance. It makes Darwinian sense, then, for a woman to be selective about the man who is going to help her build each gene machine. She should size up an aspiring partner before letting him in on the investment, asking herself what he'll bring to the project. This question then entails a number of subquestions that, in the human species especially, are more numerous and subtle than you might guess.

Before we go into these questions, a couple of points must be made. One is that the woman needn't literally ask them, or even be aware of them. Much of the relevant history of our species took place before our ancestors were smart enough to ask much of anything. And even in the more recent past, after the arrival of language and self-awareness, there has been no reason for every evolved behavioral tendency to fall under conscious control. In fact, sometimes it is emphatically *not* in our genetic interest to be aware of exactly what we are doing or why. (Hence Freud, who was definitely onto something, though some evolutionary psychologists would say he didn't know exactly what.) In the case of sexual attraction, at any rate, everyday experience suggests that natural selection has wielded its influence largely via the emotional spigots that turn on and off such feelings as tentative attraction, fierce passion, and swoon-inducing infatuation. A woman doesn't typically size up a man and think; "He seems like a worthy contributor to my genetic legacy." She just sizes him up and feels attracted to him—or doesn't. All the "thinking" has been done— unconsciously, metaphorically—by natural selection. Genes leading to attractions that wound up being good for her ancestors' genetic legacies have flourished, and those leading to less productive attractions have not.

Understanding the often unconscious nature of genetic control is the first step toward understanding that—in many realms, not just sex—we're all puppets, and our best hope for even partial liberation is to try to decipher the logic of the puppeteer. The full scope of the logic will take some time to explain, but I don't think I'm spoiling the end of the movie by noting here that the puppeteer seems to have exactly zero regard for the happiness of the puppets.

The second point to grasp before pondering how natural selection has "decided" to shape the sexual preferences of women (and of men) is that it isn't foresightful. Evolution is guided by the environment in which it takes place, and environments change. Natural selection had no way of anticipating, for example, that someday people would use contraception, and that their passions would thus lead them into time-consuming and energy-sapping sex that was sure to be fruitless; or that X-rated videotapes would come along and lead indiscriminately lustful men to spend leisure time watching them rather than pursuing real, live women who might get their genes to the next generation.

This isn't to say that there's anything wrong with "unproductive" sexual recreation. Just because natural selection created us doesn't mean we have to slavishly follow its peculiar agenda. (If anything, we might be tempted to spite it for all the ridiculous baggage it's saddled us with.) The point is just that it isn't correct to say that people's minds are designed to maximize their fitness, their genetic legacy. What the theory of natural selection says, rather, is that people's minds are designed to maximize fitness *in the environment in which those minds evolved*. This environment is known as the EEA—the environment of evolutionary adaption.[4] Or, more memorably: the "ancestral environment." Throughout this book, the ancestral environment will lurk in the background. At times, in pondering whether some mental trait is an evolutionary adaptation, I will ask whether it seems to be in the "genetic interest" of its bearer. For example: Would indiscriminate lust be in the genetic interest of men? But this is just a kind of shorthand. The question, properly put, is always whether a trait would be in the "genetic interest" of someone in the EEA, not in modern America or Victorian England or anywhere else. Only traits that would have propelled the genes responsible for them through the generations in our ancestral social environment should, in theory, be part of human nature today.

What was the ancestral environment like? The closest thing to a twentieth-century example is a hunter-gatherer society, such as the !Kung San of the Kalahari Desert in Africa, the Inuit (Eskimos) of the Arctic region, or the Ache of Paraguay. Inconveniently, hunter-gatherer societies are quite different from one another, rendering simple generalization about the crucible of human evolution difficult. This diversity is a reminder that the idea of a single EEA is actually a fiction, a composite drawing; our ancestral social environment no doubt changed much in the course of human evolution.[5] Still, there are recurring themes among contemporary hunter-gatherer societies, and they suggest that some features probably stayed fairly constant during much of the evolution of the human mind. For example: people grew up near close kin in small villages where everyone knew everyone else and strangers didn't show up very often. People got married—monogamously or polygamously—and a female typically was married by the time she was old enough to be fertile.

This much, at any rate, is a safe bet: whatever the ancestral environment was like, it wasn't much like the environment we're in now. We aren't designed to stand on crowded subway platforms, or to live in suburbs next door to people we never talk to, or to get hired or fired, or to watch the evening news. This disjunction between the contexts of our design and of our lives is probably responsible for much psychopathology, as well as much suffering of a less dramatic sort. (And, like the importance of unconscious motivation, it is an observation for which Freud gets some credit; it is central to his *Civilization and Its Discontents.*)

To figure out what women are inclined to seek in a man, and vice versa, we'll need to think more carefully about our ancestral social environment(s). And, as we'll see, thinking about the ancestral environment also helps explain why females in our species are less sexually reserved than females in many other species. But for purposes of making the single, largest point of this chapter—that, whatever the typical level of reserve for females in our species, it is higher than the level for males—the particular environment doesn't much matter. For this point depends only on the premise that an individual female can, over a lifetime, have many fewer offspring than an individual male. And that has been the case, basically, forever: since before our ancestors were human, before they were primates, before they were mammals—way, way back through the evolution of our brain, down to its reptilian core. Female snakes may not be very smart, but they're smart enough to know, unconsciously, at least, that there are some males it's not a good idea to mate with.

Darwin's failure, then, was a failure to see what a deeply precious commodity females are. He saw that their coyness had made them precious, but he didn't see that they were *inherently* precious—precious by virtue of the biological role in reproduction, and the resulting slow rate of female reproduction. Natural selection had seen this—or, at least, had "seen" it—and female coyness is the result of this implicit comprehension.

Enlightenment Dawns

The first large and clear step toward human comprehension of this logic was made in 1948 by the British geneticist A. J. Bateman. Bateman took fruit flies and ran them through a dating game. He would place five males and five females in a chamber, let them follow their hearts, and then, by examining the traits of the next generation, figure out which offspring belonged to which parents. He found a clear pattern. Whereas almost all females had about the same number of offspring, regardless of whether they mated with one, two, or three males, male legacies differed according to a simple rule: the more females you mate with, the more offspring you have. Bateman saw the import: natural selection encourages "an undiscriminating eagerness in the males and a discriminating passivity in the females."[6] . . .

[George] Williams (1966) amplified and extended the logic behind Bateman's 1948 paper. He cast the issue of male versus female genetic interests in terms of the "sacrifice" required for reproduction. For a male mammal, the necessary sacrifice is close to zero. His "essential role may end with copulation, which involves a negligible expenditure of energy and materials on his part, and only a momentary lapse of attention from matters of direct concern to his safety and well-being." With little to lose and much to gain, males can profit, in the currency of natural selection, by harboring "an aggressive and immediate willingness to mate with as many females as may be available." For the female, on the other hand, "copulation may mean a commitment to a prolonged burden, in both the mechanical and physiological sense, and its many attendant stresses and dangers." Thus, it is in her genetic interest to "assume the burdens of reproduction" only when circumstances seem propitious. And "one of the most important circumstances is the inseminating male"; since "unusually fit fathers tend to have unusually fit offspring," it is "to the female's advantage to be able to pick the most fit male available. . . ."[7]

Hence courtship: "the advertisement, by the male, of how fit he is." And just as "it is to his advantage to pretend to be highly fit whether he is or not," it is to the female's advantage to spot false advertising. So natural selection creates "a skilled salesmanship among the males and an equally well-developed sales resistance and discrimination among the females."[8] In other words: males should, in theory, tend to be show-offs.

A few years later, Trivers used the ideas of Bateman and Williams to create a full-blown theory that ever since has been shedding light on the psychology of men and women. Trivers began by replacing William's concept of "sacrifice" with "investment." The difference may seem slight, but nuances can start intellectual avalanches, and this one did. The term *investment*, linked to economics, comes with a ready-made analytical framework.

In a now-famous paper published in 1972, Trivers formally defined "parental investment" as "any investment by the parent in an individual offspring that increases the offspring's chance of surviving (and hence [the offspring's] reproductive success) at the cost of the parent's ability to invest in other offspring."[9] Parental investment includes the time and energy consumed in producing an egg or a sperm, achieving fertilization, gestating or incubating the egg, and rearing the offspring. Plainly, females will generally make the higher investment up until birth, and, less plainly but in fact typically, this disparity continues after birth.

By quantifying the imbalance of investment between mother and father in a given species, Trivers suggested, we could better understand many things—for example, the extent of male eagerness and female coyness, the intensity of sexual selection, and many subtle aspects of courtship and parenthood, fidelity and infidelity. Trivers saw that in our species the imbalance of investment is not as stark as in many others. And he correctly suspected that . . . the result is much psychological complexity. . . .

Testing the Theory

Theories are a dime a dozen. Even strikingly elegant theories, which, like the theory of parental investment, seem able to explain much with little, often turn out to be worthless. There is justice in the complaint (from creationists, among others) that some theories about the evolution of animal traits are "just so stories"—plausible, but nothing more. Still, it is possible to separate the merely plausible from the compelling. In some sciences, testing theories is so straightforward that it is only a slight exaggeration (though it is always, in a certain strict sense, an exaggeration) to talk of theories being "proved." In others, corroboration is roundabout—an ongoing, gradual process by which confidence approaches the threshold of consensus, or fails to. Studying the evolutionary roots of human nature, or of anything else, is a science of the second sort. About each theory we ask a series of questions, and the answers nourish belief or doubt or ambivalence.

One question about the theory of parental investment is whether human behavior in fact complies with it in even the most basic ways. Are women more choosy about sex partners than men? (This is not to be confused with the very different question, to which we'll return, of which sex, if either, is choosier about *marriage* partners.) Certainly there is plenty of folk wisdom suggesting as much. More concretely, there's the fact that prostitution—sex with someone you don't know and don't care to know—is a service sought overwhelmingly by males, now as in Victorian England. Similarly, virtually all pornography that relies sheerly on visual stimulation—pictures or films of anonymous people, spiritless flesh—is consumed by males. And various studies have shown men to be, on average, much more open to casual, anonymous sex than women. In one experiment, three fourths of the men approached by an unknown woman on a college campus agreed to have sex with her, whereas none of the women approached by an unknown man were willing.[10] . . .

One way to strengthen an evolutionary explanation is to show that its logic is obeyed generally. If women are choosy about sex because they can have fewer kids than men (by virtue of investing more in them), and if females in the animal kingdom generally can have fewer offspring than males, then female animals in general should be choosier than males. Evolutionary theories can generate falsifiable predictions, as good scientific theories are expected to do, even though evolutionary biologists don't have the luxury of rerunning evolution in their labs, with some of its variables controlled, and predicting the outcome.

This particular prediction has been abundantly confirmed. In species after species, females are coy and males are not. Indeed, males are so dim in their sexual discernment that they may pursue things other than females. Among some kinds of frogs, mistaken homosexual courtship is so common that a "release call" is used by males who find themselves in the clutches of another male to notify him that they're both wasting their time.[11] Male snakes, for their part, have been known to spend a while with dead females before moving on to a live prospect.[12] And male turkeys will avidly court a stuffed replica of a female turkey. In fact, a replica of a female turkey's head suspended fifteen inches from the ground will generally do the trick. The male circles the head, does its ritual displays, and then (confident, presumably, that its performance has been impressive) rises into the air and comes down in the proximity of the female's backside, which turns out not to exist. The more virile males will show such interest even when a wooden head is used, and a few can summon lust for a wooden head with no eyes or beak.[13]

Of course, such experiments only confirm in vivid form what Darwin had much earlier said was obvious: males are very eager. This raises a much-cited problem with testing evolutionary explanations: the odd sense in which a theory's "predictions" are confirmed. Darwin didn't sit in his study and say, "My theory implies coy, picky females and mindlessly lustful males," and then take a walk to see if he could find examples. On the contrary, the many examples are what prompted him to wonder which implication of natural selection had created them—a question not correctly answered until midway through the following century, after even more examples had piled up. This tendency for Darwinian "predictions" to come after their evident fulfillment has been a chronic gripe of Darwin's critics. People who doubt the theory of natural selection, or just resist its application to human behavior, complain about the retrofitting of fresh predictions to preexisting results. This is often what they have in mind when they say evolutionary biologists spend their time dreaming up "just so stories" to explain everything they see.

In a sense, dreaming up plausible stories *is* what evolutionary biologists do. But that's not by itself a damning indictment. The power of a theory, such as the theory of parental investment, is gauged by how much data it explains and how simply, regardless of when the data surfaced. After Corpernicus showed that assuming the Earth to revolve around the Sun accounted elegantly for the otherwise perplexing patterns that stars trace in the sky, it would have been beside the point to say, "But you cheated. You knew about the patterns all along." Some "just so stories" are plainly better than others, and they win. Besides, how much choice do evolutionary biologists have? There's not much they can do about the fact that the database on animal life began accumulating millennia before Darwin's theory.

But there is one thing they can do. Often a Darwinian theory generates, in addition to the pseudopredictions that the theory was in fact designed to explain, additional predictions—real predictions, untested predictions, which can be used to further evaluate the theory. . . . The theory of parental investment is a good example. For there are a few oddball species, as Williams noted in 1966, in which the male's investment in the offspring roughly matches, or even exceeds, the female's. If the theory of parental investment is right, these species should defy sex stereotypes.

Consider the spindly creatures known as pipefish. Here the male plays a role like a female kangaroo's: he takes the eggs into a pouch and plugs them into his bloodstream for nutrition. The female can thus start on another round of reproduction while the male is playing nurse. This may not mean that she can have many more offspring than he in the long run—after all, it took her a while to produce the eggs in the first place. Still, the parental investment isn't grossly imbalanced in the usual direction. And, predictably, female pipefish tend to take an active role in courtship, seeking out the males and initiating the mating ritual.[14]

Some birds, such as the phalarope (including the two species known as sea snipes), exhibit a similarly abnormal distribution of parental investment. The males sit on the eggs, leaving the females free to go get some wild oats sown. Again, we see the expected departure from stereotype. It is the phalarope *females* who are larger and more colorful—a sign that sexual selection is working in reverse, as females compete for males. One biologist observed that the females, in classically male fashion, "quarrel and display among themselves" while the males patiently incubate the eggs.[15]

If the truth be told, Williams knew that these species defy stereotype when he wrote in 1966. But subsequent investigation has confirmed his "prediction" more broadly. Extensive parental investment by males has been shown to have the expected consequences in other birds, in the Panamanian poison-arrow frog, in a water bug whose males cart fertilized eggs around on their backs, and in the (ironically named, it turns out) Mormon cricket. So far Williams's prediction has encountered no serious trouble. . . .

Animals and the Unconscious

A common reaction to the new Darwinian view of sex is that it makes perfect sense as an explanation for animal behavior—which is to say, for the behavior of *nonhuman* animals. People may chuckle appreciatively at a male turkey that tries to mate with a poor rendition of a female's head, but if you then point out that many a human male regularly gets aroused after looking at two-dimensional representations of a nude woman, they don't see the connection. After all, the man surely knows that it's only a photo he's looking at; his behavior may be pathetic, but it isn't comic.

And maybe it isn't. But if he "knows" it's a photo, why is he getting so excited? And why are women so seldom whipped up to an onanistic frenzy by pictures of men?

Resistance to lumping humans and turkeys under one set of Darwinian rules has its points. Yes, our behavior is under more subtle, presumably more "conscious," control than is turkey behavior. Men can decide not to get aroused by something—or, at least, can decide not to look at something they know will arouse them. Sometimes they even stick with those decisions. And although turkeys can make what look like comparable "choices" (a turkey hounded by a shotgun-wielding man may decide that now isn't the time for romance), it is plainly true that the complexity and subtlety of options available to a human are unrivaled in the animal kingdom. So too is the human's considered pursuit of very long-run goals.

It all feels very rational, and in some ways it is. But that doesn't mean it isn't in the service of Darwinian ends. To a layperson, it may seem natural that the evolution of reflective, self-conscious brains would liberate us from the base dictates of our evolutionary past. To an evolutionary biologist, what seems natural is roughly the opposite: that human brains evolved not to insulate us from the mandate to survive and reproduce, but to follow it more effectively, if more pliably; that as we evolve from a species whose males forcibly abduct females into a species whose males whisper sweet nothings, the whispering will be governed by the same logic as the abduction—it is a means of manipulating females to male ends, and its form serves this function. The basic emanations of natural selection are refracted from the older, inner parts of our brain all the way out to its freshest tissue. Indeed, the freshest tissue would never have appeared if it didn't toe natural selection's bottom line.

Of course, a lot *has* happened since our ancestors parted ways with the great apes' ancestors, and one can imagine a change in evolutionary context that would have removed our lineage from the logic that so imbalances the romantic interests of male and female in most species. Don't forget about the seahorses, sea snipes, Panamanian poison-arrow frogs, and Mormon crickets, with their reversed sex roles. And, less dramatically, but a bit closer to home, there are the gibbons, another of our primate cousins, whose ancestors waved good-bye to ours about twenty million years ago. At some point in gibbon evolution, circumstances began to encourage much male parental investment. The males regularly stick around and help provide for the kids. In one gibbon species the males actually carry the infants, something male apes aren't exactly known for. And talk about marital harmony: gibbon couples sing a loud duet in the morning, pointedly advertising their familial stability for the information of would-be home-wreckers.[16]

Well, human males too have been known to carry around infants, and to stay with their families. Is it possible that at some time over the last few million years something happened to us rather like what happened to the gibbons? Have male and female sexual appetites converged at least enough to make monogamous marriage a reasonable goal?

Notes

1. Darwin, C. (1871). *The descent of man, and selection in relation to sex.* Princeton, N.J.: Princeton University Press, pp. 396–97, 273.

2. Darwin, C. (1871). *The descent of man, and selection in relation to sex.* Princeton, N.J.: Princeton University Press, pp. 396–97, 273.

3. Hrdy, S. B. (1981). *The woman that never evolved.* Cambridge, MA: Harvard University Press, p. 132.

4. Bowlby, J. (1991). *Charles Darwin: A new life.* New York: Norton.

5. Tooby, J. & Cosmides, L. (1990). The past explains the present: Emotional adaptations and the structure of ancestral environments. *Ethology and Sociobiology, 11*, 375–421.

6. Bateman, A. J. (1948). Intrasexual selection in Drosophila. *Heredity, 2*, 349–68.

7. Williams, G. C. (1966). *Adaptation and natural selection: A critique of some current evolutionary thought*. Princeton, N.J.: Princeton University Press, pp. 183–84.
8. Williams, G. C. (1966). *Adaptation and natural selection: A critique of some current evolutionary thought*. Princeton, N.J.: Princeton University Press, pp. 183–84.
9. Trivers, R. (1972). Parental investment and sexual selection. In B. Cambell, ed. *Sexual selection and the descent of man* (pp. 136–79). Chicago: Aldine de Gruyter.
10. Buss, D. & Schmitt, D. P. (1993). Sexual strategies theory: An evolutionary perspective on human mating. *Psychological Review, 100*, 204–32.
11. Trivers, R. (1985). *Social evolution*. Menlo Park, CA: Benjamin/ Cummings.
12. Darwin, C. (1871). *The descent of man, and selection in relation to sex*. Princeton, N.J.: Princeton University Press, pp. 396–97, 273.
13. Trivers, R. (1985). *Social evolution*. Menlo Park, CA: Benjamin/ Cummings.
14. Williams, G. C. (1966). *Adaptation and natural selection: A critique of some current evolutionary thought*. Princeton, N.J.: Princeton University Press, pp. 183–84.
15. West-Eberhard, M. J. (1991). Sexual selection and social behavior. In M. H. Robinson and L. Tiger, eds. *Man and beast revisited*. Washington, D.C.: Smithsonian Institution Press, p. 162.
16. Leighton, D. R. (1987). Gibbons: Territoriality and monogamy. In B. Smuts et al. eds. *Primate societies*. Chicago: University of Chicago Press.

37 Gender Schema Theory and Its Implications for Child Development: Raising Gender-aschematic Children in a Gender-schematic Society

SANDRA LIPSITZ BEM

As every parent, teacher, and developmental psychologist knows, male and female children become "masculine" and "feminine;" respectively, at a very early age. By the time they are four or five, for example, girls and boys have typically come to prefer activities defined by the culture as appropriate for their sex and also to prefer same-sex peers. The acquisition of sex-appropriate preferences, skills, personality attributes, behaviors, and self-concepts is typically referred to within psychology as the process of sex typing.

The universality and importance of this process is reflected in the prominence it has received in psychological theories of development, which seek to elucidate how the developing child comes to match the template defined as sex-appropriate by his or her culture. . . .

Social Learning Theory

. . . Social learning theory emphasizes the rewards and punishments that children receive for sex-appropriate and sex-inappropriate behaviors, as well as the vicarious learning that observation and modeling can provide.[1] Social learning theory thus locates the source of sex typing in the sex-differentiated practices of the socializing community.

Perhaps the major virtue of social learning theory for psychologists is that it applies to the development of psychological femaleness and maleness the very same general principles of learning that are already known to account for the development of a multitude of other behaviors. Thus, as far as the formal theory is concerned, gender does not demand special consideration; that is, no special psychological mechanisms or processes must be postulated in order to explain how children become sex typed beyond those already used to explain how children learn other socialized behaviors.

Interestingly, the theory's generality also constitutes the basis of its appeal to feminist psychologists in particular. If there is nothing special about gender, then the phenomenon of sex typing itself is neither inevitable nor unmodifiable. Children become sex typed because sex happens to be the basis of differential socialization in their culture. In principle, however, any category could be made the basis for differential socialization.

Although social learning theory can account for the young child's acquiring a number of particular behaviors that are stereotyped by the culture as sex appropriate, it treats the child as the relatively passive recipient of environmental forces rather than as an active agent striving to organize and thereby to comprehend the social world. This view of the passive child is inconsistent with the common observation that children themselves frequently construct and enforce their own version of society's gender rules. It is also inconsistent with the fact that the flexibility with which children interpret society's gender rules varies predictably with age. In one study, for example, 73 percent of the four-year-olds and 80 percent of the nine-year-olds believed—quite flexibly—that there should be no sexual restrictions on one's choice of occupation. Between those ages, however, children held more rigid opinions, with the middle children being the least flexible of all. Thus, only 33 percent of the five-year-olds, 10 percent of the six-year-olds, 11 percent of the seven-year-olds, and 44 percent of the eight-year-olds believed there should be no sexual restrictions on one's choice of occupation.[2]

This particular developmental pattern is not unique to the child's interpretation of gender rules. Even in a domain as far removed from gender as syntax, children first learn certain correct grammatical forms through reinforcement and modeling. As they get a bit older, however, they begin to construct their own grammatical rules on the basis of what they hear spoken around them, and they are able only later still to allow for exceptions to those rules. Thus, only the youngest and the oldest children say "ran"; children in between say "runned."[3] What all of this implies, of course, is that the child is passive in neither domain. Rather, she or he is actively constructing rules to organize—and thereby to comprehend—the vast array of information in his or her world.

Cognitive-Developmental Theory

Unlike social learning theory, cognitive-developmental theory focuses almost exclusively on the child as the primary agent of his or her own sex-role socialization, a focus reflecting the theory's basic assumption that sex typing follows naturally and inevitably from universal principles of cognitive development. As children work actively to comprehend their social world, they inevitably "label themselves—call it alpha—and determine that there are alphas and betas in the environment. Given the cognitive-motivational properties of the self, . . . the child moves toward other alphas and away from betas. That is, it is the child who realizes what gender he or she is, and in what behaviors he or she should engage."[4] In essence, then, cognitive-developmental theory postulates that, because of the child's need for cognitive consistency, self-categorization as female or male motivates her or him to value that which is seen as similar to the self in terms of gender. This gender-based value system, in turn, motivates the child to engage in gender-congruent activities, to strive for gender-congruent attributes, and to prefer gender-congruent peers. "Basic self-categorizations determine basic valuings. Once the boy has stably identified himself as male, he then values positively those objects and acts consistent with his gender identity."[5]

The cognitive-developmental account of sex typing has been so influential since its introduction into the literature in 1966 that many psychologists now seem to accept almost as a given that the young child will spontaneously develop both a gender-based self-concept and a gender-based value system even in the absence of external pressure to behave in a sex-stereotyped manner: Despite its popularity, however, the theory fails to explicate why sex will have primacy over other potential categories of the self such as race, religion, or even eye color. Interestingly, the formal theory itself does not dictate that any particular category should have such primacy. Moreover, most cognitive-developmental theorists do not explicitly ponder the "why sex" question nor do they even raise the possibility that other categories could fit the general theory just as well. To the extent that cognitive-developmental psychologists address this question at all, they seem to emphasize the perceptual salience to the child of the observable differences between the sexes, particularly biologically produced differences such as size and strength.[6]

The implicit assumption here that sex differences are naturally and inevitably more perceptually salient to children than other differences may not have cross-cultural validity. Although it may be true that our culture does not construct any distinctions between people that we perceive to be as compelling as sex, other cultures do construct such distinctions, for example, distinctions between those who are high caste and those who are low caste, between those who are inhabited by spirits and those who are not, between those who are divine and those who are mortal, between those who are wet and those who are dry, or between those who are open and those who are closed.[7] Given such cross-cultural diversity, it is ironic that a theory emphasizing the child's active striving to comprehend the social world should not be more open to the possibility that a distinction other than sex might be more perceptually salient in another cultural context. What appears to have happened is that the universality and inevitability that the theory claims for the child's cognitive processes have been implicitly and gratuitously transferred to one of the many substantive domains upon which those processes operate: the domain of gender.

This is not to say, of course, that cognitive-developmental theory is necessarily wrong in its implicit assumption that all children have a built-in readiness to organize their perceptions of the social world on the basis of sex. Perhaps evolution has given sex a biologically based priority over many other categories. The important point, however, is that the question of whether and why sex has cognitive primacy is not included within the bounds of cognitive-developmental theory. To understand why children become *sex* typed rather than say, race or caste typed, we still need a theory that explicitly addresses the question of how and why children come to utilize sex in particular as a cognitive organizing principle.

Gender Schema Theory

Gender schema theory[8] contains features of both the cognitive-developmental and the social learning accounts of sex typing. In particular, gender schema theory proposes that sex typing derives in large measure from gender-schematic processing, from a generalized readiness on the part of the child to encode and to organize information—including information about the self—according to the culture's definitions of maleness and femaleness. Like cognitive-developmental theory, then, gender schema theory proposes that sex typing is mediated by the child's own cognitive processing. However, gender schema theory further proposes that gender-schematic processing is itself derived from the sex-differentiated practices of the social community. Thus, like social learning theory, gender schema theory assumes that sex typing is a learned phenomenon and, hence, that it is neither inevitable nor unmodifiable. In this discussion, I shall first consider in some detail what gender-schematic processing is and how it mediates sex typing; I shall then explore the conditions that produce gender-schematic processing, thereby providing an explicit account of why sex comes to have cognitive primacy over other social categories.

Gender-Schematic Processing

Gender schema theory begins with the observation that the developing child invariably learns his or her society's cultural definitions of femaleness and maleness. In most societies, these definitions comprise a diverse and sprawling network of sex-linked associations encompassing not only those features directly related to female and male persons—such as anatomy, reproductive function, division of labor, and personality attributes—but also features more remotely or metaphorically related to sex, such as the angularity or roundedness of an abstract shape and the periodicity of the moon. Indeed, no other dichotomy in human experience appears to have as many entities linked to it as does the distinction between female and male.

But there is more. Gender schema theory proposes that, in addition to learning such content-specific information about gender, the child also learns to invoke this heterogeneous network of sex-related associations in order to evaluate and assimilate new information. The child, in short, learns to encode and to organize information in terms of an evolving gender schema.

A schema is a cognitive structure, a network of associations that organizes and guides an individual's perception. A schema functions as an anticipatory structure, a readiness to search for and to assimilate incoming information in schema-relevant terms. Schematic information processing is thus highly selective and enables the individual to impose structure and meaning onto a vast array of incoming stimuli. More specifically, schematic information processing entails a readiness to sort information into categories on the basis of some particular dimension, despite the existence of other dimensions that could serve equally well in this regard. Gender-schematic processing in particular thus involves spontaneously sorting attributes and behaviors into masculine and feminine categories or "equivalence classes," regardless of their differences on a variety of dimensions unrelated to gender, for example, spontaneously placing items like "tender" and "nightingale" into a feminine category and items like "assertive" and "eagle" into a masculine category. Like schema theories generally,[9] gender schema theory thus construes perception as a constructive process in which the interaction between incoming information and an individual's preexisting schema determines what is perceived.

What gender schema theory proposes, then, is that the phenomenon of sex typing derives, in part, from gender-schematic processing, from an individual's generalized readiness to process information on the basis of the sex-linked associations that constitute the gender schema. Specifically, the theory proposes that sex typing results, in part, from the assimilation of the self-concept itself to the gender schema. As children learn the contents of their society's gender schema, they learn which attributes are to be linked with their own sex and, hence, with themselves. This does not simply entail learning the defined relationship between each sex and each dimension or attribute—that boys are to be strong and girls weak, for example—but involves the deeper lesson that the dimensions themselves are differentially applicable to the two sexes. Thus the strong-weak dimension itself is absent from the schema to be applied to girls just as the dimension of nurturance is implicitly omitted from the schema to be applied to boys. Adults in the child's world rarely notice or remark upon how strong a little girl is becoming or how nurturant a little boy is becoming, despite their readiness to note precisely these attributes in the "appropriate" sex. The child learns to apply this same schematic selectivity to the self, to choose from among the many possible dimensions of human personality only that subset defined as applicable to his or her own sex and thereby eligible for organizing the diverse contents of the self-concept. Thus do children's self-concepts become sex typed, and thus do the two sexes become, in their own eyes, not only different in degree, but different in kind.

Simultaneously, the child also learns to evaluate his or her adequacy as a person according to the gender schema, to match his or her preferences, attitudes, behaviors, and personal attributes against the prototypes stored within it. The gender schema becomes a prescriptive standard or guide,[10] and self-esteem becomes its hostage. Here, then, enters an internalized motivational factor that prompts an individual to regulate his or her behavior so that it conforms to cultural definitions of femaleness or maleness. Thus do cultural myths become self-fulfilling prophecies, and thus, according to gender schema theory, do we arrive at the phenomenon known as sex typing.

It is important to note that gender schema theory is a theory of process, not content. Because sex-typed individuals are seen as processing information and regulating their behavior according to whatever definitions of femininity and masculinity their culture happens to provide, the process of dividing the world into feminine and masculine categories—and not the contents of the categories—is central to the theory. Accordingly, sex-typed individuals are seen to differ from other individuals not primarily in the degree of femininity or masculinity they possess, but in the extent to which their self-concepts and behaviors are organized on the basis of gender rather than on the basis of some other dimension. Many non-sex-typed individuals may describe themselves as, say, nurturant or dominant without implicating the concepts of femininity or masculinity. When sex-typed individuals so describe themselves, however, it is precisely the gender connotations of the attributes or behaviors that are presumed to be salient for them. . . .

Antecedents of Gender-Schematic Processing

But how and why do sex-typed individuals develop a readiness to organize information in general, and their self-concepts in particular, in terms of gender? Because gender-schematic processing is considered a special case of schematic processing, this specific question is superseded by the more general question of how and why individuals come to organize information in terms of any social category, that is, how and why a social category becomes transformed into a cognitive schema.

Gender schema theory proposes that the transformation of a given social category into the nucleus of a highly available cognitive schema depends on the nature of the social context within which the category is embedded, not on the intrinsic nature of the category itself. Given the proper social context, then, even a category like eye color could become a cognitive schema. More specifically, gender schema theory proposes that a category will become a schema if: (1) the social context makes it the nucleus of a large associative network, that is, if the ideology and/or the practices of the culture construct an association between that category and a wide range of other attributes, behaviors, concepts, and categories; and (2) the social context assigns the category broad functional significance, that is, if a broad array of social institutions, norms, and taboos distinguishes between persons, behaviors, and attributes on the basis of this category.

This latter condition is most critical, for gender schema theory presumes that the culture's insistence on the functional importance of the social category is what transforms a passive network of associations into an active and readily available schema for interpreting reality. We all learn many associative networks of concepts throughout life, many potential cognitive schemata, but the centrality or functional importance assigned by society to particular categories and distinctions animates their associated networks and gives these schemata priority and availability over others.

From the perspective of gender schema theory, then, gender has come to have cognitive primacy over many other social categories because the culture has made it so. Nearly all societies teach the developing child two crucial things about gender: first, as noted earlier, they teach the substantive network of sex-related associations that can come to serve as a cognitive schema; second, they teach that the dichotomy between male and female has intensive and extensive relevance to virtually every domain of human experience. The typical American child cannot help observing, for example, that what parents, teachers, and peers consider to be appropriate behavior varies as a function of sex; that toys, clothing, occupations, hobbies, the domestic division of labor—even pronouns—all vary as a function of sex.

Gender schema theory thus implies that children would be far less likely to become gender schematic and hence sex typed if the society were to limit the associative network linked to sex and to temper its insistence on the functional importance of the gender dichotomy. Ironically, even though our society has become sensitive to negative sex stereotypes and has begun to expunge them from the media and from children's literature, it remains blind to its gratuitous emphasis on the gender dichotomy itself. In elementary schools, for example, boys and girls line up separately or alternately; they learn songs in which the fingers are "ladies" and the thumbs are "men"; they see boy and girl paper-doll silhouettes alternately placed on the days of the month in order to learn about the calendar. Children, it will be noted, are not lined up separately or alternately as blacks and whites; fingers are not "whites" and thumbs "blacks"; black and white dolls do not alternately mark the days of the calendar. Our society seeks to deemphasize racial distinctions but continues to exaggerate sexual distinctions.

Because of the role that sex plays in reproduction, perhaps no society could ever be as indifferent to sex in its cultural arrangements as it could be to, say, eye color, thereby giving the gender schema a sociologically based priority over many other categories. For the same reason, it may even be, as noted earlier, that sex has evolved to be a basic category of perception for our species, thereby giving the gender schema a biologically based priority as well. Be that as it may, however, gender schema theory claims that society's ubiquitous insistence on the functional importance of the gender dichotomy must necessarily render it even more cognitively available—and available in more remotely relevant contexts—than it would be otherwise.

It should be noted that gender schema theory's claims about the antecedents of gender-schematic processing have not yet been tested empirically. Hence it is not possible at this point to state whether individual differences in gender-schematic processing do, in fact, derive from differences in the emphasis placed on gender dichotomy in individuals' socialization histories, or to describe concretely the particular kinds of socialization histories that enhance or diminish gender-schematic processing. Nevertheless, I should like to set forth a number of plausible strategies that are consistent with gender schema theory for raising a gender-aschematic child in the midst of a gender-schematic society.

This discussion will, by necessity, be highly speculative. Even so, it will serve to clarify gender schema theory's view of exactly how gender-schematic processing is learned and how something else might be learned in its place. As we shall see, many of the particular strategies recommended for raising gender-aschematic children are strategies that have already been adopted by feminist parents trying to create what is typically called a nonsexist or a gender-liberated form of childrearing. In these cases, what gender schema theory provides is a new theoretical framework for thinking about the psychological impact of various childrearing practices. Sprinkled throughout the discussion will be examples taken from my own home. These are meant to be illustrations and not systematic evidence that such strategies actually decrease gender-schematic processing.

Raising Gender-Aschematic Children

Feminist parents who wish to raise gender-aschematic children in a gender-schematic world are like any parents who wish to inculcate their children with beliefs and values that deviate from those of the dominant culture. Their major option is to try to undermine the dominant ideology before it can undermine theirs. Feminist parents are thus in a difficult situation. They cannot simple ignore gender in their childrearing as they might prefer to do, because the society will then have free rein to teach their children the lessons about gender that it teaches all other children. Rather, they must manage somehow to inoculate their children against gender-schematic processing.

Two strategies are suggested here. First, parents can enable their children to learn about sex differences initially without their also learning the culture's sex-linked associative network by simultaneously retarding their children's knowledge of sex's cultural correlates and advancing their children's knowledge of sex's biological correlates. Second, parents can provide alternative or "subversive" schemata that their children can use to interpret the culture's sex-linked associative network when they do learn it. This step is essential if children are not simply to learn gender-schematic processing somewhat later than their counterparts from more traditional homes. Whether one is a child or an adult, such alternative schemata "build up one's resistance" to the lessons of the dominant culture and thereby enable one to remain gender-aschematic even while living in a gender-schematic society.

Teaching Children about Sex Differences

Cultural Correlates of Sex Children typically learn that gender is a sprawling associative network with ubiquitous functional importance through their observation of the many cultural correlates of sex existing in their society. Accordingly, the first step parents can take to retard the development of gender-schematic processing is to retard the child's knowledge of these cultural messages about gender. Less crudely put, parents can attempt to attenuate sex-linked correlations within the child's social environment, thereby altering the basic data upon which the child will construct his or her own concepts of maleness and femaleness.

In part, parents can do this by eliminating sex stereotyping from their own behavior and from the alternatives that they provide for their children, just as many feminist parents are already doing. Among other things, for example, they can take turns making dinner, bathing the children, and driving the car; they can ensure that all their children—regardless of sex—have both trucks and dolls, both pink and blue clothing, and both male and female playmates; and they can arrange for their children to see women and men in nontraditional occupations.

When children are quite young, parents can further inhibit cultural messages about gender by actually censoring books and television programs whose explicit or implicit message is that the sexes differ on nonbiological dimensions. At present, this tactic will eliminate many children's books and most television programming. Ironically, it will also temporarily eliminate a number of feminist books designed to overcome sex stereotypes; even a book which insists that it is wrong for William not to be allowed to have a doll by implication teaches a child who has not yet learned the associative network that boys and dolls do not normally go together.

To compensate for this censorship, parents will need to seek out—and to create—materials that do not teach sex stereotypes. With our own children, my husband and I got into the habit of doctoring books whenever possible so as to remove all sex-linked correlations. We did this, among other ways, by changing the sex of the main character; by drawing longer hair and the outline of breasts onto illustrations of previously male truck drivers, physicians, pilots, and the like; and by deleting or altering sections of the text that described females or males in a sex-stereotyped manner. When reading children's picture books aloud, we also chose pronouns that avoided the ubiquitous implication that all characters without dresses or pink bows must necessarily be male: "And what is this little piggy doing? Why, he or she seems to be building a bridge."

All of these practices are designed to permit very young children to dwell temporarily in a social environment where, if the parents are lucky, the cultural correlations with sex will be attenuated from say, .96, to .43. According to gender schema theory, this attenuation should retard the formation of the sex-linked associative network that will itself form the basis of the gender schema. By themselves, however, these practices teach children only what sex is not. But children must also be taught what sex is.

Biological Correlates of Sex What remains when all of the cultural correlates of sex are attenuated or eliminated, of course, are two of the undisputed biological correlates of sex: anatomy and reproduction. Accordingly, parents can make these the definitional attributes of femaleness and maleness. By teaching their children that the genitalia constitute the definitive attributes of females and males, parents help them to apprehend the merely probabilistic nature of sex's cultural correlates and thereby restrict sex's associative sprawl. By teaching their children that whether one is female or male makes a difference only in the context of reproduction, parents limit sex's functional significance and thereby retard gender-schematic processing. Because children taught these lessons have been provided with an explicit and clear-cut rule about what sex is and when sex matters, they should be predisposed to construct their own concepts of femaleness and maleness based on biology, rather than on the cultural correlates to which they have been exposed. And to the extent that young children tend to interpret rules and categories rigidly rather than flexibly, this tendency will serve to enhance their belief that sex is to be narrowly defined in terms of anatomy and reproduction rather than to enhance a traditional belief that every arbitrary gender rule must be strictly obeyed and enforced. Thus there may be an irony, but there is no inconsistency in the fact that an emphasis on the biological differences between the sexes should here be advocated as the basis for feminist child rearing.

The liberation that comes from having an unambiguous genital definition of sex and the imprisonment that comes from not having such a definition are nicely illustrated by the story of what happened to our son Jeremy, then age four, the day he decided to wear barrettes to nursery school. Several times that day, another little boy told Jeremy that he, Jeremy, must be a girl because "only girls wear barrettes." After trying to explain to this child that "wearing barrettes doesn't matter" and that "being a boy means having a penis and testicles," Jeremy finally pulled down his pants as a way of making his point more convincingly. The other child was not impressed. He simply said, "Everybody has a penis; only girls wear barrettes."

In the American context, children do not typically learn to define sex in terms of anatomy and reproduction until quite late, and, as a result, they—like the child in the example above—mistakenly treat many of the cultural correlates of sex as definitional. This confusion is facilitated, of course, by the fact that the genitalia themselves are not usually visible and hence cannot be relied on as a way of identifying someone's sex.

Accordingly, when our children asked whether someone was male or female, we frequently denied certain knowledge of the person's sex, emphasizing that without being able to see whether there was a penis or a vagina under the person's clothes, we had no definitive information. Moreover, when our children themselves began to utilize nonbiological markers as a way of identifying sex, we gently teased them about that strategy to remind them that the genitalia—and only the genitalia—constitute the definition of sex: "What do you mean that you can tell Chris is a girl because Chris has long hair? Does Chris's hair have a vagina?"

We found Stephanie Waxman's picture book *What Is a Girl? What Is a Boy?* to be a superb teaching aid in this context.[11] Each page displays a vivid and attractive photograph of a boy or a girl engaged in some behavior stereotyped as more typical of or more appropriate for the other sex. The accompanying text says such things as, "Some people say a girl is someone with jewelry, but Barry is wearing a necklace and he's a boy." The book ends with nude photographs of both children and adults, and it explicitly defines sex in terms of anatomy.

These particular lessons about what sex is, what sex is not, and when sex matters are designed to make young children far more naive than their peers about the cultural aspects of gender far more sophisticated than their peers about the biological aspects of sex. Eventually, of course, their naivete, will begin to fade, and they too will begin to learn the culture's sprawling network of sex-linked associations. At that point, parents must take steps to prevent that associative network from itself becoming a cognitive schema.

Providing Alternative Schemata

Let us presume that the feminist parent has successfully produced a child who defines sex in terms of anatomy and reproduction. How is such a child to understand the many sex-linked correlations that will inevitably begin to intrude upon his or her awareness? What alternative schemata can substitute for the gender schema in helping the child to organize and to assimilate gender-related information?

Individual Differences Schema The first alternative schema is simply a child's version of the time-honored liberal truism used to counter stereotypic thinking in general, namely, that there is remarkable variability of individuals within groups as compared with the small mean differences between groups. To the child who says that girls do not like to play baseball, the feminist parent can thus point out that although it is true that some girls do not like to play baseball, it is also true that some girls do (e.g., your Aunt Beverly and Alissa who lives across the street) and that some boys do not (e.g., your dad and Alissa's brother Jimmy). It is, of course, useful for parents to supply themselves with a long list of counterexamples well in advance of such occasions.

This individual differences schema is designed to prevent children from interpreting individual differences as sex differences, from assimilating perceived differences among people to a gender schema. Simultaneously, it should also encourage children to treat as a given that the sexes are basically similar to one another and, hence, to view all glib assertions about sex differences as inherently suspect. And it is with this skepticism that feminist consciousness begins.

Cultural Relativism Schema As the child's knowledge and awareness grow, he or she will gradually begin to realize that his or her family's beliefs and attitudes about gender are at variance with those of the dominant culture. Accordingly, the child needs some rationale for not simply accepting the majority view as the more valid. One possible rationale is cultural relativism, the notion that "different people believe different things" and that the coexistence of even contradictory beliefs is the rule in society rather than the exception.

Children can (and should) be introduced to the schema of cultural relativism long before it is pertinent to the domain of gender. For example, our children needed the rationale that "different people believe different things" in order to understand why they, but not the children next door, had to wear seat belts; why our family, but not the family next door, was casual about nudity in the home. The general principle that contradictory beliefs frequently coexist seems now to have become a readily available schema for our children, a schema that permits them to accept with relative equanimity that they have different beliefs from many of their peers with respect to gender.

Finally, the cultural relativism schema can solve one of the primary dilemmas of the liberal feminist parent: how to give one's children access to the riches of classical literature—as well as to the lesser riches of the mass media—without abandoning them to the forces that promote gender-schematic processing. Happily, the censorship of sex-stereotyped materials that is necessary to retard the initial growth of the sex-linked associative network when children are young can end once children have learned the critical lesson that cultural messages reflect the beliefs and attitudes of the person or persons who created those messages.

Accordingly, before we read our daughter her first volume of fairy tales, we discussed with her the cultural beliefs and attitudes about men and women that the tales would reflect, and while reading the tales, we frequently made such comments as, "Isn't it interesting that the person who wrote this story seems to think girls always need to be rescued?" If such discussions are not too heavy-handed, they can provide a background of understanding against which the child can thoroughly enjoy the stories themselves, while still learning to discount the sex stereotypes within them as irrelevant both to their own beliefs and to truth. The cultural relativism schema thus brings children an awareness that fairy tales are fairy tales in more than one sense.

Sexism Schema Cultural relativism is fine in its place, but feminist parents will not and should not be satisfied to pretend that they think all ideas—particularly those about gender—are equally valid. At some point, they will feel compelled to declare that the view of women and men conveyed by fairy tales, by the mass media—and by the next-door neighbors—is not only different, but wrong. It is time to teach one's children about sexism.

Moreover, it is only by giving children a sexism schema, a coherent and organized understanding of the historical roots and the contemporaneous consequences of sex discrimination, that they will truly be able to comprehend why the sexes appear to be so different in our society: why, for example, there has never been a female president of the United States; why fathers do not stay home with their children; and why so many people believe these sex differences to be the natural consequence of biology. The child who has developed a readiness to encode and to organize information in terms of an evolving sexism schema is a child who is prepared to oppose actively the gender-related constraints that those with a gender schema will inevitably seek to impose.

The development of a sexism schema is nicely illustrated by our daughter Emily's response to Norma Klein's book *Girls Can Be Anything.*[12] One of the characters is Adam Sobel, who insists that "girls are always nurses and boys are always doctors" and that "girls can't be pilots, . . . they have to be stewardesses." After reading this book, our daughter, then age four, spontaneously began to label with contempt anyone who voiced stereotyped beliefs about gender an "Adam Sobel." Adam Sobel thus became for her the nucleus of an evolving sexism schema, a schema that enables her now to perceive—and also to become morally outraged by and to oppose—whatever sex discrimination she meets in daily life.

As feminist parents, we wish it could have been possible to raise our children with neither a gender schema nor a sexism schema. At this historical moment, however, that is not an option. Rather we must choose either to have our children become gender schematic and hence sex typed, or to have our children become sexism schematic and hence feminists. We have chosen the latter.

A Comment on Psychological Androgyny

The central figure in gender schema theory is the sex-typed individual, a shift in focus from my earlier work in which the non-sex-typed individual—the androgynous individual in particular—commanded center stage.[13] In the early 1970s, androgyny seemed to me and to many others a liberated and more humane alternative to the traditional, sex-biased standards of mental health. And it is true that this concept can be applied equally to both women and men, and that it encourages individuals to embrace both the feminine and the masculine within themselves. But advocating the concept of androgyny can also be seen as replacing a prescription to be masculine *or* feminine with the doubly incarcerating prescription to be masculine *and* feminine. The individual now has not one but two potential sources of inadequacy with which to contend. Even more important, however, the concept of androgyny is problematic from the perspective of gender schema theory because it is based on the presupposition that there is a feminine and a masculine within us all, that is, that "femininity" and "masculinity" have an independent and palpable reality and are not cognitive constructs derived from gender-schematic processing. Focusing on androgyny thus fails to prompt serious examination of the extent to which gender organizes both our perceptions and our social world.

In contrast, the concept of gender-schematic processing directs our attention to the promiscuous availability of the gender schema in contexts where other schemata ought to have priority. Thus, if gender schema theory has a political message, it is not that the individual should be androgynous. Rather, it is that the network of associations constituting the gender schema ought to become more limited in scope and that society ought to temper its insistence on the ubiquitous functional importance of the gender dichotomy. In short, human behaviors and personality attributes should no longer be linked with gender, and society should stop projecting gender into situations irrelevant to genitalia.

Notes

1. Walter Mischel, "Sex-Typing and Socialization," in *Carmichael's Manual of Child Psychology*, ed. Paul H. Mussen, 2 vols. (New York: John Wiley & Sons, 1970), 2:3–72.
2. William Damon, *The Social World of the Child* (San Francisco: Jossey-Bass, 1977).
3. Courtney B. Cazden, "The Acquisition of Noun and Verb Inflections," *Child Development* 39, no. 2 (June 1968): 433–48; Herbert H. Clark and Eve V. Clark, *Psychology and Language: An Introduction to Psycholinguistics* (New York: Harcourt Brace Jovanovich, 1977).
4. Michael Lewis and Jeanne Brooks-Gunn, *Social Cognition and the Acquisition of Self* (New York: Plenum Publishing Corp., 1979), p. 270.
5. Lawrence Kohlberg, "A Cognitive–Developmental Analysis of Children's Sex–Role Concepts and Attitudes," in *The Development of Sex Differences*, ed. Eleanor E. Maccoby (Stanford, Calif.: Stanford University Press, 1966), p. 89.
6. Kohlberg; Lew and Brooks-Gunn; Dorothy Z. Ullian, "The Child's Construction of Gender: Anatomy as Destiny," in *Cognitive and Affective Growth: Developmental Interaction*, ed. Edna K. Shapiro and Evelyn Weber (Hillsdale, N.J.: Lawrence Erlbaum Associates, 1981), pp. 171–85.
7. For a discussion of the wet-dry distinction, see Anna S. Meigs, "Male

Pregnancy and the Reduction of Sexual Opposition in a New Guinea Highlands Society," *Ethnology* 15, no. 4 (1976): 393–407; for a discussion of the open-closed distinction, see Sally Falk Moore, "The Secret of the Men: A Fiction of Chagga Initiation and Its Relation to the Logic of Chagga Symbolism," *Africa* 46, no. 4 (1976): 357–70.

8. Sandra L. Bem, "Gender Schema Theory: A Cognitive Account of Sex Typing," *Psychological Review* 88, no. 4 (July 1981): 354–64; and "Gender Schema Theory and Self-Schema Theory Compared: A Comment on Markus, Crane, Bernstein, and Siladi's 'Self-Schemas and Gender,'" *Journal of Personality and Social Psychology* 43, no. 6 (December 1982): 1192–94.

9. Ulric Neisser, *Cognition and Reality* (San Francisco: W. H. Freeman & Co., 1976); Shelley E. Taylor and Jennifer Crocker, "Schematic Bases of Social Information Processing," in *Social Cognition, the Ontario Symposium*, ed. E. Tory Higgins, C. Peter Herman, and Mark P. Zanna (Hillsdale, N.J.: Lawrence Erlbaum Associates, 1981), 1:89–135.

10. Jerome Kagan, "Acquisition and Significance of Sex Typing and Sex Role Identity," in *Review of Child Development Research*, ed. Martin L. Hoffman and Lois W. Hoffman (New York: Russell Sage Foundation, 1964), 1:137–67.

11. Stephanie Waxman, *What Is a Girl? What Is a Boy?* (Culver City, Calif.: Peace Press, 1976).

12. Norma Klein, *Girls Can Be Anything* (New York: E. P. Dutton, 1973).

13. Sandra L. Bem, "Sex-Role Adaptability: One Consequence of Psychological Androgyny," *Journal of Personality and Social Psychology* 31, no. 4 (April 1975): 634–43; Sandra L. Bem, Wendy Martyna, and Carol Watson, "Sex-Typing and Androgyny: Further Explorations of the Expressive Domain," *Journal of Personality and Social Psychology* 34, no. 5 (November 1976): 1016–23; Sandra L. Bem, "Beyond Androgyny: Some Presumptuous Prescriptions for a Liberated Sexual Identity," in *The Future of Women, Issues in Psychology*, ed. Julia Sherman and Florence Denmark (New York: Psychological Dimensions, Inc., 1978), pp. 1–23; Sandra L. Bem and Ellen Lenney, "Sex-Typing and the Avoidance of Cross-Sex Behavior," *Journal of Personality and Social Psychology* 33, no. 1 (January 1976): 48–54.

38 Gender as Culture: Difference and Dominance in Nonverbal Behavior

NANCY M. HENLEY

MARIANNE LAFRANCE

Oscar Wilde is reported to have said about gender differences in nonverbal communication that "a man's face is his autobiography; a woman's face is her work of fiction." The implication is twofold: not only is there the assertion of sex differences (an assertion which appears obvious and unassailable), but there is also a more subtle suggestion that not all nonverbal behaviors are equivalently valued. The present paper is aimed at reviewing some of the rather substantial literature on gender aspects of nonverbal behavior. The review will show the existence and persistence of sex differences across the whole range of nonverbal behaviors. But it will also show the existence and persistence of an implicit orientation that sees differences as reflecting well on one group and poorly on another. And it will raise the question of the source of the differences and of the differential evaluation, a question of interest in any case of group differences.

The search for differences between groups is the stock in trade of social science. The discovery of large differences in apparently small behaviors is the inspiration behind research in nonverbal communication. From the outset, investigators have been actively engaged in the search for group differences. In what is now a household anecdote among researchers in the field, Edward Hall (1959) described the "UN waltz," that particular pattern of spatial approach and withdrawal, initial goodwill but resulting bad feeling, that characterizes interactions among people socialized to different proxemic preferences. The anecdote is both provocative and appealing because it implies that subtle yet observable cultural differences in nonverbal behavior could be the source of misunderstanding and miscommunication.

Twenty-plus years of active research on group differences in nonverbal behavior have turned up a host of small yet influential bits of behavior that differ between cultures. Every new finding adds to the belief that if all such differences could be catalogued and made available, then much of what to date has remained elusive and troubling about intercultural interactions might now be understood and rectified. This premise has also been adopted by those who are concerned with interactions within any one culture between people who differ with respect to race, ethnicity, or generation. And it has also been adopted by those interested in what has been termed the "longest war," the relationship between the sexes.

But how are we to view these found group differences? Are nonverbal variations between and, especially, within culture objectively neutral and benign? Are group differences typically greeted with cries of "Vive la différence"? or are they instead reflective of social patterns that are more than skin deep? The present paper intends to tackle the rather thorny issue of the meaning and function of group differences, with particular attention to gender (and culture). We propose the thesis that in many cases, group differences reflect not merely interesting variation but social function. More specifically, we argue that nonverbal behaviors convey much about the status and power distinctions within a culture and further, that nonverbal behaviors are frequently used in the service of maintaining such distinctions. Although the particular focus of this paper is with gender, it is assumed that some of the issues raised also apply to the study of group differences more generally, whether the groups be identified as cultural, ethnic, racial, or generational.

We begin then by reviewing a diverse array of studies on the gender aspects of nonverbal behavior as we work toward answering three broad and related questions: (1) What are some of the nonverbal behaviors that show differences between the sexes? (2) To what are the differences attributed? and (3) Is the attribution appropriate?

We turn first to studies that ask whether women are more nonverbally expressive than are men, move to work that investigates whether women are more sensitive to nonverbal cues coming from others than are men, and close the research review with investigations of the impact of gender on spatial and tactile behaviors. Several key issues will emerge as we proceed through the empirical studies. Our plan is to return to these recurrent themes later and at that time to consider how broader and more conceptual analyses might resolve dilemmas raised by the observed phenomena.

Empirical Studies of Gender Differences

It is virtually a cliche, of American and Canadian culture, and of their parent European cultures, that women are naturally more emotional than men, and that that fact is clearly evident in their nonverbal behavior. It appears that women have more animated faces and more agitated voices than do men. Research has tended to bear this notion out.

Facial Expression

A number of research strategies have been employed to investigate gender differences in facial expressivity. In one procedure, observers of faces are asked to identify the emotion being felt. The research method calls for women and men "senders" to look at photographic slides varying in emotional content, while their own expressions are recorded. Then another group of male and female "receivers" are shown the faces viewing the slides but without access to the slides themselves. The receivers' task is to indicate what type of slides they think are being viewed (Buck, Miller & Caul, 1974). Results indicate the existence of sex differences in expressivity; receivers are more accurate in identifying the slides being looked at by women than those being looked at by men.

Presumably, judges are more accurate because female senders show greater facial activity and/or activity that is easier to read correctly. In an extension of the previous work, Buck and his colleagues (Buck, Baron & Barrette, 1982) used a temporal segmentation procedure and demonstrated that females showed a greater amount of facial movement than males and further that receivers show greater consensus regarding the temporal location of meaningful activity in female than in male faces.

This greater expressivity by females has shown itself repeatedly. A recent review of twenty-two studies, in which groups of judges (ranging in number from two to over two hundred) viewed or listened to all manner of nonverbal stimuli produced by male and female senders, showed females to be more expressive than males in 71% of the studies surveyed (Hall, 1979).

The consistency in the findings is substantial; the consistency in the explanations given, less so. The explanation with the greatest currency has it that women are more expressive than men *because* they are more emotional. But recent research calls this association into question. For example, one study found the expected sex differences in amount of *facial activity* in response to emotionally-loaded questions, but did not find sex differences in *emotionality* (i.e., existence of the appropriate affective state) in response to these questions (Cherulnik, 1979). The author's interpretation suggested that women and men operate under different display rules (Ekman, Friesen & Ellsworth, 1972), that is, different sets of norms that dictate which private feelings are to be exposed to whom and when. For females, the norm is to accentuate; for males the norm is to inhibit.

A similar finding has been reported by Frodie and Lamb (1978), who compared male and female physiological and behavioral reactions to infants. The physiological recordings showed no sex differences, again suggesting no significant differences in felt emotion. However, when subjects were permitted to interact with the infants, females were more expressive than males. These results again suggest that sex differences in overt expressiveness may be more attributable to societal than biological imperatives.

Indeed, there are a number of other sources of variation in expressivity *within* each sex that suggest something other than biology is at work. One of these factors is the effect of sex role orientation. There appear to be notable individual differences in the degree to which women and men stay within prescribed sex role boundaries for appropriate nonverbal behavior. For example, the work by Bem (1974) and by Spence and Helmreich (1977) has shown that some people describe themselves as possessing characteristics usually associated with their own sex and not possessing characteristics associated with the other sex, while others describe themselves as having traits of both genders. The former have been termed "Sex-typed" and the latter "Androgynous" individuals.

Sex typing affects one's degree of expressivity. In a direct test of this notion, Zuckerman and his colleagues (Zuckerman et al., 1982) showed that gender orientation was more consistently related to expressivity than was gender itself. The most accurate senders of intentional facial and auditory cues were those who had scored the highest on Femininity and the lowest on Masculinity. LaFrance and Carmen (1980) also showed that smiling was related to sex role orientation. Feminine females smiled significantly more than Androgynous females, and especially so in a situation that called for interpersonal sensitivity. Apparently high facial expressivity is part of being a Feminine female. (Although see Lott, 1981, for limitations to the usefulness of androgyny as a concept and measure.)

There are also findings suggesting that differences in expressivity among men relate to gender orientation. Men whose sex role attitudes were found to be more liberal were rated as being nonverbally warmer when interacting with both men and women than were men who described themselves as being more traditional in this respect (Weitz, 1976). Apparently low nonverbal expressivity is part of being a Masculine sex-typed male.

The locus of causality for sex differences in expressivity is critical. Sex differences are frequently celebrated but then as frequently used to justify inequality. Since in North American culture women are more expressive than men and since it has been assumed that this difference in expressivity reflects a basic difference in emotionality, then it is a short step to seeing women as ill-equipped for positions that apparently require low emotionality (Kanter, 1975), such as those in management. In short, greater expressivity in women is taken as evidence that women possess biological handicaps inimical to the performance of well-paying jobs (not inimical, of course, to the performance of low-paying ones). The same argument has been used with respect to ethnic and racial groups which are more expressive than the northern European ones dominant in this culture.

Nonverbal Sensitivity

When the question turns to gender differences in receptivity to another's expressive behavior, most studies find women to be more accurate decoders of nonverbal cues than men. Using a test called the Profile of Nonverbal Sensitivity (PONS), Rosenthal and his colleagues have consistently found that women are better than men at identifying the emotional situations enacted in brief visual and vocal film segments (Rosenthal, Hall, DiMatteo & Archer, 1977). The PONS presents 220 two-second posed segments showing a young woman's face or body, or face plus body and/or voice sample treated to obliterate content while retaining tone. Viewers must choose which one of two given scenarios is being enacted.

These results confirm a tradition of research that goes back over half a century. Hall (1978) has reviewed 75 studies on gender differences in assessing another's feelings via access to facial or vocal display and found that in 84% of the studies females were found to be better decoders than males. Although the effect was clearly consistent, it was not substantial in magnitude, indicating that other processes are at work affecting individual differences in nonverbal sensitivity.

The explanation for these gender differences in sensitivity is currently under debate. The prevailing interpretation has been that women are either "naturally" more sensitive or that they have learned a role requiring them to be so. But this learning explanation raises a further question: why would women acquire finer skill than men in reading other people's nonverbal messages?

One explanation, put forward by Henley (1977) and others and explored by Hall (1979), argues that nonverbal sensitivity is required by those who are oppressed. The reason: their survival may depend on their accurately reading and predicting the behavior of the more dominant members of the society. Hall, examining this explanation, assessed "oppression" in women by measuring sex role attitudes, defining the more oppressed as those adopting more traditional sex role attitudes. She then correlated scores on this measure with scores on the PONS and obtained a negative value, apparently indicating that the *less* traditional women were the *more* sensitive. According to her prediction from the oppression hypothesis, the *more* traditional women should have been more sensitive. However, a closer look at the method of this experiment raises questions about the conclusion. The gender of the stimulus person in the PONS test is female. What the data might be better seen to reflect is that the less "oppressed" (i.e., less traditional) women are more accurate in reading another *woman's* expressive cues. This is not only not contrary to the oppression hypothesis but is entirely consistent with it: by this hypothesis more traditional women should be more sensitive to the dominant group, i.e. men. In addition, Hall reports other correlations which seem to show the relationship between traditionally of sex roles for females and sensitivity is the reverse when the stimulus person is male. In other words, the more traditional the woman, the better able she is at reading a *male's* nonverbal signs. The "oppression" explanation thus seems viable and deserves more exploration.

Greater sensitivity in women is not the unmitigated good that one might imagine it to be, or so an article by Rosenthal and DePaulo (1979) attests. These authors report that the magnitude of women's sensitivity advantage over men is greatest for the "obvious" nonverbal cues such as facial expression, but that it all but disappears for the more "covert" and generally more veridical signs, such as extremely brief signals or discrepant cues. Rosenthal and DePaulo argue that women lose their advantage in sensitivity when accurate decoding of subtle cues may be hazardous to the health of a relationship. In other words, the argument is that women have a greater investment in maintaining smooth relationships than they do in knowing what is really going on with the other person in them.

Consequently, women "accommodate" by figuratively (and perhaps literally) looking the other way when the messages are unintentionally sent. The hypothesis is certainly provocative, but again other interpretations may be more plausible. Rosenthal and DePaulo may be looking at the data through the wrong end of a telescope when instead of focusing on explaining females' greater sensitivity they turn their attention to explaining no differences on discrepant cues. The number of possible explanations for "no differences" is astronomical—among them is one that says that no one is particularly accurate when the cues are exceedingly brief or mixed.

Personal Space

The term "personal space" as coined by Sommer (1959) refers to the invisibly-bounded area by which we separate ourselves from others—areas of different size, depending on circumstances. The image is very concrete. Most people can easily visualize themselves and others housed in what are essentially invisible bubbles.

Regarding gender differences in personal space, research tends to show that the bubbles surrounding women are smaller than those surrounding men (Evans & Howard, 1973). Unobtrusive observations of people in natural settings find that male-female pairs stand the closest, followed by female pairs, and last by male pairs who sustain the greatest distances (Baxter, 1970; Nesbitt & Steven, 1974). However, in larger group settings there is evidence that people prefer the closest distances with people of the same sex (Campbell, Kruskal & Wallace, 1966).

Interpretations of these results tend to converge on the assumption that people of both sexes approach women at more proximate distances than they do men because women are more affiliative and friendly. The greater affiliation attributed to women is certainly compatible with the explanation offered by Freedman and his associates (Freedman, Levy, Buchanan & Price, 1972) to explain sex differences in response to crowded conditions. In a number of studies, they found that females were more cooperative and less aggressive than males under high density (same-sex) situations. These investigators argued that high density intensifies typical response patterns and that apparently women expect encounters with other women to be sociable and friendly, while men expect more competitive and possibly aggressive interactions with each other.

There are other data that suggest that caution must be exercised in interpreting closer distances to women as reflecting a natural or preferred state, especially when the other person is male. For example, females tend to adopt closer distances with each other than they do vis-à-vis males when they can choose their seating arrangements (Giessen & McClaren, 1979; Patterson & Schaeffer, 1977); and they allow women to approach closer than men when they are asked to indicate at what point the approach of another becomes uncomfortably close (Dosey & Meisels, 1969). Thus when women are in control of their own spacing, males are not allowed as close as other females.

Again, the *explanation* for sex differences is not, or should not be, built into the *observation* of sex differences. Greater sociability or affiliation may be partly implicated in the smaller space zones taken up around women; also likely is the assumption that spaces surrounding females are seen to be more public than private in character. In other words, there is less reservation about occupying a woman's territory than a man's territory. Spatial invasion studies support this view. For example, females react very differently to the close approach of a stranger in a library context than do males. In one study, females responded by leaving the scene altogether, whereas males were more likely to "hold the fort" (Polit & LaFrance, 1977).

Females "give up" their territory in other ways as well. Silveira (1972) found that in observations of who gets out of the other's way when passing on the sidewalk, the woman moved out of the man's way more frequently than the obverse. Similarly, another observational study asked who would more often be "in front of" in the simple matter of pairs walking together. The question stemmed from the social fact that the spatial positions of above and in front of imply superiority or status (Brown, 1965). Presumably if sex were unrelated to societal position then men and women would each be walking in front approximately half the time. Results showed this not to be so. Men were observed to be out in front significantly more often than women (Grady, Miransky & Mulvey, 1976). There seems to be a quite literal dimension to the saying that "Behind every successful man there is a woman."

It might also be argued that the different postures evidenced by men and women are part of this same phenomenon. For example, Mehrabian (1972) has shown that in general women take up less space than men as the direct result of the way they position themselves. It is not simply that women are generally smaller physically than are men, but women emphasize this difference further by sitting with arms close to their sides and legs crossed at very small angles. In contrast, men sprawl more, draping arms over backs of chairs, and either stretching legs out in front or crossing them at large angles. (See Wex, 1979, for excellent demonstrations of this phenomenon in public settings in Germany.) Expansive postures take up more space and thereby create larger personal space zones.

In like fashion, it has been found that male and female college students carry their books in consistently different ways. Women were found to wrap one or both arms around books and to rest the short edges of the books in front of their bodies. In contrast, men were more likely to support their books by one arm at the side of the body, effecting a larger territory (Jenni & Jenni, 1976).

Touch

Touch constitutes the limiting condition of personal space and has traditionally been viewed as a positive force, a means of communication that perhaps is made more special in Anglo cultures by virtue of its relative infrequency. People report liking to be touched and touch seems more intimately associated with comfort and care than it does with aggression and assault. People touch frequently at airports, certainly occasions for affirming relationships (Heslin & Boss, 1980), and here too, women touch each other more often and more intimately than do men.

In general, findings indicate that women are touched more than are men (Henley, 1977). The pattern appears to replicate the studies on personal space showing greater access to women than to men, and this pattern too suggests a number of interpretations. One interpretation states that the greater nurturance attributed to women is the cause. Another interpretation posits something quite different. Henley (1973, 1977) begins with the observation that men touch women much more than women touch men and that this pattern becomes even more clear cut when women lack status advantages such as age or social class. Henley also observes that regardless of sex, those with status advantage tend to touch those of lower status. She suggests that nonreciprocal touch is a status indicator as well as one of affection.

The critical variable is the *nonreciprocity* of touch between status unequals. Mutual touch is quite another thing, as is mutual eye contact. The point to be made here is that nonverbal behaviors such as these tend to follow the structure pointed out by Roger Brown (1965) and others regarding terms of address: the form used mutually between intimates (who are equals) is the one used by the superior person in a relationship of nonequals; and the form mutually used between nonintimates (equals) is the form prescribed for the subordinate in a status-discrepant relationship. In other words, mutual eye contact or mutual touch is informative about the level of intimacy between people; nonreciprocal gaze or touch says more about the power differences between the people.

It was in studies of touch that the relationship between gender and power was made explicit. Prior to these studies, gender and power were seldom examined together and differences between women's and men's nonverbal behaviors were almost exclusively reported as sex or sex "role" differences, but certainly not as status or power differences. A recent study affirms the connection in another way. Beginning with the assumption that status is revealed nonverbally, Schwartz and his colleagues (Schwartz, Tesser & Powell, 1982) created visual stimuli in which pairs of people were arranged in a variety of vis-à-vis positions. For example, one person was presented as being literally more elevated than another, or more in front, or standing while the other sits. Also varied were gender and right/left positioning. Subjects were asked to indicate who was more dominant. Results were significant for all five factors. The more dominant person was the one who was more elevated, standing rather than sitting, front rather than back, right rather than left, and male rather than female.

Another aspect of dominance is revealed, in an even more subtle way, in a recent study with the very proper main title of "Handedness and lateral positioning in heterosexual couples" but with the provocative subtitle of "Are men still strong-arming women?" This study examined the way in which mixed-sex couples arrange themselves while walking together. In same-handed couples, that is, when both are either right- or left-handed, significantly more females were on the males' preferred (dominant) side even when the situation might be seen to call for the male to take the outside, presumably protective position (Borden & Homleid, 1978).

A sex difference connected to dominance is also shown in a study of touching of preschool children by male and female teachers. Here the differences observed were not in the amount of touch but in the type of touch directed towards male and female children by teachers. Four types of touch were coded: friendly, helpful, attentional, and incidental. When male teachers touched girls, the touch most frequently used was of the "helpful" variety; when teachers touched boys, the "friendly" category was the most frequently coded (Perdue & Connor, 1978). Female teachers showed no differences in type of touch conveyed to boys or girls. The authors speculated that girls early on connect touch from an adult male with a dependent rather than a mutual relationship.

Moreover, there is indication that women make more perceptual distinctions about touch than do men. Women distinguish between touch signalling sexual desire and touch indicating friendliness, whereas men do not (Nguyen, Heslin & Nguyen, 1975). Also, women have been found to distinguish touch on various body parts whereas men did not. It might be argued, in line with the oppression hypothesis mentioned earlier, that with respect to sensitivity differences, sensitivity includes the ability—one might say the necessity—to make fine-grained distinctions in meaning. A wrong rendering is more costly for those in a less powerful position.

Difference and Dominance

To this point we have concentrated primarily on empirical studies of gender aspects of nonverbal behavior and we have surveyed a broad range of behaviors, including expressivity, sensitivity, personal space, and touch. For the most part, there is agreement that there are significant and manifold differences between the sexes. But as we have noted throughout, there is considerably less agreement concerning the basis or cause of these differences. We look briefly at what the predominant views have been and move from there to posing a number of hypotheses concerning the role of nonverbal behavior in status relationships. More generally it is hoped that a greater understanding of the relationship between difference and dominance will clarify not only studies of gender aspects of nonverbal behavior, but group differences more generally.

The assumed basis for sex differences in nonverbal behavior has shown an historical shift. Early on in the research in the gender aspects of nonverbal behavior, sex differences were greeted with a satisfied sigh of recognition. The findings were expected and incorporated into an existing framework that saw differences as reflecting the "natural order" of things that called for males to be assertive and females to be affiliative. The findings were unmistakable and the cause cited—mostly centering around whether the differences were due more to nature or nurture.

But this rather neat way of partitioning the world was given a rather rude awakening with the emergence of the position (Henley, 1973; Frieze & Ramsey, 1976) that argued that the differences were due not to sex but to status. There was no argument that differences existed, i.e., that males and females did different things with their heads and hands; but there was issue whether the differences reflected a gender or power base. In observations of touching behavior, Henley (1973, 1977) indicated that females were touched more than males not because they were more affiliative but because they were regarded as less worthy. Protective pats now seemed more like power plays. Nonverbal gestures could be used to put people (women) in their place.

In a similar way there was an historical shift in the past in looking at differences between cultures. Once cultural differences, including ones in national wealth and power, were explained by stereotypes founded in cultural supremacy; later and more enlightened explanations attempted to understand cultures within their own contexts and to understand behaviors as having functions within those cultures. This perspective gave a rude awakening to cultural chauvinists and required the re-evaluation of many beliefs and policies. While cultural chauvinism persists even in our scholarly and scientific community (and functional explanations can be bent to its aims), still the drive to understand cultural contexts helps us to understand behavior more thoroughly. The parallel to the effects of reinterpreting sex differences is clear. Male chauvinism too persists, but hampers our understanding of all human behavior.

Cueing Power

What has nonverbal communication to do with power? Nonverbal behavior is the major medium of communication in everyday life and power and status are major themes to be communicated. Since power is best exercised with the least overt display, nonverbal communication becomes a prime avenue for its expression. Moreover, nonverbal behaviors are significantly implicated in all manner of interpersonal regulation, and status is one of the first things to be regulated. These very small behaviors can be the stuff of very large effects.

We next propose a number of hypotheses concerning how status is manifest in nonverbal behavior. Although most of the examples used are drawn from the sex differences literature, the overall aim is to derive general principles that have potential applicability to any group difference context.

Readability With regard to the relationship between readability and status, we hypothesize that the higher status person will be less readable (in the sense of less expressive) than the lower status person. Stated somewhat differently, the conjecture is that the lower power person in a relationship is more likely to be the more expressive one and the one regarded as being more emotional, and the one of higher power will be seen as less emotional and less expressive.

Why would this be so? The hypothesis is based on the dual assumption that higher status persons need to create "distance" between themselves and their underlings and at the same time require that the underlings be "up front" with them. Nonexpressivity can mystify by generating awe. This is accomplished by limiting the amount of self-disclosure. Goffman (1979) has suggested that in advertisements featuring families, the father is often seen standing at a slight distance from the family circle. Is this protectiveness, as Goffman labels it, or status (Henley, 1980)? Looked at from the other side of the status equation, high expressivity may be expected from those occupying the lower rungs of the social ladder as evidence that they are highly impressionable, almost childlike (in our culture).

Sensitivity Looking now at the perceiver, it is hypothesized that the less dominant group will be more sensitive to cues coming from others, and particularly to those cues coming from the more dominant group, than will be the case for the dominants. Furthermore, the less dominant group is expected to be more attentive and to be better at listening than the more dominant group. Research on sex differences in sensitivity to nonverbal cues tends to bear this point out (Rosenthal et al., 1977), as does other research which shows that females tend to look more at their interactional partner than do males (Frances, 1979) and that they find conversation more difficult when they cannot see the other person (Argyle, Lalljee & Cook, 1968).

Accommodatingness There is another aspect to the attentiveness required of the less dominant group, and that has to do with the call that it be more accommodating to the more dominant group. It is important not only to know what the other is saying and feeling but also to be able to alter one's own behavior as a result. The hypothesis regarding accommodatingness is that the less dominant group is expected to adjust its verbal and nonverbal behavior to the more dominant group and not the other way around. Such accommodatingness has been shown in a study by Weitz (1976). In that study, the first minute of videotaped encounters between unacquainted men and women was coded by raters who saw only one of the interactants and therefore did not know the sex of the other person in the conversation. In male-female conversations, the nonverbal behavior of females was inversely related to the male partner's dominant or affiliative behavior. Women were found to be nonverbally more submissive with more dominant men and more dominant with submissive men. Weitz posited a monitoring process by which women adjust their nonverbal responses so as to produce a comfortable situation for their male partners. No such adjustments were noted for female-female encounters, nor were there such adaptive moves by men in either same-sex or opposite-sex interactions. Considering that all this occurs in the first 60 seconds of conversation, it suggests a vigilant sensitivity and immediate adaptation. Perhaps this is the reason Oscar Wilde called woman's face (her expressivity) her work of fiction.

Another aspect of this accommodatingness is the hypothesized greater variability overall of the less dominant group's nonverbal behavior. For example, women do not behave the same way regardless of the one with whom they are interacting. One observational study of conversational distances found that pairs of women stood closer than pairs of men (Heshka & Nelson, 1972). This difference, however, was largely accounted for by the fact that women friends stood closest and women strangers far apart. Men did not change their conversational distances in response to differences in level of acquaintance. Similarly, another study, which had male and female subjects converse for two seven-minute conversations with strangers, found that smiling, gazing, gesturing, foot movements, and postural shifts for males were more consistent across the two situations than for females (Duncan & Fiske, 1977). Lower status may call for greater code-switching.

Submissiveness A fourth factor hypothesized to differentiate groups on the basis of status is the use of cues of threat and non-threat. Smiling is one of these cues. Specifically, it is hypothesized that the less dominant group smiles more than the more dominant group. Rosenfeld (1966) found that women smiled more often than men even when they were instructed to make it clear to their partner that they disliked him or her. Frances (1979) also showed that women smiled more than men and especially so when they were listening.

Smiling appears to serve a number of interpersonal functions such as conveying warmth, creating cohesiveness, maintaining solidarity, and mending frayed relationships. But ethologists have also suggested another function, and that is to signal appeasement and submissiveness (Van Hooff, 1972). In this sense, smiles are designed to ward off possible competition or assault by indicating that no threat is intended.

The important thing to note regarding gestures of submissiveness is that they are called forth by gestures of dominance. They do not exist in isolation but in relationship to other social signals. Calling on those who display submissive signals to change and requiring that they do so before they can be admitted to the club is misplaced. As long as the power dynamics remain unchanged, the task will either be endless or if successful, grounds for exclusion because of inappropriate behavior.

The factors of readability, sensitivity, accommodatingness, and submissiveness are not intend ed to exhaust the domain of nonverbal responses to dominance. Rather they are designed to facilitate looking at nonverbal differences between groups and the possibility that some of these differences would be better conceived as status signals. Moreover, these factors are presented not as *faits accomplis* but as hypotheses deserving scrutiny. . . .

Gender as Culture

We have discussed these four areas of power cueing not exclusively in terms of gender, but in terms of group difference and hierarchy: they may apply to differences between any hierarchically-organized groups within a culture, for example to racial and ethnic group differences.

The questions of group differentiation by nonverbal cues apply broadly, and what we encounter in the study of gender differentiation both borrows from and lends to that more general study. The factor of accommodation, for example, relates to an old question for cultures in contact, that of assimilation. Differences in code may be maintained relatively easily when there is little contact between groups; but when groups with different communication forms must interact often, it becomes harder to maintain separate codes. The pattern with languages in contact has been one of exchange between languages, especially in the realms most affected by the type of contact, e.g., in commerce. When one culture dominates another, the influence of language is particularly one-sided, the dominated culture absorbing many of the terms, and sometimes some of the structure, of the dominant culture's language.

So it is too in nonverbal communication, in which adopting the "body language"—the clothing, hair style, gait, gestures, and facial expression—of the dominant culture becomes part of "making it." This may be all well and good if you want to assimilate.

But assimilation raises difficult questions. A major one is, of course, that of losing one's cultural heritage, including very important values that may be expressed in such forms. Another major question is that of effectiveness: Is it true that adopting the dominant styles will open the doors to the privileges enjoyed by those of the dominant culture?

Ethnic groups have been struggling with the assimilation question for a long time, and people of the various cultures represented in countries like the U.S. and Canada often feel strongly on the problem of loss of cultural heritage. As nations, we have at least an expressed interest in maintaining the values and richness of cultural diversity, even if that interest is not always realized in practice. For women, however, there has been little sense of a culture, and seldom any question that, especially for dealing in the halls of power, the nonverbal communication associated with males is superior.

The research on nonverbal sex differences is sometimes used to teach that women are the cause of their own subjugation, because they insist on using these gestures of powerlessness. When this point of view is presented by women you see the old problem of ethnic groups: devaluing their own style, overvaluing the dominant style; it is another form of blaming the victim.

Many of the actions characterized as feminine weakness reflect values which are core values of our society, for both females and males, supposedly. For example, sharing our emotions is honest and open; being sensitive and responsive to others' needs, moods and feelings shows sensitivity and consideration for others; not interrupting, staring, invading space, or touching when inappropriate are all signs of respect for the other person's spatial, temporal, intellectual, and bodily integrity. Of course, we know such traits may be carried to extremes and reflect self-deprecation, insecurity, or manipulativeness at times. But we should not assume that women cling to such forms only out of powerlessness; rather, it may be because of the positive values they wish to express—gender as culture.

The same, of course, is true for specific ethnic/cultural forms that are deprecated: they are not chosen to appear powerless or stigmatized, or to stand out. Rather, they may affirm values and beliefs that are at the core of one's culture and being. To assimilate is for many to pay too great a price.

For early immigrants to these countries (as to others), questions of cultural identity followed fast on the heels of questions of survival. These questions are not dead but remain difficult issues for their third- and fourth-generation descendants. And if gender acts as culture in ways, similar questions of cultural identity—of dominance of one culture by another, of pressures to assimilate—arise for women. Women are in some respects entering as immigrants into men's world. Do all immigrants who want to make it have to wear three-piece suits, hide their emotions, and incorporate aggressiveness and competitiveness into their personal styles? Or can cultural differences find their way in?

This question leads not only to discussion of change for individuals—immigrants—but to questions of change for whole cultures: a host culture cannot but be changed by those it incorporates, no matter how much it resists or seems not to change. The well-known influence of Gullah on southern U.S. dialect is one example of such cultural influence, and there are many more.

We end with questions but not entirely without answers: we have attempted to demonstrate that cultures of nonverbal behavior exist differentiated by gender, that cultural explanations serve alternatively to biological ones for sex differences in nonverbal behavior; that the issues in this cultural differentiation are the creation of difference and the existence of dominance, and the relation between the two; that the issues in sex differences are the issues for other instances of cultural differentiation; that certain general principles (readability, sensitivity, accommodatingness, submissiveness) may be abstracted to help us study and understand these cases of cultural dominance and difference; and that there is much more to explore.

We will do well in that exploration if we take off our blinders—our cultural blinders and our gender blinders as well.

References

Argyle, M., Lalljee, M., & Cook, M. The effects of visibility on interaction in a dyad. *Human Relations*, 1968, *21*, 3–17.

Baxter, J. C. Interpersonal spacing in natural settings. *Sociometry*, 1970, *33*, 444–456.

Bem, S. L. The measurement of psychological androgyny. *Journal of Consulting and Clinical Psychology*, 1974, *42*, 115–162.

Borden, R. J., & Homleid, G. M. Handedness and lateral positioning in heterosexual couples: Are men still strongarming women? *Sex Roles*, 1978, *4*, 67–73.

Brown, R. *Social psychology*. New York: Free Press, 1965.

Buck, R., Baron, R., & Barrette, D. Temporal organization of spontaneous emotional expression. *Journal of Personality and Social Psychology*, 1982, *42*, 506–517.

Buck, R., Miller, R. E., & Caul, W. F. Sex, personality, and physiological variables in the communication of affect via facial expression. *Journal of Personality and Social Psychology*, 1974, *30*, 587–596.

Campbell, D. T., Kruskal, W. H., & Wallace, W. P. Seating aggregation as an index of attitude. *Sociometry*, 1966, *29*, 1–15.

Cherulnik, P. D. Sex differences in the expression of emotion in a structured social encounter. *Sex Roles*, 1979, *5*, 413–424.

Davis, M. Morte la diffe,rence? *Semiotica*, 1981, *37*, 121–127.

Dosey, M. A., & Meisels, M. Personal space and self-protection. *Journal of Personality and Social Psychology*, 1969, *11*, 93–97.

Duncan, S., & Fiske, D. *Face-to-face interaction: Research, method, and theory.* Hillsdale, NJ: Erlbaum, 1977.

Ekman, P., Friesen, W. V., & Ellsworth, P. *Emotion in the human face: Guidelines for research and integration of findings*. Elmsford, NY: Pergamon, 1972.

Evans, G. W., & Howard, R. B. Personal space. *Psychological Bulletin*, 1973, *80*, 334–344.

Frances, S. J. Sex differences in nonverbal behavior. *Sex Roles*, 1979, *5*, 519–535.

Freedman, J. L., Levy, A. S., Buchanan, R. W., & Price, J. Crowding and human aggressiveness. *Journal of Experimental Social Psychology*, 1972, *8*, 528–548.

Frieze, I. H., & Ramsey, S. J. Nonverbal maintenance of traditional sex roles. *Journal of Social Issues*, 1976, *32* (3), 133–141.

Frodie, A. M., & Lamb, M. E. Sex differences in responsiveness to infants: A developmental study of psychophysical and behavioral responses. *Child Development*, 1978, *49*, 1182–1188.

Giessen, M., & McClaren, H. A. Discussion distance and sex: Changes in impressions and attraction during small group interaction. *Sociometry*, 1976, *39*, 60–70.

Goffman, E. *Gender advertisements*. New York: Harper & Row, 1979.

Grady, K. E., Miransky, L. J., & Mulvey, M. A. *A nonverbal measure of dominance*. Paper presented at the convention of the American Psychological Association, Washington, D.C., August 1976.

Hall, E. T. *The silent language*. Garden City, NY: Doubleday, 1959.

Hall, J. A. Gender effects in decoding nonverbal cues. *Psychological Bulletin*, 1978, *85*, 845–857.

Hall, J. A. Gender, gender-roles and nonverbal communication skills. In R. Rosenthal (Ed.), *Skill in nonverbal communication: Individual differences*. Cambridge: Oelgeschlager, Gunn & Hain, 1979.

Henley, N. M. Power, sex and nonverbal communication. *Berkeley Journal of Sociology*, 1973, *18*, 1–26.

Henley, N. M. *Body politics: Power, sex, and nonverbal communication*. Englewood Cliffs: NJ: Prentice-Hall, 1977.

Henley, N. M. Gender hype. *Women's Studies International Quarterly*, 1980, *3*, 305–312.

Heshka, S., & Nelson, Y. Interpersonal speaking distance as a function of age, sex, and relationship. *Sociometry*, 1972, *35*, 491–498.

Heslin, R., & Boss, D. Nonverbal intimacy in airport arrival and departure. *Personality and Social Psychology Bulletin*, 1980, *6*, 248–252.

Jenni, D. A., & Jenni, M. A. Caring behavior in humans: Analysis of sex differences. *Science*, 1976, *194*, 859–860.

Kanter, R. M. Women and the structure of organizations: Explorations in theory and behavior. *Sociological Inquiry*, 1975, *45* (2/3), 34–74.

LaFrance, M., & Carmen, B. The nonverbal display of psychological androgyny. *Journal of Personality and Social Psychology*, 1980, *38*, 36–49.

Lopata, H. Z., & Thorne, B. On the term "sex roles." *Signs*, 1978, *3*, 718–721.

Lott, B. A feminist critique of androgyny: Toward the elimination of attributions for learned behavior. In C. Mayo & N. M. Henley (Eds.), *Gender and nonverbal behavior*. New York: Springer-Verlag, 1981.

McDermott, R. P., & Gospodinoff, K. Social contexts for ethnic borders and school failure. In A. Wolfgang (Ed.), *Nonverbal behavior: Applications and cultural implications*. New York: Academic Press, 1979.

Mehrabian, A. *Nonverbal communication.* Chicago: Aldine-Atherton, 1972.
Nesbitt, P. D., & Steven, G. Personal space and stimulus intensity at a Southern California amusement park. *Sociometry,* 1974, *37,* 105–115.
Nguyen, T., Heslin, R., & Nguyen, M. L. The meanings of touch: Sex differences. *Journal of Communication,* 1975, *25,* 92–103.
Patterson, M. L., & Schaeffer, R. E. Effects of size and sex composition on interaction distance, participation, and satisfaction in small groups. *Small Group Behavior,* 1977, *8,* 433–442.
Perdue, V. P., & Connor, J. M. Patterns of touching between preschool children and male and female teachers. *Child Development,* 1978, *49,* 1258–1262.
Polit, D., & LaFrance, M. Sex differences in reaction to spatial invasion. *Journal of Social Psychology,* 1977, *102,* 59–60.
Rosenfeld, H. M. Approval-seeking and approval-inducing functions of verbal and nonverbal responses in the dyad. *Journal of Personality and Social Psychology,* 1966, *4,* 497–505.
Rosenthal, R., Hall, J. A., DiMatteo, R., Rogers, L., & Archer, D. *Sensitivity to nonverbal communication: The PONS test.* Baltimore: John Hopkins University Press, 1977.
Rosenthal, R., & DePaulo, B. M. Sex differences in accommodation in nonverbal communication. In R. Rosenthal (Ed.), *Skill in nonverbal communication.* Cambridge, MA: Oelgeschlager, Gunn, & Hain, 1979.
Schwartz, B., Tesser, A., & Powell, E. Dominance cues in nonverbal behavior. *Social Psychology Quarterly,* 1982, *45,* 114–120.
Silveira, J. Thoughts on the politics of touch. *Women's Press* (Eugene, Ore.), 1972, *1* (13), 13.
Sommer, R. Studies in personal space. *Sociometry,* 1959, *22,* 247–260.
Spence, J. T., & Helmreich, R. L. *Masculinity and femininity.* Austin: University of Texas Press, 1977.
Van Hooff, J. A. R. A. M. A comparative approach to phylogeny of laughter and smiling. In R. A. Hinde (Ed.), *Non-verbal communication.* Cambridge, England: Cambridge University Press, 1972.
Weitz, S. Sex differences in nonverbal communication. *Sex Roles,* 1976, *2,* 175–84.
Wex, M. *Let's take back our space. "Female" and "male" body language as a result of patriarchal structures.* Hamburg: Frauenliteraturverlag Hermine Fees, 1979. (Also available in German.)
Zuckerman, M., DeFrank, R. S., Spiegel, N. H., & Larrance, D. T. Masculinity-femininity and encoding of nonverbal cues. *Journal of Personality and Social Psychology,* 1982, *42,* 548–556.

CREDITS AND ACKNOWLEDGMENTS

Cover illustration: *Faces*, by Victoria S. Alexander. Used by permission of the artist.

1. Jeffrey Z. Rubin, Frank J. Provenzana, and Zella Luria, "The Eye of the Beholder: Parents' Views on Sex of Newborns," *American Journal of Orthopsychiatry*, 44, 4 (1974). Copyright © 1974 by the Orthopsychiatric Association, Inc. Reproduced by permission.

2. Barrie Thorne, "Girls and Boys Together . . . But Mostly Apart: Gender Arrangements in Elementary Schools" in Hartup, William W. and Rubin, Zick, eds., *Relationships and Development*, 1986, selected from pages 167–184. Reprinted with permission by Lawrence Erlbaum Associates, Inc.

3. Becky W. Thompson, "Childhood Issues: Culture Race, Class, and Sexuality" from *A Hunger So Wide and So Deep: American Women Speak Out About Eating Problems*. Copyright © 1994 by the Regents of the University of Minnesota. Reprinted with the permission of the University of Minnesota Press.

4. Laura L. Carstensen and Monisha Pasupathi, "Women of a Certain Age" in Matteo, Sherri (Ed.), *American Women in the Nineties: Today's Critical Issues*, 1993. Copyright © 1993 by Northeastern University Press. Reprinted with the permission of Northeastern University Press.

5. Natalie Angier, "Default Line: Is the Female Body a Passive Construct?" from *Women: An Intimate Geography*. Copyright © 1999 by Natalie Angier. Reprinted with the permission of Houghton Mifflin Company. All rights reserved.

6. Barbara Fredrickson and Tomi-Ann Roberts, "Objectification Theory: Toward Understanding Women's Lived Experience and Mental Health Risks," *Psychology of Women Quarterly*, Vol. 21 (1997). Reprinted with the permission of Blackwell Publishing, Ltd.

7. Amy Malkin, Kimberlie Wornian, and Joan C. Chrisler, "Women and Weight: Gendered Messages on Magazine Covers" from *Sex Roles* 40 (1999). Copyright © 1999. Reprinted with the permission of the authors and Kluwer Academic/Plenum Publishers.

8. Iris Marion Young, "Throwing Like a Girl" from *Human Studies* 3 (1980). Copyright © 1980. Reprinted with the permission of the author and Kluwer Academic Publishers.

9. Inga Muscio, excerpt from *Cunt: A Declaration of Independence*. Copyright © 1998 by Inga Muscio. Reprinted by permission of Seal Press.

10. Deborah L. Tolman, "Object Lessons: Romance, Violation, and Female Adolescent Sexual Desire" from *Journal of Sex Education and Therapy* 25 (2000). Copyright © 2000. All rights reserved. Reprinted with the permission of the author and publisher.

11. Carla Golden, "Diversity and Variability in Women's Sexual Identities" from *Lesbian Psychologies: Explorations and Challenges*. Copyright © 1987 by the Board of Trustees of the University of Illinois. Used with permission of the University of Illinois Press.

12. Natalie Angier, "What Women Really Want" from *The New York Times*, August 13, 1995. Copyright © 1995 by the New York Times Co. Reprinted by permission.

13. Sharon Golub, "Menarche: The Beginning of Menstrual Life" from *Women and Health*. Copyright © 1983 by The Haworth Press, Inc. Reprinted by permission.

14. Gloria Steinem, "If Men Could Menstruate" From *Outrageous Acts and Everyday Rebellions*, Second Edition. Copyright © 1983, 1995 by Gloria Steinem. Copyright © 1984 by East Toledo Productions, Inc. Reprinted by permission of Henry Holt & Co., Inc.

15. Joy Harjo, "Three Generations of Native American Women's Birth Experience" in *Ms.* (July/August 1991). Copyright © 1991. Reprinted by permission of Ms. Magazine.

16. Sarah Blaffer Hrdy, "Natural-born Mothers" in *Natural History* (December, 1995). Copyright © 1995 by Sarah Blaffer Hrdy. Reprinted with permission of Curtis Brown, Ltd.

17. Letitia Anne Peplau and Steven L. Gordon, "Women and Men in Love: Gender Differences in Close Heterosexual Relationships," from *Women, Gender,*

and Social Psychology, edited by Carol Tavris. Reprinted with permission by Lawrence Erlbaum Associates, Inc.

18. L. A. Peplau and H. Amaro, "Understanding Lesbian Relationships" in Paul, W., Weinrich, J. D., Gonsiorek, J. C., and Hotvedt, M. E. (Eds.), *Homosexuality: Social, Psychological, and Biological Issues*. Copyright © 1982 by Sage Publications, Inc. Reprinted by permission of the publisher.

19. Margaret Talbot, "Girls Just Want to be Mean" *The New York Times Magazine* (February 24, 2002). Copyright © 2002 by Margaret Talbot. Distributed by The New York Times Special Features.

20. Michelle Sidler, "Living in McJobdom: Third Wave Feminism and Class Inequality" from *Third Wave Agenda: Being Feminist, Doing Feminism*, edited by Leslie Heywood and Jennifer Drake. Copyright © 1997 by the Regents of the University of Minnesota. Reprinted with the permission of the University of Minnesota Press.

21. Gerhart Sonnert and Gerald Holton, "Career Patterns of Women and Men in the Sciences" from *American Scientist* 84 (1996). Reprinted with the permission of the authors and *American Scientist.*

22. Pat Mainardi, "The Politics of Housework" from *Sisterhood is Powerful: An Anthology of Writings from the Women's Liberation Movement*, edited by Robin Morgan (New York: Random House, 1970). Copyright © 1970 by Robin Morgan. By permission of the author.

23. Dana Crowley Jack, "Moral Themes in Women's Depression" from *Silencing the Self: Women and Depression*. Copyright © 1991 by Dana Crowley Jack. Reprinted with the permission of Harvard University Press.

24. Priscilla Grant, "Who Are You Calling Crazy?" from *More* (June 2001). Copyright © 2001 by Priscilla Grant. Reprinted with the permission of the author.

25. Mary Ballou and Carolyn West, "Feminist Therapy Approaches" from *Issues in the Psychology of Women*, edited by M. Biaggio and M. Hersen. Copyright © 2000. Reprinted with the permission of Kluwer Academic/Plenum Publishers.

26. Robin Warshaw, "The Reality of Acquaintance Rape" (pages 11–26 with cuts) from *I Never Called it Rape*. Copyright © 1988, 1994 by the *Ms*. Foundation for Education and Communication, Inc. and Sarah Lazin Books. Reprinted with the permission of HarperCollins Publishers, Inc.

27. Phoebe Morgan, "Sexual Harassment: Violence Against Women at Work" from *Sourcebook on Violence Against Women*. Copyright © 2001 by Sage Publications, Inc. Reprinted with the permission of the publisher.

28. Timothy Beneke, excerpt from *Men on Rape*. Copyright © 1982 by Timothy Beneke. Reprinted with the permission of St. Martin's Press, L.L.C.

29. Maxine D. Bernstein and Nancy Felipe Russo, "The History of Psychology Revisited: Or, Up with Our Foremothers" from *American Psychologist* 29, (February, 1974). Copyright © 1974 by the American Psychological Association. Reprinted with permission.

30. Naomi Weisstein, "Kinder, Küche, Kirche as Scientific Law: Psychology Constructs the Female" from *Sisterhood is Powerful: An Anthology of Writings from the Women's Liberation Movement*, edited by Robin Morgan (New York: Random House, 1970). Copyright © 1970 by Robin Morgan. By permission of the author.

31. Stephanie A. Shields, "Functionalism, Darwinism, and the Psychology of Women: A Study in Social Myth," from *American Psychologist* 30 (1975). Copyright © 1975 by the American Psychological Association. Reprinted with permission.

32. Mary Brown Parlee, "Psychology and Women," in *Signs: Journal of Women in Culture and Society*, 1979, vol 5. no. 1. Copyright © 1979 by the University of Chicago Press. Reprinted by permission of the publisher.

33. Maureen C. McHugh, Randi Daimon Koeske, and Irene Hanson Frieze, "Issues to Consider in Conducting Nonsexist Psychological Research: A Guide for Researchers," from *American Psychologist*, (August, 1986), Vol. 41, No. 8. Copyright © 1986 by the American Psychological Association. Reprinted with permission.

34. Mary M. Gergen, "Toward a Feminist Metatheory and Methodology in the Social Sciences," in M. M. Gergen (Ed.), *Feminist Thought and the Structure of Knowledge*. Reprinted by permission of New York University Press.

35. "Some Psychological Consequences of the Anatomical Distinction between the Sexes" from *The Collected Papers*, Volume 5, by Sigmund Freud. Edited by James Strachey. Published by Basic Books, Inc. by arrangement with The Hogarth Press, Ltd. and the Institute of Psycho-Analysis, London. Reprinted by permission of BasicBooks, a division of the Perseus Books Group, L.L.C. and by Random House Ltd.

36. Robert Wright, excerpt From *The Moral Animal: Why We Are the Way We Are: The New Science of Evolutionary Psychology* (New York: Vintage, 1995). Copyright © 1994 by Robert Wright. Reprinted by permission of Sagalyn Literacy Agency.

37. Sandra L. Bem, "Gender Schema Theory and Its Implications for Child Development: Raising Gender-aschematic Children in a Gender-schematic Society" in *Signs: Journal of Women in Culture and Society*, vol 8. no. 4, (1984). Copyright © 1983 by the University of Chicago. Reprinted by permission of the author and the publisher.

38. Nancy M. Henley, and Marianne LaFrance, "Gender as Culture: Difference and Dominance in Nonverbal Behavior," in N. Henley and M. LaFrance, A. Wolfgang, (ed.), *Nonverbal Behavior: Perspectives, Applications, Intercultural Insights*, ISBN 0-88937-008-7, pages 351–371. Copyright © 1997 by Hogrefe & Huber Publishers•Seattle•Toronto•Bern•Göettingen. Reprinted by permission.